THE VIRTUES OF ABANDON

The Virtues of Abandon

AN ANTI-INDIVIDUALIST HISTORY
OF THE FRENCH ENLIGHTENMENT

Charly Coleman

STANFORD UNIVERSITY PRESS

STANFORD, CALIFORNIA

Stanford University Press
Stanford, California

©2014 by the Board of Trustees of the Leland Stanford Junior University.
All rights reserved.

Printed in the United States of America on acid-free, archival-quality paper

Library of Congress Cataloging-in-Publication Data
Coleman, Charly, author.
  The virtues of abandon : an anti-individualist history of the French Enlightenment / Charly Coleman.
    pages cm
  Includes bibliographical references and index.
  ISBN 978-0-8047-8443-6 (cloth : alk. paper)
  1. Self (Philosophy)—France—History—18th century. 2. Individualism—France—History—18th century. 3. Philosophy, French—18th century.
4. Enlightenment—
France. I. Title.
  B1925.S45C65 2014
  944'.034—dc23
                                        2013047798

ISBN 978-0-8047-9121-2 (electronic)

Typeset by Bruce Lundquist in 10.5/12 Sabon

Table of Contents

Illustrations

Acknowledgments

It is a pleasure to express my gratitude to those who have contributed to this book in its several iterations. My twin interests in French history and the history of the self owe much to the mentorship of Gary Kates and John Jeffries Martin, who set standards for scholarship and teaching to which I continue to aspire. Keith Baker's critical eye and rigorous erudition strengthened several of my arguments, and Paula Findlen pushed me to flesh out the sometimes elusive ideas at their core. Paul Robinson provided me with a compelling model of scholarly elegance. My first forays into the world of scholarship were expertly guided by Carolyn Lougee Chappell, Daniel Gordon, Brad Gregory, Mary Louise Roberts, and James Sheehan. I also had the great fortune early in my career of working with Colin Jones, who has mentored a generation of British and American historians of France. He does not seem to mind that I have been bothering him ever since. Penetrating comments by Anthony LaVopa advanced my work at a critical juncture. Holly Case, Toby Jones, Chad Martin, Lara Moore, Gillian Weiss, and Brett Whalen generously shared much wisdom and good cheer.

The book's principal themes first took shape in Paris. Philippe Roger sponsored my initial research and suggested fruitful leads. Patrick Eveno and his family made me feel at home. There is no more enlightening form of sociability than that I enjoyed in my reading group with Ben Kafka, Andrew Jainchill, Rebecca Manley, Anoush Terjanian, Emmanuel Saadia, and Dana Simmons. I am also immensely grateful to Julie Coe, Paul Cohen, Amy Freund, Rita Keane, Irit Kleiman, Ellen McBreen, Jennifer Olmsted, Camille Robcis, Jennifer Sessions, Sarah Thompson, and Charles Walton for their camaraderie and support.

I refined much of the book's analytical framework during a formative period spent at the University of Chicago's Society of Fellows in the Liberal Arts. At various times, Paul Cheney, Dan Edelstein, Stephanie Frank, Aaron Hill, and Erik Thomson freely shared their ideas in and around Hyde Park. I extend a special word of thanks to Jan Goldstein, whose groundbreaking work on the history of selfhood has shaped my own. Constantin Fasolt, Rachel Fulton, Robert Morrissey, Moishe Postone, and William Sewell inspired me with searching questions—some of which I am still trying to answer.

Many colleagues have lent their support and expertise as the book took its final form. At Washington University, I was lucky to meet Cassie Adcock early on; she has helped me think more critically about religion as a historical category. Various chapters have benefited greatly from exchanges with Pannill Camp, Tili Boon Cuillé, Margaret Garb, Rebecca Messbarger, and Mark Pegg. Mark in particular became a champion for the project, as well as an astute critic and trusted friend. At Columbia, Christopher Brown, Victoria de Grazia, Marwa Elshakry, Matthew Jones, Gregory Mann, Samuel Moyn, and Joanna Stalnaker have offered stimulating insights, much-appreciated encouragement, and the warmest of welcomes. I also thank Mark Mazower and Pamela Smith for helping to make the history department such a congenial place to work.

Several institutions have contributed material and scholarly resources to this project. The Bourse Chateaubriand, the Mabelle McLeod Lewis Memorial Fund, the Mellon Foundation, and the history departments at Stanford, the University of Chicago, Washington University, and Columbia all provided essential funding. I undertook the bulk of the research for the book at the Bibliothèque nationale de France, as well as the Archives nationales, the Bibliothèque municipale de Dijon, the Huntington Library, and the New York Public Library. I am grateful to the librarians and staff members at all these institutions for their assistance in locating sources—and, more generally, for preserving the materials on which all historical scholarship is based. A further word of thanks is due to the Bibliothèque nationale de France for permission to reproduce the two images in chapter 5.

I have had the opportunity to present the ideas developed here in various forums. My thanks go to participants at meetings organized by the New York Area Group in European Intellectual and Cultural History, the MacMillan Center at Yale, the Kandersteg Seminar of the Remarque Institute at New York University, the Society for French Historical Studies, the Society for Eighteenth-Century Studies, the Modern Language Association, the American Historical Association, the France-Chicago Center, the Modern France Workshop at the University of Chicago, and the Eighteenth-Century Interdisciplinary Salon at Washington University. In sections of this book I draw on material adapted from my essays "The Value of Dispossession: Rethinking Discourses of Selfhood in Eighteenth-Century France," *Modern Intellectual History* 2, 3 (November 2005); "Resacralizing the World: The Fate of Secularization in Enlightenment Historiography," *Journal of Modern History* 82 (June 2010); and "Resacralizing the Self: Mysticism, Materialism, and Personhood in Eighteenth-Century France," in *Sacred and Secular Agency in Early Modern France: Fragments of Religion*, ed. Sanja Perovic (London: Continuum/Bloomsbury, 2012).

At Stanford University Press, I am particularly grateful to Norris Pope for expressing an early interest in the project and deftly seeing it through the review phase. As I prepared the manuscript for publication, Emma Harper, Thien Lam, Stacy Wagner, Gigi Mark, and Kate Wahl have by turns exhibited the wisdom of the Solomon and the patience of Job. Peter Dreyer's masterful editing improved the text in countless ways. Nick Koenig compiled the index with sensitivity and care. I also thank Helena Rosenblatt and Colin Jones for their thoughtful comments on the manuscript.

Writing this book would not have been possible without the support of family and friends. My mother, grandparents, and brother have sustained me with their affection. Azadeh, Minoo, and Ali Rashidi have welcomed me into their family with open arms. Adam Przeworski and Joanne Fox-Przeworski have lavished their global hospitality and delightful company on me. I owe more than I can say to the friendship of Ben Kafka and Molly Przeworski. Finally, I dedicate this book to Bahareh, whose wisdom and critical eye have strengthened every page. With her, I have an existence I prefer to all others.

THE VIRTUES OF ABANDON

Introduction

On August 13, 1698, at the dawn of what would later be christened the age of lights, the Parlement of Dijon condemned one Philibert Robert, a local priest turned fugitive from justice. Tried in absentia, he was to be burnt at the stake for professing "Quietism," a heretical form of mysticism, and for engaging in "spiritual incest," a legal term referring to sexual relations between a priest and a layperson under his direction.[1] The offenses were considered symptomatic of the Quietists' broader disregard for all spiritual goods, even salvation, with the ultimate aim of purging themselves of every trace of desire, will, and personal identity. In separate proceedings, the court turned its attention to Robert's disciples, who likewise stood accused of practicing a "prayer of annihilation" that left the soul "immobile, thinking nothing, saying nothing, doing nothing," and entirely "abandoned to God." Those who entered this state believed themselves to have become "impeccable," and thus capable of engaging in "illicit exchanges" without incurring the stain of sin.[2] At the trial's conclusion in 1700, the magistrates sentenced several local clerics and their alleged female accomplices to penalties ranging from banishment to death by hanging.[3]

Over three-quarters of a century later, in 1776, the Parlement of Paris found itself embroiled in a controversy that, at first glance, would seem quite different in nature. That year, as part of sweeping reforms aimed at liberalizing agriculture, manufacturing, and commerce, the recently crowned Louis XVI approved the plan of his controller-general, Anne-Robert-Jacques Turgot, to abolish the corporate bodies that enjoyed exclusive rights to practice specific trades.[4] The decision triggered a wave of outcries from French subjects who believed that their livelihoods, and even their identities, had come under assault. The glove makers of Paris contended that since "each person has an existence only through the corporate body [*corps*] to which he is attached," the edict did violence to their members' very sense of self.[5]

Not all petitioners, however, made their claims exclusively in terms defending the integrity of the society of orders. For instance, representatives of the powerful Six Corps of Paris (consisting of drapers, furriers, hosiers, goldsmiths, grocers, and mercers) asserted that their privileges constituted a property as real as that held in land, and thus could not be lawfully stripped from them. Drawing on a rationale influenced by John Locke, they argued that investments of mental and physical labor legitimized ownership of their possessions. A manufacturer's efforts earned him not only "honorable distinctions," such as affiliation with the crown, but also "the exclusive right" to associate his product with his own name as an extension of his personal and professional identity.[6] Echoing these protests, hat makers pleaded that a "mastership can be regarded as a property," and thus deserved protection as a "sacred thing."[7]

The Parlement of Paris vigorously remonstrated against the edicts. According to the judges, Turgot's reforms would render "each manufacturer, each artist, each worker [. . .] an isolated being, dependent on himself alone," thus compromising the moral and social cohesion of the kingdom. The measures unjustly deprived the master not only of his "estate, which was guaranteed to him by the laws," but also, as the Six Corps had alleged, of "a part of his property." The magistrates had a duty, then, to call attention to the defects in the legislation, which threatened to "alter the constitution of the state and undermine the authority of the throne."[8]

The cases before the Parlements of Dijon and Paris were considered at different times, in different places, and for different reasons. Yet the issues at stake in both centered on the same overarching problem: the self's relationship to spiritual, existential, and material possessions. Thinking about selfhood also entailed thinking about property—what one owned, or could claim to own, defined who and what one was. For increasing numbers of French subjects, the divinely ordained and royally sanctioned order appeared inadequate to the task of orienting oneself in a world of goods. Once identity was unmoored from previously sacrosanct political, social, and economic realities, it became necessary to articulate new ways of relating the human person to God, to nature, and to the body politic. The various means by which men and women in eighteenth-century France strove to do so are the subject of this book.

The self's highly contested status during the eighteenth century stemmed from profound uncertainties about the extent to which one could claim one's identity, salvation, earthly belongings, or even one's ideas and actions as one's own. This was no mere theoretical issue. It was debated in the highest echelons of Church and state in matters of crucial importance to the kingdom. It was fought over in books, pamphlets, plays, memoirs, newspapers, the corridors of Versailles, and the streets of Paris. It had a profound impact on the daily lives of men and women: what they bought and sold, their beliefs about God, their political convictions, their social identities, and, indeed, their most fundamental sense of where they stood in the world. Those who openly challenged the prevailing wisdom concerning the self's possessive character found themselves targets of religious and political persecution and were subject to imprisonment, torture, and even death.

These pressing questions related to being and having a self, I argue, can be seen as giving rise to opposing cultures of personhood that cut across doctrinal, philosophical, and political lines. On one side, orthodox Catholic theologians, mainstream philosophes, and apologists for venal officeholding and luxury consumption defended a multifaceted *culture of self-ownership*, according to which men and women were thought to possess and stand accountable for themselves and their actions. Proponents of self-ownership, despite their many differences on other fronts, shared a common commitment to notions of identity and autonomy that would, after years of controversy, underwrite the concept of the modern, individualist subject. Yet this struggle was not for individualism per se (the term did not gain wide usage in France until the nineteenth century).[9] Rather, the primary point of contention was the self's attachment to its existence as a form of property, which in turn made possible the accumulation of other goods—including spiritual gifts, moral autonomy, privileges in hereditary office, and the ever-expanding array of consumer products available in the eighteenth century.

This understanding of personhood has been commented on from various perspectives by a host of scholars, perhaps most notably by C. B. Macpherson.[10] None of these studies, however, has placed primary emphasis on the French case or examined the links between theological, existential, and material possession that gave it its distinctive dimensions. As indicated by the Quietist trials in Dijon, moreover, what I have termed the culture of self-ownership did not enjoy universal assent. On the contrary, it faced sustained criticism throughout the eighteenth century. Detractors ranged across the cultural terrain of the Old Regime and the French Revolution, to include the grandest of prelates, the most notorious of philosophes, and the most powerful of political figures. The history of the challenge they posed to the possessive, acquisitive, individualist self—from its complex origins to its enduring legacies—has never been told.

Central to my argument, then, is the recovery of a distinctively anti-individualist strain of thinking that infiltrated theology, philosophy, and politics during the long eighteenth century, from the final years of the reign of Louis XIV through the Revolution of 1789. Its partisans sought, in word and deed, to strip the subject of its property, its personality, even its very existence as an individual. Their views formed a wide-ranging but coherent *culture of dispossession* that valorized the human person's loss of ownership over itself and external objects. An unholy trinity subscribed to this position. Radical Christian mystics were aligned with radical materialist philosophes and political thinkers in denouncing as illogical and immoral all claims that the self had to property in its person or in material things. Although they diverged at many points, most obviously in matters of faith, the works of these thinkers similarly sought to reduce men and women to mere objects of totalizing forces outside the self—at first identified with the God of mystical devotion, and ultimately situated in Enlightenment conceptions of nature and the revolutionary body politic. Efforts to apply these dispossessive ideals led to extraordinary practices, scandals, and upheavals. Men and women joined illicit mystic cults that engaged in rituals of physical mortification and sexual abandon, committed suicide out of materialist fatalism, sought to induce mind-altering dreams to satisfy their lust for scientific and carnal knowledge, railed against the degrading effects of luxury, and even renounced the feudal privileges that had defined their social existence for centuries.

The Polemics of Personhood

The cultures of self-ownership and dispossession clashed throughout the eighteenth century in seminal controversies over venal officeholding, Christian mysticism, atheistic materialism, the dream state, luxury consumption, and civil and political rights. The sheer variety of concerns shows that the understandings of personhood implicated in these debates did not remain static. For defenders of self-ownership, there were significant shifts in the nature of the goods by which the human person defined itself, from the divine to the mundane. In the case of dispossession, as noted above, the totalizing force to which the self submitted changed over the course of the century from the God of Christianity, who transcended nature and ruled beyond it, to the novel political regime of the French Revolution, which its framers believed to be grounded in natural law. The chapters of this book, similarly, are organized into sections, each of which emphasizes one of the dominant frameworks—from the theological to the philosophical to the political—within which the polemics over personhood successively formed.

Part I of *The Virtues of Abandon* charts the emergence of Enlightenment-era cultures of personhood out of conflicts in the religious sphere. These conflicts were not exclusively theological in origin, but rather figured in a wider assault on corporate social structures under the Old Regime. In particular, the French crown's reliance on the sale of offices and letters of ennoblement to fund its policies of domestic and international expansion severed traditional ties linking personal virtue and social status. In response, theologians and philosophers formulated two conflicting positions. By emphasizing the self's possessive attachment to its ideas, actions, and material belongings, post-Tridentine Catholic reformers, Cartesians, and Jansenist moral philosophers affirmed that the individual person—rather than the estate—was the foundation of identity. In opposition, growing numbers of Christian mystics rejected spiritual self-ownership and enlightened self-interest, urging virtuous souls to abandon themselves entirely to God.

These developments anticipated the so-called Quietist affair, a controversy that pitted the leading theological lights of the seventeenth century, François de Fénelon and Jacques Bénigne Bossuet, against each other over the orthodoxy of the notorious mystic Jeanne-Marie Guyon. At issue in the quarrel, which preoccupied Louis XIV, Pope Innocent XII, and much of the Gallican ecclesiastical establishment, were the dispensability of spiritual goods and the limits of self-interest in Christian devotion. Bossuet held that the soul's longing to possess spiritual goods was a natural and necessary desire, fully in keeping with God's will. In contrast, Fénelon and Guyon denounced this position as mercenary, and advocated instead that the soul sever its possessive attachment to all things, even to itself and its own hopes for salvation. While Bossuet's doctrinal stance cast a relatively positive light on the Sun King's pursuit of glory and the earthly prosperity of his subjects, Fénelon surrounded himself with like-minded mystics, who sought drastic changes, not only in French economic and military policy, but also in the system of government.

Although Pope Innocent XII would ultimately condemn Fénelon in 1699, the latter's teachings continued to reverberate in subsequent trials, scandals, and causes célèbres during the first third of the eighteenth century. There were lengthy prosecutions of supposed Quietists in Dijon, Paris, Rodez, and Toulon. These episodes provide insight into how men and women attempted to put the mystical ideal of self-abandon into practice through prayer manuals, liturgical rites, and public demonstrations. Religious and scientific authorities took issue with these acts on medical as well as theological grounds. In so doing, they bore witness to a shift whereby the dispossession of self would increasingly be seen not merely as a spiritual state, but also as a somatic condition that could be treated accordingly.

By the 1730s, Christian apologists had become acutely aware of the challenges posed by radical philosophy to their doctrine of spiritual self-ownership. Part II of the book begins by exploring the ways in which

Baruch Spinoza's materialist heirs in France sought to topple God from the throne of creation and undermine human pretensions to possess distinct agency and identity. Their virulent writings so devalued the self that they even drove the occasional reader to suicide. A more measured and far-reaching response was to discern from nature's laws a new ethics and even a new social order, based on collective rather than individualist principles. Baron Paul Henri Dietrich d'Holbach's *Système de la nature* (1770), one of the most popular philosophical treatises of the Enlightenment, exemplified this approach. The writings of d'Holbach and other philosophical materialists served as primary vehicles for elaborating the culture of dispossession in the middle decades of the eighteenth century. Orthodox theologians, not unlike mainstream philosophes, deployed charges previously aimed at heretical mystics to denounce this new threat. Whereas controversies over mysticism were sparked by disputes over the virtues of spiritual abandon to God, debates surrounding radical philosophy focused on the self's indebtedness to nature, which Spinozists and materialists extended to the point of almost total dependency. This shift was recognized by Voltaire, who likened the followers of Spinoza to those of Fénelon, since both thinkers advocated selflessness as an ethical ideal.

Other radical materialists sought to construct a more positive form of dispossessive personhood. Most notably, Denis Diderot appropriated the language of Quietism in his philosophical and aesthetic writings to describe a spectrum of dispossessive states—from simple distraction to absorption to madness—with the aim of framing an alternative to the self-possessed subject of Enlightenment orthodoxy and its detached, objectifying stance toward the world. In this enterprise he was joined by expert physicians and charlatans alike, who prepared manuals on how to diagnose, induce, and direct the self in dreaming. Such approaches treated the dispossession of the self as a physiological and psychological phenomenon, not a miraculous occurrence. For Diderot in particular, altered states of consciousness offered insight into the true nature of things. He told, for instance, of how a well-crafted work of art could take him out of himself and into a scene being depicted. In response to the potentially reifying effects of objects produced for the market, Diderot developed a materialist aesthetics predicated on communion rather than exploitation.

Diderot's musings took on heightened relevance during a period when French men and women had greater access to a disorienting array of goods with which to fashion their existence. Another aim of Part II, then, is to address the implications of disputes over economic and political reform for understanding the self. The consumer revolution of the eighteenth century provoked dread as well as satisfaction. Proponents of the liberalization of trade in grain and other commodities frequently stressed the human being's status as a pleasure-seeking subject. The logic of their claims had a moral valence as well, since the enjoyment derived from consumption was regarded as a means of securing personal contentment through productive engagements with other social actors. Critics of economic self-ownership, led by Jean-Jacques Rousseau, made use of the arguments honed by Fénelon during the Quietist affair. In a series of influential publications, Rousseau criticized the possessive subject as a mere plaything of objects that were of its own making and yet beyond its control. Although he attempted to salvage self-ownership as an ideal, his ultimate political response to this problem placed stark limits on any exercise of personal autonomy that lacked the consent of the body politic as a whole.

Rousseau's halting efforts to apply the ideal of dispossessive personhood to the political sphere were taken up by his self-professed followers during the French Revolution, as men and women attempted to reconcile a commitment to individual rights with calls for self-sacrifice to the new regime. Leading politicians persistently subjected the prerogatives of individuals to the needs of the body politic, from the frenzied alienation of seigniorial privileges during the night of August 4, 1789, to the cult of martyrs that arose during the Terror. The culture of dispossession waned with the fall of Maximilien Robespierre, but its aims lived on among early socialists such as Gracchus Babeuf, who sought to reform, if not eliminate, private property and the despotic brand of egoism that it sustained.

. . .

As an interpretive prism, the culture of dispossession casts new light, not only on conceptions of the self, but also on the broader social, political, and intellectual landscapes of eighteenth-century France. Indeed, recognizing the problematic origins of individualism reveals a far more nuanced and accurate understanding of the Enlightenment, its intersections with religion, and its role in the emergence of modern economic relations. For instance, we often credit the French Enlightenment with the triumph of autonomous individualism, and the Revolution with inscribing the individual's rights into law. However, these rights arose as much out of violent self-sacrifice as out of the pursuit of happiness. Similarly, it remains a common misperception that the French Enlightenment was avowedly secular from its inception. Yet the movement's religious influences are apparent even where scholars have tended to find them most lacking: among its radical, materialist, atheistic elements. After all, the Old Regime was not only a world of freethinking philosophers, rationally calculating royal administrators, and apologists for property and commerce. It was also the domain of Christian mystics, esoteric seekers, philosophical fatalists, and self-denying republicans. The two spheres frequently clashed, with fateful consequences for both France and the wider world. Until we grasp the highly charged, contested status of the self during the period, we cannot jettison the idealized portrait of the Enlightenment for a truer history.

The Vicissitudes of Individualism

Much of the scholarship on eighteenth-century selfhood has oscillated between two interpretive extremes. In the classic accounts of C. B. Macpherson, Louis Dumont, and Charles Taylor, the eighteenth century is noted for its pivotal role in producing the modern, secular, autonomous individual—a moral agent in possession of itself and in control of its world.[11] Daniel Roche has aptly characterized the position in his summa on Enlightenment-era France. Armed with advanced scientific knowledge and a self-seeking, acquisitive drive, the individual became what Descartes had promised in his *Discours de la méthode*, the "master and possessor" of nature.[12] In sharp contrast, the Enlightenment's fiercest challengers, from Max Horkheimer and Theodor Adorno to Michel Foucault, have tended to emphasize the oppressive features of modern subjectivity, and even its impending demise.[13] This critical stance, frequently associated with "postmodern" currents in philosophy and literary criticism, has approached individualism as a recent invention with a dubious past and an uncertain future.

Writing in the wake of such pronouncements, historians have seized the opportunity to recover the highly contingent course of the modern subject's emergence. Like recent work by Jan Goldstein, Jerrold Seigel, and Dror Wahrman, this study avoids reducing the history of personhood to that of individualism, thereby allowing overlooked and neglected formulations of the self to come into focus.[14] Yet it also frames a distinct perspective. Rather than characterizing the Enlightenment-era self as indeterminate and unstable, I find French subjects attempting to base their identities on new foundations, which they regarded as more certain than those furnished by the declining corporatist order of the Old Regime.[15] This point becomes all the more apparent if one considers the sharply different alternatives offered by the cultures of self-ownership and dispossession in France. The former, espoused by Montesquieu, Voltaire, and the principal French sensationalists, promised a secure basis for staking individual claims of possession on one's ideas, actions, and identity. The latter, professed by radical spiritualists and materialists, endorsed the dissolution, and even annihilation, of one's sense of self.

My inquiry places even greater stress on the multiple, conflicting understandings of selfhood that existed outside conventional frameworks during the eighteenth century. Tentative forms of individualism arose in the seventeenth and eighteenth centuries, but so too did avowedly non-individualist currents that disputed the human person's powers of appropriation. The two positions both clashed with and influenced each other. Neither the claims in defense of self-ownership nor those in favor of dispossession would have been as extreme, or as clearly articulated, had they not developed in response to the opposing view. While the partisans of self-ownership ultimately saw their doctrines inscribed in the political order, their victory was by no means assured. Quite simply, we cannot understand the multiple twists and turns in the history of individualism without also confronting the struggles out of which it emerged.

Once eighteenth-century debates over the self are restored to their original, overarching context—the problem of relating personhood to property—the Enlightenment seems less a crucible of individualism and more a battleground for deciding its fate. From this perspective, the movement as a whole takes on a different aspect. The *Encyclopédie* famously declared the philosophe to be a rationally calculating, self-governing subject.[16] Few scholars have found reason to question this portrayal, which squares readily with the ideal of Enlightenment sociability as a free exchange between interlocutors.[17] In so doing, it lends support to Jürgen Habermas's influential descriptions of a bourgeois public sphere, the workings of which depend on participants in possession of themselves and with an acute sense of responsibility for their thoughts and actions.[18] Yet it also obscures the actual diversity of thinking about what it meant to live and work as a philosophe, even for the Enlightenment's leading figures. As we shall see, Diderot himself, the co-editor of the *Encyclopédie*, not only called into question the philosophical ideal of self-ownership; he did so by refurbishing dispossessive language derived from heretical branches of mysticism. Furthermore, his eventual understanding of matter as a blind, determining force that negated the real existence of individual beings—an understanding shared by his colleague d'Holbach—cast more than a shadow of a doubt on the axiom that human beings acted as a distinct, autonomous entities in and on the world.

The Enlightenment and the Sacred

The history of selfhood advanced here directly complicates the longstanding characterization of the Enlightenment as a secularizing force. The once-canonical interpretations of Paul Hazard, Peter Gay, and Michel Vovelle depicted the eighteenth century in terms of encroaching skepticism and declining belief.[19] Research over the past three decades, however, has signaled a return to religion as a subject of fundamental importance in the scholarship on the period. To be sure, religion has long been regarded as a means of differentiating specific national Enlightenments according to the degree of ecclesiastical participation in the movement.[20] David Sorkin has made a still more ambitious case for a pan-European, philosophically pluralist, and state-sanctioned "religious Enlightenment" that buttressed the demands of faith with support from the ideals of reason and toleration. On this view, the Enlightenment not only stood as a complement to doctrinal verities, but in many cases proved functionally indistinguishable from them.[21] Other scholars have offered various additions and correctives to this line of argumentation, by detailing the ebbs and flows of its Catholic, Protestant, or Jewish iterations.[22] Even Jonathan Israel—now perhaps the most outspoken advocate of the Enlightenment as a drive toward "rationalization and secularization"—holds that supporters of its "moderate mainstream," in contrast to their more radical contemporaries, proved all too willing to accommodate long-standing theological and political axioms.[23]

A similar recovery of religion can be detected in specialist scholarship on France, perhaps a surprising development given the notorious anticlericalism that took root there.[24] Dale Van Kley has pioneered an approach that stresses the relevance of theological controversies in the age of lights. The tendentious debates between Jesuits and Jansenists, he argues, had far more bearing than Enlightenment philosophy on the political struggles that precipitated the collapse of the Old Regime and foreshadowed the violent conflicts of the Revolution.[25] In a similar vein, Jeffrey Burson makes the case for a "Theological Enlightenment," a Jesuit-engineered amalgam of Lockean sensationalism and Malebranchian occasionalism that facilitated dialogue on topics such as the mind-body problem and the validity of revealed religion. Challenged by Jansenists on one side and skeptical materialists on the other, this precarious synthesis broke apart, however, after the abbé Jean-Martin de Prades was accused of blasphemy for submitting a naturalistic thesis to the Sorbonne, obliging him to flee to the Dutch Republic in 1752 and thence to Prussia. The Prades affair, as it became known, foreclosed possibilities for détente between the philosophes and the ecclesiastical establishment, with the latter accusing the former of plotting to subvert spiritual and political authority.[26]

On the cultural-historical front, David Bell has argued convincingly that nationalism in France emerged in the eighteenth century as a response to a theological problem—namely, the need to span the perceived distance between a transcendent God and the terrestrial sphere through the invention of new concepts and institutions regarded as independent of divine oversight or legitimation. Moreover, patriotic devotion to the nation was informed by Catholic efforts to forge affective bonds among members of a community.[27] Theology, the queen of the sciences, enjoyed a far longer and more eventful reign than scholars were once willing to recognize.

The present study also offers a new assessment of the relationship between the Enlightenment and French Catholicism, by giving sustained consideration, not only to the work of theologians, but also to the philosophes themselves. Previous scholarship has addressed similarities in the arguments made by members of the two camps on a range of issues, but not as regards the self's relationship to spiritual goods and material possessions.[28] The conflicting responses to this question reveal connections between heretical mysticism and the materialism of the radical Enlightenment. In the minds of their eighteenth-century opponents, adherents of both views sought to disseminate a form of dispossessive selfhood that threatened to undermine the basis, not only of individual property rights, but also of moral action in this life and the promise of salvation in the next. The affinities between theological and philosophical radicalism, although noted by the likes of Leibniz and Voltaire, have almost entirely escaped scholarly attention.[29]

Redressing these oversights opens new vistas for considering the theological dimensions of the French Enlightenment, and more broadly, the lines of demarcation between the secular and the sacred. The aim is not to extend the framework now closely associated with the work of Jonathan Israel, which sharply delineates the moderate and the religious from the radical and irreligious, but to reconfigure it in significant ways.[30] French mystics and materialists drew on analogous arguments, and at times identical terminologies, in their efforts to undermine the individual's claims to active self-determination. Their writings form part of a broader dispossessive culture that resonated throughout the long eighteenth century. Spinoza himself, whom Israel regards as the harbinger of modernity, equated the highest form of consciousness with the disinterested love of God. When avowed atheists had recourse to theological language, and even to mystical doctrines branded as heretical, their pronouncements would have appeared radical in a double sense. Orthodox theologians and mainstream philosophes found themselves repulsed by the spiritual excesses that marred even what Israel has held out as the purest, most cohesive strand of the Enlightenment. His characterization of the movement as fundamentally secular, then, fails to account for the ways in which religious antecedents continued to inform the thought of the period.

In reconstructing the intersections between radical theology and radical Enlightenment during the eighteenth century, I also offer an alternative account of the secularization process. Recent interpretations of the period have emphasized the extent to which theologians' growing perception of a remote God's distance from creation allowed secular concepts and institutions to emerge.[31] Divine transcendence, in other words, facilitated the rise of an autonomous and desacralized world with only tenuous links to a supreme being.[32] From this perspective, secularization no longer refers to a one-sided departure from religion, but rather to a contingent, multidimensional process that originated within religion itself.

The following study presents a more complex view of this dynamic. Proponents of dispossession responded to the problems posed by a remote and transcendent divinity by stressing that not only God, but also nature and the body politic, wielded an immediate, irresistible power over human minds and bodies. Radical mystics did so by pledging to annihilate their souls before the divine, while radical materialists claimed that it was not God, but nature, that imposed itself on one's every thought and deed. I call this countercurrent of the secularizing process *resacralization*, because it sought to reverse transcendence by valorizing the immanent relations between human beings and the world.[33] While both mystics and materialists engaged in resacralization, they did so with different aims in mind. The former hoped to draw the individual self into close, dispossessive proximity to God; the latter did the same with respect to the impersonal forces of nature. Toward the century's end, radical French political thinkers consecrated the *patrie* as an object of selfless veneration, a site where the powers of God and nature merged in communion with the collective will of the body politic. The Enlightenment did not so much jettison the divine, then, as marshal it to serve new functions. Tracing the ways in which eighteenth-century theology and philosophy endeavored to remap the sacred onto God, nature, and the body politic will serve as a red thread of analysis in the chapters to come.

Homo Economicus, Homo Consumptus

If religion in its various guises remained central to thinking about the self, it was due in large part to the positive stance toward spiritual goods affirmed by the Church at the Council of Trent. It could even be argued, as has Cissie Fairchilds, that the ensuing revitalization of spiritual life provided a crucial impetus for expanding consumption in eighteenth-century France by stimulating demand for crucifixes, prie-dieux, images, books, and other objects of devotion, which in turn introduced the faithful to a new material world. Indeed, despite the proliferation of curtains, clocks, and tea and coffee sets found in after-death inventories in Paris and Toulouse during the first third of the eighteenth century, the only items encountered with greater frequency than religious objects were mirrors.[34] It is difficult to imagine a more powerful indication of the extent to which self-regard and acquisitiveness could go hand in hand. Moreover, the arguments employed by orthodox theologians in defense of spiritual goods—that God desired souls to possess them so that they would be happy—anticipated arguments that enlightened political economists would make in favor of luxury.

Until recently, historians have tended to insist on the relative backwardness of the French economy, especially when compared to that of Britain.[35] A wealth of new research, however, has discredited this interpretation. The eighteenth century witnessed the emergence of mass markets for religious objects, along with all manner of commodities. For example, Daniel Roche's examination of Paris inventories reveals a steady growth in the total number and diversity of articles of clothing owned during the century. This increase, he argues, was part of a gradual shift from dearth to abundance, and from a "sartorial *ancien régime*," in which one's clothing manifested one's social station, to a "culture of appearances" driven by the whims of fashion.[36] Fairchilds has shown in her study of "populuxe goods" (relatively inexpensive replicas of luxury items) how the desire for objects during the period affected men and women across the social spectrum. In addition to clothing, jewelry, and other adornments, the eighteenth-century consumer increasingly gained access to new foodstuffs, as well as to addictive substances such as coffee and tobacco. One also sees a proliferation of more abstract possessions, from venal offices to stocks in colonial trading companies.[37] Reforms were made to existing property rights as well; in the 1770s, for instance, authors acquired exclusive *privilèges* over their work.[38] All these examples reinforce the impression that long before the political revolution of 1789, France underwent a consumer revolution that transformed the ways in which men and women oriented themselves toward objects of possession.

Montesquieu and Rousseau acknowledged in the eighteenth century, as Marx would later, that novel goods tend to produce novel needs.[39] They also, one might add, produce new formulations of selfhood and new ways of being in the world. Historians have become increasingly interested in uncovering how the changes in what can be owned, and how, correspond to conceptual shifts in the sociopolitical domain.[40] To cite a significant example, the widespread practice of venality in France hinged on a particular possession, the office, that exhibited its own transformative characteristics—such as the capacity to alter status—yet could also be bought and sold by individuals. Long before the mystifying effects of the commodity became apparent to Marx and other critics of capitalism, French jurists, theologians, and philosophers observed similar effects on the human subject at work in religious, intellectual, and political domains. More generally, the ways in which men and women related to spiritual and material goods show that the attractiveness of the curios of consumer culture depended not only on availability, but also on a highly charged sense among prospective buyers of living by and through possessions. The acquisitive impulse was in turn intensely scrutinized by critics, who asserted that it rested on a flawed notion of what it meant to be and to have a self.

The Self in Language and in Practice

The arguments outlined above, as well as the claims I make for their significance, rest on a series of interpretive and methodological decisions. When framing terms of art, I have placed a high premium on maintaining fidelity to the language of Enlightenment-era France. To be sure, all historical writing involves some measure of translation: no one in the eighteenth century would have spoken of "cultures of personhood." Nonetheless, my references to the "self" and the "human person" are rooted whenever possible in the usage of the period. There was no single term for "self" in eighteenth-century French: *âme*, *moi*, *soi*, and *personne* could all refer to an individual being's attributes and identity. The first of these terms, directly translated as "soul," had the most marked spiritual connotations. As such, it tended to indicate higher-order states of self-awareness, interiority, and identity. In eighteenth-century writings, *moi* (and less often, *soi*), gradually took on a similar range of meanings. Nevertheless, dictionary entries continued to refer mainly to their grammatical function as pronouns.[41]

The term *personne* simultaneously held broader and more precise connotations. It could be used to describe a being's metaphysical status, as in the cases of the three persons of the Christian God (Father, Son, and Holy Spirit) or the sacred person of the king. Like *moi*, it could also describe a particular being's sense of self. For instance *personne* could impute social and moral qualities, as in "a person of merit," "a person of condition," or "a very well-intentioned person." In this case, the term was often paired with possessive pronouns—as in the example "he loves his person, which is to say, he loves his comforts, that he looks after his health, that he has great concern for his body and his appearance."[42] *Personne*, then, could be used to describe a specific—and specifically possessive—relationship to oneself. Even before Locke's formula of the property in one's person gained wide currency, a similar notion had acknowledged precedents in French.

Adapting eighteenth-century usage, I employ the term "self" in a generic sense, to refer to one's existence as a particular being distinct from others, while, for the sake of clarity, I tend to reserve "soul" for allusions to the spiritual and religious dimensions of this existence. The terms "person" and "personhood" refer more broadly to the self's status and essential qualities—whether divine or human, spiritual or material, active or passive, noble or common, good or evil. Different authors defined these attributes in various ways, which often entailed a specific understanding of a person's capacity for possession. A man or woman could be characterized as a particular, individual self who held property in and through his or her person, and thus possessed the attributes associated with it. If a self were to lose this existential property, then the kind of person it was would change as well. Throughout the period, what it meant to be a distinctly human person provoked controversies that implicated the self's possessive relationship, not only to personal attributes and belongings, but also to more fundamental properties that defined one metaphysically as a being.

Likewise, the rubrics of self-ownership and dispossession follow from the vocabulary of the eighteenth century. Philosophers, theologians, and political thinkers made frequent reference to *propriété, possession, biens* (goods), *jouissance* (enjoyment of possession), and their derivatives when describing the human person's relationship to itself and to exterior objects. Unlike the first three of these terms, the use of *jouissance* might seem less evident, given its less pronounced economic valence. Yet successive editions of the *Dictionnaire de l'Académie française* make clear that *jouissance* was invariably defined not only as enjoyment in general, but first and foremost as the "use and possession of something" and "to have full and complete enjoyment of the possession [*la jouissance*] of one's goods."[43] Standard definitions implied not only the possession of a given thing, but also a gratifying relationship between the possessor and the possessed. Even so, *jouissance* and related terms remained a source of contention. The proponents of self-ownership employed them in a positive sense, to describe the self's legitimate property in its person. In contrast, partisans of dispossession studded their writings with allusions to *abandon, aliénation, anéantissement* (annihilation), *désappropriation* (dispossession), *distraction, renoncement,* and similar words, all of which described varying degrees of self-loss.

One reason these lexicons proved so useful in debate is that they could simultaneously convey theological, psychological, and economic meanings. A *bien* referred not only to a piece of immoveable or moveable property, but also to spiritual goods granted by God or to a desired moral aim.[44] Similarly, *aliénation* denoted mental instability as well as the loss of property, while *distraction* applied both to a state of mind (as when one's attention turned unexpectedly from the matter at hand) and, more generally, to the separation of a part from the whole. The latter definition applied directly to economic transactions, as in the case of dividing a piece of land.[45] As we shall see, Enlightenment-era polemicists frequently exploited the polysemous character of such terminology in their debates. It is precisely during these wars of words, plagued by mutual lapses in comprehension, that the cultures of self-ownership and dispossession come most clearly into view.

One of the aims of this book is to recover the linguistic constructions of personhood during the Enlightenment in their original contexts, which include attempts to put them into effect. Eighteenth-century cultures of personhood were comprised of both discourse and practice.[46] Readers sought out devotional manuals, philosophical treatises, and literary works, not to find free-floating, disembodied ideas, but to locate operational parameters for religious, aesthetic, political, and economic conduct. Likewise, authors hoped their writings would intervene in the world by directing a specific course of action: how to pray, how to love God, how to believe, how to read a novel or view a painting, how to produce or consume, and how to be a mother, father, or citizen. The cultures of self-ownership and dispossession offered ways to confer significance on these practices both through linguistic and nonlinguistic acts. To return once more to the example that opened this introduction, when Quietist spiritual directors in Dijon seduced their female penitents, they engaged in more than discursive intercourse. Their liaisons willfully exceeded the bounds of the teachings on which they drew and served to embolden critics of the mystical tradition. Their desire to embody spiritual annihilation in sexual rituals also exhibited continuities with later trends in medicine and materialist philosophy that privileged physical explanations of dispossessive states.

Enlightenment-era cultures of personhood, then, did not function as isolated, reified crucibles of meaning. Their logics and lexicons mutated over time—either by their being put into practice or through the ways theologians, philosophers, and political thinkers used them in polemics. Partisans of self-ownership responded to attacks by proponents of dispossession by escalating their rhetoric, and vice versa. It was also possible for a single author to embrace both views at different times, or even in the same work. Rather than representing absolute positions, self-ownership and dispossession operated along a broad spectrum. More generally, these conceptions stood in a dialectical relationship that frequently brought them in close proximity to each other. For example, mystical spiritualists who embraced the loss of reason or will tended to stress the subject's submission to, but also possession by, the totalizing force of divinity at once within and outside the self. Likewise, calls for self-ownership were frequently predicated upon the recognition of prior loss—such as the need for spiritual goods in the wake of humanity's banishment from the Garden of Eden, or the recovery of primordial wholeness after the collapse of the state of nature. Ultimately, the two cultures, which remained relatively distinct in theological disputes, converged in the writings of the philosophes and in the political theology of the Revolution, both of which championed the dispossession of particular individuals as a means of achieving self-ownership on a collective basis. These shifts were not preordained by logical necessity or the cunning of reason, but rather followed the exigencies of men and women seeking to define themselves in relation to spiritual, existential, and material goods.

One final caveat is in order. In deference to the aim of coherence and the limits of my own expertise, the subject matter of this book maintains an almost exclusive focus on metropolitan France. I do not mean to suggest that analogues to the French constellation of mysticism, materialism, and dispossessive thought cannot be located elsewhere in the firmament of eighteenth-century Europe. Historians of the eighteenth century have long traced the itineraries of authors, texts, and ideas across the continent. Jonathan Israel has brought renewed attention to the long shadow cast by Spinozism, and it remains difficult to overestimate the attraction of English thinkers like Locke and Isaac Newton.[47] Guyon, for her part, found followers among members of Pietist sects in the German-speaking lands.[48] She also makes a prominent, albeit unflattering, appearance in Karl Philipp Moritz's early psychological novel *Anton Reiser* (1785), where her disciples are noted for seeking the "total mortification of all so-called 'individuality' and 'self-love'" in the pursuit of "a completely disinterested love for God."[49] In addition, both Hegel and Schopenhauer productively drew on mystical influences to develop philosophies with anti-individualist consequences; the latter even expressed a certain admiration for Guyon.[50]

While the French case might one day form a chapter of a far broader and more intricate narrative, there are compelling reasons—both methodological and historical—for the extended treatment it receives here. Reconstructing cultural schemas over the course of a century, and across multiple domains of activity, not only requires close attention to detail, down to the usage of specific words and expressions, but also involves amassing a considerable store of evidence. Given these exigencies, linguistic and geographical boundaries make it possible to consider the theological and philosophical implications of debates over the self, while also attending to specific political, economic, and social developments. In addition, while French served as the literary language par excellence among intellectual elites in the eighteenth century, the polemics featured in this book were often parochial affairs. Even when participants were not French by birth— Rousseau and d'Holbach immediately spring to mind—they spent much if not most of their lives in and around Paris. Finally, and perhaps most significantly, only in France did revolutionaries launch an unprecedented drive to impose a dispossessive ethos on public life, both in restricting individual property rights and in establishing a cult of patriotic martyrdom that exalted personal sacrifice as an ultimate aim. To the extent that these factors distinguish France in a broader European context, they also raise questions that a focused study can more readily answer.

Part I

THEOLOGICAL BATTLEGROUNDS

I *Spectors of Venality*

France was at war in early 1696, as it had been for most of the preceding decade. Moreover, Europe was in the grips of a protracted financial crisis: money had grown scarce even for relatively rich states, which made it all the more difficult for the French to compensate for a succession of poor harvests by importing grain. The consequence was widespread dearth, and as many as a million and a half of Louis XIV's subjects would succumb to famine. There also remained the daunting task of concluding the War of the League of Augsburg (1688–1697), which pitted France against much of the rest of Europe. To keep his armies in the field, much of the king's gold and silver plate had been melted down, but still more money was needed.[1]

Desperate for funds, Louis followed a tried-and-true Bourbon precedent: he created a host of new nobles. He did so not to honor the martial valor of exceptional soldiers, nor to buttress the aristocratic character of the officer corps. Rather, the measure was aimed specifically at recognizing five hundred merchants whose fortunes would contribute to financing the war. Typically, men of commerce attained ennoblement through the purchase of a specific office, and in most cases, their new status would not be inheritable without the payment of yearly fees, or until the fulfillment of two generations of service.[2] In this instance, however, the nobility conferred by the king was to be immediate and perpetual. The edict echoed absolutist orthodoxy in such matters. The monarch, as the fount of honor, could bestow nobility on his subjects at will, in recognition of services rendered. This act, moreover, entailed an elevation in character. The nobles created would become "as if born of noble and ancient lineage" and were entitled to "use and enjoy the possession [*jouir*] of all the honors, prerogatives, privileges, [. . .] liberties, exemptions, and immunities of the other nobles of our realm, without distinction."[3]

Such benefits came at a price, of course. First, according to a clarifying *arrêt* issued in August 1696, the aspiring nobles were required to pay the sum of six thousand livres, along with additional fees to have the letters patent registered. Significantly, this addendum noted that those who had been stripped of their titles during Louis's sweeping campaign against false claims of nobility, which he had waged in the reformist (and relatively peaceful) atmosphere of the 1660s, were now invited to buy back their positions.[4] Many who chose to do so, however, ran into difficulties. A subsequent declaration, dated March 12, 1697, addressed the issue of court officials holding registrations for ransom by charging fees according to the personal wealth of the petitioner, rather than assessing a flat fee, which in this case had been set at twenty livres. In response, the king commanded that all the letters be registered, with no inquiries made into financial matters. Simultaneously, and without explanation, the registration fee was raised to fifty livres, and the applicant also had to pay for the requisite paper and stamps. These measures had proven necessary, according to the king, so that subjects granted letters might "fully enjoy the possession of the privileges attached to them." Clerks guilty of misconduct would henceforth be fined a hundred livres.[5]

The king's actions on this occasion were by no means extraordinary. Venality—the sale of offices and titles that empowered the buyer to fulfill a public function or to occupy a position of dignity—served as a major prop for French absolutism and sustained the Old Regime. While the practice helped to ensure the monarchy's survival during periods of extreme financial stress, it also produced political, economic, and ideological contradictions that eroded its viability from within. The funds raised from venal offices and titles allowed the French monarchy to mount wars of expansion even as it spent massive sums to affirm and extend its prerogatives as the sole source of power in the kingdom. The authority to distribute honors also made it possible to make and remake the privileged orders of society in its own image and as it saw fit. The confusion that ensued struck at the fundamental logic of the system of orders. In place of a divinely ordained hierarchy in which persons of each rank exhibited certain fixed attributes and knew their places, there emerged the possibility of uncoupling moral qualities from social standing.

This state of affairs, although overseen by the crown, also problematized the monarch's standing. If the king was set upon his throne by God to represent the essential harmony between the various members of the body politic through the exercise of his will, what did it mean when the sovereign himself desired their reorganization? On what grounds could he justify doing violence to an order that was believed to be of divine provenance?

What effects did the practice of venal officeholding have on the ways in which French subjects understood their social and personal identities? If human persons could no longer be considered first and foremost as part of an organic social whole, what function did they serve? How were individuals to regard one another? What legal framework governed their interactions? How were they to relate, not only to God, but to their prince and fellow subjects?

These questions captivated a generation of jurists, theologians, and philosophers in the final years of the reign of Louis XIV. His constant meddling in the society of orders opened a chasm of massive proportions that proved incredibly difficult to close. Although the sale of venal offices and titles would continue until the Revolution of 1789, its very persistence signaled a challenge to traditional means of fixing social and political identities. Two rival positions arose in response. As legal theorists attempted to find ways of maintaining the status quo, clerics and moralists inspired by the movement for Catholic reform affirmed that the soul was an individual agent. All humans, regardless of social origin, were equally compelled to seek spiritual goods out of a desire for salvation. The proponents of emerging philosophical currents—above all, those led by René Descartes and John Locke—sought to liberate the human person from a preordained order and enshrine it as an acquisitive, possessive subject. Their interventions laid the groundwork for a far-reaching culture of self-ownership that would serve as an organizing principle for thought and action throughout the eighteenth century.

At the same time, the mystical theologians who rose to prominence during the period denounced this solution as morally dangerous and logically unsound. It represented for them nothing less than the expansion of venality into the very hearts and minds of the French people. From the pulpit, on the printed page, and even in the political arena, they called upon the faithful to surrender their egoistic designs, not in order to return to the status quo ante, but to dispel the fiction of the self's personal, particular identity. Their pronouncements—gradually at first, then with increasing urgency—cohered into a culture of dispossession that exerted a strong influence on French religious affairs for the next several decades. Self-professed defenders of Catholic orthodoxy condemned such views as heresies that aimed to strip the soul of its mental and physical faculties and undermine the promise of heavenly redemption. The impasse between the partisans of self-ownership and dispossession would not be settled during the reign of Louis XIV or those of his successors. It was fated, rather, to establish the terms of debate for ongoing trials, scandals, and controversies that periodically erupted down to the collapse of the Old Regime.

Property, Office, and Identity under the Old Regime

Nearly every significant attempt to settle what it meant to be a self during the Old Regime responded in some way to vexing questions concerning the nature and limits of property. The leading eighteenth-century legal scholar Robert-Joseph Pothier defined property, in a seemingly direct manner, as "the right to dispose of a thing according to one's pleasure."[6] Yet the application of this principle proved complicated, not least because the exercise of property rights, and especially the rights of inheritance, could vary considerably depending on the prevailing legal code of the region (generally, customary law, but Roman law in the south). Beyond this general division, there was the matter of the extent to which a property right could be exercised. Even property in land, commonly regarded as absolute, could be placed under significant restrictions.[7] For instance, although eighteenth-century jurists tended to recognize the current owner of a plot associated with a larger seigneurial domain as its real proprietor—that is, as the *seigneur utile*—they also acknowledged that the traditional feudal lord retained the right, depending on locale and circumstances, to various goods, payments, services, and obligations.[8] Property owners thus continued to pay homage to the feudal principle of *nulle terre sans seigneur* ("no land without a lord").[9]

Corporate structures like the *seigneurie* not only altered otherwise absolute legal claims to property, but also constituted their own modes of ownership. In the most general sense, men and women identified themselves by their rank in the society of orders and their place within family life, rather than as particular individuals or members of an economic class.[10] As Charles Maurice de Talleyrand-Périgord remarks in his memoirs, "It was the *family* that one loved, much more so than individuals."[11] The nobility, as well as those who aspired to join its ranks, pursued the honor to be derived from possessions more readily than the profit to be gleaned from them. This honor, in turn, manifested itself in benefits that accrued by virtue of membership in an estate, ownership of a *seigneurie*, or the possession of privileges or other properties in right, which carried both fiscal and social advantages. For instance, noble lords were exempted from the *taille* (the basic land tax), and endowed with an array of additional prerogatives in other matters. The *seigneur* supervised the execution of justice, collected the *cens* (feudal rent, paid annually) and other dues, exercised monopolies over the mills that ground grain, enjoyed exclusive rights to hunt, imposed the *corvée* (a period of mandatory labor), and assessed fees on the sale of land in his domain.[12] Holders of these privileges regarded them as legal extensions of their original ownership of the domain—or, as Charles Loyseau put it more specifically, as a part of their "power in property."[13]

The venal office constituted one of the most pervasive and perhaps the most contested forms of nonmaterial property under the Old Regime.[14] Upon purchasing an office, the buyer acquired the authority to perform a public service and was entitled to the income derived from it. The transaction provided revenue for both parties, but it was far more than financial in character, since the office transformed the status of its holder. Certain offices—such as those of *secrétaire du roi,* or positions in the *bureaux des finances,* the *Cours des aides,* and magistracies in the Parlements—granted inheritable nobility to the buyer either after twenty years or, as was more commonly the case, after at least a generation of service. Two generations was the norm for most of the seventeenth century, but the crown eased the requirement in subsequent decades to such an extent that, by the end of the Old Regime, 70 percent of ennobling offices allowed for membership in the Second Estate after a single generation.[15] These posts reaped the greatest financial windfalls for the state—it cost up to 120,000 livres to become a *secrétaire du roi*—but the crown also sold thousands upon thousands of less expensive offices that authorized royal subjects to exercise certain functions or practice particular vocations.[16]

This practice of venality first emerged in the fifteenth century, and it quickly took root in all sectors of state and society. Nearly the entire judiciary was venal, from presiding judges down to clerks, registrars, ushers, and process servers. Municipal offices throughout the kingdom could be bought and sold, as could captaincies and other military ranks (at least until France's dismal showing in the Seven Years' War). Trade corporations generally escaped full-blown venalization; even so, it required the purchase of an office to operate as an oyster-seller, fishmonger, tin inspector, grain merchant, wigmaker, official tester of *eaux de vie,* or in any number of other professions. As this brief survey suggests, the French monarchy in the seventeenth and eighteenth centuries engaged in the creation of posts to be bought and sold on a truly gargantuan scale. According to William Doyle's calculations, approximately 70,000 venal offices existed by 1789, and at least 300,000 French subjects owed their livelihoods and status either directly or indirectly to possessing such a position.[17] The system, simply put, was too big to fail, and when it did, the Old Regime collapsed with it.

Especially during military conflicts and other periods of financial hardship, the monarchy exploited the venal system to raise badly needed funds, making little or no effort to conceal its intentions. To cite one characteristic case, in August 1696, the year in which Louis XIV issued five hundred new titles of nobility, he also created new hereditary offices for overseeing the duties levied on gold and silver work, or *marques d'or* and *d'argent.* In February 1698, however, he reversed course, ordering the suppression of the offices and the reimbursement of those who had purchased them.[18]

Although the king was under no obligation to justify the decision, he defended it by claiming that the costs of war had compelled him to create offices that he now recognized as being injurious to the "good of our state and the peace of our subjects."[19] A less magnanimous rationale clearly shone through as well. In 1696, France was still embroiled in the War of the League of Augsburg. Once peace was concluded the following year, the additional revenue that would be generated by the offices was no longer needed, and so they were abolished. In a perverse variation on the traditional service ethic of the privileged orders, exemplified by the military sacrifices of the Second Estate, the crown brazenly disposed of an entire class of subjects once it had outlived its immediate usefulness.

Venality thus gave rise to glaring contradictions for which no immediate remedy presented itself. While the abuses and absurdities inherent in the system were widely denounced, not only by those directly affected, but also by the period's most astute political thinkers, the monarchy made no serious efforts to curb it.[20] Since the crown could not do without the cash that venality raised, it remained as a glaring, towering monument both to the king's stature, as the source of all dignity, and also to the all-too-material limits of his power. Venality also problematized the standing of property rights, in creating conflicting claims of ownership by officeholders and the monarch.[21] Indeed, it fundamentally altered what it meant to be a French subject. According to the logic that governed the traditional society of orders, identity derived from status, which in turn derived from one's position in the hierarchical chain originating in God and extending down to lowliest of creatures. Venal officeholding monetarized status. It converted the attributes that determined one's identity into qualities that could not only be acquired but purchased in a marketplace. This innovation had decisive effects on both fiscal and social arrangements, not least of which was that the French nobility became the most open in Europe. In large part due to venality, two-thirds of French noble families at the end of the Old Regime had only been so since the seventeenth century, and a quarter had been elevated after 1700.[22] As in the case of offices, the crown ruthlessly exploited the demand for titles to its advantage by issuing and then rescinding orders of ennoblement as the financial situation demanded.[23] Given that bearers of nobility tended to regard it not only as a social marker, but as an essential aspect of their being, manipulating status in this manner could only serve to intensify the sense that identity was precarious, and that appearances need not necessarily correspond to reality.

Yet challenges to traditional identity could provoke a spirit of innovation as well as a paralyzing sense of despair. For instance, during the seventeenth and eighteenth centuries, enterprising aristocrats dominated mining, metallurgy, and other emerging industries.[24] More generally, as Jonathan Dewald has argued, they sought to turn the commercialization of social life to their advantage in ways that complicated but did not undermine time-honored ideals such as honor and liberality. On this view, modern values associated with individualism and consumption developed within aristocratic culture rather than in opposition to it.[25] As economic actors, nobles launched ambitious building campaigns both in Paris and in the provinces. They gambled with abandon. They bought and sold offices— not only in the Parlements, but also in the military and the royal adminis- tration. Engaging in these activities put them in control of, but also made them beholden to, forms of property in which the status of ownership re- mained contested.[26] Persistent doubt regarding the use and abuse of money engendered speculation in both the financial and intellectual domains.

Jurists in particular acknowledged the extent to which the sociopolitical ideals of the kingdom were only imperfectly reflected by the actual order of things. Among the most trenchant of these legal commentators was Charles Loyseau (1564–1627). During his tenure as *bailli*, or chief magistrate, for the county of Dunois from 1600 to 1610, he experienced the judicial and administrative problems faced by the kingdom firsthand. His voluminous writings on *seigneuries* and offices would become standard references for his contemporaries, and the oft-cited *Traité des ordres et simples dignités* (1610) bequeathed to latter-day readers clear insight into the founding principles of the Old Regime.[27]

Loyseau held that the terrestrial sphere, like its celestial counterpart, is comprised of separate but interdependent ranks. The clergy oversee spiritual needs, the nobility lead the defense of the kingdom, and mem- bers of the Third Estate provide material sustenance through labor and exchange.[28] The most binding form of identity, Loyseau observed, lies with one's "order," defined as a "species of dignity, or honorable quality, which in the same manner and by the same name belongs to several persons" and signals an "*aptitude for public power* [italics in original]." Neither wealth nor one's relationship to the means of production, much less strictly individual qualities such as personality or temperament, served as funda- mental sources of identity. Rather, a French subject's capacity to carry out a particular social function followed from his estate, which in turn defined personal characteristics.[29] What one possessed did not determine one's order. Rather, it was one's order that determined what one could possess— either materially or as moral, mental, and spiritual attributes.

Nevertheless, Loyseau makes it clear that one's order or condition was not always predestined by birth. Members of the clergy, of course, owed their authority to taking holy orders. Likewise, a nobleman could be stripped of his status by engaging in activities such as trade, and the king could create new nobles in recognition of extraordinary services rendered to the crown. The latter case, according to Loyseau, affirmed the absolutist credo that all privilege stemmed from the monarch, "who is God's ordained distributor of the secure honor of this world." A royal letter of ennoblement or the acquisition of an ennobling office made possible a fundamental change in one's status, and even in one's person. The *Traité des ordres*, echoing a formula that monarchs employed in their edicts and declarations, stipulates that the king's actions "purge the blood and posterity of the ennobled of all marks of commonness, and establish him as of the same quality and dignity" as those who claim to trace their status from time immemorial. While Loyseau noted that this transformation was more of a "fiction than a truth," he nevertheless maintained that, in general, one's place in the social matrix bore directly on one's essential being.[30] A man's social order, which "forms his condition [*État*] and imprints upon him a perpetual character," was "more inherent and inseparable from the person than the office," which was merely a function.[31]

Loyseau was careful to defend the monarch's prerogatives in the creation of offices and noble titles. He was far less sanguine, however, in his discussion of the market that had sprung up around them. The sale of offices, in particular, provoked his ire. In *Cinq Livres du droit des offices* (1609), he ridiculed the French zeal for venality as a collective mental illness, a "rage for office," which he called "archomania." Historians have continued this usage, with William Doyle even likening the practice to a form of addiction.[32] These descriptions hit their mark. Once venality was accepted into the body politic, the state seemed to require more and more of it to survive. By the time Louis XIV began his personal reign (1661), French monarchs had been engaged in the sale of offices for four centuries, and the principles underlying the trade had begun to coalesce. In particular, Louis XI's declaration of October 21, 1467 affirmed that officeholders maintained their positions for life. Another watershed measure in this regard was the so-called Paulette Edict of 1604, by which Henri IV set rules for the inheritance of offices that would remain in force until the end of the Old Regime. Previously, there had been a forty-day restriction on their transfer: if the holder died within this period, the office reverted to the king. With the introduction of the Paulette tax, however, it became possible to gain exemption from this rule by paying the *droit annuel*, a charge based on a percentage of the office's value (originally set at one-sixtieth), often supplemented by forced loans and other fees imposed by the crown.[33]

Institutionalizing inheritability created a legal basis for regarding offices as the effective property, not of the king, but of the officeholder. In addition, by mitigating the requirements for succession, the Paulette Edict increased their potential to serve as means of ennoblement. The few offices that conferred nobility typically did so after a period of service. Officers who paid the *droit annuel*—or in the cases of the sovereign courts, the *survivance*, a fee that also ensured the right to succeed to the position— could be reasonably certain that their descendants would eventually acquire noble status. Even in the case of offices that did not ennoble, the holders now had the option of making them part of their patrimony. The Paulette Edict set a significant precedent that made the purchase of offices more attractive to buyers by offering a relatively stable vehicle for social advancement and financial investment. The crown also had a clear stake in maintaining the principle of inheritability, and therefore the property rights of officeholders, since it derived revenue from exemptions granted by the *droit annuel* and additional taxes associated with it, as well as from the *finance*, or the sum for which it had sold the office originally.[34]

By the first decade of the seventeenth century, critics of venal office-holding had already begun to wrestle with the difficulties attending the practice. The Paulette Edict, in particular, raised serious legal issues. To what extent was an office to be regarded as personal property, and how should it relate to other forms of ownership? Loyseau set himself the task of resolving these problems in *Cinq Livres du droit des offices*, although he lamented that "wishing to regulate by reason the law of offices is to search for reason where there is none." Contrary to past legal opinion, Loyseau realized that, once the principle of inheritability was in place, there was little choice but to conclude that an office was a form of property, albeit of a special kind. It could not designate merely the usufruct or the temporary right of possession that had been granted by another person, since this arrangement would amount to "odious servitude." Rather, Loyseau asserted that the office assumes a unique relationship with its holder. When vacated, in his words, "it nevertheless always remains in its being, waiting to be filled by another person [. . .]. This gives offices a particular nature."[35]

The distinction between the power inherent *in* the office itself, regardless of who holds it, and the person who becomes inherent *to* the office through a financial transaction recognized by the crown, follows from Loyseau's basic premises. The first is that all honor, all dignities, and all powers derived from God, who had transferred them to the king to distribute to his subjects. Thus, all offices originated in royal concessions, which, according to Loyseau, "consist materially in certain rights of the king, which are alienated to particular persons." The theory, however, did not always conform to practice. In particular, Loyseau noted that, through a series of misinterpretations, it had become commonplace to believe that public power itself, rather than the exercise of it, actually adhered to the office and thus to its holder. To clarify the issue, Loyseau separated the office from its public function. For example, in the case of magistrates, "the officer is not the owner, but only the user and administrator of Justice; however, he is the owner and lord of his office, [. . . which is . . .] to be inherent in his very person."[36]

Nonetheless, if offices could be inherited, as stipulated by the Paulette Edict, this feature went "against their nature." Even though Loyseau railed against the practice as "the most irregular, and I dare say the most unjust sort, that could ever be invented," he was nonetheless compelled to account for it. To do so, he reverted to the difference between person and office. When one claimed to inherit an office, what was actually inherited was the legal capacity to give back the office to the crown or transfer it to oneself or another according to established procedure. Despite this attempt at clarification, Loyseau recognized that, in actuality, "it is difficult to distinguish venal from non-venal offices on a reasonable basis," since the king allowed most offices to be freely bought and sold.[37]

The transferability of these positions especially concerned Loyseau, because it made venal officeholding all the more difficult to organize in a rational way. As Loyseau noted, "gradually this traffic in offices has reached the point of infinity." The system had taken on a life of its own. The problem applied not only to offices with a clear and necessary function, but all the more so to those Loyseau described as "extraordinary and superfluous," bought "with the express purpose of selling them." Similarly, buyers were attracted to the positions not because they authorized one to exercise a public function, or even for the wages that they paid, but merely as "an external adornment." In Loyseau's view, the seemingly limitless desire for offices defied the logic of supply and demand, because increases in their number only served to stimulate the market and drive up prices. He concluded that no monarch would ever devise a better means of extracting revenue from his subjects than a "*taille* so immense yet imperceptible, [and] even voluntary and desired, on the ambition and madness of the kingdom's men of leisure."[38]

If *Cinq Livres du droit des offices* indicates the extent to which the practice of venal officeholding could confound even the most systematic of minds, Loyseau's bafflement also reveals how offices could exert so strong a hold over their buyers. Following the sometimes tortured logic outlined in his comments, one can trace changes in the office, from its origins as an alienated prerogative of the monarchy, to a bizarre, irrational thing (the venal office, which is both *meuble* and *immeuble*, a public function as well as a private belonging), to a particular subject who assumes the office in a manner that elevates his status, and back to a thing that may again be sold—indeed, that was originally bought precisely to be sold. Furthermore, in the course of circulation, offices blurred the distinction between possessor and possession, thereby distorting the moral economy of the Old

Regime in fatal ways. Most notably, they separated honor from order. As Loyseau explains, "it is difficult to attribute to vice the honor that belongs to virtue; moreover, those who have no merit whatsoever in themselves believe that they can buy honor with money."[39]

The venal office, then, was a property that could at once possess a person, thus conferring identity and attributes, and yet be owned and alienated in turn. Likewise, its status as a public function, derived from the mystical body of the king, endowed it in the eyes of others with a particular character that existed independently of its buyer, while allowing him to appropriate its attributes, at least temporarily, for himself. In addition, the "rage for office" left those in its grips unable to assess their real self-interest. These qualities—exchangeability, reification, and compulsion—suggest the appearance of a commodity capable of objectifying social relationships in terms of things that can be bought and sold.[40] The gradual and meandering process by which commodification became a governing social rule did not only follow from transformations in politics or the economy, however. Theological and philosophical developments also served to disseminate an understanding of personhood grounded in the self's relationship to spiritual and existential goods. Taken together, these various discourses and practices converged in the culture of self-ownership that became entrenched during the eighteenth century.

The Empire of Possession:
The Council of Trent and the Rise of Spiritual Self-Ownership

In *Cinq Livres*, Loyseau opened the chapter on the Paulette Edict with an anecdote. In January 1608, right before the deadline for the *droit annuel*, he had visited an agent charged with overseeing the market in offices on behalf of the crown. Loyseau's host was swarmed by officers wishing to make their payments. As the hour grew late, and he prepared to close his doors, some who had not yet paid began fretting about whether they would live to see the next day. If not, their offices could not be handed down to a successor. The incident led Loyseau to comment, "Good God, if only we were as careful to save our souls as our office! Both are put at risk at our deaths, but with one rather different factor. After death, we no longer have need for an office; then it is only necessary that our souls be saved for eternity."[41]

Loyseau was not alone, of course, in his concern for the souls of his fellow subjects. The Gallican Church's primary business was to provide access to the means of redemption through the distribution of the sacraments and the exercise of pastoral care. Official doctrine stipulated that clergymen should appeal to the spiritual self-interest of their parishioners in order to encourage and deepen their faith. This policy had been affirmed at the Council of Trent, when the Catholic ecclesiastical hierarchy settled on numerous reforms intended to respond to the challenges posed by Protestantism. Luther, Calvin, and their followers rejected the notion that human effort could ever merit salvation, but the Council determined during its sixth official session, held in 1547, that striving for redemption is efficacious. Citing Paul's epistle to the Hebrews, its decrees made clear that "in order to draw near to God, one must believe that he exists, and that he will reward those who seek him." In addition, it was expected that the devout would "also cast their eyes on eternal recompense, in order to stir themselves from languor, and to encourage themselves in the course of their career." The salvation awaiting the elect stems not only from mercy, but from justice, "as a reward that, according to the promise of God himself, must be faithfully rendered to their good works and their merits."[42]

This general position was further developed in the writings of Council participants, as well as in the new catechism adopted in its wake. In keeping with the general institutional and spiritual bearings of the Reform movement, religious pedagogy and ecclesiastical discipline involved pronouncements on the soul's relationship to its actions as well as to the spiritual gifts that derived from good works.[43] For example, the Spanish Dominican Melchior Cano (ca. 1509–1560), theological emissary of Charles V at Trent, urged the faithful to strive for self-mastery. According to his *Tratado de la victoria de sí mismo*, first published in 1550, body and spirit are possessions of unequal value, and human folly stems from excessive concern for the lesser good. To take one's desires in hand, he advised, it is necessary to approach spiritual work rather as one does its earthly counterpart: "since the capital comes from God, it is our task to furnish the labor." Cano counted grace and virtue among "the greatest goods that we can possess on earth," properties that enable the soul to turn away from worldly pleasures toward the greater reward of eternal life.[44]

The Tridentine catechism, issued in 1566, provided guidelines for putting the Council's reforms into practice. Thus, priests were encouraged to reason with their spiritual charges on the basis of a simple calculation: "all that they can experience and even desire here below that is pleasing, [. . .] they will possess entirely without exception, and with a full abundance." This logic was not, however, intended to negate the exercise of benevolence or the example set by Christ's sacrifice of himself for the world. As the catechism explained, the surest path to salvation is to "persevere in prayer and in the beneficial practice of the sacraments, and finally to fulfill all the duties of charity toward one's neighbor."[45] Possessive aspects of devotion establish the limits of disinterestedness in order to preserve the grounds for accountability. The soul's thoughts and deeds must remain its own if it is to be judged by them, while hope of eternal reward and fear of chastisement provide a clear impetus for virtuous action. This manner of framing the interior life in terms of its relationship to divine recompense recalled the natural sinfulness of the human person, while rooting the attainment of eternal life in heaven to spiritual acquisition.

Although fraught with conflict, the challenges of religious reform were vigorously taken up by French clerics. The crown withheld official sanction of the decrees of the Council of Trent out of concern for its religious independence from Rome, and violence between Catholics and Calvinist Huguenots during the Wars of Religion detracted from the government's efforts to impose a stable confessional order.[46] Nonetheless, the Tridentine program was approved by the theological faculty at the Sorbonne immediately upon its publication. Provincial councils organized between 1581 and 1590 under the auspices of the royal Ordinance of Blois (1580) exhibited clear allegiance to the dictates of Trent, and dozens of seminaries for the training of the parish clergy, while short-lived, were founded during this period. Despite opposition from the Parlement of Paris, which sought to uphold the prerogatives of the Gallican Church, the Assembly of the Clergy signaled its acceptance of the Council's decrees in 1615.[47]

The new orthodoxy stressed the need for souls to relate to themselves and to the objects surrounding them in possessive terms. Believers were accountable for their sins, but also rewarded on the basis of good works and the accumulation of divine gifts. Thus, the French ecclesiastical establishment committed itself to promoting a spiritual variant of the culture of self-ownership. In so doing, it gave at least implicit support to pursuing worldly goods and status. Moral philosophers, economic theorists, authors of comportment manuals, and philosophers also projected an image of the human person as a self-owning, possessive subject. While these developments unfolded under specific conditions and according to particular logics, the broader outcome was to characterize selfhood in terms of the acquisition of spiritual, material, and existential goods.

Although acceptance of the Tridentine reform entailed an affirmation of self-ownership, French theologians expressed their compliance in different ways. The official position, supported by the crown, maintained that men and women are capable of virtue with minimal assistance from God. As the Catechism of the Council of Trent made clear, acquisitiveness in itself poses no threat as long as it is directed toward suitable ends. Proponents of Jansenism, however, refused to concede this point. Their stance was rooted in the Augustinian conviction that the Fall of Adam and Eve had severed the ties between the created world and the heavens, leaving men and women in a state of absolute iniquity.[48] In his *Pensées*, Blaise Pascal described the abjectness of the human condition in especially stark terms. Sin has left us stranded between "nothingness" and "infinity," yet we remain deluded by evil to such an extent that we seek refuge in the depths of pride. The only "true virtue," he concluded, is "to hate ourselves (because our concupiscence makes us hateful), and to seek a being truly worthy of love."[49] This view would have sweeping consequences, not only because it was a source of persistent theological controversy, but also because it reconfigured the relationship between the earthly and heavenly spheres. More specifically, since the self's thoughts and actions could no longer be assessed by divine standards, but only on its own debased terms, it became necessary to identify the distinct laws that govern human behavior.[50]

Jansenists responded to the difficult theological quandaries they raised by making significant contributions to the field of moral philosophy. Among the more visible and influential exemplars of this trend was Pierre Nicole, a former instructor at their stronghold of Port-Royal, whose widely read *Essais de morale* (1671–1679) would be published in several editions and translated into English by none other than John Locke.[51] In his *Essais*, Nicole advanced a doctrine of spiritual individualism as the basis of a distinctly Augustinian moral philosophy. His point of departure was the fundamentally debased character of the human person. Adam's primordial sin alienated him and his progeny from God as well as from the divine aspect of their original nature, leaving a void to be filled by *amour-propre* and the conflict of earthly passions. "Man, by his sin, not only implicated himself in the death of the body and the miseries of this life, but also deprived himself of the life of the soul, that is, of grace, sanctity, and justice," Nicole asserted.[52] It was precisely these attributes that the human person must strive to regain with divine assistance.

In their fallen state, humans lack even the wherewithal for true self-knowledge, a problem that is only exacerbated by their desperate tendency to evade the pain of estrangement rather than confront its source. As a result, each person finds that he has become "a great torture to himself" and "regards himself in some sense as his own worst enemy." So profound is this antagonism that "he makes his happiness consist in forgetting himself, and in drowning himself in this forgetting." The spiritual amnesiac, evicted from Eden, is condemned to wander aimlessly in the world, seeking in the self a vain external reality. As Adam begat Cain and Abel, estrangement begets estrangement. "We are outside of ourselves from the moment of birth," Nicole lamented, "and the soul, occupied from infancy only with exterior things, and the sensations of the body, thereby gives itself up to these familiar objects and feelings and attaches itself to them so strongly that it would not know how to return to itself but by doing extreme violence to itself."[53] Deprived of the immediacy of divine love, the soul turns to its own corrupted, truncated being for consolation, thereby giving rise to the delusions of *amour-propre*. According to Nicole, the self is but a mask to conceal the misery of this fundamental lack, a graven image to worship and to have others worship, deepening the alienation around which human existence has been organized since the Fall.[54] Since human insufficiency is infinite, the depths of *amour-propre* are unfathomable. It is a desire "without limits and without measure," a "tyrannical disposition" that "desires to lord over everything," and demands that "all creatures occupy themselves only with satisfying it, praising it, and admiring it."[55]

Having articulated the state of human existence in such hopeless terms, Nicole was compelled to answer the original query of his treatise: under what conditions is moral action possible? Could the workings of *amour-propre* mimic the exercise of virtue? It is here that *Essais de morale* takes a pragmatic turn. On one hand, self-love pits each against all; on the other, the drive to accumulate "commodities and the pleasures of life" draws social actors into engagement with one another, according to rules of conduct established to protect acquired goods from the brute plundering of one's fellows.[56] Although based on flattery and deceit, these checks on unbounded greed function as if they were inspired by the opposite impulse of disinterested action. So similar are the effects of socialized *amour-propre* and the pure state of charity that the latter is all but unnecessary to assure peaceful existence in a fallen world. According to Nicole's reasoning, "in order to reform the world entirely [. . .], it would require, for want of charity, merely granting to all an enlightened self-love [*un amour-propre éclairé*], which is to discern one's real interests, and to pursue them by the paths that the straightness of reason will reveal."[57]

For Nicole, *amour-propre* and charity are nearly as indistinguishable in cause as in effect. The precarious nature of self-knowledge leaves one uncertain whether intent proceeded from one or from the other. Yet this predicament, paradoxically, establishes the basis for Christian virtue: "knowledge of one's humility makes one over proud, and knowledge of one's pride makes one humble."[58] *Amour-propre* and charity also resemble each other on a more fundamental level, as repercussions of the essential need to love and to be loved. "Love is what dominates him [the human being] and drives him," Nicole observed. "He desires and fears, rejoices and is saddened, only because he loves." It is made clear at several points in the *Essais* that the desire for worldly goods created by *amour-propre* is merely an inferior modulation of the desire for spiritual goods through charity. God "has not only subjected to us all earthly creatures in making us the masters of the world; what is more, he desires to give himself to us, and to make us happy by the possession of himself." To reject this possession amounts to "the refusal to be supremely happy," precisely because it is the only good that the soul can truly seize upon: "God is so much the essential happiness of man, that he is the sole good that man can obtain and possess." The love of God, likewise, is "the only love that is able to arrive at the possession of its object." The Gospel's dictate to surrender earthly delights for divine love, duly noted by Nicole, only reinforces the primacy of possession—in this case, of the real over the ephemeral.[59]

Jacques Esprit, who was both a devoted Jansenist and an associate of the freethinker François de La Rochefoucauld, took Nicole's reasoning to an even more extreme conclusion. His treatise on *La Fausseté des vertus humaines*, published in 1678, attempts to demonstrate that all human action is a function of self-love. Men and women, he argued, are incapable of transcending material concerns to contemplate the delights of heaven by their own power. Given the distance that separates a person from his or her "sovereign good," it would appear reasonable "to seek one's happiness in oneself, and to enjoy the possession [*jouir*] of a good that is so near and toward which one's heart naturally turns, rather than to elevate oneself to the possession of God." Only divine intervention can turn the soul toward its higher end. Self-love blinds humans to such an extent that it makes no sense for Christians to deploy pride to mitigate the other passions, as Nicole had taught. Doing so, Esprit noted, is akin to "wanting to heal the soul's ills with its most dangerous ill." The only recourse is to rely absolutely on God to direct all one's actions, knowing only that grace, and not human merit, makes true virtue possible.[60]

Jansenist moral theologians did not agree on all fronts, but the differences between them were more of degree than of kind. Both Nicole and Esprit characterize humans as compulsively possessive beings whose reactions follow from the calculation of self-interest. They underscore the difficulty of reconciling divine precepts with the workings of fallen souls, thereby necessitating the formulation of moral principles that apply strictly to the terrestrial sphere. The separation that Nicole and Esprit posit between God and humanity therefore had a secularizing effect on how the self was imagined. Their anthropological pessimism left them resigned to the intractability of self-ownership. Even their coreligionist Pascal, who tended to be less forgiving in his judgments, marveled at the "admirable rules" humans had succeeded in deriving from their sinfulness.[61] Since the vast majority of men and women would never overcome their obsession with themselves or with worldly goods, it was a matter of finding ways of coping with this state of affairs, rather than of fundamentally changing it.

These thinkers exerted considerable influence beyond their immediate circle. Historians have focused on Bernard Mandeville, whose *Fable of the Bees* (1714) drew on the lessons of Nicole and his brethren, but a wide array of commentators on explicitly worldly matters had already arrived at similar conclusions on the basis of a utilitarian and mechanistic orientation toward morality.[62] In particular, the mercantilist creeds of the period emphasized the ways in which one could put pride to work. For instance, Antoine Montchrétien observed in his influential *Traité de l'économie politique* (1615) that since its ejection from Eden, humankind has had no choice but to toil for subsistence. It is a matter, therefore, of rendering labor as productive as possible. To this end, Montchrétien called on the kings of France to foster specialization and emulation by exploiting each subject's concern for "his particular profit," a motive so engrained that it had become "a second nature." To increase crop yields and promote economic development, cultivators should therefore be allowed to possess the land they worked "as their own [*en propre*]."[63] Montchrétien's views anticipated the initiatives of Jean-Baptiste Colbert, who as controller-general and head of the navy oversaw French commercial and industrial expansion from the 1660s to the 1680s, and whose principles would continue to inform policy well into the eighteenth century. According to Colbert's mercantilist dogmas, the wealth of the nation depended on maximizing self-sufficiency in essential commodities, while achieving a favorable balance of trade with France's neighbors through the regulation of domestic production and the imposition of tariffs on foreign goods.[64]

This system for ordering the economy had no lack of either critics or champions. Upon Colbert's death in 1683, a satirist speculated that having ransacked France, "master Jean" would "pillage Paradise" for an eternity.[65] In the eyes of his detractors, it was as if Colbert's administration personified the rapacious individual described by Nicole and Esprit. For others, the late statesman had pointed the way toward the apotheosis of commerce. According to Jacques Savary, whose treatise *Le Parfait négotiant* (1675) was dedicated to Colbert, "the providence of God" had dispersed natural resources throughout the world, thus compelling humans to truck and barter in order to meet their needs. While commerce "established union and charity," it did so only through "profit and the desire to elevate oneself." Thus, Savary praised Colbert for fostering the conditions under which merchants could not only amass personal fortunes, but also use this money to purchase "the first offices of *la Robe*" for their descendants.[66] It was with a certain irony that Savary noted how venal officeholding served as a conduit to higher social status, since Colbert had struggled unsuccessfully to end the practice. Yet Savary's remarks point once again to the burgeoning belief that identity is exchangeable, albeit for those whose intelligence and industriousness allow them to excel in commercial enterprises.

The term *commerce* during the seventeenth and eighteenth centuries referred not merely to financial transactions, but to social intercourse more generally.[67] It is unsurprising, then, that conduct manuals placed great emphasis on the "art of pleasing" one's company as a way of making one's associations as profitable as possible. However, unlike many moral philosophers and economic theorists of the period, the authors of these texts tended to offer a less cynical account of human motivations. For instance, Antoine de Courtin's *Nouveau traité de la civilité*, a best-selling guide published in 1671, asserted that true *politesse* stems from humility rather than self-love, a conviction that placed mutual improvement before reciprocal exploitation.[68] Even so, other works in the genre presented a less lofty view of social interaction. To cite one telling example, C. M. D. Contière's *Élements de la politesse*, published around 1700, counseled readers that sinfulness had corrupted the human inclination toward amity. Thus, one should remain cognizant of the irresistible sway of *amour-propre*. Citing Augustine, Contière explained that "our love is nothing but the desire for something in pursuit of pleasure [*l'amour n'est en nous qu'un appétit de quelque chose pour notre plaisir*]" and that "all love is nothing but the love of oneself." Nonetheless, the modest display of one's talents and the tasteful concealment of personal defects that cause displeasure make it possible for self-interested individuals to contribute to one another's happiness while ensuring their own. Thus, although Contière recognized that human nature is by no means flawless, he also argued, as had Nicole, that self-regard could be put to beneficial ends. To do so, he counseled, one must be willing to make oneself a source of gratification for others, who would repay the favor in kind. Unlike Nicole, however, Contière did not equate this manner of relating to others as perverse or demeaning, since it led to the "true love" of one's fellows.[69]

While Jansenists such as Nicole and Esprit tended to associate the moral status quo with utter depravity, they nonetheless shared with economic thinkers and conduct manual writers a desire to show how the demands of labor and exchange could yield a relative advantage for men and women in the world. But for a tiny minority, they reasoned, the torments of hell would come soon enough. In the meantime, there is little choice but to observe the vain strivings of fallen souls with resignation. Likewise, authors such as Montchrétien and Contière, although working in different fields, noted that the change in human nature wrought by original sin is irreversible. Their writings signaled a tendency to account for acquisitiveness in terms of anthropological and social, as well as theological, necessity. If God instills into human beings the desire to pursue happiness through possessing him, it is possible to imagine that they would continue to equate appropriation and fulfillment when separated from their maker. This rationale would find further support, and additional grounding, in new philosophical currents—most notably those advanced by Descartes and Locke.

Descartes, Locke, and the Possessive Turn in Philosophy

Descartes contributed to the emerging culture of self-ownership by providing it with an epistemological framework that structured mental operations around the accumulation of ideas. In the *Discours sur la méthode* (1637), *Méditations* (1644), and other works, he described his personal struggles with doubt and disillusionment while serving as a soldier in the armies of Maurice of Nassau and Maximilian of Bavaria in the early stages of the Thirty Years' War. After casting off every so-called truth he had received, even the reality of his own being, he came to the realization that, if nothing else, he was a thinking subject, since doubt presumed thought. This formulation, the *cogito*, was initially conceived as a minimalist self, one devoid of the particularities of existence. Yet Descartes's view cannot be reduced to this initial, seemingly dispossessive, stance, since the *cogito* also furnishes grounds for identity as innate to the mind, literally "born in us," and thus impossible to deny or to alienate.[70] As Descartes observed, he is above all a *res cogitans*, "a thing that doubts, understands, denies, wills, refuses, and also imagines and feels." Since his fundamental sense of self depends on his status as a thinking subject, he held that "it is not incidental if all of these things belong to me"—a caveat that necessitated the exposition of the source of the mind's powers.[71] The absolute assurance of one's existence, Descartes argued, is the first of many "clear and distinct" ideas vouchsafed us by God, which allow humans to reconstitute and thus control reality, beginning with their own bodies. For instance, one must learn how to direct the passions, which work on the mind through physiological reactions, in ways that serve one's best interests. In addition, Descartes maintained that happiness and moral fulfillment follow from "the acquisition of all the knowledge of which I am capable," on the basis of the interest that known objects hold for the self. Adopting this instrumental stance allows humans to act on the world as artisans practice their craft, and in so doing, "to make ourselves, as it were, the masters and possessors of nature."[72]

Descartes's method made the self the subject of all knowledge and activity. This orientation is announced even in the rhetorical strategy of *Discours de la méthode* and the *Méditations*, both of which are narrated in the first person. Yet this does not entail dismissal of the divine, proof of whose existence figures prominently in Descartes's system. God is not only the first certitude attained by the self after the affirmation of its own existence, but also the guarantor that its subsequent ideas, if perceived clearly and distinctly, accurately represent the world as it is. More generally, Descartes predicated his metaphysical and epistemological innovations on a specific understanding of the relationship between the divine and terrestrial spheres. As he repeatedly makes clear in his works, "God's omnipotence over the universe is completely absolute and free," thus implying that the laws governing creation do not follow static criteria, set for all time, but rather the continual operation of divine will. Humans, despite their weakness, should cherish "the goods that he [God] has given us," and not complain that "he has not bestowed others that we know that we lack, but that he could have granted us."[73]

This line of reasoning did not originate with Descartes. It had been a theological current at least since the thirteenth century, when nominalists such as William of Ockham challenged the Thomist and Scholastic view that God's laws conform to intrinsic moral standards that can be recognized by created beings. Descartes's originality lies in his response to the assertion of divine omnipotence.[74] Since humans have no access to God's rationale in organizing the universe, they must arrive at their own understanding of creation. It was precisely this enterprise that Descartes undertook in part 5 of the *Discours de la méthode*, where he summarizes the work he had completed on *Le Monde*, a Copernican treatise on the physical and moral realms that he had abandoned in the wake of Galileo's condemnation in 1633.[75] The conceit of the discussion was to imagine "what would happen in a new world, if God created somewhere, in an imaginary space, enough matter to compose it." Descartes stipulated that the alternative universe was formed whole, but "out of chaos," and that God "did nothing more than lend his ordinary concurrence to nature, and let it act in according to the laws he had established."[76] It is God's radical transcendence, coupled with his absence, that authorizes Descartes to reconstruct material bodies as pure mechanisms that can move either by themselves or under the direction of the mind. Once humans attain a sufficient knowledge of their workings, he continued, it would be possible to put this expertise to use—for example, in curing "an infinity of maladies, as much of the body as of the mind."[77]

Descartes's manner of argumentation, then, begins with and culminates in the thinking subject. At the moment of the *cogito*, the subject is certain of nothing but its own existence, before gradually and systematically reconstituting the material world around it. A key task in charting this progression was to delineate how the self related not only to physical objects, but also to its mental operations and personal actions. Descartes held that since we have the capacity to act freely—for instance, to withhold assent to an idea until we perceive it clearly and distinctly—we must also be "masters of our actions and thereby merit praise or blame."[78] Likewise, our passions are dictated in large part by desire, which depends on "the acquisition of a good or the avoidance of an evil." Hope, fear, despair, and similar sentiments all follow from one's perceived relationship to a particular object or end, thereby triggering a change in the quantity of blood and humors in one's bodily organs. In the case of joy, for instance, the soul experiences "the enjoyment it has from possessing some good, that the impressions of the brain represent to it as its own."[79] According to this schema, the human person possesses ideas and actions in a double sense. Not only does one make moral calculations on the basis of the personal benefits that accrue from the acquisition of a good (be it moral or material), but one is accountable for the decisions that ensue.

Descartes expressed particular concern about the bounds of both immaterial and material ownership, and he markedly preferred the former to the latter. As he explains in the *Discours de la méthode*, since "there is nothing that is completely within our power except our thoughts," we should adopt a detached demeanor toward everything outside ourselves.[80] He elaborated on this advice in his correspondence with members of various European royal houses. In a letter to his final patron, Queen Christina of Sweden, he described the exercise of free will as "the greatest of all goods," on the grounds that it is the only capability fully under our control and thus "the most fully our own [*le plus proprement nôtre*]." His argument follows from a fundamental premise concerning the nature of possession. "The greatness of a good," he reasoned, "must not only be measured by the value of the thing in which it consists, but principally by the manner in which it is related to us." Similarly, he counseled Elizabeth of Bohemia that "the true office of reason" requires careful consideration of all potential goods within the orbit of our possession in order "to procure for ourselves those that are, in effect, the most desirable."[81]

Descartes's logic promoted self-ownership as an intellectual and moral ideal rather than as justification for the pursuit of worldly riches. He scrupulously applied this standard to his own conduct. His family had risen in status through the purchase of ennobling offices in the Parlement of Brittany, and his father Joachim wished him to pursue a legal career, as did his elder brother Pierre. They failed to convince him to do so, although he later made an unsuccessful bid to purchase the post of lieutenant-general of Châtellerault, which had previously belonged to his maternal grandfather. In the end, Descartes embraced philosophy as his vocation.[82] He explained his decision as a matter of choosing a higher form of possession. While admitting that law and medicine (another subject in which he had trained) "bring honors and riches to those who cultivate them," he added that "I place very little value on the glory that I could not hope to acquire except through false titles."[83] The life of the mind, Descartes indicated, offers the surest means of refining one's will, and therefore of extending the knowledge of oneself and of the outside world around to its utmost limit. In Cartesian terms, the *cogito*, after prevailing over the doubt that once plagued the reality of its very existence, must not risk staking its identity on the dubious foundation of an office that can be bought and sold, or on a profession that sacrifices intellectual purity to social standing. By rejecting traditional sources of honor, whether in military exploits or the exercise of public power, Descartes identified the self and its operations as the most valuable of our belongings, to be guarded before all other considerations.

The refusal to seek the status to which his family aspired fitted squarely within the moral framework that Descartes designed for himself—one that adhered to the principles undergirding his philosophical method. He aimed, above all, to discover the truth according to his own reason. If, as he held, free will "renders us in some fashion similar to God in making us master of ourselves," then the philosopher's duty lies in developing his rational and moral faculties to the greatest possible extent.[84] At the same time, Descartes took care to assure his readers—sympathetic and hostile alike—that his system posed no threat to religious and moral orthodoxies. In correspondence with Marin Mersenne, he confessed the pride he had in his proof of the existence of God, which he believed surpassed those previously advanced. He also acknowledged his willingness to suppress his treatise *Le Monde* out of deference to the Church.[85] In addition, the *Discours* that he published in its stead features a guide to morality based on his desire to "obey the laws and customs of my country," and to remain steadfast in his devotion to "the religion in which God has given me the grace to have been instructed."[86] Although he rebelled against his family's wishes, he held that the imperative to exercise self-control in all things places limits on what the philosopher can outwardly profess, even in the name of reason.

Descartes hoped that his system would win wide acceptance. Yet it continued to attract dogged criticism, especially in the country of his birth, both during his lifetime and long after his death. His attempt to explain the Eucharist in light of his physical theories earned him lasting rebukes from the Gallican ecclesiastical establishment, while the association of Cartesianism with Jansenism did little for either doctrine in the eyes of the authorities. Despite resistance, Descartes's views nevertheless circulated in various salons and other venues where enthusiasts debated the ramifications of the new philosophy for theology, mathematics, physics, and medicine.[87] There was no official, monolithic strand of Cartesianism, but rather a synthesis of a broad range of related positions with different, if intersecting, emphases and adherents. Nicolas Malebranche lent further theological credence to many of Descartes's teachings by adapting them in occasionalist form.[88] During the same period, François Poulain de La Barre marshaled arguments from Cartesian dualism to argue for the intellectual equality of women, on the basis that "the mind has no sex," and that physical differences between the sexes have no bearing beyond the mechanics of reproduction.[89] Charles Perrault, to cite one final instance, upheld Descartes's innovative style of philosophizing as evidence of the superiority of the moderns in the famous Quarrel of the Ancients and Moderns that occupied the republic of letters in the final decades of the seventeenth century.[90]

Between 1700 and 1720, Cartesianism even made significant inroads in two institutions where hostility toward it had been most entrenched: the Jesuit *lycée* and the Sorbonne. His mechanistic philosophy never entirely supplanted the Aristotelian curriculum, however, and it would, by the 1720s and 1730s, begin to lose ground to the ascendancy of Newtonian physics and Lockean sensationalism in France.[91] Although Cartesianism had peaked as a force in natural philosophy, the specific arguments that its founder had advanced regarding spiritual substance came to be seen by theologians as a bulwark against the encroaching tides of radical mysticism and philosophical materialism, two movements that called into question the sanctity of the self as an autonomous, thinking subject. Bossuet lauded the divinely ordained preeminence of the human mind in Cartesian fashion, for example, prior to his involvement in the Quietist affair. By the middle decades of the eighteenth century, Christian apologists had come to rely on Descartes's dualism in upholding the soul's separation from, and superiority to, the teeming mass of matter that surrounded it.[92] Although leading philosophes expressed a marked preference for Locke, while acknowledging the contributions of Descartes, theologians found in the latter's meditations on personhood a source of renewed strength and solace. Cartesianism thus continued to exert a significance influence on Enlightenment-era debates concerning the self.

According to the *Encyclopédie*, Locke's philosophical career was spurred on by his reading of Descartes. He would later claim to surpass his predecessor in method, and his work would ultimately attract an equally stalwart following.[93] His original aim in the *Essay Concerning Human Understanding* (1689) and other writings was to promote the cause of tolerance in the face of mounting sectarian competition, to extend the lessons of Baconian induction to the study of human psychology, to provide justifications for an emerging commercial society, and to settle lingering questions regarding political obligation in the wake of the English Civil War and Restoration.[94] In so doing, he conceptualized the human person as more sensitive to external conditions, while providing a new basis for self-ownership that found enthusiastic reception among the dominant intellectuals in eighteenth-century France.[95]

What attracted Locke's followers, above all, was his sensationalist understanding of the human person, one rooted in its interactions with the external world of things. In contrast to the Cartesian method, which posited the *cogito* as a deductive base from which to extrapolate the workings of the natural world, Locke sought to understand the human mind through an empirical psychology grounded in sensory experience. There are no innate notions, he argued, implying that all thoughts must be acquired, either in the form of simple ideas derived directly through the senses or through the mind's active reflection, which fashions ideas of a complex nature.[96]

While Locke recognized that physical, psychological, and social conditions affect one's experience as a self, he preserved a place for personal identity in terms of the continuity of consciousness.[97] He made his case, however, in a meandering fashion, through a series of thought experiments that considered the possibilities of detaching personal identity from consciousness. For instance, to discredit the Cartesian theory of the *res cogitans*, which holds that, since thought is the essence of spiritual substance, the soul must never cease to think, he considered whether one remains the same person while waking and sleeping if one retains no awareness of the thoughts that occur to the mind in the latter state. Locke's intention in doing so was not to advocate a bifurcation of identity, but to point out the contradictions inherent in the Cartesian system. "To suppose the Soul to think, and the Man not to perceive it, is," he claimed, "to make two Persons in one Man." He likewise found fault with the argument that the mind's attachment to the same body assures the identity of the slumbering subject, since, as he observed, the body's physical constitution undergoes constant change. The defects in his opponents' reasoning lent support to his own position, that ideas originate in the senses, and that the mind, "by compounding those Ideas, and reflecting on its own Operations, [. . .] increases its Stock as well as Facility, in remembering, imagining, reasoning, and other modes of thinking."[98]

Locke confronted these issues in greater depth in "Of Identity and Diversity," a chapter appended to the second edition of the *Essay.* There he defended his view that consciousness provides the fundamental subjective criterion for moral action. "That with which the consciousness of this present thinking thing can join it *self*, makes the same *Person*, and is one *self* with it, and with nothing else; and so attributes to it *self* [emphasis in original], and owns all the Actions of that thing, as its own, as far as that consciousness reaches, and no farther; as every one who reflects will perceive," he observed. This depiction establishes an intimate, possessive relationship between the self and those things that consciousness makes a part of it. Conversely, Locke reasoned that "for whatsoever any Substance has thought or done, which I cannot recollect, and by my consciousness make my own Thought and Action, it will no longer belong to me, whether a part of me thought or did it, than if it had been thought or done by any other immaterial Being any where existing."[99] In other words, one can only own up to that which one already owns. Orthodox theologians and mainstream philosophes would recurrently employ arguments similar to Locke's in their defense of moral agency. They held that self-ownership by definition involves not only the self's appropriation of recognizable ideas and actions, but also accountability for them to other persons and before God.

While it is incorrect to read the *Essay* as establishing a direct epistemological basis for Locke's celebrated account of property in the *Second Treatise of Government* (1690), both texts lend crucial support to the notion that the self maintains a possessive attachment to its existence.[100] The noted natural law theorist Jean Barbeyrac—who translated and commented on the works of Samuel von Pufendorf, an equally eminent figure in the tradition—had no doubt on this point. "Mr. Locke means by the word 'property,'" he observed, "not only the right which one [has] to his goods and possessions, but even with respect to his actions, liberty, his life, his body; and, in a word, all sorts of right."[101] In the *Second Treatise*, Locke developed his own version of natural jurisprudence by arguing that God had granted possession of the world to humankind in common, rather than to Adam alone, as his adversary Robert Filmer and other defenders of absolutism contended. Since humans owe their existence to God as his "workmanship," they are bound to sustain their lives according to "his, not one anothers [*sic*] Pleasure." Their common origins, likewise, prove their natural equality vis-à-vis each other. On the basis of the universal duty of and right to self-preservation, Locke contended that it is necessary and just for humans to appropriate parts of the donation God had granted to them.[102] For instance, "the Fruit, or Venison, which nourishes the wild *Indian*, [. . .] must be his, and so his, *i.e.*, a part of him, that another can no longer have any right to it, before it can do him any good for the support of his life." Locke insisted that each individual retained an unassailable, inalienable "*Property* in his own *Person* [emphasis in original]."[103] Through labor, this property could extend to material possessions beyond the self. While the dictates of natural law originally limited personal appropriation to use—that is, one could only own what one could enjoy without spoilage—Locke recognized that the invention of money made unbounded accumulation possible, up to and including the labor of others. This development did not, however, alter the original dynamic of ownership of the self, "that though the things of Nature are given in common, yet Man (by being Master of himself, and *Proprietor of his own Person*, and the Actions or *Labour* of it) had still in himself *the great Foundation of Property* [emphasis in original]."[104]

Scholars continue to debate the possible implications of Locke's position, in particular the nature of property as defined in the *Second Treatise*,
and the extent to which it served as a justification or critique of economic
exploitation.[105] One conclusion remains certain. In Locke's verbal constitution of the individual, whether in its moral or political guises, being
a self now definitely entailed having a self. Even if property in external
things is conditional, as James Tully has argued, rather than an absolute
right derived from nature, one's property in one's person is nonetheless
inviolable.[106] Through God's creation, individuals come to own their existence by virtue of the exertion of their minds and bodies. As authors of all
their conscious thoughts and actions, they are accountable for them before
civil and spiritual authorities. The self-owning subject stands as the rightful proprietor of both the material and the moral goods it produces.

For Locke's French readers, the theory of property in one's person
held startling implications both in its political and philosophical guises.
The social imaginary of the Old Regime made corporate entities—such
as the three estates, the Church, manufacturing and commercial guilds,
even the king's two bodies—the basis of identity. The *Two Treatises of
Government*, and the tradition of natural law on which it drew, turned
this order on its head. Now the individual became the fundamental, foundational element of society. The same dynamic held in the *Essay*, insofar
as it argued that philosophers and theologians should henceforth ground
personal identity in the self's conscious, possessive relationship to its
thoughts and actions. Thus Voltaire and Condillac, perhaps Locke's two
most conspicuous disciples among the philosophes, would follow him in
insisting upon the moral accountability and rational self-governance of
the human person. The latter would even seek to recruit Jesuit theologians such as René-Joseph Tournemine into a broad intellectual front for
the propagation of mainstream Enlightenment ideals.[107]

Locke's vocabulary also found perhaps more surprising uses. During
the campaign to abolish trade corporations in the 1770s, a royal edict an-
nouncing the measure drew on Lockean language to defend the government's position, which held not only that God had founded "the property
of all men" on "the right to work," but that "this right is the first, the most
sacred, and the most imprescriptible of all."[108] The crown's argument here
echoed those of Bigot de Sainte-Croix in his treatise calling for reform,
where he asserted that the economic right to buy and sell freely derived
from the "right of property, of which it is at once the effect and the guarantee."[109] At the same time, members of a corporation could turn such
an argument against the crown, as when the *Six Corps* of Paris asserted
that their privileges constituted both a property and an extension of their
professional identity, which they could not rightfully be compelled to alien-

ate.[110] Members of the Paris Community of Booksellers and Printers also utilized a related rationale against challenges to what they maintained was an exclusive right to publish works that had been purchased from their original authors.[111]

On a number of fronts, the culture of self-ownership informed how French subjects viewed themselves and understood their existence. While those in possession of a venal office or financially backed privilege could draw on Lockean arguments to support their rights to them as owners, they also had recourse, as did their contemporaries, to parallel lines of reasoning. The Cartesian aspiration to render the human person a "master and possessor of nature" conditioned men and women to regard the world around them in terms of appropriation. Although the writings of Descartes remained out of reach for most people, the teachings of pastors and confessors were far more accessible, and Catholic orthodoxy of the period stressed the desirability, even the necessity, of accumulating spiritual goods. All these factors, taken together, suggest the extent to which the human person was increasingly defined by the ideas, actions, and other belongings that it could make its own.

Descartes's writings, and those of Loyseau, Nicole, and other French contemporaries, confronted the same problematic that Locke later took up in his epistemological and political works: that of fixing the self's relationship to its possessions. The task became all the more urgent as traditional hierarchies became increasingly less authoritative and less directly relevant to the actual functioning of the social order. The origins of this lapse involved both the crown's manipulation of the system of venal officeholding, and, on a conceptual level, a new mechanistic philosophy that contested the Aristotelian ideal of a harmonious cosmic hierarchy. More and more, the individual emerged as a credible alternative to the estate as the ultimate source of identity.

Theologians, philosophers, and jurists not only reflected on this state of affairs in their writings, but also intervened in it. In so doing, they fostered the coalescence of a culture of self-ownership that could furnish meaning and direction to the desire for control over one's ideas and actions, along with the accumulation of material objects. Their efforts encompassed an array of positions rather than a single platform. Descartes tended to stress the possibilities for self-mastery more than did his Jansenist counterparts, even if he was careful to note that the passions of the soul and the body could never be completely brought under control. His moral views, then, more closely resemble those of mainline representatives of post-Tridentine orthodoxy, and especially its Jesuit variants, which tended to give individual believers a considerable degree of latitude. Locke, for his part, emphasized the acquisitive nature of identity to an even greater degree than had Descartes, since he asserted, against the doctrine of the *cogito*, that the self was founded not on its innate ideas, but on the accumulation and appropriation of experience.

These pronouncements represent a range of opinions despite their agreement on an essential tenet: the self's possessive attachment to its person. The point did not go unchallenged. On the contrary, it triggered a virulent backlash that ultimately developed into a rival culture of personhood—one based on dispossession—that would continue to challenge the legitimacy of self-ownership until the end of the Old Regime and beyond.

French Mysticism and the Origins of the Culture of Dispossession

Like self-ownership, the culture of dispossession emerged in a somewhat halting fashion. It originated in Counter-Reformation theological developments, which themselves had a long doctrinal history, before entering into Enlightenment-era political, economic, and philosophical debates on a wide array of issues. The Council of Trent's admission of the soul's self-interested desire for salvation coincided with a surge in devotional fervor, most notably among followers of mysticism. In the aftermath of the Wars of Religion, committed French Catholics increasingly turned away from violence and toward engendering a deeper sense of spiritual intimacy. This "mystic invasion," as Henri Bremond characterized it, was spearheaded by the translation in the first three decades of the seventeenth century of works by Catherine of Siena (1347–1380), Teresa of Avila (1515–1582), John of the Cross (1542–1591), and other prominent theologians.[112] In addition, members of the Society of Jesus, beginning with the order's founder, Ignatius Loyola (1491–1556), composed numerous prayer manuals that included advice on how to achieve exalted states of spiritual abandon.[113] An indigenous current of mystical spirituality began to take form during this period, represented by theologians such as Laurent de Paris (1563–1631) and Benoît de Canfield (ca. 1562–1610), whose writings exhibited particular concern for the soul's union with God through the suppression of the intellectual faculties.[114] The arrival of Teresa's Carmelite order in 1601 sparked a mystic revival behind the walls of the cloister, and figures such as Marie of the Incarnation (1566–1618) became models of devotion.[115] This "French school" of mysticism reached its apogee in the theology of the founder of the Congregation of the Oratory, Cardinal Pierre de Bérulle (1575–1629), with its emphasis on how Christ's Incarnation conditioned the possibilities for human deification.[116] It was perhaps François de Sales (1567–1622), the bishop of Geneva and founder of the Order of the Visitation of Holy Mary, who most deeply informed the preoccupation with saintly indifference that would come to characterize French mysticism as professed by its two most visible advocates, Jeanne-Marie Guyon and François de Fénelon, during the Quietist affair of the 1690s.[117]

Decades before this controversy, French mystics had already come under fire for making pronouncements that appeared to deviate from post-Tridentine orthodoxy. During the 1640s, Jean-Pierre Camus, the former bishop of Belley, then serving the archdiocese of Rouen, sparred with the Jesuit theologian Jacques Sirmond over the limits of the pure love of God. Camus's position, which he elaborated in works such as *De la Gloire de Dieu* (1637) and *La Défense du pur amour* (1640), distinguishes between true charity, which he considered to be a "gift of God," and "interested love," which is "entirely turned back toward the self." Actual charity describes the soul's love of God, "for the sole good and interest of God," without reference to oneself. In contrast, to love God "in order to be compensated" exposes "a servile or mercenary mind," whose calculations would ultimately prove self-defeating.[118] Sirmond, however, asserted in his response to Camus, *La Défense de la vertu* (1641), that perfect charity is impossible in this life. In addition, the scriptural injunction to love one's neighbor as oneself led him to conclude that "I must love myself" out of concern for salvation. To this end, fear of chastisement and hope of redemption gives us the patience to await the "possession" of eternal happiness that God has promised. As for Camus's charge that to keep one's reward in view is to harbor evil motives, Sirmond countered that it would apply only if one desired temporal incentives to the exclusion of supernatural benefits, which God also desires for us.[119]

Both Sirmond and Camus appealed to the Council of Trent and to the authority of Augustine in support of their arguments, but the two theologians arrived at drastically different conclusions. They diverged, first and foremost, in their contrasting notions of how the soul should relate to God—and, by extension, what it means for the self to possess an object in general. Sirmond maintained that there is a form of "self-love [*amour-propre*]" that allows one to love God entirely while not losing sight of "one's own particular good."[120] According to Camus, claiming a middle ground between disinterestedness and self-regard is untenable. He defined the "possession [*jouissance*]" of God as "uniting oneself to something, for the good and the advantage that reverts to the thing to which one is united."[121] Thus, while Camus believed that the soul should be joined with the divine, and that grace serves as a conduit for their union, he maintained that human beings could not view the benefits that followed from this outcome as accruing to them personally. Otherwise, one would succumb to the fallacy that the soul could in some way make use of God in order to obtain salvation. As Camus was well aware, Augustine had rejected this position in *De Doctrina Christiana*, asserting that the soul must distinguish enjoyment, which means "to hold fast" to a thing "for its own sake," from use, or the employment of "whatever it may be to the purpose of obtaining what you love." On this view, one should strive to enjoy and to attach oneself to the divine persons of the Trinity, while merely making passing use of the things of this world.[122]

In clarifying his argument, Camus did not limit himself to theological and scriptural allusions. He also translated his views into terms with which his readers would be more immediately familiar: property in things and offices. One should not hope to "possess God [. . .] like the moveable or immovable goods that we possess here below in ownership." Rather, the true way to possess God is to be possessed by him, "to want to be God's." In his discussion of mystical concepts such as "dispossession" and "annihilation," Camus explained that believers should surrender their wills to divine command in the manner of "resigning an office or a benefice"— that is, by returning them to their divine source, just as those who vacated an office or benefice allowed their former positions to revert back to the crown or the Church.[123] In contrast to Descartes, then, Camus did not regard the soul's intellectual faculties as its most precious possession. These powers are of a transitory nature and thus alienable to God, with the promise that doing so leads to greater closeness with the divine. His understanding of the human person's relationship to its potentially defining elements, such as the will, bears a resemblance to Loyseau's claim that offices cannot logically be considered the absolute property of their holders. In both instances, the ideal self is required to be capable of surrendering attributes that it once held dear.

Camus's analogies between spiritual and material goods show that, like many of his contemporaries, he was committed to establishing at least a semblance of order with regard to how men and women defined themselves in terms of what they could claim to possess. As his passing comments about officeholding suggest, he also held venality in grave suspicion. During the convocation of the Estates-General in 1614, the last such meeting before 1789, Camus proved to be one of the more vocal critics of the practice. His speeches bemoaned the fate of "venal France," and he demanded that his listeners contemplate the disaster that would ensue "if she finds a buyer." The king's "sacred and inviolable house," he went on, "is profaned by this monster of simony; this venality of duties and offices takes hold of its entryways, doors, rooms, [. . .] indeed even reaching to those who guard the sacred person of Your Majesty." Camus's warning had a real, but short-lived, effect. In the wake of massive protests from members of all three orders, Louis XIII promised in March 1615 to suspend the sale of offices. However, he reversed himself less than two months later.[124]

In hindsight, Camus's efforts to uproot venality appear to foreshadow the culture of dispossession that only emerged as a full-fledged alternative to prevailing doctrines of self-ownership during the controversies surrounding Quietism. In denying the soul's possessive attachment to God and divine gifts, Camus anticipated Fénelon's defense of the pure love of God, a stance that triggered controversy on a far more massive scale. The following two chapters trace the repercussions of the Quietist affair in late seventeenth- and early eighteenth-century theological polemics over how the soul should relate to spiritual goods as well as to its own desires and actions. Fénelon, like his spiritual mentor Guyon, advocated a form of mysticism that made self-annihilation an explicit ideal. In sharp contrast, Bossuet and his supporters alleged that this view introduced heretical elements into the mystical tradition. They also believed that it threatened to deprive the soul of the impetus to love God, since devotion should be motivated in part by the contentment that spiritual gifts, and ultimately salvation, bestow. Despite repeated opportunities for rapprochement, the prelates could not settle their differences. This failure stemmed not only from their adoption of opposing logics of personhood, but also from their relative positions on the style of governance pursued by Louis XIV, a matter that in turn involved the nature of the monarchy and the status of its subjects.

2 The Challenge of Mysticism

To all appearances, on the eve of the Quietist affair (1694–1699), Christian mystics held a privileged position in France. They had permeated not only the Carmelite and Jesuit orders, but also the *dévot* circle at court. Their numbers included pupils of the Maison royale de Saint Louis at Saint-Cyr, the school for noblewomen established in 1686 by Louis XIV's morganatic wife, Françoise d'Aubigné, marquise de Maintenon. A prelate of the highest rank—François de Fénelon, the royal tutor and future archbishop of Cambrai, the wealthiest diocese in the kingdom—also immersed himself in the new spirituality.

Yet the golden age of Christian mysticism would prove not long for this world. By the 1680s, religious authorities had come to suspect its followers of heretical perversions of the faith. The tradition became tainted by associations with the Spanish priest Miguel de Molinos (1628–1696), whose *Guía espiritual* (1675), according to the papal bull *Coelestis pastor* (1687), advocated indifference toward salvation and a passivity toward the desires of the flesh.[1] It was Molinos's belief, so his critics charged, that "natural activity" is "the enemy of grace," since "God wants to act in us, and without us." This ideal of devotion entails a total diffidence toward spiritual goods: "the soul must think of neither recompense nor punishment, neither heaven nor hell." As for self-comportment, Molinos was accused of teaching that if free will is truly surrendered to God, along with "the care and the knowledge of our soul," then it would be "no longer necessary to be troubled by temptations, or to put up any active resistance to them."[2]

Mysticism was by no means a novel presence—the tradition has a history longer than Christianity itself—but its advocates fell under intensified scrutiny in the seventeenth century. This change in attitude stemmed from shifts in both doctrinal content and the context. Clerics like Molinos appeared to extend the ideal of indifference, long an element in mystical devotion, to a reductio ad absurdum. His assertion that the "life of renunciation" left the soul uncertain if "it is living or dead, if it is lost or saved, or if it consents or resists, for it makes reference to nothing," gave the impression of total disregard for one's spiritual condition or fate.[3] In contrast, "orthodox" mystical theologians rarely claimed that the soul should jettison all interest in the gifts granted by God, much less in the promise of salvation. Thus François de Sales encouraged penitents in his *Introduction à la vie dévote* (1609) to purge themselves of the "taste for sin" by meditating, not only on the chastisements awaiting the wicked, but also on "what goods from God" those granted eternal life "have from God to enjoy."[4] In like manner, Cardinal Bérulle's *Discours de l'état et les grandeurs de Jésus* (1623) waxed poetic concerning the sublime delights awaiting souls when Christ "lifts them even up to the sight and possession of his goods and grandeurs, giving them access, entry, and standing in his palace, in his paradise, and in his eternity."[5]

In light of the post-Tridentine affirmation of spiritual goods and the soul's status as a self-owning subject, mystic doctrines that cast even a shadow of a doubt on the desire for beatitude struck terror into the hearts of ecclesiastical authorities. Vigilant clerics railed against perceived affronts to the Church's teachings on the need to participate in one's own redemption through acts of faith and the exercise of moral responsibility. In 1682, Cardinal Innico Caracciolo, archbishop of Naples, sounded the alarm against "Quietists" (his term) for their pursuit of absolute tranquility, or quietude, during which all active striving effectively ceases.[6] Pope Innocent XI's judgment against Molinos, though partially coerced, gave additional impetus to a burgeoning anti-mystic movement throughout Europe.[7]

The challenge of mysticism assumed a particularly threatening aspect in France. The popular teachings of Jeanne-Marie Guyon coupled a call for passivity with a sustained assault on the self's appropriation of spiritual goods and material objects. This radical form of spirituality—which Guyon held to be accessible to all, and which came to hold sway over Fénelon—aggravated tensions at the heart of the Catholic Reform movement. It exemplified the intensification of devotion encouraged by the reformers, but at the cost of undermining the soul's interest in salvation, a key component of the Tridentine catechism. Its disdain for traditional forms of religious observance also challenged the Church's campaign to reinforce the role of a morally and intellectually engaged priesthood in the lives of believers. Moreover, in the hands of her disciple Fénelon, Guyon's theology upset the careful balance between God and Mammon that prevailed in Bourbon France, where the Church provided liturgical trappings and technical expertise—as well as access to lucrative benefices and other forms of material support—in exchange for the government's vigilance in enforcing the doctrinal status quo.[8] With this arrangement under siege, the noted theologian Jacques Bénigne Bossuet, bishop of Meaux and former tutor of the king's eldest son, took up the cause of Gallican orthodoxy.

The ensuing conflict between Fénelon and Bossuet over Guyon's mysticism, known as the Quietist affair, represented the first major clash between competing views of personhood that had arisen around the problematic of being and having a self. For Bossuet and his supporters, it was imperative to defend the soul's prerogatives of self-ownership, which justified the accumulation of theological virtues and other divine gifts as personal effects. In sharp contrast, Guyon and Fénelon opposed these views in radically dispossessive terms. For them, the absolute desire for God eclipsed the soul's hopes of eternal recompense and even compromised the ability to govern one's thoughts and actions.

This ideal of mystic abandon found expression in treatises, prayer manuals, letters of spiritual direction, and political writings that put forth an alternative vision of God's place in the world. Not unlike his Jansenist and Cartesian contemporaries, Bossuet regarded divine transcendence as authorizing human self-ownership in both religious and temporal matters, whereas Fénelon sought to mitigate—if not extinguish—the separation between creator and created. More was at stake in the Quietist affair, then, than the doctrinal status of mysticism. The conundrums that emerged out of the debate would not be resolved with Bossuet's apparent triumph over Fénelon in 1699. Rather, their contradictory stances toward the self's possessive capacities set the battle lines along which the nature and attributes of personhood would continue to be contested throughout the eighteenth century.

Madame Guyon and the Conversion of Fénelon

But for Madame Guyon's teachings, the contest between Fénelon and Bossuet would not have unfolded in the manner it did, and might perhaps never have occurred at all. Voltaire would later dismiss Guyon in Le Siècle de Louis XIV (1751) as hopelessly "lost in mystic reveries;" nonetheless, her life and works served as models for contemporary and latter-day followers to emulate, even in the face of severe persecution.[9] Fénelon—theologian, archbishop, and courtier—counted among the most notable of her disciples. His unwavering commitment to her cause would trigger his dispute with Bossuet, during which the differences separating the cultures of self-ownership and dispossession would become strikingly evident.

Madame Guyon was born Jeanne-Marie Bouvier de La Motte in 1648, the daughter of Claude Bouvier, a minor nobleman who served as *procureur*

du roi in the town of Montargis. After a perfunctory education, she was
married in 1664 to Jacques Guyon du Chesnoy, the scion of a wealthy family whose father had helped to oversee the construction of the Canal de
Briare, connecting the Seine and Loire rivers, under Henri IV's chief minister Maximilien de Béthune, duc de Sully. The marriage was plagued by
grief—not only over Guyon's loss of two of her five children in infancy, but
also owing to her parents' premature deaths and her family's prolonged
struggles with illness.[10]

Guyon had in her youth attempted to enter the Order of the Visitation,
although her parents had forbidden her to do so. Now, during her trying
years of marriage, she sought solace in mystic devotion. Her autobiography (composed 1682–1709; published 1720) describes a transformation
she underwent after a chance encounter with a Franciscan on the feast
day of Saint Mary Magdalene in 1668. Upon hearing his counsel, she was
immediately overcome by the presence of the divine. In terms resembling
the famous depiction of ecstasy in Saint Teresa's *Vida*, Guyon likened the
piercing sensation to a "very deep wound, as exquisite [*délicieuse*] as it
was loving."[11] That evening she first felt the self-annihilating effects of
God's love, which she claimed to have supplemented with a brutal regime
of torment aimed at hastening estrangement from her own body, by rendering its functions as unpleasant as possible. She tells of wearing beneath
her clothes a belt studded with iron points, wrapping her body in burrs
and thorns, keeping a piece of wormwood in her mouth, and tainting what
little food she ate with colocynth (*Citrullus colocynthis,* an extremely bit-
ter-tasting fruit with strong purgative effects).[12]

Yet Guyon would not be satisfied with the mere mortification of the
flesh, no matter how apparently rigorous. The *Vie* recounts the gradual
surrender of her mental and spiritual capacities, or the "annihilation of
powers," in which the soul "finds itself little by little void of any particular
will [*volonté propre*], [. . .] in order to want only what God does and
wills."[13] She consummated this union with the divine by entering into a
contract with the Infant Jesus, whom she now regarded as her "divine husband."[14] Her spirit of renunciation ultimately extended to an inability to
perceive her own sense of self. In the final passages of her autobiography,
she reported that "my state has become simple and invariable. Its source is
a profound annihilation, that finds nothing nameable [*nominable*] in me."
She likened her very being in this condition to "a drop of water engulfed
by the sea, [. . .] with no interest in, memory of, or occupation with oneself, except in God."[15]

Familial obligations often kept Guyon from her spiritual exercises. She
received encouragement, however, from François La Combe, a Barnabite
spiritual director whom she met in 1671, and who would go on to exert

a powerful influence on her subsequent career. The death of her husband in 1676 freed the twenty-eight-year-old widow to devote herself entirely to God. In 1680, on the anniversary of her first mystical experience, all her doubts regarding her vocation miraculously subsided.[16] This newfound sense of purpose entailed abandoning her surviving children to the care of her family, which, she explained in a letter to her half-brother, the cleric Dominique de La Motte, was a matter of defying "the sentiments of nature for those of grace." To this end, she granted him control over most of her fortune, which at the time amounted to 70,000 livres in yearly income. For herself she reserved a pension of 1,200 livres, along with several thousand more in ready funds, much of which she apparently gave away as alms, thus necessitating additional requests for money.[17]

Guyon decided to take her daughter with her on her travels and left instructions on how her sons were to be raised.[18] Her message to her elder son explained that God was now his father and the Virgin Mary his mother, and that she had surrendered her material possessions to provide for his education. To her younger son, who she hoped would enter the priesthood, she left a cross, a portrait of the Virgin, and relics. She wrote to him that these mementos were intended "to encourage you by their example to spill your blood, if necessary, to support our faith and religion."[19] Although Guyon would later visit her children for brief periods, she never resumed primary responsibility for their care. By rejecting her role as mother, she cast off a dimension of her personality and prepared to serve as a spiritual mentor to others. In so doing, she advanced her campaign to abandon everything to which she felt a personal, emotional, and therefore possessive attachment.

Severing ties with her family, Guyon headed first to Paris, where she donated a large sum of money for the support of the *nouvelles catholiques*— young women who had recently converted from Protestantism. She then set out on a peripatetic journey through Savoy, eastern France, and surrounding areas. At Gex, she was reunited with La Combe, whom Jean d'Arenthon d'Alex, bishop of Geneva, appointed as her spiritual director.[20] Not content with privately advising those she met on her travels, she sought out a wider audience through the writing and publication of devotional guides. One such text, *Règle des associés à l'Enfance de Jésus*, most likely compiled at Grenoble in the mid-1680s, established the guidelines for a new religious confraternity. Initiates resolved to extinguish all remnants of possessive self-love, or *propriété*. Guyon defined this as a call "to renounce ourselves, and to strip ourselves of all the rights that we have to ourselves and to our actions."[21]

As its name suggests, the aim of the Associés à l'Enfance de Jésus was to imitate the Infant Jesus, with prayer serving as the conduit. The manual outlined the degrees of spiritual meditation through which the soul must progress, through which one gradually surrenders one's words, thoughts, and feelings to divine will. Penitents were directed to seek a quiet space for turning inward toward themselves and beyond the reach of worldly distractions. With practice, they would learn to allow "God to act in them without involving themselves in his work, and without willing it or realizing it." The liturgy accompanying these exercises anticipated the desired end. The *Règle* outlined model prayers for followers to recite, such as "O Jesus my divine Master! [. . .] Make of me what you please. I give myself to you without reservation. [. . .] I abandon myself forever to your whim." While the provision would appear to contradict the message that the soul must suspend its will, the instructions also allowed for the simple repetition of words and phrases as they came to the mind. The overarching aim of the exercises was to arrive at a state in which all "care for oneself" would be replaced by "the direction of God," thus leaving one "indifferent" toward both "worldly and eternal goods."[22]

Along with advice regarding prayer, the *Règle* told how to conduct oneself while engaged in other activities. Associates were expected to keep regular hours, attend mass daily, and take the Eucharist frequently. Time was set aside for prayer at midnight, then upon rising, and once more in the evening—a regime that suited those who had obligations during the day. The twenty-fifth of each month was reserved for more intense devotions, which included fasting. Each member also embarked on an annual spiritual retreat. At all times, talk of frivolous matters was forbidden, as was excessive attention to one's appearance. There were financial duties as well. Wealthy followers were called on to give generously to the needy, while those of lesser means were to donate their time and labor. Clergy affiliated with the order were implored to cultivate the "interior life" of their parishioners by preparing catechisms that emphasized prayer led by the heart rather than the mind.[23] Those who followed these rules, and were thereby transformed into the children of Christ, would differ in marked ways from the corrupt offspring of Adam and Eve. They would also depart from strict adherence to the tenets of post-Tridentine Catholicism. In particular, Guyon called on her followers to adopt a stance of indifference, not only toward "every personal inclination," but also toward "all temporal or eternal goods." Since divine will, rather than human impulses, determined the movements of the soul, mind, and body, it followed that "one who is truly abandoned can no longer sin."[24]

Guyon now began to convey the experience of pure love in detailed theological terms. Correspondence from the 1680s, her most active period, endlessly promoted renouncing one's place in the world in preparation for dispossessing the self. Progress in the mystical vocation, she taught, entails passage from "a love that possesses its object" to "a love that destroys its subject."[25] The use of grammatical metaphor is especially apt, because it captures the principal effect of mystical devotion on the self—to reduce the soul to a mere object, fated for destruction. Gradually, but definitively, the soul's sense of "possessive self-love [propriété]" narrows as the flow of charity expands, to the point that no obstacles remain to "losing oneself in the divine ocean."[26] The self, then, is not merely misplaced or forgotten. Rather, it is absorbed into God. Abandoned entirely, with no faculties of its own, "the soul is left without distinctions: God is the soul, and the self [moi] is no longer me."[27]

Although Guyon often addressed herself to male disciples, La Combe and Fénelon being the most notable, she regarded women as more readily adept at the mystical vocation. Whereas men "usually desire to accord reason, science, and experience with that which God gives to them," the natural humility of women renders them "more suitable for allowing free rein to naked truths."[28] To illustrate God's preference for the poor and the weak, the Illuminist theologian Jean-Philippe Dutoit-Membrini, a devoted admirer of Guyon, included in his 1767 edition of her correspondence a letter from a woman whom she had met during her travels around Grenoble in the mid-1680s.[29] In the sprawling five volumes of Guyon's correspondence that he assembled, this woman's testimony is a rare interpolation of another's voice—other than excerpts from Fénelon's correspondence with Guyon—and offers a telling glimpse of how others received and implemented Guyon's counsel.

The woman began by praising the virtues of deprivation. If God happens to grant a novice certain favors in the preliminary stages of mystical devotion, it is only a temporary indulgence, which, once withdrawn, reveals the fundamental destitution of the self. The annihilation of the soul is necessary precisely because its poverty is incommensurate with the pricelessness of the spiritual goods entrusted to it. Grace functions to purge the soul of "all earthly things," precipitating the destruction of the soul within the divine. As if to replicate this union in her text, the anonymous writer seems compelled to convey to God himself, rather than to Guyon, the effects of divine love on a creature now resigned to its own negation: "You have created *something* of the soul by your grace, but through yourself you have created of it a *nothing*. [. . .] [Y]ou came yourself to pull it from the nothingness of your grace, that is to say, from the assurance and the support that it found in this same grace."[30] Despite this reversal, the dynamics of mystical transformation move once more from extreme want to the fullness of being facilitated by the absence of self-ownership. The soul ultimately exists, then, merely as an effect of pure love. In this state, Guyon's interlocutor confessed, "There is no longer a self [moi]. [. . .] It is a thing that I neither worry over nor assume any knowledge of, and I do not know what spirit governs it." Incapable of regard for, or even awareness of, the existential site that she once occupied, the woman related to the divine in forgetting herself: "You take the place of everything in the soul, and I am unable to linger over any object but you alone."[31]

Guyon's attention to the states induced through prayer typifies in certain respects the highly charged yet systematic tendencies of post-Tridentine spirituality.[32] However, it also departs from orthodox standards when denying the soul's interest in gleaning benefits from proximity to God. In contrast, the anonymous *Secret de l'oraison mentale* (1680) warns of the dangers inherent in spiritual "quietude" and advises readers to assess the value of prayer by "the profit that you derive from it."[33] The distinctions between Guyon's methods and those of her contemporaries could hardly be clearer. She counseled that advanced stages of prayer give way to a state of utter passivity; the soul, having been seized by God, ceases to function as itself. Orthodox guides, in contrast, affirmed the active role of one's mental faculties even in the presence of the divine.

Guyon's fullest treatment of mystical prayer—*Le Moyen court et très facile de faire oraison* (1685)—continued to assert the virtues of abandon, defined as the "stripping of all care for ourselves," which extended to possessions of any kind.[34] For novices, Guyon recommended the practice of "meditative reading," during which one deliberately assimilates passages into the mind, as if physically digesting them.[35] As she further advised in a letter to Pierre Poiret, the editor of her autobiography, reading presents more than an opportunity to appropriate a series of truths. Rather, it is precisely one's lack of comprehension that indicates the need of "working toward dying to oneself" until the meaning of the text becomes clear.[36]

This way of consuming texts accompanies the first stage of prayer, "meditation," the aim of which is to place oneself before God. In the next stage, the "prayer of simplicity," one seeks to sustain divine presence, "not to enjoy the possession [*jouir*] of God but to be as he wishes." While so engaged, she noted, the soul may experience periods of "drought," when God seems absent, but such trials serve to foster the lack of self-regard necessary for advancing to true self-abandonment. In describing the effects of this state, Guyon had recourse to a formula employed in writings such as the *Règle*. It leads to "the donation of all of oneself" to God—not only during prayer, but permanently—so that the soul is deprived of its individual powers of reflection, reason, and will. Such indifference knows no bounds; it extends "both physically and spiritually, toward all worldly and eternal goods." Once the soul enters into the "prayer of simple presence," its activity conforms to divine dictates. The ultimate end of mystical observance, Guyon repeatedly asserted, is to uproot "possessive self-love [*pro-*

priété]" and "all that is human and of one's own industry."[37] Nothing else ensures that God alone, rather than one's particular, mercenary designs, governs one's conduct in all matters.

Guyon's definitive endorsement in the *Moyen court* of mysticism's dispossessive effects provoked fears that her theology might undermine the basis for Christian morality. As if in anticipation of this reaction, she took care to stipulate, albeit in somewhat ambiguous terms, that her advice did not promote laxity toward sin. Her method, she claimed, aided followers in "defeating every vice and acquiring every virtue," because a soul that surrenders its own will "cannot desire to do anything that could displease the beloved."[38] At the same time, she also made clear that the soul had to be rendered completely passive in order to surrender its faculties; otherwise, one "would never consent to it."[39]

According to her detractors, such admissions bore a disturbing resemblance to the doctrines for which Molinos had been condemned. Total passivity, they feared, left one susceptible to corrupting influences with no recourse to the powers of the will. Guyon's association with La Combe, whose teachings were even more extreme, further compromised her credibility. As La Combe argued in his *Maximes spirituelles*, composed during the same period as the *Règle*, the purpose of prayer is to effect a "union of essences" between the human and the divine, so that God assumes complete power over one's soul. Penitents thus lose all concern for the esteem of others, and even more significantly, for the course of their thoughts or actions, which no longer bear any relationship to the self as a subject of experience. La Combe encouraged his followers to enter into this "void without distinction," even if it floods the soul with "the deepest, and I dare say most uncomfortable temptations." What is more, ridding the soul of all vestiges of self-ownership requires a willingness to "die to virtue," and to be led from "precipice to precipice, and from abyss to abyss, as if lost." In a bizarre turn of logic, La Combe asserted that it was precisely the infinite magnitude of God's grandeur that rendered "even impurity a means of glorifying himself."[40]

Despite assurances to the contrary, critics could find at least indirect evidence linking Guyon's and La Combe's views to those of Molinos. The pair soon began to attract the attention of ecclesiastical authorities. While they were in Geneva and Savoy, rumors emerged concerning the nature of their relationship, and these suspicions caught up with them in Paris. The scandal that had erupted over Molinos's writings provoked Guyon's brother to share with François Harlay de Champvallon, archbishop of Paris, his concern that La Combe was a Quietist heretic and involved in sexual impropriety with his sister. Guyon speculated that La Motte had betrayed her out of resentment, since she had declined to grant him control over a sum of money that she had allotted to a former acolyte to begin a religious vocation. At all events, La Combe was taken into custody in October 1687, and would remain in prison until his death in 1715. The following month, the bishop of Geneva publicly condemned Guyon's *Moyen court*, which led to her arrest in January 1688 and detainment in the convent of the Visitation on the rue Saint-Antoine for the next few months, during which time she was repeatedly questioned about her views.[41]

Guyon's *Vie* notes that the torments she endured drew her into even closer identification with the divine. Despite the malicious intent of her persecutors, she remained "abandoned to God" and without "particular interest [*intérêt propre*]," so that her pains could not be said to be hers, but rather the wounds of Christ himself.[42] Harlay de Champvallon offered to free her if she allowed her daughter to marry his nephew, but she rebuffed the gesture as extortion. Despite the archbishop's findings against her, Guyon was nonetheless released in September 1688 owing to the efforts of Madame de Maintenon, who had become convinced of her innocence.[43] Soon thereafter, in October 1688, she first encountered Fénelon. The meeting would prove to be a decisive event not only in their personal and public lives, but also for the future of theological polemics in France on the orthodox limits of mysticism.

The future Archbishop Fénelon, born in 1651 at his family's ancestral château in Périgord, outside the town of Sarlat, descended from a long line of prelates, soldiers, and royal governors. He received an excellent education, first at home and then in Paris at the Collège du Plessis, before entering the seminary of Saint-Sulpice in late adolescence. In 1677, he attained the degree of doctor of theology. The following year he was appointed superior of the Maison des Nouvelles-Catholiques in Paris.[44] By the mid-1680s, he had met Bossuet, who became his patron and commissioned one of his first major works, the *Réfutation du système du Père Malebranche* (1683–1684).[45] In 1687, Fénelon published his *Traité de l'éducation des filles*, which further cemented not only his literary reputation but also his standing as a pedagogue.

Fénelon's talents on these fronts would soon bring him in contact with Madame de Maintenon, who made him spiritual director of the Maison royale de Saint-Louis at Saint-Cyr, an establishment for daughters of aristocratic families of relatively modest means. His views on education, which set the virtues of domesticity above the values of courtly *politesse*, complemented Maintenon's hopes of restoring the nobility.[46] In part because of her confidence, Fénelon was named preceptor to Louis XIV's grandson, the young duc de Bourgogne, in 1689. Through Maintenon, Fénelon also made Guyon's acquaintance. In an ironic turn of events, the author of *De l'Éducation des filles* would soon come to the defense of a woman who had forsaken her children to adopt the mantle of a self-appointed prophet.

Released from confinement, Guyon began to frequent Saint-Cyr, where she acquired a following among the residents and their director. With Fénelon, as with La Combe, the usual dynamic between teacher and pupil reversed itself, and he eventually placed himself under her spiritual tutelage.[47] Their correspondence testifies to the deep theological, intellectual, and emotional bonds they forged in the months after their initial meeting. Guyon sounded the constant refrain that God had ordained an "intimate union" between them. "[I]t seems to me that my soul is consumed before him for your sake, [. . .] and my heart expands within yours without difficulty," she wrote to Fénelon in November 1688.[48] She thus advised him to prepare for future struggles, since God replaced "every proprietary tendency with reference to himself" through the stages of mystical self-abandonment.[49]

As Louis Cognet has observed, Guyon's counsel encouraged Fénelon to overcome his regimented intellectualism in theological matters and to seek a more immediate sense of God's presence.[50] While she deferred to his superior learning in doctrinal matters, she nonetheless submitted her own experiences as authoritative. She claimed, for instance, that God had granted her immediate insight into the state of his soul, which revealed his hesitation to submit to the loss of self that pure devotion required.[51] In subsequent letters, she attempted to ease his apprehensions with the assurance that it was God's design to "destroy in the greatest men that which he seemed to have given to them most profusely."[52]

Guyon's claims to predict not only the course of Fénelon's spiritual development, but also other events—such as his appointment as preceptor to the duc de Bourgogne—affected him deeply. In May 1689, he wrote of reaching at last the depths of self-annihilation that she had promised. Having done "all that you order me," he announced, "I want no longer to have anything, nor to have myself."[53] Guyon answered approvingly, and their relationship entered a phase of even greater intensity. In the spring of 1690, when he suffered an acute bout of malaise, his letters called out to her as his "doctor" and "mother." She attempted to quell his fears by observing that "the more you are lost and forgotten, the more I find you in the manner that God alone knows and brings about." He should therefore cease all striving, even in matters of salvation, and divine will would at last eclipse his own.[54]

By the autumn, her hopes for Fénelon's spiritual development had been fulfilled. He had passed from a reliance on his own intelligence to unquestioning acceptance of her advice and complete resignation to God. Even his passivity had become automatic, rather than a conditioned, measurable response, and he expressed gratitude to Guyon for her support. She recognized this momentous transformation with both a benediction and a prophecy. "You are the son of the right hand of the Most High," she declared, and "you will assemble his elect. [. . .] It will be in me that you do these things. It is I in you who will bring down the enemy. It will be in you through me that the Most High will take his pleasure."[55]

Guyon's account of what had come to pass in her relationship with Fénelon was based on a specific understanding of spiritual dispossession. In keeping with the devotional practices she endorsed, self-abandonment served to neutralize the remnants of self-ownership in their souls. They ceded their claims to material and spiritual goods. Their mental faculties and bodily reactions no longer inhered in themselves, but rested with God alone. The divine had come to permeate the space they occupied as individual beings, thereby effacing the distinctions between them. Merged as if sharing a single soul, together they would transmit and enact God's will in the world. As Guyon had seemingly predicted, their mission posed a challenge to those who could not countenance her ideal of mystical self-annihilation, much less a woman's exertion of authority in religious matters. She did not anticipate, however, how fierce this opposition would prove to be.

The Quietist Affair (1694–1699)

Guyon's status in the autumn of 1690 appeared secure. While doubts over her views persisted in some quarters, she counted both Madame de Maintenon and Fénelon as patrons. The former had the ear of the king, and the latter was tutor to a royal prince. At Saint-Cyr, she was hailed as "an oracle" and "a saint," and her teachings were regarded as divinely inspired.[56] In addition, Guyon had been welcomed into the circle of reform-minded nobles—Paul, duc de Beauvilliers, and Charles-Honoré d'Albert, duc de Chevreuse, among them—who shared Fénelon's hopes for political reform together with his commitment to mysticism.[57]

This state of grace would not long endure. The mystical devotions inspired by Guyon among the school's pupils raised concerns for Paul Godet des Marais, bishop of Chartres, who resented her undue influence and feared that her doctrines bore the mark of Quietist heresy. Maintenon, who was fiercely protective of the school's reputation, sought advice from Louis-Antoine de Noailles, then bishop of Châlons, as to the orthodoxy of Guyon's teachings. He reiterated the suspicions of the bishop of Chartres, and on the basis of their judgments, Maintenon banned Guyon from Saint-Cyr. Fénelon, now implicated in the emerging scandal, recommended that she seek the arbitration of Bossuet. The latter at first appeared favorably minded toward Guyon, but under pressure from Maintenon, he adopted a more critical stance. Seeking exoneration, Guyon then requested a complete official inquiry into her life and work. Maintenon and the king approved the request, and deliberations commenced in July 1694 at the Sulpician seminary in Issy, outside Paris.[58]

Bossuet was joined at the conferences by Noailles and Louis Tronson, superior-general of the Congregation of Saint-Sulpice at Issy. Guyon remained sequestered at the convent of the Visitation in Meaux, Bossuet's episcopal seat. Fénelon felt himself to be under personal attack, given his well-known relationship with the subject of the investigation. Fearing the worst from Bossuet, who had relatively little knowledge of mysticism, he sent the examiners a clutch of texts on the history and orthodoxy of the tradition. Then, in February 1695, Louis XIV named Fénelon archbishop of Cambrai. On the advice of Maintenon and the bishop of Chartres, the newly appointed prelate was given a seat on the commission at Issy, where he succeeded in mitigating the severity of Bossuet's criticisms.[59]

Although the two clerics remained on amicable terms, Guyon's case had exposed serious theological differences between them. Fénelon's attempts to defend the mystical theology of self-abandonment only bolstered Bossuet's defense of spiritual self-ownership as enshrined in Counter-Reformation Catholicism. He was not even deterred by the imposing presence of Fénelon, who at the time was held in such high regard by Louis XIV that the king refused his request to leave his position as royal tutor upon appointment as archbishop of Cambrai.[60] Commentators on the Quietist controversy since the eighteenth century have claimed that political ambition—the desire to supplant Fénelon at court—was the primary impetus for Bossuet's actions.[61] While such an intention can only be surmised, it is possible to reconstitute the theological and philosophical dimensions of the debate between Bossuet and Fénelon, which also gave ample motivation for the former's charges against the latter.

Bossuet's anti-mystic stance was grounded in a range of sources, including Jansenism and Cartesianism. While critical of Port-Royal's challenges to ecclesiastical authority, he nonetheless, as Voltaire put it, "was nourished on their fine writings."[62] In particular, Bossuet shared Pierre Nicole's belief, as expressed in *Réfutation des principales erreurs des quiétistes* (1695), that Guyon's mysticism erroneously conflated "concupiscence" and "possessive self-love [*propriété*]," thereby prompting a heretical disdain for "personal operations and activities," as well as "temporal and spiritual goods."[63] Also like his Jansenist interlocutors, Bossuet had an acute sense of the debasement of existence after the Fall of Adam and Eve.[64] In rarer moments, Bossuet even flirted with the Pascalian doctrine of self-hatred, although generally he tended to emphasize the human potential for virtuous action.[65] For instance, in *Traité de concupiscence* (1694), he duly acknowledged that "there is nothing more beautiful, or more like God, than the reasonable creature who is sanctified by his grace" and capable of "living in accordance with reason and God, making good use of his free will." However, he repeatedly denounced pride, the soul's inclination "to attribute and to appropriate to itself every good that it has," as the source of all sinfulness. Glory should not lull one into a false sense of self-importance, then; what the soul has, it has received from its creator. In an uncustomary lapse into mystical language, he went so far as to declare before God that "all light that is created and therefore not you, although it comes from you, owes you this sacrifice of being annihilated, of disappearing in your presence, and, above all, to our own eyes."[66]

This is an atypical passage, written before the debate with Fénelon, after which Bossuet tended to avoid such rhetoric as advocating spiritual and intellectual passivity to an excessive degree. It was more characteristic of him to express faith in reason as a palliative for human defects, as he did in the treatise *De la Connaissance de Dieu et de soi-même*, originally written for the dauphin in the 1670s, and revised around 1701.[67] He began with the premise that the human and the divine are intricately bound in mutual affection—a relationship that in turn presumed mutual possession. God stands as "the sovereign good," which "has the right to possess all of our love." The supreme being transmits to the believer favored with election the capacity to desire and to possess in kind, "since it is for him to give to his creature every good that it possesses, and therefore the most excellent of all goods, which is to know him and to love him." The quest to acquire knowledge of God, moreover, originates in our "intelligent nature," which aims to seek happiness and evade misfortune.[68]

To buttress these claims, Bossuet followed Descartes in his insistence that God endows humans with the faculties necessary to exert rational control over the movements of their bodies. The mind's powers of reason allow it to accumulate knowledge, and its freedom of will allows it to master passions and sensations. The soul, then, functions as a subject that not only lays claim to physical objects, but also directs them with quasi-divine force. As Bossuet observed, "our muscles act, our members move, and our body is transported at the moment that we will it. This empire is an image of the absolute power of God, who turns the entire universe by his will." Bossuet thus affirmed, as had Descartes, the dual character of personhood, and he expressed a clear preference for the "spiritual and divine part, capable of possessing God," over the material aspects of being.[69]

Applying these propositions to the orthodoxy of mysticism led Bossuet to dismiss the strictures of Guyon and Fénelon on self-ownership. Losing sight of the benefits accruing from divine love could undermine the rationale for charitable action, which is inseparable from the promise of eternal reward. Bossuet claimed that his opponents' denial of this precondition of Christian virtue compelled them to accept a host of related errors. As he observed, the Gospel's most basic injunction, to love one's neighbor, follows from the love of self. Thus, "one does not love oneself as it is necessary, without procuring, or at least desiring, all the goods that God has proposed for our faith."[70] Souls in the grips of Quietist delusion, however, falsely distinguish between love and happiness, and between God and the spiritual goods emanating from him. In contrast, the Church teaches that "all those who desire beatitude at bottom desire God," rather than acknowledging a difference between the two objects. However, Bossuet further specified that spiritual goods do not exist for the human person alone, but serve as "the remainder [*regorgement*]" and "excess portion [*redondance*] of the possession of God."[71] If Quietist heresy leaves the soul irredeemably impoverished, true devotion leads to heavenly riches—and even the extravagance of luxury.

Bossuet's attack on Fénelon was not simply a matter of political posturing. Rather, it stemmed from the prelates' respective conceptions of spiritual economy. Drawing on Jansenist and Cartesian precedents, as well as on the possessive premises of post-Tridentine theology, Bossuet held that self-ownership depends on the workings of a rational mind that has mastered itself and its ideas, and on the accumulation of spiritual goods. Possession does not arise from a self's wanton attachment to a thing, but from the mutual identification of God and the soul. Human persons are the earthly heirs to divine sovereignty over the universe. Their prerogatives are not, however, without limit: for example, it would be impossible to exchange or to alienate hope of salvation.[72] On the contrary, believers are bound up in a circular relation of goods that both limit and define their existence as persons. If God guarantees the soul and its faculties, and the soul possesses God and his grace, then the soul also owns itself.

The self's complete dispossession, as professed and practiced by Guyon and Fénelon, was thus excluded from Bossuet's theological system. Under different circumstances, the conflict between the two camps might still have been defused.[73] Fénelon would have had to acknowledge that Bossuet's understanding of charity also presumes the reconciliation of divine and human ends, so that the desire for salvation does not devolve into self-interest. For his part, Bossuet might have admitted that his opponent's doctrine, as we shall soon see, permitted the unconscious and unintended acquisition of spiritual goods. Although the settlement on Guyon's theology issued from Issy on March 10, 1695 raised hopes that further strife might be avoided, it proved to be merely a truce. As Bossuet and Fénelon would soon realize, the discursive structures and practical implications of their pronouncements established an impasse that neither could breach.

The thirty-four articles signed at Issy reaffirmed the Church's condemnation of the Quietist heresy. Seeking to avoid an interpretation of Guyon's *Moyen court* that might validate Molinos's errors, the participants stated that "every Christian, in any state and in every moment, is obligated to conserve the exercise of faith, of hope, and of charity." Believers were likewise reminded of the need "to will, to desire, and to demand explicitly [their] eternal salvation." It was asserted that one should not regard prayer as a conduit to prophecy, and that all "extraordinary paths" require pastoral oversight.[74] Guyon's views, while escaping direct reprimand, were refined in a manner that placed limits on passive devotion and affirmed the authority of the male priesthood.

The compromise allowed each side to interpret the articles in a favorable light, but it satisfied no one. The détente came to an abrupt end when Bossuet published his *Ordonnance et instruction pastorale sur les états d'oraison* on April 16, 1695. Departing from the conciliatory tone adopted at Issy, the pronouncement formally condemned the "new mystics" for advocating "a kind of disinterestedness" that denigrates seeking from God "anything for oneself, not even the remission of one's sins, the coming of his kingdom, and the grace to persevere in goodness." Guyon's works in particular struck Bossuet as among "the aberrant expressions and exaggerations of certain ill-considered, or even presumptuous, mystics," whose ravings deviated wildly from the doctrines of Teresa of Avila, François de Sales, and other orthodox representatives of the tradition.[75] Bossuet's voice was soon joined by a chorus of criticism. The bishop of Chartres castigated Guyon for her tendency to reduce true virtues to "so many vices in disguise." He noted, for instance, her view that limiting "possessive self-love [*propriété*]" requires one not only to place checks on egoism [*amour-propre*], but also "to renounce all reflection and all human effort, [. . .] even if it stems from a principle of grace." Similarly, he denounced her understanding of self-abandonment for suggesting, not "submission to the will of God," but a "misguided acquiescence to all that which occurs in us, with no discernment whatsoever." These "monstrous maxims," he argued, could dissuade a soul from resisting "the state of its corruption."[76]

The interventions of Bossuet and Godet des Marais established arguments in defense of self-ownership that their allies would subsequently develop. First, they contended that the hope of acquiring spiritual goods does not stem from sinful self-regard. On the contrary, the soul's interest in recompense is inseparable from its wish to conform to God's will, which is to ensure the happiness of his creations through communion with them. "Every Christian in every state," Bossuet affirmed, "is obliged to want, desire, and explicitly demand his eternal salvation, as a thing that God wants."[77] Second, as Godet des Marais intimated, to deny oneself the benefits of grace amounts to a deluded tempting of fate, by which the soul concedes to an utter passivity that hastens moral, spiritual, and physical degradation.

Bossuet hoped that Fénelon, as one of the major participants in the conferences at Issy, would join in the salvos against Guyon. Madame de Maintenon urged him to do so, or at least to compose an approbation for a major anti-Quietist work to be authored by Bossuet. Fénelon rejected these overtures. He spent the summer of 1696 drafting his own mystic apologia, *Explication des maximes des saints sur la vie intérieure*, and unsuccessfully lobbying for support from Noailles and Tronson. Since he feared that approval of the text for publication would be revoked, it was hastily printed in January 1697.[78]

Fénelon's principal aim was to legitimize the mystical understanding of *pur amour*, and in so doing, to vindicate Guyon's position as part of "the general tradition of Christianity."[79] In open defiance of the other clerics from Issy, he enumerated five degrees of divine love—ranging from the "purely servile" to the "love of God alone"—each distinguished by the extent to which the soul relates its affections to itself. The fifth and highest stage of devotion requires the total absence of particular self-interest in regard to "the fear of punishment and the desire for recompense," even if one were damned to hell. While a soul continues to view God as the source of spiritual advantages, it surrenders all possessive attachment to them. The abstract recognition of salvation as "our personal good [*bien personnel*]" is thus no longer associated with "our *own* happiness and our *own* reward [emphasis added]."[80] While Fénelon noted that only the most exalted saints experience this highest form of divine love, the caveat left the implications of his schema fully intact. God had conferred a state of absolute dispossession on souls in the past, and could do so in the present. Guyon, who remained in custody, deserved not punishment, but veneration.

In order to parry the charges against her teachings, Fénelon found it necessary to address the potential conundrum of how the soul could remain devoted to God, "insofar as he is one's good," with no vestige of self-interest. In doctrinal terms, how could one defend Guyon's ideal of self-abandonment without advocating the heretical degree of passivity associated with Molinos, whose doctrines Fénelon had himself previously condemned?[81] Fénelon offered a paradoxical response. He admitted that "God wants that I desire him, insofar as he is my good." At this point the exposition takes a serpentine turn, with the added proviso that "I do not want him by [reason of] the precise motive that he is my good." As Fénelon explained, "[t]he object is my interest, but the motive is not at all interested, since it only considers the pleasure of God."[82] Thus, one loves because it is God's will that one do so, without regard for any advantages that might accrue to the soul due to this love. Fénelon grounded his claim in a distinction between two kinds of "possessive self-love [*propriétés*]." The first, pride, is defined as "a love of one's own excellence insofar as it is one's own." The other form of *propriété* is also "a love of our own excellence," but with the crucial difference that it involves a consideration of our "principal end," which is "the glory of God." Thus, we may desire virtue on behalf of God's glory, yet also to gain "merit and recompense." Although Fénelon lauds even this second *propriété*, he insists that it is inferior to the truly "saintly indifference" made possible by an act of "dispossession [*désappropriation*]," which seeks God's glory with no reference whatsoever to ourselves.[83]

To be sure, Fénelon's enigmatic position presumes a rarified—if not contorted—understanding of the relationship between object and motive, between *what* is possessed and *how* it is possessed. More specifically, his doctrine recasts the will so that it no longer relates directly to a particular self. If the soul acknowledges an interest in the reward (or object) derived from God without claiming it as its own, then the rationale (or motive) for devotion remains devoid of self-interest. This operation displaces the desiring subject—from the soul who desires for itself and on its own behalf, to God who wills through it and for it. Fénelon's theology of *pur amour*, articulated in dispossessive terms, distances the hope for spiritual goods—and even their attainment—from the orbit of human ownership. The soul is stripped of "every perceptible grace, every inclination, every faculty," and left unable even to want anything for itself.[84] In this way, Fénelon's notion of indifference preserved the essential contours that Guyon had outlined in *Le Moyen court*: "Abandonment is a stripping away [*dépouillement*] of all care for ourselves, in order to give up ourselves entirely to the direction of God."[85]

The *Explication des maximes des saints* provoked the ire of Bossuet, who had hoped that Fénelon might support his campaign against Guyon. His response appeared six weeks later as *Instructions sur les états d'oraison*, to which Fénelon refused his official sanction.[86] Bossuet alleged that Molinos, Guyon, and other alleged Quietists had corrupted the sanctity of the tradition they claimed to represent. Repeatedly, he condemned those he referred to as "new mystics" for assorted crimes against Christianity.[87] Fénelon had anticipated this line of attack, which typified theological polemics, by constructing a long lineage for his doctrines that extended from Clement of Alexandria in the second and third centuries to François de Sales in the seventeenth.[88] Yet denying Bossuet's charge of theological novelty involved more than historical verification or rhetorical strategy. With the Quietist controversy, mysticism had come to occupy a new cultural position. Once a repository of spiritual wisdom, the tradition now provoked a referendum on the virtues of self-ownership. If Fénelon could succeed in demonstrating the authenticity of his views on dispossession, post-Tridentine justifications of spiritual acquisitiveness might lose their legitimacy. It was imperative, then, for Fénelon's enemies to seize on the recent provenance of his errors, with marked emphasis on his refusal to acknowledge the possessive elements of Christian devotion.

In particular, Bossuet found the heretical source of Quietist doctrine to be in its disdain for active devotion, to that point where "one pushes indifference to the eternal possession of God." This fatal error, he argued, stands in direct opposition to Catholic dogma, which teaches that "one must absolutely demand [. . .] the most efficacious favors," including "all the goods possible in relation to God." Even damned souls should not passively accept their fate, because "excessive abandon" cultivates diffidence toward sin.[89] In sharp contrast, "a false idea of the new mystics" is to distort "the goodness of God as the object of charity"—that is, an object to be possessed—by "excluding from the state of perfection all relation to ourselves." According to Bossuet, the soul's love of God is inseparable from the rationale for loving. The presence of a divine object, then, presumes a human subject to desire it. To assert otherwise, Bossuet observed, is to neglect Jesus's command in the Gospel of Luke to love God with all one's power and one's neighbor as oneself, since, "the word 'Lord' bears relation to us." It follows that the transitive properties of devotion assume a possessive form. If this were not so, "it would be necessary to scratch out the term 'The Lord your God'" from the passage "since it is not *our* God without this relation [emphasis in original]."[90]

This argument departed in significant ways from Fénelon's view that the object of divine love is distinct from its motive, so that concern for the self must likewise remain detached from the workings of *pur amour*. For Bossuet, the soul's longing for salvation conformed to the dictates of charity, since it is a good that God "wants us to want."[91] Even "the idea of recompense does not make charity more interested," so long as one "wants as one's recompense God himself and all the goods of the soul and body that follow from possessing them." On these grounds, Bossuet denied "that he who loves God sovereignly in making use of the motive of recompense or eternal beatitude can fall into the vice of relating [*rapporter*] God to the self"—or, more specifically, of reducing the divine to its relation to the soul. On the contrary, he stipulated that "it is the nature of this *perfecting* recompense [emphasis in original] and of this possessing love [*amour jouissant*] to attach the soul to God more than to itself."[92] Despite appearances to the contrary, then, the desire for spiritual goods draws the faithful away from their petty cares and closer to the divine.

Key to Bossuet's doctrine was a rhetorical sleight of hand. He maintained that a charitable soul may continue to love itself, but in a manner that justifies self-regard as a means of fulfilling God's will. As Gabriel Joppin described his position, "the more I love God as good in itself, the more, by correlation, I love him as good for me, since in his work these two perfections are inseparable."[93] Once allowance is made for the harmony of human and divine interests, this essential logic could be applied to related considerations. Bossuet argued that even the most refined soul should ask for both temporal and spiritual goods, like the Church as a whole, but for others as well as for oneself.[94] He could not acknowledge the validity of Fénelon's central premise, that there is a more perfect love of God that does not involve the self. The two sides in the debate would continue to clash over this fundamental difference. If critics insisted that Fénelon's *Explication des maximes des saints* undermined morality by questioning the soul's desire for recompense, their opponents believed that Bossuet's *Instructions sur les états d'oraison* seemed to legitimize a possessive love of self under the aegis of an acquisitive God.

The *Instructions* badly hurt Fénelon's cause. Not only did Bossuet support his arguments with passages from the Fathers of the Church and other authorities (Fénelon had been persuaded to forgo such a strategy), but he also had backing from Madame de Maintenon and much of the *dévot* circle at court.[95] Increasingly isolated, Fénelon requested and received permission from Louis XIV to appeal to the pope as to the orthodoxy of the views expressed in the *Explication des maximes des saints*.[96] He reiterated his position in an *Instruction pastorale*, issued on September 15, 1697, which now featured proof-texts culled from François de Sales and other prominent mystics.[97] While its publication briefly rallied support to his cause, the effect was not decisive. Forbidden to travel to Rome to act as his own advocate, Fénelon left Versailles for Cambrai, where he would remain in exile for the rest of his life.[98]

The conflict now reached critical mass, and a volley of texts followed, many highly critical of Fénelon's *Explication*. Reviews of the work by Godet des Marais and Noailles predictably rehearsed their original complaints.[99] Noailles, for instance, again denounced the innovations that "the new mystics" had introduced into the doctrine of Christian perfection.[100] Rather than endorsing "the fervent practice of virtues" and "the ardent desire for beatitude," as approved by the Church, the Quietists advocated renunciation of "every voluntary desire for even our eternal interest." This heretical form of indifference likewise extended to "every good and every evil," leaving the soul devoid of a basis for moral action.[101] Their many errors, Noailles argued, could be traced to a flawed conception of "self-ownership [*propriété*]." Orthodox mystics rightly saw nothing untoward in the active desire for spiritual goods. The likes of Molinos and Guyon, in contrast, sought to reduce this impulse to simple "greed," as if it applied merely to some "personal possession."[102]

Concerned clerics beyond the center of power likewise endeavored to steel their charges against the temptations of Quietist heresy in ways that defended self-ownership with perhaps unintended candor. For instance, Hilarion Monier, prior of the Abbey of Luxeuil, argued against Fénelon that experience testifies to the power of "a desire that follows from our estate, that God has imprinted in us," which he described as that "of being happy, of enjoying the possession of [*jouir*] God, of possessing him."[103] Another supporter of Bossuet's, Père Loir from Bourges, made his case through appeals to the language of interest, profit, and exchange, albeit in reference to spiritual rather than economic goods. God desires that we love him "as our promised recompense, as our personal good," he contended. At odds with Noailles's assurances to the contrary, he openly admitted that he found a duty impossible to fulfill if he could not at the same time embrace "a thing that promises me pleasure." Since "it is the pleasure that a thing is capable of producing that is the essence of the good in that thing," he argued, "I could not love it if it were not for me a true or apparent good, a thing that did not promise me, or had not given me, pleasure." Loir described the mechanics of this impulse on an epistemological level. When forming its sentiments of love, the soul first pictures the divine as a "corporeal species." The resulting image, he explained, furnishes the mind with a visceral representation of "all the goods that God has made for us."[104]

This line of argument came tellingly close to proving Fénelon's case against spiritual self-interest. So difficult was it to separate hope of eternal possessions from the longings of one's baser nature that Bossuet's supporters were obliged to express themselves in terms resembling sensationalist psychology (in this case, that of Aristotle, rather than Locke) nearly as much as post-Tridentine theology. As we shall see, their claims would resonate strongly with subsequent defenses of luxury consumption by enlightened political economists.

Bossuet himself was not above resorting to a rather different kind of sensationalism. Wishing to press his advantage, he turned to ad hominem attacks that exploited Guyon's alleged moral improprieties with her former director La Combe in order to implicate her current defender. Bossuet's *Relation sur le quiétisme* (June 1698) ridiculed Fénelon for cavorting with a spiritual temptress "who prophesies and who intends to seduce the entire universe." In a seeming parody of the *Explication des maximes des saints*, he even likened Fénelon and Guyon to Monatus and Priscilla, second-century mystical heretics believed to have engaged in an illicit affair.[105] Despite the scandalous nature of the attacks, Guyon was denied the opportunity to defend herself publicly. In the spring of 1698, partly on the basis of the confession extracted from La Combe, she was transferred to the Bastille.[106]

The matter was now beyond Fénelon's control as well. In Rome, Innocent XII organized a commission to investigate his *Explication*. Like his predecessor in the case against Molinos, the current pope did not seek a definitive condemnation of the work. But under pressure from Louis XIV and his agents, as well as a delegation of French clerics, which included Bossuet's nephew, he finally issued the brief *Cum alias* (March 12, 1699), which denounced twenty-three propositions from the *Explication* as "reckless, scandalous, offensive to pious ears, dangerous in practice, and even erroneous."[107] The Gallican Assembly of the Clergy approved the measure in July of the following year. Fénelon duly submitted to and even participated in the action, censuring his own work from exile in Cambrai and swearing to form "an interior judgment against the condemned book."[108] As for Guyon, she remained imprisoned until 1703, when she was finally released into her son's care.[109]

Quietism's long afterlife was due in part to the provocative form of Innocent XII's verdict against Fénelon. Its wording was surgically precise: only twenty-three propositions of the treatise were explicitly censured; none were specifically approved. Neither Fénelon's other mystical writings nor the term "heretic" were mentioned.[110] The tone of the brief reflected the pope's reluctance to impugn Fénelon any more than was necessary to appease the French court. Furthermore, Francesco Albani—a sympathizer of Fénelon's, who, as Pope Clement XI, would later contemplate appointing him a cardinal—ensured that the Sun King's victory came only at the expense of his and Bossuet's Gallican sensibilities. On Albani's advice, Innocent XII issued *Cum alias* not as bull (a ruling offered on the recommendation of a Church body), but as a brief—that is, as proclamation made *motu proprio* (of his own accord)—without the participation of the bishops of the kingdom.[111] This affront to the prerogatives of the French Church was noted in the deliberations over accepting the decree. Noailles, now the archbishop of Paris, grumbled that the papal declaration was "not as compliant as could be desired with the customs [*mœurs*] and norms [*usages*] of the Kingdom," but excused the lapse since the judgment pertained to "a purely spiritual matter."[112]

Although Fénelon never recovered the status he had once enjoyed at court, and Guyon languished in prison for nearly a decade, neither was condemned to perpetual silence. Their elaboration of the culture of dispossession in treatises, prayer manuals, correspondence, and other writings— which continued to be published in new editions throughout the eighteenth century—offered compelling models for mystical self-abandonment, not only in theology, but also in philosophy and politics. This confluence was inevitable in a state where God, government, and the good derived legitimacy and force from one another, rendering their respective spheres difficult, if not impossible, to distinguish. The same year as Fénelon's condemnation, his *Aventures de Télémaque*—a utopian sequel to Homer's *Odyssey*—was being read by an astonished and, as time would tell, receptive public. Fénelon remained engaged in politics, secretly corresponding with the heir to the throne, passing damning judgments on Louis XIV, and conspiring with like-minded nobles to reform the monarchy after the latter's long and disastrous reign. In these efforts, Fénelon's commitment to mystical spirituality remained apparent, and even decisive, as he elaborated a vision of divine totality to frame the metaphysical and political dimensions of his system. Mysticism, he continued to assert, encompassed a worldview.

From Mysticism to Metaphysics

The intent behind Fénelon's formal theological works and spiritual correspondence was to instruct readers as they advanced in the practice of mystical self-dispossession. His advice, then, tended to emphasize the most appropriate manner, time, and place to retreat into oneself in order to allow God to bring about the transformation—and ultimately, the self-abandonment—of the soul. Yet, when writing to intimates, Fénelon complemented this view by turning to the productive elements of spiritual renunciation—what the human person, once it ceases to belong to itself, gains for God. His philosophical and political works likewise placed considerable emphasis on what the surrender of self-interest might accomplish in the lives of individual subjects and in the kingdom at large. Nonetheless, he maintained that to perceive the divine as it is—the immutable wholeness of being—first requires one to recognize the contingency of the self's partial, particular existence.

The positive, constructive aspects of Fénelon's mysticism cannot be understood apart from the sacrificial impulse that animated it. *Sentiments de piété*, a compilation of the archbishop's counsel first published in 1713, exalts spiritual poverty as the precondition of Christian virtue. One must regard the self not as one's own, but as a trifling object lent one by God. "All that is yours and all that is yourself is but a possession [*bien*] on loan," Fénelon asserted. "It is this spirit of dispossession [*désappropriation*] and of simple usage of one's self, in following the movements of God, that is the only true property of his creature."[113] This view, which he would expound upon in his metaphysical writings, defines human personhood in terms of what it lacks. While the soul does not entirely cease to exist, it loses all possessive attributes in relation to its particular being. The divine then emerges to fill the place that debased souls once vainly coveted as their own.

As a devotional manual, *Sentiments de piété* carefully charts the successive stages leading to the loss of self-regard. From the "prayer of faith," in which one meditates on divine wisdom and power, one progresses to the "prayer of hope," which inspires a longing for the spiritual goods promised to the faithful. The soul adopts this vantage point, however, only to grasp more fully what it must renounce. After passing from prayer devoted to Christian virtues, the penitent advances to that of "the presence of God," which concentrates one's thoughts on the divine to the exclusion of all else. This process culminates in the mystical "prayer of union," a perpetual state of indifference in which the soul "lives only by its divine life."[114]

The possibility of spiritual self-abandonment, according to Fénelon, stems from the bifurcation of the human person. In keeping with the soul's desire for union, God "separates me from myself," wanting "to be closer to me, by his love, than even I am." Above all, divine will dictates that "I depart from the narrow limits of this self [*moi*], that I sacrifice it in its entirety, and that I return it to the Creator from whom I have taken it." Yet this itinerary is fraught with psychological snares that can entrap the soul at every turn. Even acts of virtue can provoke the machinations of a secret pride, since "the forgetting of oneself is so noble that *amour-propre* seeks to imitate it."[115]

Veritable disinterestedness, in contrast, requires the total alienation of all personal properties—physical, moral, spiritual—so that the self is divorced even from its own negation. In Fénelon's zero-sum wager, "there is no middle ground: we must return everything either to God or to ourselves." The former case requires the complete "renunciation of ourselves," while the latter entails absolute usurpation, since one would have "no other God but the self [*moi*]." To become perfect, the soul is obliged to renounce not only "criminal pleasures," but also "goods that have been legitimately acquired, the pleasures of an honest and humble life." Yet, if God grants these possessions for the conservation of virtue, how could one be expected to surrender them? Fénelon's response poses a distinction between the self-interested acquisition of belongings and the resolution "to make sober use of them, without the wish to take pleasure in possessing them [*jouir*] or to place them in one's heart." Since this stance applies to all goods, both human and divine, the scope of dispossession has no bounds. It is necessary that "every Christian renounce all that he possesses [*possède*]," but in a specific sense. Fénelon did not demand that one eschew all association with family, companions, or worldly goods. The task, rather, was to break the self's possessive fixation on persons and things, so that their abundance or paucity did not hinder the workings of the divine.[116]

This exaltation of the virtues of self-detachment in the world found a receptive audience at court, where distractions from the spiritual life could scarcely be avoided. Madame de Maintenon, when Fénelon was still a favorite, confessed her persistent struggles with overdependence on companions, the burdens of her social duties, and her haunting fear of criticism. Fénelon replied that adversity serves an important function, since the helplessness it engenders "purifies the heart" and "breaks one's own will." He advised Maintenon "to die to everything without reservation, not even possessing one's virtue in relation to oneself." Accordingly, it should be of no consequence whether one is "despised" and "hated" by all the world.[117] Yet dispossession holds still other advantages, in that it returns all that it has stripped away. This, he stipulated, does not constitute a gift from God, but is, rather, "God himself, immediately alone, that one sees, and who, without being possessed by the soul, possesses it according to his good pleasure."[118]

Fénelon perhaps best captured the dynamic between dispossession and plenitude in a letter written to Guyon on August 11, 1689, in which he traces six degrees of annihilation, culminating in the merger of the human and the divine. "As soon as the soul goes out of itself," he asserted, "it enters immediately into God [. . .], for I maintain that it only goes out of itself insofar as it enters into God, and that it does not completely realize the loss of itself in God." While grace affects a passage from "privation" to "possession," "one is not emptied of the self but to the extent that one is filled with God." According to this logic, the annihilated soul cannot subsist outside God; rather, divinity immediately reoccupies the position left vacant by the self. As Fénelon observed, "God opens it to himself by pushing out the *amour-propre* that once occupied the space. To be in God is to be entirely dispossessed [*désapproprié*] of one's will and to want only by means of purely divine movement."[119] On this view, God and self—as well as self-ownership and dispossession—converge in a dialectical relation. When the human person at last surrenders completely to the divine, it does so, not merely through loss (which would entail the restoration of its primordial nothingness), but as an effect of resacralized being—annihilated in the particular, but expansive in its subversion by, and identification with, God alone.

In its purest form, the love of God is conceived of as an immediate, immanent force that detaches the self from its individual existence. This ideal became the point of departure for Fénelon's metaphysical speculations, which he articulated in a work most likely drafted during the time of his correspondence with Maintenon, *La Nature de l'homme*.[120] The treatise presents the human person as a vacuum to be filled by God and subsumed in unity with him. As in *Sentiments de piété*, Fénelon maintained that the existence of individuals depends purely on divine largesse. God, as "Being by itself," contains within himself "the universality and the plenitude of Being." Created entities cannot "possess" this being, however, "except within a certain limit that renders its difference essential."[121] All particular selves, substances, or material forms are thus emanations of God, distinguishable by what individual elements of the whole they contain. Following these premises, the natural world and its mental representations offer a conduit, however imperfect, to the divine. Even so, personal existence is defined not by its positive attributes, but by what it lacks.

Fénelon's philosophy of immanence raised troubling questions about the bounds of selfhood. Above all, how is one to distinguish the human from the divine? This difficulty was taken up in the *Traité de l'existence et des attributs de Dieu*, a work Fénelon completed in two stages, the first dating from 1689 and the second from 1712.[122] In it, he attacked the pantheistic understanding of God as a limitless being coexistent with the whole of nature, recently made notorious by Spinoza. However, the author of the *Ethics* was not cited by name.[123] The challenge for Fénelon was to conceive of a being that is perfect, and thus absolutely indivisible, while also allowing for the existence of finite created entities. Initially, he may have been almost willing to entertain Spinoza's view, since it avoided having to segregate creation from a presumably infinite divinity. Yet he soon abandoned this approach, on the grounds that a supreme being comprised of a limitless array of mutable parts would violate the principle of God's perfection. Fénelon could not, however, jettison the "real and reciprocal identity of all the beings in the universe" without similarly rejecting God's essential unity.[124] In order to salvage his convictions, he found it necessary to establish the parameters of a being that could entirely encompass creation without being reduced to it. What he needed, above all, was a metaphysical stance that could accommodate his mystical sentiments.

Fénelon resolved this problem by applying the principles of spiritual self-abandonment. Faced with contradictory tenets—that the apparent whole represented by the universe is comprised of compound matter, and that no perfect being can exhibit such a trait—he recoiled from attempting to reconcile them through rational demonstration. He drew instead on his personal experience of a God who is "a simple and indivisible infinity, immutable and without modification." If he could not find this being in nature, then the God who had so moved him could not be identical to nature. Having dispensed with the technical issue of how the creator relates to creation, he then applied his understanding of the human person—that it has no independent existence, but is rather a mere pseudo-being, with which the mind needlessly occupies itself—to the material universe in general. "There is nothing but unity," he argued, "it alone is all." The apparent dualism of spirit and matter is only "a misleading image of being." Fénelon went so far as to endorse the quasi-pantheistic axiom that God "is everywhere," while conceding that this merely gestured at "popular and imperfect notions." His difficulty with the phrase "is everywhere" stemmed not from the sentiment per se, but from the implied constraints that it placed on the divine. "Everywhere," he reasoned, still limited God to a finite set of locales.[125]

Once Fénelon felt persuaded that his understanding of divinity was legitimate, he could address its attributes in more explicit, and affecting, terms. The wisdom that had been imparted to him emanated from the "light of God," a source of illumination found directly in one's person that "places within us that which is of the farthest distance." Fénelon's gratitude and praise for this light was similarly vast. "It is not ourselves or our own," he admitted in wonder, yet so "familiar and intimate that we never fail to find it as near to us as we are to ourselves," and therefore, as "nothing distinct from us." This final qualification laid the ground for Fénelon's next observation: since God is the source of all being, then he must also "have all the being of the body" and "all the being of the spirit" without sharing in the limited existence of separate substances. Thus, Fénelon was assured that he had come face to face with the "true infinity" that was the object of his quest. God, who does not contain, but purely and simply is "the totality of being," operates at all possible times and spaces. In the midst of divine light, Fénelon described himself as merely a passing shadow—not a *je*, but rather a "*je ne sais quoi* [. . .] who cannot for a single moment find myself fixed and present to myself."[126]

Three features stand out in this exposition. At the rhetorical level, there is a fundamental tension between the content of Fénelon's metaphysics and its form.[127] To seek to codify experiences that by their very nature evade human consciousness and the reach of analytic description is to court futility. Fénelon thus felt compelled to borrow from philosophical currents that threatened, not only to distort, but to reverse his meaning. The challenge posed by Spinoza's pantheism could not merely be set aside. Despite himself, Fénelon moved to incorporate a logic that he knew to be of dubious provenance. Thus, his God is a singular, totalizing all, not unlike that of Spinoza, but one that, he insisted, wielded a distinct, creative power over the physical world. Also like Spinoza, Fénelon accepted the proposition that there could be but one substance in the universe—that is, divine substance—which he described in both spiritual and material terms. If he rejected Spinoza's extended infinity as unviable, he was nonetheless obliged to postulate something no less improbable: a perfectly unified infinity of merely apparent composites.

In the end, Fénelon settled on a mystical variant of monist philosophy as the basis of his metaphysical system—a decision that carried profound implications for its original orientation and subsequent reception. Among the most striking features of Fénelon's characterization of the divine is its lack of specificity. To claim that the divine alone truly exists complicated its equivalence with the God of Christian scripture and doctrine: the creator of the world, the lawgiver of the Israelites, the Word made flesh in the person of Jesus of Nazareth.[128] Noailles in fact chastised the "new mystics" precisely on this point during the Quietist controversy. It was a pernicious error to recommend, as they did, a "state of pure contemplation in which one must exclude the God-Man"—or, the "crucified Jesus, my sovereign good," as Noailles described him, citing Teresa of Avila—"by whom alone we have access to God."[129] Fénelon did not lapse into this error, however, and he took issue with Noailles for imputing it to him.[130] Nevertheless, as we shall see, there was more than a ring of truth to the charge that Quietism could lead to atheism. Fénelon's embrace of totality made it possible for later commentators to align his views with those of Spinoza and to apply his articulation of dispossessive personhood to avowedly anti-Christian visions of the cosmos.

Finally, the mystic monism of Fénelon's *Traité de l'existence et des attributs de Dieu* offered a radical alternative to the dominant view of the relationship between the human and the divine. The growing insistence among theologians and philosophers on God's absolute transcendence over creation cast doubt on a perceptible continuity between the heavenly and terrestrial spheres. Paradoxically, this conceptual state of affairs required the notion of an independent, autonomous subject capable of organizing the natural and social worlds according to its distinct purposes. In this way, divine transcendence was concomitant with human self-ownership. Fénelon's metaphysics deviated from this formula in significant ways. While religious conviction kept him from denying the distance that separates the supreme being from inferior creatures, his understanding of divine totality led him to emphasize the immanence of God in the world. This tendency was nowhere more pronounced than in his ideal of spiritual self-abandonment, according to which the divine grows so intimately near to the soul that the provisional existential space that it occupies is overtaken by the absolute presence of God himself.

The corollary of an immanent stance toward the divine is the dispossession of the self. Fénelon affirmed this logic most pointedly in his theological and devotional writings, as evidenced by his correspondence with Guyon. A similar dynamic prevailed in his politics as well. If God could come to reside in the world through the soul's self-effacing devotion, then temporal authority could likewise be resacralized—that is, instituted as an absolute power that operates, not for its own sake, but as the instantiation on earth of the pure love of God. It was this belief that guided Fénelon's endeavor to transform the French monarchy.

The Soul of Télémaque

Fénelon began both *La Nature de l'homme* and *Traité de l'existence et des attributs de Dieu* in 1689, the year he was appointed preceptor to the duc de Bourgogne. These treatises would have confounded a seven-year-old prince, but the tutor prepared several other works—most famously *Télémaque*, but also *Dialogues des morts* and *Examen de conscience sur les devoirs de la royauté*, among other writings—aimed at teaching the art of kingship. Through them, the archbishop hoped to exert an influence on affairs of state, much as Cardinal André-Hercule de Fleury would do under Louis XV. Not content to await his pupil's ascension to the throne, Fénelon sought to intervene in policy-making in conjunction with the members of his religious and political circle. Together, they held fast to the conviction that the unity between God and the soul could also find expression in the relationship between the ideal monarch and his subjects. This attempt to redeem the French body politic by instilling the virtues of self-denial into the soul of the duc de Bourgogne preoccupied Fénelon during his years in exile.[131] Long after the prince's death from measles in 1712, and Fénelon's passing three years later, *Télémaque* would continue to inspire readers and became one of bestselling works of the eighteenth century.[132]

Fénelon's official responsibilities as royal tutor involved overseeing the duc de Bourgogne's political, philosophical, and literary education, as well as his religious instruction. The unofficial duty he took upon himself, as evidenced by *Télémaque*, was to turn the prince away from his grandfather's glory-mongering. Fénelon urged the prince to cultivate an air of disinterestedness in all things. This injunction entailed immediate acceptance of one's condition for both a monarch and his subjects. According to Fénelon's vision, divine will dictates the social order, which the prince must maintain over and above his place in it. Similarly, the lowly status of his most humble subjects does not confer "baseness." On the contrary, contentment with their lot reflects "true grandeur."[133] In *Télémaque*, the eponymous character's Mentor—who by the novel's end reveals himself to be Minerva, and who is clearly based on Fénelon himself—praises the inhabitants of Crete for their commitment to civic virtue, which leads to "the liberty of all citizens, the abundance of material necessities, contempt for the superfluous, a penchant for working and loathing of idleness, emulation of virtue, submission to the laws, and fear of just Gods."[134]

The contrast between this utopian setting and the France of the Sun King was glaring. Since the ministry of Colbert (1665–1683), the reigning principles in statecraft, diplomacy, and political economy had favored the expansion of economic and political dominance. The campaign to strengthen rural industry and favorable balances of trade went hand in hand with the centralization of absolute monarchical authority and the display of its power at home and abroad. In this system, the consumption of domestically produced luxury items could no longer be regarded as superfluous, but was an essential means of preserving the kingdom's self-sufficiency.[135] Fénelon denounced these strategies on both economic and moral grounds. The Mentor of *Télémaque* puts the matter succinctly: "Men wish to have everything, and they make themselves unhappy by the desire for excess," whereas attending to their "true desires" would lead to "abundance, joy, peace, and unity." In place of wasteful investment in luxury goods, the government should encourage the development of agriculture, the legitimate material basis of the state. Likewise, military action might at times prove necessary, but for kings to wage war in pursuit of their "own glory" is dehumanizing for both the perpetrators and victims of violence.[136] This indictment of Bourbon policy was not lost on Louis XIV, who officially dismissed Fénelon from his position as royal tutor soon after the unauthorized printing of *Télémaque* in 1699.[137]

Fénelon had not intended the work to be published, but he confronted his king directly, if anonymously, in a letter written in the mid-1690s. As he would do in his conflict with Bossuet, Fénelon criticized Louis's self-interested faith. Since "it is hell, and not God, that you fear," he charged, "you relate everything to yourself [alone]." Fiscal and moral bankruptcy were the price to be paid for the king's blasphemous worship of "the idol of glory." The only means of escape from the abyss into which Louis had sunk, Fénelon advised, was to submit his will to God. Until then, not only his territories but his very soul would be in jeopardy.[138]

Fénelon alleged that the kingdom owed its troubles to the same pathological acquisitive impulse that marred French Catholicism. The War of the Spanish Succession (1701–1714), the devastation of which he observed firsthand, provided him with damning evidence. In an effort to secure the position of his grandson, Philippe, duc d'Anjou, as heir to the childless and witless Charles II, thereby extending the Bourbon dynasty's power across the Pyrenees, Louis XIV had drawn Austria, the United Provinces, and England into military action against France. Cambrai was ravaged by enemy troops, leaving the local population without grain and other essentials.[139] Such a dereliction of duty, Fénelon argued, undermined the monarchy's very reason for being. As he put it in a political memoir from 1710, since the king could not consider the throne as his personal "property," but rather as a "usufruct" entrusted to him, he was not entitled to risk the lands and lives attached to it for the self-serving design of tipping the balance of power in Europe to his advantage.[140]

A new political orientation was needed to save France from ruin. Since the current king proved recalcitrant, all hopes were staked on the duc de

Bourgogne. With the ducs de Chevreuse and de Beauvilliers, Fénelon drew up plans for reform in 1711, while the War of the Spanish Succession was still waging. The death earlier in the year of the king's eldest son strengthened the trio's determination to prepare a set of policy prescriptions for his grandson, who was now the immediate heir to the French throne.[141] After more than a decade in political exile, Fénelon assembled his circle to make arrangements for their eventual rise to power. Years earlier, when Fénelon had been named Bourgogne's preceptor, Guyon had predicted that the future king would be a "saint," destined to "restore that which is nearly destroyed [. . .] through the true spirit of the faith."[142] Influential courtiers held a rather different view of the new dauphin. They ridiculed his lack of military prowess and lampooned him as the archbishop's "disciple" and "a true Quietist" who lacked the mettle to be king.[143]

Fénelon set down plans for his pupil's reign in the *Tables de Chaulnes*, named for the locale where he and his collaborators held their deliberations. Above all, the manifesto advocated the resurgence of the aristocracy as defenders of political morality. He implored the crown to slash spending on both the military and the royal household. The state's chaotic finances were to be put in order through the rationalization of the tax system. Provincial assemblies, composed of members of all three orders, would ensure fairness in the collection of revenue. In other matters of local administration, representatives of the nobility and the clergy were to replace the royal intendants. The Estates-General, which had not met since 1614, would be convened every three years. Fénelon and Chevreuse also advocated a more rigorous division between secular and temporal authorities, in defiance of Gallican orthodoxy. The Church would be allowed to select its own ministers, while also contributing to the monetary needs of the state. The nobility was to be purged of all false claimants, and each aristocratic house assured of fiscal viability through endowments and access to traditional service positions in the court and in the military. While freedom of commerce would be respected, the *Tables* called for sumptuary laws for each estate, and usury would be abolished wherever possible.[144]

Fénelon and Chevreuse based this schema for "republican monarchism"— to adopt Patrick Riley's expression—on principles that also informed *Examen de conscience sur les devoirs de la royauté*, another text written for the duc de Bourgogne.[145] The prince was exhorted to participate in a Christian social totality that reached far beyond the geographical and political confines of the French crown. "All the nations of the earth," according to Fénelon, "are but different families of the same republic, of which God is the common father." He matched this disregard for mercantilist autarky with deviations from the main currents of natural-law theory, which enshrined self-interest and the instinct for appropriation as transhistorical attributes.

In contrast, Fénelon contended that the first human communities had followed the divinely issued imperative "to prefer the public good to particular interest." This Edenic state had been shattered by the emergence of *amour-propre*, thus necessitating a single authority to regulate human affairs. However, Fénelon distinguished the absolute character of legitimate monarchy from arbitrary government, since the former is bound to serve "the general interest of society." While the king alone exercises sovereignty, he also has the duty to strive, as much as possible, to extinguish his particular wills or desires. "It is not for himself that God has made him king," the archbishop instructed Bourgogne. Rather, he is not worthy of royalty, "except insofar as he forgets himself for the public good."[146]

Fénelon's ideal monarch, then, only fulfills his duties to the extent to which he becomes "a slave who has sacrificed his liberty and repose for the happiness of the public," according to *Télémaque*.[147] Rather than possessing two bodies—one mortal, the other mystical and everlasting—the king loses all claims to his own being. Power does not inhere in his person or in his dynasty; nor does it coincide, except in passing, with his individual will. The monarch must surrender all interested designs and desires in the name of a public good with which he can never identify as a particular self. This is not to say, however, that Fénelon believed that a prince in power would fully achieve the level of disinterestedness championed in his writings. Although the archbishop counseled Bourgogne to emulate his predecessor Saint Louis (Louis IX), God does not require "the renouncement of legitimately acquired possessions." It suffices that "one be just, sober, and moderate in the appropriate use of all these things."[148]

At the same time, Fénelon's rejection of Bourbon absolutism should not be confused with a proto-liberal defense of individual rights. While the king was expected to rule in concert with provincial assemblies and the Estates-General, these institutions could not bind the crown to a course of action. Nor did Fénelon argue that subjects have a right to rebel against tyrannical rule. As he explained in a letter to Charles Auguste d'Allonville, marquis de Louville and tutor to Bourgogne's younger brother, the duc d'Anjou (later Philip V, king of Spain), good government requires that a monarch "keep all intermediate bodies [*corps*] and individuals [*particuliers*], however powerful they are, in subordination."[149] If sovereign personhood belongs exclusively to neither king nor people, it resides ultimately in a divine order beyond them, the laws of which are governed by the Gospels, the "rule of kings."[150] The effects of depersonalization that characterize Fénelon's mysticism thus bear on his political values as well. It is on this front that Fénelon once again diverges from Bossuet and his supporters.

.   .   .

Despite their many differences, it is important to note that the politics of Bossuet and Fénelon resembled each other in several respects. Both believed ardently in the divine right of kings and emphasized the distinction between absolute and arbitrary government. Both warned against the dangers of unbridled luxury consumption and the horrors of war.[151] More generally, both called on the king to reign in the common interest. "The prince is not born for himself, but for the public," Bossuet declared in *Politique tirée des propres paroles de l'Écriture sainte* (1709).[152] Yet, as Lucien Jaume and other scholars have noted, Bossuet's overall system tended to subsume the public within the person of the prince.[153] According to Bossuet, the monarchy functions as the embodiment of divine power on earth. As such, the king should not submit himself to an external standard; rather, this standard remains directly accessible within his person, as a representation of God's wisdom. "Majesty is the image of the grandeur of God within the prince," Bossuet asserts in his *Politique*. Just as "God is all," so it is with the king: "All the state lies in him, the will of all his people is enclosed within his own. [. . .] What grandeur that a single man may contain so much!" Even royal self-denial does not preclude recompense, since the "public good" it yields constitutes their "earthly reward while awaiting the eternal possessions that God reserves for them."[154] Bossuet's ideal monarch, then, exists simultaneously on an exalted, quasi-divine plane and as a human soul who legitimately strives for the material prosperity of his people in this life and salvation for his own soul in the next.

While Bossuet and Fénelon shared similar views about the aims of kingship, they differed significantly in their respective conceptions of what constitutes the *self* of a prince. For Bossuet, the king is distinguished by the capacity to encompass the state within himself. Fénelon, however, sought to restore the position of the aristocracy, the Church, and even the Estates-General as independent institutions. Immutable divine law, diffused throughout the body politic rather than accumulated in the royal will, is to determine the king's actions. Both ruler and ruled must live according to "the pure love of order," which "is the source of all political virtues, as well as all the divine virtues."[155] Whereas the bishop of Meaux asserted that this order is contained within the person of the king, the archbishop of Cambrai held that order contains the king, sustains him, and is his reason for being.

Fénelon's hopes for political reform, then, cannot be divorced from his preoccupations as a mystical theologian and metaphysician. Indeed, he frequently made use of the rhetoric of one domain to amplify his exposition in another. For instance, in a devotional guide explicating the pure love of God, he cited with approval "the idea of perfect disinterestedness" that animated the law of the ancient Greek polis. For Fénelon, it was not merely a matter of reconciling self-interest and the public good. As he explained, political morality called on the virtuous citizen "to devote oneself, to perish, and to leave oneself no other resource, for the love of this order." Citing Plato, the archbishop further specified that "what makes a man a God is preferring, in the name of love, another over oneself to the point of forgetting oneself, sacrificing oneself, counting oneself for nothing."[156] This union of God and soul, the ultimate goal of Fénelonian mysticism, likewise furnished a model for social relations in an ideal body politic. The dispossession of the self could also serve as a conduit to regenerating the world.

In the realm of politics, as in the spiritual domain, Fénelon and Guyon clashed with Bossuet and his partisans over the nature of personhood, both human and divine. The archbishop of Cambrai captured the crux of the dispute with striking clarity. Taking aim at Bossuet's argument that, in its purest form, the love of God extends "insofar as he transmits to us beatitude," Fénelon objected that this rationale effectively instrumentalizes devotion. "What is distressing," he explained, "is that M. de Meaux speaks not of God, but of the beatitude that he transmits to us [. . .]. He regards God only as its cause, its principle, its object." This formula followed from the erroneous premise that "possession and beatitude are the same thing," and that "to love is to desire to possess, and consequently, to desire to be happy in the beloved object."[157] If *pur amour* requires the absolute suppression of possessive impulses, as it must for Fénelon, Bossuet's stance fails to meet this standard. At issue in their debate, then, are the relative natures of God and self. Either one engages the other through the medium of possessions—an array of spiritual gifts culminating in salvation—or the human person surrenders to God its grasp on all belongings, even the self. In the latter case, the individual human soul would effectively cease to exist as an autonomous entity and be subsumed within the divine.

To defend their respective positions, the antagonists in the Quietist affair elaborated opposing cultures of personhood, each of which generated distinctive lexicons as well as philosophical and political practices. Drawing on post-Tridentine Catholic orthodoxy, Cartesian rationalism, and the anti-mystic propositions of Jansenist theologians such as Pierre Nicole, Bossuet held that denying the attractions of divine love severed the soul's interest in obtaining it. In so doing, he and his supporters codified a theological culture of self-ownership that exalted the human person as a possessive subject who consciously directs its ideas and actions in the world and relates to God through the accumulation of spiritual goods. This view entailed conceptualizing the human person as a distinct being who acts with self-awareness in matters theological and political. The soul could not lose sight of itself in desiring God; nor could the king surrender the majesty of his person. In both cases, the individual self remains transcendent over other selves as well as the things of this world.

For Fénelon and Guyon, *propriété*, defined in mystical theology as the impulse to relate ideas, actions, and goods to oneself, invariably impedes pure devotion. Thus they made persistent demands for the alienation of the human person, not only from spiritual and material belongings, but even from itself. Existentially bankrupt, the soul owes its being entirely to God, who in turn is justified in dictating its every impulse. Theological articulations of this view, as well as various efforts to implement it in liturgy and spiritual direction, informed a culture of dispossession that valorized self-loss and sought the revitalization of divine immanence in the world.

The culture of dispossessive personhood thus posed a double challenge to the logic of self-ownership, which stressed the essentially transcendent character of both the creator God and the created subject. To varying degrees, Fénelon's and Guyon's mysticism, metaphysics, and politics represented God as an immediate, absolute, and totalizing force that detached the human person from any independent claim to autonomous action. The individual self, in turn, was evacuated from its position in favor of God. These movements effectively resacralized the self and the body politic as extensions of divinity on earth. As his critics noted, Fénelon often demurred from personifying the divine. *Télémaque*, for instance, hails Minerva rather than the God of Abraham and David or Jesus of Nazareth, while philosophical works such as the *Traité de l'existence et des attributs de Dieu* generally avoid Christological references.[158] So dispossessed a soul as Fénelon's, it would seem, proved largely incapable of imagining God as a distinct person.

Finally, the divine immanence portrayed in the writings of Fénelon and Guyon constituted a concrete aim, not only in the direction of souls, but also in affairs of state. Fénelon's tutelage of the duc de Bourgogne was but one element in a sweeping project to reform France's domestic and foreign policy. On the spiritual front, in defiance of orthodox norms limiting the religious authority of women, Guyon had sought to show Fénelon the means of achieving dispossession as a habitual psychological state rather than a passing supernatural act. Priests and laypersons who followed in their wake attempted to apply these principles to a broad array of liturgical practices that hastened union with the divine through spiritual self-abandonment and the mortification of the flesh. Their experiments confirmed suspicions that, despite Fénelon's fall from grace, mystical heresy had yet to be vanquished. In response, the defenders of self-ownership renewed their campaign against Quietism throughout the kingdom, provoking new clashes with the disciples of dispossession.

3   *The Curse of Quietism*

The papal brief that censured Fénelon's *Explication des maximes des saints* did not sound the death knell for Quietism. Not even the thunderous advance of the Enlightenment could drown out the tradition's lasting resonance. For the next four decades, clerics, theologians, and jurists continued to wage war on mystic heresy throughout France. Quietists, they charged, committed brazen acts of debauchery with ceremonial pomp, performed bizarre healings that required the contortion of limbs, raved prophetically about the destruction of their enemies, and enshrined an alternative pantheon of saints. These spectacles attracted the scrutiny of ecclesiastical and civil officials and captivated the attention of the wider public, ultimately transforming the practice of dispossession and extending its scope beyond the theological sphere.

Quietism's long afterlife problematizes the once-commonplace view that the eighteenth century witnessed an irresistible turn toward rationality and a concomitant decline in religious belief.[1] Mystical devotion persisted on the cultural landscape, not only because it remained a target of attack, but also because its logic and lexicon were continually refitted and redeployed in an array of configurations and for wide-ranging ends. Directors of conscience in Burgundy and Provence devised rituals aimed at hastening the sacrifice of their penitents' virtue to God. According to critics, this disavowal of spiritual goods betokened doctrinal heterodoxy as well as mental instability. In the provincial city of Rodez in southern France, Jansenist priests colluded against Jesuit professors of theology whom they suspected of perpetuating the errors of Fénelon and Guyon. In the capital, theologians raised the specter of Quietism to denounce the *convulsionnaires*, a sect whose outrageous prophecies and miraculous healings threatened to undermine its professed cause, the revocation of Pope Clement XI's anti-Jansenist bull *Unigenitus* (1713).

As these events unfolded, the parties involved did not follow a consistent pattern of doctrinal alignment. Jansenists and Jesuits, while sworn enemies on other fronts, found themselves fighting on both sides of the mystic divide. Given these variations, what cultural force, if any, drew these scandals into a shared orbit of meaning? The few recent studies of the topic suggest that Quietist trials contributed to the development of public opinion in eighteenth-century France. In exploiting the sensational crimes of their enemies to rally opposition to overreaching clerical power, it is argued, the guardians of law and order also lent support to the rising notion of personal autonomy.[2]

Aspects of this interpretation are borne out by eighteenth-century commentators on the Quietist affair who sought to retry the case before the tribunal of public opinion. The historian Hyacinthe Robillard d'Avrigny exalted Fénelon as "the victim and martyr of pure love," while condemning the verdict against him as "the work of intrigue and cabal, the fruit of the solicitations of secular powers, and the most evident proof of the ignorance and the prostitution of the Examiners."[3] Jean Phélypeaux, a close associate of Bossuet's, published a lengthy rejoinder to Robillard d'Avrigny's account in 1732, which renewed the charges of sexual impropriety against Fénelon and Guyon. Phélypeaux warned that their doctrines remained a serious threat to the faith and morals of the kingdom, citing as evidence recent trials in Burgundy and Provence.[4] If it now fell to readers to assess Quietism's prospects and legacy, they would have no lack of evidence on which to base their judgments.

Yet the emphasis that historians have placed on the public sphere fails to take fully into account a fundamental issue: what attributes and faculties must the human subject possess in order for such a sphere to operate? Jürgen Habermas, whose work has exerted profound influence on eighteenth-century studies, describes the category along Kantian lines as the "public making use of its reason." In order to fulfill the dual ideological function of individualism in modern commercial society, the subject had to employ its own rational faculties, not those of an external authority. The "bourgeois public sphere," he argues, "was based on the fictitious identity of the two roles assumed by privatized individuals who came together to form a public: the role of property owners and the role of human beings pure and simple."[5] It was precisely the human person's capacity to own and to be held accountable for its thoughts, actions, and belongings that the conflicts surrounding Quietism called strikingly into question. To grasp the significance of these debates, then, it is essential to take the self's relationship to spiritual, material, and existential goods as a point of departure.

Radical mysticism—and, above all, its endorsement of the soul's dispossession—furnished a template for early eighteenth-century polemics involving the human person. The antagonists did not merely echo the positions articulated by Fénelon and Bossuet in their disputes over Guyon's theology. Rather, they gradually came to view novel situations and untried fields of inquiry through the prisms of self-ownership and dispossession. As the Quietist threat radiated from Paris to the provinces and back again, its primary point of contention also moved from the debasement of the soul to the defilement of the body. While Guyon and Fénelon intended their elaborate theological positions to inform devotional practice—and for the latter, philosophy and politics as well—they also stressed that abandoning one's soul to God entails rejecting the physical world as far as possible. Despite frequent accusations that this stance left them ruefully vulnerable to temptation, there is no proof that either engaged in or advocated illicit conduct.

The men and women who followed in their wake, however, ardently embraced this possibility. Quietist clerics in Dijon and Toulon, along with *convulsionnaires* in Paris, professed that God works both in the world and by unseemly means. From this perspective, error, confusion, and profligacy yield truth, insight, and atonement. To be annihilated in spirit, one had first to abandon the soul to the imperatives of the flesh. These teachings, and the various rituals that brought them to life, redefined dispossessive personhood from a state of passivity into a mode of action, and from an avowedly spiritual state to an all-too-corporeal condition.

For the enemies of the "new Quietists," it was imperative to uphold the self's privileged grasp of, and control over, its thoughts and actions.[6] The king and the Parlements, despite their frequent clashes on other matters, joined forces with the ecclesiastical establishment to stamp out mystical heresy wherever it occurred—in the confessional, in the seminary, and in the streets of Paris. So vital did they judge their cause that no measure seemed disproportionate to the threat. In the coming decades, practitioners of mystical self-abandonment would be pursued, imprisoned, and even sentenced to death for their beliefs.

The Sacrifice of the Spirit and the Flesh

As we saw in the Introduction, the Parlement of Dijon imposed a sentence of death on a *curé* from the neighboring town of Seurre, Philibert Robert. The judgment was rendered on August 13, 1698, at the height of the controversy between Fénelon and Bossuet. Robert was ordered to be taken with a rope tied around his neck to the main entrance of the Church of Notre-Dame in Dijon, where he was to kneel and beg the forgiveness of God and king for his crimes, which included "impiety," "irreligion," teaching "the false doctrine of Quietism," and practicing "spiritual incest"— that is, engaging in sexual relations with women under his pastoral care.[7]

Robert had previously been condemned to life imprisonment by the *offici-*
alité, or ecclesiastical court of the diocese. However, the crime of spiritual
incest fell under the king's jurisdiction rather than that of the Church, so
the Parlement's order took precedence.[8] The condemned cleric was therefore to be conveyed to the public square in Seurre, bound to a stake, and
burned alive, before the executioner scattered his ashes to the winds.[9]

Robert had no intention of submitting to the sentence. In hiding when
the verdict against him was issued, he made his escape. Aided by followers, he fled in a small craft down the Saône River. He stopped for a time
in Avignon before making his way to Italy, where he was recognized by a
nobleman from Franche-Comté. The Holy Office of the Inquisition thus
learned of his whereabouts and arrested him in Florence. He died in a
Roman prison, the sentence of the Dijon Parlement having been implemented in effigy.[10]

The magistrates further announced a new operation targeting other
Quietist priests and their accomplices, which won support in certain quarters, but also encountered obstacles.[11] Although sympathetic to Fénelon,
the Jesuits were particularly keen to combat heretical mysticism in Burgundy, at least partly out of a desire to gain an advantage over the secular clergy, whose members dominated religious life in the region. Local
curés enjoyed considerable latitude in managing their affairs, particularly
since the presiding bishop had his seat in Langres, rather than Dijon.[12]
This lack of oversight impeded ongoing efforts to root out moral laxity
among clergymen, which had become a priority not only in Burgundy,
but throughout France. As John McManners has remarked, the ideal of
the *bon prêtre*—sensitive, professional, and above reproach—rose to
prominence in the late seventeenth and early eighteenth centuries: priests
throughout the kingdom were growing more sober and less licentious.[13]
The possibility that spiritual directors in and around Dijon were not only
preaching doctrinal error, but also seducing their female penitents, seemed
all the more egregious in this context.

In December, the ecclesiastical court of the diocese of Dijon issued an
official letter of instruction (*monitoire*) commanding all those with information to answer questions regarding doctrinal and sexual improprieties.
A central concern was "the prayer of quietude," described as leading to a
"passive state" in which the soul is forbidden to "demand anything from
God, because doing so would be self-interested." The authorities inquired
whether suspected priests discouraged orthodox spiritual exercises, such as
fasting during Lent and preparation for communion, or claimed that it was
permissible to engage in "illicit relations without sin." They also sought
to substantiate rumors of concealed pregnancies.[14] The investigation soon
yielded a list of Robert's known associates: Philibert Peultier from Beaune

and Chalon-sur-Saône, Claude Quillot and Étienne Carme Duchailloux from Langres, Claude Rollet and Maurice Roussel from Besançon, and Pierre Regnier from Seurre. The charges against them ranged from instructing their female penitents in the practice of Quietist prayer to flagrant sexual abuse.[15]

The proceedings against this cohort of priests, which began on January 12, 1699, attracted considerable interest.[16] Bossuet, still embroiled in the controversy with Fénelon, was kept apprised of the affair unfolding in his native city. As he noted in his correspondence with the archbishop of Paris, reports of Robert's associations with Guyon strengthened his resolve to combat her teachings. His supporters also seized on the news to discredit their opponents.[17] Étienne Filsjean de Grandmaison—doctor of the Sorbonne, councilor to the Parlement, and the *officiel* (chief ecclesiastical judge) who oversaw the diocese's case on behalf of the bishop of Langres— took a more sanguine view. He believed that the heresy originated in the misguided longing for a "union with God that is only promised to us in the hereafter." Exploited by unscrupulous spiritual directors, this desire led to a pernicious disregard for "the saving fear of the judgments of God" and "respect for the commandments." While he believed that the threat was being contained, the sheer number of participants in the trial lends some credence to Bossuet's suspicions. Over five hundred witnesses were deposed, and it took the court two years to reach a verdict. Quietism had become a spiritual scourge in Burgundy—and like Jansenism, it infected even members of the judicial elite.[18]

Nevertheless, the Dijon trial departed in notable ways from the scandal implicating Fénelon. The beleaguered archbishop of Cambrai emphatically denied both knowing Robert and any responsibility for Guyon's suspected cavorting with dubious characters.[19] Furthermore, unlike in Fénelon's case, the sexual charges against the accused were extensively documented, although Filsjean de Grandmaison at times doubted their veracity.[20] Despite his reservations, the witnesses who came forward provide the fullest account on record of the ways in which practicing Quietists understood and implemented their theological system. They described how the annihilation of the soul was inculcated through carefully crafted liturgies: not only prayers and fasts, but also devotions involving sexual liaisons. In these rituals, the violated body and alienated mind bore witness not only to the dispossession of the human self, but to the efficacy of God's presence, which could transform even seemingly sinful acts into the means of mystical union.[21]

. . .

The evidence against Peultier, Quillot, Rollet, and their associates centered on the accounts of women who claimed to have been under their spiritual tutelage. Their testimonies told of intense, long-standing relationships and concerted efforts to formalize the soul's surrender of personal autonomy. One Elizabeth Chenu, who had confessed to Peultier for over a decade in the 1670s and 1680s, claimed that his penitents regularly assembled in a house dubbed "the little seminary," in which the cells were separated only by rugs. The devotees who flocked there, mainly young women of high status, referred to themselves as the "Sisters of the Heart," an order that required a vow of absolute obedience to their director. Peultier would hold formal sessions to instruct them in the ways of mystic prayer; the aim, he taught, was to be transported "into the presence of God without thinking of anything, without demanding anything, or worrying about anything in the entire abandonment of their will."[22] Several times a year, Chenu added, the sisters were joined by a woman known as Prudence, who aided them during worship and whose writings Peultier read aloud for their edification. She also had a hand in arranging clandestine meetings between Peultier, Robert, and their penitents.[23]

Peultier continued his ministrations in private services at the Church of Saint-Pierre in Beaune, where he served as cantor. Within the consecrated space of a chapel, the priest led his followers in a ceremony called "the communication of mystic love." Each woman would retreat with Peultier behind a small cupboard. While Chenu apparently did not engage in the ritual herself, she related the descriptions of the initiates. The women were made to loosen their clothing and press their bodies tightly against Peultier as he kissed them on the mouth. Then he would recite a formula adapted from the Song of Songs, such as "My beloved is entirely mine, and I am entirely hers," before sighing a breath that sent them into an ecstasy during which "they were so forcefully transported by pleasure that they no longer knew themselves."[24] Peultier taught that these rituals induced an "illuminative and unitive" state. Mutual self-loss of priest and penitent thus reflected the more fundamental submission required by God. The divine enters into and assumes control over the individual soul's mind and will, thus rendering one incapable of sin. Chenu inquired why, if this was the case, the women so frequently attended confession. The reason, they informed her, was that the purpose of the sacrament was no longer atonement and reconciliation, but rather immediate contact with God.[25]

Chenu's claims were supported by statements from several other women, who confirmed Peultier's penchant for kissing and groping his followers while in the confessional or behind closed doors at the seminary. One witness, Marie Durand, described a conversation during which Peultier defended "the lapses of the devout"—in this case, of a woman who had had a child out of wedlock—as necessary for the "annihilation" of one's individual nature. Peultier's views on morality were in keeping with his advice regarding prayer. He taught that devotion required no conscious desire or act of will, but merely "placing oneself in the presence of God, to let him act, and to remain tranquil in the face of thoughts, whether good or evil." The cleric recommended manuals for the further edification of his followers, including two works by Guyon: *Règle des associés à l'Enfance de Jésus* and *Le Moyen court et très facile de faire oraison*.[26]

In addition to Peultier, witnesses implicated several other priests in the scandal. The most notorious was Claude Quillot, widely recognized as a ringleader of the Quietist clique in Burgundy. Born in Arnay-le-Duc to a poor family, Quillot had first served as a preceptor in the household of a magistrate in the Parlement before taking holy orders. At the time of his trial, he served at the Church of Saint-Pierre in Dijon. From early in his career, he was apparently an enthusiastic reader of Molinos, and he met Guyon and La Combe in the mid-1680s. Like Robert, Peultier, and the other priests charged in the case, he soon gained a reputation as an able confessor, and a group of women sought him out for spiritual direction.[27]

Quillot's spiritual teachings are well documented in the depositions. While he professed doctrines associated with the Quietism of Molinos, he also devised specific innovations in style and substance. Marie Marthe de Jésus, a Carmelite nun, testified to his belief that it is "not necessary to have a desire for one's salvation in doing good works," and that vocal prayers are a defective means of communicating with God. Likewise, he maintained that "sins become virtues and virtues sins among souls who have reached a certain degree" of sanctity, in which one no longer needs "to reflect on temptations." This statement suggests a radical interpretation of the Quietist principle that the soul in abandon can neither lay claim to nor be held accountable for actions that are beyond its control. For instance, he argued that pregnancies resulting from spiritual incest could be viewed from two perspectives, for which he developed a distinctive terminology. The first, that of the flesh alone [*chair chair*], corresponds to sexual offenses in the usual sense, or, in Quillot's words, a "sin of brutality." Yet there also exists a rare and less-understood state, that of the "spirit and flesh [*esprit chair*]," which he described as a "sacrifice of purity that a young woman makes against her own will in abandoning herself to impurities." He counseled that it is an offering that one should never refuse, because struggle is tantamount to "resisting the humiliation of the loss and destruction of one's self [*sa propre perte et sa destruction*]" that God desires. Marie Marthe knew well that Quillot's ideas did not rest on merely hypothetical foundations. Bertrande Soulié, a young woman who moved in Quietist circles, was widely believed to have conceived a child with Philibert Robert. The priest had the child baptized and arranged for its care.[28]

Armed with the testimony of Quillot's former penitents, the authorities set about building a case against him. The deliberations considered not only the guilt or innocence of the accused, but also the question of whether the *officialité* or the Parlement would have the ultimate responsibility of judging him. On July 17, 1700, the ecclesiastical court found Quillot and his accomplices guilty of preaching Quietism.[29] The Parlement announced its verdict on August 27, not only regarding the charges of heresy, but also of the priests' "having seduced and corrupted" their penitents. In determining Quillot's fate, five magistrates in the Parlement voted for capital punishment, two others advocated banishment, and another three jurists suggested a term in the galleys. Nine officials, however, declared that the matter concerning Quillot, Regnier, and Roussel fell outside the court's jurisdiction. Ultimately, the cases against the men were dismissed.[30] Filsjean de Grandmaison, for his part, had already handed down a sentence: Quillot was to pay thirty livres and ordered to spend three years confined in a monastery, where he would be required to perform weekly acts of penance. Upon release, he would be allowed to return to the priesthood, provided that he no longer served as a confessor.[31]

Quillot remained a fugitive for the next several months, while his supporters lobbied strenuously on his behalf. He finally surrendered himself on the first Friday of Lent of the following year and was incarcerated—not in a cloister, but in the prison of the Hôtel de Ville in Dijon, where his penitents and other visitors were free to visit him. He was also granted the opportunity to contest the accuracy of witnesses who had testified against him. Upon review of this evidence, Filsjean de Grandmaison and the bishop of Langres ultimately decided to drop the charges against Quillot, who was released on April 21, 1701.[32]

His codefendants faced sterner treatment. Peultier remained under the Parlement's jurisdiction and was banished from the kingdom for eight years. His associate Claude Rollet was ordered to be hanged. This final sentence could be carried out only in effigy, since Rollet had fled during the proceedings. Prudence, the woman suspected of arranging the traffic in penitents between Robert and Quillot, was found guilty of this charge and of teaching Quietist heresy. For her crimes, the Parlement fined her fifty livres and exiled her from the kingdom for life, stipulating that she would be hanged if ever again found on French soil.[33]

While Quillot's followers were shocked by the harshness of his original sentence, Filsjean de Grandmaison's clemency equally disillusioned his critics. Their outrage found powerful expression in the *Histoire de Quillotisme*, published in 1703, which soon became an illicit bestseller. The author, commonly thought to be Hubert Mauparty, the *procureur-général* in the case, blamed the outcome on the incompetence of the Parlement's commission, and more sinisterly, on the undue influence wielded by those sympathetic to Quillot.[34] This exposé, which reproduced selections of the more damning testimony against the accused, was formally condemned by the bishop of Langres in April of the same year, and by the Parlement of Dijon in June. The rationale for doing so, according to the bishop, was twofold. First, the work impugned the integrity of both the secular and ecclesiastical authorities by claiming that Quillot had exploited their laxity. Second, the bishop also reasoned, with some irony, that the book's salacious accounts threatened to infect readers with the very heresy that the trial had sought to eradicate.[35]

Despite such repression, Quietism persisted in Burgundy and elsewhere. The trial foreshadowed a gradual shift in the culture of dispossession that broadened its influence and attracted new adherents. Peultier, Quillot, and their accomplices introduced illicit methods by which the discursive logic of self-abandonment came to be embodied in ritual. Like Bossuet, at least certain judges in the case tended to view the crimes they punished as stemming from the doctrinal errors of Molinos and Guyon: to abdicate self-ownership, they suggested, inexorably led to physical and spiritual corruption. However, the testimony of witnesses like Elizabeth Chenu and Marie-Marthe de Jésus also offers a glimpse into an elaborate set of practices that had no precedent, even in Guyon's influential guides to mystic prayer. According to the testimony against Peultier and Quillot, such spiritual directors aimed to coordinate their penitents' thoughts and actions to maximize the effects of self-annihilation, in the full knowledge that a soul that surrenders its will also loses the capacity for moral agency.

Their teachings also confronted the central issue of the limits of divine immanence. How can God come to replace the self in this world? How does the self, once abandoned, exemplify a state that aims to defy all concerted action? How does one demonstrate pure passivity without negating it? Is it possible to indicate loss of will without willing it? In response, the Quietists of Dijon purportedly staged ceremonies that required the bodies of both director and penitent to register their abandon to each other and to God. There were rituals, such as the communication of mystic love, that radically altered the function of confession. No longer a sacrament of penance, since the perfectly abandoned soul was free from sin, it now manifested the union of human and divine. According to this logic, the prayer of quietude had already stripped the participants of their particular voices and desires; the movements that passed between them could then embody their lack of individual existence. What remained of their being was now possessed by another—the director by the penitent, and the penitent by the director—hence the resonance of the declaration in Song of Songs 2:16, that "my beloved is entirely mine, and I am his . . ."

According to this doctrine, the physical body, rather than the *corpus mysticum* of Christ, functions as a privileged site of transformation—of flesh into spirit, of impurity into beatitude. Peultier and Quillot taught that the desire to abolish all claims of ownership over one's self and one's actions culminates in virtue becoming vice, and vice virtue, a state of affairs that effectively renders questions of intent and accountability null and void. Quillot's musings about the sacrifice of *chair-esprit* seemingly rests on this fundamental paradox. A penitent desiring true purity, a state that requires the abolition of all human desire, even for purity itself, must first submit to defilement, orchestrated in the name of divine will and by the hands of the spiritual director. In this way, God could be seen as working through the body to eradicate one's flawed and partial will. Deprived of all that is particular to it, the soul enters a state of perfection, since sin originates not in actions alone, but in appropriating their consequences to oneself.

Officials who prosecuted Quietism regarded it as a ruse by which clerics seduced penitents, whether willing or unwilling. This is almost certainly accurate, but it fails to contend with the complexity of the situation. In particular, it does not explain why the Sisters of the Heart maintained their commitments over a period of years despite fears of detection and criminal sanction. Priests and penitents engaged in spiritual incest before the advent of Quietism, and they have continued to do so for a wide range of reasons. Whatever the other motives of Robert, Peultier, Quillot, and their followers, they understood their actions not merely in terms of personal desire, but also in relation to the dispossessive stance that they adopted toward the self.

Jansenists, Jesuits, and the Quietist Challenge

Whereas the Burgundy scandals unfolded against the backdrop of the Quietist affair, the case of the *convulsionnaires* in Paris originated in the long and violent conflict between Jansenists and Jesuits for the soul of the kingdom. The struggle threatened to undermine the theological and political foundations of the monarchy itself. Underpinning French absolutism was the king's pledge to end the confessional strife of the Wars of Religion and to perpetuate the spiritual peace of the realm by his intercession. The crown regarded Jansenism—named for Cornelius Jansen (1585–1638), bishop of Ypres, whose writings revived the Augustinian emphasis on predestination and the essential function of grace in post-Tridentine Catholic theology—as an insidious attempt to reestablish Protestantism on French soil. For critics, these suspicions seemingly found confirmation in the Jansenist belief that spiritual power of the Church flowed upward, from the parish priest to the papacy, rather than descending hierarchically.

Louis XIV's commitment to stamping out any vestige of religious dissent had become apparent by 1685, when he revoked protections extended to Protestants by the Edict of Nantes. No less alarmed by the threat emerging from within the Church itself, the king doggedly pursued Jansenists even into the cloister: their stronghold in the abbey of Port-Royal-des-Champs, southwest of Paris, was closed in 1709 and demolished the following year. This measure coincided with efforts to impugn Jansenism on doctrinal grounds. Louis prevailed upon Pope Clement XI to issue the bull *Unigenitus* (1713), condemning the Oratorian Pasquier Quesnel's *Réflexions morales sur le Nouveau Testament* as a virtual primer for Jansenist distortions of the faith. Also known as the Constitution, Clement's order singled out 101 propositions for censure, including those related to grace and ecclesiastical organization.

Opposition to the bull set off an intense struggle that pitted Jansenists and their supporters in the Parlement of Paris against the crown and its spiritual bulwark, the Society of Jesus. For Jansenists, royal absolutism and its Jesuit defenders posed a dire threat not only to the holy remnant of the faithful, but also to the body politic's legitimate representatives—the magistrates of the court. Their militant defense of Gallican liberties, both spiritual and temporal, gradually eroded public faith in the crown's claims to embody the national will. The casualties in this campaign of desacralization would include the Jesuits, who were to be expelled from France in 1764, and ultimately, the monarchy itself. As Dale Van Kley and Catherine Maire have argued, from different perspectives, Jansenism intensified the religious contradictions of the Old Regime to such an extent that there remained no way out of the conceptual and institutional impasse save its dissolution.[36]

These religious and political conflicts were grounded in opposing views of human nature and its relation to divinity. The Jesuits' moral theology, as codified in Luis de Molina's *De concordia liberi arbitrii cum gratiae donis* (1588), valorized the individual's spiritual and mental faculties and promoted the exercise of personal agency. They held that the exercise of reason and attention to the sacraments permitted individuals, although born of sin, to participate with God in the quest for eternal beatitude. Divine grace counts as "sufficient," rather than absolutely indispensable, in the pursuit of this end.[37] The soul's prerogatives follow from its exalted status in the great chain of being that cascades from the celestial to the material realms. In the words of the French Jesuit Louis Richeome (1544–1625), the soul reigns as the "mistress of the universe," bearing "the living image of God, and the signs of his bounty, power, and wisdom."[38]

This highly anthropocentric theological optimism sharply contrasted with the neo-Augustinian bearing of the Jansenists. Pascal, Nicole, and Esprit, as we have seen, insisted that original sin opened a nearly unbridgeable chasm between creator and created. In perpetual exile, the corrupt soul is left to its own miserable devices. Without the succor of "efficacious" grace, bestowed by God upon the elect, salvation remains utterly beyond one's grasp. Alienated from themselves and one another, men and women blindly substitute love of self for love of the divine. Nevertheless, Jansenist moral philosophers recognized a perverse utility in this predicament: consumed by the desire to have their bottomless self-regard reflected by the eyes of others, humans attempt to mask their faults to gain social esteem. In a curious logical turn, even vicious motives could give rise to actions mimicking the effects of charity. The depths of human wickedness even necessitated such an argument; otherwise, it would be impossible to account for the workings of human society.[39]

At first glance, the Jesuit-Jansenist divide appears to reenact the age-old contest between Pelagianism and Augustinianism. However, these orientations assumed new forms and new meanings during the eighteenth century, when the human person—and more specifically, its capacity to accumulate spiritual and material goods—became a matter of intense speculation. From this perspective, the differences between the two camps in their professions of self-ownership are of degree rather than of kind, and markedly distinct from the theology of dispossession advanced by Fénelon, Guyon, and their followers. It would be difficult, for instance, to reconcile the Quietist ideal of abandon with the Jesuit Richeome's encomiums on the soul, or his clarion call "to enjoy the possession of the world, to possess it in the most noble fashion possible," through both body and mind. This injunction, he made clear, entails both self-knowledge and self-possession. If "the man who knows the world possesses the world," he must likewise "know himself as the finest part of the world."[40]

For the devotees of Port-Royal, the soul was likewise animated by possession, for good and for ill. The soul resorts to the love of self and of ephemeral objects out of its longing for the divine, the superior good removed beyond its grasp as a consequence of original sin. The sole hope for fulfillment, however, lies in actively seeking the love of God. This conviction informed Nicole's vehement disdain for Quietists such as Guyon, whom he accused of defying God's will for our happiness.[41] Both Jansenists and Jesuits, then, asserted that the dictates of self-ownership condition the soul's relation to the temporal and the divine, albeit to varying degrees. If Quietism represented the extreme pole of dispossessive personhood, Molinism marked the extreme pole of self-ownership—with Augustinianism occupying a relative position closer to the latter than to the former.

The divergent stances adopted by Jesuits and Jansenists followed from their respective understandings of the relationship between the temporal and celestial spheres. While Jesuits located the self along a continuum of being that extends from God to the physical world, so that the divine remains accessible to reason and wisdom, the Jansenists maintained that original sin had severed the links between this world and a "hidden god," whose motives and intentions are necessarily occluded.[42] The latter understanding—which found expression in the writings not only of Jansenists, but of Cartesians and Enlightenment philosophes—posited the human person as alone in a universe that operated according to independent, discernible laws. Paradoxically, this sense of abandonment also fostered a new understanding of self-ownership, predicated on the human person's need to define its distinct place in the world without immediate reference to God.[43] For the partisans of dispossession, in contrast, the ultimate goal was immanence: to close the gap between heaven and earth, even at the expense of the self's independent existence.

. . .

The Quietist epidemic next flared in Rodez, a prosperous market town with about five thousand inhabitants located in the Guyenne. At the center of the controversy stood the Society of Jesus. Since the order's arrival in the 1560s, its members had founded a *collège* and expanded their presence in the region by acquiring numerous benefices, as well as secular and ecclesiastical properties. These efforts did not go unopposed, and the Jesuits repeatedly clashed with local nobles and the bishop over the payment of *rentes* and other financial matters.[44] By the 1720s, the dispute shifted to the theological front, with Jansenist clerics in the diocese agitating against the pernicious doctrines that appeared to stream from the Jesuit *collège* and the seminary attached to it.

The source of the heresy, according to the formal denunciation submitted to the bishop of Rodez, was the *Traité des actes humains*, a work dictated first by one Père Charly, and further elaborated by his colleague Père Cabrespine. Initially, the priests charged the Jesuit professors with propagating a vulgarization of Molinist theology, which, in its classic form, asserts that sufficient grace, if seized upon and amplified by the believer's free will, provides an adequate basis for Christian virtue, and ultimately justifies the reward of salvation. On Charly's view, according to his detractors, this doctrine authorized the wanton embrace of egocentrism, with no necessary consideration of divine or natural law. He taught his pupils that if one rationally pursues a laudable end, even though "solely out of self-love," one's actions remain "good in every sense and merit the approval of God."[45] Jansenists also appealed to the *procureur-général* in the Parlement of Toulouse to intervene, on the grounds that the Jesuit curriculum justified all manner of criminal activity—including theft, murder, and sedition. Charly denied all the charges against him.[46] The bishop, Jean-Armand de la Vove de Tourouvre, duly issued a pastoral order condemning the *Traité des actes humains*; however, the Congregation of the Holy Office nullified it. The Parlement then countered with an *arrêt* overturning the decision on classic Jansenist grounds: the action infringed upon the prerogatives of the Gallican Church.[47]

By the 1730s, the controversy at Rodez shifted focus—from attacks on Charly and Cabrespine to criticism of Père Lamejou, an instructor at the Jesuit seminary, and from the charge of Molinism to Quietism. As the clerics themselves admitted, a change in course was necessary, since previous attempts to contain the Jesuits had proven as ineffectual as they were brash, and "the simple people realized that all of these invectives fell back down on us like lead."[48] If Molinism remained sufficiently acceptable to avoid reproach, Quietism would surely prove beyond the pale. The priests warned the bishop of Rodez that Lamejou's writings endorsed "the principal foundation of Quietism" regarding the pure love of God. They feigned regret for again coming to their superior about Jesuit misconduct, and expressed a willingness to coexist with the order, "if it were possible for truth to make an alliance with error."[49]

The clerics' formal complaint, published in 1732, set out to prove Lamejou's guilt by association. If it could be established that he subscribed to views on pure love that had been condemned during the clash between Bossuet and Fénelon, it would be apparent that he was likewise guilty of Quietism. In particular, the *curés* found Lamejou's teachings to echo Fénelon's definition of pure love. They submitted as evidence the Jesuit's proposition that "actual charity toward God is an act by which one effectively loves God above all for God himself, [. . .] independently of those perfections that are or would be a good for us."[50] Furthermore, Lamejou justified this rarified form of charity as the basis for a "perpetual state" of spiritual abandon, a position clearly condemned in the papal brief *Cum alias*.[51]

In contrast, the *curés*' doctrine of the theological virtues (faith, hope, and charity) emphasized their fundamentally possessive character, as well as the crucial role of human happiness in Christian devotion. Citing the ruling against Fénelon, they noted that Lamejou's propositions were "contrary to the essence of the love of God, which always desires to possess its object, and to the nature of man, which necessarily desires to be happy." Salvation was desirable precisely "because there is nothing that one can love with more profit." It followed that "profit and usefulness [. . .] are part of the reason to love God for his own sake." No contradiction existed for the Rodez clerics between the self-regard required for salvation and the pure love of God, since "the interest that he [God] offers to us, is to have the one we love." Their rationale depended on the soul's just desire for beatitude. Citing Bossuet, the priests affirmed that "one cannot disregard oneself [*se désinterésser*] to the point of neglecting in even a single act, whatever it might be, the will to be happy."[52]

Lamejou's system thus endangered the faith of his pupils. Its radical interpretation of pure love cast aspersions on the saints and even on the Virgin, by suggesting that they held a "mercenary" interest in salvation. Even more critically, its exaggerated sense of spiritual abandon threatened to collapse the distinction between the human and the divine, and to obviate the need for God altogether. The belief that "God is no longer the essential and sovereign good [*bien*]," the priests argued, "allows him his divinity only as a spectacle."[53] Left unchecked, the cult of pure love ultimately risked devolving into "deism," by dissociating spiritual goods from Christ's redemption and thereby reducing God to a faceless, meaningless entity. "The absolute sacrifice of one's salvation," finally, dissolved the relationship between love of God and love of virtue, paving the way for other "horrible excesses" in thought and deed. Like the authorities in Dijon, the *curés* of Rodez traced a clear line from the doctrine of indifference to "foolish acts capable of causing scandal throughout the Church."[54] The prospect of Jesuits steeped in this doctrine serving as teachers and directors of conscience caused them considerable alarm.

However, the clerics faced a vexing obstacle in prosecuting their case. Lamejou did not repudiate theological or moral virtues, although he distinguished them from the pure love of God. Instead, he argued that the soul is capable of experiencing two forms of charity—one disinterested, the other infused with self-interest. The believer's hope of salvation stems from the latter, lesser form of charity, which remains wholly separate from the superior ideal of loving God as divinity in itself. Regardless of this distinction, the role in salvation that Lamejou assigned to free will (in contrast to the pure love of God) only served further to offend his critics' Jansenist sensibilities, since it implied that the efforts of fallen souls could somehow contribute to the redeeming actions of grace. The qualification appeared all the more dubious, they added, coming from "the mouth of a Molinist."[55]

The joint denunciation of Fénelon and Molina insinuated compatibility between Quietism and the Jesuits' *humanisme dévot*.[56] While Lamejou apparently followed Fénelon in acknowledging a form of "mixed charity" that fused self-interest with the love of God, both regarded this sentiment as inferior to absolute charity, which did not depend on the desires of the individual believer.[57] Moreover, Lamejou's association of pure love with total spiritual abandon sharply diverged from the Molinist emphasis on self-directed activity. This difference became more apparent as the conflict in Rodez progressed. The latitude of human action described in Charly's writings depended on an image of a self that governs its actions without necessarily having recourse to grace.[58] Lamejou accepted this position in part, but only as it applied to motivated acts. In contrast, he maintained that pure spiritual disinterestedness comprises a separate case, in which the love of God bears no relation to the human person.

The synthesis of Molinism and Quietism—toward which Lamejou ostensibly gestured, and which his critics attempted to exaggerate—was a theological novelty that the Jansenist clerics at Rodez felt compelled to denounce. To their minds, it was the worst of all possible errors, combining the heedless self-interest of the Molinists with Quietist disdain for desiring one's salvation. They also bristled at the implication that theological hope—which they regarded as the sole means by which the soul, through the workings of grace, could love God as its own highest good—could itself be a mercenary form of devotion. At issue was a distinctly Augustinian form of self-ownership. Its tenets allowed, and even required, the soul to exercise maximum control over itself, and to take absolute responsibility for all lapses in doing so. While believers are incapable of attaining salvation except as a free gift from God, they are nonetheless expected to desire its possession as their highest good.

Yet it could be argued that the Jansenists clerics protested too much—their criticisms exhibit a curious resemblance to the views they sought to refute. Despite differences regarding the operations of grace, both Augustinian and Molinist theology asserted that beatitude constitutes a good to be possessed by the soul. As for the doctrine of Père Charly, his defense of self-interest without regard to divine will closely approximates Pascal's and Nicole's descriptions of how humans conduct themselves in the world. The Jesuit's formulation ran afoul, however, of the Jansenist insistence that egocentric actions, while potentially beneficial to society, should differ starkly from one's devotions to God. Fénelonian mysticism, in contrast, removes concern for the self—and likewise, for spiritual gifts—to a lower order of Christian perfectibility. It would seem, then, that despite the doctrinal discord between adherents of Jesuit Molinism and Jansenist Augustinianism, their respective assumptions about the necessity of self-ownership resembled one another more than either side would be willing to acknowledge. In contrast, the mystic ideal of pure love found in the works of Fénelon and Lamejou belonged to a separate culture of personhood that privileged dispossession above all else.

The controversy in Rodez, like the scandal in Dijon, both confounded and transcended partisan doctrinal lines. It was not merely a matter of Jansenists cynically raising the specter of Quietism in an effort to neutralize Jesuit influence in ecclesiastical affairs. Nor was the sanctity of theological tradition per se of decisive, or even primary, significance. The fundamental point of contention had to do with opposing understandings of the human person—not only between partisans of self-ownership and dispossession, but also among militants within the same camp. Whether the Jesuit seminary in Rodez propagated Molinism, Quietism, or some amalgam of the two positions was of less importance than the possibility that its teachings discounted the soul's possessive relationship to the actions for which it was accountable, or to the ultimate beatitude afforded it by God. When Jansenists themselves began to embrace either or both of these possibilities—as the *convulsionnaires* in Paris did—their leadership swiftly moved against them.

God Trespasses on Saint-Médard

In July 1735, the *procureur-général* received a petition on behalf of Marguerite-Catherine Turpin, a woman of thirty then confined in the Hospice de la Salpêtrière, who claimed that divinely inspired convulsions had miraculously straightened her deformed spine and limbs. She had been accused of spiritual imposture, and her mother now appealed to the Parlement of Paris's Grand'Chambre to quash the charges. According to the statement of facts, in October 1731, Turpin had visited the grave of François de Pâris, a Jansenist deacon around whom a popular cult had emerged after his death in 1727. While at the tomb, Turpin's body was seized by violent spasms, which persisted for several months with no improvement in her condition. In July of the following year, however, she felt her atrophied limbs take on new strength, so much so that her arms and then legs began to lose their twisted appearance. However, the accompanying seizures left her in such agony that she begged to be restrained and even to have her muscles struck as a means of relief. These requests grew progressively more extreme, with the instrument of choice advancing from a wooden bat to a piece of iron; the latter, she claimed, had been broken on her body without harm. Another therapy involved her being drawn between two stools, supported only by her head at one end and her feet at the other. With a rope around her neck fastening her to the first stool, another rope was slipped around her feet and pulled tight, as if to straighten her body. Lest the magistrates not recognize the severity of this treatment, the request noted that it "should not only have strangled her, but even torn off her head."[59]

How to account, then, for these supernatural effects? Turpin's advocate called on the Parlement to embrace her healing as the work of the divine. If God stood as "the author of the felicitous change that has occurred in the limbs of this girl," then there could be no basis on which to condemn "the convulsion that he chose as the means for it." Turpin had in no way misrepresented the miraculous nature of her recovery, and so had been unlawfully imprisoned.[60] Some magistrates counted themselves among the devotees of the cult of François de Pâris, and the court as a whole ruled the matter to be outside its legal competence. Turpin remained at the Salpêtrière, however, and there is no record as to her eventual fate.[61]

Turpin's case was no isolated incident. Scores of suspected *convulsionnaires*—so named for their tendency to convulse when experiencing miraculous healings or prophetic visions—were interrogated or imprisoned for assorted crimes. In the late 1720s and early 1730s, the infirm, the devout, and the curious flocked by the thousands to the tomb of François de Pâris in the cemetery of the Church of Saint-Médard. They were drawn from all stations in life, ranging from commoners like Turpin to Marie-Thérèse de Bourbon-Condé, princess of Conti, who sought a cure for her failing eyesight.[62] Cardinal Louis-Antoine de Noailles, the archbishop of Paris and ally of Bossuet during the Quietist controversy, had long harbored Jansenist sympathies, which also extended to the burgeoning cult of François de Pâris. But his successor, Charles-Gaspard-Guillaume de Vintimille du Luc, showed no such mercy for the *convulsionnaires*.[63] Faced with increasing harassment, they retreated to secret conventicles. A gendered division of labor tended to prevail at the meetings, with female disciples frequently succumbing to tremors and related states of ecstatic agitation, overseen and aided by male participants (known as *valets de chambre*), who would answer their calls for relief through the exercise of bodily mortifications. The therapies frequently involved torture, during which the patient was beaten, bound, stabbed, and dragged across the floor.[64] Reports of the *convulsionnaires*' methods shocked professional theologians, who criticized them as the work of libertines engaged in "eroticism, covered under the veil of religion."[65]

Yet these detractors should not obscure the cult's prominence. The events at Saint-Médard marked a defining moment in the conflict between the crown and its Jansenist critics in the Parlements and among the clergy. The *convulsionnaires* appeared on the public stage as resistance to *Unigenitus* reached a fever pitch. On March 24, 1730, Cardinal André-Hercule Fleury, Louis XV's unofficial first minister, declared the bull to be French law. The Parlement of Paris interpreted this decision as an assault on its prerogatives. The ensuing struggles occurred not only in the chambers of the court, but in the pages of *mémoires judiciaires* issued by rebellious magistrates and in the pro-Jansenist periodical *Nouvelles écclesiastiques*. As the historian B. Robert Kreiser has amply demonstrated, the affair served as a lightning rod for publicity around which the *appellants*—as the Jansenist critics of *Unigenitus* were also known—could reanimate support for their cause.[66]

Beneath the surface of these struggles there seethed a preoccupation with what it meant to exist and function as a rational human subject. To their critics, the *convulsionnaires*' activities offered frightful evidence of the dangers posed by the overcharged imaginations of religious enthusiasts.[67] The post-Tridentine Gallican Church continually affirmed the duty of bishops, spiritual directors, and parish priests to police both doctrine and observance. During the Quietist controversy, Bossuet had mounted a wide-ranging, highly publicized campaign against Guyon for preaching the virtues of saintly indifference in defiance of clerical interdiction. Now the archbishop of Paris, with Fleury's support, sought to stamp out the *convulsionnaires*' fanatical adherence to a theology that threatened to overthrow self-governance, and with it, all institutional forms of authority.

The scandal revealed the underlying conflicts regarding the limits of human self-ownership in the world and divine transcendence beyond it, while again redrawing the battle lines of the struggle. Initially, Jansenists had regarded the seemingly miraculous events in Paris, where the *convulsionnaires* first made their appearance, as evidence of God's intercession on their side.[68] However, they soon grew disenchanted with the sight of men and women flailing about in ecstatic agony during staged healing sessions and making startling pronouncements on the fate of the Church. Desperate to restore their credibility, Jansenist theologians denounced the *convulsionnaires*, their supposed brethren in the fight against *Unigenitus*, as a troupe of "new Quietists" who idealized the alienation of the soul as an exalted spiritual state. Physicians also joined the fray, diagnosing convulsions not as signs of demonic possession or mystical abandon, but as symptoms of underlying mental and physical disturbance. Dispossessive personhood, once the subject of theological speculation, had become a matter of corporeal pathology.

· · ·

The humble origins of the *convulsionnaire* crisis little foretold the spectacular events that would soon engulf Paris. François de Pâris, the disowned son of a counselor in the Parlement, had turned his back on a legal career for a life of holiness. He received minor orders in 1715 and was made a deacon. His stalwart commitment to Jansenism barred him from a higher position in the Church, but he found his calling in martyrdom, offering his body as a sacrifice to God for the evils of the Church. He retreated to the faubourg Saint-Marceau—a destitute quarter that had long been a center of Jansenist spirituality—and devoted himself to serving the poor. His regime of intense spiritual and physical mortifications steadily ruined his health, and he died in May 1727, on the eve of his thirty-seventh birthday.[69]

His reputation for piety in life was transformed into cause for veneration after his death. Witnesses came forward describing miracles performed through Pâris's intercession. One Pierre Lero, a dealer in secondhand clothes, testified that he had sought treatment for ulcers that had formed on his leg, leaving him incapacitated. A surgeon's efforts were ineffective, and in 1727, desperate for a cure after nearly two years of suffering, he went to Pâris's grave at the cemetery of Saint-Médard. His lesions gradually began to improve during a novena that he had a woman there pray on his behalf, and the wound was perfectly healed after he returned to the tomb to say a second novena. Similarly, a dressmaker named Marie-Jeanne Orget claimed to have been cured of a fallen uterus and a badly infected leg wound after doctors had declared both conditions incurable.[70]

Another woman, Anne Lefranc, experienced a still more spectacular miracle. For nearly three decades, she had suffered from a mysterious affliction that caused her to lose consciousness, her tongue to swell into her throat, and her entire body to convulse with such fury that she had to be restrained for fear that she would injure herself. Despite brief periods of abeyance, new symptoms would continuously appear, until she was left unable to leave her house. Lefranc claimed that she had received last rites on at least twenty occasions, had been bled over three hundred times, and for several years had been unable to sleep more than an hour at a time. Finally, in 1728, a friend advised her to seek the aid of Pâris, but she doubted his powers. When her pastor, a Jansenist, was forced to resign, her indignation compelled her once more to seek Pâris's assistance, so that her recovery might prove "the justice of my *curé*'s cause." God blessed her petition, and she was soon completely delivered from her illness.[71]

The authorities lost no time in discrediting the miracles at Saint-Médard. Vintimille, recently installed as archbishop of Paris, issued an order in July 1731 pronouncing Lefranc's testimony to be invalid and censuring its publication. He declared a ban on worship at Pâris's tomb and condemned the miracles there as hoaxes orchestrated to generate support for Jansenism. This repressive measure failed to have the desired effect, and it was soon overshadowed by more incredible events. Larger, ever more partisan crowds poured into the cemetery seeking divine assistance. The spectacles assumed increasingly elaborate and violent forms. During this period, convulsions became commonplace among the devotees, thereby giving the sect its name.[72] For supporters like the Oratorian abbé Pierre Boyer, an early biographer of Pâris, the new phenomenon was a continuation of the first miraculous healings at the tomb, and "a triumph of the cause of God."[73] For Vintimille and Fleury, the bizarre displays suggested a new rationale for legal proceedings, on the grounds of religious imposture. René Hérault de Fontaine, the tenacious lieutenant general of police, assembled a jury of physicians to investigate the matter. Upon examination, several purported *convulsionnaires* admitted that they could produce their symptoms at will.[74] The forced closing of the cemetery, on January 29, 1732, led one anonymous wit to scribble the following couplet: "De par le roi défense à Dieu/De faire miracles en ce lieu" (By royal order, God may not/Perform miracles on this spot).[75]

The affair now entered a new, even more radical stage. The closing of the Saint-Médard graveyard had the unintended consequence of causing the sect to metastasize into a cluster of small, underground cells, whose members engaged in ever more outlandish rituals of healing and prophecy. By the mid-1730s, the *convulsionnaires* lost their support among the Jansenist elites, who were now willing to cooperate with the authorities in order to avoid further scandal. The Grand'Chambre of the Parlement of Paris authorized the counselor Aimé-Jean-Jacques Sévert to renew the judicial campaign against Pâris's followers, leading to numerous arrests. The magistrates then refused to consider the appeals of Marguerite-Catherine Turpin and other imprisoned *convulsionnaires*, a decision amounting to a condemnation.[76]

The alliance between Jansenist leaders and the government made its definitive foray into doctrine with the *Consultation sur les convulsions*, issued in January 1735 by thirty *appelant* doctors of the Sorbonne. The report was unequivocal in its denunciation of the Pâris cult, and took specific aim at the heresy that men and women incapacitated by convulsions or other ailments could nonetheless uncover heavenly truths. For the authors of the *Consultation*, it was absurd and obscene to attribute such ravings to supernatural causes, equating "hideous contortions, [. . .] indecencies, flashes of every sort of madness, falsehoods, and calumnies" with "the order of miracles." There could be no doubt that the spectacles were the product of terrible *aliénations*, a pointed term that carried economic as well as psychological meanings. It could refer to the surrender of ownership over a piece of property, to the estrangement of one person from another, or to a descent into madness. In this case, the doctors used it to describe the self's separation from its mental and physical faculties, and thus its loss of control over its thoughts and actions. In contrast, they employed the lexicon of self-ownership to describe the fundamental requisite of divine inspiration. "To be included in the ranks of those who speak through the spirit of God," the doctors made clear, "one must be master of one's mind and one's senses."[77]

No longer content to dismiss convulsions as the folly of credulous laypersons, the *convulsionnaires*' opponents now specifically targeted the self-dispossession advocated by members of the sect. This was partly a reaction to the scandalous teachings of Jean-Robert Causse, a layman who claimed to be able to see into the future and even to raise the dead. Christening himself Frère Augustin, and purporting to be the fourth person of the Trinity, Causse maintained that the present order would soon give way to a new dispensation. The impending upheaval made itself apparent through

the movements of his body and those of his followers. In the grips of convulsions, men and women delivered ecstatic prophecies and engaged in
sexually charged rituals. As the *Consultation* reported, participants were
seen "trembling in all their limbs" and "placing themselves in all manner of immodest and truly shocking positions." Some "flung their heads
against the wall" or were beaten by their fellow devotees with sticks, while
others held forth in speech, their words appearing "to predict the future,
discover hidden things," and lay open "the secrets of hearts."[78]

Augustinistes, as Frère Augustin's devotees were known, shared with so-
called *mélangistes* and other *convulsionnaire* factions the belief that seemingly ungodly means could serve godly ends. To justify this position, and
to give it legitimate meaning, their supporters prepared detailed considerations of the alienability of the self. For instance, the tract *Nouveau Plan de
réflexions sur la Consultation* took explicit aim at the thirty doctors' argument that "the character of alienation alone" provided sufficient proof that
"God has no hand in the convulsions." In response, the anonymous author
cited the ecstasies of Saul as a scriptural precedent justifying the dispossessive effects of divine illumination. As for the authorities' prosecution of
convulsionnaires, the work reversed the charges to implicate those who had
leveled them. "If the *convulsionnaires* are ill," he reasoned, then "they are
not criminals," but rather unfortunate souls in need of consolation. Therefore, the actions taken against them should be regarded as specious in their
rationale and unjust in their execution. More generally, since "there is nothing to lose and everything to win in attributing the convulsions to God,"
the author asked how one could dismiss them out of hand. "Who could not
align himself on the side of the *convulsionnaires*," he demanded, if doing
so could usher in a new and better world?[79] The premise of the text is clear:
for God to make his immanent presence felt, it is necessary for the human
person to surrender itself with abandon to the movements of the divine, no
matter the repercussions for the religious and legal status quo.

This argument in favor of dispossession was also in keeping with the
venerable Jansenist hermeneutics of figurism, which strove to interpret
both scriptural and contemporary events in prophetic terms. For the keep-
ers of the tradition, the sight of convulsing bodies served as a clear allegory of the upheaval necessary in the last days to purify the Church, and
in so doing, to vindicate the Jansenist faithful as God's elect.[80] The abbé
de Saint-Jean, a provincial cleric who spent several weeks in Paris observing the *convulsionnaires* at close range, saw in their violent movements
a premonition of "some grand object, or some significant event." To his
mind, "the *œuvre* of convulsions is thus an enigmatic *tableau*," in which
one "discovers characters of greatness that make one sense that God is
there, and that it is his hand at work." His account is studded with vivid

descriptions of the torturous ministrations, or *secours*, to which the *convulsionnaires* voluntarily submitted as a paradoxical way of lessening the pain of their ordeal. Several were splayed out on the floor, while seven or eight assistants—or *secouristes*, as they were called—trampled upon their limbs and torsos and stomped on their throats and faces. These physical convulsions were amplified through prophetic statements that testified to the "current desolation of the Church" and foreshadowed the "brilliance of its renewal"—no doubt a reference to the Jansenist mission of ecclesiastical and doctrinal reform.[81]

Pierre Boyer, who had personally met with Frère Augustin, ascribed even greater significance to the grotesque scenes that accompanied the convulsions.[82] He noted that since the barring of access to Pâris's tomb, the emphasis of the miracles had shifted from healing to more extravagant enactments of the present and the future. He likened the flailing of the *convulsionnaires* to Christ's passion, a testament to the degradation that the devout must now endure. Such "representations," he made clear, "take place in an alienation of the senses," marked by "speechless gestures" that nonetheless "bear a general relation to the present situation of the Church," which was marked "by the corruption of all estates, and by errors impugning the efficacy of grace and the purity of morals." Boyer did not hesitate to admit that the practice of *secours* seemed to go against the standards of decency, and that the *convulsionnaires* made false prophecies. But he remained convinced that these lapses were God's way of "confounding the false wisdom of political authorities" as he revivified the Jansenist cause. It was a test of faith, then, that would distinguish those who "love the truth in itself," without regard for reputation, from those vainly concerned with "public esteem."[83]

Saint-Jean's and Boyer's figurative exegeses of the phenomena they observed supported the view that the soul's dispossession served as a conduit for God's work in and on the world. If the thrashing movements of *convulsionnaires* in a state of radical self-estrangement simultaneously depicted both the pain of Jesus's crucifixion and the current divisions within his Church, they also heralded its regeneration. The two clerics embellished their accounts with tales of prophecy, speaking in tongues, and sudden illuminations. Certain *convulsionnaires* experienced so profound a derangement of the senses that they "read with eyes closed and bandaged, using smell to distinguish the letters."[84] Other members of the cult, having lost their physical sense of sight, fell under the sway of apocalyptic visions, during which they foresaw the coming of Elijah and the conversion of the Jews in anticipation of the return of Christ. On their bodies were lavished the purifying tortures of the "lethal assistance [*secours meurtriers*]" that God required of his chosen people before the predictions on their lips

would come to pass. Saint-Jean, for instance, told of a woman who requested that she be savagely beaten and stabbed with hatpins around her
head in the form of a crown. Another was seen to lie on the floor while a
secouriste put the heel of his shoe in her eye, and then shifted his entire
weight upon it.[85] However gruesome these chastisements might seem to the
uninitiated, Boyer contended, God did not forsake his children in moments
of tribulation. Through the "dark cloud" that obscured their sacrifice, his
voice could be heard demanding "whether they love the humiliations by
which he desires to make his cause victorious," and "whether they are
willing to take on the appearance of madness under which he hides his
wisdom and his power."[86]

For the *convulsionnaires'* supporters, as for the defenders of the Quietist priests in Dijon and Toulon, the dispossessed soul performed a sacred
function. Miraculously alienated from mind and body, at once anointed
and debased, it stood as God's agent in the world. As Saint-Jean explained, convulsions were necessarily "an adulterated work [*une œuvre
mêlée*]," constituted by the "shadows and obscurities" of truth alongside
"its lights and its evidence."[87] A prophet's nearness to the divine did not
preclude false utterances or scandalous comportment. At the same time,
it was not a matter of personal culpability, since a mind subject to the
alienating effects of convulsions could not sensibly claim responsibility
for its actions. Boyer too sustained this *mélangiste* position, arguing that
"there are times when God more carefully conceals his works, and covers
them with denser clouds, because men are more unworthy of knowing
his secret." He reasoned that the outlandish and even salacious character
of certain *secours*, during which a *convulsionnaire* might rip her clothing or assume a provocative pose with the men assisting her, contributed to the efficacy of the scene, being "necessary to awaken attention
to the general upheaval of all law, of all order, of all decorum within the
Church." Thus, even as the *convulsionnaire* experienced enlightenment
through alienation, rendering her prone to truth as well as to error, her
loss of self-control exposed the confusion prevailing beneath the thin veneer of ecclesiastical discipline.[88]

Jansenist opponents of the *convulsionnaires* challenged the validity of
the movement on both theological and medical grounds. Among their immediate points of reference was the Quietist affair, which spelled out in
no uncertain terms the perils of dispossession for both mind and body.
Representative of this strategy is the treatise *Vains efforts des mélangistes
ou discernants dans l'œuvre des convulsions*, published in 1738. Its author, Abbé Jacques Vincent d'Asfeld (1664–1745), was a doctor of the
Sorbonne and signatory of the *Consultation sur les convulsions*. Although
initially hopeful about what the events at Saint-Médard might portend for

the *appellant* cause, d'Asfeld soon came to view the spectacle of writhing bodies and wayward prophets as an incontrovertible sign of mass lunacy.[89] His refutation of the Pâris cult hinged upon defining the limits of mental and spiritual *aliénation*. "I speak of wisdom and of madness," he declared, "according to the ideas that subsist in every nation of the earth, and that God has engraved in all men." At the outset, then, d'Asfeld placed himself on the side of universal reason. He depicted the defenders of convulsions not only as the pathetic victims of enthusiasm, but also as agents of "a new Quietism."[90]

According to d'Asfeld, rationality and alienation correspond to distinct modes of personhood—one valorizing self-ownership, the other dispossession. "The wise man," he noted, "has always been defined as the master of himself," one "who remains continually in a state to submit his affairs and conduct to reason." For the "madman," conversely, mind and matter exceed the bounds of his dominion. This lapse could manifest itself in several ways and with more or less severity, including "a type of madness erroneously named," which d'Asfeld identified with "enthusiasm," or "a presumptuous weakness of the mind, which takes for the light and inspiration of God the effects of an inflamed imagination." There was also the still more serious condition of the *convulsionnaires*, which involves both "the loss of reason" and the "disruption of the economy of the human body." Such a state was entirely incommensurate with revelation, because "if ever man must be master of his reason, it is when he claims to speak for God." More generally, d'Asfeld cited the Fathers of the Church in support of his claim that "the alienation of the mind" is incompatible with the truth. Communication with the divine presumes the active participation of human consciousness, since "there is nothing more opposed to the alienation of reason than intelligence." Prophetic statements, therefore, must necessarily issue from a self-possessed spiritual subject, rather than circle like an imperious swarm of ideas that debase the mind in seizing control over it. The soul's constant vigilance ensured that its utterances were faithful both to God's direction and to the actual content of one's own thoughts. The errors of the *mélangistes*, on the contrary, stem from the absurd conviction "that one may be mad and reasonable at the same time," and thus operate outside the order of rational thought.[91]

D'Asfeld singled out for rebuke the speculations of Jean-Baptiste Poncet Desessarts (1681–1762), a collaborator on the *Nouvelles ecclésiastiques*, who had published a series of letters criticizing the *Consultation*. Desessarts related the experiences of a young *convulsionnaire* named Marie-Jeanne, whose seizures occurred at regular intervals and progressed from one part of her body to another. The woman claimed that she remained conscious of what befell her, although unable to speak. For Desessarts, the case offered proof positive that Marie-Jeanne was "possessed of complete liberty," even though, by his own admission, "her soul was displaced at the onset of the convulsion, so that it was rendered a mere spectator" of the movements of her body. The division between the spiritual and physical aspects of her existence, Desessarts held, lent support to the claim that the *convulsionnaires'* visions could not be explained as a naturally occurring disorder. It also neutralized the *Consultation*'s argument that, since their states involved an "alienation of the mind," one could not attribute them to God.[92]

D'Asfeld dismissed Desessarts with unconcealed contempt, claiming that his tortured justifications betrayed a heretical source. In particular, the defense of spiritual dispossession struck him as reminiscent of "certain Quietists of the last century." The abbé justified this comparison on moral as well as theological grounds. The *convulsionnaires*, like the spiritual libertines who had come before them, sought "a pretext for excusing men of the shameful actions that they are capable of committing." Citing Bossuet's *Instruction sur les états d'oraison*, d'Asfeld prepared an extensive list of parallels between the heresy combated by the bishop of Meaux and that professed by the *mélangistes*. Both asserted the existence of a "state of perfection," during which "the soul," or "superior self [*moi*]," becomes "so absorbed in God that it loses its independence from the actions of its body," or "inferior self." The *convulsionnaires*, like the annihilated souls of Quietist devotion, believed themselves subject to "transports that deprive them of all use of free will to such a degree that even if they lapse into grievous sin, they nonetheless are not at all inwardly culpable." From these and other similarities, a common threat emerged to the exercise of spiritual self-ownership: the subversion of moral agency and accountability "through the alienation of the mind and the senses" and the embrace of an unholy "indifference" to sin as a divine means of mortifying the soul.[93]

To be sure, d'Asfeld's claim that the *convulsionnaires* had resurrected Quietist error was one of imputation rather than demonstration. *Augustinistes*, *mélangistes*, and other radicals in the movement did not, and would not, profess affinities with a doctrine that had been so roundly condemned. Nevertheless, the characterization was neither baseless nor incidental. The strategy reveals once more how the culture of dispossession, now under the watchword *aliénation*, made intelligible the self's loss of control over its thoughts and actions. This was no less true of the *convulsionnaires'* supporters, who sought to neutralize the charge of spiritual or sexual excess with the counterclaim that God alone imposed such mortifications upon his suffering servants against their personal will. Their emphasis on spiritual abandon and self-forgetfulness led d'Asfeld to insist on the fundamentally possessive relations that bind together memory and experience, mind and body, thought and deed. Otherwise, the individual soul would not remain accountable for its actions during altered states of consciousness.

Although the *convulsionnaire* controversy resembled previous scandals, it also introduced a new line of argument in debates over the limits of self-ownership. In particular, d'Asfeld and other theologians who signed the *Consultation* attributed the conduct of their opponents not merely to religious enthusiasm, which might have originated in ignorance or demonic possession, but also to mental illness. He thus appealed to the spirit of reason, and concluded that "the alienation of mind and senses recognized in the *convulsionnaire* is true madness," rather than being evidence of spiritual overexertion.[94] This diagnosis pointedly contradicted his opponents' distinction between the ecstatic and the insane. For instance, Desessarts had argued, on the basis of evidence drawn from the Fathers of the Church, that God could reveal himself to souls without inducing actual mental illness or "delirium."[95]

D'Asfeld was not alone in accusing the *convulsionnaires* of reprising the errors of Molinos, Guyon, and other radical spiritualists, or in linking this heresy to mental derangement. His fellow skeptic Jacques Fouillou—an ardent Jansenist and historian of the movement's demolished stronghold, the abbey of Port-Royal-des-Champs—chastised commentators for ignoring the role of disorders such as epilepsy in precipitating the spectacles at Saint-Médard. It bewildered Fouillou that symptoms of illness produced by "the alienation of the senses and of reason" could be mistaken for signs of revelation. The supposed visionaries' pronouncements were riddled with absurdities, discrediting their claims to divine provenance. Insofar as these outrages passed for theology, the scrupulous mind could find nothing more in them than a "dogmatic basis for the most corrupt Quietism."[96]

The noted Jansenist physician Philippe Hecquet (1661–1737) offered the most exhaustive assessment of the physiological aspect of convulsions. Hecquet followed d'Asfeld and Fouillou in describing the epidemic's victims as "new Quietists," but his analysis in *Le Naturalisme des convulsions* (1733) privileged physical causes over spiritual effects.[97] Hecquet regarded the human body in avowedly mechanistic terms, as a "string instrument" composed of "an immense quantity of nervous fibers" that, when working properly, moved in concert.[98] Yet the system's equilibrium was most delicate, hanging on "almost nothing, the least atom, a grain of sand." Disruptions occurring when "the nerves lose their natural firmness, in slipping from their normal ducts," were thus abnormal but not uncommon, resulting in altered states "that can hide the mind from the body, or the soul from the functions that govern it." By way of example, Hecquet cited the case of a "man of letters" whose mental overexertion "instantly triggers a kind of rapture, with the result that, no longer being the master of his body, he falls into convulsions."[99]

Hecquet was known first and foremost as a physician, and was later named professor and dean of the Paris Faculty of Medicine. His reputation was such that he counted as patients the prince of Condé and the duchesse of Vendôme. That is not to say, however, that his religious convictions had no bearing on his medical views. For instance, he was admired for his abiding concern for the poor and abject, a preoccupation that on occasion also informed his scientific writings.[100] Theological sensibilities are also apparent in *Le Naturalisme des convulsions*. In Hecquet's view, the human nervous system remained forever perched on the edge of collapse. Bombarded by stimuli, the mind's delicate balance could falter at any time, with little warning. Such pessimism was befitting of a devout Jansenist. Hecquet's emphasis on the physical frailty of the body recalls, with proper Augustinian rigor, the debased nature of the soul tainted by original sin.

Inasmuch as Eve had corrupted Adam, it did not surprise Hecquet that women were highly susceptible to convulsions and other nervous conditions, a weakness that he believed might account for their overrepresentation in the Pâris cult. Moved by the desire for recognition or other passions, he argued, female penitents succumbed to overexcitement of the imagination, which in turn caused their mental faculties to exceed normal bounds. In healthy individuals, the soul commands thoughts like a general in the field, ordering its "spirits" effortlessly "to the places in the body where [it] wants to send them." During illness, however, the soul is displaced from its "natural and voluntary seat" and thus left at the mercy of the objects on which it fixates. In the case of the *convulsionnaires*, Hecquet surmised, these impulses frequently manifested themselves in the sexual organs—hence the "impertinent *secours*" demanded by female members of the sect, which served "to relieve the swelling" experienced in their "lower stomach." Likewise, he explained cases of paralysis in terms of "melancholy ecstasies," during which blood accumulated in the brain to such an extent that the rest of the body became numb owing to the lack of circulation.[101]

In all these cases, Hecquet concluded, the same dynamic was at work. The soul or the mind, incapacitated by nervous disorder, had lost its ability to govern its thoughts, desires, and actions. It followed that the *Augustinistes*, *mélangistes*, and other religious enthusiasts required medical rather than spiritual attention. Hecquet went so far as to blame theologians who "erect a religious cult to what is the object of natural remedies" for perpetuating the epidemic. The first line of medical treatment included doses of opium, sulfur, saltpeter, and other tonics to slow the racing mind. Bleeding was found to have a similar effect. Another approach called for removing the patient from environments that might overexcite the imagination. All of these methods, the doctor noted, proved effective in restoring the function of the nervous system.[102]

Nevertheless, Hecquet did not intend to dismiss religion out of hand. He expressed reverence toward the first miracles at Pâris's grave, in contrast to the "epidemic convulsions" that followed. To qualify as a miracle, a phenomenon must clearly contravene the laws of nature. The *convulsionnaires* displayed no symptoms that met this standard. Moreover, their afflictions did not warrant supernatural explanation even on theological grounds, since God could not be the cause of "an illness that defiles the body."[103] With this remark, Hecquet's Augustinian leanings once more come into view. Given the Jansenist stress on human depravity and divine transcendence, it followed that God would not employ natural means—and particularly not a physical disorder, which was a consequence of sin—to bring about a sacred, otherworldly end.

Hecquet classified convulsions as manifestations of a physical pathology by virtue of their alienating effects. On this view, a soul that had abdicated self-governance corresponded to a brain overwhelmed by the impulses that it would direct when healthy. Whatever the parallels between the *convulsionnaires* and other heretical sects, Hecquet believed that theological rehabilitation was not enough to keep their illness in check. Moreover, his efforts to translate the lexicon of dispossession into physical terms presaged a decisive shift in polemics over the self. Hecquet noted that "the human body carries in itself a natural propensity for convulsions," implying that altered states of consciousness posed a threat that needed to be closely monitored.[104] As we shall see in subsequent chapters, eighteenth-century physicians and philosophers pursued this broad mandate with remarkable zeal.

By the time Hecquet published his findings, the coalition against the *convulsionnaires* had begun to succeed in their aims. The *Consultation* made it clear that Jansenist theologians were willing to lend their support to the government's crackdown. Likewise, the Parlement and police pressed on with their efforts to disperse the sect. Frère Augustin went into hiding, and many of his followers found themselves incarcerated in the Conciergerie prison. Infighting among the various factions kept them from mounting an effective defense of their views, and their movement entered a period of gradual decline.[105] Religious enthusiasts believed to exhibit unorthodox leanings and unsound minds increasingly attracted solicitude rather than reprisals. Yet the ideal of dispossession that they valorized did not pass away quietly, but found new adherents in unsuspected quarters—especially among the philosophes of the radical, materialist Enlightenment. Their persistent denials both of human agency in the world and of divine presence beyond it met with even stauncher resistance than that faced by Quietists, *convulsionnaires*, and other heretical mystics, thus intensifying the debate over the human person's status as a willful, self-owning subject.

From Cadière quiétiste to Thérèse philosophe

In *Le Naturalisme des convulsions*, Hecquet alluded to a highly publicized scandal that had reached its apex two years earlier. In 1731, the Parlement of Aix had decided the fate of Jean-Baptiste Girard, the Jesuit rector of the Collège Royal of Toulon, accused of Quietism and the seduction of one of his penitents, a young woman named Catherine Cadière. For Hecquet, the trial fit readily into his schema as another instance of the "endemic disease of convulsions or hysterical vapors" that impressed "pious persons and learned men" at the expense of true religion.[106] Among historians, the case has been seen as a notable incident in the protracted power struggles between Jansenists and Jesuits, during which public opinion emerged as a determining factor in both ecclesiastical and national politics.[107] In light of the recurrent debates and proceedings involving Quietists throughout the kingdom, the Cadière affair also appears as a crucial link between earlier theological disputes and emerging concerns over the implications of Enlightenment materialism for the human person's claims to moral agency and autonomy.

In certain respects, the events in Provence followed the formula laid down in Dijon and later adapted in Rodez and Paris. Cadière, a young woman from a devout family with pretensions to spiritual acumen, alleged that she had fallen under the spell of a confessor who had plied her with Quietist heresy and directed her to engage in sordid rituals, leading to the loss of her virtue. She testified to the magistrates in Aix that she had begun her association with Girard in the spring of 1728. The priest's advances had first taken the form of an unholy kiss blown across her lips. The gesture triggered a state that left her, she claimed, "outside of myself and without consciousness." In matters of doctrine, Girard taught that prayer was of little use for advanced souls. Instead, she was ordered to "accept a state of obsession" that would allow her "to annihilate myself in myself [*m'anéantir en moi-même*], and to resign myself to God's will, without concern for all that happened in me." He further claimed that their encounters would serve as "humiliating trials to lead [her] to perfection." Tales of Cadière's extraordinary visions and prophetic statements eventually aroused the suspicion of the bishop of Toulon. She admitted Girard's indiscretions to him, and subsequently to the civil authorities.[108]

The ensuing trial produced a mountain of evidence for the Parlement to consider. Girard was formally accused of spiritual incest and suspected of propagating Quietist heresy. Cadière's lawyers prepared a series of damning briefs, including an extended commentary claiming to demonstrate that the Jesuit shared with Molinos a liking for doctrines emphasizing self-abnegation and indifference. They also suggested that Girard practiced sorcery, and that he had made a pact with the devil to bring him souls in exchange for spiritual gifts.[109] The accusation bore striking resemblance to a case from the 1610s involving the priest Louis Gaufridi, who had confessed that Satan had granted him the power to seduce women at will by blowing his breath upon them.[110] Girard denied the accusations of similar conduct. His lawyers argued that, since the charge of demonic possession "was not serious enough to persuade minds in an age as enlightened [*éclairé*] as the one in which we live," his enemies had stooped to adding Quietism to the litany of his supposed crimes.[111] The conflicting accounts polarized the magistrates. After intensely fractious deliberations, including a split decision to condemn both parties to death, the Parlement acquitted Cadière and Girard in an *arrêt* dated October 10, 1731.[112]

It was partly because the trial of Cadière and Girard did not reach a definitive conclusion that it lived on, both in the memories of those involved and as a trope in the collective imagination. In particular, the case provided ample fodder for one of the most widely read libertine works of the eighteenth century, *Thérèse philosophe* (1748), which was likely written by Jean-Baptiste de Boyer, marquis d'Argens. As Robert Darnton has argued, the novel appeared during a decisive period, when the Enlightenment in France emerged as a publicly definable movement on the cultural scene.[113] That Quietism figures centrally in its plot already suggests the degree to which radical spirituality and radical philosophy were intertwined. The author had still stronger reasons for his engagement with heretical mysticism. Its essential message about the self, as readers who had followed the news of Quietist trials in Dijon and Toulon would have recognized, found further corroboration in the doctrines propagated by the Enlightenment's most audacious popularizers.

Thérèse philosophe not only offers salacious details about the relationship between a debauched priest and his penitents, but also a seductive introduction to materialist thought. In the opening scenes, Thérèse overhears Father "Dirrag," with whip in hand, instructing his pupil, "Mademoiselle Éradice," that "it is in forgetting the body that one succeeds in uniting oneself with God." All three names are clear allusions to mystic theology and ritual: "Thérèse" recalls the exalted life of Saint Teresa of Avila, while "Dirrag" and "Eradice" are obvious anagrams of Girard and Cadière. As the story progresses, Thérèse loses her virginity and receives instruction from one Abbé T., who maintains that "all is of God" and thus that "there is nothing evil in the world from the perspective of divinity." Revealed

religion, he teaches, is the "work of men," who foolishly endow the supreme being with petty passions and desires. Among humans, it is neither
good nor evil, but blind impulse that reigns. The happiness of each person
depends upon "seizing the type of pleasure that is appropriate to him,"
although not without considering the happiness of one's fellows. While
this doctrine would appear to justify license, Abbé T. makes it clear that
men and women do not actually exercise liberty even over their own minds
and bodies. On the contrary, "we are no more able to think in this or that
manner, to have this or that will, than we control whether or not to have
a fever." Indeed, "the soul is not master of anything" and "only acts as
a result of the sensations and faculties of the body." There is no spiritual
subject, only flesh, the dictates of which control our every movement.[114]

   At first glance, it would appear that the author of *Thérèse philosophe*
parodied Cadière's experiences simply for the purpose of entertainment.
The exploits of a notoriously corrupt cleric would have made good copy
for those who wished to discredit the spiritual and moral authority of the
Church. Yet one can also detect a more substantive rationale behind his
allusions to mystic heresy. The character Thérèse, like Catherine Cadière
and the disciples of Robert, Peultier, and Quillot before her, is taught that
sexual defilement serves as a conduit to perfection. To be sure, the novel
departs from the doctrines professed by Fénelon and Guyon in emphasizing the role of pleasure in the attainment of happiness. Nevertheless,
the writer makes clear that men and women do not strive for an ideal or
an object through the exercise of free will or other faculties thought to
belong to a particular person. Rather, one's will becomes incidental, even
illusory—a function of the natural order that determines all things, not
from on high, but immediately in the world.

   Although now translated into a materialist idiom, these tenets echo
mystical claims that the divine effectively replaces an annihilated soul's
mental and spiritual powers. While Quietists generally advocated the
total neglect of the flesh, some took a decidedly more carnal approach to
self-renunciation. For the confessors of Dijon and Toulon who led their
followers in rituals of spiritual and sexual abandon, as for the Parisian
convulsionnaires, mystic dispossession was a bodily act. If, in this way,
mystics were becoming more inclined toward the physical world, so too
materialists turned more and more to the kinds of speculative inquiries
once dominated by theologians and metaphysicians. As we shall see, what
drew the two movements together was a mutual tendency to enshrine the
annihilated self as a void to be filled with the immanent power of a totalizing force, whether God or nature.

   Remarkably for us, contemporaries recognized the links connecting
mystics and materialists, despite their starkly different views regarding the

existence of God. Beyond the example of *Thérèse philosophe* and similar works, some of the most influential minds of the period were quick to point out similarities in the two camps' disdain for the individual.[115] In opposition, orthodox theologians and mainline philosophes struggled to uphold the imperatives of divine transcendence and human self-ownership, and to overturn the dispossessive ideal now championed by Spinozists, materialists, and other philosophical radicals.

Part II

PHILOSOPHY, ECONOMY, AND THE BODY POLITIC

4 Spinoza's Ghost

In 1773, on Christmas Day, two young dragoons shot themselves at an inn outside Paris. It was a premeditated act. The men, named Bourdeaux and Humain, left notes explaining their motives in terms that echoed materialist teachings, even if the only authors they acknowledged were the poets Jean-François de Saint-Lambert and Claude-Joseph Dorat, both of whom had eulogized suicide. The soldiers labored under no illusions as to the significance of their actions. "At the moment I write this," Bourdeaux calmly remarked, "a few specks of powder are going to destroy the mechanism of this mass of moving flesh that our proud fellows call the king of beings." He had simply lost all interest in life, and therefore, all attachment to himself as a being: "I have had more than enough of every possible state, of men, of the entire universe, of myself." Once his existence had become a burden, reason dictated that he surrender it. The logic was brutally direct. "When one has grown weary of everything, one must renounce everything," he claimed. "[O]ur disgust with life is the only motive leading us to end it." He described his life as a mere "title [*brevet*] to existence that I have possessed for twenty years," of which the only attraction left was to surrender it. In a joint testament with Humain, he encouraged others to follow their example, which entailed no more than "giving up an outfit whose color is no longer pleasing." Well aware that they were committing a criminal offense, the pair bequeathed their remains to the authorities, and remarked that "we despise them too much to bother ourselves with their fate."[1] Upon their discovery by the police, the Parlement of Paris ordered the men's bodies to be hanged in effigy, their property to be seized, and the writings found at the scene to be burned by the king's executioner. These penalties were in keeping with the letter of the law against suicide, but were not commonly imposed in the eighteenth century.[2]

What drove Bourdeaux and Humain to die by their own hands—not owing to a sudden, overwhelming emotional trauma, but out of simple malaise? They did so during a wave of suicides in the capital that left government officials, clergymen, and journalists both baffled and alarmed. It was widely alleged that the blame rested with the vogue for materialist philosophy, which undermined faith in religion and the sanctity of human life. Without the belief in God to sustain them, so went the theory, unsuspecting readers would succumb a state of anomie that made them a threat to themselves.[3] After all, what did it matter if so insignificant a being ceased to exist? What was the individual, if not an assemblage of physical parts that had formed by chance and meant nothing in the scheme of the universe as a whole?

These questions preoccupied theologians and philosophers as they struggled with the ramifications of Enlightenment thought for understanding the human person. Their clashes signaled a decisive shift in terrain for the partisans of self-ownership and dispossession. By 1750, the focus of the polemics, once primarily an internecine Catholic quarrel over the value of spiritual goods and the dangers of alienation, had turned to the self's relationship to nature. Yet, as the example of *Thérèse philosophe* suggests, this development did not follow a linear process of secularization, in which religious concerns inexorably gave way to worldly affairs. Orthodox theologians remained at the forefront of debates, although they increasingly had recourse to arguments drawn from the era's dominant philosophical orientations—above all, Cartesian dualism and Lockean sensationalism. These appropriations brought them into dialogue with mainstream philosophes, who, despite their resistance to traditional doctrine, proved no more inclined to countenance attacks against personal agency and moral accountability. Now, however, the immediate threat to the ideal of self-ownership no longer issued from Christian mystics, but from unrepentant materialists who embraced the philosophical monism of Baruch Spinoza, the Dutch lens grinder who has come to be regarded as the founder of the radical Enlightenment. Like the devotees of Quietist heresy, these radical philosophes characterized the self as a passive being entirely determined by immutable forces beyond its control.

To be sure, mystics and materialists held substantially divergent views, especially regarding the existence of divinity. Yet so too did radical and mainstream philosophes. Whereas even the most debauched Quietist claimed to serve a supernatural, omnipotent creator, Spinozists and materialists toppled God from his heavenly throne and declared grace and salvation to be irredeemable figments of a bankrupt religion. Their common enemies—who included prominent philosophes such as Voltaire, Montesquieu, and Condillac—seized upon the striking affinities between spiritual and philosophical radicals. Both, it was argued, aimed to sever the self's possessive attachment to ideas and actions, thereby nullifying its prerogatives as a thinking subject. The philosophical mainstream, in contrast, upheld the self's property in its own person to be vital for reasonable and sociable comportment in the world. They considered this ideal so fundamental to their cause that they joined the Gallican Church in denouncing their heedless brethren.

Peter Gay's once-dominant interpretation notwithstanding, the Enlightenment was not a unified, if unruly, party devoted to promoting "modern paganism."[4] Multiple, even conflicting, positions were taken by philosophes working across Europe, in different countries and under different political, social, and religious conditions. Jonathan Israel, while committed to portraying the Enlightenment as a singular movement, nonetheless maintains that it consisted of two principal factions. The "moderate mainstream," inspired by Descartes, Leibniz, Locke, and Newton, pursued gradual reforms in natural philosophy, theology, and confessional relations. In contrast, partisans of the "Radical Enlightenment"—Spinozists in the Dutch Republic during the seventeenth century and French materialists in the eighteenth—rejected the traditional European culture rooted in "the sacred, magic, kinship, and hierarchy," adumbrating the secular, individualist, and democratic values guiding the modern world.[5]

This way of configuring the Enlightenment, however subtle in detail, remains overly monolithic in substance. It leaves little place either for religion, except as a doomed source of atavism, or for non-individualist understandings of the self. Eighteenth-century polemics resounded with a concatenation of heresies that scandalized even the most liberal-minded of eighteenth-century clerics, jurists, and philosophers. They reveal an Enlightenment that was even more radical than scholars have imagined. Quietists demanded that the soul relinquish control of its mind and body to the divine. Spinoza and his philosophical heirs—including Paul Henri Dietrich, baron d'Holbach (1723–1789), a central figure in this chapter—advocated the self's degradation in markedly similar terms. The line separating mystics and materialists from the cultural mainstream was even more impermeable, then, than that between priests and philosophes. This divide is nowhere more apparent than in debates over the human person. Radical philosophy converged with radical spirituality in its calls for self-dispossession, while both Enlightenment and Catholic orthodoxies defended self-ownership. Given these intersections, it is all the more difficult to valorize one side as progressively modern while condemning the other as hopelessly retrograde.

Even so, Spinoza and d'Holbach did not simply reoccupy the position once held by Fénelon and Guyon. The invectives of self-professed atheists against Christian spirituality entailed the displacement of the sacred from

God to nature, and the demotion of the self from active subject to passive object. Radical philosophes advanced a new understanding of the natural world as an agent, but of a distinct kind. Whereas orthodox Christian theologians viewed divinity as a person (or, more specifically, the union of three persons), Spinozists and materialists accepted nature as a complex whole with no fixed center or particular will. This understanding presumed a dramatic resacralization of the physical realm, according to which it exhibits the immanent power wielded by the God of Christian mysticism, but without creative intelligence. Nature could have extraordinary effects on those who submitted themselves blindly to its dictates. In rare cases, the sense of being at its mercy induced suicidal tendencies, as was the case with Bourdeaux and Humain, the two dragoons who took their own lives in 1773. D'Holbach instead chose to embrace the possibilities that materialism offered to imagine the world anew. His *Système de la nature* (1770), reduced the individual human person to its underlying corporeal functions, while also calling attention to what he considered essential to redeeming the species as a whole.

The efforts of d'Holbach and his contemporaries to come to terms with nature as a totalizing force had wide repercussions in the cultural landscape of eighteenth-century France. After all, theirs was a world with a highly charged awareness of the power of things. One could marvel at Jacques Vaucanson's famous inventions, like his flute-playing automaton. Or one could lose oneself in the panoply of newly accessible commodities—ranging from culinary novelties to clothing, jewelry, and works of art—which Montesquieu describes in *Lettres persanes* (1721) as "invisible nets in which every customer gets snared."[6] Cultural historians have enriched our understanding of how scientific and economic innovations impacted the individual subject's views of consumption, a difficult task given the paucity of direct evidence. In particular, recent work has focused on how sensationalist psychology, with its tenet that all knowledge derives ultimately from physical experiences, informed arguments on both sides of the eighteenth-century debates over luxury. Proponents held that superfluous consumption arises from the basic drive to maximize pleasure, while detractors countered that it divorces appearance from reality and leads to the confusion of social ranks.[7]

These clashes suggest that men and women had begun to relate in unprecedented ways not only to their belongings, but also to their very minds and bodies, as objects that could elude their willful control. It is tempting to recognize in these developments the alienating illusions of the capitalist commodity form, or the instrumentalist worldview associated with modern science. Yet it is no less crucial to grasp, wherever possible, how French subjects understood the changes going on both around and within themselves. At least from the perspective of the radical Enlightenment, there was nothing to fear from the rule of nature. Rather than self-estrangement or the drive for domination, it inculcated a deeper, more immediate bond with one's fellows and with the wider world—but only at the price of renouncing false titles of possession over oneself and creation.

Deus sive Natura

In *Questions sur l'Encyclopédie* (1770–1774), Voltaire made a provocative observation. To his mind, Spinoza, a Jewish heretic and alleged atheist, had put forward an idea of God that resembled none so much as that of Fénelon, archbishop of Cambrai and committed mystic. Remarking upon the belief that divine love "banishes fear, inquietude, defiance, and all the failings of a vulgar or interested love," Voltaire feigned confusion as to its provenance: "Is it the virtuous and tender Fénelon, or is it Spinoza who wrote these thoughts? How could two men so opposed, with such different notions of God, come together in the idea of God for himself?"[8] Voltaire did not pose the question in jest. No less a thinker than Leibniz, his philosophical foil in *Candide,* had likened Spinoza's metaphysics to the views of "Molinos and several new Quietists," on the grounds that both assert the existence of a "single, universal spirit" that jeopardizes the principle of individuation.[9] Conceiving the love of God as a wholly selfless sentiment set Spinoza apart, as it did Fénelon, from theological and philosophical conventions.

Voltaire's reflections indicate a fateful turn that had already occurred in Enlightenment polemics over personhood. Spinoza warranted discussion because his early impact prepared the way for philosophical assaults on received wisdom along a wide range of fronts. At first, police surveillance confined the scourge to underground traffic in illicit manuscripts. By the middle decades of the eighteenth century, as the monarchy's censorship apparatus fell under more lenient direction, the tide began to turn against the sentinels of the status quo. In rapid succession there appeared Condillac's *Essai sur l'origine des connaissances humaines* (1746), La Mettrie's *L'Homme-machine* (1747), and Montesquieu's *De l'Esprit des lois* (1748). These works were followed in 1751 by the publication of the first volume of the *Encyclopédie,* which announced the arrival of a cohesive intellectual movement committed to the reconceptualization of all human knowledge.[10] As the philosophes ventured into the world of print, Christian apologists launched their own campaign to distract public opinion from the Enlightenment's allure. From 1730 to 1770, the number of works produced in defense of religion rose exponentially, from a low of around twenty to a high of nearly ninety books per year.[11]

While defenders of the faith might mobilize against philosophes of any stripe, they saved their fiercest rebukes for writings believed to be Spinozist or materialist in inspiration. In terms of the self, what put philosophical radicalism beyond the pale was its derogatory treatment of persons both human and divine. Spinozists and materialists, it was charged, strip the soul of its most worthy faculties. God is likewise pulled down from heaven, thus eliminating providence and hope of eternal reward, both in the present and in the life to come, as guiding forces. For critics, this two-pronged attack heralded nothing less than complete moral and metaphysical dissolution. To combat it, Christian apologists and mainstream philosophes reasserted the powers and prerogatives of self-ownership. Drawing on a wide range of sources, from traditional theology to elements of Cartesianism and Lockean sensationalism, they hoped to save impressionable minds from Spinoza, who haunted the Enlightenment like an inexorable ghost.

Spinoza's French critics seized upon what they perceived as his three most pernicious errors. Each originated in his understanding of substance, or "what is in itself and conceived through itself" and thus can have no external determining cause.[12] First, they condemned the monist doctrine that a single substance constitutes all that exists, since it leaves no distinction between the spiritual and material realms. This understanding departed from the philosophical dualism made famous by Descartes, with its assertion that mind and matter are animated by fundamentally distinct attributes: the attribute of mind is thought, or intellectual and spiritual activity, while that of physical bodies is extension, or dimensionality in physical space. Next to come under fire was Spinoza's imputed espousal of pantheism, which was believed to reject the real existence of individual beings, and thus of distinct human souls. Finally, he was accused of denying free will and personal agency. Although his actual views remain a source of contention, eighteenth-century detractors repeatedly examined his work for incriminating statements on all these points.

Insofar as Spinoza articulated a coherent theory of selfhood, it proceeds along the strict monist lines of the *Ethics*, first published posthumously in 1677. The propositions sustaining his arguments are introduced with geometric precision, each leading to the next with measured tenacity. The foundational unit of analysis is substance, which Spinoza identified with God. Substance is self-sufficient, infinite, and unique, so no distinction can hold between spirit and matter, or between thought and extension. Nor is it possible to separate substance from its modes, or particular manifestations: "Whatever is, is in God, and nothing can either be or be conceived without God." Despite his recourse to theological language, Spinoza repeatedly stressed that nature co-existed with the divine—either as "*Natura naturans* (naturing Nature)," its eternal and infinite essence, or as "*Natura naturata* (natured Nature)," the sum of substance's properties as actually perceived in physical and mental phenomena.[13] The prescriptive elements of this view require humans to grasp these phenomena in order to arrive at an understanding of the whole of nature, and therefore, of God.

The divinity of Spinoza's *Ethics* is decidedly not the redemptive creator of scripture, possessed of free will and absolute sovereignty. Revelation and providence are dead letters, since Spinoza's universe has neither independent purpose nor design. Nature exhibits no contingency, and no intervening force can alter it. The term "volition," even in reference to the divine, merely denotes cognizance of determination. Being ultimately constrained by his own nature, Spinoza's "God does not produce any effect by freedom of will."[14]

If God cannot be thought to act freely, the notion of a binding human will is even more illusory. According to Spinoza, the principal errors of orthodox theology stem from projecting onto God a mistaken sense of human subjectivity. The thoughts of individuals are not unique to themselves, but merely the consequence of God thinking through the mind. As stated in the *Ethics*, "when we say that the human Mind perceives this or that idea, we are saying nothing but that God [. . .] has this or that idea." One can only conclude that our intellect, rather than being the faculty of a particular species, instead forms "part of the infinite intellect of God."[15]

Spinoza thus deviated markedly from the individualist tenets of self-ownership. The dictates of nature make ethical conduct thinkable within a determinist metaphysics, but only because he taught that all things should seek to preserve themselves in accordance with universal reason.[16] Yet his framework also undermines the self's proprietary claims to its thoughts or actions—a position that, for his enemies, implied abdication of moral responsibility. Tellingly, Spinoza failed to define the human person in the rigorous terms he applied to other elements of his philosophy.[17] While nature and divinity cast imposing shadows, the individual subject passes through Spinoza's system like an apparition.

Contemporary claims that the *Ethics*'s dispossessive stance carried mystic or even Quietist overtones were based on Spinoza's descriptions of the love of God, which call to mind Fénelon's view of salvation. He maintained that the search for divine knowledge should be fundamentally disinterested, undertaken purely for its own sake, for "he who loves God cannot strive that God should love him in return."[18] This longing further approximates the mystic ideal of spiritual self-abandonment, in that it reverses the relationship between lover and beloved—and, more generally, between the subject and object of thought. It culminates, according to Spinoza, in the realization that "true liberty is to be and to remain chained by the bonds of [God's] love."[19] Unlike our mistaken notions about the world, which have been marred by the passions, "clear and distinct" truths produce an awareness of God within the self, as coextensive with the self. Such pure knowledge, Spinoza asserts, "begets a love toward a thing immutable and eternal, which we really fully possess," and which "can always be greater and greater, and occupy the greatest part of the mind, and affect it extensively."[20] Yet these pronouncements, seen in light of Spinoza's system as a whole, quickly double back on themselves. If what we think derives ultimately from divine thought, the same should apply to what we have. In grammatical terms, the love of God gives the lie to the subject by reducing it to the object of divine possession.

This understanding of things led Spinoza to embrace the "intellectual love of God," a devotion without beginning or end, in which the mind becomes "endowed with perfection" and achieves "blessedness." It is a state identical to God's love for himself, "not insofar as he is infinite, but insofar as he can be explained by the human Mind's essence, considered under a species of eternity." Only when grasped at this level does the truth conveyed early in the *Ethics*, that "all things (and consequently the human Mind also) depend on God both for their essence and existence," achieve its fullest clarity.[21] For Spinoza, intellectual love can only be radically self-referential—not to the human subject, but to divine substance. The beatified self persists merely as an effect of God's, and nature's, totalizing subjectivity. The mind's operations reflect divinity thinking of itself, through a part of itself. The difficulty of imagining humanity *qua* humanity exemplifies the conundrum of personhood posed by Spinoza's monism: the subject cannot point to itself because its existence does not possess a substantiality of its own. To posit "God, *or* Nature" leaves no distinct position for the human subject to occupy, so that the Spinozist ideal of the self comes into view at the very moment its ostensible existence disappears.[22] Under the sway of intuitive knowledge, the mind achieves beatitude, abolishing the myth of the autonomous, individual person.

Voltaire's assertion that Spinoza and Fénelon understood the pure love of God in a similar way is essentially correct, although certain qualifications are in order. Both emphasized the virtues of disinterestedness, but they parted ways when conceiving the relationship between divine and human forms of personhood. Whereas the mystics held the self in sufficient regard to demand its extinction, for Spinoza the nonexistence of the atomistic, independent individual followed logically from the equation of God, nature, and selfhood in his philosophical system.

The matter is somewhat more complicated in that, as discussed previously, Fénelon scripted a refutation of Spinoza in his *Traité de l'existence et des attributs de Dieu*. He did not undertake a rigorous study of the *Ethics* in that work; nor is Spinoza referred to by name. The engagement was necessarily fleeting. Even so, it offers a telling glimpse into how the archbishop arrived at a position that differed from that of his interlocutor in degree rather than kind.[23] In particular, the exposé inadvertently sheds light on the affinities between Fénelon's theology and the Spinozist philosophy it seeks to overturn.

Fénelon endorsed a mystical monism that stressed divine immanence and the transitory nature of individual beings. His stance resembles Spinoza's claim that if substance is by nature infinite, it is necessarily singular. There can be only one such substance in the universe: God or nature, God as nature. Tellingly, Fénelon did not retreat into Cartesian proofs of material versus spiritual substances or the Leibnizian theory of the monad. Instead, he stipulated that beyond the phenomenal world, but encompassing it, there is an immovable entity that is properly infinite and divine. The marvels of nature, then, are not to be confused with nature in itself. Fénelon lingered over this idea in the *Traité*, as if faced with compelling aspects of Spinoza's thought that resist decisive criticism. "Why add to the universe that seems to surround me," Fénelon wondered, "another incomprehensible nature that I call God?" The answer lay in the character of infinite divinity's perfection as "a simple and immutable being, which has no modification" but still "contains all the perfections of all the most varied modifications in its perfect and immutable simplicity."[24]

Fénelon rejected the *Ethics* for affirming the infinity of extended substance—that is, of matter. Spinoza's identification of God and purely physical nature proved too bold for the archbishop, since it obviates the need for a divine creator. A mere "assemblage of parts" could not comprise the "sovereign unity" whose existence he set out to prove, unless each part were identical to the whole of infinity. This proposition struck Fénelon as absurd, on the grounds that the "composite infinity" associated with Spinoza's understanding of God is hopelessly contradictory. From this statement Fénelon leapt to a daring conclusion. "All that is not really being," he claimed, is "nothingness." The reference to dualist elements might distinguish his thought from Spinoza's, but not without reinforcing the monist framework he shared with his adversary.[25]

The essential difference that Fénelon posed between himself and Spinoza on the nature of God thus turns back on itself. In the *Traité*, Fénelon recounted his discovery of divinity through the ideas of the mind—manifestations of God that, he realized at last, were not his own. If ideas are infinite, and the mind and body are inherently finite, then it follows that the former originate in a being "which is not within me and is not me, but which is superior to me"—that is, in God. Since ideas function as the conduit to divinity, God emerges in Fénelon's mind as at once the subject and object of all thought. "The same God who makes me be," he argued, "also makes me think, for thought is my being." Similarly, "the same God who made me think is not only the cause that produces my thought, he is also its immediate object."[26] This formulation, which recalls Spinoza's intellectual love of God, further distances Fénelon from the Cartesian credo, "I think therefore I am." According to Descartes, it is the human subject's cognition that constitutes unshakable evidence of its existence. Fénelon insisted, on the contrary, that we have been caused to think; therefore, we have been caused to exist. If the archbishop is correct, then Descartes had pronounced the *cogito* in the wrong grammatical voice.

Nevertheless, even if Fénelon shared with the *Ethics* a monist perspective on the universe and a dispossessive attitude toward the self, he could not bring himself, as a Christian, to accept Spinoza's repudiation of a divine creator. For Fénelon, God exists beyond nature, and spiritual abandon entails the surrender of reason and the soul's total submission to divine ownership. In contrast, Spinoza's naturalism displaces the divine from its otherworldly position in denying its absolute autonomy vis-à-vis the universe, while also affirming the sufficiency of human reason—not as the defining attribute of the mind, but as a function of God's determined thought in the world. His quarrels with Spinoza aside, Fénelon's conception of divine totality led him to emphasize immanence over transcendence to such an extent that it could overtake the existential space occupied by the individual soul. This possibility, which reduced the self to a mere figment of the imagination, found new life in the teachings of eighteenth-century Spinozists and materialists, and it would continue to provoke orthodox theologians and mainstream philosophes long after the archbishop's death. If Spinoza should be considered the "messiah of the Enlightenment," then Fénelon stands as one of its most penetrating prophets.[27]

. . .

The affinities between mysticism and Spinozism are thrown into even sharper relief when contrasted with the responses that the *Ethics* elicited among moderate philosophes in France. While admiring Spinoza's quiet bravery, Voltaire found his atheism reprehensible, and lamented his influence over "audacious and misguided scholars who reason poorly, and who, unable to understand creation, the origin of evil, and other difficulties, have recourse to the hypothesis of the eternity of causes and necessity."[28] Condillac, deemed the foremost Lockean in France, professed utter bewilderment at the *Ethics*, which he found so abstract as to be almost incomprehensible. Its object, however, struck him as sufficiently clear. Spinoza set out "to prove that there is but one substance, of which all beings [. . .] are merely modifications," and "that all that happens is an equally necessary result of the nature of this unique substance, so that there is no difference between what is morally good and what is morally evil," Condillac observes in his *Traité des systèmes* (1749). He asks his readers' pardon for "attacking the phantoms that issue" from such speculations, likening the task to that of a "knight errant." A preferable strategy, he concludes, is to "destroy the enchantment" at its source.[29]

Perhaps the most arresting criticism came from the pen of Montesquieu, whose denunciation of the *Ethics* attempts to counter Spinozist philosophy with a defense of individualism. In fragments from his unfinished *Traité des devoirs*, Montesquieu explores the logical ramifications of Spinoza's determinism. In the absence of a providential God, the idea of death becomes unbearable, since the soul is either left with "nothingness" or with an eternity without consolation. Our very being offers adequate proof of a benevolent creator, "for he gave us life, a thing that no one among us could wish to lose. He gave us existence, and what is more, the sentiment of our existence." Providential logic dictates that the notion of a divine creator cannot be reconciled with the despoilment of that creation. Since "our happiness costs him nothing," Montesquieu reasoned, God could not fail to desire it without also admitting to being "more imperfect than men themselves."[30]

Montesquieu's discovery of the *Ethics* compelled him to consider what would become of the human person if nature were God. Spinoza, whom Montesquieu sarcastically lauded as "a great genius" who "has promised me that I will die like an insect," sought nothing less than to deplete the self of its metaphysical riches. In exchange for the "immense space that my mind covers" in reality, Spinoza offered "an area of four or five feet in the Universe." This radical act of dispossession, Montesquieu concluded, degrades the moral subject and threatens to neutralize its distinctive elements:

According to him [Spinoza], I am not a being distinguishable from any other. He strips me of all that I believed was the most personal in me. I do not know where to find again this self [*moi*] that interested me so much, since I am more lost within extension than a drop of water in the sea. Why glory? Why shame? Why this modification which does not exist? Does it want, therefore, to create a body that is apart from the Universe? It is neither here nor there; it is nothing distinct from being. The lion and the insect, Charlemagne and Chilperic: they have been and have passed without distinction in the universality of the Universe.[31]

This passage expresses how Spinoza's philosophy could unsettle a partisan of self-ownership by offering the prospect of completely losing one's personal identity. More striking still is Montesquieu's likening of the effects of totalizing substance to the mystic's surrender to divinity. Not unlike Fénelon's spiritual mentor Guyon, but in a thoroughly negative sense, he deployed the metaphor of dissolution—a drop of water swallowed by the sea—to convey the existential abandonment that Spinoza's metaphysics entails.[32]

Despite this forceful critique, Montesquieu's later work is not without its own deterministic elements. In particular, the chapters on climate in *De l'Esprit des lois* suggest that political institutions follow from complementary social and physical conditions according to fixed natural laws. Although Montesquieu was careful to preserve a function for revealed religion that would have had no place in the *Ethics*, orthodox critics denounced the treatise as a vehicle for Spinozism—a charge that he vehemently denied. In defending his work, Montesquieu claimed that it confirmed the superiority of Christianity as the most advanced state of religion, the tenets of which gave credence to his views on the state and its subjects.[33]

The uproar over *De l'Esprit des lois* could not drown out the striking resonance of Montesquieu's fears for the self with those of his clerical detractors. In theological terms, the efforts of Christian apologists to defend the spiritual possessions of the human subject echoed his sentiment that true religion must appeal to the natural human interest in recompense.[34] In economic matters, his stature as a theorist of *doux commerce* placed him in a position to emphasize the mutually beneficial effects of exchange among self-owning subjects. This claim mitigated Catholic suspicions of economic egoism on grounds not far removed from the "enlightened self-interest" thesis articulated by the Jansenists such as Pierre Nicole.[35] Whatever their differences concerning the nature of God or the organization of states, both Enlightenment philosophes and resolutely Catholic theologians showed intense interest in saving the self from the threat posed by radical philosophy. Their respective arguments for doing so proved remarkably consistent, even if the rationales behind them did not: depriving the human person of its possessive claims over its existence in this life, and of divine consolation in the next, leaves the self with no basis for concerted moral action.

Exposing the Impostors

The specter of Spinozism loomed far beyond the intricate propositions of the *Ethics*. Spinoza's works were banned throughout Europe almost upon publication, but the clandestine manuscript trade disseminated his ideas among social and cultural elites—especially those with international connections, such as courtiers, military officers, and diplomats—despite intermittent police crackdowns and the lingering fear of arrest. The most notorious of these illicit works, which were mainly composed in French, is the *Traité des trois imposteurs*, also known as *L'Esprit de Spinosa*. Although the exact origins of the text remain uncertain, it appears to have been a compendium made up of synopses of part 1 of the *Ethics* and Spinoza's *Theologico-Political Treatise*, amplified by selections taken from the works of seditious authors such as Lucilio Vanini, François de

La Mothe Le Vayer, Gabriel Naudé, and Thomas Hobbes. Jan Vroesen, a freethinker from a prominent Rotterdam family who had served as a diplomat in Paris, likely produced the original version during the waning years of the seventeenth century. The work circulated widely in manuscript form (around 200 copies have been identified) and first appeared in print in 1719.[36] This vulgarization of Spinoza's system not only introduced a wider circle of readers to the doctrine of monist determinism, but also signaled a materialist turn in radical thought that would bear significantly on the development of French philosophy in the second half of the eighteenth century.

The compiler of the *Traité des trois imposteurs* refitted the *Ethics*'s geometric expositions as a weapon against traditional authorities. The aim was to expose the claims of revealed religion and absolute monarchy as insidious plots fabricated to suppress free thought and to maintain the illegitimate power of Church and state. The masses, on this view, had little chance to liberate themselves, since truth was controlled and obscured by priests, kings, and a host of "false savants with base and self-interested souls." The true philosopher, then, must endeavor to strip away the prejudices of the multitude, in the hope that "their eyes open little by little and their mind be convinced of this truth, that God is not as usually imagined."[37]

Like Spinoza's philosophy, *Traité des trois imposteurs* criticized monotheism for conflating human sentiments with the divine. Dispelling the "lofty speculations" of theologians leads to the realization that "God is neither angry nor jealous, that justice and mercy are false titles that one attributes to him, and that what the Prophets and Apostles say of him teaches us nothing about his nature or his essence." The anthropomorphization of God binds the faithful to a fictitious divinity by appealing to their self-interest. Since the supreme being is thought to operate with some end in mind, it seems reasonable to profess that "God made everything for man, and reciprocally that man was made only for God." This illusion conceals the true nature of moral categories, as well as the position of the human person in the universe. For instance, the belief that the soul is cast in the image of God leads to the erroneous conclusion that "in order to be free, it suffices to sense in oneself that which one wills and wishes, without calling into question the causes that dispose one to will or to wish." Christianity thus encourages a cult of spiritual individualism in which men and women exercise ownership of the world by right of their privileged relationship to divinity. Surrounded by objects they can exploit to their advantage, humans presume that "there is nothing in nature that has not been made for them, and which they cannot possess [*jouir*] and use [*disposer*]." The idea of God functions as a means of authorizing these ill-gotten gains, and religion sustains the illusion of their validity.[38]

The *Traité des trois imposteurs* denounced this arrangement as a devious conspiracy of "mercenary souls" who unjustly monopolize religious and political power. The truth of the matter is that "nature offers no end" for our existence and that "all final causes are merely human fictions." The idea that there are motives for divine action defies all logic, since it presupposes "an indigent God" who somehow lacks the objects or conditions that he desires. Christianity, then, is little more than a cabal for illegitimate possession. Convinced of the untruth that "all that they see is made for them," believers strive "to apply everything to themselves, and to judge the price of things by the profit that they extract from them." The architects of the system ensure its perpetuation by distinguishing righteousness and iniquity on the basis of "that which turns to their profit and the divine cult." The doctrines of providence and revelation are not testaments to God's grace, but merely reflect the extent of human self-regard. Against the siren song of Christian utility, the voice of reason teaches that an object's moral value does not depend on momentary desires. On the contrary, "one cannot judge the perfection or imperfection of a being, except to the extent that one knows the essence of nature." Good and evil have no inherent meaning, since "everything is necessarily as it is, and in nature there is no imperfection since everything follows from the necessity of things."[39]

The treatise's anonymous author mocked religious authorities for preferring to consult their "book of magic" rather than recognizing the law of necessity that "God—that is to say, nature, insofar as it is the principle of all things—has written in the heart of men." Scripture bears witness not to divinely inspired truths, but to "the politics of princes and priests." The teachings of Moses, Muhammad, and Jesus—the "three impostors" for whom the treatise is named—ultimately serve to strengthen the hold of fanaticism on the poor and the ignorant as an instrument of control. Only "a free and disinterested mind" can extricate itself from this tangle of lies. Yet the truth to be gained does not set one free. Rather, it reveals the minor, wholly determined position of the human person in the universe.[40]

The remaining chapters of the *Traité* proceed from the critique of monotheism to an understanding of God and the human person freed from the prejudices of dogma. The ensuing account owes much to Spinoza's writings. God and nature are regarded as synonymous, "the immanent and non-distinct cause" of phenomena that bear no relation to human notions of good and evil. The impartial observer must deny the existence of a supernatural dispenser of spiritual goods, since the "idea of punishment and recompense can only seduce the ignorant." As Montesquieu feared, the self has no exalted standing in such a world. God is the blind, indiscriminate source of all things, with no particular creature "preferable to another in his regard, and man costing him as much to produce as the smallest earthworm or the least plant." The soul consists entirely of matter, so that the substance animating human beings is indistinct from that of any other entity. In contrast to Spinoza's view that substance subsumes thought and extension to parallel degrees, his successor held that all beings owe their existence to a purely physical "soul of the world" that can be found "diffused to a greater or lesser degree in other bodies according to their nature."[41]

This dismal portrait of the materialist soul thus excludes communion with nature under the guise of the intellectual love of God. Although the work shares Spinoza's monist framework, it makes no attempt to scale the metaphysical heights explored in the *Ethics*. The efforts in the *Traité des trois imposteurs* to discredit orthodox claims regarding divine sovereignty and the centrality of the human person in creation signaled a new iteration of the self's dispossessive relationship with nature that had no place for God or for religion in any guise. The vulgarizing tendencies of the work suggest that Spinozist philosophy had moved beyond the rarefied intellectual circles that had initially contained it. Over the next several decades, the *Traité* would go through several editions, including one in 1768 overseen by d'Holbach and Jacques Naigeon, that rendered the text relatively more literary in style, but also more uncompromising in message.[42]

Ecclesiastical authorities faced the mounting threat of radical philosophy at a time when political and religious absolutism could no longer disguise the dogmas and ideologies warring beneath its fragile veneer. As the king struggled against intransigent magistrates in the Parlements, and Jesuits railed against Jansenists, orthodox tradition began to collapse before the eyes of a reading public whose critical sensibilities grew sharper with each passing conflict. On the doctrinal front, Christian apologists were confronted with the most tendentious countermovement to emerge since the Wars of Religion. Galvanized by the organizational prowess of Diderot and d'Alembert, the philosophes marshaled their forces as "a society of *gens de lettres*," which, despite internal tensions, claimed to represent a new intellectual and cultural elite.[43] Menacing philosophical currents surged in a flood of subversive writings, from clandestine texts such as the *Traité des trois imposteurs* to the thinly veiled, cross-referenced impieties of the *Encyclopédie*. In response, theological polemicists unleashed a bombardment of texts—almost 950 appeared in the years from 1670 to 1802.[44] According to the historian Darrin McMahon, these works formed the basis of a powerful "anti-*philosophe* discourse" that underwrote an eighteenth-century counter-Enlightenment, presaged the violent reaction against the French Revolution, and even laid the ideological foundations for the modern political Right.[45] Yet the religious opposition to the Enlightenment was not above appropriating the sources and methods of its purported enemies in an effort to keep the tide of radicalism from sweeping away the ideals of intellectual activity and moral agency that it shared with philosophical moderates.

As the number of both seditious and apologist works continued to grow, their rhetorical strategies came more and more to resemble one another. Instead of monotonously citing the Fathers of the Church on the existence of God and providential design, Christian apologists sought to settle doubts about the nature of divinity while sparing readers the tedium of theological hair-splitting. More remarkable still was their tendency to interpolate long passages from Spinozist and materialist authors in their works. Paradoxically, the dissemination of heretical ideas accompanied their refutation, so much so that critics wondered aloud on whose side religious controversialists were fighting.[46]

More commonly, Christian counterattacks against radical philosophy employed a terminology similar to that found in orthodox denunciations of mystical heresy earlier in the century. For instance, the theologian Benoît Sinsart (1695–1776) charged that Spinozism and materialism, not unlike Guyon's theology, "undermines morality and the hope for another life, by the annihilation of the soul." Furthermore, the assertion that the human mind is merely the modification of a single substance presumes its divisibility, and therefore its incapacity for thought. If one accepts the materialist view, Sinsart intoned, "the soul will cease to think; it will be destroyed."[47] Like the cults of the Quietists and the *convulsionnaires*, materialism was "a public plague."[48] For François-André-Adrien Pluquet (1716–1790), who held chairs in moral philosophy and history at the Collège de France, it also manifested signs of spiritual pathology. He held that curing radicalism required an evaluation of its "symptoms" and "causes." The disorder presented itself as a monist determinism that denied both human free will and hope of divine recompense—fallacies that had previously been decried as the logical outcome of Quietism.[49] To defuse these threats, it would be necessary to undermine materialism's most scandalous element, its denigration of God and self.

According to Laurent François (1698–1782), Spinoza's supreme being was a debased entity, the monster of a corrupt imagination. If movement is inherent in substance, and nature organized according to self-perpetuating, necessary laws, divinity no longer has a purpose or reason for being. Stripped of the prerogatives of the creator of the universe, the God of the *Ethics* turns instead to self-destruction: he "hates himself, he pleads mercy for himself and is refused it, he persecutes himself, he kills himself, he eats himself, he slanders himself, he condemns himself to the scaffold."[50] The Jansenist curé Guillaume de Maleville (1699–1756) likewise stressed that divinity without autonomy is a contradiction in terms. In particular, the denial of God's power to bestow spiritual goods on the righteous and to deprive the wicked of them renders moral virtue a meaningless ideal. Maleville defended divine transcendence on the grounds that "God has perfect liberty and independence, so that neither his own needs nor any exterior cause can impose necessity on him." "His wisdom and his pleasure," therefore, "are his unique laws." Active motives stand behind the design of the universe. Otherwise, God would seem to be an impoverished deity, "deprived [*destituée*] of goodness" and unworthy of worship. In reality, Maleville claimed, "the possessions [*biens*] that he has distributed with such profusion throughout nature prove that he has our interest in view."[51] The principal directive of creation is thus to increase spiritual and temporal prosperity.

Maleville's critique, like those of his fellow apologists, wedded moral arguments to metaphysical speculations on the nature of the soul. He feared that reducing existence to a single material substance, as did radical philosophers, theorizes away the thinking subject, since matter is incapable of cognition, and therefore of moral action. "A free being," he asserted, "has in itself an interior principle of action, which it can exercise at will." This liberty is void, however, "if its determinations come to it from a foreign cause," as the materialists claimed in relation to nature, and the Quietists in relation to God.[52] Beyond these considerations of the properties of matter, simple reflection on our "constitution" suffices to prove that the soul is not a passive being. Divine law itself confirms human agency by authorizing reward and punishment. Echoing Sinsart's sentiments on the necessary desire to accrue spiritual goods, Maleville charged that unbelievers unwittingly place "all their resources on the hope of their destruction."[53]

To refute the materialist position, Christian apologists asserted the essential distinction between the spiritual soul and the physical body. The union of these separate substances, François argued, is purely contingent on the will of God, who desires to grant the soul the means to rule over the temporal sphere. The spiritual component of the self—residing in the soul or the mind—governs its physical component, while the human person imposes its will on the world of lesser creation. Our relation to material bodies, including our own, thus replicates God's relation to the soul. The mind clearly concerns itself with the pains and pleasures of the body. In turn, the body serves the soul as a means of appropriating that which it desires to possess in nature:

From the most distant stars of the firmament to the surface of the Earth, all that is visible is for our eyes. [. . .] All manner of sounds are for our ears. Every odor is for us to smell. Fruits and plants are for us to taste. The animals of every species, whether they live in the water, in the air, or on the earth, are at our service. Thus the entire world is reduced to our use, and through this use comes its unity, for everything is included within the expanse of the sensations, whose organs belong to the body, and whose end is the mind.[54]

Nevertheless, God grants humankind stewardship over creation for benevolent ends. The physical world sustains members of a society founded on the natural right, and therefore duty, to love and to be loved in return.[55] The divine mandate for acquisitiveness does not, therefore, sanction antisocial conduct.

François's emphasis on enjoying the possession of things did not keep him from utilizing one of the prevailing accusations of the counter-Enlightenment, that the new philosophy promoted unbridled egoism and threatened the continued existence of humankind.[56] Yet in his hands, this tactic took a curious form. Since Spinoza did not advocate the unqualified pursuit of self-love, François turned to supposed logical inconsistencies in his argument. "How are *amour-propre* and the passions sure and infallible guides," he inquired, "if they must be ruled by reason?" Quoting the *Theologico-Political Treatise* on the imperative for citizens to "defend the interest of others as our own," François concluded that Spinoza's thought is at war with itself. The exercise of reason is incompatible with a thoroughgoing determinism that regards egoistic behavior as a dictate of nature.[57] Christian apologists, as François's critique suggests, claimed to speak a language of self-ownership that starkly differed from that of their opponents. However, confusion arose over Spinoza's views on selfishness, since his system tends to efface rather than enhance the status of the individual. The dispossessive elements of radical philosophy were, then, a stumbling block for its refutation.

Pluquet addressed this problem by distinguishing between two types of fatalism. The "egoists," exemplified by Descartes, Malebranche, and Leibniz, "believe that they alone exist, and there is not, outside themselves, an earth, a sky, or other men." Spinoza, however, belongs to "the partisans of the universal soul," who believe that "an infinite multitude of intelligences [. . .] are emanations of a single soul that is in the world." According to Pluquet, discord between these positions becomes apparent when listening to the voice of God, which rises above the murmurs of human reason. The egoists' arguments falter on the existence of the body, and therefore of multiple substances. The devotees of the universal soul fail to see that each substance possesses fundamentally different capacities, since spiritual substance exercises dominion over bodily substance. Although Pluquet judged Spinoza more fairly than his contemporaries—even exonerating the *Ethics* of the charge that it preaches materialism in disguise—he spurned its implications for human subjectivity. In keeping with the moderate Enlightenment, he maintained that Spinoza's system grossly underestimated the soul's agency and even seemed to deny it a distinct identity.[58]

The charge that Spinoza and his materialist progeny held the self in disdain followed from the individualist principles of Christian orthodoxy.

For Sinsart, as for Descartes, spiritual substance assures the existence of distinct selves in possession of their thoughts: "I know, then, that I exist and that I am a particular being; consequently, I recognize my individuality. [. . .] I cannot doubt that these impressions are real, or that they are my own." The self is its own master, and free will is "an essential property of our soul," which by nature cannot belong to matter. Whereas spiritual substance forms an active, indivisible, and indestructible thinking entity, matter is defined by passivity, divisible extension, and temporal finitude. Thus, the soul is not, and can never be, a material form. If it were, the self would lose its unity, and therefore its unique existence: "I would no longer be an individual, a singular person who feels, but in reality several persons."[59]

To an even greater extent than Maleville, Sinsart insisted that individuality presumes the ownership of a given body by a particular soul. For him, the spiritual self relates to the material world through a process of appropriation. First, the mind translates physical sensations into "immaterial objects," from which it constructs reality. Thus, "the images the body transmits to the soul, which are properly our ideas, all that we feel, this entire universe—the heavens, the earth, the seas—are merely in ourselves." Likewise, "all these varied sentiments that we have of them are only the modifications of our soul, and belong to us alone."[60] Sinsart's opposition to Spinoza could not be clearer. Fearing that the monism of the *Ethics* reduces the human subject to an object of thoughtless matter, he responded with a full-blown idealism that makes the self the sole possessor of all its senses encounter. The move would seem to qualify him for a place among Pluquet's egoists, who likewise dissolved the universe in a sea of immateriality.

. . .

Sinsart's views, while idiosyncratic, still fall along the continuum of justifications for self-ownership that moderate philosophes and theologians formulated in tandem. As noted above, Montesquieu shared religious concerns that Spinozism and materialism undermined the very basis for the self's personal identity. Likewise, the notion that a divine creator had designed the universe according to a moral order was commonplace among both Christian apologists and leading figures of the mainstream Enlightenment. According to Louis de Jaucourt, the most prolific contributor to the *Encyclopédie*, "all that which is in God, all that which is in man, and all that which is in the world, leads us to providence."[61] His fellow *Encyclopédiste* Abbé Jean Pestre also held that "Nature has fashioned for all a law of our own happiness." He placed particular emphasis on the relationship between ownership and contentment: "The possession of goods is the foundation of our happiness, but it is not happiness itself, for what would happiness be if we possessed goods but lacked the sentiment of possessing them?"[62] Notwithstanding that it championed an anticlerical position that he have might otherwise supported, Voltaire, for his part, publicly denounced the *Traité des trois imposteurs*. As a "restraint on the villainous" and "the hope of the just," belief in a providential deity constitutes "the sacred bond of society," he asserted. His faith in the sheer usefulness of religion led him famously to quip, "If God did not exist, it would be necessary to invent him."[63]

To be sure, Voltaire's writings could provoke horror and scorn among the devout.[64] It is thus all the more striking that certain Christian apologists would come to count him among their number—if only in hindsight. In 1826, Abbé Athanase-René Mérault de Bizy, grand vicar of the diocese of Orléans, published an extensive list of passages that proved Voltaire's fundamental orthodoxy to him. According to Mérault, the philosophe had never abandoned the lessons of his Jesuit education, in particular regarding the necessity of religion "for the happiness of the earth."[65] While Mérault wisely refrained from hailing Voltaire as "a Father of the Church," he held that one could find in the philosophe's work "the makings of a book of devotion, and almost a catechism."[66] For instance, he cited an excerpt from Voltaire's *Lettres de Memmius à Ciceron* summarizing his defense of religion: "What I cannot understand is the disdainful, foolish indifference in which almost all men languish in regard to the object that should interest them the most. [. . .] Nearly everyone says, 'What does it matter?' and having spoken thus, they go count their money or run to the theater."[67] In the struggle against radical philosophy, figures associated with both the moderate Enlightenment and Christian apologetics maintained that the soul should seek those goods that bring it happiness, and that this pursuit is in conformity with reason and the founding principle of human society.[68] Even if the Catholic faith needed reform, Mérault preferred its myth of providence to the atheistic credo of d'Holbach, whom he regarded as "a devil of a man inspired by Beelzebub."[69]

The example of Voltaire shows that eighteenth-century polemics over the nature of divinity and the status of the human person were not organized exclusively around the contest between Enlightenment and counter-Enlightenment. Rather, an operative distinction crystallized between the defenders of individualism, whether on Christian or deistic grounds, and the partisans of dispossession in radical circles, who called for the annihilation of the self. While the antagonists in these clashes drew on arguments first articulated during controversies over mystical heresy, the stakes had grown considerably higher. Spinozists and materialists called into question not only human self-ownership, but even the very existence of God.

From the Human Machine to the Goddess of Nature

Spinoza's influence on Enlightenment thought has been a subject of debate among intellectual historians. According to Ernst Cassirer, Pierre Bayle's critique of the *Ethics* made Spinoza persona non grata—his ideas could only be acknowledged obliquely, if at all.[70] More recent accounts, however, demonstrate that Spinozism remained a touchstone of eighteenth-century philosophy, even if Spinoza himself never attained the exalted status of Locke and Newton.[71] Jonathan Israel extents this interpretation to the utmost degree, canonizing Spinoza as the progenitor of the radical Enlightenment, if not the very soul of its philosophy. The period's most astute observers, while highly conscious of his influence, offer a somewhat more nuanced view. Of the two articles in the *Encyclopédie* devoted to the subject, the anonymous entry on Spinoza's thought tends to follow Bayle's line, with the quip that, even among ardent students, its meaning remains "incomprehensible," and an "enigma." In a separate article, "Spinosiste," Diderot observes that the development of French materialism marked both a continuation and a departure from the monist vision elaborated in Spinoza's metaphysics.[72] Unlike their forbearer, Diderot notes, "modern Spinozists" hold that the universe is comprised exclusively of material forms, whose properties must be understood through empirical observation rather than logical reconstruction. Nevertheless, "they follow the older Spinozism in all its consequences"—namely, in their arguments for singular substance and the determined nature of reality.[73]

Spinoza's heirs claimed a universal knowledge that could at last fix the essential attributes of God and the human person. In schematic terms, Enlightenment materialism can be regarded as a powerful synthesis of Lockean empiricism and Spinozist monism that applied the innovations of both thinkers to new purposes. Influenced by the rising tide of scientific vitalism, which emphasized the dynamic, self-perpetuating activity of natural forces, radical materialists such as d'Holbach went far beyond their predecessors in denying the existence of both God and the soul.[74] They argued that the self depends for its existence not on the grace of a divine creator, but on sensory experiences gleaned from the external world. Since matter is endowed with the cause of its own movement, it requires nothing in the way of supernatural direction or subjective agency to control its functions. D'Holbach believed that nature alone directs the universe, and should thus serve as the guide for all social action. Against the Cartesian doctrine that the soul acts on the body as a subject on its object, radical materialists emphasized the mind's passive role as the register of sensations—with limited allowance for memory as a site of internalized activity and source of self-identity.[75] Christian apologists found these tenets appalling in theory and acutely dangerous in practice. As evidence, they pointed to an epidemic of suicides in Paris by desperate souls who believed that philosophical fatalism authorized their acts of self-destruction.

Despite its enemies' claims to the contrary, eighteenth-century materialism never attained strict uniformity as an intellectual current. The historian Alan Charles Kors has noted diverse and even contradictory views even within a single grouping of materialist thinkers—in this case, the *coterie holbachique*.[76] Their squabbles were not confined within the walls of the radical salon. Diderot and d'Holbach publicly denounced the mechanist physician Julien Offroy de La Mettrie (1709–1751), whose writings, which included the notorious *L'Homme-machine* (1748), forced him out of France and eventually to the court of Frederick the Great of Prussia, where he died in 1751. In their estimation, La Mettrie's work distorted materialist principles by portraying human beings, not as nature's humble servants, but as incorrigible criminals kept in check only by the stern hand of social convention.[77] Among the issues involved in this dispute was the self's capacity for possessing things in a manner that privileged the natural whole over the conflicting interests of individual beings. D'Holbach sought to redeem possession along radical, collectivist lines, as an effect of the self's surrender to the dictates of nature, in contrast to La Mettrie's defense of egoism and political absolutism.

According to La Mettrie, the human person—not unlike Vaucanson's celebrated flute-playing automaton, whose system of axles, strings, and bellows produced realistic music—consists of an assemblage of parts engaged in an array of mental and physical operations.[78] While decidedly mechanist in orientation, like the Cartesian medical science of the day, this view rejected the primacy of spiritual substance that had informed Descartes's model of the universe. Personal identity, according to *L'Homme-machine*, is merely the fluctuating sum of effects of physical factors—climate, diet, and the general state of health. For instance, a mind racked by illness might oscillate between genius and imbecility. All knowledge, likewise, originates in the brain's ability to reproduce impressions originally derived from the senses, which function "like a violin string or a harpsichord key" when played.[79]

So constituted, the human person remains, from cradle to grave, determined by the bodily imperative to seek its own pleasure. Yet one can do so in a deliberate, calculated way. In *L'Art de jouir* (1751), La Mettrie breathlessly describes sexual bliss as an experience of such intensity that "the soul seems to leave us in order to pass into the adored object," and that "two lovers form but one mind animated by love." Yet he also cautions that these sentiments "are merely pleasures," and that one must await "the sweet state that follows" to feel fully "all the charms of sensual delight."

While such a state might seem to resemble a form of spiritual abandon, it paradoxically marks when the soul "is its own [*est à elle-même*], precisely inasmuch as is necessary in order to enjoy the possession of itself [*jouir d'elle-même*]." True "voluptuousness" differs from baser pleasures in its sense of economy. For instance, while the gourmand stuffs himself indiscriminately, the voluptuous soul samples modestly from each dish, because "he wants to profit from everything."[80] In the latter case, pleasure does not reduce the human person to sensual experience so much as serve as a means for one to possess oneself more deeply. This ideal, moreover, requires a degree of detachment and control in keeping with individual self-ownership rather than with dispossession.

Yet La Mettrie made clear that his art of voluptuousness was suitable only for an enlightened elect, the rare *honnête homme* who graced society. Lurking behind his hedonism was a pessimistic understanding of human nature retained from his upbringing in the Jansenist stronghold of Saint-Malo.[81] As he explained in *Anti-Sénèque, ou Discours sur le bonheur souverain* (1748–1751), "men are born wicked," and education can improve but not fundamentally alter human nature. For the hapless majority, virtue is a matter of coercion rather than choice, since "without the fear of laws, no wicked man would be restrained." The aim, then, should be to find "peace in the midst of crime."[82] If Christians seek entry to the city of God, *hommes-machines* content themselves with more transitory pleasures. For the mass of humans, self-ownership regresses to mere acquisitiveness, and licentiousness proves the necessity of strict social controls. The state exercises the right to punish, even arbitrarily, crimes stemming from unchecked desire, lest selfish creatures destroy each other in a rush to satisfy their whims. Thus, while La Mettrie resembles the caricature of the radical philosophe sketched by Christian apologists perhaps more than any other major figure, he remained a defender, albeit in a rather idiosyncratic manner, of the existing sociopolitical order.[83]

La Mettrie's writings met with condemnation from every side. Even fellow materialists were scandalized by his disregard for moral conscience. Tellingly, d'Holbach compared La Mettrie to Mandeville, another defender of egoism who borrowed heavily from Jansenist moral philosophy. Like his predecessor, La Mettrie also assumed the worst of human nature, although he expressed even less confidence in the possibility that self-interested means could serve social-utilitarian ends. D'Holbach thus reserved his harshest judgment for La Mettrie, whose affronts to virtue he called the ravings of "a true frenetic." Philosophers who obscured the distinction between good and evil, d'Holbach claimed, failed to understand "the nature of man" and "the true source of his duties."[84] It is precisely the need to maintain social unity without recourse to traditional power structures that distinguishes the totalizing *système de la nature* from the atomistic *homme-machine*. In elaborating his philosophy, d'Holbach framed the relationship between the particular self and the natural whole in terms that owe more to Spinoza's tranquil universe than to Mandeville's swarming hive.

The baron d'Holbach, wealthy scion of a Rhenish noble family and naturalized French subject, was celebrated for the hospitality he showed fellow intellectuals at his Paris salon, where he regaled them with fine food and heady conversation. His regular guests, among them Jean-François Marmontel, André Morellet, Jean-François de Saint-Lambert, Friedrich-Melchior Grimm, Denis Diderot, and Jacques-André Naigeon, represented an array of philosophical views. Only the last two identified themselves as atheists.

D'Holbach was less widely known for *Système de la nature*, a work published anonymously in 1770 and not formally attributed to him until after his death in 1789. The treatise sent immediate shock waves through the reading public and became one of the best-selling philosophical works of the century.[85] An avid amateur scientist who hosted physicians of the Montpellier school and contributed learned articles on chemistry, mineralogy, and related topics to the *Encyclopédie*, d'Holbach developed a theory of matter that melded mechanist determinism and vitalist dynamism.[86] Of more immediate and abiding interest for him were questions related to metaphysics, religion, and social obligation. Accordingly, *Système de la nature* utilized materialist arguments to construct a rigorous defense of atheism on naturalistic grounds, which in turn informed a determinist vision of politics and morality. D'Holbach contended that human misery stems from ignorance of the laws of nature, a state perpetuated by the "phantoms" of religious imagination. The task of philosophy, then, is to awaken humankind from these "reveries" and induce it to find fulfillment in recognizing the dictates of necessity.[87]

This means of liberation paradoxically begin by acknowledging one's determined status. Human beings have no divine origins, d'Holbach contended, but are rather "the work of nature." As such they remain within its parameters and without chance of escape. The thoughts, motives, and actions of every being are all "equally natural effects, the necessary result of its own mechanism, and of the impetus that it receives from the beings that surround it." On a broader scale, nature operates as the guiding force in the universe, comprised of self-perpetuating matter organized into particular forms according to its "immutable laws."[88]

Like Spinoza, d'Holbach follows a monistic vision that has neither a place nor a need for the designs of a divine creator or the desires of mere mortals. Since the totality of nature is "but a chain of causes and effects that ceaselessly follow from one to the other," individual beings can never be said to possess "independent energy" or the wherewithal for "detached action." Their role, properly understood, is to fulfill a "necessary task in the general work." For humans in this system, being a self entails not agency but submission. D'Holbach seeks to explode the myth that the universe remains "under the empire of an intelligent cause whose model was and always will be man." God had not created humanity; the human mind had invented God to justify its illegitimate claims to sovereignty over the terrestrial sphere. D'Holbach insisted that we reconsider our existence as nature determines it, rather than imagine nature on the basis of a flawed conception of the self.[89]

The first task is to recognize that all material forms share equal status before a universal law. No being stands above it. Man deludes himself with a false vision of the soul as an independent agent—capable of acting "always by his own power" and standing "independent of the general laws of nature and of objects that, often knowingly and always despite himself, nature causes to act on him." An empirical investigation of the natural world suffices to prove that "man is in each instance of his life a passive instrument in the hands of necessity." D'Holbach reasons that, since the movements of the universe are determined in a great interlocking chain of causality, no single being can be thought to possess a particular will outside it. Accordingly, nature alone "signals to man each point of the trajectory that he must follow." Duped by the false promises of revealed religion, however, the individual—"only an imperceptible point in the immensity" of matter—clings to the belief that "the universe was made for him" and therefore continues to claim the ridiculous title of "king of the universe." D'Holbach takes precise aim to shatter these delusions of grandeur. "O man!" he mocks. "Will you never grasp that you are but an ephemeral thing?" The chance displacement of a single atom could "rob you of this intelligence of which you are so proud."[90]

On materialist and moral grounds, d'Holbach refutes the belief that the soul exists independently of the physical body. The faculties of judgment, memory, and will, which theologians had designated as the province of a distinct spiritual substance, merely pertain to the particular organization of matter in the brain, which reacts to stimuli as a harp responds to its player's touch. The mind generates no innate ideas of its own, but depends absolutely on sensory experience for its operations. Personal identity, likewise, proceeds from the succession of sensations that the mind recollects, rather than from an intrinsic self-consciousness. The Christian doctrine of free will is thus merely a ploy to convince believers that God metes out rewards or punishments justly, as a consequence of one's deliberate actions. In reality, the system of nature determines how the mind functions: the individual is "necessarily guided at every step by the real or fictive advan-

tages that he attaches to the objects that excite his passions." In contrast
to La Mettrie, however, d'Holbach places self-striving within a totalizing
framework that renders the good of an individual being inseparable from
the good of all.[91]

Nature, d'Holbach argued, dictates that the force of "self-gravitation"
binds men and women to seek ways of preserving and improving their individual existence, but not at the expense of their fellow creatures. Reason
directs the self toward ends that are "truly of concern for ourselves and
others" because they lead "necessarily to the real and durable well-being
of society." Human social relations, then, should reflect the determined
interdependence of things in nature. Individuals must pursue their interests
as part of the common cause. Mutual aid and coordinated effort are indispensable, since the isolated self does not possess all that is necessary to
fulfill its desires. As d'Holbach noted, "the most impractical project for a
being who lives in society is to wish to make oneself exclusively happy."[92]
At first glance, these pronouncements would seem to resemble Nicole's
doctrine of enlightened self-interest, by which egoism could be converted
into sociability. D'Holbach, however, rejects this formula. According to
Système de la nature, love of self is not a "tyrannical disposition" symptomatic of the fallen status of humankind.[93] On the contrary, it refers to a
psychological determination shared by all for the good of all, proof positive of the essential benevolence of the human person once freed from the
influence of religious pessimism.

These metaphysical and moral observations culminate in d'Holbach's
doctrine of "fatalism," which serves as the foundation of a naturalistic
social order that "procures for all members their physical needs, security,
liberty, and the possession of their natural rights." Against the persistent
charge that atheism is incompatible with virtue, d'Holbach maintains that
his system would establish morals on "an unshakable base." Those who
reconcile themselves to the "system of necessity" subsist in a state of "con-
tented apathy" that follows from "a reasoned resignation to the decrees of
destiny." True fatalists come to realize that the individual "possesses nothing that he has not received" and that one's will remains free only insofar as it conforms to nature. "Let us submit ourselves then to necessity,"
d'Holbach implores, "let us resign ourselves to nature. Only this disposition
allows one to embrace "the goods that nature offers us" while combating
"the necessary evils that it makes us endure with the necessary remedies that
it consents to accord us."[94] Under such an arrangement, the human person
owes its possession of moral goods to an acute awareness of its shared existence with all the other beings that together constitute the system of nature.

Ironically, d'Holbach's efforts to smash the false idols of Christian devotion do not prevent him from swaddling fatalist doctrine in quasi-religious

imagery. The final pages of *Système de la nature* depict nature as a goddess worthy of adoration, the singular force that reconciles the individual to humankind as a whole, and humankind to the universe. Assuming the role of high priest, d'Holbach envisions nature summoning her charges to find repose in their collective being:

Cease contemplating the future. Live for yourself, live for your fellows. Descend within your self [*ton intérieur*], consider the sensitive beings that surround you, and leave behind those gods who can do nothing for your felicity. Enjoy [*Jouis*], and have others enjoy, the use of the goods that I have placed in common for all the children who have come equally from my womb. [. . .] Thus be happy, O humanity! Nature beckons you, but remember that you cannot be happy alone. I invite all mortals to happiness as well as you; it is only in making them happy that you will be happy yourself. Such is the order of destiny.[95]

To stress the binding force of the covenant between nature and humanity, d'Holbach summarizes his moral program in the form of ten commandments: to exhibit in all things justice, goodness, magnanimity, gentleness, gratitude, modesty, forgiveness, chastity, humanity, and love of country. Then the goddess nature turns to the matter of civic duty. With Rousseauian ardor, she reminds citizens that the laws "are the expression of public will to which your particular will should be subordinated." The virtuous citizen, attentive to the presence of nature in all its forms, rightly deserves happiness. So proclaims the deity in her parting words, which promise eternal esteem to the righteous, while the wicked languish in self-contempt and public scorn.[96]

Despite these rhetorical flourishes, which some commentators have sought to attribute to Diderot, d'Holbach repeatedly stresses that nature should not be regarded as a distinct body, divine or otherwise. As he declares in first chapters of his treatise, "When I say that nature produces an effect, I do not at all claim to personalize it. [. . .] We cannot call nature intelligent in the manner of some of the beings it encompasses."[97] This caveat is essential for understanding the implications of his system for the relationship between the human person and nature, and between the transcendent and immanent. D'Holbach seeks to resacralize nature, so that it performs functions analogous to that of Christian divinity, but in a radically different manner. The goddess nature is not an omniscient and omnipotent subject but an amorphous, disinterested, and totalizing force, which paradoxically retains her own regulatory principle but expresses no conscious, willful design. This position explains d'Holbach's strategic recourse to theological language in an attempt to capture nature's singular form of agency. Human beings, as a part of nature, must come to see themselves as an effect of its power. Philosophical fatalism, then, can be regarded as doubly dispossessive. It describes, on the one hand, a

presumably immutable condition—our intrinsic dependence on nature—
that demolishes theological claims concerning the soul's personal identity
and agency. Yet, as d'Holbach makes clear, we can lose sight of the true
source of our existence. Thus, on the other hand, his system also requires
an act of self-surrender in the present to establish the code of nature as the
basis of the social order. In contrast, revealed religion has alienated the self
from nature by imposing an array of fictitious spiritual goods that assure
salvation to believers at the cost of debasing their essential being, which it
deems inherently fallen or sinful.

By casting aside deism in all its forms, D'Holbach also jettisons transcendence from his materialist system. His concept of resacralized nature
drastically alters the relationship between God and soul as understood
in orthodox spirituality. What theologians regarded as an exchange between two distinct, albeit unequal persons is now an arrangement in nature among objects that can never be truly extricated from each other. The
meaning of immanence likewise changes. As Christian apologists felt compelled to defend the self's transcendent status in the created world, atheist
philosophes such as d'Holbach reacted by asserting nature's intimate presence around and within the self in order to repudiate the conventional understanding of God. Having banished the idea of a transcendent supreme
being, the materialist profession of faith likewise rejects the principles of
hierarchy and dominion. The self's concerted resignation to its determined
being enshrines a new, immanent force in the universe. At the conclusion
of his work, d'Holbach appeals to nature as the "Sovereign of all beings"
and the source of "virtue, reason, and truth." "Be forever our only divini-
ties," he enjoins them, and "concentrate your power in order to conquer
our hearts."[98]

D'Holbach's musings may assume a devotional air, but he did not share
the mystic sensibilities that figure in the *Ethics*. Nor did his reliance on Spinozist arguments for monism preclude him from dismissing the identification of nature with a nonexistent God on atheist and materialist grounds.[99]
Nevertheless, d'Holbach's and Spinoza's shared skepticism of the human
person's possessive relationship to itself eroded individualist claims to personal autonomy. For neither thinker, however, does such an outcome entail
absolute loss. Rather, what the self surrenders to God or nature is returned
to it under the guise of collective ownership, as part of the totality of beings that comprise the universe. For d'Holbach, in particular, knowledge
of our determined nature is concomitant with a strong sense of solidarity
with our fellow humans. While the self's existence remains subordinate to
the dictates of nature, so too its designs find true fulfillment only in keeping with the will of the multitude.

Exorcising d'Holbach, Saving Souls

The guardians of philosophical and religious orthodoxy moved swiftly against *Système de la nature*, not only for its espousal of atheism, but also for the threat it posed to belief in the self's very existence. Testifying before the magistrates of the Parlement of Paris, *avocat-général* Antoine-Louis Séguier denounced the work's reduction of free will to "the necessary consequence of the laws of nature" as a sacrilege that stripped the human person of its "most noble prerogative." The court duly issued an *arrêt* in August 1770 outlawing the work's publication and ordering all copies to be burned, a judgment mockingly reproduced in the next clandestine edition of the treatise.[100]

Voltaire prepared his own scathing response. He recoiled in horror from d'Holbach's axiom that "matter, blind and without will, produces intelligent animals." This view is entirely insufficient, he claimed, because it fails to account for the status of the self as a conscious, self-owning subject. Human intelligence becomes comprehensible only in relation to the workings of an "intelligent cause." Voltaire further argued that social order requires belief in the existence of a supreme being. To deny "a remunerative and vengeful God" effectively condemns humankind to face "our calamities without hope" and "our crimes without remorse."[101] In his correspondence, he went on to denounce the work to d'Alembert as "a dreadful evil to philosophy," to Bernard-Joseph Saurin as "a crime against nature," and to the Prussian heir-apparent Frederick William as "pernicious for princes and peoples alike."[102]

These indictments pale in comparison with those of one Père Laliman, a Dominican priest, who warned of the Enlightenment's highly lethal edge. As proof, he pointed to the wave of suicides that had swept over Paris in the late 1760s—there were 147 officially recognized cases in 1769 alone. The English, owing to their insalubrious climate, diet, and philosophical tradition, were believed to be especially prone to taking their own lives, and many attributed the rise in self-murder to Anglophilia. Laliman concurred, noting, "it is from them that the *Enlightenment* [*lumière*] has come down to us, and from them we have learned to make use of our *liberty* [italics in original]." The French had proceeded to drag these ruinous ideas down to new depths. Laliman identified the prevailing cause of suicide in France as the "irreligion" of the philosophes. His accusation did not distinguish between the moderate and the radical: Montesquieu, d'Holbach, and Rousseau were equally to blame for disseminating the falsehoods that God did not exist and that the soul perishes with the body. Without a concept of the divine, Laliman insisted, there is ultimately nothing to hope for and nothing to fear, so that one is left "accountable only to nature, to which the diverse modifications of matter are equal." Similarly, denying the existence of the immortal soul fostered the illusion that suicide ended one's misery once and for all.[103]

Among the tragedies that Laliman described was the joint suicide of Bourdeaux and Humain, the two soldiers who, as noted at the start of this chapter, killed themselves in late 1773.[104] The *Correspondance littéraire*, which published their testament in defiance of the Parlement of Paris, took the case as evidence of "the ravages that too audacious a philosophy can cause in ill-disposed minds." The task of the legitimate philosopher, in contrast, was to demonstrate that "the sentiment of our existence, the enjoyment of the possession [*jouissance*] of our being, is our first happiness."[105] Laliman posed his own corrective. As if responding to the deity who appears at the end of *Système de la nature*, he invoked the image of Jesus as God incarnate, whose essential message to his followers is "*Possess your soul in peace* [italics in original]."[106] If radical philosophy facilitated suicide by demeaning human existence, thereby making it appear transitory and disposable, the necessary response would be to affirm the grandeur of the soul and the pleasures of self-ownership in the strongest possible terms.

This strategy guided one of d'Holbach's most able opponents, the abbé Nicolas Bergier (1718–1790). At Séguier's request, and with the support of the Assembly of the Clergy, Bergier applied his talents to a definitive refutation of *Système de la nature*. Recently appointed canon of Notre-Dame, he already enjoyed a reputation as a slayer of philosophical dragons. His previous targets included Rousseau's *Émile* and d'Holbach's anonymously published *Le Christianisme dévoilé*. He could also claim firsthand knowledge of his adversary. Since 1767, he had been a frequent guest at d'Holbach's salon, and he even shared with his host, along with Diderot, a draft of his work.[107] Whatever his personal sentiments, when called upon to defend the tenets of the faith, Bergier harbored no sympathy for the devil. His *Examen du matérialisme* (1771) synthesized the stock arguments of Christian apologetics into a cogent and rigorously thorough challenge to d'Holbach's treatment of the human person.

Like other scholars associated with the second wave of Christian apologists that emerged in the 1760s, Bergier adopted a subtle approach, which involved close readings aimed at exposing his rival's factual errors and logical inconsistencies.[108] The doctrine of fatalist necessity came under particularly harsh scrutiny. If the human person has no free will in thought or action, how is the mind to cast off the supposed prejudices of religion and acquire an awareness of its true state? And, if matter is inherently active, how could the human person, as an exclusively material form, be described as "*a passive instrument* [italics in original]"?[109] From the abbé's perspective, d'Holbach's grasp of theodicy appeared rather casual, even naïve, given the determinist bent of his thought. Yet it is precisely this supposed lapse that brings to the fore their different assumptions about human agency—one rooted in the powers of the individual person, the other in that of nature as a whole.

The sin of materialism—that "absurd and murderous system," in Bergier's description—is to impugn the prerogatives and sanctity of the human person. In response, he reaffirmed the central tenets of Christian dualism, which emphasize the superiority of spiritual substance. Matter is "essentially divisible," and thus too variable to sustain personal identity and concerted thought. The mind, then, maintains separation from the body, which it directs "by a simple act of its will." According to Bergier's logic, "since I act and have the sense of acting, the agent [*suppôt*] or *self* [*moi*] [italics in original] is therefore active and spiritual."[110] With these claims, Bergier reinstated the faculties of self-ownership that d'Holbach had so vehemently denied. He professed awe toward the image of the person that emerged: "The majestic visage that you lift toward the Heavens, the variety of your thoughts, [. . .] and the breadth of your hopes all attest to the dignity of your being, the nobility of your origins, and the grandeur of your destiny."[111]

Bergier contrasts his admiration for the self with d'Holbach's groundless faith in nature. With both God and logic on his side, he dismisses his opponent's atheistic posturing as a mask for quasi-religious fanaticism. No other doctrine, in his judgment, "contains more mysteries and unbelievable elements, or more absurd and contradictory dogmas." Then he goes further still, asserting that "matter, such as the materialists understand it, is a being more *mystical* [italics in original], more unknown, and more inconceivable than a spiritual God."[112] This choice of words is suggestive, not least because the term *mystique* in eighteenth-century usage referred to explicit spiritual doctrines.[113] The fraught status of mystical spirituality in the wake of the Quietist controversy only strengthened the damning implications of the abbé's remark: d'Holbach and his partisans had substituted an ill-defined, illusory deity masquerading as nature for the substantial God of Christian orthodoxy.

It is uncertain whether Bergier wished his reader to identify the materialism of d'Holbach specifically with the mysticism of Fénelon, since he makes no direct allusion to the latter's theology. Even so, in the context of eighteenth-century polemics over the human person, his observations point once more to profound affinities between philosophical and spiritual radicalism. Enshrined in both movements was the imperative that men and women surrender their sense of self, the spiritual and existential goods to which they falsely laid claim—and even their very lives—to the totalizing forces of God or nature. In so doing, the Quietist and the philosophical fatalist each offered French subjects an alternative, anti-individualist stance from which to regard themselves, one another, and their world. To be sure, significant differences persisted between these factions, beyond the question of belief in a supernatural creator. D'Holbach took a conceptual leap that neither Fénelon, nor even Spinoza, would have dared. His radical materialism endowed the assembled objects of nature, even the most humble and finite among them, with the all-encompassing power that had once belonged to God alone. It did so, moreover, without privileging certain states such as Spinoza's love of God, in which the self could be said to gain a rarified form of knowledge by participating in—and submitting itself to—the divine intellect. Nevertheless, Voltaire and Bergier condemned all three thinkers on similar grounds. If divine and human persons lost their status as self-owning subjects, these critics contended, the heavens would crumble, societies collapse, and dynasties fall.

The Fate of the Self in the World of Things

D'Holbach's materialism emerged on the scene at a moment when nature—and by extension, what could be considered natural—appeared very much in flux. From the peasant's plot to the merchant's stall and at all points in between, objects everywhere had begun to assume new aspects. The monarchy attempted to liberalize the trade in grain, the commodity that provided the essential link between humans and the physical world.[114] During the same period, French subjects found themselves confronted with a vast array of novel economic goods, as well as ways of relating to them. Government officials, political economists, and cultural commentators all set about making sense of what these changes entailed for personal identity and the social order. The eighteenth century witnessed a gradual decline of the aristocratic politics of representation, which conceived of the display of wealth as a direct projection of social power, to a view that focused instead on the physical and moral properties of the individual self.[115] The rise of luxury could be seen either as an overwhelmingly positive advance, on the basis of the freedom from want it delivered to consumers of all stripes, or as a harbinger of new forms of oppression. The latter view was taken up most prominently by Rousseau, who claimed that material possessions had a dangerous tendency of turning against their owners and engendering dependence rather than self-determination.[116] The government's drives in the 1760s and 1770s to implement laissez-faire policies met with even stronger resistance, and officials ultimately failed to overcome the Old Regime's obsession with scarcity.[117]

The transition from subsistence to abundance was neither automatic nor preordained. It required dizzying reorientations in the conceptual realm that at times bounded ahead of material conditions, and at other times lagged behind them. These shifts in direction are discussed at greater length in subsequent chapters, but it is worth noting here how d'Holbach's writings pointed the way. He sought, above all, to overturn the relationship between the human person and the natural world as conventionally understood. In stark opposition both to orthodox religion and to the incipient doctrine of political liberalism, his writings vehemently denied that God had made the world for men and women to use for their own advantage. On the contrary, the self existed as a mere function of nature, beholden to interior impulses and external forces over which it exercised no direct control. To be human meant to be a thinking, feeling object among others, rather than an individual subject of divine lineage that governs its thoughts and stands accountable for its actions. Individuals owed their existence to nature alone, which disposed of them as it saw fit. In the extreme, this view made it thinkable to cast off the self, like the benighted Bourdeaux and Humain, with the same disregard shown for unwanted possessions.

Like theologians and philosophers in the eighteenth century, scholars have contested the impact of cultural and economic transformations on how the human person was conceptualized during the period. For instance, Max Horkheimer and Theodor Adorno famously alleged that the Enlightenment's struggle for emancipation from received wisdom culminated in humankind's enslavement to its own technical prowess. Crucial for this reversal was the rise of instrumental reason, which rendered nature a disenchanted site of domination. By the end of this process, the alienating power of abstraction came to subsume the mind itself, so that "even the human individual [. . .] is converted into the repeatable, replaceable process, into a mere example for the conceptual models of the system."[118] Michel Foucault likewise described the effects of Enlightenment rationality as a means of constructing the individual to serve a determined function in the social order. "We are neither in the amphitheatre, nor on the stage," he observed, "but in the panoptic machine, invested by its effects and power, which we bring to ourselves since we are part of its mechanism."[119] At the other end of the ideological spectrum, Jonathan Israel has attempted to salvage the Enlightenment project—and its radical materialist wing in particular—as a highly contested but ultimately victorious movement for human freedom. Without it, he claims, the modern ideals of "equality, democracy, individual liberty, and freedom of thought" might never have emerged from the dark shadows of the Old Regime.[120]

Neither critical nor triumphalist accounts of the Enlightenment adequately capture the dynamics of dispossessive personhood that pulsed through Spinozist and materialist currents in eighteenth-century France. Again, the work of d'Holbach proves instructive. His metaphysics aimed at subjecting the human person to the dictates of nature, not, as Hork-heimer and Adorno or Foucault would have it, at reducing nature to hu-manity's self-imposed domination. In contrast to Israel's portrayal of the radical Enlightenment as avowedly secular and individualist in orientation, d'Holbach's political ideals denied the prerogatives of particular selves in favor of the good of all. This guiding principle followed from a commit-ment to the existential interdependence of all beings that for critics such as Voltaire and Bergier resonated with mystical devotion.

In *Système social* and *Politique naturel*, both from 1773, d'Holbach contended that humans could only find fulfillment in society.[121] While each individual seeks "his own happiness" in everything, it is equally the case that "the exclusive preference of ourselves is madness, because it prevents us from seeing that we need others for our own well-being." Social con-sciousness extends well beyond the instinct to truck and barter; there is no invisible hand that miraculously reconciles personal and collective ends. The very substance of positive law, therefore, "must be the just wills of all, founded on the interests of all, opposed to particular wills, to the in-terests, passions, and caprices of the individual." On the economic front, d'Holbach blamed France's woes on the blind pursuit of commerce, which only satisfied "imaginary needs," even as agricultural lands, which he called "the true foundation of the state," suffered from neglect. It is better, he reasoned, "to prefer the well-being of the greatest number to that of a handful of amoral idlers."[122]

This salvo of prescriptions echoed the hopes expressed by the most vocal philosophes of the radical Enlightenment. As we shall see, Rous-seauian politics gave even fuller expression to the possibility that the self's dispossession as a distinct individual could give rise to a form of collective self-ownership in which the desires of particular persons find fulfillment only in satisfying the needs of the multitude. D'Holbach's collaborator Diderot seized on another of his preoccupations, the effects of nature on the self, to articulate a highly nuanced defense of dispossessive personhood in the aesthetic and scientific domains. His writings on the self, moreover, openly employed Quietist rhetoric to describe altered states of conscious-ness induced by encounters both with nature and representations of the natural world. Like Rousseau, Diderot imagined not only innovative con-figurations of the cultures of self-ownership and dispossession, but also unprecedented possibilities for men and women to commune with one an-other, and with the material and existential goods surrounding them, with-out falling prey to the exigencies of domination and exploitation.

5   *The Sleep of Reason*

"To dream that you have changed your sex," directed the anonymous manual *L'Art de se rendre heureux par les songes* (1746), boil in two pints of wine spirit "two handfuls of fresh scurvy grass, a handful each of fresh watercress, wormwood, greater celandine, and fumitory, a half-ounce or dram of scabwort and horseradish roots, an ounce of juniper berries and six drams of the seeds, a dram of prepared black hellebore root, two or three drams of prepared leafy spurge, two drams each of anise and fennel seeds, a dram each of ginger, cinnamon, and white turmeric root, and finally, three drams of salt of tartar." Once the mixture is reduced by half, the user must dilute a spoonful into a half pint of water and bathe his or her "private parts [*parties naturelles*]" in it. The recipe aimed to induce the bodily sensations of the opposite gender. As with the other experiments outlined in the manual, it required mental as well as medicinal preparation. The subject was to begin by "meticulously disengaging the mind from all impressions" with the aid of purgatives. This procedure reinforced the moral stance of the purported author, a French chemist and botanist. He claimed that since sleep removed the dreamer from the orbit of real sense impressions, one could avoid accountability even when imagining highly transgressive acts. The Church, he confidently assured the reader, condemned only actions, not "desires for themselves"—even if these happened to be purposefully aroused.[1]

The age of Enlightenment produced many such pseudoscientific guides, along with more serious meditations on various aspects of the dream state. The sleep of reason elicited both curiosity and dread during the eighteenth century, as evidenced by Francisco Goya's famous portrayal of the subject, "El sueño de la razón produce monstruos" (fig. 1), which depicts an exhausted writer collapsed on his desk, his face hidden from view

FIGURE 1. Francisco Goya, *El sueño de la razón produce monstruos* (1799). Print. Source: Bibliothèque nationale de France

and shrouded in darkness. Out of the shadows emerges a swarm of flying beasts. Closest to the sleeping figure is the owl, the perennial symbol of wisdom, in the act of taking flight, while perched beside him is a cat, crouching in wait. Behind these figures lurks a cloud of bats, ominously signifying the grotesque thoughts that imperil the slumbering mind. Goya's image confronted the fear that sleep and other states of altered consciousness have the potential to overthrow one's command over ideas and actions. These experiences threatened from within the prevailing ideal of the moderate philosophe movement, which was predicated on the rigorous application of self-ownership in thought and action.

In the struggles to combat this menace, which were joined by an eclectic assortment of credentialed scholars and charlatans alike, Denis Diderot emerged as a surprising partisan of dispossession. In so doing, he consciously appropriated the taboo rhetoric of Quietism to question man's powers of volition, rationality, and individual consciousness. His wide-ranging contributions to the *Encyclopédie* provide a perspective from which to observe how contemporaries employed the idioms of religious excess to diagnose and denounce a range of conditions, from the dream state to spiritual ecstasy to madness. Defying the status quo, he made frequent allusions to philosophers and artists as adepts of self-alienation who in turn created images intended to draw their audiences outside and beyond themselves. His musings on psychology, metaphysics, and aesthetics culminated in the "mystic materialism" of *Le Rêve d'Alembert*, in which he attempted to make a science of the self's radical dispossession in an ever-shifting physical world.[2] This dialogue speculates on the limits of identity with far deeper nuance than the *Système de la nature*, while sharing many of the latter's monist and determinist tenets. D'Holbach wrote little that does not apply to the waking person. Diderot, however, suggested that the suspension of particular identity while dreaming reflects the real status of the self in the totality of nature. His views refined and elaborated an understanding of the self that is indicative of the radical Enlightenment. The measure of self-ownership attributed to the individual is determined by, and made dependent on, a prior experience of dispossession—whether through nature or its human representations.

The stakes in this enterprise ranged widely, extending to the medical status of dreaming, the intellectual and social roles of the philosophe, and the fundamental character of the Enlightenment. Religious and political authorities frequently suspected that the *Encyclopédistes* intended their work to serve as a Trojan horse for the smuggling in of philosophical materialism. Diderot thus courted disaster by adding to his purported crimes a tolerance for mystical heresy. Among members of his own faction, the willingness to entertain and even embrace the possibility that a wayward mind could grasp the true nature of things ran counter to the philosophe's self-image as a rational subject with a duty to dispel the illusions of religious fanaticism. At a time when the advocates of Enlightenment were striving against unfavorable odds to assert themselves on the cultural scene—as a new intellectual vanguard, as independent authors in possession of their ideas, and as a compelling source of moral authority—their acknowledged leader was also expending considerable effort to contemplate not the progress to be gained by the mastery of reason, but the self to be lost in the alienation of the senses.

The Philosophe, the Dream State, and the Enlightenment's Cult of Wakefulness

The *Encyclopédie* article "Philosophe"—based on the work of the grammarian César Chesneau Dumarsais (1676–1756), but with various modifications—sought to define the attributes of a new elect. The text opens grandly, with the proclamation that "reason is to the philosopher what grace is to the Christian." Accordingly, the philosophe should not speak without thinking, or think without feeling. He is to be sensible in an Enlightened manner, which includes remaining open to the mutual influence of intellectual and moral concerns. His consciousness should remain deliberate, anchored by the effect of sense impressions on the mind as it observes, classifies, and orders the objects that give it cause to reflect. Reason must guide him even through wayward passions and creeping uncertainties—"he walks at night, but is preceded by a torch." Rather than resting on claims of total knowledge, the "perfection of the philosopher" lies in pronouncing only on matters where there is a "clear motive for judging" on the basis of "an infinity of particular observations." This self-possessed figure is set in clear contrast to the fanatically devout souls who "fall asleep under the yoke of superstition," as well as to pseudo-philosophes like the ancient Stoics, who "madly desired to annihilate the passions, and to elevate us beyond our nature by a chimerical insensibility." Rather than renounce the world, the philosophe is exhorted to take his place in it with sympathy and humanity, so that he may "enjoy with sage economy the possession of the goods that nature offers him."[3]

If bearers of false knowledge lived with their eyes closed, the truly enlightened philosopher could be identified by his wakefulness, sociability, and self-control. Voltaire—who reprinted "Le Philosophe" in his tragedy *Les Lois de Minos* (1773), and who also had a particular fondness for coffee—saw himself as an exemplar.[4] To be enlightened meant appropriating and then recasting aristocratic ideals of *honnêteté* and *politesse*, which placed great emphasis on personal restraint and social grace, in the service of a republic of letters founded on open but critical intellectual exchange.[5] The philosophe was to be an adept in the art of conversation, possessed of a pleasing natural style of speech, and receptive to the views of his interlocutors, whom he engaged as equals. It often fell to the hostess of the Enlightenment salon to ensure that these ideals reigned supreme—or, in Dena Goodman's apt phrase, that "mastery of the word" did not "become the basis of mastery over persons."[6] While harmonizing the voices of sometimes unruly participants required the *salonnière* to function as a social cipher, it did not necessarily entail complete self-denial. Marie-Thérèse Rodet Geoffrin (1699–1777), at whose gatherings the likes of Voltaire, Diderot, and d'Alembert were *habitués*, described her vocation in terms of both intellectual and existential fulfillment. "Do not believe that my nothingness, which I recognize in regard to others, negates me in regard to myself," she wrote to an unnamed correspondent. "I sense in myself an elevated soul, reason, and virtues. The knowledge of these advances [. . .] makes me see and feel clearly that they are useful only for my personal happiness."[7]

The Enlightenment's republic of letters extended beyond the salon, through epistolary correspondence, to be sure, and by 1750, increasingly in philosophical, political, and dramatic works produced for a broader public. Roger Chartier, Carla Hesse, Gregory Brown, and other historians have charted the attendant rise of authorial self-consciousness during the period. This development took place within a cultural milieu in which aristocratic patronage remained an essential, if waning, element, and within a literary market dominated by the Paris Community of Booksellers and Printers. Enlightenment authors expressed their aspirations with reference both to the aristocratic *honnête homme* and to the modern *homo economicus*, with the ideals of the former frequently serving to justify the interests of the latter.[8] Both positions drew on facets of the culture of self-ownership, in that the author's claims to be a civilized subject in possession of himself and his comportment, and thus motivated by more than the desire for profit, also supported his status as a worthy recipient of both social and economic benefits accruing from his work.

In a seeming paradox, the corporatist body of booksellers played a key role in the development of individualist literary property rights. According to legal tradition, the *privilège* to publish a given work was granted by royal grace. Lawyers for the Booksellers' and Printers' Community, however, employed Lockean arguments to buttress their claims to hold real property in the works appearing under their imprints. On their view, a *privilège* reflected not a dispensation that could be granted or revoked by the crown, but a transfer of legal possession from the original author, whose rights derived from his or her efforts to compose the work, to the publisher, who likewise expended labor in producing the printed edition. Thus, the author sold all future commercial rights to the title in question, which were transferred to the bookseller. In emphasizing the capacity of authors to sell their intellectual work, the Community also recognized their right to treat it as a form of individually held property. It remained a theoretical rather than actual prerogative, however, because authors were forbidden by law to publish their own writings. This state of affairs changed in 1777, when the government issued a series of edicts reforming the book trade. The provisions included an order stipulating that henceforth, the writer was to enjoy perpetual *privilège* in a work, unless he or she chose to sell the rights to a publisher.[9]

Diderot considered the dynamics of literary property in his *Lettre historique et politique sur le commerce de la librairie*, composed in 1763 on behalf of the Booksellers' and Printers' Community. Characteristically, his position represented various points of view. First, he maintained, in Lockean fashion, that an author held an original and unassailable claim to his or her writings on the basis of the labor invested in them. "What property," he asked, "could be said to belong to a man if the work of his mind [. . .] does not belong to him?" There could be no doubt that "the author is master of his work," unless "no one in society is master of his property." As lawyers for the Community also argued, it was precisely the author's property in his or her work that established the right to alienate it, in which case the publisher "possesses it as it was possessed by the author," with an "incontestable right" to produce new editions.[10] Although Diderot would later denounce the tawdry commodification of the art world, he expressed little resentment toward the *librairies* that had consistently paid him meager wages—and, in the case of André-François Le Breton, even tampered with his work on the *Encyclopédie*. As he once admonished Sophie Volland, "do not speak ill of my publishers; they have done all that I have required of them. There is the fairness that one should expect from everyone."[11] At the same time, he observed, somewhat enigmatically, "I also know how to alienate [*aliéner*] myself, a talent without which one does nothing of worth."[12] Perhaps Diderot's claim that nothing valuable comes without alienation implied a double meaning—one commercial, the other creative. As we shall see, he at times championed the destabilizing, even dispossessing effects that a work of art could have on readers and viewers in an aesthetic, rather than economic, sense. In any event, he proved more sanguine about the literary market than the Enlightenment's "low-life" chronicled by Robert Darnton, members of which railed violently against their treatment in an exploitative system controlled by literary grandees and unscrupulous publishers.[13]

In the salon, in correspondence, and in the literary market, the philosophes sought to exhibit a highly refined sense of self-governance, and thus of self-ownership. The rules of Enlightenment sociability dictated that they express themselves with precision, while remaining attentive to the views of others. As purveyors of the printed word, they frequently championed the cause of the author as proprietor of his works, and thus legally capable of transferring ownership of them to another party. To adopt the Lockean terminology then in wide currency, the property individuals held in their persons compelled them to respect the same right in their fellows. For the philosophe, this imperative applied in a double sense. He was expected not only to rein in his thoughts and actions when interacting with others, but also to construct through his writings a public persona through which the ideals he advocated could be identified both with himself as an author and with the Enlightenment as a social and cultural force.

· · ·

Under such conditions, any mental or physical disorder that might compromise this careful balance threatened to disrupt the internal workings of the republic of letters. It also challenged the integrity of the philosophe movement, since lapses in self-governance remained associated with religious excess. Both Descartes and Locke fixated on dreaming and related lapses in consciousness as aberrations that cast the mind's proper workings into sharper relief.[14] Their eighteenth-century progeny viewed such experiences with utter contempt. For instance, the biographer, historian, and philosophical critic Louis-Antoine de Caraccioli (1719–1803) sharply contrasted the slumbering mass of humanity with the man of truth, who "remains awake in the meditation of himself, and of God." Caraccioli found this preoccupation with wakefulness to be so intense that such a man "resents seeing himself interrupted by sleep," a state likened to "a kind of annihilation."[15]

More generally, somnolence posited a limit case of the sensationalist paradigm championed by the moderate Enlightenment, whose proponents often equated being a self with having a self. During the eighteenth century, sensationalism emerged from its Lockean chrysalis to take flight as a dominant mode of inquiry and expression, which influenced not only the sciences, but the arts as well.[16] Few figures personify this development as much as Diderot, who expounded upon the operations of sense experience as fervently as he advocated a new aesthetics with the capacity to move both body and mind. In so doing, he drew upon the ideas of Théophile de Bordeu to articulate his vision of how sense organs register and respond to stimulation. Bordeu himself was a major exponent of medical vitalism, a movement that originated in Montpellier, but soon gained a wider audience, partly due to its prominence in the *Encyclopédie*. Vitalists rejected the iatromechanist axiom that organisms function like machines. Instead, they gave pride of place to an indefinable force that pulses through living beings and conditions their existence. This approach privileged sensibility as the conduit between the various nerves, glands, and other organs that together constitute the body.[17] In developing their views, Bordeu and his colleagues contributed to innovations in medical knowledge that broke with both Galenic and Cartesian orthodoxies regarding the mind's relationship to the body. More generally, their work opened new possibilities for approaching the human person as an array of sensations that could be charted, manipulated, and directed under the right conditions.

Yet the shift toward sensibility created new notions of abnormality in the process of redefining health; through overstimulation, sensibility could deteriorate into nervousness, hypochondria, delirium, and other disorders.[18] A body understood in terms of sensations could also be regarded as living at their mercy. There were potentially alarming consequences to viewing the self as a bundle of nerves. In diagnosing pathological disruptions of consciousness, it became abundantly clear that even the minds of philosophes might wander, and perhaps falter as well. On a nightly basis, as Diderot himself considered at some length, they certainly slept. This physical necessity raised troubling uncertainties for the ideal of philosophical vigilance. For instance, Diderot's published diary of impressions gleaned from the Salon of 1767 recalls a day spent contemplating the landscapes of Claude-Joseph Vernet and the restless night that followed. The next morning, Diderot came to a realization. "No philosopher that I know," he observed, "has yet determined the real difference between waking and dreaming. Am I awake when I think that I am dreaming? Am I dreaming when I think I am awake?" Perhaps with the article "Philosophe" in mind, he demanded to know "whether the veil will not be one day torn open," thus revealing that "I have dreamt all that I have done and in reality done all which I have dreamt."[19]

Diderot's meditations figure within the broader efforts of physicians, philosophers, and theologians to classify—and more often than not, to corral and to neutralize—forms of altered consciousness. In the Christian tradition, these states had long been regarded as possible conduits to revelation, albeit of dubious provenance.[20] By the eighteenth century, qualified skepticism had turned to sheer disdain. Even churchmen rushed to sanitize the prophetic tradition by limiting its scope to the apostles, the early fathers, and a rarefied cohort of saints.[21] As the abbé d'Asfeld's rebuke of the *convulsionnaires* makes abundantly clear, reasonable clerics showed no quarter for coreligionists who claimed that their visions heralded a new stage in sacred history.

While priests began to gird themselves against the charge of peddling superstition, amateur oneirologists began to produce manuals on dreaming. These guides explore the possibilities of self-consciously manipulating dreams to a specific end. For instance, the anonymous author of *L'Art de faire des songes* (1750) advises a young woman suffering from nightmares that just as "the will depends perfectly on ourselves" while awake, so can one learn to direct the soul during sleep, by keeping "the movement of the fibers in the brain [. . .] regular and uniform." To do so requires one merely to concentrate on pleasant thoughts until retiring, so that "the fibers, following the same direction that has been imprinted on them, continuously depict our object to us" in our dreams.[22] With preparation, the author confidently affirmed, one's powers of self-ownership could lead the darkened mind until it regained consciousness at first light.

L'Art de se rendre heureux par les songes seeks to establish this axiom on a purportedly scientific basis, through the practical application of naturally derived medicines. A foreword from the author's supposed nephew claims him to be a chemist and "great philosopher" who eschewed "chimerical projects."[23] To ward off readers' skepticism, he notes that the physical world has its share of "marvels," such as the auto-regeneration of sea anemones and other polyps.[24] The author himself relates how he honed his methods during an expedition to Canada. To treat what he believed to be a poisonous animal bite, he developed an ointment consisting of scammony and dried cod, which induced sleep and a vivid dream of seducing a woman who had cared for him during his illness. Eager to reproduce the effect, he received further instruction from a native of the Illinois Confederation.[25]

Armed with new-found knowledge, the chemist set out to discover preparations that could reliably affect the content of dreams, while also developing moral justifications for doing so. He argued that it is a natural, divinely authorized inclination to seek one's own happiness.[26] The art of dreaming allows one to fulfill this imperative even in the case of sinful longings. In contrast to the spiritual vigilance of wakefulness, during sleep "divine and human laws no longer demand anything of us." The only commandment is to "enjoy the possession [*jouissez*] of all that you can imagine."[27] Ironically, then, allowing oneself to succumb to experiences that mitigate one's responsibility for thoughts and actions exonerates the soul of wrongdoing.

In this seeming paradox lies the crux of the author's method. The conscious manipulation of mind and body makes it possible to determine the content of dreams in advance, yet the exercise is undertaken while unconscious, and thus when dreamers are no longer in immediate control of themselves. The pleasure of having indulged any and all of one's deepest-seated desires during sleep effectively neutralizes the compulsion to pursue them in the real world. Nevertheless, the greater sense of mastery and self-ownership thereby achieved depends on a prior—and previously prepared for—state of dispossession.

The author's professions of innocence betray the heterodoxy of this line of reasoning, which theologians had long condemned in their dealings with Quietists, *convulsionnaires*, and other heretical mystics. Despite its recourse to medicinal elixirs, *L'Art de se rendre heureux par les songes* approaches dreams in a like manner to spiritual abandon, at least to the extent that adequate mental preparation is required to ensure that the subsequent visions and sensations take the desired form. Guyon, like many of her mystic contemporaries, taught followers to adopt a passive stance toward the world of physical sensations in order to occupy themselves wholly with God. Similarly, the author of *L'Art de se rendre heureux par les songes* instructs readers to begin by "disengaging one's brain from all impressions" for one lunar month. To facilitate the process, he prescribes various emetics and herbal concoctions, as well as the mental exercise of "strongly pointing one's imagination toward the idea of this person or this thing" about whom or which one wishes to dream while drifting off to sleep.[28]

The experiences depicted in this work range from sensual pleasures to the longing for social esteem to intellectual fulfillment. The first several recipes deal with desires of a sexual nature. For example, the author provides a formula for sleeping with a woman, which calls for two ounces of scammony and Roman chamomile root, and three ounces each of cod bones and tortoise shells mixed in five ounces of beaver fat. One then adds to the preparation two ounces of the oil of blue scammony flowers during an early spring morning, and boils the mixture with an ounce of honey and six drams of dew gathered on a poppy flower. A small amount of opium can also be included at this stage, if desired. The mixture must rest in the sun for two months and then be stored in one's cellar over the winter. Given the laborious process of fabrication, the author advises the reader to make up several bottles of this "precious ointment," which he claims has given him "my tranquility, my innocence, and the entire system of the new art of happiness that I have the good fortune of being able to present to the human race." For "delightful effects," one simply applies it each evening to the feet, hands, temples, and nape of the neck.[29]

As implicit testimony to the efficacy of his recipes, the author also provides a remedy for counteracting the "exhaustion" stemming from nocturnal emissions of semen during "lascivious dreams." The treatment involves, among other ingredients, salt of tartar, powered dog's penis, and the user's own dried urine. One collects the mixture in a sachet, which is to be applied to one's groin for a week.[30] Such a hands-on approach complicates the author's claim that dreaming provided a wholly innocent means of fulfilling one's desires. While Saint Augustine had taught that the soul held no moral responsibility for physical reactions during sleep, it would be a different matter to anticipate, and even facilitate, those reactions in a deliberate, conscious way.[31]

Other recipes in the manual cater to an array of social and physical experiences, including glory in war, gastronomic indulgence, and the accumulation of great wealth.[32] Its final pages turn to the affairs of the mind. Like many of his contemporaries, the author expresses concern over the pathological excesses of intellectual life, such as "metromania" (or the obsession with composing poetry) and "the rage to write and to pass oneself off as a *bel esprit*."[33] As treatment, he proposes an elaborate concoction involving buckthorn, bay leaves, wormwood, and other plants cooked in the urine of a woman who has recently given birth. After further preparation, the solution is to be boiled in cow's milk and divided into thirds: one is to be drunk by the patient, another used to wash one's head and stomach, and the remaining quantity is poured over one's bedstead. According to the author, the elixir's effects are "so astounding" that it allows him, at the age of eighty, to compose "quite beautiful" lines of verse—even though he has trouble remembering the specifics of these "nocturnal productions" upon waking.[34]

The attention paid to intellectual life in the anonymous guide resonates with clinical reports by physicians during the period. Medical professionals, however, tended to take a sterner view of errant night-time thoughts. Jean-François Lavoisier's *Dictionnaire portatif de médecine* (1764) describes a constellation of disorders, from dreaming to madness, believed to stem from the same source: a total physical inability to control internal and external reactions to stimuli. Dreams are deemed inherently pathological, "a kind of delirium in which the things that most struck the imagination during the day, appear to our soul when it is at rest." In turn, delirium, or "the alienation of mind, an imagination or rational faculty that is depraved," entails a lapse in the mind's capacity to govern itself.[35]

Sleepwalking and related conditions triggered strong reactions by complicating the sensationalist psychology dominant in the eighteenth century. According to this model, all knowledge originally derives from sight, hearing, touch, smell, and taste. The nervous system transmits sense experiences to the brain, which uses them to forge ideas. In Condillac's influential restatement of the paradigm, sensation also accounts for the successive formation of the faculties of imagination, memory, and reflection through the conversion of bodily impulses into abstract signs. Despite the materialist elements of his system, Condillac did not regard the mind as a mere accumulation of physical reactions. Rather, at each stage of development, the human person acquires a greater degree of control over its senses and itself. As he first explained in the *Essai sur l'origine des connaissances humaines* (1746), the formation of memory allows one to restrain the imagination. Reflection, or the "manner of applying, on our own, our attention to various objects one by one," then empowers the mind to take possession of its thoughts and actions. Conversely, if the individual "does not direct his attention on his own," he remains "subject to his surroundings, and has nothing except by virtue of an outside force." Only after the mind prevails as "master of its attention" does it become self-sufficient; it thus develops ideas "that it owes to itself alone" and "enriches itself from its own resources."[36]

During sleep, however, the self's ownership of its ideas can falter as the mind's loses of contact with the sensual world, leading in turn to a destabilization of the proper balance between its faculties. As Voltaire described the conundrum, the soul "is free, and it is mad!"[37] A 1788 report on somnambulism issued by the Society of Physical Sciences in Lausanne approaches the matter in similar terms, but with greater precision. Its authors, Louis Levade, Jean-Louis-Antoine Reynier, and Jacob Berthout van Berchem, likened madness to a "more durable" form of sleepwalking, which is regarded as "madness of a short duration." As they defined it, somnambulism is "a nervous condition [. . .], during which the imagination represents objects to us that struck us while in a wakeful state, and with as much vigor as if they were really affecting our senses." A sleepwalker thus shows interest in external objects only when he or she "excites the imagination to turn attention to it," rather than through a process of willful reflection. Sleepwalkers also lose the faculty of memory, with no subsequent recollection of what transpired during the night.[38] Unfettered imagination, therefore, effectively overwhelms the sleepwalker's mental apparatus, and operates beyond the individual's conscious control for the duration of the episode.

Levade and his colleagues attempted to submit the unruly nature of sleepwalking to the rigors of empirical investigation. They admitted that this task posed considerable difficulties, since it required physicians to follow afflicted patients into "the workshop of illusions." They arranged their experiments carefully, choosing as their subject a thirteen-year-old boy named Duraud who suffered from involuntary movements during sleep. He was subjected to a battery of tests intended to measure the effects of "electrical and magnetic currents" on his behavior. For instance, the application of magnets caused Duraud to react violently when sleeping, but not when awake. More generally, their observations revealed that the child's senses had, in effect, taken on a life of their own. While asleep, he could distinguish between objects he had seen before and those he had not.

In one instance, he even recognized that a book the doctors had left behind did not belong to him. On another occasion, he rose to visit a local church, but quickly returned. He seemed under the impression that he had reached his destination, spoke excitedly to friends who were not there, and even acted out the gesture of sounding the bells in the tower. He also performed assorted feats while sleepwalking, such as practicing handwriting, doing arithmetic, and locating information in an almanac.[39]

The Lausanne physicians offered explanations for Duraud's behavior in sensationalist terms. They noted that he would open his eyes slightly when searching for objects, but only for an instant, since in his mind's eye the objects would have continued to appear as they did in real life. From this observation they concluded that Duraud's "overexcited imagination paints objects with which he is familiar for him," and that "all his senses, subordinated to his imagination, seem to be concentrated on the object that it is struck by, and at that moment have no perceptions except those relating to it."[40] The actions of sleepwalkers, then, confirmed the axiom that the mind cannot distinguish between physical objects if it has not previously experienced them through one of the senses.[41]

Above all, the physicians intended their report to explain the curiosities of sleepwalking as a purely physical phenomenon, stripped of all supernatural trappings. "The marvelous ceases," they declared, "as soon as the flame of experiment can light the path of reasoning." On these grounds they dismissed Franz Anton Mesmer's "magnetic somnambulism," then making waves in Paris. Rather than contemplate the existence of a subtle, omnipresent electric fluid, which the Mesmerists believed could be manipulated to allow access to the spiritual realm, they preferred to speak of how imagination disrupts the workings of the nervous system, and how charlatans could exploit this defect to their advantage. "The fever of animal magnetism," they predicted, would dissipate as surely as "the dreams of the night subside upon waking."[42]

Despite these efforts to cast a cold light on the feverish world of dreams, religious referents continued to inform how its inhabitants were understood. For instance, the treatise *Du Sommeil* (1779) fuses discursive strands from medicine, philosophy, and spirituality in explicating its subject. The author, known only as P.F.L.M., described sleep in sensationalist terms typical of the scientific literature, as a "weakening or collapse in the fibrous parts" thought to convey impressions from the external world to the brain. Not unlike the philosophes who wrote on the topic, he identified loss of consciousness with the suspension of reason. Exiled from the world of sensation, the dreamer enters "a theater of enchantment," where, deprived of his "judgment and liberty," "objects appear confused and form bizarre tableaux." Even in less intense states, such as distraction, "one belongs neither to others nor to oneself," while the artist or scholar in meditation might lose "sight of the universe" as a whole. All these "derangements of the brain," according to P.F.L.M., have the same cause: the mind's inability to govern the imagination by grounding thought processes in sense experience. The greater the separation from external reality, the deeper the delirium, until one descends into the throes of madness.[43]

P.F.L.M. also ruminated on the metaphysical and even theological implications of his findings. While he pledged to avoid "the language of bad faith and superstition," he failed to contain his awe. On his telling, the dreamscape encompasses "the cells [*réduits*] of Bedlam," but it also permits a glimpse of "the most august and sublime scenes." In particular, out of the ruins of mental disorder, he recognized the visage of the divine as it "advances toward the place it has chosen to stage its most illustrious favors," and where "the sovereign author of the universe lays bare his supreme power, and makes his immortal voice understood to humankind." The dream state, P.F.L.M. surmised, allows one to witness the transformative effects of God's power in and on the world. Accordingly, he proposed an "inspection of the interior and purely human modification" that attends "these celestial phenomena." His aim in doing so was to uncover "the origin and site of these *mystic* [emphasis added] operations within the center of sensibility"—the site he had previously defined as "the seat of consciousness and the self [*moi*]."[44]

Du Sommeil makes common cause with the Lausanne report on somnambulism, in that it seeks to place "even the sphere of faith" under "the jurisdiction of reason" by applying sensationalist categories. Yet it would be inaccurate to claim that the text, or the cult of *sensibilité* more generally, signals a direct turn toward secularization.[45] P.F.L.M. did not attempt to sequester the supernatural as a category or to dismiss the power that divinity exerts on the world. Among the work's stated aims is to see that "the duty [. . .] to believe and to adore is reconciled with the right to observe and to analyze."[46] Fulfilling this objective required bringing the human person in closer proximity to the divine through careful scrutiny of experiences during which the mind surrenders its ability to govern its thoughts and actions. The author sought a deeper understanding of the experience of mystic communion with God, not to undermine its relevance. In so doing, he formulated a position that diverges from historical accounts of the rise of modern science and religion, with their frequent allusions to the decline of enchantment in a secular age of reason.[47] From his perspective, demystification does not disenchant; on the contrary, it expands the possibilities of observing the sublime mechanics of the divine at intensely close range—within the nerves and muscle fibers that constitute the human body.

P.F.L.M. was not alone in evoking the spiritual abandon of the mystics alongside the dream state and other forms of altered consciousness. Most notably, and perhaps most shockingly, Diderot himself adopted Quietist rhetoric to extol the self's dispossession in the resacralized material universe theorized by d'Holbach and other radicals. This move can be understood only in light of the fraught terminologies employed to depict the human person's alienation from itself. In the eighteenth century, the dream state fell along a continuum extending from a momentary distraction to incurable madness. The lexicon available to describe these conditions, such as *aliénation, rêve, rêverie, distraction, enthousiasme,* and *inspiration,* carried both religious and economic connotations, adding semantic ambiguity to conceptual disarray. This tangle of meanings looms large in Diderot's masterwork. While heralded as a testament to human reason, the *Encyclopédie* also explores the shadows of the Enlightenment—the spiritual experiences, bodily sensations, and states of mind during which the thinking subject loses sight of itself and veers dangerously close to the fallacies that the work intended to combat. Across its pages unfurled a struggle for the soul of the philosophe—as either an active, wakeful, self-owning subject, or as an object under the ecstatic sway of forces beyond its control.

The Encyclopédie as a Dictionary of Dispossession

The *Encyclopédie* was, to adopt John Lough's phrase, the Enlightenment's *machine de guerre.* It was also heavily armed.[48] The sprawling twenty-eight volumes comprise nearly 72,000 articles and 3,000 plates. Its production required the labor of hundreds of printers, bookbinders, papermakers, engravers, and other craftsmen, in addition to the work of the 160 contributors of articles and millions of livres in financial capital.[49] Yet in their assault on authority, the Encyclopedists generally engaged in guerrilla warfare rather than frontal attack. Constant threats to ban the project necessitated this strategy. Church and crown joined forces against the perceived threats that the Enlightenment posed to France as it confronted foreign and domestic enemies during the Seven Years' War. Amid a barrage of criticism—especially concerning Abbé Jean-Martin de Prades, a young cleric and contributor accused of propagating blasphemous views in a thesis he submitted to the Sorbonne—an *arrêt du Conseil* denounced the first two volumes of the *Encyclopédie.*[50] Then, in 1759, the government revoked its *privilège* outright. Publication only resumed in 1765, owing to the intervention of Chrétien-Guillaume de Lamoignon de Malesherbes, the director of the book trade, who proved a stalwart supporter of the cause.[51]

Despite these challenges, the *Encyclopédie* continued its transformation of France's intellectual terrain. The *Discours préliminaire* that prefaced the work announced the editors' intentions to revolutionize epistemology on the basis of Baconian induction and Lockean empiricism, with the implication that theology would henceforth remain subject to philosophy, and the sacred would defer to the social. Historians have often recognized in this shift the workings of secularization. According to Robert Darnton, Diderot and d'Alembert's "morphological and epistemological arguments combined to cut orthodox religion off the map, to consign it to the unknowable, and thus to exclude it from the modern world of learning."[52] For Jonathan Israel, the publication of the *Encyclopédie* ruptured the moderate "physico-theological" alliance between Jesuits, Lockeans, and Newtonians, opening the way for pro-Spinozist and pro-materialist elements to seize control of the Enlightenment.[53]

Yet as eighteenth-century supporters and detractors of the *Encyclopédie* well knew, a devil lurked in the details. The work did not advance a unified platform of ideas, despite the appearance of cryptic cross-references that instructed the reader, for instance, to read the article on cannibalism in light of an entry on the Eucharist.[54] Nor did the contributors share a common intellectual orientation even on so fundamental a matter as religion. While Diderot and d'Holbach denied the existence of God outright, the chevalier Louis de Jaucourt, with some 17,000 articles to his credit, could be described as either "a very latitudinarian Calvinist or even a deist," but decidedly not as a materialist or an atheist. In addition, as many as 25 percent of contributors professed orthodox Catholic beliefs.[55] To the extent that the disparate views of these authors informed their contributions, the Enlightenment's *machine de guerre* could also be seen as at war with itself.

As in their views on God, prominent authors associated with the *Encyclopédie* also differed drastically in their conceptions of man. Replicating the fissures within the philosophe movement as a whole, a moderate faction remained fiercely protective of the individual's claims to self-ownership, while the radicals proved receptive to the dispossession of minds and bodies. Diderot in particular showed an intense fascination with the discoveries made possible by the loss of self, which he described in terms of alienation and even mystic experience. In contrast, Voltaire was among the host of philosophes and theologians who feared the mind's loss of conscious control over itself while in the grips of imagination, and who expressed qualms with reference to the dangers of religious enthusiasm.

In his article "Encyclopédie," Diderot notes how the project aimed at stabilizing the usage of problematic and contentious words.[56] It is telling, then, that he chose to contribute to the articles on *distraction* and *rêver* (distraction and dreaming), since these terms presented the semantic challenge of applying both to economic and legal operations as well as to mental states. According to the *Dictionnaire de l'Académie française*, one definition of *distraction* concerned "the separation of the part from the whole," as when paying an advance on a salary or fee, or when a magistrate surrenders competency over a legal matter to a colleague.[57] Similarly, the word *rêve* could mean the sum levied on goods brought in and out of a territory in addition to the thoughts and visions one experienced in sleep. Remarkably, the terms shared the same polyvalence with *aliénation*, which referred alternatively to the transfer of ownership over a property, the loss of another person's esteem, or the loss of one's reason.[58] This terminological ambiguity between economic and psychological deprivation implied another, deeper meaning—that the faculties constituting the human person could also be lost provisionally or permanently, depending on the circumstances.

While Diderot restricts himself to adding the moral and metaphysical components of this lexicon, his entries argue that the self constitutes both a thinking subject and an object that, like physical property, could be alienated. In the article "Distraction," for instance, he offers a separate definition that is analogous to the term's economic meanings, as "the application of our mind to an object other than the one with which the present moment requires us to continue occupying ourselves."[59] All the term's definitions, then, point to the same phenomenon: the separation of a part, be it mental or material, from the whole. Deducting an advance from a payment due, or a parcel of land from an estate, could be likened to the estrangement of the distracted mind. In the latter case, errant mental functions break the continuity between the self's psychological attention and bodily presence.

As with the economic and legal dimensions of the term, the loss of self-governance during distraction could produce a desirable outcome if kept within certain bounds. Diderot specifies that "distraction has its source in an excellent quality of understanding," which emerges when ideas come to govern the mind. In this reversal of the rational exercise of the intellect, "the distracted man follows [ideas] indistinctly as they show themselves." In contrast, the thinker who remains "master of his mind" fixes his attention only on those ideas that serve his aim. Upon establishing the essential distinctions between the conscious subject in possession of himself and the distracted mind that has ceded control of its thoughts, Diderot acknowledges a middle position between these two extremes. "A sound mind," he notes, "must be capable of *distractions* without, however, being *distracted*." This prescription stems from a concern with sociability. Distraction is thought to produce "a lack of regard for those with whom we are conversing," although infelicities might be avoided with "a little attention to oneself, to guarantee against this libertinism of mind." Otherwise, as when asleep, the wandering intellect would be lost to itself, with no sense of the duration of its virtual absence or what had transpired.[60]

Diderot elaborated distraction's typological likeness to dreaming in the article "Rêver." After briefly considering the dream state in general, as "the mind occupied during sleep," the entry unexpectedly shifts to the related term *rêverie*, defined as "any idea that comes to us during the day in waking, as we imagine that dreams come to us during sleep." For Diderot, reverie signals the mind's loss of self-mastery, "allowing our understanding to go as it pleases, without taking pains to lead it." This diagnosis reflected the normative view of cognition outlined in "Distraction," with its presumption that the mind should deliberately order its thoughts. Then, as if catching himself in the act, Diderot inquires of himself, "What are you writing there? I don't know—a reverie passed through my mind and it will become something or nothing." Reverie, he suggests, could replicate the products of intellection, while evading—literally "passing through"—the governance exerted by a thinking subject. At this point Diderot returns from his semantic (and actual) foray into reverie, with an unanticipated mention of distraction serving as an abrupt conclusion: "Dreaming is also synonymous with being distracted. [. . .] On other occasions, it signifies a profound consideration [of some subject]."[61] The form of the entry for "Rêver," then, would seem to reflect its content, passing errantly from the dreams of sleep (*rêve*) to waking dreams (*rêverie*) to *distraction*, before the demands of intellectual sociability interrupt Diderot's musings.

The mind's tendency to stray outside the bounds of reason posed a problem all the more difficult to resolve in that the lexicon employed to describe it subverted the philosophe's rationalist creed. Like *distraction* and *aliénation*, the most common terms for the dream state—*songer* and *rêver*—implied an array of meanings extending from the momentary loss of self-governance during profound contemplation to a more permanent derangement of the senses.[62] Eighteenth-century investigations into these phenomena took place against the backdrop of ecclesiastical and philosophical campaigns against popular superstition, as well as more esoteric movements in mystical theology.[63] The terms *imagination* and *enthousiasme*, along with *rêver*, *songer*, and *rêverie*, thus became implicated in the status of revelation and God's proximity to humankind. The cultural clashes that ensued signaled far more than a secularizing impulse, or a direct departure from religion.[64] Rather, enlightened abbés joined forces with moderate Encyclopedists who sought to discredit spiritual excess on empirical grounds.

As the *Encyclopédie* entries for "Songe" and "Songer" show, critics who equated the Enlightenment with philosophical, mental, and spiritual wakefulness regarded all lapses in self-governance with open hostility. The first article was based on an essay by Johann Heinrich Samuel Formey (1711–1797), a German-born Huguenot and author of *Le Philosophe chrétien*

(1750), while the second was by Jaucourt alone (although the seemingly omnipresent chevalier was responsible for completing the other entry as well).[65] According to the literary scholar Robert Morrissey, the fact that there were separate articles for "Songer" and "Rêver" reflected ambiguities in French usage, which tended to blur the lines between nocturnal dreaming, musing, meditating, and other forms of potentially errant thought.[66] Notably, the two sets of articles also advanced different interpretations of dreaming. While Diderot's article "Rêver" appeared to endorse a related state, *rêverie*, in the very process of composing it, "Songe" and "Songer" expressed an explicitly damning view, revealing their authors' essential commitment to the values of self-ownership.

Formey and Jaucourt regarded the human need for repose as no less than a nightly fall from empiricist grace; their hope was that death would "elevate us to a state in which the clear and perceptible continuation of our ideas will no be longer interrupted by any sleep or dreams at all."[67] This disdain echoed Locke's judgment in the *Essay Concerning Human Understanding*: "'Tis true, we have sometimes instances of Perception, whilst we are *asleep*, and retain the memory of those *Thoughts*: but how *extravagant* and incoherent [emphasis in original] for the most part they are [. . .], those who are acquainted with Dreams, need not be told."[68] Likewise, Formey's contribution describes dreaming as "a state that is bizarre in appearance, in which the soul has ideas without reflexive consciousness of them, and feels sensations without exterior objects seeming to make any impression on it." Jaucourt further stipulates that these ideas arise "without being chosen or determined in any way by the understanding," since during sleep the mind is by definition "alienated from the senses."[69]

Lockean psychology held that the self coalesced in active engagement with the sensible world. The loss of consciousness, therefore, raised fears about the continuity of existence. During sleep, the self ceases to function as the subject of its thought. The mind cedes possession over its ideas, which in turn come to possess their purported master. As we have seen, this deviation from sensationalist norms prompted French epistemologists in Locke's wake to characterize dreaming as a form of cognitive malfunction precipitated by the imagination's overthrow of rational thought.

Formey and Jaucourt departed from Locke, however, in rejecting his proposition that the mind or soul suspends activity during sleep. They retorted that, even in the deepest slumber, "the soul has, without interruption, a constant stream of representations and perceptions."[70] Their position resembled the fundamental criticism that orthodox theologians leveled against radical mystics and radical materialists alike: both were regarded as demeaning the self by casting doubt on its status as an active, thinking, willful subject. Consider, for instance, d'Asfeld's shock at the *convulsionnaires*' praise of alienation, or Bergier's assault on d'Holbach's doctrine of mental passivity. Yet Formey and Jaucourt consistently professed the sensationalist dictum that dreaming stems from natural causes alone, to the point of explicitly refuting biblical accounts of prophetic dreams as inconsistent and in all likelihood fraudulent.[71]

Christian apologists would not dare challenge the integrity of revealed religion, but their writings on the dream state frequently exhibit misgivings resembling those of the philosophes. Nicolas Lenglet Dufresnoy (1674–1755), a veritable polymath employed by turns as a theologian, diplomat, historian, and Encyclopedist, shared a measure of Formey's and Jaucourt's willingness to cast doubt on certain aspects of the Christian tradition. A member of Bossuet's circle during his studies at the Sorbonne, the abbé shared his mentor's contempt for Quietism.[72] Once settled in his career, he came to advocate a critical stance toward revelation that acknowledged the skeptical tendencies of Enlightenment empiricism as consonant with the spirit, if not precisely the letter, of Catholic orthodoxy.[73]

In *Traité historique et dogmatique sur les apparitions, les visions, et les révélations particulières* (1751), Lenglet professed a "reasonable and prudent doubt" regarding his subject. His work outlines a method for classifying supernatural events either as perceptible to the senses or as communicated directly to the intellect. The greater the physical tangibility, the less reliable the experience, since the body is more prone to error than the mind. Visions that occur while sleeping should be scrutinized with particular care, since, as long as the imagination reigns, "the functions of the soul and of the understanding remain suspended," giving rise to "extraordinary dreams" that defy authentication. Lenglet considered intellectual apparitions, which are subject to the mind's powers of discernment, less suspect, although he maintained that vigilance is nonetheless required in determining their veracity.[74]

While Lenglet exempted scriptural and patristic accounts from these criteria, the claims of latter-day mystics fell short in his eyes. He even considered the testimonies of orthodox figures like Saint Catherine and Saint Teresa unverifiable, since "in the case of facts that depend on human authority, it is necessary to employ the legal maxim: a single witness does not suffice for proof." Guyon provided him with a far more egregious instance of spiritual self-deception. Following Bossuet's judgment and Phélypeaux's scathing account of the Quietist controversy, he condemned the author of the *Moyen court* as a lost soul who had fallen into "the snares of the Devil"—while still expressing admiration for the volume of writings she produced.[75]

The Encyclopedists' position on prophetic dreaming bore an even more striking resemblance to the views of Abbé Jérôme Richard (1720–ca.1800), canon of Vézeley, who later embarked on a literary career in Paris.

Richard's *Théorie des songes,* which favorably cites Formey's writings on the subject, appeared in 1766, a year after the publication of the *Encyclopédie*'s articles "Songe" and "Songer." In his preface, Richard denounces the practice of dream divination, which he regards as an affront not only to ecclesiastical statutes, but to the laws of reason. He did not hesitate to implicate notable figures from the Church's past, whether poets or popes, who fell under superstition's sway. To entertain such illusions is "to shut voluntarily one's eyes to enlightenment [*lumière*]," while one's guiding motive should be "to strip from a subject of little consequence in itself all that which smacks of the marvelous, of the supernatural, and often of dread for the vulgar persons who seriously occupy themselves with it."[76]

Richard's *Théorie des songes* employs an empirical approach characteristic of Encyclopedists as well as of enlightened clerics. Richard contrasts the rational mind with the imagination and recognizes the need for the former to govern the latter. In the normal order of things, it should be "the soul, or the spiritual substance, that directs the imagination and pulls from it images or ideas upon which it wants to reflect or act." Richard adopts the sensationalist view that sleep interrupts the chain of impressions from the external world to the brain and suspends the mind's powers of reason, memory, and will. Not unlike Condillac, he also claims that "the soul never forms any thought without the imagination representing to it at the same time the appropriate signs and names." Yet in contrast to the imagination, which "only produces confused and disordered images," the soul is free to combine and recombine the ideas it fashions from sensations "as it pleases and without restriction." Thus, the mind operates willfully, while also remaining grounded in reality. During sleep, however, there is a "general slackening of the strings and springs of our machine." As a result, "the soul is deprived of its interactions [*commerce*] with external objects," thereby leaving the imagination without oversight, and thus becoming prone to strange visions and illogical turns that "throw the soul into a tumultuous and confused activity." The thinking subject must, then, remain vigilant when taking possession of ideas from the repository of the imagination, or else may stray beyond the bounds of reason. Richard cites no less a figure than Locke to demonstrate his point. "To say that one doubts whether one has had thoughts the night before," as did Locke, "only proves that the greatest geniuses are given to lapses, toward which they have so much indulgence and commitment that they regard them as particular productions of their transcendent minds."[77]

While Richard was keen to deny an interpretation of Locke that opposed the immateriality of the soul, he reserved unequivocal criticism for devotees of Christian mysticism. To his mind, religious ecstasy strongly resembled the dream state, and thus shared its pathological tendencies. The mystic "transported outside himself by the force of his imagination—plunged in the most profound abstractions in broad daylight and while wide awake—was in a state resembling that of a deep sleep during which one dreams." Spiritual dispossession is for Richard predicated on division: the mind alienated from itself by imagination also abdicates sovereignty over its thought, which in turn loses all connection to physical reality. He allowed that altered states of the soul might convey divine revelation, but he notes that even mystics believe it to be "a source of illusion and error."[78]

This derogatory allusion recalls not only Jaucourt's discussion of dreams, but also his contention, in the article "Quiétisme," that Guyon's spiritual comportment issued from an "overexcited imagination" and "mystic reveries."[79] Richard likewise notes that "centuries enlightened by reason and philosophy have done little for the case of visionaries." As in Lenglet's *Traité historique et dogmatique*, "the illustrious Bossuet" appears in Richard's *Théorie des songes* as a paragon of Christian rationality, whose "superior lights" exposed the deceptive charms of Guyon's system, in particular its cult of "disinterestedness," as leading not to spiritual illumination, but rather to "the depravity of morals."[80] For Richard, then, the heroes of orthodoxy contributed to the project of true Enlightenment, while mystic heresy warranted dismissal as a product of errant imaginations.

Voltaire, who like Lenglet, Richard, and Jaucourt attacked Guyon's religious folly, also shared his contemporaries' suspicion of altered states in which the mind loses command over its ideas.[81] His article "Imagination" for the *Encyclopédie* characterizes the faculty as an essential, yet potentially dangerous element in higher orders of thought and an analogue to dreaming. According to Voltaire, imagination can take either a passive or an active form, depending on the extent of the mind's self-governance. During passive imagination, the mind is incapable of availing itself of the "aid of our will, neither during sleep nor while waking." Rather, it surrenders to "an interior sense that acts with empire," confirming Voltaire's axiom that "*one is not the master of one's imagination* [italics in original]." The mind wields somewhat greater control of the active imagination, but only through the exercise of "judgment," which serves to make the ensuing ideas its own. Even though imagination can facilitate acts of intricate conceptualization and creativity, it still threatens to elude the surveillance of human reason. Sublime verse can turn grotesque, and a penetrating formula can degenerate into absurdity, with alarming ease. For Voltaire, imagination was a "gift of God"—but one to be held at arm's length.[82]

Jan Goldstein has argued that, in contrast to the criticisms of religious enthusiasm commonplace in Protestant areas, the tendency in Catholic France, where the Reformation had not bombarded *enthousiasme* with negative meanings, was to vilify *imagination* in its place.[83] Yet the semantic choice between "enthusiasm" and "imagination" did not exhaust the possibilities for theologians and philosophes seeking to classify subjective experiences defined by the lapse of reason. A constellation of terms arose from the *Encyclopédie* that expressed the social and cultural tensions between partisans of self-ownership and dispossession. Under the sway of dreams, distraction, reverie, and imagination, it was feared, the mind ceased to govern itself or give order to its sensations and ideas in dialogue with other persons. Even if Encyclopedists had less frequent recourse to enthusiasm than to related terms, its associations of spiritual excess still informed its usage in apparently secular contexts, as in the articles "Enthousiasme" and Diderot's "Génie" and "Éclectisme." These entries pointed the way not only toward a rehabilitation of altered states that had been widely impugned, but also toward a reimagining of the sacred within the human person.

.   .   .

In contrast to Voltaire's article on imagination, Louis de Cahusac's entry for "Enthousiasme" asserts the compatibility of altered states of consciousness with the function of reason. The author, a playwright and librettist of noble birth, contributed over 120 articles to the *Encyclopédie* on matters related to dance, music, and festivals.[84] Faithful to these interests, Cahusac devoted much of the article to artistic creation. Its opening lines echo the ancient Greek etymology of the term (which referred to being possessed by the gods), as "a type of furor that takes hold of the mind and masters it, which inflames the imagination, elevates it, and renders it fertile." Yet this definition proved unsatisfactory to Cahusac, since furor implies madness, which stands in opposition to the rational aesthetics he sought to elaborate. His article advanced a new, enlightened form of enthusiasm that could stand as "the masterwork of reason" and extend its scope into the unseen. In Cahusac's rendering, enthusiasm becomes "a pure fire that illuminates in moments of the highest superiority," that "supposes an infinite multitude of previous combinations," and that "can only be made with reason and through reason." To demonstrate the validity of his argument, Cahusac calls on the reader to imagine the "soul of a man of genius." Even if stunned by "a crowd of objects which simultaneously occupy it," his soul would be "soon restored to its activity." With the order of self-governance reimposed on the senses, the faculties of memory and judgment oversee the conversion of enthusiasm into the workings of genius. Rather than designating an irrational state, enthusiasm thus functions for Cahusac as "the indispensable instrument of production."[85]

The exposition proceeds to a revised definition of enthusiasm as "*a moving emotion of the soul toward the appearance of an original and well-*

ordered composition that strikes it, and that reason presents to it [italics in original]." Cahusac asserts that a work of genius surpasses the enthusiasm from which it has sprung, in that inspiration, reason, and the artist's technical prowess merge to create a form that had nowhere existed before. Gifted artists partake in divinity by virtue of their nearness to reason—which Cahusac describes as "an emanation [. . .] of the supreme being"—as well as by their power to bring being out of nothingness. The mind under the sway of enthusiasm, then, is called on to reproduce God's transcendent act of creation in the world. Likewise, the human subject possessed by reason emerges more fully in possession of itself and its powers. Once these ideals were in place, Cahusac believed, artists would achieve a status co-equal with philosophers. While he acknowledges that men of genius at times deviate from convention, he holds out hope that, among the multitude, "the artist and man of letters might assume in the order of things a superior rank to the intendant who subjugates and ruins them," or a "cashier who refuses them their money for his own gain."[86]

Cahusac's article includes two cross-references to entries by Diderot pertaining to genius, enthusiasm, and reason.[87] These links, however, do not preclude significant differences between the Encyclopedists. The first cross-reference directs the reader to "Génie," in which Diderot distinguishes between men of genius and philosophers of reason not on the basis of intellect or perspicuity, but according to degrees of self-governance. Philosophy requires "men who are able to make use of the order and the succession of their ideas." The genius, however, is "struck by everything" and "carried away by a torrent of ideas" that acquire "an existence independent of the mind that made them." To exemplify the differences between these archetypes, Diderot contrasts Locke with Shaftesbury. Whereas the former possessed "an expansive, penetrating, and just mind," the latter was "a genius of the first order," a visionary prone to error. Just as enthusiasm advances the arts, genius contributes to "the progress of philosophy" by drawing "a fecund principle from the shadows," which must then be examined more fully in the light of reason.[88] Unlike Cahusac, however, Diderot makes no effort to reconcile the rational and the irrational. As he remarks in the entry for "Théosophes," an informal coterie of philosophical enthusiasts from Socrates to the alchemists, "Oh, how very close genius and madness are to one another!"[89]

The other article by Diderot that Cahusac references, "Éclectisme," further explores the incommensurability between rational knowledge and unfettered speculation. It charts the rise and fall of the Neoplatonist schools of philosophy led by figures such as Plotinus (205–270 C.E.), who informed Saint Augustine's knowledge of Plato; Porphyry (ca. 232–305 C.E.); Plutarch of Athens (ca. 350–433 C.E.); and Proclus (ca. 409–ca. 487 C.E.).

Uniting these various currents was a belief in the ecstatic return of the soul to its source, the One, as a radically depersonalizing act. Diderot devotes several lines to the role that enthusiasm plays in human invention, noting that "it is impossible in poetry, painting, or eloquence to produce anything sublime without enthusiasm." Yet he also warns, in contrast to Cahusac, that enthusiasm poses an undeniable obstacle to reason. According to Diderot, "enthusiasm is a violent movement of the soul, which transports us into the midst of objects that we have to represent," so that "as long as this illusion lasts, all existing entities are annihilated, and our ideas gain reality in their place." He emphasizes that enthusiasm severs the self's ties to external reality and even to the realm of rationality. "If this state is not madness," he remarks, "it is closely akin to it." The risk of losing oneself in a crowd of images, therefore, warrants constant vigilance by a mind "prepared by and submitted to the force of reason."[90]

Diderot raises the specter of enthusiasm in the case of the eclectics because he reads their history as a morality tale of its dangers. He alleges that they deviated from the dictates of reason in courting, and even imitating, the vagaries of religious inspiration. This tendency culminates with the later eclectics, who according to Diderot, "nearly succeeded in passing for Christians," while "the Christians were not far from confessing themselves eclectics." As with enthusiasm, Diderot feels at liberty to generalize the point: "All is lost when theology degenerates into philosophy, and philosophy into theology. It produces a ridiculous monster rather than a compound of one and the other." Deluded by their theological aspirations, the eclectics sought "the essence of understanding," not through "natural intelligence," but in the recognition of God within the soul. As a result, they taught that "the most worthy occupation of man is thus to separate his soul from all tangible things, to draw it profoundly into itself, isolate it, lose it in contemplation to the point that it entirely forgets itself and all that it knows." If Cahusac's reasoned enthusiasm fulfilled the *Encyclopédie*'s credo of philosophical orthodoxy, to abuse the capacity for losing oneself, Diderot suggests, led to heresy. His references to annihilation and self-forgetfulness—which hearkened back to the subversive propositions advanced by Fénelon and Guyon—were by no means casually placed. Diderot sharpens the point with a quip: "*Quietism is quite ancient, as one can see* [italics in original]."[91]

Even while recoiling from these doctrines as "absurd pretensions," Diderot implicates himself in eclecticism's ideal of dispossession. First, he offers a general definition of the eclectic that bears a striking resemblance to the eighteenth-century philosophe, as one "who, trampling underfoot prejudice, antiquity, authority, [. . .] dares to think for himself" and "to admit nothing unless by proof of experience and reason."[92] Moreover, his own experiences, as reflected in his *Encyclopédie* articles, had convinced him that philosophes could become the objects of their own iconoclasm, with positive results. In this respect, Diderot could be considered a philosophical eclectic in his own right, daring to challenge the axioms of his movement before they ossified into mere dogma.

Tellingly, Diderot also notes that the "profound contemplation" advocated by the eclectics gave way a "delightful repose in which ceases all the dissonance that surrounds us and keeps us from experiencing the divine harmony of all intelligible things."[93] These terms precisely echo an altered state valorized previously in the *Encyclopédie*, where he himself had asked, "but what is a *delightful repose* [italics in original]?" In response, his article "Délicieux" describes a "moment of enchantment and weakness" in which the self experiences "neither memory of the past, nor desire for the future, nor concern with the present." The suspension of time indicates a lapse in the continuity of exterior sensations, so that one proceeds "by an imperceptible movement from waking to sleeping."[94]

For the duration of this liminal state, one remains "entirely in oneself," but reflection and memory no longer secure the possession of ideas that the mind exercised when fully awake. Rather, "in the midst of the failure of all his faculties," the person under sway of delight might return to a state of semi-consciousness, "if not to think of some distinct thing, then at least to feel all the sweetness of his existence." Yet in hindsight, it becomes clear that this existence, while perceptible, would be rendered impossible to call one's own, since the self "enjoyed the use [*jouissoit*] of it from an entirely passive possession [*jouissance*], without being attached to it, without reflecting upon it, without delight in it, without being pleased by it."[95] In repose, then, the dreamer surrenders his powers of self-ownership to find himself incorporated into the totality of existence, with no attachment even to his own person.

This valorization of use without attachment recalls the lack of self-referentiality that characterizes Spinozist beatitude, the radical passivity of d'Holbach's naturalism, and even more immediately, the mystical experience of self-abandonment. As Fénelon had once declared of spiritual goods, "one must do what one can to conserve these things, moderately and without passion, in order to make sober use of them, without the wish to take pleasure in possessing them [*jouir*] or to place them in one's heart."[96] In a like manner, the existential stasis elaborated in the article "Délicieux" depends on indeterminacy and indifference: between past and future, slumber and wakefulness, being and nonbeing. Whereas Fénelon maintained that the soul's communion with the divine occurs only in fleeting moments, Diderot speculates on its value as a perpetual condition, "in which all the faculties of the body and of the soul are living without being active." He goes on to observe that, if one could "attach to this *delightful Quietism* [emphasis added] the idea of immutability, one would form the greatest and purest happiness that humankind could imagine."[97]

For eighteenth-century readers, Diderot's allusion to Quietism could not be construed as an innocent gesture. The term referred almost exclusively to mystical spirituality, its usage being confined mainly to descriptions of the heretical doctrines professed by Molinos, Fénelon, and Guyon.[98] That he would employ so fraught a term, and in an article describing a state of altered consciousness in which the mind loses possession of itself, suggests that he did so for a specific purpose. The *Encyclopédie* declared the philosophe to be an autonomous, wakeful, self-owning subject, and the Enlightenment a bulwark against the tide of religious excess. Diderot's contributions, however, experiment with an alternative ideal, one steeped in the language of alienation, and even of Quietism, that considers the revelations to be gained from self-loss. In so doing, he seemingly gestures toward a resacralization of the human person in a world without God. While Cahusac's article "Enthousiasme" extols the enlightened artist as a transcendent, creative agent worthy of quasi-divine status, Diderot seeks to reduce the self to natural impulses beyond its control. He explicates the possibilities of dispossession at greater length in both the aesthetics of detachment that inform the *Salon de 1767* and the materialist epistemology of *Le Rêve de d'Alembert*. From his meditations, there emerges a model for a positive form of alienation that allows the suspension of particular identity, consciousness, and will, and that ultimately gives way to a deeper understanding of the self's true status in the world.

The Aesthetics of Dispossession

Diderot's aesthetic writings appeared at a transitional moment in French art. Prominent figures had begun to turn toward ideals of intellectual and moral regeneration and break with the aristocratic *bel esprit*, which they regarded as frivolously self-centered. The age of Scarron and Watteau was giving way to that of Rousseau and David. France was awash with new styles, genres, and media—like the *Encyclopédie* itself—that drew in an ever-expanding public.[99] To captivate his readers, Diderot posed not only a theory of art, but a system of reading and viewing to guide performance as well as reception. His method, as he intimated in the article "Génie," occasionally required the artist to cede control of his mind while in the throes of inspiration. Likewise, the ideal work of art must succeed in transporting its audience beyond the quotidian and into the sublime. Diderot articulated both models in dispossessive terms, consonant with his works on the dream state and sharing the same end: to reduce spectators to a state of transfixed passivity under the sway of the scenes unfolding before them. He did so in part as a response to the commercialization of art, but in a manner that sought to intensify and reconfigure, rather than diminish or conceal, the alienating effects of aesthetic experience.

The vogue for socially conscious art followed the sensationalist credo that changes in environment could alter thoughts and feelings. In keeping with their didactic mission, artists and critics alike began to focus on the reception of works by viewers resistant to taking their cues from academic officialdom.[100] Paradoxically, their participation was bolstered by attempts to create works that appeared oblivious to the gaze of their audiences. In the case of painting, the art historian Michael Fried has characterized this dynamic in terms of "the primacy of absorption," a mid-century reaction against the earlier ideal of having figures on the canvas gesture toward the spectator to attract his or her gaze. For Diderot and other critics, this outdated approach had the opposite effect, estranging the audience from what they were meant to behold. Only by effacing their implied presence, it was argued, could an artist ensure his work's ability to enchant its spectators. A canvas depicting philosophical reverie or peaceful slumber, for instance, could overcome viewers and induce a similar state of absorption.[101]

The principal theorists of these transformations included Abbé Jean-Baptiste Dubos (1670–1742), whose *Réflexions critiques sur la poésie et sur la peinture* (1719) prefigured several of the innovative criticisms elaborated by Diderot.[102] For Dubos, art's function lies in the psychological need to occupy the mind, which would otherwise succumb to the debilitating effects of ennui. One can be occupied either by thinking or by feeling. Excessive engagement in abstract thought diminishes the capacity to relate to the exterior world of sensations. The mind then enters a state in which "the imagination, too forcefully stimulated, no longer distinctly presents any object," and its victim becomes overwhelmed by "an infinity of unconnected ideas" before lapsing into listless reverie. Concentration on physical perceptions, Dubos argued, offers more grounded diversion through the senses. He deemed art's facility at provoking "artificial passions" especially advantageous, in that the effects are temporary and thus "incapable of causing us real pain."[103]

In contrast to Cahusac, Dubos maintained that the creation and reception of art follow not from rational deliberation, but from precognitive sense impressions. Artists of genius exhibit a particular talent for enthralling viewers, which he defined in loose physiological terms, as well as in reference to religious folly. To achieve the desired effect, the artist must also succumb to a loss of self-governance, described in the *Réflexions* alternatively as a "furor," "real madness," "intoxication," and "enthusiasm." Diderot would eventually break with Dubos on this point and instead argue for the necessity of self-command in aesthetic production, but he shared with Dubos a commitment to a kind of art that engaged feeling before thinking in the audience. In Dubos's words, "sentiment teaches far better whether the work touches us [. . .] than all the dissertations written by critics to explain its merit." This "sixth sense," moreover, bypasses conscious thought, "in a movement that precedes all deliberation."[104] The viewers' response, then, should echo the enthusiasm of the artist.

Diderot expressed this dynamic even more forcefully. "Touch me, surprise me, torture me; make me quiver, cry, tremble," he urges painters. "Outrage me first, then you will amuse my eyes, if you can."[105] His commentary on the salons, the highly popular exhibitions held by the Academy of Painting and Sculpture in Paris, illustrates a phenomenon that he considered throughout his work on painting and other media of creative expression: art's capacity to alter the viewer's consciousness and sense of self. He upholds sublime transport and moral edification as desired effects, whether before the canvas or the printed page. This end requires artist and audience to lose the specific, individual identities assigned to them in the aesthetic division of labor and to place themselves under the sway of a created object that, in the correct conditions, manifests its own creative force. The work of art, here resacralized as an immediate, immanent source of power, acquires the status once reserved for divine revelation.

In works like *Jacques le fataliste* and *Le Rêve de d'Alembert*, Diderot privileged forms that demand the intimate participation of the reader to complement his diffuse authorial voice.[106] Similarly, he related the personal experience of reading himself into the novels of Samuel Richardson as a means of intellectual enthrallment. His *Éloge de Richardson*, first published in the January 1762 issue of the *Journal étranger*, lauds the novelist for establishing conditions that allow one to assume "a role in your works" so integral that "one joins in the conversation" of the characters.[107] To advocate this manner of deep reading, as Roger Chartier has noted, meant to forsake the warnings, most often directed at women, about the physical and mental disturbances to which an excessive identification with the world of fiction might lead.[108] Diderot claims, however, that Richardson's novels are as morally improving as they are engrossing. He learned from them that virtuous action demands a double "sacrifice of oneself": first, by surrendering to the narrative during "moments in which the disinterested soul is open to the truth," and then by emulating in real life the examples that have been realistically composed on the page. For instance, Diderot identified so intensely with the character of Clarissa (from Richardson's eponymous novel) as to avow, "I would gladly give my life to resemble her."[109] To lose oneself in the narrative, it would seem, also imparts a poignant lesson about the ideal of selflessness.[110]

Diderot acknowledged that his devotion to the "Divine Richardson" was by no means unusual. Indeed, during this period, English fiction became widely available in translation, in part owing to efforts of bilingual French immigrants in Britain—an unintended consequence of the revocation of the Edict of Nantes. Richardson's stories in particular gained a large and fervent following.[111] His enthusiasts became so absorbed in the fantasies unfurling before them that they apparently confounded the real and unreal, reason and unreason, waking and dreaming. Diderot reported an incident involving a man who, after reading of Clarissa's burial, fell into a trance, during which he paced aimlessly back and forth and raved about the injustice of her fate. As Diderot recognized, such profound empathy with the character inspired a style of reading more typically associated with "a still more sacred book"—that is to say, the Bible.[112] Not unlike figures depicted in the scriptures or prayers manuals, Richardson's creations were seen as worthy of spiritual emulation. Observing the doctrines conveyed in his novels required readers to refashion themselves in the image of the characters, for whom the surrender of self-love is the highest good. Diderot found these transformative effects of aesthetic identification within himself, and sought to codify the experience in his aesthetic writings.

The sacredness of artistic creation is a recurrent theme of Diderot's review of the Salon of 1767, an abridged version of which appeared in Melchior Grimm's *Correspondance littéraire* even as the Academy was redoubling its effort to silence unauthorized criticism of the event.[113] The opening pages of the work fault artists who content themselves with imitation, whether of static models derived from nature or of the classic works of antiquity. The reason for their mediocrity, Diderot explains, is that "they study nature as perfect and not as perfectible." In support of his position, he turns to the tableaux of Claude-Joseph Vernet, whose arresting landscapes, according to an abbé in Diderot's dialogue, demonstrate that "the work of man" could be "sometimes more admirable than the work of God!" Diderot responds that in the physical world, "there is a law of necessity that is executed without design, without effort, without intelligence, without progress, and without resistance."[114] Like Richardson, whose gripping scenarios Diderot found more compelling than the dreary bustle of real life, Vernet could be seen as improving upon the productions of a supposedly divine, but most likely nonexistent, creator.

Vernet's work also figures in Diderot's invectives against the corrupting effects of luxury on moral and artistic life. Another of his extended dialogues in the *Salon de 1767*, this time featuring his friend and colleague Grimm, decries ruinous taxes that bankrupt agriculture, thus obstructing the flow of wealth needed to support painting, sculpture, and music. Unscrupulous dealers and collectors, meanwhile, have taken command of the art market, driving up prices while driving down the quality of work. Their manipulative avarice, he charges, is symptomatic of a wide-ranging "depravity of manners [*mœurs*]," an "unchecked taste for universal gallantry that can only support images of vice, and that would condemn a modern artist to beggary although surrounded by a hundred masterworks with subjects borrowed from Greek or Roman history." For Diderot, cultural degradation set in once "money, with which one could acquire everything, became the common measure of everything." Like Rousseau, he does not hesitate to link the abuses of luxury to the "nearly general misery" afflicting painter and peasant alike.[115]

Yet Diderot's response to commodification is enigmatic, at least in light of subsequent critiques of political economy.[116] In the *Salon de 1767*, he goes so far as to consider the edifying insights to be gleaned from the form of alienation that prevails in aesthetic displacement. As he argues, the painter's strategy of eschewing individual likeness for a totalizing perspective complements the viewer's desire to abandon the particularities of existence—even to the point of dissociating self-consciousness and the individual mind. According to Michael Fried, Diderot suggested that absorption could overcome the distance between art and audience to such an extent that the spectator would not only lose awareness of his presence before the canvas, but also, paradoxically, come to recognize himself in the scene.[117] He likened this state to dreaming, madness, and to "being absorbed in God, or in the contemplation of some object, when one loses oneself in the entire expanse of thought, without allowing the least distraction."[118] Like the mystic abandoned to the divine, the beholder can commune with a painting only by separating himself from his individual existence and becoming absorbed in the site being depicted. Paradoxically, then, Diderot found a remedy for estrangement, not merely in the reconciliation of viewing subject and viewed object, but in the dispossession of the former before the latter. When the self that has been lost ultimately reappears, it does so with a profound awareness of its negligible place in the sweeping flux of existence.

Vernet's landscapes apparently fulfilled this paramount criterion. Diderot provides Grimm with a sophisticated account of his impressions of the artist's work. The narrative hinges on the conceit that Diderot, having left Paris to visit a friend in the countryside, is describing real scenes from nature rather than canvases at the Salon. He embellishes his account with allusions to dreaming in its various manifestations, including reverie, repose, and—as foreshadowed in the article "Délicieux"—spiritual self-abandonment. At one site, modeled on a now lost painting, Diderot finds himself overcome by the view of a lake situated between two groups of mountains: "I was immobile, my gaze wandered ceaselessly without seiz-

LES OCCUPATIONS   DU RIVAGE.

Dedié à Son Excellence Monsieur   Le Marquis de Felino grand-croix
de l'Ordre Royal et Militaire de S.t Louis   Conseiller d'État du Roi tres Chretien
Ministre et Secretaire d'État etc.   S.A.R. L'Infant Duc de Parme.

FIGURE 2. Joseph Vernet, *Les Occupations du rivage* (1766). Print. Source:
Bibliothèque nationale de France

ing on any object, my arms fell to my side, and my mouth came open." His eyes saw, but his mind did not comprehend. His senses of time and self were paralyzed by quietude. "I could not tell you how long my enchantment lasted," he recollects in the *Salon*, since "the immobility of beings, the solitude of a place, its profound silence suspend time. There is no longer any measure of it, and man becomes eternal."[119]

By the fourth Vernet scene, *Les Occupations du rivage* (fig. 2), Diderot has reached a "delightful state" of transfiguration. He recounts feeling overcome by "the pleasure of belonging to myself, [. . .] and the still sweeter pleasure of forgetting myself." This paradoxical reference to both possessing and surrendering oneself signals a desire to surpass the confines of self-ownership as typically understood. Exploiting the religious and psychological inflections of the *Salon*'s dispossessive lexicon, he juxtaposes references to madness and the dream state with mystical imagery. Not unlike a soul surrendered to the divine, he has lost sight of his own distinct person, along with the landscape it has supposedly entered. "Where am I in this moment?" he wonders. "What surrounds me? I don't know." Yet his confusion gives way, not to panic, but to perfect tranquility: "What do I lack? Nothing. What do I desire? Nothing." To these questions one is tempted to add, "What am I?"—which would presumably elicit the following response: "Everything, yet nothing." It is as if Diderot's presence before the tableau-as-nature effaces his personal motives and identity, rendering the individual self consubstantial with the wholeness and plenitude of being as represented on the canvas. "If there is a God," Diderot confesses to Grimm, "this is what he is like. He enjoys possession of [*jouit de*] himself."[120]

In a stunning reconfiguration of Enlightenment (and Catholic) orthodoxy, the dreaming Diderot detaches possession of himself from his own particular existence, imputing it instead to a hypothetical God. Of course, his pronouncement should not be taken as an impromptu expression of traditional religious faith; nor should his reference to *jouissance* be confused with a direct valorization of self-ownership. Indeed, Diderot's entry for the term in the *Encyclopédie* does not follow the definition of the Académie française ("the usage *and* possession of a thing"). Instead, he stresses the possibility of taking pleasure in an object without necessarily possessing it. According to the article, "one often possesses without enjoyment." For instance, a king may construct elaborate residences and gardens—and would thus own them and be their reason for being—yet it is the lowly subject who takes real delight in them when strolling the grounds. While *possession* signals the defining attribute of an individual owner, *jouissance* properly adheres to the whole of existence. "Let's leave these magnificent palaces," Diderot counsels the reader, "and linger on the voluptuousness that perpetuates the chain of living beings, and to which the word *jouis-sance* is devoted."[121]

The contrast between the unfettered sentiment of being and the exercise of property in one's person becomes all the more apparent in light of the marquis Louis-Antoine de Caraccioli's celebrated treatise *La Jouissance de soi-même*, published six years prior to Diderot's article. Caraccioli explicitly defends the possessive relations that should reign between human subjects and the object of their desires, a position predicated on the inseparability of self-ownership, self-governance, and existential fulfillment. The word "oneself," he observes, signifies "all the faculties of the body and of the mind, and one enjoys possession [*jouit*] of neither except insofar as one becomes the master of them." He excoriates the unsociable morality of "a refined Quietism"—a term Diderot was all too willing to apply when lauding dispossessive delight. (Tellingly, Formey, author of the entry "Songe," elicited praise from Caraccioli as a "Philosophe *Chrétien*" who counted among the holy remnant of "enlightened persons.") Whereas the *Salon de 1767* paints an alluring portrait of the viewer adrift in the quasi-divine immediacy of Vernet's landscapes, *La Jouissance de soi-même* implores readers to maintain their transcendental distance as thinking subjects at all times. "The soul," Caraccioli states, "guarding always in itself the essential thought of itself, and feeling itself thinking of a certain object, is not in the least such a thought, but rather the being of thought."[122]

Immersed in Vernet's *Occupations du rivage*, Diderot claims to have been startled from his reverie by the rustling of the laundress depicted in the scene. "Farewell my divine existence," he laments, before turning to reflect on his experience. "If I forget myself too much and for too long," he explains, "the terror is too strong, but if I don't forget myself at all, if I always remain one, the terror is too weak." To achieve the golden mean requires a doubling of the self; one has to exist both within and outside the work of art. One must lose consciousness before the painting, only to regain oneself vicariously through the recollection of what one has seen. For Diderot, the aim of aesthetic dispossession is not to prepare the way for man to secure his own self per se, but to gain an awareness of one's place in the totality of nature—hence his allusions to the depersonalizing aspects of spectatorship. Likewise, the mind of the artist must oscillate between forgetfulness and consciousness to create the desired effect: "All beautiful compositions, all true talent in painting, in architecture, in sculpture, in eloquence, have supposed a certain temperament of reason and enthusiasm, judgment and imagination."[123]

Vernet's talent for channeling his creative fervor allowed him to produce landscapes that captivated, even enveloped their beholders. What had Diderot gained from the experience of viewing them? His account alternates between depictions of self-loss and philosophical observations on the power of nature. After surveying one of the Vernet scenes, Diderot rebukes his friend for complaining of a bit of dust irritating his eye. In "the universe," he declares, "all is connected, in its place, and there is not a single being whose position, production, and effect lack a sufficient reason."[124] There is no sense in grumbling, then: the human person exists within and for nature, not vice versa.

Diderot would elaborate this view, and the role of the dream state in achieving an awareness of our true place in the world, in his meditations on nature—and above all in *Le Rêve de d'Alembert*. This work illustrates, in provocative terms, Diderot's understanding of the human person as a mutable being adrift in a sea of matter. It does so, moreover, by parodying contemporary musings on the dream state. Unlike his fellow Encyclopedists Jaucourt and Formey or the Lausanne doctors Levade and Reynier, Diderot refused to approach the slumbering mind as a necessary but unfortunate deviation from the sensationalist ideal. He instead adopted a strategy more akin to that of *L'Art de se rendre heureux par les songes*. The dreamer's errant thoughts, Diderot suggests, may serve as a conduit to deeper understanding. However, rather than championing the deliberate manipulation of dreams by dreamers themselves, *Le Rêve de d'Alembert* argues that the individual mind operates not so much as a subject exerting its will on itself and the world, but as an object in the throes of physical and metaphysical flux.

Diderot's Fable of the Bees

As early as 1749, the date of the publication of the *Lettre sur les aveugles*, Diderot had started on a trajectory that would lead to the atheistic materialism evidenced in his later works.[125] Yet he was often circumspect in expressing his views, at least when compared to his more brazen contemporaries. This was in part a sign of his aversion to intellectual stasis, which occasioned Ernst Cassirer's Diderotian reading of Diderot as one whose "thought can only be grasped on the wing, that is, in the stages of unceasing transitions."[126] A more immediate explanation lies in his harrowing brushes with the legal system. Diderot had been jailed for several months on charges of having authored seditious writings, and he lived in fear of arrest during the campaign against the *Encyclopédie*. While his published works did not avoid confrontation with political and religious orthodoxy, he professed more openly radical views in texts that circulated among a limited readership and through his contacts with other philosophes. *Le Rêve de d'Alembert*, a dialogue that Diderot first drafted in 1769 and revised in

1776 or 1777, serves at once as the summa of its author's thought and as a testimony to his elusiveness.[127]

In his private dealings, Diderot was said to have been responsible for converting d'Holbach to atheism. The two men frequently collaborated. D'Holbach wrote for the *Encyclopédie*, and Diderot attended the baron's salon in Paris, as well as visiting his country house.[128] They also shared key philosophical and scientific principles, particularly with regard to the passive nature of the mind in the face of physical forces. And while both thinkers at times made disparaging remarks about Spinoza, his monistic framework nevertheless added structure to their respective renderings of materialism, as confirmed by Diderot's *Encyclopédie* article "Spinosiste."[129]

In *Le Rêve de d'Alembert*, Diderot set forth his most profound explication of how unitary matter operates in the universe and on the individual human person, and his most detailed commentary on the relationship between dreaming and philosophical inquiry. These aims were inexorably linked, for Diderot regarded the study of nature as itself a process within nature. To rephrase Marx's famous dictum, he believed that philosophers must actively engage in interpreting the world in order to understand how constantly, and ineluctably, it changes.[130] This awareness derives most immediately not from the waking perceptions of the active mind, but from the depths of delirious slumber. Even the most fastidious of philosophes, when lost in dreams, could alight on the realization that the individual self is but a figment to be dispossessed, and consciousness a mere shadow cast by the totality of nature.

Le Rêve de d'Alembert takes the form of a dialogue on the limits of consciousness in a materialist account of existence. Much of the plot revolves around d'Alembert's anxiety concerning the precariousness of personal identity. In the opening scene, the character Diderot antagonizes d'Alembert with his assertion that the difference between inanimate objects and thinking subjects is merely one of physical organization, and that memory alone makes self-awareness possible from one moment to the next. Disturbed by this doctrine of universal motion, which upends the Cartesian theory of substances, d'Alembert retires for the evening, with Diderot predicting that their conversation will haunt him in his sleep.[131] Thus, the opening exchange both serves to draw the reader into the story that will unfold and also signals its form and content. If, as Diderot's character alleges, the preservation of identity depends on memory, then sleep entails a temporary suspension of consciousness. D'Alembert's skepticism may be overturned along with his self-governance, leaving him receptive to a materialist critique of individualism just when he himself ceases to be an individual who possesses reason and will. *Le Rêve de d'Alembert*, then, problematizes the conviction that Descartes's *Méditations* had so forcefully affirmed, that no onslaught of deception should be capable of annihilating the dreamer's sense of self.

Returning to the residence he shares with Julie de Lespinasse, d'Alembert collapses into his armchair and falls into a profound, feverish sleep.[132] His ravings seem so bizarre that she decides to record whatever she can decipher. In the morning, she calls for the physician Théophile de Bordeu, in real life a mutual acquaintance and proponent of medical vitalism—a tradition that Diderot drew upon and adapted to his purposes.[133] She reads to Bordeu from her transcription, while d'Alembert persists in mumbling about the primacy of individual existence: "Listen, philosopher, I can well see an aggregate, a tissue of tiny sensitive beings, but an animal! . . . a whole! A system in itself, having consciousness of its unity! I don't see it; no, I don't see it."[134]

A related metaphor—that of a swarm of bees—not only conveys the relative insignificance of the individual in the universe, but also depicts the interactions between the characters themselves. Lespinasse relates how d'Alembert had likened an individual being to a swarm that moves as a single body, along with his demands that she take part in a thought experiment to organize and reorganize its component parts. The tale so captivates Bordeu that he lapses into distraction, prompting Lespinasse to ask, "Are you also dreaming?" Now in a state parallel to d'Alembert's, Bordeu proposes to see what the patient sees, and to divine the end of the fable. Lespinasse replies that, if he succeeds, "I promise to take you for the greatest madman the world has ever seen." Her pledge conjures up the associations that link the dream state, prophecy, meditation, and mental derangement, not only in Diderot's work, but in eighteenth-century theology and philosophy more generally. Bordeu momentarily assumes d'Alembert's place as the dreaming philosophe by imagining the swarm, with the insects' feet grown together, as analogous to an animal composed of interconnected organs. Lespinasse marvels at this suggestion, which almost exactly mirrors d'Alembert's original instructions. Compelled to remark on the strange interchangeability of the two men, she declares, "There is no difference between a waking doctor and a dreaming philosopher."[135]

The confusion deepens when the narrative returns to Lespinasse's account of the experiment. If one takes a pair of scissors to the conjoined cluster, what is one left with? What becomes of the unity of the whole? The characters discover that the remaining bees hold their pattern; the swarm does not perish, despite its physical separation. As Bordeu observes, "you could push the division as far as you please without killing a single one, and this whole formed from imperceptible bees will be a veritable polyp that you will not destroy except by crushing it."[136] The metaphorical swarm of bees, he concludes, represents the principle of organization that fashions cells into tissues, tissues into organs, and organ systems into animal bodies.

The principle of unified alienability extends further still, as suggested by the melding of consciousness among Bordeu, d'Alembert, and a figment of Diderot that Bordeu projects, with whom d'Alembert argues even while asleep. The characters of the dialogue are another swarm unto themselves.[137] Their minds, like the bees, fuse in the act of collective dreaming. At other times, they appear disconnected, standing apart and speaking apart, yet their essential wholeness prevails despite and because of its divisibility. The characters lose sight of themselves in the dream state only to reappear in one another's thoughts. The subjects of their musings—"general sensibility, the formation of a sensate being, the origin of animals and their duration"—are so many "follies" befitting only the philosophical dreamer, since, according to Lespinasse, "a man who is awake and in his right mind would never occupy himself with them."[138]

The text again considers the ephemeral nature of individual identity when Lespinasse recounts d'Alembert's awe over the English biologist John Turberville Needham's experiments with microscopic organisms. D'Alembert regards Needham's test tube of water as representative of the entire universe, in which the human person is as inconsequential as a single transitory particle. "Everything changes, everything passes," d'Alembert remarks, and "only the whole remains. [. . .] In this immense ocean of matter, there is no molecule that resembles another, none that for an instant resembles itself."[139] The only constant in the universe, then, is infinite mutability; all particular beings are bound to lose themselves in it.

This implicit critique of the delusions of human grandeur owes much to Needham's findings, but it resonates with other sources as well. In particular, d'Alembert's allusion recalls Guyon's description of abandoning oneself to the love of God like a drop of water in the sea and Montesquieu's fear that Spinoza's monism reduced the soul to nothingness, similarly devaluing individualist selfhood.[140] In both cases, the immensity of a totalizing force, whether divine or natural, can unmoor the human person from its distinct identity. "There is nothing except drinking, eating, living, making love, and sleeping," the slumbering d'Alembert says—and, Lespinasse obliquely recounts, he starts masturbating.[141] In a strange reversal of the scenario played out in *L'Art de se rendre heureux par les songes*, it is while dreaming that d'Alembert appears to prepare himself for sensual experience in actual life.

While Bordeu develops Diderot's side of the argument against self-sufficient individuality, Lespinasse adopts the sleeping d'Alembert's skepticism, contending that "it is not necessary to carry on so in order to know that I am myself, that I have always been myself, and that I shall never be another." Bordeu pretends to accept this truism, while undermining its basis in fact. As he makes clear, all material bodies are comprised of a single substance organized in various configurations, extending from a single cell to the entire universe. The identity of an individual form, whether a particular organ or an animal, depends on a complex of alienation, by which particular units are subsumed into more general entities. However, the question arises: "Each sensitive molecule has its self [*moi*] before the application, but how was it lost, and how do all these losses result in a consciousness of the whole?"[142]

"Why am I thus?" the slumbering d'Alembert eventually asks, and he proceeds to invoke the determinate nature of particular beings: "I am thus, because it was necessary that I be thus. Change the whole, and you necessarily change me. But the whole is always changing . . ." With this observation, d'Alembert suggests that the self he once claimed as his own has no inherent specificity, and "thus nothing is in essence a particular being." Individuality does not belong to organs or bodies or selves, but only to material nature in its entirety. D'Alembert reaches the climax of his delirium, and lashes out at his prior faith in independent self-consciousness. "And you speak of individuals, poor philosophers! Leave behind your individuals and answer me this . . ." Apparently still dreaming, he forcefully expresses what his newfound convictions imply. Since "everything adheres in nature," he demands of his fellow philosophers, "what do you mean to say by your individuals? There is no such thing. . . . There is but one great individual, and that is the whole." In the "general mass" that comprises the totality of nature, a being (including the human person) is equal merely to "the sum of a certain number of tendencies," which emerges from and then disintegrates into the constant flux of which it is a part.[143] The self, therefore, has no unique value, no fixed boundaries, no inalienable essence.

D'Alembert's virtuoso performance, which Bordeu praises as "truly lofty philosophy," plays up the lack of particularity within materialist monism. In explicating the meanings of this view for the human person, however, the doctor shifts emphasis. Rather than dwell on the changeability of selves and other beings, he seizes upon Lespinasse's reference to the common sensationalist trope likening the brain to a spider in its web, with nerve fibers running throughout the body. Bordeu adds that the mind owes its unity to "the constant, invariable link of all impressions to this common origin," the site of memory and rational comparison. As such, it is "susceptible to everything, it is the register of everything, [. . .] and the animal is trained from its first experience to relate the self to it."[144]

Bordeu's account of cognition goes on to describe the various circumstances in which one's sense of self is suspended. Indeed, the dialogue often turns to abnormal cases that fascinate the characters—Siamese twins, various anatomical abnormalities, and the like. More often, however, the interlocutors focus their attention on the immediate case of the philosophe slumbering before them. While external sensations typically give grounding to the self, Bordeu warns Lespinasse, "in the shadows, when you dream of something abstract, and even during the day, when your mind is occupied," these limits are removed. She gives her own account of this experience: "I exist at a single point. I almost cease to be matter and feel nothing but my thought." Then, in terms that recall Diderot's descriptions in the *Salon de 1767*, she observes: "There is neither place, nor movement, nor body, nor distance, nor space for me. The universe is annihilated for me, and I am nothing for it." At other moments, this sense of existing without time and place gives way to the opposite extreme—a feeling of immensity in which one is no more oneself, but instead diffused within the totality of matter. Bordeu explains these phenomena as resulting from disturbances in the "tension" of nerve fibers that govern "the real or imaginary expanse of the body." Even during normative states of consciousness, this pressure fluctuates, so that "our body does not always have the same volume."[145]

As if roused by remarks relevant to his condition, d'Alembert awakens at last, but he is immediately ordered to go back to sleep by the good doctor, who is now preoccupied with seducing Lespinasse. Although ostensibly unaware of what has transpired during his mental absence, d'Alembert speaks directly to the subject at hand. "Through all the vicissitudes to which I have been subjected over the course of my life," he demands, "how have I remained 'me' for myself and for others?" Bordeu knowingly replies, "You told us while dreaming."[146] The answer, in effect, is that the self exists as an inconstant, mutable, and alienable entity, ebbing and flowing in relation to the material totality to which it belongs. As a manner of being and method of inquiry, dreaming makes this order visible, precisely because it exposes the fleeting nature of particular existence, and thus the fragility of all pretensions to individual self-ownership.

The final part of the dialogue both complicates Diderot's moral and extends it to a more radical conclusion. Bordeu suggests that d'Alembert's fitful dreams might have been produced by an overcharged sensibility, such as that affecting "the man in deep meditation," and more generally, during experiences of spiritual "ecstasy" or "voluntary or involuntary insanity [*aliénation*]." In contrast, the "man of greatness" must stave off this threat "to make himself the master of his movements and to preserve the center of the network in all its empire." This call for self-possession, however, soon gives way to an ironic recognition of its limits. For one thing, Bordeu's insight comes to him while daydreaming about Voltaire. His meandering conversation occupies him longer than he intends and keeps him from an appointment with a patient. Furthermore, he acknowledges that during sleep, a state to which everyone succumbs, "all coordination, all subordination ceases" between the brain and the nervous system, so that "the master is abandoned to the whims of his vassals and to the unbridled energy of his own activity." Finally, even the mind of genius is given to dreamlike lapses marked by the loss of conscious sovereignty over thought. Bordeu apostrophizes d'Alembert as embodying the continuum between wakefulness and slumber, self-ownership and dispossession: "delivered over to profound speculations" he has "passed two-thirds of [his] life dreaming with [his] eyes open and acting without willing."[147] With this pronouncement, Diderot leaves his readers with the indelible impression that to philosophize is to dream. Likewise, the enlightened practices identifying the universe's physical laws culminate in an understanding of the thinking subject's profoundly determined nature as a physical object—a drop of water in the ocean, a bee in the swarm—and as the dynamic product of interactions with other changeable selves.

From Mystical Science to the Materialist Dream

D'Alembert was not at all flattered by the work that now bears his name. His response is perhaps unsurprising, given the irreverence Diderot showed toward his ideal of the self-possessed philosophical subject, who, far from losing himself, assumes "an elevated point of view from which he can perceive at once all the principal sciences and arts, and see at a glance the objects of his speculations."[148] Lespinasse was no less displeased by the unserious manner in which she had been portrayed. D'Alembert apparently asked that the manuscript be destroyed.[149] The impetus behind the request is understandable. The *Rêve* shines an unflattering light on characters who brazenly flirt with each other, swap incredible tales about the marvels of nature, and rave unconsciously about the expanse of the universe and the comparative insignificance of individuals. As Diderot admitted to Sophie Volland regarding the work, "it is impossible to be more profound and more insane," even if "it is often necessary to give wisdom the air of madness."[150]

Behind the brash façade, however, stood a subtle reworking of the philosophe's identity. For Diderot, the Enlightenment subject must be by turns a rational being capable of self-governance and an intellectual vagabond whose occasional lapses from self-mastery might reveal as much as the scrupulous application of empirical method or geometric reasoning. This ideal departed in significant ways from those of Voltaire, d'Alembert, and other moderate philosophes. In Diderot's view, wakefulness and dreaming, and self-ownership and dispossession, stood in dialectical collusion rather than in binary opposition. In keeping with his materialism, the two manners of being a self, and the cultures of personhood to which they correspond, pass from one to the other like night and day.

Diderot elaborated his vision of the philosophical dreamer in both theory and practice, with a constant eye to the status of the self as a fully material entity. In so doing, he had recourse to a lexicon used to describe a range of altered mental states, all characterized by varying degrees of the self-alienation. These terms originated in an array of settings, from the experiments of professional physicians to the liturgies of mystical heretics. Diderot's *Encyclopédie* articles traverse these registers in tracing the commonalities shared by the slumbering mind, the inspired genius, and the spiritual enthusiast, all capable of losing their places in the here and now and existing as if beyond themselves. Yet he did not limit his efforts merely to describing the effects of distraction or dreams or existential delight. The article "Rêver" and the dialogue *Le Rêve de d'Alembert* chronicle his attempts to demonstrate, not only the inevitability, but also the productivity, of experiencing dispossession.

The aesthetic and philosophical works that followed saw Diderot developing, in concrete detail, methods for inducing self-loss and ensuring its positive outcome. He explored these possibilities from a perspective that could no longer accommodate a supernatural creator. In its place, matter came to function as a powerfully immanent force, but one, in keeping with his atheistic convictions, deprived of divine agency or title. Where orthodox theologians exalted the soul in its likeness to a spiritual, omnipotent, and sovereign God, Diderot proposed the self-effacing identification of individual human consciousness with the totality of material objects, or with their representation in works of art. The use of mystical tropes in the article "Délicieux," the *Salon de 1767*, and *Le Rêve de d'Alembert* provides a semantic cue for the dispossessive nature of subjective experiences that this stance entailed. If Diderot did not employ an avowedly secular vocabulary to express his designs, it was not merely because elements of Catholic religiosity lingered in his system, but also because an appropriate lexicon did not exist. Thus, he was compelled to adopt terms with spiritual, and even mystical, connotations. The language of Quietist abandon, refitted for aesthetic, philosophical, and scientific use, captured the dynamics that he sought to evoke: nature's resacralization as an immanent, totalizing force, and the dream state, broadly conceived, as a means of charting its dispossessing impact within and against the self.

Diderot's creative fusion of mystical rhetoric and materialist philosophy resonated with broader developments in theology, aesthetics, and scientific thought. The dream state was a source of fascination for many, as shown by the attention it garnered from physicians as well as amateur oneirologists, and by the polemics surrounding prophecy and other forms of revelation among theologians and Encyclopedists (sometimes one and the same). Whereas d'Alembert resented the depiction of himself as a raving, alienable being, Jean-Jacques Rousseau lauded the sublime effects of reverie in terms strikingly similar to the language of the *Salon de 1767*. Unlike Diderot, however, whose intellectual project encompassed a truly encyclopedic scope, the self-styled citizen of Geneva defined his mission in more strictly social and political terms. In a series of writings on the oppressive effects of luxury, he produced the eighteenth-century's most intricate reflections on the relationship between human persons and material goods, and in so doing, intervened crucially in the major sociopolitical upheavals of the final decades of the Old Regime.

6   The Politics of Alienation

In January 1762, the year in which he would publish both *Du Contrat social* and *Émile*, Rousseau reflected on the origins of his philosophical vocation. Echoing the tale of Saint Paul's vision on the road to Damascus, he told of his illumination in 1749 on the way to visit Diderot during his imprisonment at Vincennes. Rousseau had paused to read an announcement in the *Mercure de France* for the Academy of Dijon's essay contest of 1750, on the question of progress in the sciences and the arts. He recalled how, at that moment, his mind was "dazzled by a thousand lights," while his body convulsed in "a violent palpitation." Although the enthrallment lasted a fleeting half-hour, he at once became cognizant of "all the contradictions of the social system," as well as the axioms "that man is naturally good, and that it is due to institutions alone that man becomes wicked." The writings he produced to elaborate this vision were born of a revelation, as was Rousseau the philosophe: "I saw another universe and I became another man."[1]

The world that Rousseau perceived on that fateful day stood on the brink of collapse. France, even at the zenith of the Enlightenment, reflected a vast, corrupting darkness set to eclipse the faint glimmers of virtue that still emanated from his native city of Geneva and elsewhere around the world. He traced the source of the disaster to the fractured relationship between human selves and the moral and material goods they claimed to possess. All his major works fixated on some aspect of this predicament, from the *Discours sur les sciences et les arts* (1750), the prize-winning critique of luxury he composed for the Academy's competition, to *Du Contrat social*, the political treatise for which he would be driven from France in 1762. Even the novel *Julie, ou La Nouvelle Héloïse* (1761)—his most acclaimed work, and one of the century's bestselling titles in any genre—exalted the character Wolmar as a righteous man who "does not enrich himself by new acquisitions" but by "possessing better what he has."[2]

Rousseau's meditations were admired and criticized in equal measure. Readers of *La Nouvelle Héloïse* professed their strong identification with its tale of unrequited love and well-tempered virtue. The young Charles-Joseph Panckoucke, later the publishing impresario who would mastermind the *Encyclopédie méthodique*, described Rousseau's "divine works" as "a devouring fire" that "penetrated my soul, fortified my heart, and enlightened my mind." He extolled their author as "a god who has come to perform this miracle." Another devotee wrote that she "would have erected altars" in honor of Rousseau's "sublime genius."[3] Provincial elites, as his success in Dijon made clear, embraced the message that moneyed interests threatened to undermine the social order from within.[4]

Moderate philosophes and theologians alike disdained the enthusiasm, imagination, and ardor of Rousseau's "ravings." The former tended to regard him as an apostate to Enlightenment orthodoxy. Voltaire wondered if he had become "absolutely mad," while d'Alembert adopted a more solicitous tone: "Jean-Jacques is a sick man of great intellect, but only when he is feverish. One must neither heal nor offend him." According to his estranged colleague Diderot, Rousseau's enthusiasm emboldened his rhetoric while overwhelming his mind. "Propose to him two means," Diderot claimed, "one peremptory but didactic," the other "capable [. . .] of capturing the mind, of moving the heart, of arousing a flood of passions. It is the latter that will hold him."[5] Critical clerics echoed such sentiments. D'Holbach's nemesis Nicolas Bergier contrasted the reasonableness of his methods with Rousseau's "dangerous talent of dazzling readers." The anti-Spinozist Guillaume Maleville also derided his spiritual excesses and logical fallacies. "Rousseau spouts the most perfect fanaticism," he protested, "without renouncing the privilege of declaiming against fanaticism."[6]

Even among those most familiar with his work, Rousseau remained an enigma. Although he at times upheld the ideal of the self-owning philosophe, he also exceeded even Diderot's praise of dispossession. "My entire life is nothing but a long reverie," he noted, "divided into chapters by my daily walks."[7] An avowed follower of both Locke and Fénelon, he regarded the self as an entity to be gained and lost in a variety of circumstances, and to multiple ends. He was equally convinced that domination had come to threaten personal freedom at every turn, and yet, paradoxically, that the way out of this predicament must begin with alienating one's particular will to more expansive forces beyond the self. Nature itself had fallen prey to insatiable avarice. Only radical regeneration could save humans from devolving into witless, hapless automata.

The twin menaces of despotism and exploitation, Rousseau charged, originated in a dangerous propensity to treat persons as mere objects—to be directed, consumed, or taxed according to the demands of the powerful. The *Discours sur les sciences et les arts* decries the corrosive effects of luxury, along with economic doctrines that equate acquisitiveness and dominance with prosperity and contentment. His next major work, the *Discours sur l'origine et les fondements de l'inégalité* (1755), constructs a history of the emergence, decline, and fall of natural humanity in order to condemn the alienating effects of social organization, a theme developed further in the *Lettre à d'Alembert sur les spectacles* (1758).

In his later writings, Rousseau formulated a series of responses intended to overcome the fatal contradictions that had arisen between seeming and being. The first, in *Émile*, proposes the reconstitution of primordial existence in society as a means of neutralizing man's estrangement from himself and others. Yet, by Rousseau's own admission, the experiment failed. In *Émile et Sophie*, the unfinished sequel to the original novel, lingering dependence compromises the ideal of individual self-ownership. Émile suffers one misfortune after another, including the loss of his freedom.

Rousseau then maneuvered toward the opposite solution in *Du Contrat social*, devising a political model in which the denaturing and dispossession of particular wills assures the fulfillment of civic existence. His final work, *Les Rêveries du promeneur solitaire* (1776–1778), testifies to Rousseau's retreat from the world into subjective experience. Whereas *Du Contrat social* endows the body politic with a totalizing power over the citizens who constitute it, the *Rêveries* signals his idiosyncratic return to nature as a form of communion with God, beyond the reach of the social obligations that had once ensnared him.

Rousseau drew on divergent traditions in an attempt to assess the effects of luxury and to devise strategies for humans to live within their material and existential means. Perhaps more than any major figure of the period, he recognized and experimented with the logics and lexicons of both self-ownership and dispossession, combining and recombining them in artful and influential ways. His writings extol Fénelonian mysticism in one passage, Locke's political voluntarism in the next. To his critics, this paradoxical approach lent support to accusations that Rousseau had fallen under the spell of philosophical and religious heterodoxy, if not mental disorder. Yet he never lost faith in the virtue of his enterprise. The contradictions that passed before his eyes on the way to Vincennes would not find resolution, he claimed, until men and women were compelled to reform their possessive attachments to themselves, to each other, and to the world around them.

Rousseau's Fénelonian Inheritance and the Wages of Luxury

Rousseau, the self-professed exile and solitary walker, defied and continues to defy classification. He cultivated a public persona as a citizen of Geneva and maintained an intense interest in the city's affairs, but he also kept his distance, never spending more than brief periods there after his departure in 1728, while still an adolescent.[8] He made his name in Paris during the 1750s. A confidant of Diderot's, he submitted several articles to the *Encyclopédie*, although his arguments in the *First Discourse* cast profound doubts on the work's moral efficacy. His entire corpus, according to the historian Mark Hulliung, formed an "autocritique" of the Enlightenment, which challenged, among other tenets, its faith in the reconciliation of interest and virtue through the redeeming powers of natural sociability. When Rousseau railed against the rising tide of vicious self-love, he also aired the philosophes' secret fears about their own designs.[9]

Perhaps the literary scholar James Swenson's view of Rousseau's relationship to the French Revolution—that he bequeathed to his heirs an intense desire for unity, which by its own criteria was incapable of realization—could also apply to his contemporaries.[10] By fixating on the self-defeating tendencies of the Enlightenment project, his writings had the paradoxical effect of sustaining it. A movement locked in constant struggle with itself might fail to arrive at the means to institute its ideals, but neither could it ever come to an end. Rousseau's life and work bear witness to the Enlightenment's perpetual need to enlighten anew.

From this perspective, Rousseau's stance vis-à-vis individualism takes on critical significance as a key for understanding his work, both on its own terms and as a crucial intervention in the cultural and political realms. Previous commentators have advanced widely divergent views on how or whether to reconcile the individualist ideal of self-sufficiency enshrined in the *Second Discourse* with the collectivist designs of *Du Contrat social*.[11] To avoid this dilemma, Rousseau scholarship has trended toward adopting a dialectical perspective on the antinomies that structured his life and thought.[12] The following analysis similarly charts the manner in which Rousseau incorporated elements of both self-ownership and dispossession into his philosophy of existence. Given his professed devotion to Fénelon, it takes as a point of departure his engagement with the latter's theology, aspects of which he synthesized into an alternative Enlightenment. In particular, Rousseau's valorization of *rêverie* as a quasi-mystical style of life and work challenged the ideal of philosophical self-governance, which vaunted wakefulness over waywardness, and sociability over solitude. Like Fénelon's, Rousseau's political commitments appropriated classical republican values to fashion a modernized form of patriotic self-sacrifice that renounced luxury in favor of austerity, and the will of all over the whims of one.

. . .

Despite the shifting sands of his religious identity, Rousseau acknowledged his enduring debt to Fénelon. Converted from his native Calvinism to Catholicism upon leaving Geneva in 1728, he later noted in the *Rêveries* how he was "devout almost in the manner of Fénelon" while under the tutelage of his lover and surrogate mother, Françoise-Louise de Warens, herself steeped in the Pietist tradition shaped by Guyon. Writing of the idyllic days he had spent by her side, he described the Fénelonian delights of "meditation during retreat" and "the study of nature," during which "the contemplation of the universe forces a solitary soul to soar incessantly toward the author of things" and to turn away with indifference from "fortune and honors."[13] Rousseau reconciled with Geneva's Reformed Church in 1754. As Helena Rosenblatt has demonstrated, his writings both before and after that date show signs of the "enlightened Orthodoxy" popular there, with its stress on human liberty and rational devotion.[14] His pronouncements on theological matters, however, continued to exhibit mystical tendencies, as when the Savoyard vicar in *Émile* declares to his God that "the most worthy usage of my reason is that it be annihilated before you."[15] The work's publication in 1762 led to Rousseau's definitive excommunication from the Genevan religious establishment. Despite also being forced to flee Paris after the condemnation of *Émile*, he insisted, "I have many friends among the French clergy, and I have always lived very well with them."[16]

The ambiguous nature of Rousseau's religious convictions in no way detracted from his singular admiration for Fénelon. His friend Jean-Henri Bernardin de Saint-Pierre, author of the popular novel *Paul et Virginie* (1787), recalled how Rousseau had once answered the charge that if "Fénelon were alive, you would be Catholic," by exclaiming: "I would seek to be his lackey, in order to deserve becoming his valet!" Of his taste in authors, Rousseau confided that he "preferred Fénelon to everyone," especially for having "turned the spirit of Europe toward agriculture, the foundation of the people's happiness."[17] He likely had in mind the reforms outlined in Fénelon's *Examen de conscience sur les devoirs de la royauté*, republished with considerable fanfare in 1747 as *Directions pour la conscience d'un roi*, as well as *Les Aventures de Télémaque*, the classic tale of political virtue, with sales that rivaled Rousseau's *Nouvelle Héloïse*.[18] In *Émile*, *Télémaque* is one of two books in the eponymous pupil's library.[19]

Rousseau could also attribute his early prominence to a resurgence of Fénelonian discontent during the culture wars that erupted over luxury in the middle decades of the century. This barrage of criticism was triggered in part by the spectacular rise of Madame de Pompadour as Louis XV's mistress in the 1740s, and by the expanding power at court of professional financiers, whom the provincial elite viewed with contemptuous dread. The latter's pessimism was rooted in deeply held anxieties over economic transformations seemingly beyond their control, even if they could themselves be regarded as beneficiaries.[20] In their eyes, according to the philosopher and naval official André-François Boureau-Deslandes, the lust for lucre not only squandered "expenditures that would be better employed for useful and essential things to pay for baubles," but also threatened to consume "the charity due to other men."[21]

Yet luxury had no lack of defenders in the government and in the public sphere. Jean-François Melon, former advisor to the Conseil des finances during the early Regency and a secretary to John Law, defined commerce in general terms as "the exchange of superfluities for necessities" between persons or economies. Melon's *Essai politique sur le commerce* (1734) unabashedly locates the source of human progress in the desire "to put oneself in a state to enjoy the possession [*jouir*] of life voluptuously." Luxury serves as the engine of "wealth and security of a government," secures the provision of grain and the defense of the realm, and follows as "a necessary consequence of all well-ordered societies."[22] Melon's views won the praise of Voltaire, who shared his belief that the instruments of happiness could be bought and sold. "I love luxury, even laxity," he declared in *Le Mondain* (1736). He could see no end on the horizon to the joys of "scrupulousness, taste, and ornaments," and affirmed that every "*honnête homme* has such sentiments."[23]

Other philosophes, however, took more circumspect views. Jean-François de Saint-Lambert, in his article on luxury for the *Encyclopédie*, reasoned that since superfluous consumption remained essential for "the strength of states" and "the happiness of humanity," it fell to government, not merely to "encourage it," but even "to enlighten" and "direct it." This approach, which Diderot adopted as well, aimed to reconcile opulence with equity, and self-interest with virtue. The *Observations sur le Nakaz* (1774), his commentary on a proposal for a new fundamental law for Russia by the empress Catherine the Great, his patron, contrasts unprofitable luxury that demands incessant labor with luxury that, by "excellent administration," promotes not only "the wealth and ease of every station" but "the splendor of the sciences and the liberal and mechanical arts."[24]

Diderot was also aware, as he made clear in the discussion of semantic confusion in his article "Encyclopédie," that luxury was contentious because it referred to a disorienting social fact lacking an adequate signifier.[25] From the final year of Louis XIV's reign to the outbreak of the Revolution, the kingdom's population increased from twenty-two to twenty-eight million, despite fears of a decline disseminated by Montesquieu and other contemporaries.[26] This growth stoked total demand, stimulated production, and supported the extension of markets. Foreign trade in particular exploded by a factor of five, while outputs of foodstuffs, textiles, and metals all rose significantly. Yet the new economic realities also engendered social strife. While the propertied classes reaped the rewards of greater demand for agricultural produce, real wages were left moderately depressed in the 1760s, and inheritances divided into less robust shares.[27]

These pressures, however, did not lead inevitably to economic constriction and mass immiseration. Increased expenditures on the part of landowners, industrial entrepreneurs, merchants, and prosperous peasants sustained commerce, as did the contributions of women and other household members who opted to enter the marketplace or join the work force.[28] French subjects across the social spectrum threw themselves into consumption as never before, even if it meant accumulating debt alongside the comforts purchased with borrowed money.[29] The rush to acquire was predicated not only on the expansion of the material base: that incomes tended to fall in relation to prices, especially for basic commodities, suggests that cultural and psychological factors played a crucial role in the consumer revolution. Recent histories by Daniel Roche, Cissie Fairchilds, Colin Jones, Rebecca Spang, and many others point to a palpable shift in tastes and expectations during the eighteenth century. It was not only that style began to trump subsistence, but that subsistence itself came to be widely perceived as a historically mutable and contingent criterion. For every critic who denounced luxury, a hundred buyers registered their enthusiasm in the bustling shops that lined the rue Saint-Honoré. Cutting-edge fashions in dress, gastronomic delicacies like coffee and chocolate, inexpensive replicas of status symbols such as watches and umbrellas, and the latest medical remedies caught the eye, not as mere trifles, but as goods no less indispensable than bread—whether in its natural or transubstantiated form.[30] Louis-Sébastien Mercier described the situation with arresting concision in *Tableau de Paris*: "luxury torments them, I believe, as need torments the indigent."[31] It was as if the logic of subsistence, with its systemic dread of scarcity, applied to fine clothing and accessories as readily as to grain.

Luxury thus posed a dual problem of definition—both quantitative and qualitative. Consumers and commentators faced the challenge of fixing the true threshold of need and determining which goods should count as necessary (or superfluous), and for whom. In France, one's belongings projected one's social standing, with silks, swords, and other pieces of sartorial finery serving as manifestations of aristocratic power. This logic was reflected in the intermittent renewal of sumptuary laws—even if enforcement remained haphazard.[32] As John Shovlin has argued, the relentless flow of luxury contributed to the erosion of the Old Regime's fragile system of material signs. "It brings great pleasure to a bourgeois to be able to dress up like a lord," Mercier lamented, so that to the "untrained eye," it seems as if "everything is confused," and "no one any longer knows anyone else."[33]

Nobles in particular found it difficult to maintain a collective sense of identity. They were assailed not only by the crown's efforts to monopolize authority from above, but also by pressures from below, since wealthy commoners could secure ennoblement through the purchase of venal offices, and in any case possessed the means to look the part. By 1789, a quarter of the nobility had acquired their status only in the past generation or two, and even scions of the most ancient dynasties married into the financial sphere and threw themselves into commercial and industrial ventures. In keeping with these trends, the allures of ancestry gave way to ideals bound to the individual rather than his social order. The concept of merit, traditionally understood in terms of service rendered to the king, came to encompass utilitarian and patriotic impulses toward the nation as a whole.[34]

Yet identity and social function—merit in whose eyes, and to what end—remained vexing concerns, as evidenced by the controversy surrounding the publication of Abbé Gabriel-François Coyer's *La Noblesse commerçante* (1756).[35] Coyer contended that France's economic vitality— and that of less prosperous members of the Second Estate—depended on the participation of nobles in commerce, a route that remained unpopular, despite the government's removing the ban on wholesale trade in 1701. He assured his readers that "commerce has been considered honorable by all nations during their golden age [*beau siècle*]," citing cases from Ptolemaic Egypt to Periclean Athens to Medici Florence. The same should be true for France, as it was for Britain and the Dutch Republic. The growth in trade would increase agricultural production, population, and the consumption of goods, with the effect of "endowing the body politic with all the strength it is capable of attaining,"[36] making commerce a worthy pursuit for a nation's elite. This apparent defense of avarice shocked Philippe-Auguste de Sainte-Foix, comte d'Arcq, who published his rejoinder, *La Noblesse militaire*, the same year. A commercial nobility, he claimed, would undermine the crucial distinctions between the "principal classes," since it was the duty of the nobility to "sustain the glory and interests of the prince and the nation, and to spill all its blood to defend those whose daily labors contribute to subsistence." Unlike merchants, who, d'Arcq believed, were driven primarily by "egoism [*amour de soi-même*]" and "personal interest," officers "continually sacrifice their fortune, their comforts, and their peace of mind for glory," in order to "attract to themselves the esteem" of their fellows.[37]

At issue, then, was not only the legitimacy of the society of orders, but also the mental and spiritual constitution of its members. As John Shovlin has made clear, neither Coyer nor d'Arcq challenged the supposition that the aristocracy existed to defend the *patrie*—either economically or militarily. Nor did they fail to denounce the fiscal and moral excesses of luxury.[38] They diverged on whether commerce qualified as a noble calling, despite the financial profits it generated, and whether a truly noble status required a willingness to lay down one's life on the field of battle. In other words, could self-interest directly serve patriotic ends, or did such ends require the countervailing measure of glorious self-sacrifice to one's king and to one's lineage? Even more essentially, to what extent did the desire to accumulate objects through commerce or consumption serve to complicate, if not negate, one's sense of self as a member of the nobility or of another estate?

Insofar as the debate over luxury involved political and economic considerations, it also pertained to personhood. It was here that Rousseau chose to intervene with his two *Discourses*. Unlike those of Coyer and d'Arcq, his writings did not directly address the problem of how or whether to reform the social order in France. In addition, as Helena Rosenblatt has shown, Rousseau composed his texts with the political situation of Geneva—where pro-French elites struggled with the middling classes for the soul of the city—very much in mind.[39] Yet he also believed that threats to Genevan liberty emanated from Paris, and he submitted his findings to a provincial institution, the Academy of Dijon, which expressed its approbation by awarding him first prize in its annual essay competition.[40]

Rather than commenting openly on discrete points of social conflict, Rousseau chose to pursue a more sweeping strategy. It did not suffice to attack luxury without also scrutinizing the self's relationship to material and existential goods, which he recognized as a dire and immediate threat to personal freedom. The two *Discourses* and the *Lettre à d'Alembert* thus reaffirmed previous criticisms of frivolous display (in particular, Fénelon's *Télémaque*), while also casting new light on the psychological effects of unfettered consumption.

Impoverishing Luxury: The First Discourse

Rousseau's thesis in *Discours sur les sciences et les arts* can be summarily stated: enlightened societies are doomed to collapse under the weight of their own avarice. The occasion for this claim was the Academy of Dijon's asking whether "the reestablishment of the sciences and the arts served to purify or to corrupt manners and morals?"[41] Taking a position strongly reminiscent of Fénelon, Rousseau maintained that "the evils caused by our vain curiosity are as old as the world."[42] In so doing, he refracted the

Enlightenment's ideal of progress through the prisms of seeming and being. This analytic frame, which he would further elaborate in subsequent writings, reads the discontents of civilization as duplicitous signs of a modern barbarism as oppressive as it is insidious.

The argument of the *First Discourse* advances along two fronts—one historical, the other psychological. Rousseau traced the course of ancient civilizations along cultural and material lines. While the Athenians descended into luxury, the Spartans protected their civic virtue behind the ramparts of simplicity and temperance. The fortitude of republican Rome gave way to the decadent grandeur of the Empire. The same dynamic was fated to prevail in Rousseau's own century, since "luxury, dissolution, and slavery have been in all times the punishment for the arrogant efforts that we have made to leave the unhappy ignorance in which eternal wisdom has placed us." Rousseau pointedly identified advances in the arts and sciences with the encroachment of luxury. As an example, he cited Voltaire, "the celebrated Arouet," whose literary genius surrendered "strong and manly beauties" in exchange for "false decency." Thus, intellectual posturing had not merely supplanted martial virtues. Rather, *doux commerce* degraded opposing ideals from within, as it did to all goods in which it trafficked.[43]

The corrupting influence of the arts and sciences stems in part from their exploitation for egoistic purposes. Knowledge in itself remains a neutral force until deployed in the fabrication of false appearances. Rousseau alleged that courtly sycophants, whose eloquent declarations "spread garlands of flowers over the iron chains with which they are burdened," circulate deceit throughout the system of human relations. By turns of phrase and changes of heart, appearances and reality fall into impossible contradiction. "One no longer dares to seem what one really is"; as a result, "no one will ever really know with whom one is dealing." While the tenets of enlightened self-interest justify the art of pleasing on utilitarian grounds, the "uniform and treacherous veil of politeness" blinds social actors to the possibility of meaningful interaction.[44]

In Rousseau's mind, the debate over progress coalesced around opposing assumptions about human nature, and by extension, about the prerogatives of selfhood. Defenders of instrumental knowledge acquired expertise to elevate their status, whereas true citizens simultaneously existed within and beyond themselves. Rousseau made the contrast explicit: "In a word, who would want to spend his life in useless contemplation, if each person, consulting only the duties of man and the needs of nature, had no time but for the homeland, the unfortunate, and his friends?" In place of the luxurious trappings that embellished the cult of learning, Rousseau sought the austerity of divine knowledge. "Almighty God," he prayed, "deliver us from Enlightenment and the lethal arts of our fathers, and restore our ignorance, innocence, and poverty, the only goods which might secure our happiness and which are precious in your sight." Rousseau called on his fellows to seek contentment not in the things of the world, but in the self alone. The "sublime science of simple souls" requires one "to withdraw into oneself and to listen to the voice of one's conscience in the silence of the passions."[45] This formula implies a reversal of the Enlightenment's *esprit systématique*, in which elements of Baconian induction, the Cartesian *cogito*, Lockean psychology, and Newtonian physics merged in a search for meaning that passed from outside the self, whether in divine knowledge or sense experience, to within the self and its cognitive faculties, and then outward toward engagement with the world. Rousseau, in contrast, advocated a return to the ideals of ancient civic virtue, Stoic resignation, and Christian retreat, in which meaning and the fulfillment of duty originate within the disinterested self.

Its author's claims to singularity notwithstanding, the *First Discourse* was no isolated cry in the wilderness. According to Darrin McMahon, the Rousseauian refrain against material and cultural goods resonated throughout the anti-philosophe writings penned by Christian apologists during the period.[46] Even among enlightened minds, the Citizen of Geneva held spectacular sway. "Monsieur Rousseau has converted almost all the philosophes here," Melchior Grimm remarked of Parisian circles. "They all agree, with some qualifications, that he is right."[47] Diderot, whom Grimm explicitly mentioned in this regard, defended the pursuit of luxury within reasonable bounds but did not hesitate to rip away its embroidered veil and expose the corruption seething underneath. "An empire cannot subsist without manners [*mœurs*] and without virtue," he later warned the newly crowned Louis XVI, and "splendor adds nothing to the majesty of the throne."[48] Fittingly, the *First Discourse* appeared in time for d'Alembert to comment on it in the *Encyclopédie*'s *Discours préliminaire*. To Rousseau's charge that "men are perverse, and they would be even worse if they had suffered the misfortune of being born learned," d'Alembert answered that, even if deprived of knowledge, "our vices would remain, and we would be ignorant as well." It followed, then, that the source of moral decline must be sought elsewhere than in an acquisitive impulse that led from learning to luxury. Despite their differences, d'Alembert maintained a measured tone that exhibited the *politesse* he regarded as the means to sociability—not least because Rousseau had promised to contribute articles to the *Encyclopédie*.[49]

Other critics proved less magnanimous. The provincial luminary Charles Borde, whose charismatic style had earned him a reputation as the "Voltaire of Lyon," published a spirited refutation of the *First Discourse*. In a work read before the Académie des Sciences et Belles-Lettres in his native city, Borde unrepentantly privileged Athens over Sparta, erudition over ignorance, and sumptuousness over austerity. The arts and sciences, he argued, produce an "enlightened wisdom" that "purifies material goods [*biens*] and extracts happiness from them," guiding the subject "by turns to abstain from and take possession of" desired objects "within the bounds it has prescribed."⁵⁰ Likewise, Johann Heinrich Samuel Formey— who would later popularize the Lockean ideal of wakefulness in the *Encyclopédie* article "Songe"—attempted to neutralize Rousseau's arguments by denying any correlation between science and morals, either positive or negative. He held that human subjects act freely on the basis of acquired facts and theories, neutral in themselves, which are then "subordinated to either sound or corrupt moral maxims" adhering to individual conscience. Scientific inquiry, therefore, serves a purely instrumental function. It is a means for the thinking subject "to appropriate a share" of dispensable knowledge, "out of which he makes his object" and submits it to be assessed by the "republic of letters."⁵¹

The attack on luxury made notorious by Rousseau's stance against the arts and sciences continued to warrant attention long after the original controversy over the *First Discourse* had begun to wane. Georges-Marie Butel-Dumont's *Théorie du luxe* (1771) identified the *homo economicus* as the protagonist in an unfolding epic of material, moral, and intellectual progress. The author of the treatise, a former royal censor and diplomat, whose previous writings dwelled on the commercial development of England's American colonies, made no effort to conceal his sources of inspiration: the title page bears an epigram from Voltaire's *Le Mondain*, and the first words of the text pay homage to J.-F. Melon.⁵² Nor did Butel-Dumont's arguments fail to rehearse the familiar themes established by various predecessors. The *Théorie du luxe* offered readers a telling glimpse into how apologetics for luxury not only followed current philosophical trends, but also related to the theological position on spiritual goods that formed an inseparable part of the eighteenth-century culture of self-ownership.

Butel-Dumont defended superfluous consumption on the paradoxical grounds of necessity, stating that "luxury is a spring without which everything would languish." It was therefore his duty to enlighten government ministers as well as the public. Opulence particularly suited a country rich in territory and resources such as France, whose inhabitants "have at their disposition many substances and diverse materials, by means of which they are capable of executing the inventions of their genius." Left to the impulses of nature, each subject of the realm would gravitate toward "the kinds of enjoyable possessions [*jouissances*] analogous to his being." The crown had a sacred duty to liberate trade and property from antiquated prejudices and institutions. By attending not only to agricultural subsistence, but also to commerce and the arts, France would at long last live by "the most sacred maxim of good government," defined as the imperative "to favor all that which can increase its subjects' enjoyment [*jouissances*]." Such a course of action promised immense rewards. Where luxury reigned, one would find "an immense quantity of cities, an innumerable population, and vast cultivated fields"; in addition, "human nature attains the highest degree of happiness of which it is capable."[53] The contrast with Rousseau could hardly be more pronounced. Where the latter saw perversity, oppression, and degradation, Butel-Dumont envisioned a limitless horizon of moral and material progress.

Théorie du luxe goes beyond political economy strictly defined, venturing into the social and psychological dimensions of acquisitiveness. In so doing, it clashes sharply with the framework adopted in the *First Discourse*. According to Butel-Dumont, "the taste for luxury" is nothing less than "the essence of man." God himself had endowed his creatures with instincts of both self-preservation and self-improvement. Any innovation or augmentation beyond what is absolutely necessary to sustain life—including perfunctory shelter and food cultivation—falls within the domain of luxury, which Butel-Dumont regarded as a morally neutral category. As he explained, "all is relative" in this realm, since "one need [. . .] engenders other needs." With the passage of time, "to the primitive necessities to which nature has submitted us, we have added a thousand secondary, almost equally urgent necessities." The useful and the pleasing are equally valid categories of luxury, since both apply during various periods to the same referent, "superfluous things."[54] Attempting to impose an arbitrary threshold on historically evolving categories thus struck Butel-Dumont as meaningless.

If the number and kinds of objects that humans pursue tend to change over time, the impetus of desire does not. Butel-Dumont held that normative human action should be regarded, in keeping with Enlightenment orthodoxy, as the pursuit of fulfillment through self-ownership. On this view, true happiness does not follow fashion and opinion, whether public or private. Rather, it derives from "positive bases," which Butel-Dumont identified as "the extension of the enjoyment of possessions [*l'étendue des jouissances*]." This criterion transcends all efforts at contradiction. The stoic pauper who claims to be at peace with his fate can make such a pronouncement only after satisfying his physical needs, and even then he would fail to achieve happiness. Conversely, to harbor discontent "in the bosom of honors and opulence" amounts to "manifest lunacy." From these observations, Butel-Dumont posited the existence of a general complex of attributes, consisting of "health, independence, a right mind," and "the pleasant exercise of the sentiments of the heart and of all the faculties of the soul as well as the body."[55]

In this scheme, luxury operates at both metaphysical and material levels, with self-ownership corresponding to self-governance, which in turn presumes a mind capable of deriving pleasure from the objects within its grasp. The historian Michael Kwass has convincingly argued that Butel-Dumont grounded his defense of luxury in the sensationalist psychology of the period, thus rendering it a universal, natural, and even salubrious desire, rather than a symptom of social disorder. Butel-Dumont's strategy also had the effect of detaching economic consumption from the question of rank and fixing it instead to the individual.[56] Indeed, he explicitly states that "happiness consists in agreeable sensations," both physical and intellectual. A properly enlightened philosophy, then, should instill not resignation or self-denial, but a rational longing for those experiences most capable of producing contentment.[57]

Butel-Dumont's statements show that he had sensationalist categories in mind when composing his *Théorie du luxe*. Yet, as contemporary controversies over mysticism, materialism, and the dream state make clear, this stance figured in a broader theological and philosophical context— Enlightenment-era polemics over the self's relationship to goods. Butel-Dumont recognized and even lauded the possibility of delaying base gratifications in favor of "the satisfactions of the soul, which are born of magnanimous action, charity, and the fulfillment of duties."[58] His account of luxury, while grounded in the operation of the senses, also employs arguments strikingly similar to those found in theological criticisms of Quietism from the 1690s, especially in their more unguarded versions.[59] Clerics who extolled the riches to be accumulated in spiritual life shared in the same overarching culture of self-ownership as philosophes who advocated enlightened luxury. Despite drawing on distinct sources and traditions, their respective arguments feature affinities of lexicon and theme—in particular, the equation of *jouissance* with the fulfillment derived from acquiring desired goods. Furthermore, their claims rest on similar logics governing how men and women should relate both to God and to lesser things as objects to be possessed, and to be incorporated into the very being of one's person. This rationale informed a system of action, dictated by the priest from his pulpit and by the philosopher to his readers. It remains difficult to quantify the frequency with which communicants at the altar, or consumers at the market stall, understood their desires in the terms established by Butel-Dumont, or by Bossuet and Voltaire. That these authors felt compelled to address the issue suggests the contested nature of their ideals. Nevertheless, their interventions offer a rare blueprint of the discursive and practical possibilities for how French subjects in the eighteenth century believed themselves, and all selves, to engage with their possessions.

Spiritual and economic rationales for self-ownership developed within a treacherous field of binaries that opposed reason and madness, wealth and poverty, possession and dispossession. Tellingly, Butel-Dumont denounced his critics as victims of "enthusiasm" (with all the term's negative religious and epistemological connotations) and insisted that those who find despair in riches suffer from "the torments of mind experienced while dreaming or in the agitation of delirium." The opponents of opulence, he continued, declare war on progress as well. Although Butel-Dumont did not refer to Rousseau by name, he was clearly thinking of the *Second Discourse*'s praise of primitive humans when he quipped that "the lot of an orangutan" serves as a lamentable precedent for readers sufficiently deluded to follow the text's prescriptions. The nostalgia for less-advanced stages of civilization suggests "the mind of a melancholic lost in his reveries," who, despite the "magic" of his literary styling, fails to lure opinion to his side.[60] This final slight makes the allusion to Rousseau undeniable, even if it underestimates the scope of his influence. Nonetheless, the damning epithets Butel-Dumont hurled at him, and at critics of luxury more generally, point to the philosophical stakes of challenging the self's possessive nature. Rousseau, meanwhile, had set to work on successively more elaborate judgments against worldly riches, crafting a new array of moral and spiritual properties for human persons to make their own.

The Nature of Property: The Second Discourse

Rousseau submitted the *Discours sur l'origine et les fondements de l'inégalité parmi les hommes* to Dijon's Academy in the hope of once again winning its essay prize. In 1754, it was devoted to the question "What is the origin of inequality among men, and is it authorized by natural law?"[61] Rousseau dismantled the operative categories of the problem as stated, substituting a conjectural history of personhood that posited the experience of inequality, as well as the faculties of thought and feeling more generally, as the products of social relations, rather than as inherent attributes of the species. His approach implicitly undermined the academicians' premise, based on prevailing doctrines, that natural law transcends time and place, thereby challenging the status of property as a fundamental right. Not surprisingly, the *Second Discourse* failed to win the Academy's approbation. Even so, the intervention could hardly have been more timely, arriving on the eve of the physiocrats' efforts to popularize the doctrine that the property held in one's person could serve as the guiding principle of self and state. Rousseau sought to sever this line of argumentation at its root by reducing the scope of ownership to the self, by the self, so that exterior objects became the source of estrangement of the self, from the self.

The subject of the Academy's essay competition touched on both practical and theoretical issues of pressing importance to its members. The issue of inequality resonated with provincial elites, who believed their fortunes to be in decline, and who shared in a more general concern over the havoc that wanton consumption had wreaked on the social order. They also bristled at the ever-greater demands that the cash-strapped crown was making on their property: in addition to the capitation (a tax by head), introduced in 1695, it had imposed the *dixième* (literally, the "tenth," or a 10 percent income tax) in 1710. After several suppressions and reinstatements, the *dixième* was replaced in 1749 by the *vingtième* (the "twentieth," or a 5 percent tax), with a second vingtième to be levied in 1756, and a third in the years 1760–64 and 1782–86.[62]

The stipulation that candidates for the Dijon prize respond with reference to natural law reflected its standing as a source of political and intellectual wisdom that stressed the virtues of sociability, the harmonization of mutual interests, and the sanctity of personal property. While the tradition lacked support from official institutions like the Paris Law Faculty, it nevertheless found its way to prominence via the printed page. The French jurist Jean Barbeyrac's translations of Samuel Pufendorf's works, including his magisterial *Droit de la nature et des gens*, appeared in numerous editions. With the *Encyclopédie*, Pufendorf's ideas gained an even wider audience, as Jaucourt and other contributors drew on his writings, along with those of Barbeyrac himself and Jean-Jacques Burlamaqui.[63] Locke's formulation of the state of nature as the basis of political liberty in the *Second Treatise of Government* also held wide appeal, as did his insistence that property rights stemmed from the ownership that humans exert over their own existence.

The Lockean understanding of self-ownership, along with the more general dictates of natural law on it which drew, crystallized into a new science for governing human relations. Physiocracy—a term coined from Greek, meaning the rule of nature—advocated the preeminence of agriculture over other forms of economic activity, the free circulation of goods, and the agency of individual producers. Its vanguard of *économistes*, as they styled themselves, elaborated this vision in an onslaught of literary and political activity. Their principal theorists, led by François Quesnay, held that an economy followed the laws of nature only when it maximized the enjoyment of property, both within the self and beyond it, and that this divinely ordained objective justified government's existence.[64]

The physiocrats preached a gospel of *jouissance*, a testament to the private pleasures and public benefits of possession, whether of ideas, actions, rights, or material belongings.[65] They fervently believed that the whole of the law of nature was fulfilled in this imperative. In Quesnay's words, "*The perfection of economic management lies in obtaining the greatest possible augmentation of the enjoyments of property* [jouissance], *by the greatest possible diminution of costs* [italics in original]."⁶⁶ His colleague Victor de Riqueti, marquis de Mirabeau, specified three types of property. The first, "the property in our person," derives from "nature itself" and thus cannot be abrogated by the laws of civil society. In addition, labor entitles persons to hold moveable property, or non-landed capital, as well as property in land. Even seemingly abstract rights constitute possessions to which one holds title, on the basis of "one's original right to oneself, and therefore of one's prerogatives of self-preservation."⁶⁷

The sacrosanctity of property rights bolstered the physiocratic tenets that agriculture provides the source of all real value and the free exchange of goods facilitates the expansion of national wealth. According to Pierre-Paul Le Mercier de La Rivière, landed property reigns supreme, not only as the material base that supports other economic activities, but also because it follows directly from the inviolable "right to exist." The desire to expand enjoyment through possession, he reasoned, could be harnessed to spur wider cultivation, the profits from which could drive the purchase of manufactured goods. Since the natural order of things "necessarily renders each man the exclusive owner or sole master of his individual self [*individu*]"—and with it, following Locke, his labor—economic subjects must also remain free to employ possessions where and how they see fit.⁶⁸ Thus, all artificial efforts to control trade not only contravene the order of nature but also stymie productivity, thereby entrenching scarcity rather than assuring true wealth.

Such sentiments reflect the liberalizing tendencies of physiocracy, but it was equally committed to absolutist government. This disposition cannot be attributed to mere political opportunism; rather, it was a tactic with elaborate philosophical underpinnings. As Quesnay made clear in his *Maximes générales du gouvernement économique d'un royaume agricole* (1758), it is essential that "*sovereign authority be singular, and superior to all the individuals of society and to all the unfair undertakings of particular interests* [italics in original]." Absolute authority thus provides for "the security and legitimate interests of all." Division and balance of power, and even the organization of society into distinct orders, is contrary to "the general interest of the nation." The unity of power, likewise, should reflect the uniformity of the "general laws of the natural order, which obviously constitute the most perfect government."⁶⁹

The implications of this stance were abundantly clear. Since the credo of reason and nature comprised a monolithic body of truth, it required a similarly monolithic state to impose it. Otherwise, civil society would fracture into a pernicious array of corporate and individual interests that might serve a privileged few, but at the expense of the common good. To be sure, Quesnay's maxims did not challenge individual rights. He readily designated property as the "essential foundation of the economic order of society," without which land, the source of all true wealth, would cease to be assiduously cultivated. Similarly, the free exchange of commodities was to be encouraged, since it allowed for the proper balance between prices and wages.[70] The justification for these policies stemmed not only from the sanctity of individuals—that is, from their autonomy, agency, and independence—but also from their conformity with an abstract system of laws that transcended the perspective of any particular subject and could be imposed, if necessary, against one's express will.

The physiocrats' defense of individualism, and especially its possessive character, remained robust despite their stance on absolute sovereignty. Quesnay and his acolytes realized that the reforms they sought, even in the name of free trade, would require government intervention. After years of struggle, their proselytizing efforts began to gain traction when the crown, facing bankruptcy in the financial fallout of the Seven Years' War, wagered on the redeeming virtues of liberalization. Louis XV's initial plan faltered owing to poor harvests, opposition from the Parlements, and the rousing success of Abbé Ferdinando Galiani's *Dialogues sur le commerce* (1770), which challenged physiocratic views on free trade. Rousseau also pronounced judgment on their doctrines during this period, asking, in a letter to Mirabeau, "what will become of your sacred rights of property in times of great danger and extraordinary disasters, when your available resources are no longer adequate, and when it is the tyrant who will declare, *salus populi suprema lex esto* [Let public safety be the supreme law]." Although Rousseau praised aspects of the physiocrats' economic thought, he found their general system to be as incomprehensible as it was unrealizable, suitable for "the people of Utopia," but not "the sons of Adam."[71]

In the first years of Louis XVI's reign, the controller-general Anne-Robert-Jacques Turgot, a fellow traveler who appointed the physiocrat Pierre-Samuel Du Pont de Nemours inspector-general of commerce, revived the liberalizing campaign in his decrees abolishing restrictions on trade and the monopolistic privileges of the guilds. These policies provoked the ire of thousands of French subjects, who believed that their subsistence, their livelihoods, and even their very identities had been rendered obsolete with the stroke of a minister's pen. Tellingly, their petitions turned the language of self-ownership against the reformers, in asserting just title to the prerogatives that they had purchased, along with the status and reputation that adhered to them. The reforms, they claimed, would strip them of the property for which they had labored their entire lives, leaving them a "confused multitude that jostles, clamors about, and humiliates itself to attract the wages of consumers."[72] Bowing to intense pressure from courts, corporations, and consumers alike, the king dismissed Turgot in 1776, and his realm reverted once more to the status quo.

These disputes over the nature of the sociopolitical order found impetus in the even broader conflict over the relationship between persons and possessions. Two decades before the impasse of the 1770s, with the publication of the *Second Discourse*, Rousseau had taken a definitive stand against all manifestations of blind faith in the power of property—whether in its corporatist or liberal guises. The tragic fate of humankind left him in no doubt that the cult of avarice that property sustained would lead inexorably to dependence, dearth, and despotism. He chose to confront the menace directly, on the discursive field where his adversaries made their most fundamental claims. By exposing the errors in logic that underwrote natural-law theory, he hoped to a generate a scathing indictment of self-ownership in society on the basis of its ignoble origins and the myriad crimes it continued to legitimize.

Rousseau's first task in the *Second Discourse* was to devise an alternative account of the state of nature. He was fully cognizant of the impediments to "knowing thoroughly a state which no longer exists, which perhaps never existed, and which will probably never exist." Natural law, he asserted, rings hollow because it reflects in actuality not primitive but present conditions—the human condition before the advent of society.[73] He accordingly set out to reconstitute the prehistory of humankind without reference to learned pronouncements "that teach us only to see men as they have made themselves." Significantly, the method he adopted unfolds along dispossessive lines. Rousseau sought to reconstruct man's original state by imagining a human person that had been deprived "of all the supernatural gifts that he might have received, and of all the artificial faculties that he could have acquired only through a long process of time."[74] This procedure also cast doubt on Adam's creation in God's image and humankind's divinely granted dominion over the terrestrial sphere. Instead, the *Second Discourse* depicts the first humans as unthinking creatures who belonged to nature alone—a portrait that repulsed Rousseau's theological critics on the grounds that it debased the status of selfhood.

Standard interpretations of natural law tended to identify fatal flaws in the state of nature—"avarice, oppression, desires, and pride," as Rousseau observed—that necessitated the rise of civil society and formal political institutions in order to reconcile individual interests with the commonweal.[75] This metanarrative rested on the premise that human nature, however defined, remains fixed from one epoch to the next. Rousseau accused the philosophers who held these views of endorsing a fallacy of composition. It defies the principles of logic and evidence, he contended, to attribute the wickedness that humans exhibit in society to their primordial, presocial existence. Under normal circumstances, they exhibited neither belligerence, as Thomas Hobbes had asserted, nor fearfulness, as Richard Cumberland and Samuel Pufendorf had claimed.[76] Rousseau argued instead that man was born and remained naturally good, at peace in abundant surroundings, "without industry, without speech, without a fixed home, [. . .] without relationships."[77] Rather than presume a continuity between nature and civil society, he posited a radical break, treating qualities his predecessors regarded as immutable as entirely artificial and contingent.

Rousseau's history of human origins bore even less resemblance to the biblical account of creation—a lapse he defended with the caveat that religious authority "does not forbid us from forming conjectures [. . .] about what the human race could have become, if it had remained abandoned to itself." Thus, on Rousseau's telling, there was no Adam to claim sovereignty over his fellow creatures, no Eve made of his rib to precipitate their downfall. In the absence of mutual needs or even language to express them, human interactions were fleeting and unmemorable. Not even the bonds between fathers and mothers, or mothers and offspring, lasted beyond the satisfaction of drives that assured the reproduction of the species. There was no God to worship, no law to follow, no tragic fall from grace for which to plead mercy. Primitive humans had lived in an Edenic state of ignorance in which the fruits of the tree of knowledge held no allure. "Savages are not evil," Rousseau declared, "precisely because they do not know what it is to be good."[78]

Nor could primitive humans claim to possess an individual self in distinct relation to other persons. They lacked the faculties of speech, reason, or imagination necessary to form a personal identity, and their capacity for self-perception and self-improvement, which would later be their undoing, was essentially dormant. "We seek to know," Rousseau claimed, "only because we desire to enjoy some possession [*jouir*]." It followed that self-sufficient creatures would have no need either for knowledge or for the rational faculties with which to acquire it. Their desires also remained strictly circumscribed, since one did not long for things already within one's grasp.[79]

Rather than reason or the passions, the "first and most simple operations" of the soul conformed to the dictates of self-preservation and pity. Rousseau regarded the latter drive as an extension of the former. Here he departed from Hobbes, who, on his reading, had taught that "man is naturally vicious" and "foolishly imagines himself to be the sole proprietor of the universe." For Rousseau, prior to "the usage of all reflection," the sight of suffering drew humans beyond their isolated bounds. The act of commiseration expresses "a sentiment that puts us in the place" of another being—an idea of sympathy further elaborated by the narrator in *Émile*, who inquires, "How are we to allow ourselves to be moved by pity, if not in transporting ourselves outside ourselves?"[80] Since the first humans lacked a well-defined sense of the future, they rendered aid without concern for reciprocation, and therefore without their own interests in mind.

In the state of nature, then, one retained the capacity to extend the love of self, and the drive to preserve one's life, to encompass another person. Rousseau calls this form of self-love "amour de soi-même" (love of oneself), "a natural sentiment that moves every animal to watch over its own preservation," without reference or regard to other selves. In contrast, the "relative, artificial" sentiment of "amour-propre" (pride or vanity) "leads each individual to value himself more than all others."[81] The distinction between these two ways of relating to oneself hinges on the question of proprietorship, as Rousseau's terminology makes clear. *Amour de soi*, the mere care of self, is not limited to a single being, but instead facilitates identification with the whole of nature—hence its compatibility with pity. Conversely, *amour-propre*, the exclusive love of one's *own* being, engenders a struggle between belligerent proprietors whose claims can never peacefully coexist.

The rise of *amour-propre*, and with it the loss of our freedom, did not stem from innate imperfections or a willful act of rebellion, but from the development of rational faculties that emerged, through no fault of our own, with society.[82] "Reason [. . .] is what turns man in upon himself," Rousseau asserted, thereby repudiating the doctrines of *doux commerce*, and "it is philosophy that isolates him." Yet how this change came about remains unclear, since a central conceit in the *Second Discourse* involves Rousseau's professed incomprehension of how men and women could exit the state of nature under their primordial conditions. For instance, language and abstract ideas could not have developed without frequent social interaction, which the first humans neither needed nor would have desired. "The little care Nature took to bring men together through mutual needs" convinced Rousseau of "how little she prepared them for sociability," since "what chains of dependence could exist among men who possess nothing?" In the end, he laid the blame on "several bizarre causes" that brought people into regular contact for the first time. This new state of affairs activated the latent potential "to perfect human reason in deteriorating the species," which in turn made "a being vicious in rendering him sociable."[83]

Rousseau launched his invective against the tragic decline of the species with a salvo against private property: "The first man who, having enclosed a piece of land, dared to say, 'This is mine,' and found people simple enough to believe him, was the true founder of civil society."[84] He described this development as the culmination of a series of material and psychological transformations that together altered how the man related to himself, to other persons, and to external objects.[85] First, the invention of rudimentary tools allowed for the production of new goods, but at the cost of dependence, since "being deprived of them became much more cruel than possessing them was sweet," so that their possessors "were unhappy about losing them without being happy about possessing them." Even the earliest superfluous inventions, then, had the capacity to take control of their would-be masters. The move to permanent dwellings gave rise to contests over rightful occupation. Intense emotional bonds evolved between the inhabitants of these early domiciles, establishing a setting in which vanity and pride could take root. Along with material possessions, humans began to forge "ideas of merit and beauty," and thus a sense of personal identity in relation to others. Rousseau called this period "a golden mean between the indolence of the primitive state and the exuberant activity of our *amour-propre*," but the latter had prevailed in the wake of "some fatal accident"—the nature of which remained uncertain.[86]

The rise of personal property corresponded to the entrenchment of a corrupting form of self-ownership. The moral stratification that emerged in domestic life soon became manifest with regard to material possessions. "As soon as one realized that it was useful for one person alone to have the provisions for two," Rousseau contended, "equality disappeared, property was introduced, labor became necessary." With the development of agriculture as a distinct vocation came the need to establish formal property rights over land, which, Rousseau specified, were "different from that which results from natural law," since they no longer derived immediately from the expenditure of labor.[87]

Alongside these developments, the regard of others gradually became a value to be exchanged and expressed in objective and subjective terms. Inequality intensified on all fronts. Rousseau describes this process as one of reification, by which human beings were reduced to the products of social circulation. "The rank and destiny" of individuals coalesced around their "quantity of possessions and the power to serve or to injure," as well as their "intelligence, beauty, strength or skill, merit or talents." Each person was compelled to acquire such attributes at the cost of his or her original identity, so that "being and appearance became two entirely different things, and from this distinction arose dazzling pomp, deceptive cunning, and all the vices that follow in their wake." An individual who defines others according to material and moral possessions is himself reduced to a mere possession, "subjugated by a multitude of new wants [. . .] to his fellows, to whom he has become in a sense a slave, even in becoming their master."[88] In Rousseau's eyes, then, the apparent logic of self-ownership ultimately turned against its subject, whose dependence on the judgment of others ossified into an insurmountable barrier. Men and women found themselves leading utterly alienating lives, so that their existence depended entirely on what they could appropriate in cruel competition with others.

The oppressive, fraudulent character of human interactions was enshrined in the first social contract, which likewise came about through a ruse. Although formal government promised to mitigate inequality, it merely codified the rights of the strong and rich at the expense of the weak and the poor. The rule of force posed as the rule of law. The original contract, by which the people ostensibly "united all of its wills in a single will," served as justification for the despot's unassailable power. Paradoxically, the force of inequality culminated at the self-negating point where "all particular individuals become equal again because they are nothing."[89] A "new state of nature" arose in which social vices dominated personhood rather than natural virtue. Rousseau left the possibilities of redemption as vague as the invention of language out of primordial silence.

The tyranny of civilization appears in the *Second Discourse* as the mirror image of the original state of nature. Equality in freedom returns as equality in servitude, and the emotional transport of the self under the sway of pity is recast as a debilitating reliance on external measures of value. "The savage lives in himself," Rousseau concluded in the final pages of the work, while "the sociable man, who is forever outside of himself, only lives in the opinion of others. It is, in a word, from their judgment alone that he draws the sentiment of his own existence."[90] The loss of self-ownership under despotism perversely parallels the self's lack of goods in the state of nature. The dialectical relations that structure Rousseau's analysis—master/slave, subject/object, and nature/society—offered contemporaries arresting insights into the stakes involved in polemics over luxury. Whereas writers like Voltaire and Butel-Dumont exalted *jouissance* as the path to existential fulfillment and enlightened autonomy, Rousseau regarded it as a means of self-objectification. Under these conditions, any quest for wealth—whether in material goods or in the esteem of others—only estranges one further from one's true, original nature.

For Rousseau's critics, his image of the first humans, shorn of the trappings of reason and sociability, was an affront to the individual's dignity as a child of God, or alternatively, as a representative of the Enlightenment. A priest from Paris, one Abbé Pilé, classed Rousseau among "the philosophes of our century" who conspired against all forms of legitimate knowledge. This cabal wantonly distorted the self's status in creation and place in the world, and exhibited "no shame in preferring impious illusions and ridiculous and disjointed [*mal-cousues*] reveries [. . .] to the solid, unshakable, and infinitely consoling proofs of a religion capable of satisfying sound reason." Pilé counted humility among the spiritual virtues, but this did not detract from his confidence in humanity's likeness to God. Nor could he resist lampooning Rousseau's distinction between *amour de soi* and *amour-propre*. "In the name of God," he sneered, "strip from me once and for all any return to and any way around this horrible monster of pride!" Scripture offered sound affirmations of man's exalted position, he countered. It had been known since the time of Moses that the supreme being had "animated him with a divine breath, that he filled his soul with light and intelligence, that he granted him dominion over all the animals." Rather than a spiritual being made in the image of his divine creator, however, Rousseau's primitive man resembled nothing so much as a *"swine,"* who *"neither knows, nor perceives, nor feels* any other *goods in the universe* but his trough and his girth." Despite Rousseau's professions of faith, his state of nature, with its lawlessness, godlessness, and sexual promiscuity, struck Pilé as tantamount to materialist heresy, designed "to strip man in general of every *passion* and *duty*," leaving a "pure automaton" in place of a soul capable of redemption [italics in original].[91] Even if Rousseau denounced atheism and materialism as roundly as a vicar (as he would do in *Émile*), his account of humanity's impoverished origins left him vulnerable to the charge of fraternizing with the enemies of religion.

Voltaire, no stranger to the criticisms of Christian apologists, shared their view that the *Second Discourse* devalued personhood. He penned a caustic note on the matter, which appeared in the *Mercure de France*. "I have received, Monsieur, your new book against the human race," it began, "and I thank you for it." He claimed to be so impressed with Rousseau's performance—"No one has ever expended so much intelligence in wanting to render us beasts"—that he was overcome by a "desire to walk on all fours."[92] Remarkably, when Rousseau replied to the letter, he passed over these barbs in silence. Voltaire continued the harangue at greater length in *Questions sur l'Encyclopédie*. The article "Homme" dismissed Rousseau's ideal of self-sufficient primitivism. Voltaire instead contended that instinct has always been "fortified by reason," a quality that led the first humans into society. To have remained in isolation would have jeopardized "the faculty to think and to express oneself," ultimately causing one "to metamorphose into a beast." Like Pilé, Voltaire also expressed his revulsion at the conjecture of sexual freedom in the state of nature.[93]

Turning to the origins of property, which Pilé treated sparingly, Voltaire ridiculed Rousseau's account as that of "a rogue who wants all the rich to be robbed by the poor, in order to better establish fraternal unity among men." In an obvious parody, he presented his own tale about the first honest soul to enclose a parcel of land. A neighbor followed the man's example upon seeing the benefits reaped for security and productivity, thereby moving the nascent community toward a system of "distributive justice."[94] The anecdote typifies Voltaire's political sensibilities. He had no qualms about inequality. "Not all peasants will be rich; nor is it necessary that they be," he pronounced in *Questions sur l'Encyclopédie*. The case of England bolstered his confidence in the willingness of elites to pursue the common good, and he lavished praise on Frederick the Great of Prussia and Catherine the Great of Russia as strict but sufficiently enlightened authoritarians.[95] His tolerant disposition toward crowned heads set Voltaire apart from Rousseau, and to a lesser extent, from Diderot, who, while snubbing Frederick, agreed in 1765, out of financial desperation, to sell his library to Catherine.[96] Yet, at the time of the *Second Discourse*, Diderot was still close to Rousseau, who remarked of the work that it "was more to Diderot's taste than all my other writings, and [the book] for which his advice was the most useful to me."[97]

Within a year of its publication, however, a chain of events unfolded that would lead to Rousseau's estrangement and self-imposed exile from the republic of letters. Even the personal aspects of this break carried significant social implications for Rousseau, who heaped his scorn on "an entire generation" that "gladly agrees to extinguish all natural wisdom [*lumières*], to violate all the laws of justice and all the rules of good sense, [. . .] only to satisfy a fantasy." In 1756, he fled Paris with his companion Thérèse Levasseur and her mother to stay at the Hermitage, a retreat on the grounds of the estate of his patron and confidante Louise d'Épinay. He believed that Diderot had betrayed him by revealing his love for the comtesse d'Houdetot, then Saint-Lambert's mistress, and the two had quarreled over his relationship with d'Épinay.[98] The final indignity, however, was d'Alembert's *Encyclopédie* article on Geneva, which called for the construction of a theater in the self-consciously austere capital of Calvinist devotion. Rousseau was scandalized. His vitriolic response, published in 1758 as *La Lettre à d'Alembert sur les spectacles*, announced his formal renunciation of the philosophes. The work also made a poignant allusion to the loss of Diderot's friendship. "I had a severe and judicious Aristarchus," he noted, alluding to Aristarchus of Samothrace, the famed editor of Homer. "I no longer have him or want him, but I shall miss him always—in my heart still more than in my writings."[99]

The *Lettre à d'Alembert* also signaled the end of a formative period in Rousseau's career and a shift of emphasis. He had risen to fame with the two *Discourses*, works that diagnosed the individual and social ills that stem from the culture of luxury. His rebuke of d'Alembert renewed these arguments with particular vehemence. The desire for wealth and frivolous distinction would lead to the total destruction of virtue in Geneva, he predicted, as it did for the unwitting victims portrayed in the *Second Discourse*. Seeking perhaps a more relevant example, he considered the hypothetical dissolution of a hamlet near Neûfchatel, whose inhabitants once exhibited "an amazing combination of delicacy and simplicity." Upon constructing a theater, he warned, this community gradually succumbs to falling productivity, rising costs, economic decline, oppressive taxes, and morally compromising emulation. In this way, "a prosperous people, but one that owes its well-being to its industry, in exchanging reality for appearance, ruins itself at the moment it wants to shine."[100]

To sharpen his warning to Geneva, Rousseau extended the analysis of alienation presented in the *Second Discourse* to the subjective experience of losing oneself in a world of appearances. The *Lettre à d'Alembert* makes clear that, to his mind, theater operates according to the same principles as the despotic second state of nature that accompanies the rise of inequality. Like consumers in thrall to material objects, and citizens under an unjust social contract, actors and spectators alike surrender possession of themselves to external forces. In so doing, they lose not only moral autonomy, but also their sense of self and even their humanity. The actor's profession thus amounts to a form of psychic prostitution: "He gives himself away in performance for money," "puts his person publicly on sale," and ultimately exchanges his own identity for "a mixture of baseness, duplicity, ridiculous pride, and disgraceful degradation, which make him appropriate for all sorts of characters except the noblest of all, that of man, which he abandons." The wrenching conversion from being to seeming promoted by the theater reduces the individual actor—on stage as in society—to a state of nonexistence. To assume the identity of a "chimerical being" requires casting aside one's own, so that the actor "annihilates himself, or negates himself with his hero, and if something remains in this state of self-forgetfulness, it becomes the plaything of the audience."[101]

In his critique of d'Alembert, Rousseau employed the lexicon of dispossession to capture the cruel dynamics of estrangement. Actors on the stage and in society *forget* themselves, *annihilate* themselves, *negate* themselves—surrendering, not to the sanctifying force of divine will or the powers of nature, but to the mercurial regard of others. At first glance, his usage resembles that of Christian apologists' invectives against radical materialists, with "society" as a whole replacing philosophy as a source of egoism to be combated. Yet Rousseau was most inventive in his use of this language, reconfiguring terms and logics to serve novel ends. The *Second Discourse* asserts that depraved social relations both engendered and have been perpetuated by the corruption of the property held in one's person. Self-ownership was therefore irrevocably compromised at its inception, with *amour de soi* giving way to *amour-propre*. Devising a strategy for salvaging this manner of existence in a way that approximates the natural goodness of humankind preoccupied Rousseau for the rest of his days. Over the next several years, he formulated a series of solutions to the problem of alienation. The first, elaborated in *Émile*, offers speculations on the fate of "a savage made to live in the city" who nevertheless retains the liberty of his primitive state.[102] *Du Contrat social*, in contrast, sets forth a theory and practice of political communion that requires individual citizens to surrender their particular wills to an all-powerful general will, made sustainable in part by a quasi-divine legislator. Rousseau insists that only absolute force can assure freedom, and only virtuous dispossession can rehabilitate the exercise of self-ownership. In formulating these paradoxes, he had recourse to the language of selflessness that abounds in Fénelon's writings, now pressed into service to describe the resacralization of the body politic.

Émile in Chains

Rousseau's *Émile, ou De l'Éducation* rests on the dual premises that the state of nature differs radically from civil society, and that human nature can change. Pedagogy must aim for either "making a man or a citizen, for one cannot do both." Rousseau regarded "natural man" as "everything for himself," like the primitive creature of the *Second Discourse*, describing him as a "numeric unity" and "absolute whole." The "civil man," in contrast, resides on a wholly separate plane of existence. He is "nothing but a fractional unity dependent on the denominator," and "his value" can only be "determined by his relation to the whole, which is the social body." In order to fashion virtuous citizens rather than isolated individuals, it is necessary "to denature man, to take his absolute existence from him in order to give him a relative one, and to transport the self [*moi*] into the common unity, so that each individual believes himself no longer one but a part of the unity, and no longer feels except within the whole." Given that, in France, "the public institution" or *res publica* no longer existed, Rousseau has Émile's all-knowing tutor set out to instruct the child in the ways of individualism.[103] Above all, the virtues of self-ownership in matters physical and metaphysical are to be instilled into him.

Yet this commitment to autonomy was not absolute. Rousseau allowed elements of dependence to enter into the child's education. For instance, a form of spiritual abandon figures in the child's religious sensibility, especially as it relates to the question of divine assistance in the guise of miracles and revelation. This stance attracted considerable criticism from Christian apologists, who argued that it too closely resembled that of atheists, materialists, and other enemies of religion. Moreover, Rousseau made it abundantly clear that even an education designed to foster independence did so through potentially self-defeating means. The student's apparent freedom of mind follows from the highly manipulative and artificial conditioning on the part of the tutor, whose influence Émile never succeeds in escaping entirely. Far from declaring that unfettered agency is sustainable in a hostile world, Rousseau left open the possibility of constructing a new citizen along dispossessive lines. The road not taken decidedly in *Émile*, then, would lead to *Du Contrat social*.

The tutor's objective of in *Émile* is to direct his pupil toward an approximation of the self-sufficiency that reigned among the first humans, while facilitating the development of rational and moral faculties that his ancestors lacked. Among the first truths taught to Émile is justice, inculcated through the discovery of property. The lesson proceeds according to Lockean axioms. Having observed others tend their fields, the child soon feels a natural desire to acquire his own. The tutor helps him grow a crop of beans, and the child becomes convinced that "he has put his time, his labor, his effort, finally his person there," and is thus entitled to possess it. Émile's dreams are shattered, however, when he discovers one day that his plants have been destroyed by the gardener. The man protests that the boy has wrongly interfered with his own crop, but then agrees, on the tutor's suggestion, to allow them a corner of his plot for their own use. Through direct, albeit staged experience rather than abstractions, the child comes to understand "how the idea of property naturally goes back to the right of the first occupant by labor," which he can then exchange if desired.[104] Moreover, as Patrick Coleman has observed, it is precisely through losing control of an unjustly held possession that Émile begins to regard himself as an individual worthy of just treatment himself. Material dispossession, paradoxically, reinforces in this case a sentiment of self-ownership.[105]

Indeed, it gradually dawns on Émile that the property he holds in his person is far more durable and free from constraint. The tutor's ruses, as in the episode with the gardener, leave the child "forced to learn from himself," so that he "makes use of his reason and not that of another," and whatever ideas he possesses count as "truly his own." Émile also discovers, through the exercise of pity, how to identify his interests with those of his fellows. The aim is to convert *amour-propre* into virtue by expanding its scope. "The less the object of our cares is attached immediately to ourselves," Rousseau observed, "the more one generalizes this interest, the more equitable it becomes." In developing a "love of justice," the child can mature into a "man of nature" who, although "caught up in the social whirlpool," still "sees with his own eyes" and "feels with his own heart," without imposing his will on the vision and sentiments of others.[106] Reflecting on his education before taking leave of his tutor at the end the treatise, Émile proclaims that he has internalized these principles fully. Unlike other men, who, "to avoid yielding to the flood of things, form countless attachments," he understands that true freedom comes from "not wanting to cease being free." Resigned to the ebb and flow of fortune, he swears off dependence on any possession, even his inheritance, with the declaration that "I shall loosen all the bonds that tie me to it. [. . .] Rich or poor, I will remain free."[107]

In the course of his travels, Émile has also learned that moral obligation, and religious devotion in particular, stem not from received wisdom but from the voice of his own conscience, aided by reason. These lessons are imparted by way of a Savoyard vicar, the character Rousseau introduces to express Émile's idea of spiritual being. As the cleric professes, "I exist and I have senses by which I am affected." If this sensationalist credo lacks the infallible certainty of its philosophical model, Descartes's *cogito*, it nonetheless suffices to justify the self's position as an active, feeling subject endowed with will and the power to reflect upon and judge between the objects of sensation. Since matter is inherently passive, it requires a "supreme intelligence" to set it in motion, which the vicar identifies with God, the divine presence that exists at once within and outside the self. Rousseau avoids stating the exact relationship between spiritual and corporeal substances, but he clearly distinguished Émile's beliefs from those of the materialists, whom the vicar chastises for ignoring the unassailable truth that "a machine does not think, there is no movement or figure that can produce reflection."[108]

Yet the vicar also teaches Émile that the exercise of spiritual faculties alone cannot bring the soul into communion with the divine. It is impossible for the human mind to grasp the logic behind God's designs, even regarding the immortality of the soul or the possibility of redemption or chastisement after death. One can only hope that those who pursue virtue will be compensated for their earthly sufferings in the next life. Nor can the vicar imagine the divine in relation to himself, "as if God and my soul were of the same nature." Praying to the "Being of beings," he declares— in a decidedly mystical register—that "the most worthy usage of my reason is that it be annihilated before you: it is my rapture of spirit, and the charm of my weakness to feel overwhelmed by your grandeur."[109] The subject's status as a spiritual entity allows, and even dictates, its being rendered an object acted upon by God's will. Although to a lesser extent than Fénelon and Guyon, Rousseau also suggests that the promise of future reward should have no bearing on the love or devotion felt toward one's creator.

The soul's capacity for dispossession, moreover, engenders an altruistic impulse, perceived through the sentiment of pity and manifested in the tenets of natural religion. Echoing Émile's tutor, the Savoyard vicar acknowledges that "the first of all our cares is that of oneself," while also marveling at "how many times our interior voice tells us that in securing our well-being at the expense of another we commit a wrong!" The source of morality lies not in rational thought, which is oriented toward egoism, but in one's conscience, a "divine instinct" that directs desire away from the oneself and toward "the common interest." The power of conscience to direct virtuous action obviates the need for miracles, revelation, and all manner of "particular dogmas" that force their defenders into "absurd contradictions." Through the "spectacle of nature" and one's "interior voice," God instructs souls on how to conduct themselves. While the Savoyard vicar acknowledges that the faithful have a civic duty to practice the official religion of their country outwardly, the Gospel merely teaches the love of God in accordance with one's understanding.[110] Only the supreme being—acting directly upon and within an individual soul, rather than through spiritual intermediaries—may demand the suppression of reason and the proofs it demands for belief.

This assault on revealed religion provoked a violent response from both Church and state. The Parlement of Paris issued an *arrêt* on June 9, 1762, shortly after the publication of *Émile*, condemning the work to be publicly burned and its author imprisoned. Rousseau's treatise sought to deny "the truth of Holy Scripture and of the Prophecies, the certitude of miracles, [. . .] the infallibility of revelation, [and] the authority of the Church," in favor of a "purely human faith," according to the *avocat-général*, Jean-Omer Joly de Fleury.[111] Immediately upon receiving word of the order, Rousseau fled France. Over the next three years, he sought refuge in a series of Swiss locales—including Yverdon, Môtiers, and the island of Saint-Pierre in Lake Bienne (Biel)—before embarking in 1766 on a disastrous journey to England as the guest of David Hume.[112]

Having seen Rousseau driven into exile, and despite his professed hostility to godless philosophes, theologians continued their campaign to discredit *Émile*. According to the abbé Bergier, Rousseau was in essence fighting against himself. "In rejecting the mysteries on the grounds of their obscurity," he charged, "you return to the atheists and the materialists the very weapons that you wanted to strip from them." Rousseau was actually worse than an atheist, Bergier suggested, since he concealed his godlessness under the mantle of deism. Staging an imaginary meeting between a devotee of Spinoza and the Citizen of Geneva, he had the former confess that "the most powerful motive that keeps me an atheist is the fear of resembling you."[113]

Bergier, who a few years later would set his sights on d'Holbach's work, took particular offense at Rousseau's doctrine of natural virtue, which threatened to undermine the Church's role as mediator in the exchange of spiritual goods between God and human creatures. To justify the orthodox view, the abbé recalled the king's power to endow or rescind noble status. After the Fall, God likewise "did nothing but deprive the posterity of Adam of a privilege that he had accorded freely to our first father." Yet Christ's sacrifice makes it possible to reinstate the soul's former grandeur in the life to come. The means to salvation is a prize from "which a great number have already profited," which the Savoyard vicar in *Émile* seeks to render worthless by denying its necessity.[114] To Bergier's mind, then, what distinguished his position from Rousseau's, as well as from that of materialist critics of revealed religion, was his belief in the power of supernatural gifts and their effects on the believer.

Other Christian apologists who had fought the war against radical philosophy also seized on this latest challenge to spiritual individualism. Maleville, for instance, stressed the violence that Rousseau had perpetrated against human autonomy and personal identity. First, he accused the Savoyard vicar of repeating the error of the "greatest fanatics," that "the heart counts for everything in religion." Then, citing Diderot's article "Éclectisme," he claimed to have discovered a secret lurking beneath Rousseau's apology for natural religion, an unorthodox desire for immediacy with the divine. He likened this dispossessive impulse to elements in ancient philosophy that Diderot regarded as harbingers of Quietism. Christianity had long taught that "we exist individually and personally after death." Rousseau's doctrine, however, struck Maleville as tantamount to positing an all-encompassing "soul of the world," which leaves one like "the water of a vial plunged into the sea," the content of which "no longer subsists separately, as a particular individual." It is a view that undermines all rationale for devotion, since "there is nothing to gain or to lose" if "one believes our soul annihilated."[115]

In surveying the similarities between Neoplatonism and Rousseau's pronouncements, Maleville deployed arguments that he and colleagues like Bergier used to incriminate Quietists, Spinozists, and materialists. As a rhetorical tactic, this approach exaggerated the dispossessive features of Rousseau's theology to render it more vulnerable to charges of irreligion. Furthermore, in his fervor to defend human individuality and divinely granted possessions, Maleville overlooks the fact that the tutor seeks to instill into Émile the existential ideal of self-possession, albeit on unorthodox grounds. Rousseau appeared to disparage one of the spiritual subject's chief prerogatives—access to efficacious supernatural gifts—with all the vehemence he used to condemn worldly luxuries. Such an affront proved sufficient in the minds of Christian apologists to characterize him as an apostle of atheism. To these critics, then, it mattered little that *Émile* aimed to restore the human person's natural independence in the midst of social evils—such as wanton egoism and disdain for God—that they themselves found reprehensible.

Ironically, Rousseau himself perhaps provided the most damning criticism of his plan for rehabilitating self-ownership. He intended his pedagogy to serve as a means of overcoming the negative effects of alienation. It is thus only fitting that at the end of the book, Émile proclaims his desire for absolute freedom, to be shared only with his wife Sophie, now that he has completed his education. Yet, by the author's own account, the success of this experiment is far from assured. The pupil's cultivated self-sufficiency is compromised by the coercive methods employed to achieve it. "There is no more perfect form of subjection," Rousseau claims, "than that which maintains the appearance of liberty. By this means, one makes the will itself captive." Seemingly aware of his tutor's designs, Émile declares his intention to "remain what you have made me, and voluntarily to add no other chain to that which nature and the laws impose on me [. . .] As long as I live, I shall need you." This admission, however, suggests that Émile's autonomy remains a paradoxical function of his tutor's continued presence, both in his thoughts and at his side.[116]

It is perhaps fitting, then, that Rousseau began drafting a sequel to the novel, entitled *Émile et Sophie, ou Les Solitaires*. It recounts not Émile's ultimate independence, but his unhappy fate, from Sophie's infidelity and the collapse of their relationship to the misfortunes he suffers upon fleeing his family.[117] The most spectacular scene in this curious fragment involves Émile's capture by Barbary pirates, which leads him to meditate on the true nature of liberty. As he recounts to his tutor, these experiences impressed upon him a difficult lesson: "If liberty consisted in doing what one wants, no man would be free." He has come to realize to extent to which "we are all weak, dependent on things, on hard necessity," so that one who follows where fate leads is in reality "the most free, since he is never forced to do what he does not want."[118] Like the individual at the end of the *Second Discourse*, and in anticipation of *Du Contrat social*, Émile finds himself in chains, with only resignation to console him.

This admission announces the failure of the experiment to recreate, on new terrain and in new terms, the attributes of the state of nature. Émile's misfortunes in *Les Solitaires* depict the fragility of freedom, its ultimate dependence on external forces. Seeming free, Rousseau now reveals, does not amount to being so; indeed, the former condition may offer greater fulfillment than the latter.[119] Yet it is not enough to conclude, with Jerrold Seigel, that Rousseau's thinking about selfhood suffered from a fatal inability to save *amour de soi* from the ravages of *amour-propre*, or to overcome the contradictions between freedom and subjection.[120] The eighteenth-century cultures of personhood to which his philosophy contributed were not exclusively individualist in orientation or in application. He drew from the discourse and practice of dispossession—which valorized the surrender of spiritual, material, and existential goods—as much as he advocated the principles of personal identity and agency associated with self-ownership. By the time of *Émile*'s publication, Rousseau had begun to adopt a quiet fatalism toward the possibility of recovering individual autonomy. His views veered toward the opposite extreme, already intimated in the self-effacing act of pity, by which the loss of particular will makes possible a form of freedom beyond one's own efforts. He would now commit to purging the ideal citizen of all possessive attachments, even to himself, that jeopardized the realization of political immediacy.

From Dispossession to Collective Self-Ownership: Du Contrat social

As part of Émile's education, his tutor leads him on an extended voyage, during which he studies moral conditions under various forms of government. The similarities between Rousseau's and Fénelon's political mythologies are made obvious in that the adolescent's reading includes the tale of Telemachus, "so that he learns to resemble him." During his travels, Émile discovers the nature of the legitimate social contract, which dictates that *"each of us places in common his possessions, his person, his life, and all his power under the supreme direction of the general will, and we receive into the body each member as an indivisible part of the whole* [italics in original]"[121] Yet the vicissitudes of Émile's life prevent him from fulfilling his duties as a citizen; nor is it clear how deeply he might have desired to do so. Instead, Rousseau codified his political ideals in *Du Contrat social*—a work written concurrently with *Émile*, published in the same year, and doomed like its predecessor to official condemnation in Paris and Geneva.[122]

With *Du Contrat social*, Rousseau added his voice to a chorus of opposition that, by the middle of the eighteenth century, threatened to drown out the absolutist refrain of incontrovertible royal prerogative and *raison d'état*. The French crown found itself beleaguered on all sides—by humiliating military reversals and territorial losses in the Seven Years' War, debilitating government debt, the failure of fiscal reform, and the waning personal popularity of Louis XV. On the ideological front, the partisans of Port-Royal decried royal despotism and championed the orthodoxy, and therefore legality, of Jansenist doctrine in avowedly constitutional terms, gradually eroding the king's symbolic power as the guarantor of religious order.[123] These calls for justice were joined by appeals to the exempla of ancient polities in the writings of Rousseau, Gabriel Bonnot de Mably, and other commentators working in the classical republican tradition. Although these militants stopped short of demanding the end of monarchy, classical republicanism furnished a critical lexicon for depicting the kingdom's decline—to adopt Keith Baker's terminology—as a failure of political will.[124]

Rousseau asserted in *Du Contrat social* that recovering a people's virtue entails submitting the interests of particular citizens to the exigencies of the common good. His distinctive formulation of this ideal, *la volonté générale* (the general will), while inspired by classical republican sources, originated in Paris as much as in Sparta or Rome. According to Patrick Riley, Rousseau's political philosophy draws deeply from seventeenth-century theological speculations on the dynamics of salvation. Antoine Arnauld and his fellow Jansenists had surmised that God's essential desire to save human creatures remains constant even if original sin deprives the soul of a particular right to redemption, a position that Malebranche supplemented with his view that God governs the world through the exercise of a general will. Rousseau was well-versed in this tradition, which he applied to an equally vexing problem: the reconciliation of political authority and personal autonomy. *Généralité*, Riley contends, allowed him to maintain the will as the act of an individual, while at the same time rejecting its particularity. The citizen wills for himself, and by himself, insofar as he strives for the common good as determined by the sovereign authority of which he is a part.[125]

Yet Rousseau pursued these possibilities to still greater extremes, by detaching the particular from the individual in ways that fundamentally altered the locus and exercise of individuality, and in so doing, radically transformed the nature of political association.[126] In *Du Contrat social*, the operations of *généralité* proceed from, and are complemented by, the effects of *aliénation* on individual citizens. The prominence of this term and the transformation it represents bore the influence, not only of the broad French tradition of *généralité*, but also of the distinctively Fénelonian ethos of dispossession. According to Rousseau, the act of voluntary self-surrender gives rise to a collective moral being that absorbs all particular motives in public life into its own totalizing force. Rather than a sum of social beings, there exists under the social contract a singular, abstract individual—a "common self," in Rousseau's parlance—whose unalienable will must correspond to the wills of all flesh-and-blood citizens under its direction.[127] The emergence of such a sovereign power endows the body politic with the immanent powers of dispossession once attributed to the God of Fénelon's mystical metaphysics. For Rousseau, the ideal of *généralité* does not entail a mere secularization of a theological concept, now applied to matters of justice and obligation, but rather a resacralization of the political domain as a whole.

Rousseau assumed two distinct positions, then, on the matter of political individualism. The first, which Riley has duly emphasized, makes freedom contingent on the exercise of individual will. Volition depends in turn, however, on the continuous alienation of individuality from the citizen's own desires to the general will. If this paradoxical configuration has perplexed Rousseau's latter-day commentators, it was met with sheer hostility by eighteenth-century theologians and political philosophers, who feared that it violated the right of individuals to their own persons and possessions.

Rousseau devoted *Du Contrat social* to elaborating a theory of governance that would avoid the despotism of luxury described in the *Second Discourse,* according to which guileless subjects lose true possession of themselves and their belongings even in the rush to secure them. Its opening chapters describe a people on the threshold of entering into civil society, but before their enslavement to the conditions of the illegitimate social contract portrayed in his earlier work as the subterfuge of the rich against the poor. Sparing them this fate, Rousseau stipulated, requires altering the relationship individual subjects have to themselves and to one another. A truly just "social compact" must simultaneously preserve the contractants' liberty as well as their common interests, so that "each person, in uniting himself to all, nevertheless obeys only himself and remains as free as he was before." Such a union can be made possible, however, only by "the *total alienation* [emphasis added] of each member, with all of his rights, to the entire community."[128]

Rousseau's formulation transposed the so-called natural right of conquest, which he denounced as an illegitimate basis for authority, into a laudable act of self-surrender.[129] Upon entering into the compact, men and women cede their natural prerogatives and powers to an abstract subjectivity that bears no relation to an existing individual. As the repository of rights surrendered in common, it is everything. As a particular entity that stands apart from the whole, it is nothing—hence the claim that "in giving himself to all, each person gives himself to no one." Rousseau considered the attributes of this hyperbolic agent closely. "The private person of each contractant" must give way to "a moral collective body composed of as many members as there are voices in the assembly," and from whose existence it should derive "its unity, its common *self* [moi *commun*], its life and liberty." The *moi commun* functions as the sovereign, which possesses a general will that is perfectly unalienable, indivisible, and infallible. Even so, each individual remains free to pursue his or her own perceived interests. In the event that this activity clashes with the common good, the entire body mobilizes against the wayward citizen until he is "forced to be free." It is within such a framework that one should approach Rousseau's understanding of the transformation humans undergo in entering the social contract. He emphasized that whatever the newly forged citizen has lost in terms of freedom, he will gain in terms of moral capacity: "His faculties are honed and developed, his ideas expand, his sentiments are ennobled." This passage from "stupid animal" to "intelligent being" occurs, not in isolation, but only in concert with other citizens, who as a body stand ready to buttress the virtue of their fellows when they falter in their duties.[130]

The relationship that Rousseau envisioned between the sovereign and the particular citizen is predicated on an uneven exchange. The moral faculties and material possessions of all members are to be subsumed within the collective body, which then returns them to individuals as emanations of the general will. Rousseau assured readers that the generality of the sovereign's power is precisely what prevents it being unjustly imposed on a particular individual, thereby fulfilling his directive of shielding each citizen from tyranny of any other and preserving his or her freedom. Yet even the procedure for calculating the general will—not as the aggregate of particular wills, but as the canceling out of the minor variations between them—testifies to its nature as a predetermined consensus. The body politic retains "a universal and compulsory force to move and dispose of each part"—that is, each individual citizen—"in a manner most suitable to all."[131]

This absolute directive regulates the exercise of property rights, which, like all rights, stem from an act of dispossession: "Each member gives himself to the community at the moment it is formed, just as he actually is, himself and all his forces, including all the goods that he possesses." Property originates neither in the natural rights of the first occupant nor in prerogatives derived from labor. Only with the authorization of the sovereign can the belongings surrendered to it be allocated on a legal basis to individual citizens, so as to "change usurpation into a true right, and possession [jouissance] into property." Even then, the exercise of ownership remains "forever subordinate to the right of the community over all," thereby preserving the equality stipulated by the social contract.[132]

Rousseau's restrictions on individual property rights, it should be noted, pale in comparison with those of his more radical contemporaries. For instance, Étienne Gabriel Morelly, whose Code de la nature (1755) was once attributed to Diderot, considered avarice, or "the desire to have [emphasis in original]" as "the base, the vehicle of every vice." It followed that "where no property exists, there could be no pernicious consequences."[133] Léger-Marie Deschamps, a Benedictine monk with whom Rousseau had a brief correspondence while working on Du Contrat social, expressed similar views.[134] In his treatise Le Vrai Système (1762), he called for the establishment of a "state of morality [mœurs]," a new order in which the "spirit of dispossession [désappropriation]" would reign. Men and women "would have nothing of their own" and "all would be held in common among them." This social program corresponds to Deschamps's metaphysical claim, which drew on both mystical and materialist sources, that the "individual" is an illusory being, a mere element that "stems directly" from an all-encompassing "universal whole."[135]

Rousseau refrained from taking a stance that might in retrospect be characterized as proto-socialist. Indeed, his article on political economy in the *Encyclopédie* designated property as "the most sacred of all the rights of citizens, and more important in some respects than liberty itself," not least because it is "the true foundation of civil society, and the true guarantee of the citizen's commitments.[136] Yet he also made his wariness of unfettered ownership clear. For instance, his *Projet de constitution pour la Corse* (1772)—solicited by the fighters for the independence of an island he praised as "the one country in Europe still capable of receiving legislation"—strictly curtails private property.[137] The proposals concerning the exercise of ownership aim to "give it a measure [. . .] that subjugates it and always keeps it subordinated to the public good," in the hope that "the property of the state will be as great and powerful, and that of citizens as small and weak, as is possible."[138] As these recommendations indicate, Rousseau did not regard property as a natural right based on self-ownership. Citizens bear legal title to their possessions only by virtue of convention and as determined by the exigencies of the common good.

Du Contrat social asserts as a general principle that whatever limits apply to the sovereign must be decided by the sovereign itself. Even in matters of conscience, citizens can practice the faith of their choosing only if they also abide by the dictates of the established civil religion. Those who refuse to do so risk banishment, and defectors court a death sentence. Nevertheless, Rousseau remained cognizant of challenges posed to the institution of just laws by "the seduction of particular wills." Christianity could never provide the moral edification or cohesion necessary to sustain the body politic. Even in its purest form, the Gospel's otherworldly orientation renders it "contrary to the social spirit." Rousseau thus has recourse to a mythic, quasi-divine legislator modeled on figures such as Lycurgus and Numa. This "extraordinary man of state," whose work "constitutes the republic" but "does not enter into its constitution," strives "to transform each individual, who by himself is a perfect and solitary whole, into a part of the great whole from which this individual in some fashion receives his life and his existence."[139]

In defining the functions of the legislator, *Du Contrat social* turns once again to the dispossessive forces that sustain collective identity. To succeed in his task, the founder of a republic "must feel that he is in a position to change, so to speak, human nature." He must deprive the individual of "his own forces in order to give him forces that are alien to him and that he cannot make use of without the help of others." As with property rights, self-surrender produces an assemblage of moral goods to be possessed in common, under the auspices of the body politic. The more one's "natural forces" become "dead and annihilated," Rousseau observed, "the greater and more lasting are those acquired, and the more solid and perfect is the institution." The "great soul of the legislator"—the figure who, operating outside the formal bounds of law, inscribes in the hearts of citizens the alienating effects of their union—bears witness to "the true miracle that must prove his mission."[140] The social contract serves as the testament to his feat. The dispossession of particular members engenders a collective sense of self-ownership that alters the experience of agency. The *moi commun* becomes an unassailable subject in displacing the individual citizen, who now exists, not only as one self among many, but also as an object of regeneration, exercising his faculties in tandem with, and as part of, the general will.

· · ·

Du Contrat social did not have the immediate impact of *Émile*—Diderot gave it little attention, despite having previously expressed his own views on the general will—but it elicited critical responses from less radical philosophes as well as theological traditionalists.[141] Perhaps the most thorough engagement was that of Paul-Louis de Bauclair (1735–1804), advisor to the landgrave of Hesse-Darmstadt and author of a sympathetic biography of Peter the Great, whose *Anti-Contrat social*, published in 1765, refutes Rousseau's treatise section by section, and nearly line by line. On certain points Bauclair found himself in accord with his adversary, especially regarding the dangers of excessive luxury and the role of alienation in the founding of political associations.[142] Yet his alternative account of the general will departs significantly from that of Rousseau. Bauclair refused to accept the notion that sovereignty can reside in an abstract *moi commun*, rather than in a particular institution (in the case of a republic) or person (in a monarchy). Like Rousseau's clerical critics, he feared that granting the body politic so total an authority over its members denies the essential nature of the human person as a distinct moral and spiritual entity—in a word, as an individual.

Bauclair also took issue with Rousseau's assaults on property rights. According to the *Anti-Contrat social*, the sovereign should give free rein to its subjects' powers of acquisition. The "felicitous inequality" that inevitably emerges in society "makes for the finest arrangement of a state," by allowing for a division of labor, with the poor destined to apply themselves to the most arduous work. Similarly, Bauclair found Rousseau's defense of the community's claims to individual holdings to be hopelessly paradoxical. How, he demanded, could particular citizens stand in relationship to their possessions as both "proprietors and trustees"? This ambiguity would make it impossible to determine just rules for the buying and selling of property, or for its transfer upon the death of the original owner.[143]

These doubts extend to the metaphysical basis of the social contract. Bauclair concurred with Rousseau that "the general will alone can direct the forces of a state, according to the demands of the public good." Even so, he could not imagine a polity capable of transcending the particular desires of individual citizens, since "interest everywhere divides the will of unfortunate mortals" and sows "seeds of discord that the wisdom and virtue of a small number will never be able to quell." The sovereign *moi commun* is thus a chimera: "It is a being of reason that can act, but will never act." The impossibility of realizing the general will within a collective form of subjectivity sounds a leitmotif among Rousseau's detractors, as when Bauclair turned to the function of civil religion. Refuting the claim that Christian doctrine clashes with temporal virtues, he observed with no little irony that the same should be admitted of Rousseau's social contract, which is "not made for fragile humans, but for celestial spirits."[144]

Pronouncements made on religion in *Du Contrat social* provided clerical skeptics with a pretext for denouncing Rousseau's work as a whole. After attacking the denial of miracles and revelation in *Émile*, Laurent François, a veteran of battles over radical philosophy, turned to the issue of civil religion. First, he rejected Rousseau's claim that Christianity is a purely spiritual religion. On the contrary, François noted, its teachings call for "diligent work" on the part of the believer, according to "the talents he has received from the author of his being." Rather than denying the world, the devout soul "neglects nothing in order to procure happiness from it." François also balked at granting equal status to all established faiths while demanding allegiance to the civic religion, a stipulation that struck him as flagrantly incongruous with Rousseau's declarations that its apostates should be put to death. "Materialists, Spinozists, fatalists," he quipped, "should congratulate themselves on not having you as their sovereign, for they would not live long."[145]

François found further fault with the principles behind the social contract. The notion of a people formed by the alienation of each citizen under the direction of the general will is nothing but a "work of the imagination." If the original contract binds together "a particular individual with the whole," a formulation that presumes the prior existence of both parties, then where should one locate the source of the whole, since, as Rousseau suggested, it owes its existence to the contract itself? This problem of origins led François to conclude with Bauclair that Rousseau's ideal polity was purely "fictive." Equally preposterous was his contention, as restated by François, that "the will of each member, or at least the majority," has "no object but the common good, even at the expense of his own interests."

This would only be the case if charity "reigned in the hearts of an entire people"—a possibility François deemed too unlikely to countenance.[146]

For François as well as Bauclair, the incomprehensibility of *Du Contrat social* stems from the dispossessive elements in its ideal of political subjectivity. Particular interests, love of self, and attachment to one's person can be tempered, but not fundamentally altered. But Rousseau, like his ideal legislator, sought to endow humans with a second nature. Under the social contract, self-ownership applies first to the *moi commun*, before its mediated reinstatement among individual citizens, whose proprietorship over themselves and their possessions is protected from other persons only by virtue of their submission to the body politic. For Rousseau, this arrangement depends on the surrender of "natural liberty, which has no limits but the powers of the individual," for "civil liberty, which is limited by the general will."[147] The restrictions placed on property rights and religious expression confirm beyond all doubt that the pursuit of self-interest by each citizen extends only so far as it is reconcilable with the interests of all. In place of a society comprised of atomistic persons, there remains a unitary, generalized, and transfigured "self" with totalizing force, in which the multitude of citizens share equally, and to which they equally belong. In this sense, Bauclair's remark about "celestial spirits" revealed more than he intended. Toward the end of his life, Rousseau himself lost faith in the politics of alienation, only to return to the ideal of dispossession as a solitary walker who communes with the God of nature as deeply as his idealized citizens do with their invisible sovereign.

Last Words: Reverie and Divinity

Rousseau's final work, the *Rêveries du promeneur solitaire*, depicts a dreamer who is isolated, crestfallen, and impoverished. The years following the publication of *Émile* and *Du Contrat social* had been harrowing for their author. Fearing arrest by both French and Genevan authorities, he fled the countryside outside Paris for Switzerland, only to be driven from the asylum he sought in the principality of Neuchâtel when another work, *Lettres écrites sur la montagne* (1764), provoked the ire of the local clergy. After a sojourn in England, which featured a highly publicized falling-out with Hume, Rousseau returned to France in 1767. He spent three years in the provinces before settling in the capital that he believed had brought him so much torment.[148]

That the *Rêveries* is not a political treatise—but rather, the musings of a dejected exile—should not detract from the expansive insights it offers into the subjective experiences of an estranged citizen. In *Rousseau juge de Jean-Jacques*, he lamented that "Our sweetest existence is relative and collective, and our true *self* [moi] is not entirely within us." It follows, like an echo of *Du Contrat social*, that "such is man's constitution in this life that one is never entirely able to enjoy the possession of oneself without the cooperation of another." Rousseau claimed that the intransigence of his fellows, rather than a lack of commitment on his part, had induced him to surrender his hopes of collective regeneration. "The idea of private happiness never touched my heart," he admits in the *Rêveries*, "until I saw my brothers seeking their own in my misery."[149]

Rousseau's turn toward autobiography—in the years from 1770 to 1778, he completed *Rousseau juge de Jean-Jacques* and the *Confessions*, leaving the *Rêveries* unfinished at his death—deepened his speculations about the human person, in particular vis-à-vis the conflicting yet inseparable ideals of self-ownership and dispossession. As the *Confessions* show, Rousseau had come to see his life largely as an internal struggle over appropriation. Among his most deep-seated memories of childhood, later revisited in the tale of Émile's ill-fated bean crop, was witnessing a caretaker's destruction of an irrigation system that he and a friend had devised for a sapling they had planted. So decisive was this episode that Rousseau surmised that he owed his "disinterestedness" toward worldly things in later life to the feeling that "the pleasure of possessing is not worth the trouble of acquisition." The same conviction held true in his personal relationships, most notably with Madame de Warens, whom he loved both spiritually and physically, but without sexual attraction. Tellingly, their most blissful time together was spent at the rural estate Les Charmettes. Of the house and grounds Rousseau remarked, "I did not even need the property; the enjoyment of possession [*jouissance*] was enough." The same could be said of the state of existential fulfillment he discovered during this period: "Happiness followed me everywhere; it lay in no definable object but it was entirely within me" and "would not leave me for a single moment."[150]

Rousseau spent his life attempting to recreate this sense of wholeness both within himself and in his relations with others. Time and again, his overtures were rebuffed, and his reforms proven defective. He believed that Diderot and d'Alembert had betrayed him, while Émile, a character of his own invention, had failed to achieve true self-sufficiency. Geneva, he feared, had fallen into the clutches of despotism, and even the ideal citizens of *Du Contrat social* were doomed to decline. "The body politic," he ruefully observed, "carries within itself the causes of its own destruction."[151] Resigned to permanent exile from the social world, Rousseau turned to the mystical power of divinity as it emanated from the physical world, and sought fulfillment in submission to and radical identification with nature. This last, desperate hope compelled him to surrender ownership of his person, and to seek solace as a partial, dispossessed element in the totality of existence.

The path to redemption in the *Rêveries* begins with detaching oneself from all persons and things. "All is finished for me on earth," Rousseau declared. "There no longer remains for me anything in the world to fear or hope for, and I remain tranquil in the depths of the abyss—a poor, unfortunate mortal, but as impassive as God himself." This pronouncement recalls the Christian tradition of religious retreat. As with Fénelon's uncontested retirement in the wake of the Quietist controversy, a profound sense of resignation characterized Rousseau's final years in the capital, and then in the more-distant Ermenonville. His desire to cast off "all the painful objects with which I have occupied myself" also evokes the spiritual direction of the archbishop of Cambrai.[152]

Rousseau broke ranks with his predecessor, however, when considering the fate of the self given over to renunciation. Whereas Fénelon emphasized the destruction of the subject along with the objects in his possession, for Rousseau, retreat prepares the way not for existential demise, but for a higher form of being, in which "my only desire, and only duty, is to remain occupied with myself." Commentators, most notably Marcel Raymond, have seized on such statements as marking the limit of Fénelon's influence on the philosophy of existence elaborated in the *Rêveries*.[153] Yet Rousseau describes the self's subsistence in terms that evoke scarcity more than plenitude. "Reduced to myself alone," he observes, "it is true that I feed on my own substance, but it does not diminish, and I am self-sufficient even though I ruminate, so to speak, on nothing, and although my desiccated imagination and lifeless ideas no longer provide nourishment for my heart."[154] As he continued to compose the *Rêveries*, his account of dispossession took on even stronger similarities to the liminal state between existence and nonexistence described by Fénelon and Guyon as the precursor to total spiritual abandon, which leaves the soul deprived of all contentment not granted by God. Even if Rousseau did not idealize the self's annihilation, he nevertheless found value in its impoverishment.

The solitary walker perceives the world through the experience of reverie—or, in Abbé Joseph-Adrien Lelarge de Lignac's all-too-fitting phrase, *rêver à la suisse*.[155] In this dreamlike state between waking and sleeping, the errant mind forgets the burdensome particularities of existence. Rousseau captures this dynamic in the strange tale of a Great Dane charging him on the way back from a walk to Ménilmontant, at the time a village outside Paris. He fell, struck his head on a cobblestone, and lost consciousness. Upon waking, his mind lapsed into reverie, the effects of which he describes in intricate detail. He recounts how, suffering from amnesia, "I still had no feeling of myself except as being 'over there.'" Yet, rather than estrangement, he had the sense of having been "born into life at that instant": "It seemed to me that I filled all the objects I perceived with my frail existence." Despite the apparent expansion of his being, he continues, "I had no distinct notion of my person" and "knew neither who I was nor where I was."[156] The mind in reverie, Rousseau suggests, loses all proprietary attachments, even to its own operations. Self-consciousness yields to a sense of dislocation—of being "over there"—that facilitates communion with all existence. From this perspective, Rousseau regarded himself not as a solitary, independent person, but rather as a fraction of the whole of creation, immutable in the eternal present. He no longer possessed the world as a self-owning subject but had instead become an object possessed by the world, seized in its grasp. All aspects of his individual identity—his thoughts, actions, and memory—suddenly faded to nothing.

The transposition of self and nature in reverie reflects a shift in Rousseau's interest from philosophy to botany in the wake of the scandal over *Émile*.[157] Abandoning the project of reforming society and the citizen freed him to immerse himself in the study of nature and its sublime operations. In the *Rêveries*, he recalls the transformative experiences he had had on the remote Île de Saint-Pierre after being driven from Neuchâtel. Although Rousseau hoped to pass the remainder of his days on the island, the Petit-Conseil of Bern, which had jurisdiction over the territory, ordered him to leave after only a month. Nevertheless, the *Rêveries* idealizes the site where its author had achieved his most complete identification with the natural world. Near the edge of Lake Bienne, "the ebb and flow of this water and its noise, continual but at intervals magnified [. . .], superseded the internal movements which reverie extinguished within me and was enough to make me feel my existence with pleasure." Supersession and extinction—these semantic cues intimate the process of abandon as Rousseau's self melded with his surroundings. The mutability of the tides, he realized, followed the "constant flux" of the material universe, which swept away his distinct thoughts and movements in its wake. Communing with nature, lost in an eternal present, one at last "enjoys the possession [. . .] of one's own existence." He adds, tellingly, that "as long as this state lasts, one is self-sufficient like God."[158] Reverie, then, suspends personal identity by severing the self's attachment to distinct objects—from material things to thoughts and actions—so that only pure, undifferentiated being remains.

The full "sentiment of existence," Rousseau discovered, ultimately inheres not in one's person, but in nature itself. He captures this dispossessive dynamic with an arresting observation:

The more sensitive a soul a contemplator has, the more he gives himself up to the ecstasies this harmony arouses in him. A sweet and profound reverie takes hold of his senses, and he loses himself through a delightful intoxication within the immensity of this beautiful system with which he identifies himself. Then, all particular objects elude him; he sees and feels nothing except within the whole.[159]

Rousseau's memory of these transformative experiences concentrates on the loss of personal identity. Reverie seizes one's person in both mind and body. Time and space are suspended, and the thinking subject becomes the object of a totalizing force beyond its control. The self endures, but as a barely distinguishable aspect of creation. If only for a moment, Rousseau found here the plenitude that had so long eluded him, once the demands of self-ownership could no longer infringe upon him. As he confesses at the end of the *Rêveries*, "the idea and word 'own' [*propre*] equally escape me."[160] Yet he also observes that the surrender of personhood in turn gives rise to reappropriation within the sublime system of an immanent God, who, like the self, is synonymous with nature.

. . .

Like much of Rousseau's political philosophy, the *Rêveries* advances a positive ideal of alienation. In place of the enlightened proprietorship espoused by defenders of luxury, who define happiness as a function of the intimate relations between an acquisitive subject and the objects in his possession, the *First* and *Second Discourses* chart the tragic loss of primitive self-sufficiency and the human person's enslavement to material goods. This primer on objectification culminates in the moral and psychological estrangement portrayed in the *Lettre à d'Alembert*. For this all-consuming malady, Rousseau sought an array of remedies, beginning with the exploration, in *Émile*, of a pedagogy that could salvage natural autonomy. While Rousseau's ill-fated pupil remains dependent on others despite his tutor's emphasis on autonomy, *Du Contrat social* seeks virtue in necessity. Only by depriving citizens of their natural, individual prerogatives can their collective force be preserved under the guardianship of a *moi commun*. In a like manner, the solitary walker under the depersonalizing sway of reverie surrenders his will in communion with nature, allowing him to overcome the debilitating dependencies inherent in social existence. Rousseau's oscillations between the cultures of self-ownership and dispossession allowed him to articulate a mode of subjective experience beyond the bounds of individualist personhood as typically conceived, and to posit that the surrender of particularity gives way to the fullness of being, thereby rendering the communal subject—whether in the political or natural realms—a manifestation of divinity on earth.

Rousseau recognized with rare acuity the extent to which the social and political ramifications of luxury figured in far-ranging and deep-seated uncertainties concerning the self's relationship to spiritual, material, and existential goods. His writings trace the gamut of positions in favor of dispossessive personhood. The deification of the self in the *Rêveries*, for instance, echoes and extends Fénelon's speculations concerning the soul's repossession by God in the aftermath of annihilation. Moreover, the Spinozist hope of beatitude through identification with the divine, which d'Holbach refashioned along materialist lines, finds novel expression in Émile's resignation to fatalism, as well as in Rousseau's subsequent quest for the immediacy of the divine through reverie. With Diderot, Rousseau shared not only a devotion to the general will, but also a desire to rehabilitate the dream state as a conduit to revelation with purely terrestrial origins. After his death, the architects of the French Revolution would look to his legacy as a guide in their efforts to remake the human person in the image of a new body politic.

7 Revolutionary Reveries

In the wake of Robespierre's ouster in the coup of 9 thermidor Year II of the French Revolution (July 27–28, 1794), the long-held plans to rebury Rousseau in the Pantheon at last came to fruition. A resurrection more than a funeral, the proceedings spanned three days, from 18 to 20 vendémaire Year III (October 9–11, 1794). For the final ceremony, soldiers, artists, musicians, a deputation from the Paris sections, mothers with babes in arms, dignitaries from Ermenonville and Geneva, and members of the Institute of Music assembled ahead of deputies from the National Convention. The representatives marched with "the beacon of legislators," a copy of Rousseau's *Du Contrat social*, guiding their way. Upon reaching the Pantheon, the participants listened to hymns chosen for the occasion.[1] In the words of one librettist, Théodore Desorgues, the scene provoked not only a rush of gratitude but also a palpable desire for communion. "Come out of your funeral urn," the musicians sang, and "see this liberated people, who implore you as their father." According to the lyric, Rousseau's ashes, like a burnt offering, function as a conduit between the celestial and temporal spheres. Addressing the Citizen of Geneva, Desorgues expectantly awaited the moment "when your soul is reunited in the bosom of the universal being." "Let us offer it new honors," the poet implored the assembly, "and by our unanimous consent, consecrate his sublime remains."[2]

Rousseau's pantheonization had been delayed for years due to the chronic instability faced by the nascent Republic. The political leadership in France sought to regenerate the body politic from within, while facing the dual existential threat of war and civil war. This transformative enterprise led to intense speculation about the nature of citizenship—and therefore about the kind of self that the new regime should engender. In light of the polemics over personhood examined in this book, it can reasonably be asserted that the French Revolution marked the eighteenth century's last and most explosive clash between the cultures of self-ownership and dispossession. On the one hand, successive revolutionary governments enshrined the rights-bearing citizen in the legal framework its members designed and strove to implement. On the other hand, there was a simultaneous drive to eschew political individualism in favor of an ideal of civic virtue privileging the collective needs of the *patrie*. The tensions between autonomy and abandon explored in Rousseau's writings struck a chord with the revolutionaries, who found their own preoccupations reflected in this work.

To be sure, ever since Louis-Sébastien Mercier pronounced him the "first author of the Revolution," Rousseau's relationship with the events of 1789 has been contested. Some commentators, most notably Roger Chartier, have even inverted the genealogy. On this latter view, Rousseau's intellectual and political stature, and the prestige of the philosophes more generally, becomes *la faute de la Révolution*, with their writings serving to invent origins for, and thereby legitimate, the new regime.[3] Rousseau abandoned five children to foundling hospitals, and it would seem that, in death as in life, he remained adept at evading paternal responsibility. The homage paid him by Desorgues, however, suggests a more subtle form of filiation. Rousseau did not cause the Revolution or establish the conditions that made it possible. Rather, his legacy was built into the Revolution, of which he was both a precursor and an apostolic overseer. In other words, he came to embody its spirit and ideals. It followed, then, that Rousseau's impact on the Revolution would change in tandem with the experiences of the revolutionaries themselves. The report outlining the Convention's plans for his pantheonization, drawn up by Joseph Lakanal, a leading member of the Committee of Public Instruction, stated the matter succinctly. "It is the Revolution," he observed, that "has explained the *Social Contract* to us."[4] More recently, James Swenson has elaborated this dynamic of reciprocal influence with particular sensitivity and deftness. In his words, what drew the revolutionaries to Rousseau, and made Rousseau's legacy integral to the Revolution, was a "shared constitutive instability," produced by "the combination of a passionate longing for unity and a rigorous experience of division."[5]

Rousseau and his latter-day disciples faced similarly daunting conundrums with much the same sense of hope and dread: how to overcome the corruption of social relations, and to how to recover, or at least to approximate, the natural goodness of humankind. To be sure, the revolutionaries broke with Rousseau, at times vehemently, on points of both theory and practice. For instance, as Keith Baker has pointed out, the abbé Emmanuel-Joseph Sieyès openly defied Rousseauian principles with the claim in *Qu'est-ce que le Tiers-État?* that the general will could be determined through the deliberation of representative bodies.[6] In a similar vein, Dan Edelstein has drawn attention to how Louis-Antoine-Léon Saint-Just's interpretation of natural law led him to criticize the social contract on the grounds that it only applied to the regulation of affairs between states, not between citizens of the same polity.[7]

Despite such differences, Rousseau and the revolutionaries seized on similar prescriptions for revivifying the body politic. Rousseau located the tragic nature of modern civil society in the institution of private property, along with the pathological forms of self-ownership to which it gave rise. In its way, so too did the nascent National Assembly, with its spectacular abolition, on the night of August 4, 1789, of *privilèges*—and, with them, of the means of fixing one's identity within the framework of corporatist rights. The Declaration of the Rights of Man and Citizen made explicit guarantees of property as "natural, inalienable, and sacred."[8] Nevertheless, defining the rights of ownership continued to invite both contestation and experimentation, especially among political radicals, who in the ensuing years proposed restrictions on the private accumulation of resources that would not have been out of place on the pages of *Du Contrat social*.

Although the Revolution would ultimately establish private property— in particular, property owned by individuals—as axiomatic, this outcome was by no means preordained. It required considerable effort to dismantle the byzantine structures that regulated ownership under the Old Regime and to devise new institutional arrangements. In November 1789, the National Assembly confiscated ecclesiastical property, creating a mass of *biens nationaux* destined for sale and redistribution. Successive revolutionary legislatures added former common lands (*biens communaux*) and the holdings of émigrés to this patrimony.[9] The liquidation of properties once held by the crown and the First and Second Estates led some deputies and the citizens they represented to question whether private individuals should have exclusive ownership of the means of subsistence.

In parallel, the revolutionaries launched a project to redefine the self as citizen and to regenerate the body politic. Religion, like property, remained an issue of crucial importance, even after the settlement presumably established by the Civil Constitution of the Clergy, which made Gallican bishops and parish priests functionaries of the state.[10] Political morality became an abiding preoccupation of the Jacobins, of course, and especially of Robespierre, as did the task of infusing France with patriotic fervor for the new regime. Calls to devote oneself to the public good tended to rest on a fundamental dichotomy—found in Rousseau, to be sure, and in the classical republican tradition more generally—between love of self and love of country. Already in 1789, an anonymously published *Discours sur le patriotisme* had cast the sentiment in pointedly anti-individualist terms as a "total abnegation"—"the sacrifice of one's possessions, of one's parents, and of one's family" to the common good. True patriotism, then, implied "the forgetting of man, in order to be nothing but a citizen."[11]

By the Year II, radical Jacobins had launched a sweeping campaign to resacralize politics, to endow the nation with an immanent, quasi-divine force to which citizens were compelled to sacrifice their particular existence. Under Robespierre's leadership, the ideals of dispossessive personhood carried the force of law. The ethos of self-sacrifice extended not only to one's possessions but to one's very life. However, like d'Holbach's pronouncements in *Système de la nature* and Rousseau's in *Du Contrat social*, these directives entailed not the absolute surrender of self-ownership, but rather its reconfiguration along communal lines. The prerogatives and properties stripped from the individual were assumed by the body politic, to which all members owed their regenerated identity and existence as parts of the same indivisible whole.

For all Robespierre's commitment to unanimity, his vision for France failed fully to convert the people in whose name he claimed to speak. Its underlying rationale did not translate easily into an internally consistent mode of administration. The government, ostensibly founded on the principles of popular sovereignty and the rule of law, eschewed elections and suspended its own constitution. It established revolutionary tribunals that, operating outside the rules of due process, sent thousands of men and women to their deaths. Robespierre himself resorted to paradoxical phrases in explaining his position—such as his justification of the Terror as the "despotism of liberty."[12] Former prominent supporters of the Revolution defected from the cause or fell victim to it. Sieyès, having survived the ordeal, registered his discontent in hindsight. Since "the purpose of the political order is individual liberty," he reasoned, it was folly to uphold "a public happiness that belongs to no one." For the Jacobin administration, he astutely noted, "the commonwealth is [. . .] nothing other than an abstract being, a superstition, an idol to which one must offer victims." Or, as he once described the situation with even greater precision, under the Jacobins, the *république* had become a *"ré-totale* [italics in original]."[13]

As this quip about totalizing forces suggests, the political thought of the French Revolution lurched violently between the principles of self-ownership and dispossession. Both positions animated political discourse after 1789—at times within the work of a single figure or faction. Sieyès, whose famous pamphlet *Qu'est-ce que le Tiers-État?* had seemingly predicted the early course of the Revolution, upheld the Lockean maxim that "all men are inviolable proprietors of their persons, and of their affairs"; hence, "all rights are contained with this real and personal property."[14] At the same time, however, the opposition to *privilège* fomented by his writings gave rise to a flurry of acts of dispossession: the suppression of seigneurial rights on August 4, the expropriation of Church lands, and a host of similar measures. Not only social reorganization, but also the regeneration of the human person, was, moreover, seen as necessary to institute the new regime. Parallel efforts to construct *le nouvel homme* reached a fever pitch during the Terror, when the demands of political morality oscillated between the virtuous self-sacrifice of faithful martyrs and the death on the guillotine of alleged apostates of the republican credo. The Jacobins dictated a cult of martyrs and revolutionary festivals that not only instilled a heightened sense of civic duty but also sought to envelop the *patrie* in a sacred—indeed, resacralized—aura. Whereas absolutist kings had reigned from on high as transcendent representatives of Christ's power on earth, the Republic would emanate from the hearts and minds of citizens willing to sacrifice their property, and even their very lives, on its altar. Although Robespierre and his supporters met with a swift and gruesome end, the ideal of personhood that they attempted to institute would persist in subsequent movements and events that challenged the sanctity of property held in the self or in the abstract rights and material possessions to which it laid claim.

Dismantling the Old Regime, Constructing the New Order: Property and the Rights of Man and Citizen

Even more, arguably, than the Tennis Court Oath of June 20, 1789, or the fall of the Bastille on July 14, it was the abolition of *privilèges* on the night of August 4 that signaled the advent of the Revolution. Those decisive hours established a trajectory that the new regime would follow for several years. Although successive revolutionary legislatures worked to institutionalize self-ownership, they did so via immediate, sweeping, and at times violent acts of dispossession. Once the self-proclaimed National Assembly abolished the exercise of privileges that had legitimized economic transactions and personal identity under the Old Regime, it became imperative to recast civil society as an autonomous sphere, comprised no longer of interdependent corporate bodies, but of individual agents—the sum of whose interests amounted to the commonweal.[15] Within a month, the deputies had produced the definitive statement enshrining the rights of these agents as fundamental law. Tellingly, the Declaration of the Rights of Man and Citizen, approved on August 26, 1789, specifically cited property in Article 17 as "a sacred and inviolable right." Neither liberty, nor security, nor resistance to oppression—the other rights expressly named—received so exalted a title. The Constitution of 1791, for which the declaration served as preamble, further entrenched property as a qualification for the exercise of political authority: only men with sufficient assets (the amount varied according to the population of one's locale) were eligible to stand for office, and to be entitled to vote, citizens had to pay a tax equivalent to three days' unskilled labor.[16]

Previous attempts at reform, especially Turgot's abolition of the guilds in 1776, had shown that severing the ties that bound French subjects to their respective social orders could produce a highly disorienting effect. For many, the notion that private property should be held mainly, if not exclusively, by individuals did not appear as natural or as inviolable as the Declaration of Rights heralded it to be.[17] Dismantling the Old Regime required the citizens of the new regime to sacrifice not only an array of ancient rights, but also the socioeconomic identity that stemmed from their possessions. At its inception on the night of August 4, this process of double alienation assumed the form of communal reverie, in which "enthusiasm seized every soul."[18] The logic of dispossession informed the deputies' activities, as the sacrifice of privilege converged in patriotic rapture with the loss of self-mastery. More generally, the drama established a powerful template for subsequent developments, whereby the demolition of traditional structures gave rise not to individual self-assertion, but to an effusion of patriotic self-sacrifice. The apparent triumph of self-ownership as an axiom of revolutionary political culture in fact originated in an act of collective abandon.

Given the spontaneous political virtue that the night of August 4 came to characterize in the public imagination, it is ironic that the event began as a ruse.[19] By the summer of 1789, rural unrest over taxation and feudal obligations, along with persistent fears of pillaging, had triggered panic on a broad scale. At Versailles, alarming reports circulated that peasants were ransacking their seigneurs' châteaux in search of feudal records and other symbols of the traditional hierarchy. With the National Assembly paralyzed by infighting over the declaration of rights and other matters, a cadre of deputies who belonged to the Breton Club (predecessor to the Jacobins) concluded that the most effective means of neutralizing the crisis would be a direct assault on aristocratic privilege. To prod the Assembly into action, Armand de Vignerot du Plessis de Richelieu, duc d'Aiguillon, decided that he would renounce his feudal rights as one of the nation's largest landowners in exchange for indemnification. Before he could take the floor, however, Louis-Marie, vicomte de Noailles, came forward with a similar offer. Caught unawares by the turn of events, d'Aiguillon proceeded with his original plan. "In this century of Enlightenment," he observed, when the nation's representatives had been "gathered together for the public good, and freed from all personal interests," it was necessary "to establish as promptly as possible the equality of rights that should exist among all men, and that alone can assure their liberty."[20]

What occurred next was nothing short of extraordinary. According to the account of events reported in the *Moniteur universel*, the de facto journal of record during the revolutionary decade, the proposals of de Noailles and d'Aiguillon "were welcomed with a transport of indescribable joy." When d'Aiguillon declared his commitment to nonfeudal property—as when he envisioned a new social order "composed exclusively of proprietors"—his voice was drowned in the din of "motions without number, each one more important than the last." A host of deputies arose to demand the suppression of all legal and fiscal distinctions based on estate, including personal obligations imposed on the peasantry under the guise of *mainmorte* and the *corvée*, aristocratic hunting privileges, the tithe, venal officeholding, and the particular rights conferred upon *pays d'état* and other locales. The meeting did not adjourn until two in the morning, after the Assembly had passed articles abolishing the corporatist order and instituting a system of progressive taxation and uniform justice. Members also adopted the proposal made by Alexandre-Frédéric-François, duc de Liancourt, to strike a medal commemorating "the sincere union of all orders, the abandonment of all privileges, and the ardent devotion of every individual to public peace and prosperity." The *Moniteur* praised the "holy enthusiasm of personal disinterestedness" that held sway, as the mass of representatives "experienced the manner of intoxication that elevates the soul above the senses and allies itself so advantageously with the effervescence of patriotism and generosity."[21]

From the outset, the collective memory of the night's events harbored deep-seated contradictions. The surrender of corporatist rights was related not only to the liberation of the individual from unjust feudal restrictions, but also to the galvanizing sense of political communion made possible by patriotic self-sacrifice. The divergent ideals of personal autonomy and political immediacy clashed in the years that followed—in the text of the Declaration of the Rights of Man, in the halls of the National Assembly and the Convention, and in the streets of Paris. The difficulties besieging representatives and the represented alike defied resolution, in part because they had already been inscribed in the founding acts of the Revolution. If property was an "inviolable and sacred" right, as the Declaration of the Rights of Man affirmed, then to what extent and with what justification could its ownership be limited? Was the body politic composed of individuals, or did it itself constitute them? Could liberty reign in the absence of equality, or equality in the absence of liberty?[22] Property—as a right, source of authority, and form of identity—figured crucially in these dilemmas.

Despite the breathless sweep with which the deputies sacrificed their aristocratic privileges on the altar of the nation, the implications of their actions emerged only gradually. The scope of legal expropriation was broadened on November 2 to encompass ecclesiastical domains. The sale of these *biens nationaux*, as they came to be designated, was intended to address the financial strains that had precipitated the fall of the Old Regime. To these would soon be added properties confiscated from the émigrés, as well as the *bien communaux*, or common lands that peasants traditionally used for pasture, firewood, and other needs. Yet the policy did not have the effect of redistributing wealth to unpropertied members of the former Third Estate. While poor peasants in certain areas fared well, the *biens nationaux* were mainly bought up by their richer brethren. With this substantial transfer of property from the Church to individual holders came a series of changes to the nature of ownership itself. The National and Constituent Assemblies gradually eliminated various restrictions on the sale, rent, and use of landed property in an effort to ensure that self-interest did not override the general welfare.[23]

After the collapse of the monarchy in August 1792, when the Revolution entered its most radical phase, the possibilities of socioeconomic transformation merged with the Montagnard rationale of the right to subsistence. The most strident calls were those of Jean-Paul Marat, the incendiary author of the journal *L'Ami du Peuple*. His election as a deputy to the Convention gave him an institutional platform for expressing his views. As early as 1780, in his *Plan de législation criminelle*, he had stipulated that the property rights of individuals remain valid only insofar as the needs of all had been met. Setting aside Locke's celebrated argument in defense of the privatization of ownership, he argued that not even the exertion of labor necessarily formalized possession. Unless there was an "equal repartition" of the entire land, one's claims extended only to what was needed for subsistence. "The right to possess stems from the right to live," Marat reasoned. Therefore, "all that is indispensable to our existence is ours, and nothing superfluous can legitimately belong to us so long as others lack what is necessary."[24]

This principle foreshadowed Robespierre's plan for a new declaration of rights in 1793, his colleague Jacques Nicolas Billaud-Varenne's reflections on republican government, and the ambitions of deputies who allied themselves most closely with the radical movement. Likewise, it underwrote Marat's denunciations of "capitalists, stockjobbers, monopolists, luxury merchants," and other undesirables, whom he accused of exploiting the people's material desperation for their own rapacious ends. In February 1793, he implored the Convention to adopt "revolutionary measures" to combat the scourge, which included empowering the Committee of General Security to haul economic "traitors of the *patrie*" before a special tribunal composed of "the most upright and severe" judges. A related scheme called on wealthier citizens to import vital commodities from abroad in order to replenish local supplies and lower prices.[25] Despite the hyperbole of Marat's rhetoric, he sought to restrict private property on humanitarian grounds rather than abolish it, even if his disciples among the representatives-on-mission declared social leveling as an explicit aim.[26]

The question of property enthralled the Convention during debates over the republican constitution. In part to shore up support from the popular movement in Paris, Robespierre took aim at the Girondins, with whom he and his Montagnard colleagues were locked in a fierce struggle, vilifying his opponents as "souls of mud, who only value gold." He further questioned why, in their bid to revise the original declaration of rights, they placed explicit limits on liberty, "the first of man's goods," while eschewing qualifications in the case of property, which he defined as a mere "social institution." As a result, their proposals struck him as "made not for men, but for the rich, [. . .] and for tyrants."[27] In response, he offered his own draft declaration, published by order of the Convention, elements of which found their way into the final version in the Constitution of 1793.

Robespierre's amendments differed markedly from those of the Girondins in their treatment of property and its relation to other rights. His elaboration of fundamental prerogatives began neither with liberty (like the declaration of 1789) nor with equality (like the Girondins'), but with "the conservation of one's existence." This imperative, he suggested, justly determined the exercise of all rights, including property, which should be limited by "the obligation to respect the rights of others." Any "dealing"—or "possession," to cite the version of the proposal published by the Jacobins—that contravened these principles was declared "illicit and immoral." In keeping with his commitment to public assistance as a natural right, Robespierre also drafted a separate article, affirming that "society is obliged to provide for the subsistence of all its members," so that "essential aid to those who lack what is necessary is a debt of those who possess more than is necessary." His message was clear: individual property rights rest purely on convention, and the true moral purpose of ownership is to ensure the provision of all, with contributions from every citizen with the means to render aid.[28]

While Robespierre relativized the status of property, he also assured skeptics in the Convention of his awareness that, in practice, "equality of ownership is a chimera."[29] Indeed, although he advocated the redistribution of excessive or unjustly acquired wealth, his arguments favored small and middling property holders. As he had previously put the matter, during the debates over the Constitution of 1791, "one's interest in the conservation of a thing is proportional to the modesty of one's fortune."[30] According to this rationale, the exigencies of subsistence could be reconciled with respect for property rights—albeit not of individuals, but of the body politic en masse. If "the first law of society is therefore that which guarantees to all members of society the means of existence"—a position he articulated in a speech on December 2, 1792, and later codified in his draft declaration—then "all others are subordinated" to it. The right from which this most fundamental law derives, the right to existence, applies to all and depends on the support of all, since "everything that is indispensable for conserving it is a common property of the entire society."[31] In Robespierre's schema, the subject of political and social rights no longer corresponds to the abstract individual of the first declaration, but to a collective self manifested in the sovereign people. This, ultimately, is the meaning behind his subordination of property, along with all other rights, to the imperatives of existence. It reflects a concomitant move toward subsuming the pursuit of personal happiness in the *patrie*'s struggle for self-preservation.

Robespierre's revisions were not incorporated directly into the approved text of the new Declaration of the Rights of Man and Citizen, but the causes he advocated nonetheless left their mark on the document and on subsequent legislation. For instance, while the final version of June 24 omitted his proposals concerning property, its first article stated unequivocally that "the goal of society is the happiness of all." A subsequent article proclaimed that "public assistance is a sacred debt," and that "society owes a living to unfortunate citizens."[32] As William Sewell has observed, this constitutional mandate for subsistence resonated strongly with militant sans-culottes, who drew on a wealth of traditional arguments accumulated during previous struggles to denounce the injustice and unnaturalness of dearth.[33]

The Girondins persistently refused the demands of the popular movement, thereby drawing the ire of Marat and Jacques Roux, a looming presence among the so-called *enragés*. The Montagnards leapt into the breach. Their anti-institutional stance and activist economic policies galvanized sans-culotte support, leading to the violent expulsion of the Girondins from the Convention during the events of May 31–June 2, 1793.[34] While the factions subscribed to similar economic views in principle, the Jacobin endorsement of decisive intervention to assure subsistence during a period of rising costs and fear of famine rallied popular support to their side. The Montagnard-dominated Convention proceeded to pass a wave of social legislation even as it sought to rein in potential critics like Roux, who had an insatiable appetite for agitation. Perhaps most notably, the legislature authorized the partial return to economic paternalism in the form of the so-called Maximum, a limit on the price of grain and bread first decreed in May 1793 and then expanded in September to include all foodstuffs. There were also efforts, much resisted and only partly successful, to establish a nationwide system of granaries to provision the Republic in a time of domestic insecurity and foreign war.[35]

Even with these measures in place, tensions between the dual imperatives of subsistence and property continued to provoke discontent as well
as renewed speculation. Sans-culottes took to the streets to demand a wider
application of the Maximum, which, they charged, failed to encompass the
full range of necessary goods.[36] For the Convention, the issue of how to dispose of confiscated lands occasioned a broader debate on the limits of private property. For instance, during the debates over the *biens communaux*,
the deputy Julien-Joseph Souhait deployed the sans-culotte rhetoric of subsistence to argue that holdings should be left intact as a collective resource
for public assistance. "When the poor demand bread and work, they do
not require property," he asserted, but rather "possession [*jouissance*]" and
the "means of subsistence." Besides, to divide properties into small plots
risked obliging beneficiaries who faced financial ruin to sell them to wealthier parties, thereby undermining the rationale of the program.[37] In contrast,
Claude-Dominique-Cosme Fabre, deputy from Hérault, argued for the creation of individual tracts, since "all inhabitants are equally owners of the
commons." Land in which no one had invested "the idea of property," he
added, tends to suffer from neglect. This view carried the day, and the Convention voted on June 10, 1793, for division per capita.[38]

Nevertheless, leading Montagnards remained committed to the axiom
that property, like all social institutions, should be subject to the needs
of the community as a whole. From this perspective, individualist appropriation—ownership conceived as first and foremost the prerogative of the
individual—could not fail to pose formidable problems both from a theoretical and a practical standpoint. Billaud-Varenne, soon to join Robespierre on the Committee of Public Safety, devoted himself to arriving at a
definitive solution. In the spring of 1793, he published his *Éléments du
républicanisme*. This "political profession of faith," as he called it, bore
witness to the inexorable distinctions between the rich and the poor, the
wicked and the virtuous, the individual and the citizen. Billaud-Varenne
pointedly rejected Rousseau's contention in the *Second Discourse* that
early humans were, as asocial beings, incapable of *amour-propre*, but he
embraced the distinction posed in *Émile* between fashioning men and citizens. The first task of legislators must be to minimize the devastation unleashed by self-love. *Amour-propre* is not only a natural sentiment—it "is
to morality what hunger is to the physical world"—but also one conducive
to cultural, social, and economic development. To harness its power while
avoiding its corrupting tendencies would require nothing less than neutralizing the individualism that had been its most pernicious manifestation.
The true citizen, according to Billaud-Varenne, "naturally confounds his
interests with those of the *patrie*," "the whole of which he is an integral
part." However, this "noble devotion" can only hold sway where "the peo-

ple and the sovereign are united." In sharp contrast, atomistic, possessive, and self-interested "individuals [. . .] are those who isolate themselves" and "seek to upset the equilibrium of equality in order to expand their personal well-being."[39]

The aim of political regeneration, then, must be to ensure that the virtues of the citizen triumph over the prerogatives of the individual. To reach this goal meant submitting property to the exigencies of the common rather than particular good. "In a century of Enlightenment," Billaud-Varenne explained, "during which the Declaration of the Rights of Man has been promulgated," entering civil society presumes a surrender of "one's exclusive well-being to that of all the members of the same association." The time had come for a political and economic about-face from what had once passed for the march of progress. Billaud-Varenne acknowledged that "property is the pivot of civil associations" and should thus be protected, but he also held that it should be complemented by an effort "to establish, as far as possible, a redistribution of goods, if not absolutely equal, then at least proportional among all citizens." Although he did not advocate a reversion to primitive conditions, he made it abundantly clear that an enlightened government should seek to eradicate luxury and the "furor for possessing [*jouir*]" that it inevitably arouses. This obsession could only serve to enrich a wealthy minority, while further impoverishing the masses. Since "the interest of all," or "public safety," is the "imprescriptible title of the equal rights of each citizen, [. . .] before which the exclusive claims of individuals vanish," the law of nature itself prescribes restrictions on the accumulation of property. Billaud-Varenne argued that land holdings and the right to inheritance should be limited by the state, according to the dictum that "if the right to property is inviolable, this principle must be applied to the advantage of all persons who compose the nation."[40]

Billaud-Varenne's proposals did not fall on deaf ears. Many of his fellow deputies shared his view that, if property was to remain sacrosanct in principle, it must also be regulated and even curtailed in practice. In the Year II, the Convention passed a series of measures to this end. For instance, previous legislation equalizing inheritance was extended to all children and all forms of property. In February and March 1794, Saint-Just mitigated his oft-stated commitment to property rights by spearheading what became known as the Vêntose decrees, which called for confiscating the possessions of political suspects and other potential counterrevolutionaries on behalf of indigent citizens. "The property of patriots is sacred," he argued, "but the goods of conspirators exist for the needy."[41] In actuality, however, officials stopped short of mandatory expropriation and redistribution; some even chose to ignore the decrees. Instead, land

and other valuables were made available to the poor for fixed terms, with the stipulation that they would be returned to former owners found innocent of treason.[42]

In the end, the Convention proved unwilling to engage in a systematic reform of private property. Yet many deputies also believed that an individual's right to ownership could be suspended in times of political and economic duress. Others found it necessary to balance the defense of this right with moral and material restraints on its exercise.[43] Their convictions lent weight to the cause of political morality championed in Billaud-Varenne's *Éléments du républicanisme*. On this front, word proved more forceful than deed. Out of the speeches of Robespierre, Saint-Just, and their allies among the Jacobins and in the legislature there emerged a distinctive ideal of revolutionary citizenship that sought to displace the individual—and with it, the nascent doctrines of individualism—in favor of the body politic. The protracted, ultimately inconclusive debates over the *biens nationaux*, *biens communaux*, subsistence, and related matters thus were of a piece with a still more expansive campaign to affix the property in one's person to an indivisible, sovereign, and totalizing force beyond the individual self. The Montagnards remained acutely aware of the need to overcome the invidious effects of the 1,700-year reign of tyrannical *amour-propre* if French citizens were to become true patriots who would unhesitatingly surrender their personal interests to those of the nation. It fell to their representatives to oversee the establishment of institutions—revolutionary festivals, schools, a cult of martyrs, and even a deity—that would bring about this glorious end. Their task went far beyond the project of remaking France as a social and political entity. It would also be necessary to regenerate the citizenry, and to resacralize the *patrie*, by dispossessing the individual of unjust prerogatives that rightly belonged to the people as a collective, self-owning body.

Valorizing Self-Sacrifice: The Cult of Martyrs

The political culture of the Year II resonated strongly not only with concurrent debates over property and one's relationship to possessions, but also with the broader cultures of self-ownership and dispossession that coalesced during the eighteenth century. In addition to the debts of the Old Regime, the Revolution inherited—to adopt Hans Blumenberg's evocative phrase—a "mortgage of prescribed questions."[44] If the new regime was to endure, its leaders recognized, they would need to reconcile competing claims of liberty, based on individual rights, and of sovereignty, which required forging a collective, national, irresistible will. As we have seen, Rousseau faced a similar difficulty in *Du Contrat social*. Fénelon and d'Holbach likewise struggled to define the self's relationship to external forces, whether to God and to nature, respectively, and both went on to elaborate the political implications of their views.

In confronting the urgent tasks before them, the Montagnard-led Convention and its allies relied on tactics developed in previous struggles over mysticism, materialism, and radical republicanism. It is especially revealing that patriotic self-sacrifice found affirmation at a time when Fénelon was enshrined by revolutionaries with Cato and the Gracchi as an exemplar of political morality, notwithstanding his noble birth and ecclesiastical career. As we have seen, Fénelon himself extolled Plato and Cicero as practitioners of the disinterestedness that characterized his spiritual and political ideals.[45] For Marie-Joseph Chénier, Jacobin delegate to the Convention and librettist for the revolutionary festivals, he was a "model of virtue without blemish" as "a philosophe and a patriot." Even the notoriously irreligious Sylvain Maréchal praised the author of *Télémaque* in his *Almanach républicain*, while suggesting that citizens disregard his clerical status.[46] As we shall see, d'Holbach also earned his share of accolades for writing *Système de la nature*.[47]

To record these genealogical connections is neither to privilege the direct influence of individual authors, however celebrated, nor to reserve pride of place for their views. Nor is it sufficient merely to acknowledge the religious antecedents of modern political culture. Fénelon was no republican in the Jacobin sense; nor were the Jacobins mystics in a Fénelonian—or even in a specifically Christian—sense. The chain of affinities that linked them extended across a far broader terrain. Rhetorical tropes and liturgical practices drawn from the mystical, materialist, and classical republican traditions constituted an anti-individualist culture of dispossession that acquired coherence gradually over the course of the eighteenth century. Radical revolutionaries who sought to challenge what they regarded as an excessive, politically immoral attachment to one's self and one's possessions creatively employed the logics and lexicons of this culture in formulating their distinctive vision for the Republic. These appropriations signal not the causation of ideas, but rather the contingencies inherent in all social modes of expression, which depend on preexisting resources as their point of departure.[48]

In the case of revolutionary political theology, the king's trial and execution radicalized the original act of conjuring the nation, which Sieyès had defined partly by excluding the Second Estate. Deciding Louis's fate marked a turning point in this logic, insofar as the regicides passed down their death sentence not merely as a penalty for past crimes, but also as a means of expiation with immediate and future consequences.[49] With the cult of martyrs and Festival of the Supreme Being, the imperatives of self-sacrifice took on an unprecedented prestige and intensity. The Terror, for all its iconoclasm, was predicated on the sacredness of politics and driven by the compulsion to manifest this quality everywhere—in the laws of the Republic, in the hearts of republicans and the bonds they shared, and even in the corpses of their fallen brethren.[50] In such a climate, Fénelon's exhortation that virtuous leaders must die to themselves took on greater significance than he could have predicted or even countenanced. The pure love of God was recast as the pure love of *patrie*.

Embracing the virtuous present required severing all ties with a corrupt past. As we have seen, by abolishing seigneurial and corporate privileges, the night of August 4, 1789 announced the end of the Old Regime. A little more than three years later, on January 21, 1793, the first act in the drama of the nascent Republic culminated in killing the king, the traditional font of all privilege. Louis's continued presence threatened to negate the existence of the French Republic. Only his sacrifice to the polity—and by the polity—ensured the promise of its regeneration. Robespierre, speaking before the Convention as it deliberated the king's fate in November and December 1792, propounded this logic with arresting clarity. "Louis was king, and the Republic is founded," he declared, before concluding: "Louis must die so that the *patrie* may live." Saint-Just echoed his mentor's sentiments exactly: "The Revolution begins when the tyrant is finished."[51] By translating the absolutist credo of succession into Christological terms, their rhetoric expressed what were, to their minds, the symbolic and practical implications of dispatching Louis the Last. Regicide enacted a solemn transfer: the monarch's former sovereignty, and with it his sacrality, now came to reside in the body politic.[52] At the same time, these attributes underwent a radical transformation. The king's claims of exalted status were a perversion of justice, because it set him apart and outside the polity he claimed to govern. As Robespierre reminded his fellow delegates, "Louis alone was sacred."[53] His death did not mark the eradication of this force, however, but rather its expansion to a totalizing scale. What had once belonged to a single man now was imbued in the people as a whole.

Already in 1790, royalists had begun to predict that the king's demise would usher in even more sweeping disarray, "when the tombs will open, not to facilitate the resurrection of the dead, but on the contrary, to swallow up the innocent with the guilty, the one and the other sacrificed by blind and frenetic desire."[54] Their prophecies would prove at least partly accurate. On January 20, 1793, on the eve of Louis's execution, the Jacobin deputy Michel Le Peletier de Saint-Fargeau was stabbed to death by an outraged ex-bodyguard of the former monarch.[55] He was immediately hailed as a martyr of republican liberty, and his body lay in state for four days. Jacques-Louis David, who had emerged as the Revolution's most celebrated iconographer, drew a sketch depicting his wound like a sanctified gash. The painter also organized Le Peletier de Saint-Fargeau's funeral, during which his body was displayed in the Place Vendôme on a pedestal that had once supported a statue of Louis XIV. The passion play concluded when the remains were deposited in the Pantheon, in the underground crypts that already held the body of Voltaire, and would later serve as Rousseau's final resting place. Robespierre hailed his former colleague as an "incorruptible friend of truth," and, addressing himself to the fallen hero's memory, vowed to uphold "the holy cause of which [he was] the apostle."[56]

Le Peletier de Saint-Fargeau's death marked the birth of a new republican cult of martyrs, one that would reach its zenith when Marat, the voice of sans-culotte political aspirations, was assassinated in his bathtub on July 13, 1793. The news electrified Paris and triggered a wave of popular enthusiasm. David hastily arranged the funeral, which drew throngs of mourners to the Cordeliers Club on July 16. Nearly six months later, on 20 nivôse of the Year II (January 9, 1794), the members of the Paris section of Beaurepaire gathered at the former Church of the Sorbonne, now converted into a Temple of Reason, to commemorate the unveiling of busts of both Le Peletier de Saint-Fargeau and Marat. Marat's assassin, Charlotte Corday, had Girondin and émigré ties and was suspected of participating in a vast plot against the Republic. Given such trepidations, the proceedings of the Beaurepaire section assumed a somber, defiant tone. The decision was subsequently made to print the speeches given in the martyrs' honor, which included an address by A. C. N. Closquinet de La Roche. Reflecting on the examples of Le Peletier de Saint-Fargeau and Marat, La Roche exhorted the virtuous patriot not only "to submit his mind to the absolute empire of reason," but "to have no other interest in view but that of his *patrie*, to be occupied with it more than with himself, and to consider it as his only fortune." Revolutionary sacrifice also encompassed material goods. "One must renounce the passions, pride, presumption, and above all avarice," La Roche made clear. Citizens had a duty to "learn how to dispense with the superfluous, and not to hesitate to share with the poor even what is necessary for oneself."[57]

The celebrations in the capital were replicated throughout France in the months following Marat's death. An elegy delivered at events in Schiltigheim and Strasbourg paid him a lavish compliment typical of the times. "Such was his burning love for the *patrie*," remarked Célestin Morel, "that one said of him: he had the fever of patriotism." His virtue, surpassing that of the ancients, found few precedents. "Like Jesus," the speaker continued, "Marat was extremely sensitive and humane; he had the sublime soul of Rousseau."[58] The flood of veneration swept along thousands in its wake.

In addition to the participants themselves, the services drew sculptors, poets, musicians, and other artists who contributed their talents. Seemingly everywhere, one could see and touch various effigies (busts, medals, rings, paintings, engravings, even hairstyles) or hear songs of praise devoted to the great revolutionary martyr.[59] Citizens demanded not only that he be granted the honors of the Pantheon, which the Convention duly approved on 24 brumaire Year II (November 14, 1793), but also that streets, squares, and cities be given his name. One such petition went so far as to request that Montmartre be rechristened "Mont-marat" (an ironic proposal in hindsight, given the subsequent construction there of the Sacré-Cœur Basilica, conceived of as penance for the sins of the Paris Commune during the revolutionary uprising in 1871).[60]

For devotees of the Marat cult, it was not enough to see representations of their hero everywhere they turned. They longed to feel his spirit from within. The president of the Popular Society of Uzès-La-Montagne, one Citizen Dumas, captured this zeal in a speech. He invoked Marat's name as one would that of a saint, pleading in reverent tones: "Inspire me, let your beautiful soul penetrate my own. May your deified soul [*mânes*] make all my fellow citizens understand that man is born, and must live and die, for the *patrie!*" Dumas then gave a sermon intended to explicate the true import of his exhortations. For him, patriotism implied "imitating nature, which, in its constant and invariable march, inevitably reaches its goal." To be a citizen meant "to be born for a determined end and to fulfill one's civic duty without deviation." Morality was not the charge of priests, whom Dumas denounced as false witnesses in their claim to be "the intermediaries between divinity and humanity." Rather, it was a code found "engraved on every heart in ineffaceable characters," both rational and sacred in that following its dictates made one "useful to society."[61]

The apotheosis of Marat continues to fascinate, not least because it exhibits in dramatic style the myriad contradictions behind the monolithic façade of Jacobin political culture. For one, the cult appeared on the eve of dechristianization.[62] This concurrence has led historians such as Frank Bowman to minimize, even to disavow, the religious dimensions of the cult.[63] Nevertheless, its most fervent adherents employed Catholic forms, albeit devoid of their original content, to express reverence for a revolutionary hero and saint.[64] They offered prayers and hymns to a martyr, whose death held for them the blessed hope of redemption in this life—as David suggested by depicting Marat entombed in his bath, the limp Christ of a republican pietà.[65] Nonetheless, their aim was not to substitute Marat for a divine savior, but to replace a transcendent deity with an immanent, all-too-human referent of ideal citizenship. Dechristianization—a form of desacralization—reflected a corresponding urge to resacralize the *patrie* as an object worthy of devotion. Marat's assassination, rendered as sacrifice, embodied this desire, and Christian referents served to make it more widely comprehensible during a moment of religious upheaval. The Republic, having become sacred upon the king's death, now acquired martyrs of its own.

The cult's following among sans-culotte radicals in the Paris sections aggravated preexisting tensions between the Montagnard leadership and the popular movement. Although Marat's funeral was carefully staged by David, the ensuing demonstrations materialized with relative spontaneity and in the absence of significant government oversight.[66] For precisely this reason, the cult drew the mistrust of Robespierre and like-minded colleagues in the Convention, who launched a campaign to rein in the forces that had propelled them to power. In such a fraught climate, Lucien Jaume has claimed, "the question of how the citizen could achieve a mediation between the particular and the universal [. . .] was no longer posed." Instead, the Convention set the Republic on a course of officially sanctioned regeneration—one that aimed, paradoxically, to return humankind to its original, natural state of virtue through decidedly manufactured means.[67]

Historians have long noted that the term *régénération* held strong theological connotations during the eighteenth century. It referred not only to the purifying effects of baptism and the anticipated resurrection of the Christian faithful, but also to Catholic devotional practices recalibrated by the revolutionaries to disseminate the gospel of *liberté, égalité, et fraternité*.[68] Jaume even recognizes a certain continuity between Jansenist spirituality and Jacobin expressions of disdain for the individual self as a bastion of *amour-propre*.[69] However, this thought-provoking conjecture overlooks the extent to which Jansenist moral philosophy, taken as a whole, aimed to convert self-centeredness into social virtue with its stipulation that the corrupt soul's bottomless vanity and pride could only find fulfillment by appealing to the same desires in other persons. Yet the Jacobins, at least in unguarded moments, proved fearful of any manifestation of individual will, lest it disrupt the transparent unity that bound together all citizens as one in a single body politic.

Marat's death and apotheosis offered an opportunity to elaborate this new state of symbolic affairs in positive terms, fulfilling another of Saint-Just's axioms from the previous November: "The spirit in which the king is judged is the same as that with which the Republic will be established."[70] Or, in the words of La Roche in his address to the section of Beaurepaire, "this crime was necessary for the salvation of France," as was the imperative to "punish traitors and wisely follow the revolutionary impulse."[71] With France struggling for its very existence against the combined forces of Austria, Prussia, Britain, and the Dutch Republic, and against counter-revolutionary rebellion in the Vendée, the Convention took decisive action to neutralize these threats. It created the Revolutionary Tribunal (March 1793) to prosecute political enemies. The month following Marat's assassination, on August 23, the deputies decreed the *levée en masse*, which mobilized the entire French populace for the war effort and increased the army's strength by 300,000. In September, the government passed the Law of Suspects, which provided legal justification for the investigation and detention of purported political enemies on a massive scale.

The "cult of the martyrs of liberty," as it became known, had by that time become a fixture on the political and cultural scenes.[72] No doubt, it offered the regime's true believers solace in a time of war and economic insecurity. It also provided a forum in which to reflect upon the spiritual and metaphysical aspects of the patriotic abandon to which all citizens had been called, and which appeared as a directive of the general will. According to the amateur homage in verse delivered before the members of the Popular and Revolutionary Society of Dunkirk (renamed Dune-Libre), martyrdom was not merely a civil act. It served as a means of worshipping the "soul of the world," which alone "furnishes the seed of the supernatural pleasures [*jouissances*] of love for the *patrie*." Nature itself, in which "all beings contribute to the universal harmony," serves as the model for reciprocal edification. The individual accordingly "owes to the world as much as he has received from it." Plenitude entailed immeasurable debt. It followed, then, that "the man who sacrifices himself to his brothers fulfills his task in the universal order." Self-renunciation thus constitutes a sacred duty that determines one's actions in all things. Rather than the "desire for glory" or the "ambition of honors," virtuous republicans should follow the "ardent passion" that strives for "the complete abnegation of themselves." For the citizen under this sentiment's powerful sway, "possessions" and "affluence" count for nothing as "one forgets oneself in its contemplation." In such a state, even poverty is "a means to be more virtuous and useful." The anonymous bard imagined the souls of martyrs as entirely consumed with the common good, "like a burning flame that absorbs every other hearth," until all "ordinary and partial affections" are annihilated.[73]

Meditating further on this interior state, the writer continued his account in patently dispossessive terms. For patriots, "the love of a single being has been extinguished by the love of all." In a similar manner, the "pleasures of the senses" give way to and are "redeemed [*amortis*] by those of the soul."[74] The self-sacrifice of martyrs involved not so much a simple negation as a dual transformation. Purged of the artificial sentiment of *amour-propre*, zealous citizens came to identify no longer with their individual interests and identity, but with those of the body politic, which in turn maintained its perfect correspondence with nature as a whole.

This republican adaptation of Neoplatonism would find more nuanced elaboration in the works of philosophically minded dechrististianizers like the geometer and amateur classicist François Peyrard, whose curious treatise *De la Nature et de ses lois* appeared in 1793. After providing a survey of ancient pantheism from Pythagoras to Epicurus, the author paid homage to d'Holbach's *Système de la nature*, which he praised as "the most beautiful monument that philosophy has elevated to reason." He fully endorsed the thesis of his notorious predecessor that "all the effects that the universe presents to us are the necessary results of the combination of matter." If the Christian deity was an "invisible tyrant" who "carried desolation and madness in the souls of mortals," then the general welfare depended on eradicating this scourge from the earth. To this end, Peyrard reaffirmed one of central tenets of radical philosophy, that the "eternal circle" of nature, and not a God with intelligent aims and desires, encompasses the existence of every being. A series of notes appended to the body of his text intimated the practical significance of his views. Peyrard charged that superstition remained an insidious source of social ills, along with despotism and "the excessively unequal division of wealth." Unfortunately, he did not specify how these spiritual, political, and economic injustices related to each other. He did, however, approvingly cite Lycurgus's equal division of Spartan territory, which each inhabitant possessed as a "simple usufructer" rather than legal proprietor, as a possible model for France.[75]

The implications of rejecting conventional religion were spelled out in grandiose if quixotic terms by Anacharsis Cloots, a Prussian nobleman who had been naturalized as a French citizen and elected to the Convention. "The attributes of a fantastical divinity," he stated in *Bases constitutionelles de la République du Genre Humain* (1793), "really belong to the political divinity." If one could only dispense with the fiction of a supernatural, transcendent creator, it would become evident that "Humankind is God, the aristocrats are atheists," and worship is due to the "People-God of which France is the cradle and the rallying point." Thus Cloots set his beliefs squarely against those embraced by followers of traditional religion, with their blind faith in "the Eternal outside the world, [. . .] an incomprehensible *Theos*" that in some mysterious fashion created the universe. His God was resolutely "in the world," and his testament stemmed from "the revelation of nature."[76] Given these premises, as well as the foreign-born Cloots's cosmopolitan sensibilities, a deified polity could not be confined to a single nation. "The universal Republic," he predicted, "will replace the universal Church." He had every faith that its time was near. If the French people could regenerate their own *patrie* in a matter of years, there was no limit to what "the totality of humans" would accomplish in extending the principle of "the subordination of the part to the whole" around the world.[77]

Cloots allied himself with a circle of radicals, including Jacques-René Hébert, creator of the notoriously irreverent newspaper *Père Duchesne*, and Pierre-Gaspard (Anaxagoras) Chaumette, procurator of the Paris Commune. This group went on to advocate for and then to oversee the Festival of Liberty and Reason, which was held at the cathedral of Notre-Dame in Paris on 20 brumaire Year II (November 10, 1793). Although Robespierre later portrayed the movement as essentially an atheist plot, theist references abound in its iconography and liturgy. During the festival, Reason was depicted as a goddess, with the role being played by an actress from the Paris Opera.[78] To reject Christ, then, did not at all involve rejecting God altogether. According to Jacques-Antoine Brouillet, member of the Society of Friends of the Republic, reason is the "precious emanation" of the divine, and "the Supreme Being has cast within us this marvelous ray of light in order to enlighten us in the discernment of good and evil." God's ubiquity, moreover, was reflected for him in the power of the body politic. Law-breakers not only rebel against the "omnipotence of the nation," but fall into self-contradiction by defying their own representatives. The "public functionary," for his part, "must forget every particular interest" in fulfilling his duties; indeed, his personal self must "disappear," so that "one sees only the public man." The patriotic passion for self-sacrifice forms a precept of "pure, universal morality, drawn from the bosom of the divinity itself," on which all "republican virtues" are founded.[79]

Brouillet pronounced this lofty homage to the divinity of reason during a violent surge in the dechristianizing movement. In the weeks around the festival, iconoclasm had become the order of the day. Churches were desecrated, relics vandalized, and priests forcibly defrocked. Even time, at least as measured under the Old Regime, became suspect. On October 5, France had adopted a new calendar, purged of references to saints or the liturgical seasons. In Paris, section upon section came forward to renounce Catholicism, and the Commune ordered the closure of all houses of worship, as well as the expulsion of all clergyman from public functions. Anti-Catholic spectacles were staged on the floor of the Convention. Deputies heard letter after letter sent by priests renouncing their vocations, and the bishop of Paris, Jean-Baptiste-Joseph Gobel, even came before the assembly to do so in person. The representatives-on-mission carried out the dechristianizing campaign in the provinces, where local citizens held their own festivals and built their own temples.[80] The period also witnessed the incorporation of the cult of martyrs into the Hébertistes' so-called Cult of Reason, opening the possibility for revolutionary anti-religion to succeed the reformed Gallican Church established by the Civil Constitution of the Clergy in 1790.[81]

For a time, Robespierre kept silent about these initiatives. A committed deist in the Rousseauian tradition—or, on Françoise-Alphonse Aulard's telling, "a mystic soul"—he rejected dechristianization not only on principle but also on the grounds that it would harden the resolve of the regime's enemies at home and abroad.[82] He launched his counteroffensive with a speech to the Jacobins on 1 frimaire Year II (November 21, 1793) in support of religious freedom. In *Bases constitutionnelles*, Cloots had referred to aristocrats as atheists in spirit. Robespierre corrected his colleague: atheists were in fact the true aristocrats.[83] He then prepared an assault on his opponents in the Convention, where on 17 pluviôse Year II (February 5, 1794), he denounced them as "internal enemies of the French people." The speech rallied the assembly to his side. The deputies soon approved the arrest, not only of Hébert, Cloots, and others Robespierre deemed "ultra-revolutionary," but also of Georges-Jacques Danton and the dissimulating faction of political "moderates" that took its cues from him. Robespierre presented his remarks as a report on "political morality," the subtext of which shone through clearly. The Hébertistes proved too fanatical; the Dantonistes exhibited bad faith. Only he himself, and those who supported him, could be counted on to oversee "the development of this mainspring of the Republic, virtue."[84] In the months that followed, Danton and Hébert, along with their respective allies, were swiftly rounded up, tried, and guillotined. Once the Convention had rid itself of these pernicious elements, it set its sights on upstaging the Cult of Reason and restoring religious convictions with a ceremony of Robespierre's own design: the Festival of the Supreme Being.

As a political maneuver, Robespierre's performance was a stunning success. Yet the tactics that he employed also drew on deep-seated philosophical and religious convictions about the logical and spiritual relations connecting God, nature, and the human person. Dan Edelstein has made a compelling case for approaching Jacobin political culture as an effort to construct a "natural republicanism," whereby fidelity to constitutional principles (according to the classical republican tradition, strictly defined) gave way to the imperative of adhering to natural law.[85] Yet it is also crucial to recognize that the revolutionaries by no means agreed on what constituted nature, or what was required in following its dictates. For instance, as we saw in the preceding section, the deputies could be of rather different minds on the question of whether private property originated in an inviolable law of nature. At an even more fundamental level, they had radically varied understandings of nature and of its relationship to divinity. This conflict precipitated Robespierre's struggle to the death against Cloots and his allies—which, in terms of genealogy, could be likened to a clash between Rousseauian and Spinozist conceptions of God *qua* nature.

Even if the representatives could have reached a consensus on the metaphysical and religious dimensions of the problem, there remained uncertainties as to how, or even to what extent, it might be possible to strip away the artificial veneer of human conventions and recover nature in its purest form. The Jacobin gusto for cultural demolition and institution-building bears witness to their belief that human nature stood in dire need of regeneration, and even of reconstruction. To recapture the virtue supposedly natural to them, Robespierre suggested, citizens must be willing to undergo a two-stage process of dispossession. The first, a trial by fire, would purge them of all remnants of aristocratic values that remained in their hearts and minds. The second, a consummation, would make manifest their willingness to sacrifice their personal desires to the survival of the *patrie*. With his plan for a new regime of revolutionary festivals, Robespierre intended to ensure the triumph of both these ends.

Staging Regeneration: The Cult of the Supreme Being

Robespierre began to publicize the lineaments of the new republican gospel, with himself as its evangelist, during the proceedings against Hébert and Danton. His address to the Convention on 17 pluviôse declared the Revolution's solemn aim, to secure "peaceful enjoyment of the possession [*jouissance*] of liberty and equality." Attaining this end, however, would require a host of paradoxical transformations. Robespierre stressed the vast scope of the changes he envisioned. The Revolution would fundamentally alter the experience of personhood, substituting "morality for egoism, probity for honor, principles for customs, [. . .] that is to say, all the virtues and all the miracles of the Republic for all the vices and all the absurdities of monarchy." The "fundamental principle of democratic or popular government," he affirmed over and again, is "virtue," defined in avowedly patriotic terms as a "sublime sentiment" that "supposes the preference of the public interest to all particular interests." He called on his fellow deputies to rally around the enterprise, by promoting "all that which tends to excite love of the *patrie* [. . .] and direct the passions of the human heart toward the public interest," while eradicating "all that which tends to concentrate them in the abject nature of one's own self [*le moi personnel*]." At other moments, however, Robespierre seemed to take a narrower view. The people, he suggested, required little direct guidance "in order to love justice and equality." Otherwise, he would have found it difficult to explain how a nation that had descended into monarchy could suddenly have found the strength to "break the chains of despotism."[86]

The collective subject of the body politic posed relatively few difficulties for Robespierre. The individual citizen, however—and even the individual magistrate, who, he specified, was "obliged to sacrifice his interest to the interest of the people"—remained a source of potential opposition. All who dared defy the principles of political morality courted nothing less than "terror," or the application of "prompt, severe, inflexible justice." Robespierre thus defined revolutionary government as the "despotism of liberty against tyranny."[87] In a similar logical turn, regenerating self-ownership also required an unflinching commitment to dispossessing the individual of egoistic attachments to his particular interests, belongings, and even his own existence, when the exclusive claim to these material and existential goods threatened republican transparency and unity.

Robespierre developed this formula further in his speech of 18 floréal Year II (May 7, 1794), which offered his justification for the Festival of the Supreme Being. Again, he proclaimed that "everything must change in the moral and political order," before offering up his own life to hasten the completion of this crucial task. "O sublime people!" he pleaded, "receive the sacrifice of my entire being. Happy is he who has been born among you! More happy still is he who may die for your happiness!"[88] Although the pronouncement was by no means out of character for Robespierre, it took on an even greater immediacy given his concrete objective. He intended to substitute a civil religion of his own design for the cults that had sprung up around Marat and the goddess of Reason. It was only fitting that he too should present himself as a surrogate for Marat, the author of *L'Ami du peuple*. In life, the latter had frequently prophesied his own violent end, and in death, he had emerged as the consummate revolutionary martyr.[89] Robespierre intimated his desire not only to succeed Marat, but also to exceed him in devotion to the *patrie*. "He who can replace the divinity in the system of social life," he noted, "is to my eyes a prodigy of genius."[90]

With the Cult of the Supreme Being, Robespierre aimed to initiate nothing less than the moral reconfiguration of God as well as the human person. In particular, the new civil religion was to supplement the citizen's natural proclivities by "creating in him a rapid instinct for moral things, which, without the slow aid of reasoning, should lead him to do good and avoid evil." The rationale behind such a project, as Robespierre made clear, stemmed from an awareness that citizens, if left to their own devices, would prove incapable of submitting themselves freely and at the right moment to social ends. Since "the individual reason of each man, led astray by his passions, is often merely a sophist who pleads their cause," it was necessary to situate the impulse for benevolent action on a higher plane. However, the appeal to God alone would not suffice for this transfer of agency. Engendering the political subject with republican virtue also depended on the resacralization of communal life. If natural religion dictates that "man is the greatest object in nature," then "the most magnificent of all spectacles is that of a great people assembled."[91] The call to worship the god of nature, therefore, extended to the nation itself, in its function as the divinity of the Revolution.[92] On this view, the will of the people in no way derived from the accumulated interests of individual citizens; rather, the former was to subsume, even predetermine, the latter.

The Festival would inscribe the tenets that Robespierre had elaborated on 17 pluviôse in the Republic's moral, if not legal, constitution. In this enterprise, he claimed to follow illustrious predecessors such as Socrates and Cicero, but especially Rousseau, whose struggles against the double-headed scourge of tyranny and atheism made him the "precursor" of the Revolution.[93] While Robespierre's fidelity to the letter of Rousseau's doctrines proved far from absolute, he maintained a personal allegiance to the Citizen of Geneva throughout his political career. In one of the first texts attributed to him, for instance, he lauded Rousseau as a "divine man" who "has taught me to know myself," to "appreciate the dignity of my nature and to reflect on the great principles of the social order." Although the date of this composition is uncertain, Robespierre's stated intention to "follow in [Rousseau's] venerable footsteps" during his own venture into "the perilous career of an extraordinary revolution" appears to date to his time as deputy in the National Assembly.[94] Now in the Convention, despite his vacillation on other matters, he remained committed to the sanctity of human existence—or at least that of a virtuous citizenry.

On 18 floréal, Robespierre framed his Rousseauian idylls in sharp contrast to the nightmarish tableaux offered by his opponents. To deny the existence of God like Hébert and the dechristianizers only served to "justify egoism, harden the heart, and efface the idea of the moral beauty that is the sole rule by which public reason judges the defenders and the enemies of humanity." At the same time, Robespierre showed equal disdain for the divinity of traditional religion, which he believed to be as "jealous, capricious, avid, cruel, and implacable" as the priests who had invented him. Betraying their despotic sensibilities, they "relegated him to heaven as if in a palace," only approaching him for "tithes, wealth, honors, pleasure, and power."[95] Robespierre's pairing of atheists and aristocrats, then, was more than rhetorical sleight of hand to reduce the Revolution's enemies to a single type for the sake of political and moral clarity. To his mind, the comparison followed a discernible religious logic. A distant divinity was no better than an absent one; both served to justify a cult of self-interest that had no place in a republic of virtue.

If the gods of kings merely reflected the brutal arrogance of the men who invented them as deities, the god of the Revolution would provide celestial confirmation of the people's virtue. "The true priest of the Supreme Being," Robespierre proclaimed, was nature itself, which bore witness to the "the joy of a great people assembled under his eyes to renew the bonds of universal fraternity."[96] He refrained from offering any logical or metaphysical arguments for the existence of God, and his repeated allusions to the social utility of religious belief invite speculation as to how firmly he believed his own rhetoric. Nevertheless, his devotion to Rousseau and admiration for the Savoyard vicar in *Émile* suggest that the speech of 18 floréal constituted a profession of faith as much as a political ploy. The distinctions Robespierre emphasized between himself and his opponents made clear that whether or not the divine existed in heaven, it would make its presence decisively felt on earth.

Like Rousseau's deity in *Émile*, Robespierre's Supreme Being offered crucial support for the conscience, to the extent that it comprises a sort of second human nature, or "rapid instinct" in moral matters. If the "Incorruptible," as Robespierre came to be called, had intended religion merely to provide a check on antisocial conduct by assuring recompense for the faithful and chastisement for the reprobate, then it would have been sufficient to maintain a version of orthodox Catholicism under a constitutional guise, or to adopt a Voltairean stance toward the need for theism on strictly moral grounds. Yet he definitively broke with these available traditions, not only because they fostered egoism rather than disinterestedness, but also because they perpetuated the idea of an aloof, monarchical, unacceptably transcendent God. Robespierre's understanding of virtue as patriotic abandon required an immanent, ever-present Supreme Being that would support a civic ideal demanding the dispossession of individuals. "Citizens owe everything to the *patrie*," he had asserted in defense of the events of August 10, "and the *patrie* owes nothing to citizens."[97] The promise of a spiritual divinity, then, validated the sacrifice owed to a resacralized body politic as it faced the existential threats of internal unrest and foreign invasion.

Robespierre concluded his speech of 18 floréal with a series of sweeping proposals, all of which the Convention enthusiastically approved. The recognition of God's existence and the duty to worship him now carried the force of law. A Festival of the Supreme Being was proclaimed for the following month of prairial, under the direction of David. Henceforth, the celebration of the divine would have pride of place each *décadi*, the period of rest to be observed every ten days under the new calendar. The festivals planned during a year-long cycle were to honor a particular revolutionary ideal, including nature, humankind, martyrs to liberty, love of the *patrie*, and disinterestedness. The decree was sent to public officials, political societies, and armies in the field, as well as posted prominently on every street. Robespierre's staunch ally Georges Couthon, a fellow member of the Committee of Public Safety, went so far as to demand that it be "translated into every language and distributed across the universe."[98]

The announcement of the decree also included a request that the public compose "civic hymns and songs" dedicated to the Supreme Being.

The Committee of Public Safety was charged with judging the contest and remunerating the authors of the most worthy submissions.[99] The response was resounding. The Committee soon found itself inundated with contributions that, along with the pieces eventually selected for the festivals in Paris and throughout France, rapidly furnished the Cult of the Supreme Being with a voluminous liturgy. To be sure, these works cannot be separated from the forceful (and initially successful) effort to popularize Robespierre's designs.[100] Nevertheless, they offer a rare glimpse, however partial, into the religious and political sensibilities of those citizens willing to pledge themselves to the new revolutionary faith.

The Supreme Being was a newly invented deity, whose creators and followers alike drew on previous theological and philosophical traditions in expressing their ideals. A Citizen Lortie, who sent in a series of couplets after reading an announcement in the *Moniteur*, emphasized the grandeur of the "master of the heavens" as manifest in the wonders of nature.[101] This motif marked many of the contributions emphasizing God's status as a benevolent creator and protector of humankind. "You, who shower us with gifts," begins an "Oraison républicaine," "we adore you without ceasing. [. . .] Author of nature, without you what would become of your poor creature?"[102] For the aspiring hymnist who submitted the "Cantique à l'Être suprême," the most compelling point of reference appears to be the Song of Songs. "You pierce my soul," he wrote to God as his beloved, "it is you who enflame me." The statements of devotion were punctuated by a repeated chorus of "my life is in you."[103] Other submissions, such as the prayer sent by Citizen Deshayer, petitioned the "supreme divinity" to ignite the "sacred fire of patriotism, which burns by the pure love of liberty, equality, justice, and obedience to the laws." "Enlighten every people of the world," he implored, by "annihilating fanaticism, superstition, despotism, and tyranny with truth, philosophy, and reason."[104] Tellingly, both Deshayer and the author of the "Cantique" had recourse to rhetoric associated with mystical spirituality—that of pure love and the eroticism of the Song of Songs, respectively—in depicting their reverence for the Supreme Being. At a moment when forms of mainstream Christian observance had fallen precipitously out of official favor, those of Quietist heretics remained remarkably salient.

Some of the more elaborate productions seized upon and amplified the mystical elements in the Incorruptible's Rousseauian refrains. Citizen Collandière, who prepared a speech for the Festival of the Supreme Being held in Villejuif, proceeded from denunciations of materialism and atheism to calls for a regenerated natural religion that disposes of the need for mediators between the human and the divine. The script for his intervention was Rousseau's "Profession de foi du vicaire savoyard." The simple contemplation of our own ignorance regarding the sublime expanse of nature, he assured his audience, instills an acute awareness of the perfect being beyond ourselves. Or, as Étienne-Louis Bézout of the Popular Society of Nemours put it, the "enchanting spectacle of nature has announced to the people the existence of a Supreme Being," and the "luminous globes that revolve ceaselessly above their heads make them feel its power."[105] These captivating sights provoke a desire for unity with the being who created them, which Collandière expressed, as did Bézout, with an unattributed reference to the vicar's prayer for self-annihilation: "Being of beings, I am because you are. [. . .] The most worthy use of my reason is to be debased before you. It is the rapture of my spirit, and the charm of my lowliness, to feel myself overcome by your grandeur."[106]

This sense of dispossession, moreover, produced insights into human existence. For Bézout it proved that the soul "emanates from Divinity," at once "subjected to the immutable laws of an intelligent being" and exerting its "empire" over material bodies. Collandière emphasized how the immortality of the soul assured by God should embolden citizens in the sacrifice of themselves for the *patrie*. "You can expose yourself to danger," he told his listeners, "you can face death, if you know that it cannot destroy you."[107] The revolutionary credo could be seen as employing spiritual principles drawn from *Émile* to revise Rousseau's position on civil religion in *Du Contrat social*.[108] In contrast to the latter work, which held that the Christian emphasis on otherworldly ends stifled love of country, the likes of Collandière and Bézout charted the two domains along the same physical and metaphysical continuum. Enlightened souls must surrender themselves to the exigencies of the *patrie* as readily as they would to the dictates of God as inscribed in nature. The human person's exemplary status made possible the momentary exertion of will in the service of spiritual and patriotic dispossession.

Whereas Collandière and Bézout emulated the Savoyard vicar, Plaisant de La Houssaye's *Hymne à la Nature*, a prose poem devoted to the elements of nature in all their manifestations and symbolic force, recalls Rousseau's *Rêveries*. Replaying the solitary walker's wanderings between hyperbolic self-sufficiency and existential lack, the lyricist marvels at how "it is in the heart of woods and forests that a profound silence purifies all the thoughts and lulls all the passions of man, and renders him to himself, to his nothingness, and carries the immortal soul toward the heavens." Fixing his gaze on the sky, Plaisant de La Houssaye recounts being dazzled by the sight and sound of a lightning storm—"I lose myself in space," he declares—when the fundamental unity of nature is revealed to him in a flash of inspiration. The tumultuous mutability of the atmosphere in no way diminishes the scope of its presence within and around all material forms. "Air, O universal fluid," he exclaims, "when the longest and most violent effort succeeds in separating you from other bodies, you nonetheless lose none of your characteristic properties." On the contrary, the transformations stemming from such disturbances sweep away "destructive vapors," and are thus "necessary in the general order of the government of the universe."[109]

These meditations, ostensibly gleaned from nature, also provide an allegory of the circumstances facing France, which was now likewise in the throes of casting off the sinister forces that conspired against it. Even in moments of silent retreat, the violence of the Terror marked the experiences of citizens. Reflecting on God or nature was inseparable from reflecting on the status of the citizen as an emanation—rather than a mere constitutive element—of the body politic. Rousseau had once turned to nature as solace in the face of the irredeemable social corruption that surrounded him. Plaisant de La Houssaye awaited the dawn of the peaceful and glorious era announced by the Festival of the Supreme Being. "Your cult will be eternal among us," he proclaimed—not only "like the love of liberty," but also "like the Republic, which your all-powerful arm will continue to protect."[110]

The Festival of the Supreme Being, first staged in Paris on 20 prairial Year II (June 8, 1794), enacted the confluence of divine and political power imagined by the revolutionary faithful. The proceedings commenced at first light, with men, women, and children emerging from their homes to join their fellow citizens at the meeting places of their particular sections. The entire city—private homes, government buildings, public monuments—was adorned in flags and garlands. At the sound of a drum roll, family members dispersed and took their places among the various divisions organized by gender and age. One by one, the sections assembled at the Jardin National (as the garden of the Tuileries was known after the fall of the king). There they were met by the deputies of the Convention, led by Robespierre in his capacity as president. The Incorruptible cut a resplendent figure in his azure-colored costume. Before those assembled stood a statue depicting the "monster" of atheism, surrounded by representations of "ambition, egoism, discord, and false simplicity." Robespierre approached the rostrum to address the people and their representatives. In their name he consecrated the occasion to the Supreme Being, who "from the beginning of time, decreed the Republic," and destined "for every age and every people, liberty, good faith, and justice." God, he intoned, "has created men to assist and to love one another," and "silences the passions [. . .] before the sublime love of the *patrie*. It is he who has covered nature in charms, riches, and majesty. All that is good is his work, or himself." Calling on every citizen to surrender to "the just transports of pure elation," Robespierre then advanced toward the statues in their midst, torch in hand, and set them ablaze. From the flames there emerged another figure, that of Wisdom, although perhaps not to the dazzling effect that David had intended; witnesses claimed that it had been slightly scorched in the fire.[111]

After a second speech from Robespierre, in which he bid an unfond farewell to scourge of godlessness that "the genius of kings had vomited on France," the procession made its way to the Festival's second station at the Champs de Mars, renamed the Champs de la Réunion. The spectator-participants assembled in designated groups around and upon an imposing mountain fashioned out of cardboard and plaster and crowned with a liberty tree. Taking their places, those gathered listened to a performance of Marie-Joseph Chénier's *Hymne à l'Être suprême*. They then broke into song, reciting the chants composed for the occasion and arranged in parts, with the stanza of each chorus answering the last. The ceremony reached its climax with a discharge of artillery, at which point, according to the official report in the *Moniteur*, "All the citizens, their sentiments melding in a fraternal embrace, ended the festival by raising toward heaven this cry of humanity and civic-mindedness: 'Vive la République!'"[112]

Robespierre and David had hoped that the wonders and rousing lyrics of the spectacle would serve as grounds for the communion of expansive selves at once occupying the same spiritual, sentimental, and political space. Under the sway of patriotic enthusiasm, the particular, individual, atomistic subject surrendered his mental and physical faculties and spoke in a voice belonging no longer to himself alone, but to the *patrie* in its entirety. Robespierre's ecstatic vow of martyrdom in his address of 18 floréal Year II invoked the spirit of Marat and announced his willingness to join the revolutionary fallen. In so doing, it also reminded his listeners of the ultimate test of political morality—self-sacrifice. In times of crisis, the citizen must die so that the *patrie* may live. Reverie as much as reason, and sacrifice as much as salvation, attended republican devotions. If, as Mona Ozouf has argued, revolutionary festivals celebrated a monumental "transfer of sacrality" from the old regime to the new, the individual citizen was destined to take part in this shift, not only as a determining subject who acted within the political field, but also as a determined object acted upon by the forces of God, nature, and *patrie*.[113]

The proselytizing mission to mold the French body politic into a single, indivisible whole was conceived in thought, expressed in word, and executed in deed as an unprecedented act of dispossession by all private citizens that would ultimately regenerate self-ownership as an attribute of collective, rather than individual, existence. Hébert and Cloots had deviated from Robespierre and Couthon on the means of affecting this sovereign end, but the two factions shared the same fundamental aim. Their ambition suggested not so much a turn toward theocracy, conceived of as clerical rule in the name of the divine, but toward the direct apotheosis of the people itself through its identification with God or nature. The political theology of the Terror thus marked the culmination of successive eighteenth-century movements to resacralize the world—to close the chasm between the human person and a transcendent God by reimagining the natural and political domains as absolute, totalizing forces with determining power over the self.

Radical Jacobins approached persistent challenges facing the new Republic—the limits of private ownership, the locus of sovereignty, and the observance of civil religion—in terms of fixing the human person's relationship to property, both within and outside the self. The first National Assembly had thrust this problem onto center-stage during the events of August 4, 1789, and it continued to vex subsequent legislative bodies as they struggled against economic dearth and popular demands for a fair share of the national wealth. While the Jacobin position defended individual property rights in name, its support was conditional on the subsistence of the body politic as a whole. In a similar manner, the Cult of the Supreme Being sought to affirm the dignity of human existence, yet moored it inextricably to the sacrifice of individual desires, and even individual identities, for sustaining the sacred bonds of the *patrie*. On both the spiritual and material fronts, self-ownership adhered first and foremost to the body politic as a whole, and dispossession remained the individual's perennial cross to bear.

The experiments launched during the Year II produced unforeseen dilemmas for the leaders of the revolutionary government. At the Festival of the Supreme Being, a heckler is said to have taunted Robespierre with a now-notorious epithet. "Look at the bugger," he supposedly grumbled. "It is not enough to be the master, he has to be a god as well."[114] The slight, although made in passing, captured a dangerous tension within the Jacobin political orthodoxy of the time: the Incorruptible, in seeking to cast out the demon of egoism, could also appear to be lording it over the body politic he sought to exorcise.[115] No matter how often or how loudly Robespierre proclaimed the need for representatives to sacrifice their particular interests on the altar of the *patrie*, his star turns in the Convention and at the Festival were bound to elicit accusations of Caesarism. Ironically, he had himself, in his report on political morality, described how the decline of republics led to the concentration of power in the hands of a single man.[116] Rousseau had good reason, it would seem, for relegating the quasi-divine legislator of *Du Contrat social* to a distant, mythical past.

More generally, the aspiring founders of Jacobin economic and religious institutions repeatedly discovered that the professed cornerstone of their work—the people—could also be their most formidable stumbling block. In a key speech before the Convention defending festivals as an integral part of public instruction, Billaud-Varenne observed that "the establishment of democracy in a nation that has long languished in irons can be compared to nature's effort in the surprising passage from nothingness to existence. [. . .] *It is necessary, so to speak, to recreate the people that one wants to restore to liberty.*" Representatives could not look upon this transformation as mere observers. Their duty required "strong action" toward "developing civic virtues and constraining the passions of cupidity, intrigue, and ambition." Billaud-Varenne beseeched his colleagues to instruct their fellow citizens in how "to cast off this baneful egoism, the impure remnant of the divisive monarchical system." The new republican regime embodied a radically different kind of order, predicated on "the fusion of all wills, interests, talents, and efforts." The ultimate aim, he argued, was to ensure that "each finds in this ensemble of common resources a portion of property equal to his stake." Patriotic festivals, such as that held in honor of the Supreme Being, performed a crucial function in this regard. Their aim was to inspire in the people a profound sense of civic ardor, defined by Billaud-Varenne as a "sublime principle of the abnegation of oneself," and to establish the impetus "to place their greatest pleasure in their union, and their joy in the general participation in the same transports and the same enjoyments [*jouissances*]."[117]

The Cult of the Supreme Being, proposals for economic reform, and calls for the establishment of political morality all became ensnared in an underpinning contradiction, inherited from Rousseau—that of striving to return to nature by meticulously directed, artificially imposed means. Human nature in particular could not safely be left to its own devices; it required constant oversight and intensive effort to transform self-absorbed individuals into self-abnegating citizens. The transformation would simultaneously have to be imposed from above and yet immediately work from within the deepest selves of representatives and represented alike. The proper operation of the republican institutions envisaged by Robespierre, Saint-Just, and other leading Jacobins depended on the prior existence of the very citizens they were designed to engender.[118] Unsurprisingly, their initiatives often failed to win over public opinion. The sans-culottes cursed the Maximum once it came to apply to wages as well as to commodities, and the Cult of the Supreme Being, while widely observed, seems never to have attracted sincere belief.[119] Ultimately, the Jacobin Republic's failure to break through its conceptual impasses doomed it to lethal vacillation between the ideals of Terror and virtue, property and subsistence, self-ownership and dispossession.

A Requiem for Equality

The people whose will Robespierre claimed to worship stood idly by during his fall. Two days after the Festival of the Supreme Being, the Convention passed the Law of 22 prairial Year II (June 10, 1794), which simplified almost to the point of nonexistence the legal procedures for dealing with political suspects. Henceforth, read the measure, the Revolutionary Tribunal would accept "any kind of document, whether material, moral, verbal, or written" in its campaign against the "enemies of the people."[120] The machinery of the Terror had begun to spin with such abandon that it threatened to run off its rails. During the months of June and July alone, the Tribunal sentenced more than 1,500 persons to the guillotine.[121] With the accelerated pace, the government risked dispatching its citizens with greater speed than it could devise institutions for fashioning their political morality.

By midsummer, deputies began to suspect that Robespierre was preparing another purge of the Convention. In the wake of the executions of the Dantonistes and Hébertistes, few harbored illusions as to what a new wave of repression would bring. Heartened by the resounding military success at Fleurus in June, which made Robespierre's renewed cries of *la patrie en danger* sound all the more estranged from reality, the legislators decided to take their stand. On 8 thermidor (July 26), Robespierre rose to denounce plots in the Committees of General Security and Public Safety and criticize the ruinous policies of the Finance Committee. He neglected, however, to draw up a specific list of traitors, which terrified many of those in attendance and satisfied none. The Convention split on whether to accept or to challenge his findings, and the conflict soon came to subsume the Jacobins as well. At the assembly's next session on 9 thermidor, Saint-Just was silenced as he began to read a report on the state of the government, and chaos ensued. That afternoon, the deputies voted for Robespierre's arrest, along with that of his younger brother Augustin, Saint-Just, Couthon, and Philippe-François-Joseph Lebas. A bizarre night and day ensued, which saw the captives escape to the Hôtel de Ville to join an insurrection haplessly staged by the Commune. As forces loyal to the Convention closed in, Lebas shot himself, while both Robespierre and Couthon botched their attempts at suicide. The following evening, the Incorruptible and his followers were guillotined, falling victim to the Terror that they had done so much to orchestrate.[122]

The anti-Robespierrist deputies who took charge of the Convention quickly set about dismantling the institutional and conceptual apparatus of the Year II. The Law of 22 prairial was rescinded on 14 thermidor (August 1), and the Revolutionary Tribunal fell into abeyance on 12 prairial Year III (May 31, 1795), once the deputies had concluded the business of score-settling with the fallen Robespierristes. Previously, on 4 nivôse

Year III (December 24, 1794), the government had decreed the abolition of the Maximum on prices and wages, presaging a return to economic liberalism.[123]

The Constitution of the Year III, ratified on 5 fructidor (August 22, 1795), affirmed the sanctity of individual property rights over and above the right of all to subsistence, references to which were withdrawn from the revised declaration of rights.[124] One of the chief architects of the document, François-Antoine de Boissy d'Anglas, specified that power no longer belonged to the people in accordance with the dictates of the general will, but to "those who possess property."[125] The constitution defined as citizens all men aged twenty-five and older who met a residency requirement, were inscribed on the civic register, and had paid taxes or a monetary sum equivalent to three days' wages. These men were entitled to participate in the primary assemblies, which chose the delegates to the electoral assemblies that determined who would sit in the bicameral national legislature. The second-degree electors were required to meet a substantial qualification—the equivalent of 150 to 200 days' labor, depending on the population of their locale, or the rent of a house or land of commensurate value. Executive power was vested in a rotating five-man Directory—the name by which the regime became known.[126] Although the fall of Robespierre did not put an end to republican government (on the contrary, it allowed a republican constitution to be enacted), it brought the attempts at social reorganization considered by some of his more experimentally minded colleagues to a grinding halt.

In religious matters, the Directory vainly sought to define a middle ground between Robespierre's plans for a state civil religion and a return to a Catholic status quo ante. Theophilanthropy, a self-proclaimed "institution of religious morality" codified by the bookseller Jean-Baptiste Chemin-Dupontès, received qualified support from the government, not least because of its embrace of the more moderate leanings of the new political establishment.[127] In his writings, Chemin-Dupontès presented the theophilanthropist as an industrious patriot, not a self-denying martyr. "Virtue," he held, "does not consist in the total renunciation of self-love [amour de soi]," but in "loving oneself truly," which entails calculating one's personal interests in light of the needs of one's fellow citizens. Similarly, he located happiness "neither in what one desires nor in what one lacks, *but in what one possesses* [emphasis added]"—that is, in oneself above all, but with a view to the felicity of others.[128] Although Chemin made a point of distancing himself from Robespierre and the Terror, the following that his movement attracted in Jacobin circles raised the suspicions of the government.[129]

The Directory thus kept vigilant guard against a resurgence of Jacobinism, and with it demands for the reinstatement of rights and securities promised in the Constitution of 1793.[130] The most spectacular attempt to revive the politics of the Year II—and the most disastrous—was the Conspiracy of Equals. As its name suggests, this movement aimed at ousting the Directory, restoring the previous constitution, and, after a period of revolutionary dictatorship, establishing a new government committed to political and economic equality. Its name is now synonymous with that of Gracchus (François-Noël) Babeuf, a former specialist in feudal law turned agrarian revolutionist and political agitator. During the early years of the Revolution, he served as a municipal and departmental official around northern France, but in 1794, he was arrested on suspicion of fraud. Released from prison on the eve of Thermidor, he had welcomed Robespierre's overthrow. Nevertheless, he continued to idealize the Incorruptible's proposed declaration of rights.[131] An enigmatic figure, Babeuf sought virtue without terror, and spiritual regeneration without recourse to traditional faith. Like those of many of his fellow radicals, including Robespierre and the adherents of Marat's cult, his political views found inspiration in religious sources. The historian Eric Walter has shown how Babeuf, although a committed atheist, drew on strands of "millenarian prophecy" in articulating his egalitarian vision for France and his role in its regeneration. He regarded himself as a visionary, even an apostle of a sacred cause—that of the "paradise of equals"—for which he was willing to sacrifice himself if necessary.[132]

Babeuf's journal *Le Tribun du peuple* preached this gospel. After a series of run-ins with the new authorities, including another stint in jail, he published a "Manifesto of the Plebians" in late November 1795. The work virulently denounced the Thermidoreans' commitment to private property as an affront to natural right. "The happiness of the people," Babeuf asserted, depended on circumscribing the exercise of individual ownership within truly social bounds. Drawing on the precedents of Rousseau, Morelly (whom he confused with Diderot, owing to the widespread belief that the latter had written *Code de la nature*), and Robespierre, Babeuf championed the "equality of fact" over merely formal rights. This new order of things would be both spiritual and material in character. It would usher in a "religion of pure equality," with the "first code of nature" as its animating moral principle. Redemption would take the form of a massive "equalization" in society, so that each citizen and his family could expect to receive "what is sufficient, but nothing more." Achieving these ends, he argued, depended on establishing a "common administration" to coordinate labor and to distribute goods and revenues in a fair and rational manner across the economy.[133]

A call to arms composed by the inveterate radical Sylvain Maréchal, who became a fellow traveler in Babeuf's movement, also sought to prepare the ground for an impending revolt. For centuries, Maréchal observed, enemies of the people had preached that "equality of fact is only a chimera," so that one should remain content with a "conditional equality [. . .] before the law." Now was the time, at last, for "another revolution," the watchwords of which would be "real equality or death." The plotters proclaimed their willingness not only to lay down their lives for their cause, but "to make a tabula rasa" of the social order. "If it is necessary," Maréchal admitted, "let all the arts perish, provided that real equality remains." Not satisfied with the proposals for agrarian reform discussed during the Terror, he and Babeuf called for nothing less than communism, or "the Community of Goods," and the abolition of "individual property" in land. They declared open war against "the egoist" and "his exclusive enjoyment of possessions [*jouissance*], solitary pleasures, and personal comforts." In place of a regime installed by "lovers of absolute power," they championed a return to the Constitution of 1793 as a prelude to establishing a true "Republic of Equals."[134]

Babeuf and his circle, which now included a Montagnard faction of former deputies of the Convention, hammered out the details for their insurrection, which they planned to launch by staging a "Day of the People" at the end of floréal Year IV (late May 1796). To publicize their goals, they distributed thousands of copies of *L'Analyse de la doctrine de Babeuf*. The tract was less radical than Babeuf's and Maréchal's manifestos in that rather than proclaiming communism to be an outright aim, it merely advocated a return to the Constitution of 1793, which the militants claimed had been illegally repealed.[135] Although Babeuf is unlikely to have been the author of the document, it nonetheless expressed the substance of his platform—even if the means of its execution remained unclear. "Nature has given to each man an equal right to the enjoyment of possession [*jouissance*] of all goods," the first article read, declaring that "no one is able, without crime, to appropriate the goods of the earth or of industry exclusively to himself." Additional articles called for social egalitarianism in the form of the mandatory redistribution of wealth, the right to work, and universal education, as well as retaliation against those responsible for imposing the current constitutional regime.[136]

The Equals, despite their name, were by no means all of uniform political cast. While Babeuf and his Italian comrade Filippo Buonarroti were essentially communists who demanded the socialization of the means of production, the Jacobins among them dreamed of a reversion to the policies pursued under Robespierre. This lack of ideological cohesion, coupled with poor tactical coordination and material support, would soon undermine their plans for revolt. The "Insurrectional Directory" in charge of the plot appointed agents in each arrondissement of the capital and attempted to recruit supporters from the army and the police. All the while, however, the government, aided by an informer, was closing in on the group. When the leaders of the insurrection assembled on 21 floréal Year IV (May 10, 1796) to make final arrangements for the Day of the People, they were met by the police. Babeuf and his codefendants stood trial for advocating the overthrow of the Constitution of the Year III, a crime that had been declared punishable by death. On 7 prairial Year V (May 26, 1797), the court finally rendered its verdict: Babeuf and another conspirator were to be executed, the others deported.[137]

Although Babeuf's plot met with no practical success and an ambivalent response even among self-professed Jacobins, his supporters predicted that their ideals would live long after him.[138] It would be left to the adherents of later movements—romanticism, socialism, and anarchism, in particular—to derive from the lessons of the Year II other methods for recasting dispossessive personhood as a positive ideal that could also accommodate the individualist imperatives for self-expression and autonomy. For the most part, however, such efforts were fated to remain on the cultural and ideological defensive. Among proponents of self-ownership, such as Sieyès, the Thermidorean Boissy d'Anglas, and the leaders of successive postrevolutionary regimes, the Terror imparted a grave lesson: the human person's capacity for dispossession threatened to unleash a destructive furor that only the strong hand of political, social, and intellectual authority could contain. Yet even with the apparent victory of the cause of individualism, its champions could never fully be free of the opposing forces against which they had defined themselves over the course of the eighteenth century.

Epilogue

Constructing the postrevolutionary order required politicians, jurists, scientists, and philosophers to elaborate in intricate detail the connections between individual subjects and the property they claimed. Despite significant variations in emphasis, epistemology, and disciplinary orientation among the authors who committed themselves to this enterprise, all took it as axiomatic that the right to property derived from the self's natural and inalienable ownership of and accountability for its own existence. Similar formulations could be found in the work of Descartes and Locke, and French theorists of modern individualism made liberal use of their writings. Yet they also took the arguments gleaned from these predecessors in original directions. Whereas seventeenth- and eighteenth-century proponents of self-ownership often found themselves in embattled positions, their nineteenth-century heirs could proceed without having to defend their central premises at every turn. What had once been a debatable, even dubious proposition—the human person's status as an autonomous, possessive subject—became the obligatory point of departure for thinking about the self. The language and logics of dispossession did not simply fall into abeyance, however, but were appropriated and adapted by latter-day thinkers who sought to mitigate, if not neutralize altogether, the effects of rampant individualism.

Although the Directory had already turned away from the Jacobin ideal of equality, Napoleon Bonaparte's Civil Code of 1804, which realized long-held hopes for a nationwide legal apparatus, made clear that this repudiation would become permanent. The master category of the new fundamental law was property, defined as "the right to enjoy the possession [*jouir*] and to dispose of things in the most absolute manner." Despite allowing certain restrictions, such as the enforcement of eminent domain, the Code expounded at length upon the axiomatic status of ownership. Following the tradition of natural jurisprudence exemplified by Locke's *Second Treatise of Government*, property was rooted in the right to self-preservation. A report appended to the Code clarified the matter further, by rejecting arguments for an original community of goods in the state of nature. If "Providence offers its gifts universally," it does so strictly "for the utility and needs of individuals, for there are only individuals on the earth." Individuality and property were to be regarded as logically and metaphysically inseparable. Since "the principle of the right is in us" alone, it followed that "it is not the result of a human convention or a positive law." On the contrary, it is located "in the constitution of our being, and in our different relations with the objects that surround us." According to the commentators, the scope of ownership had expanded over time in terms both of quantity and quality, thereby "completing the great work of creation." Property was the institution that "founded human societies," and, as a moral force, it "has enlivened, extended, and enlarged our own existence."[1]

This account was intended to forestall opposition to the Napoleonic regime, especially by critics who claimed that possession in common represented a natural state of affairs that could and ought to be restored.[2] Donald Kelley and Bonnie Smith have observed how, to combat this heresy, the legal profession consecrated itself as the "high priests" of the "religion of property" enshrined in the Civil Code.[3] Among the most esteemed members of this juridical clergy was Jean-Baptiste-Victor Proudhon, professor of law at the University of Dijon and, as fate would have it, a cousin of the prominent socialist Pierre-Joseph Proudhon. His highly influential *Traité du domaine de propriété* (1839) sought to defend property, not only as a legal convention, but also as an institution in conformity with God's dictates and the standards of morality. At the center of these concentric justifications stands the figure of the self-owning individual, proclaimed on the first pages of the treatise to be the "king of nature," with "all other beings [. . .] destined for his service and use." According to Proudhon, property refers by definition to an exclusive relation between the self and an object, or "that which is our own to the exclusion of all others." No good, properly speaking, falls under collective ownership; rather, each proprietor should be said to hold "his numerical portion."[4]

Proudhon appealed explicitly to divine authority as well as to worldly reason in describing the ties that bind individuals to their properties. Since the "author of nature" orders that the "personal qualities of man [. . .] belong to him alone," it would be sacrilege to define the precise status of these existential goods. The emphasis of the *Traité* turns instead to answering the question of why the earth, which has been given to humankind in general, should be subject to private property. Individuals, Proudhon observed, are naturally inclined toward "covetousness" and other manifestations of self-love. Even so, the recognition that one's desires cannot be fulfilled without the assistance of one's fellows leads, not only to the division of property, but also to mutual respect for the rights of others. Thus, even before the institution of formal laws, claims to the possession of an object derive from the prerogatives of first occupancy or the investment of labor.[5]

Although these arguments draw on precedents established in scriptural tradition and natural law, Proudhon was innovative in his understanding of the political and moral functions of property. According to the "public administration," he noted, one's belongings serve as a "visible sign" of personal virtue, since propertied citizens can be expected also to possess estimable moral attributes, such as "probity, morality, the love of public tranquility, [and] the love of work." Thus, political power should be reserved for these citizens alone. In contrast, those without property tend to lack the qualities necessary, not only to lead, but even to follow. Proudhon justified this claim by citing the tumult of the Revolution, which he blamed on "fanatical proletarians in their clubs."[6] For decades, theologians and philosophers had argued that moral accountability, and therefore moral conduct, depended upon possessing a self that could maintain vigilance over thoughts and actions. In affirming their views, Proudhon lent credence to the legal status quo. The "juridical individual"—increasingly seen, not only as propertied, but also as married and male—would henceforth be the foremost subject of the French body politic.[7]

Despite the plethora of arguments Proudhon and his colleagues generated, the very presence in the Civil Code of a codicil defending property—not only as an incontrovertible right, but also as grounded in the nature of human personhood—serves as a stark reminder of both propositions' beleaguered past. This book has sought to demonstrate that the self's relation to property remained a vehemently contested issue throughout the Old Regime and the first years of the Revolution. The possessions in dispute were not limited to material objects or financial instruments, but also included the spiritual and existential goods believed necessary for exercising moral agency in this life and obtaining salvation in the next. In some cases, French citizens struggled to assert their rights of ownership despite the government's resistance. In particular, the holders of ennobling posts and other *privilèges* found their status repeatedly challenged by the crown, which maintained that it had granted these rights provisionally, and thus could rescind them.

The human person's possessive inclinations emerged as a crucial problematic in the late seventeenth century, with the explosion of venal office-holding in the fiscal domain and the surge of mysticism in post-Tridentine Gallican spirituality. In response, an array of views—expressed in works by theologians such as Bossuet and Bergier, moderate philosophes such as Montesquieu and Voltaire, and theorists of luxury such as Butel-Dumont— gradually coalesced into a culture of self-ownership. Its proponents, who also included consumers of new ideas and novel goods across the social spectrum, envisioned the human person as the proprietor of its being, its actions, and all other possessions that it might legitimately acquire. In vitriolic opposition to such claims, an anti-individualist culture of dispossession, propagated by Christian mystics, materialist philosophes, and radical republicans, valorized the abdication of ownership over oneself and external objects. Devout souls abandoned themselves to God out of Quietist fervor, and patriotic martyrs surrendered their lives for the glory of the nation. These were not spontaneous occurrences, but concerted actions undertaken with a preconceived end in mind—the submission of the self to totalizing forces capable of negating its identity and directing its will.

The competing ideals of self-ownership and dispossession structured a wide range of polemics that erupted over matters of fundamental significance to the spiritual, cultural, and political orders of Enlightenment-era France, including the role of personal interest in Christian devotion, the nature of free will, the limits of moral agency, the dangers of luxury consumption, and the location and exercise of national sovereignty. These controversies and scandals ran the gamut of movements that captivated public opinion in the eighteenth century, from Quietism to Spinozism and materialism, from royal absolutism to democratic republicanism, and from proto-capitalist visions of political economy to the first modern articulations of socialism. The main antagonists in debates over the self did not respect the partisan lines that scholars have commonly associated with the Enlightenment. Orthodox theologians and mainstream philosophes could and did find common cause—in the defense of self-ownership—against the efforts of radical mystics and materialists to dispossess the individual of its prerogatives and status as an autonomous, thinking subject.

From the perspective of these debates, the Enlightenment no longer appears exclusively secular either in its origins or orientation. On the contrary, it was as much a movement within theology as a reaction against it. Every thinker writing about the self during the period—even self-professed atheists—formed his views with theological questions in mind. At the conceptual level, moreover, the affinities shared by mystics and materialists in their elaborations of the dispossessed self reveal another aspect of the secularization process. Unlike defenders of self-ownership, whose growing perception of divine transcendence compelled them to stress the fundamental autonomy of the human person, advocates of dispossession invoked God and nature as immanent, totalizing forces with absolute dominion over the self. Their efforts to resacralize the world culminated in the French

Revolution, when politicians and citizens alike devoted themselves to self-sacrifice for the *patrie*—a polity that in their eyes radiated the authority of natural and divine law combined with the people's indivisible will.

As this study has shown, the modern subject had a long and painful birth. Individualism arose neither fully formed nor without opposition, but through intense conflicts and unprecedented conjunctures. Indeed, as late as 1840, Alexis de Tocqueville could still remark on the sheer novelty of the term *individualisme* in French.[8] The gradual acceptance in France of the idea of the individualist self—defined by personal identity, autonomy, and agency—hinged on the matter of the human person's relationship to spiritual, existential, and material goods. Without establishing the self's ownership of its thoughts and actions along with its belongings, property in all its forms would remain insecure. The Thermidorean reaction neutralized the dispossessive politics that dominated France for a brief, bloody phase during the Year II, and the regimes that followed reaffirmed their commitment to the institutionalization of property rights established in 1789. During the postrevolutionary period, defenders of self-ownership set about fashioning their ideals into a coherent political, economic, and pedagogical framework. It is more than telling that "individualism" only entered into common usage at this time. Even then, the term carried mainly negative connotations.[9] The modern self—whether known as the *moi*, the *individu*, or by any other name—would continue to bear the ambiguities of its origins.

. . .

The defense of self-ownership remained a constant refrain through the numerous and often sudden shifts in philosophical fashion that attended the rapid regime changes of the first half of the nineteenth century. For instance, Antoine-Louis-Claude Destutt de Tracy, the chief exponent of the philosophical system of *idéologie* that dominated intellectual life during the Directory, saw clarifying the nature and status of property as indispensable for consolidating the sensationalist school of psychology in France. He reminded students who read his *Éléments d'idéologie* (1801–1815) that man should not be regarded merely an impression-receiving machine. As a being endowed with will, he also has active "needs and means" and "rights and duties." Destutt de Tracy considered these attributes to be ways of *"having"* or *"possessing* a thing," and he defined them accordingly as "forms of *property* [*espèces de* propriétés], to adopt the most general sense of the term" [emphasis in the original]. Thus conceived, property stems to a significant degree from the "idea of personality." As Destutt de Tracy explained, "if an individual did not have consciousness of his own existence as distinct and separate from all others, he could possess nothing; he would be unable to have anything that belonged to him alone [*qui lui fut propre*]." Although Destutt de Tracy equated the self (the *je* or *moi*, in his parlance) with one's personal faculty of sensation, rather than with a purely noncorporeal entity, doing so reinforced his central point: property (in this case, the possession of a faculty) is the essential quality of individual human existence. As if to underscore the strength of this equation, and the durability of the relationship it defines, he granted that the term "soul" (*âme*) could also be used to describe a person. "The *self* [moi] of each of us," he asserted, "is for him his own sensibility, [. . .] or that which is called the soul [*âme*]" [emphasis in the original].[10]

The *Éléments d'idéologie* elaborated his position still further, arguing that the tendency to conflate one's will with oneself galvanizes a sense of personal identity. "As soon as this individual knows clearly his *self* [moi] or his moral person," an awareness fostered through the exercise of the will, "he also sees clearly that this *self* is the exclusive proprietor of the body that it animates, of the organs that it moves, of all its faculties, of all its forces, [and] of all the effects they produce" [emphasis in the original]. One's sense of self, then, entails moral accountability for one's actions. It also gives rise to "the idea of property" in its conventional, legal forms. In Destutt de Tracy's system, these two "orders of things"—the moral and the economic—remain "intimately united" as manifestations of self-ownership. Even if the exigencies of analysis require that they be examined separately, it remains the case that "we would not have ownership of any of our possessions whatsoever, if we did not have ownership of our needs, which is nothing other than ownership of our sentiments."[11] The essential constitution of the human person, then, determines the essential constitution of the social order, which likewise turns on the capacity to appropriate ideas, actions, and material objects to one's person, as extensions of one's self. For Destutt de Tracy and his fellow *idéologues*, the *cogito* could be more aptly described as a *possideo*. This idea of the self brought the sociopolitical domain in line with the operations of the human mind and body.

As the Civil Code makes clear, Destutt de Tracy was by no means alone in associating individuality with property. Yet despite the prominence of the *idéologues* in intellectual life after Thermidor, their account of personhood failed to achieve canonical status. As Jan Goldstein argues in her study of the self during the period, it was rather the philosopher Victor Cousin who, more than any other figure, succeeded in enshrining individualism as a key component in the French educational system during the first half of the nineteenth century. Cousin blamed the deadly upheavals of the Revolution on the inability of sensationalist psychology to support a stable, cohesive, and self-governing subject. In its place, he and his supporters advanced a neo-Cartesian understanding of the human person as inherently spiritual and metaphysically prior to the vicissitudes of material existence. The July Revolution of 1830 catapulted Cousin into the upper echelons of the political establishment. From posts in the Royal Council of Public Instruction, the Institute, the French Academy, and the Chamber of Peers, as well as in his capacity as president of the jury overseeing the *aggrégation* in philosophy, he set about disseminating the ideal of the willful, autonomous, introspective individual with remarkable success. Soon his doctrines held sway over the École normale supérieure and the Faculty of Letters in Paris, and permeated the instruction of philosophy in *lycées* throughout France.[12]

In keeping with Cousin's pronounced antipathy for sensationalism, Goldstein has stressed the sharp divisions between his philosophical vision and the system professed by the *idéologues*.[13] Yet both sides shared similar views on two fundamental and related points: the human person's possessive relationship to itself, and the status of this relationship as the linchpin of the social order. In his lectures for a course on the history of eighteenth-century moral philosophy taught at the Faculty of Letters during the academic year 1819–1820, Cousin defended the power of a "free being" to resist the "blind forces" of sensation. "The self [*moi*]," he countered, "draws from itself alone its movements and its actions." Although he admitted that "I can and even must enter into communication with the objects that surround me," it remains the case that "my eternal law is the independence of the person in the face of things." Nevertheless, to act on the outside world and manifest its will, the self needs its body, a "property" that shares in "the inviolability of my person" through the work performed on and through it.[14]

In a similar vein, Cousin expressed dissatisfaction with the Lockean tabula rasa, which on his view inaccurately portrays the mind as lacking its own faculties prior to sense experience.[15] However, such criticism did not prevent Cousin from endorsing a brand of epistemological self-ownership that bears close resemblance to the labor theory of property featured in the *Second Treatise of Government*. "Our first property is ourselves," he declared in the introduction to his course at the Faculty of Letters. The individual's thoughts form "the first product of the intelligence and of the will"; it is from this initial act of appropriation that all others derive. The body and additional material objects together "participate in some manner in my personality by my acquiring them," so that they become extensions of their owner and share in the liberty that defines him.[16]

Thus, while Cousin departed significantly from the sensationalists when delimiting the corporeal aspects of selfhood, he followed them and their predecessor, Locke, in taking the rights of man in a most literal sense, as part of the store of personal possessions that accrued to the human person by its very nature.[17] Furthermore, the existential reality codified in these rights is to his mind not merely natural but, in its own way, holy. Since "the person is free, sacred, [and] inviolable," he explained, "all that which depends on him is equally inviolable and sacred."[18] No intellectual argument, social convention, or political obligation can mitigate the human person's intimate attachment to himself or to his rightful belongings. Within this scheme, self-ownership functions as a bulwark against any attempt—such as the efforts of both radical mystics and radical philosophes—to resacralize nature and the political domain by endowing them with immanent precedence over the will of individuals. Cousin contended that to dispossess the self in this way is not merely anathema but a physical and metaphysical impossibility.

For all his emphasis on individual autonomy, Cousin nonetheless openly recognized the limits imposed by external forces. Thus, one has a "person," which functions by "ceaselessly colliding with things," as well as a "soul that acts on itself within the fetters of a body." While acknowledging these burdens, he also held that the self retains its own spiritual and intellectual resources, independent of sense experience or matter.[19] In particular, reason exerts a formidable influence—and in Cousin's taxonomy, one beyond suspicion. This faculty, he maintains, "speaks to me with an absolute authority" and "dictates to me all my duties and all my rights." Since it "commands and governs me," reason is "superior to me" and thus must also originate not from within the self or from the vantage point of any particular individual, but "from on high."[20] On this reckoning, the self is the paragon of freedom, yet beholden to laws explicitly foreign to it. Goldstein has aptly described this paradox in both practical and genealogical terms. Not only does Cousin's "combination of 'personal will' and 'impersonal reason'" allow for "a thrilling degree of individuality" that buttresses the bourgeois male subject's sense of social superiority, but it also conceals "a decidedly self-abnegating model of selfhood" that could restrain subversive behavior. The Cousinian formula, she argues, offers a near-classic example of the dynamic that Foucault would later describe in *Discipline and Punish,* by which individuals, despite but also by virtue of their autonomous natures, become the constituted "objects" as well as the constitutive "instruments" of the power that produces them.[21]

When describing the "substance" of the "necessary, universal, [and] absolute truths" conveyed to the mind by reason, Cousin cited Fénelon, whose *Démonstration de l'existence de Dieu* offered proof of their divine provenance.[22] It is telling that he would have recourse at such a juncture not merely to a "mystic," but to a convinced "Quietist" whose thought verged on "heterodoxy."[23] Yet the dispossessive stance toward the self for which Fénelon had been condemned marked the limit of self-ownership for Cousin, even if he had no intention of advocating the sacrifice of individual will to the divine. On the contrary, the identification of God with reason reinforces the human person's nature as a possessive subject, and corroborates Cousin's view that reason originates outside the self, in the heavens.

Cousin's curious appropriation of Fénelon provides further confirmation of a far more fundamental shift in the cultural terrain. Enlightenment-era France witnessed a long chain of controversies pitting the partisans of self-ownership against those of dispossession. Yet by the mid-nineteenth century, dispossessive personhood had lost significant ground. A defender of self-ownership could feel at liberty not only to allude to one of its most notorious exponents, but to do so in support of a dramatically antithetical characterization of the self. It is not as if religious models of interiority—even those with mystic elements—had suddenly ceased to have appeal. Cousin's model of the self is deeply spiritual in orientation. Furthermore, as Goldstein has shown, prominent figures such as Ernest Renan could find ways of reconciling Catholic influences with the new political and metaphysical orthodoxy.[24] Rather, the problematic that triggered and then sustained the eighteenth-century debates—the human person's relationship to spiritual, existential, and material goods—no longer engaged public debate as it once did. The self's possessive attachments had gained acceptance as what Cousin and his theological predecessors both proclaimed them to be—sanctified and entirely beyond dispute.

. . .

One final example illustrates this reconfiguration of the stakes involved in contesting the nature of selfhood. Among Cousin's detractors, not surprisingly, was Pierre-Paul Proudhon, a leading French socialist of the era and author of *Qu'est-ce que la propriété?* (1840), a sweeping attack on the political order of the July Monarchy, perhaps most celebrated for introducing the enigmatic and oft-misinterpreted axiom "Property is theft."[25] Proudhon aimed not merely to denounce the poverty and hardship caused by economic stratification, but also to redefine the category of property itself. In particular, he dismissed as both illogical and immoral the notion that property should be regarded as a natural right. For instance, the supposed privileges of first occupants might account for the origins of simple possession, but they cannot justify exclusive claims of ownership. This difficulty, Proudhon claimed, derives from a slippage in the linguistic use of the term "property," which could refer both to a metaphysical attribute or a legal and social fact, "the quality by which a thing is what it is," as well as "the right of dominion of a free and intelligent being over a thing." Whatever their differences on other fronts, Proudhon condemned Destutt de Tracy and Cousin together for conflating distinct and separate meanings of the term. This error, he continued, led both thinkers to defend private property on the specious grounds that material acquisitions hold the same exalted status as innate personal qualities. In their works, Proudhon alleged, "the possession of things was likened to property in the powers [*avantages*] of the body and the mind, and on this false analogy was based the right to property."[26]

Qu'est-ce que la propriété? takes direct aim at arguments equating personhood and private property. "Man is not even the proprietor of his faculties," Proudhon retorted; nature is their original source. To universalize the subjective, qualitative right to material property only complicates matters, especially given the finite quantity of worldly objects. Likewise, the thesis that labor leads to ownership collapses with the acknowledgement of scarcity, especially in the case of land. Claiming a plot for oneself deprives one's fellows of a resource necessary for their survival, thereby infringing on the natural right to self-preservation. It is futile, moreover, to demand that individuals live off the proceeds of their personal labor when their subsistence requires the contributions of hundreds, if not thousands, of others. Proudhon asserted that these and all other rationales for exclusive property actually lead to the opposite conclusion—the necessity of equality.[27]

Notwithstanding his criticism of contemporaries such as Destutt de Tracy and Cousin, Proudhon had no wish to do away either with property or with the concept of individualism on which it was based. Even in *Qu'est-ce que la propriété?*, perhaps the most strident of his texts on the subject, Proudhon rejects the establishment of a "systematic community" to socialize the means of production. Such an arrangement, he argues, would leave the citizen "stripped of his *self* [moi; emphasis in original], his spontaneity, his genius, [and] his affections" and under the obligation to "annihilate himself before the majesty and the inflexibility" of the collective. He called instead for a third way between the regimes of private property and communism, where "the respective independence of individuals, or the autonomy of private reason, deriving from differences in talents and abilities," can coexist with the "equality of conditions." Among members of such a society, the possession of each to the benefit of all, rather than the rapacious designs of the rich against the poor, would be the guiding principle.[28]

In his later works, Proudhon dramatically revised his position to include a prominent place for property once it has been purged of the potential for abuse. According to the posthumously published *Théorie de la propriété* (1866), property serves as "the greatest revolutionary force that exists and that can oppose the power" of an ever-expanding state. When moderated through social institutions that decentralize power and redistribute wealth, it forms the crucible in which "the individual self—asocial, avaricious, envious, jealous, full of pride and bad faith—is transfigured and makes himself like the common self, his master and model." In elaborating these developments, Proudhon had no desire to "combat individualism as the enemy of liberty and equality." Not unlike Cousin, he held that the ideal of freedom "is essentially, if not exclusively, individualist." Even if one could dispense with the individual as the basis for society, doing so would ultimately lead to a "barbarous communism."[29] As his commentators have observed, and he explicitly acknowledged, individuals and their property are not to be overthrown, but rather revamped in a social system that strives to render the benefits of being and having a self accessible to all its participants.[30]

It is tempting to regard the project outlined in *Théorie de la propriété* as yet another effort to conjure up the forms of communal self-ownership gestured toward, albeit on different grounds, in d'Holbach's *Système de la nature* and Rousseau's *Contrat social*. Yet the terms of synthesis are markedly different. The radical philosophes advanced their claims by first dispossessing the self of false pretensions to agency and autonomy before elaborating an alternative sociopolitical order. Proudhon reversed their procedure, and thus modified their intended outcome. For him, meaningful change begins with the reform of property. Yet there is little need, in his eyes, to undermine the specific understanding of the human person that had come to justify private ownership. Although he had expressed opposition to the self's possessive attachments in *Qu'est-ce la propriété?* with his remark that individuals cannot even be said to own their own bodies, his subsequent criticisms of communism in the same work recoil from a doctrine that would too brazenly dispossess the self of its intellectual and physical faculties. Also noteworthy is his discussion of the Quietist controversy in one of his final writings, *De la Justice dans la Révolution et dans l'Église* (1860), where he explicitly sides with Bossuet over Fénelon on the grounds that "the most powerful love is that which is most ardently possessive [*le plus ardent à la possession*]." The latter's condemnation, he opines, "was one of the wisest and most fortunate acts of the Holy See."[31] Proudhon contents himself with identifying the lapses in the logical sequence that binds the individualist subject to corrupt elements in the institution of private property. He does not go so far as to deny the legitimacy of self-ownership as a fundamental attribute of personhood. On the contrary, he evidently viewed it as a natural, permanent fixture that could be modified, but never abolished.

The unexpected similarities between Cousin and Proudhon indicate the degree to which the culture of self-ownership, now under the guise of full-fledged individualism, stood as an insurmountable bulwark in French politics and philosophy. Even those who, like Proudhon, desired radical social change also sought to preserve individualism in a rehabilitated form. To admit the existence of property in one's person did not necessarily entail defending exclusive ownership in the material realm. It was possible to criticize injustice in the legal and political order without undermining the forms of personhood on which it was based. The self, at least for the time being, was no longer in question.

Note on Abbreviations and Translations

AN   Archives nationales, Paris
BN   Bibliothèque nationale de France, Paris
BMD   Bibliothèque municipale de Dijon

For the titles of works published before the twentieth century, I have generally retained the original spelling and punctuation in the Notes and Bibliography. Unless indicated otherwise, all translations from French into English are my own. Wherever possible, I have relied on English translations of primary and secondary sources originally published in languages other than French.

Notes

1. *Arrest de la cour de Parlement rendu contre Maistre Philibert Robert* (Paris: Jean-Baptiste Langlois, 1698), 3–6; quotations, 3–4. For further discussion of this case, see chapter 3.

2. BMD, Fonds Patrimoine, Ms. 335/MIC 528, f.4.

3. Ibid., Ms. 333/MIC 527, f. 19, and Ms. 335/MIC 528, f. 51. On these trials in Dijon, see also Henri Pensa, *Sorcellerie et religion: Du Désordre dans les esprits et dans les mœurs aux XVIIe et XVIIIe siècles* (Paris: Félix Alcan, 1933), 197–238.

4. *Édit du Roi, Portant suppression des Jurandes & Communautés de Commerce, Arts & Métiers* (February 1776) (Paris: Imprimerie royale, 1776). On the corporations and Turgot's attempt to suppress them, see William H. Sewell Jr., *Work and Revolution in France: The Language of Labor from the Old Regime to 1848* (Cambridge: Cambridge University Press, 1980), 25–39, 72–77, and Steven Laurence Kaplan, *La Fin des corporations*, trans. Béatrice Vierne (Paris: Fayard, 2001), 77–165.

5. BN, Manuscripts, Collection Joly de Fleury, vol. 596, f. 114, *Observations des maitres-gantiers*, quoted in Jan Goldstein, "Foucault and the Post-Revolutionary Self: The Uses of Cousinian Pedagogy in Nineteenth-Century France," in *Foucault and the Writing of History*, ed. Goldstein (Cambridge, Mass.: Blackwell, 1994), 100. See also Goldstein, *The Post-Revolutionary Self: Politics and Psyche in France, 1750–1850* (Cambridge, Mass.: Cambridge University Press, 2005), 38–43.

6. Jacques-Vincent Delacroix, *Mémoire à consulter, sur l'existence des six corps, & la conservation de leurs privilèges* (Paris: P. G. Simon, 1776), 12–16; quotations, 16, 12 . For Locke's argument, see John Locke, *Second Treatise of Government*, in *Two Treatises of Government*, ed. Peter Laslett (Cambridge: Harvard University Press, 1988), 287–288.

7. BN, Manuscripts, Collection Joly de Fleury, v. 462, fol. 112, *Mémoire à consulter, pour la communauté des Fabriquans de Chapeaux, établie à Paris, sur l'extinction des Jurandes & Communautés* ([Paris]: Cailleau, 1776), 5.

8. *Rémonstrances du Parlement de Paris au XVIIIe siècle*, ed. Jules Flammeront (Paris: Imprimerie nationale, 1898), 3: 346, 370, 385.

9. For an overview of historical semantics of the term *individualisme* in France, see Steven Lukes, *Individualism* (Oxford: Basil Blackwell, 1973), 3–16.

10. See C. B. Macpherson, *The Theory of Possessive Individualism: Hobbes to Locke* (Oxford: Oxford University Press, 1962), and Louis Dumont, *Homo Aequalis I: Genèse et épanouissement de l'idéologie économique* (Paris: Gallimard, 1997), esp. 68–75. For an overview of recent scholarship on self-ownership, see Duncan Kelly, *The Propriety of Liberty: Persons, Passions and Judgement*

in Modern Political Thought (Princeton, N.J.: Princeton University Press, 2011), 261–269.

11. In addition to Macpherson's work, see Charles Taylor, *Sources of the Self: The Making of Modern Identity* (Cambridge: Cambridge University Press, 1989), esp. 127–198; Louis Dumont, *Essais sur l'individualisme: Une Perspective anthropologique sur l'idéologie moderne* (Paris: Éditions du Seuil, 1991), esp. 35–133. These prominent examples represent only a sample of the scholarship on eighteenth-century individualism. Other notable studies include Ian Watt, *Myths of Modern Individualism: Faust, Don Quixote, Don Juan, Robinson Crusoe* (Cambridge: Cambridge University Press, 1996); J. B. Schneewind, *The Invention of Autonomy: A History of Modern Moral Philosophy* (Cambridge: Cambridge University Press, 1998); Stephen Darwall, *The British Moralists and the Internal "Ought," 1640–1740* (Cambridge: Cambridge University Press, 1995); and, more recently, Kelly, *Propriety of Liberty*.

12. Daniel Roche, *France in the Enlightenment*, trans. Arthur Goldhammer (Cambridge, Mass.: Harvard University Press, 1998), 485–578; quotation, 517.

13. The oppressive character of modern subjectivity is, of course, a major theme in Michel Foucault, *Discipline and Punish: The Birth of the Prison*, 2nd ed., trans. Alan Sheridan (New York: Vintage Books, 1995). See also Max Horkheimer and Theodor W. Adorno, *Dialectic of Enlightenment*, trans. John Cumming (New York: Continuum, 1999). On the emergence and potential death of man, see Foucault, *The Order of Things: An Archeology of the Human Sciences* (New York: Vintage Books, 1994), 385–387.

14. See Goldstein, *Post-Revolutionary Self*; Jerrold Seigel, *The Idea of the Self: Thought and Experience in Western Europe since the Seventeenth Century* (Cambridge: Cambridge University Press, 2005); and Dror Wahrman, *The Making of the Modern Self: Identity and Culture in Eighteenth-Century England* (New Haven, Conn.: Yale University Press, 2004). Other notable studies include John Martin, *Myths of Renaissance Individualism* (New York: Palgrave Macmillan, 2004) and Scott Paul Gordon, *The Power of the Passive Self in English Literature, 1640–1770* (Cambridge: Cambridge University Press, 2002).

15. See Goldstein, *Post-Revolutionary Self*, 15–17, 117–115; Wahrman, *Making of the Modern Self*, xiii–xv, 34–44, 168–185; and Jean Perkins, *The Concept of the Self in the French Enlightenment*, Histoire des Idées et Critique littéraire, vol. 94 (Geneva: Droz, 1969), 69–72, 146–147. Seigel makes a somewhat different case. On the one hand, he sharply criticizes Charles Taylor for characterizing Locke and his followers as paragons of a "punctual self," predicated on the self's adoption of a standpoint removed from its physical body, the material world, and the world of other selves. On the other hand, he recognizes in both thinkers' efforts to ensure personal identity by recourse to God, reason, and memory. Similarly, he argues that philosophes such as Condillac, Diderot, and Rousseau tended to oscillate, to varying extents and for different reasons, between giving assurances of the individual's self-sufficiency and emphasizing its significant dependence on external forces. See Seigel, *Idea of the Self*, 87–109, 171–246; for Taylor's argument about Locke and the punctual self, see *Sources of the Self*, 159–176.

16. *Encyclopédie, ou Dictionnaire raisonné des sciences, des arts et des métiers, par une société de gens de lettres* (1751–1780; repr., Stuttgart: F. Frommann, 1966–

1988), s.v. "Philosophe," 12: 509–511. On this theme, see also Daniel Brewer, *The Enlightenment Past: Reconstructing Eighteenth-Century French Thought* (Cambridge: Cambridge University Press, 2008), 49–74.

17. Daniel Gordon, *Citizens without Sovereignty: Equality and Sociability in French Thought, 1670–1789* (Princeton, N.J.: Princeton University Press, 1994), esp. 61–85, 94–128, 177–241. Tellingly, André Morellet, whom Gordon cites as one of the prime theorists of Enlightenment sociability, later shifted his emphasis to the defense of property, including property held in one's person; see Gordon, *Citizens without Sovereignty*, 237–240.

18. Jürgen Habermas, *The Structural Transformation of the Public Sphere: An Inquiry into a Category of Bourgeois Society*, trans. Thomas Burger, with the assistance of Frederick Lawrence (Cambridge, Mass.: MIT Press, 1989). See also Sarah Maza, *Private Lives and Public Affairs: The Causes Célèbres of Prerevolutionary France* (Berkeley: University of California Press, 1995); Dena Goodman, *The Republic of Letters: A Cultural History of the French Enlightenment* (Ithaca, NY: Cornell University Press, 1994); *Habermas and the Public Sphere*, ed. Craig Calhoun (Cambridge, Mass.: MIT Press, 1992).

19. Paul Hazard, *The European Mind, 1680–1715*, trans. J. Lewis May (Cleveland: Meridian Books, 1963); Peter Gay, *The Rise of Modern Paganism*, vol. 1 of *The Enlightenment: An Interpretation* (New York: Norton, 1966–1969); and Michel Vovelle, *Piété baroque et déchristianisation en Provence au XVIIIe siècle: Les Attitudes devant la mort d'après les clauses de testaments* (Paris: Éditions du Seuil, 1978).

20. See, e.g., the essays collected in *The Enlightenment in the National Context*, ed. Roy Porter and Mikuláš Teich (Cambridge: Cambridge University Press, 1981).

21. David Sorkin, *The Religious Enlightenment: Protestants, Jews, and Catholics from London to Vienna* (Princeton, N.J.: Princeton University Press, 2008).

22. For a survey of this literature, see *Religion and Politics in Enlightenment Europe*, ed. James E. Bradley and Dale K. Van Kley (Notre Dame, Ind.: University of Notre Dame Press, 2001); *A Companion to the Catholic Enlightenment in Europe*, ed. Ulrich L. Lehner and Michael Printy (Leiden: Brill, 2010); and Shmuel Feiner, *The Jewish Enlightenment*, trans. Chaya Naor (Philadelphia: University of Pennsylvania Press, 2004).

23. Jonathan Israel, *Radical Enlightenment: Philosophy and the Making of Modernity, 1650–1750* (Oxford: Oxford University Press, 2001), 7–12; quotations, 7, 11.

24. For overviews of this development in French history, see Thomas Kselman, "Challenging Dechristianization: The Historiography of Religion in Modern France," in *Church History* 75, 1 (2006): 130–139; Dale Van Kley, "Christianity as Casualty and Chrysalis of Modernity: The Problem of Dechristianization in the French Revolution," *American Historical Review* 108, 4 (2003): 1081–1104; and Darrin M. McMahon, "Happiness and *The Heavenly City of the Eighteenth-Century Philosophers*: Carl Becker Revisited," *American Behavioral Scientist* 49, 5 (2006): 681–686.

25. See Dale Van Kley, *The Religious Origins of the French Revolution: From Calvin to the Civil Constitution of the Clergy, 1560–1791* (New Haven, Conn.: Yale University Press, 1996).

26. Jeffrey D. Burson, *The Rise and Fall of Theological Enlightenment: Jean-Martin de Prades and Ideological Polarization in Eighteenth-Century France*, foreword by Dale Van Kley (Notre Dame: Ind.: University of Notre Dame Press, 2010); quotation, 13.

27. David A. Bell, *The Cult of the Nation in France: Inventing Nationalism, 1680–1800* (Cambridge, Mass.: Harvard University Press, 2001).

28. On the intersections between Catholic and Enlightenment ideas in eighteenth-century France, see also Carl Becker, *The Heavenly City of the Eighteenth-Century Philosophers* (New Haven, Conn.: Yale University Press, 1932); Robert Mauzi, *L'Idée du bonheur dans la littérature et la pensée françaises au XVIIIe siècle* (1960; repr. Geneva: Slatkine, 1979), esp. 12–17 and 180–221; Bernard Plongeron, *Théologie et politique au siècle des lumières (1770–1820)* (Geneva: Droz, 1973); and R. R. Palmer, *Catholics and Unbelievers in Eighteenth-Century France* (Princeton, N.J.: Princeton University Press, 1939).

29. Previous scholarship has commented, however, on similarities between Fénelon and Spinoza. See Léon Bruschvicg, *Spinoza et ses contemporains*, 5th ed. (Paris: Presses universitaires de France, 1971), 225–236 and Paul Vernière, *Spinoza et la pensée française avant la Révolution* (1954; repr., Geneva: Slatkine, 1979), 270–278. In addition, one can find references to the borrowings of radical utopians such as Dom Deschamps from the mystic tradition; see Plongeron, *Théologie et politique*, 31–32, and Jean Deprun, *La Philosophie de l'inquiétude en France au XVIIIe siècle* (Paris: J. Vrin, 1979), 120.

30. Aspects of Israel's overarching thesis, especially concerning the relationship between the moderate and radical factions of the Enlightenment, are also found in Margaret Jacob, *The Radical Enlightenment: Pantheists, Freemasons, and Republicans* (London: George Allen & Unwin, 1981).

31. Key examples of this approach include Keith Michael Baker, "Enlightenment and the Institution of Society: Notes for a Conceptual History," in *Main Trends in Cultural History: Ten Essays*, ed. Willem Melching and Wyger Velema (Amsterdam: Rodopi, 1994), 95–120, and Bell, *Cult of the Nation*, 6–17, 22–48. Both Baker and Bell draw explicitly on theses put forward by the French political philosopher Marcel Gauchet in *The Disenchantment of the World: A Political History of Religion*, trans. Oscar Burge, foreword by Charles Taylor (Princeton, N.J.: Princeton University Press, 1997), 47–176.

32. On desacralization, see also Roger Chartier, *The Cultural Origins of the French Revolution*, trans. Lydia Cochrane (Durham, N.C.: Duke University Press, 1991), 105, 109–110.

33. See also Charly Coleman, "Resacralizing the World: The Fate of Secularization in Enlightenment Historiography," *Journal of Modern History* 82, 2 (June 2010): 368–395.

34. Cissie Fairchilds, "Marketing the Counter-Reformation: Religious Objects and Consumerism in Early Modern France," in *Visions and Revisions of Eighteenth-Century France*, ed. Christine Adams et al. (University Park: Pennsylvania State University Press, 1977), 31–52. For Fairchild's statistical overview, see 36–38, 41, 45–46.

35. For a stimulating survey of new directions in French economic history, see

Colin Jones and Rebecca Spang, "Sans-culottes, sans café, sans tabac: Shifting Realms of Necessity and Luxury in Eighteenth-century France," in *Consumers and Luxury: Consumer Culture in Europe, 1650–1850*, ed. Maxine Berg and Helen Clifford (Manchester: Manchester University Press, 1999), 37–62.

36. Daniel Roche, *The Culture of Clothing: Dress and Fashion in the "ancien régime,"* trans. Jean Birrell (New York: Cambridge University Press, 1994). See also Roche, *The History of Everyday Things*, trans. Brian Pierce (Cambridge: Cambridge University Press, 2000).

37. Cissie Fairchilds, "The Production and Marketing of Populuxe Goods in Eighteenth-Century Paris," in *Consumption and the World of Goods*, ed. John Brewer and Roy Porter (London: Routledge, 1993), 228–248; David D. Bien, "Property in Office under the *ancien régime*: The Case of the Stockholders," in *Early Modern Conceptions of Property*, ed. John Brewer and Susan Staves (London: Routledge, 1996), 481–496; and William Doyle, *Venality: The Sale of Offices in Eighteenth-Century France* (New York: Oxford University Press, 1996).

38. On literary property, see Raymond Birn, "The Profits of Ideas: Privilèges en librairie in Eighteenth-Century France," *Eighteenth-Century Studies* 4, 2 (Winter 1970–1971): 131–168; Gregory S. Brown, *Literary Sociability and Literary Property in France, 1775–1793*, Studies in European Cultural Transition, vol. 33 (Aldershot: Ashgate, 2006), 17–18, 36–38; and Geoffrey Turnovsky, *The Literary Market: Authorship and Modernity in the Old Regime* (Philadelphia: University of Pennsylvania Press, 2009).

39. Charles Louis de Secondat, baron de Montesquieu, *De l'Esprit des lois*, ed. Laurent Versini (Paris: Gallimard, 1995), 1: 232–233; Jean-Jacques Rousseau, *Discours sur l'origine and le fondement de l'inégalité*, in *Œuvres complètes*, ed. Bernard Gagnebin and Marcel Raymond (Paris: Gallimard, 1959–1995), 3: 168–171; and Karl Marx, *The German Ideology*, in *The Marx-Engels Reader*, 2nd ed., ed. Robert C. Tucker (New York: Norton, 1978), 156.

40. See Michael Kwass, "Ordering the World of Goods: The Consumer Revolution and the Classification of Objects in Eighteenth-Century France," *Representations* 82 (Spring 2003): 87–116; Kwass, "Consumption and the World of Ideas: Consumer Revolution and the Moral Economy of the Marquis de Mirabeau," *Eighteenth-Century Studies*, 37, 2 (2004): 187–213; and John Shovlin, *The Political Economy of Virtue: Luxury, Patriotism, and the Origins of the French Revolution* (Ithaca, N.Y.: Cornell University Press, 2006).

41. See, e.g., *Dictionnaire de l'Académie française*, 4th ed. (1762), s.vv. "Âme," "Moi," and "Soi." All citations from the various editions of the Academy's dictionary are from "Dictionnaires d'autrefois," the electronic database of the ARTFL Project at the University of Chicago, http://artfl-project.uchicago.edu/content/dictionnaires-dautrefois. For a succinct discussion of uses of *âme, moi*, and *soi* in eighteenth-century French, see Goldstein, *Post-Revolutionary Self*, 115–118.

42. *Dictionnaire de l'Académie française*, 4th ed., s.v. "Personne."

43. Ibid., 1st ed. (1694), s.v. "Jouissance." See also Pierre Rétat, "La Jouissance physiocratique," in *Ordre, nature, propriété*, ed. Gérard Klotz (Lyon: Presses universitaires de Lyon, 1985), 179–180. On the basis of this evidence, I translate *jouissance* as "the enjoyment of possession."

44. *Dictionnaire de l'Académie française*, 4th ed., s.v. "Bien."

45. Ibid., s.vv. "Aliénation" and "Distraction."

46. This definition of culture offered here is indebted to Keith Michael Baker, *Inventing the French Revolution: Essays on French Political Culture in the Eighteenth Century* (Cambridge: Cambridge University Press, 1990), 4–7, 13–20, and William H. Sewell Jr., *Logics of History: Social Theory and Social Transformation* (Chicago: University of Chicago Press, 2005), 152–174.

47. On the influence of Locke and Newton, see John W. Yolton, *Locke and French Materialism* (Oxford: Clarendon Press, 1991) and J. B. Shank, *The Newton Wars and the Beginning of the French Enlightenment* (Chicago: University of Chicago Press, 2008).

48. For overviews of Guyon's influence on German mysticism, see Hans-Jürgen Schrader, "Madame Guyon, le piétisme et la littérature de langue allemande," in Josesph Beaude et al., *Madame Guyon: Rencontres autour de la vie et l'œuvre de Madame Guyon, Thonon-les-Bains, Château de Ripailles, septembre 1996* (Grenoble: Jérôme Millon, 1997), 83–130, and Christof Wingertszahn, *Anton Reiser und die "Michelein": Neue Funde zum Quietismus im 18. Jahrhundert* (Hanover: Wehrhahn Verlag, 2002).

49. Karl Philipp Moritz, *Anton Reiser: A Psychological Novel*, trans. John R. Russell (Columbia, S.C.: Camden House, 1996), 3.

50. Glenn Alexander Magee, "Quietism in German Mysticism and Philosophy," *Common Knowledge* 16, 3 (Fall 2012): 457–473; esp. 467–471.

CHAPTER 1. SPECTORS OF VENALITY

1. See Andrew Lossky, *Louis XIV and the French Monarchy* (New Brunswick, N.J.: Rutgers University Press), 246–247.

2. See Doyle, *Venality*, 12.

3. *Édit du Roy, Portant Annoblissement dans nostre Royaume de cinq cens personnes* (n.p., n.d. [March 1696]), 3–4.

4. *Arrêt du Conseil d'État concernant les 500 lettres de noblesse accordées par l'édit du mois de mars 1696* (n.p., n.d. [August 1696]), 3–4.

5. *Declaration du Roy, Portant Reglement pour les Enregistrements des Lettres de Noblesse crées par Edit du mois de Mars 1696* (Paris: Estienne Michallet, 1697), 1 and 4; quotation, 1.

6. Robert-Joseph Pothier, *Traité du droit de domaine de propriété* (Paris: Dubure père; Orleans: Veuve Rouzeau-Montaut, 1772), 1: 6.

7. On the status of landed property, see Thomas E. Kaiser, "Property, Sovereignty, the Declaration of the Rights of Man, and the Tradition of French Jurisprudence," in *The French Idea of Freedom: The Old Regime and the Declaration of Rights of 1789*, ed. Dale Van Kley (Stanford, Calif.: Stanford University Press, 1994), 301–303, and Sewell, *Work and Revolution*, 115.

8. On the rights of the *seigneur utile* and the *seigneur direct*, see Pothier, *Traité du droit*, 4–5, and Preudhomme, *Traité des droits apparetenans aux seigneurs sur les biens possédés en roture* (Paris: Froullé, 1781), 1–4, 7–18.

9. Preudhomme, *Traité des droits*, 1.

10. See Roland Mousnier, *Les Institutions de la France sous la monarchie absolue*

(Paris: Presses universitaires de France, 1974), 1: 47–69, and Yves Durand, *L'Ordre du monde: Idéal politique et valeurs sociales en France, XVIe–XVIIIe siècle* (Paris: Sedes, 2001), 33–38, 74–76, 167–185.

11. Charles Maurice de Talleyrand-Périgord, *Mémoires du prince du Talleyrand*, ed. Albert de Broglie (Paris: C. Lévy, 1891–1892), 1: 7–8.

12. Mousnier, *Institutions de la France*, 1: 371–411.

13. Charles Loyseau, *Traité des seigneuries*, quoted in Mousnier, *Institutions de la France*, 1: 372.

14. On the venal office system, see Doyle, *Venality*, and Roland Mousnier, *La Venalité des offices sous Henri IV et Louis XIII* (Paris: Presses universitaires de France, 1971).

15. On the service requirements for ennobling offices, see Michael Bush, *Rich Noble, Poor Noble* (Manchester: Manchester University Press, 1988), 68–69.

16. For the price of the office of *sécretaire du roi*, see Doyle, *Venality*, 71, 79–81.

17. Ibid., 58–151.

18. *Édit du roy, Portant création des Offices de Controlleurs de la Marque d'or & d'argent* (Paris: E. Michallet, 1696) and *Édit du roy, Portant suppression des Offices de Visiteurs & Controlleurs de la Marque de l'or & de l'argent, des Offices de Distributeurs du Papier & Parchement Timbré, & de ceux de Vendeurs de poisson d'eau douce* (Paris: Estienne Michallet, 1698).

19. *Édit du roy, Portant suppression des Offices de Visiteurs & Controlleurs de la Marque de l'or & de l'argent*, 1.

20. On criticisms of the venal system, see Doyle, *Venality*, 239–274.

21. Kaiser, "Property, Sovereignty, the Declaration of the Rights of Man," 305–306.

22. Guy Chaussinaud-Nogaret, *The French Nobility in the Eighteenth Century: From Feudalism to Enlightenment*, trans. William Doyle (Cambridge: Cambridge University Press, 1985), 28–30.

23. See Mousnier, *Institutions de la France*, 1: 106–107.

24. Chaussinaud-Nogaret, *French Nobility*, 87.

25. Jonathan Dewald, *Aristocratic Experience and the Origin of Modern Culture: France, 1570–1715* (Berkeley: University of California Press, 1993), 1–13.

26. Ibid., 146–173.

27. On Loyseau's life and influence, see Brigitte Basdevant-Gaudemet, *Aux Origines de l'état moderne: Charles Loyseau (1563–1627), Théoricien de la puissance publique* (Paris: Economica, 1977), 1–10.

28. See Durand, *Ordre du monde*, 26–35, 220–225, and Mousnier, *Institutions de la France*, 1: 14–23.

29. Charles Loyseau, *Traité des ordres et simples dignitez*, in *Les Œuvres de maistre Charles Loyseau* (Lyon: Compagnie des Libraires, 1701), 2–3.

30. Ibid., 25.

31. Ibid., 3.

32. Charles Loyseau, *Cinq Livres du droit des offices*, in id., *Œuvres*, 152; Doyle, *Venality*, 8.

33. Doyle, *Venality*, 1–8; Mousnier, *Venalité*, 223–243.

34. Doyle, *Venality*, 6–7, 42–44, 50–51, 74–75, 162–166; Mousnier, *Institutions de la France*, 2: 46–62.

35. Loyseau, *Cinq Livres*, in id., *Œuvres*, 1 and 14.

36. Ibid., 95–108; quotations, 104 and 97.

37. Ibid., 159–165; quotation, 160.

38. Ibid., 151–159; quotations, 158, 152.

39. Ibid., 43.

40. On this development, see Karl Marx, *Capital, Volume One*, in *The Marx-Engels Reader*, 302–312, and Georg Lukács, *History and Class Consciousness: Studies in Marxist Dialectics*, trans. Rodney Livingston (Cambridge, Mass.: MIT Press, 1971), 83–92.

41. Loyseau, *Cinq Livres*, in id., *Œuvres*, 143.

42. *Le Sainte Concile de Trente œcuménique et général, célébré sous Paul III. Jules III. et Pie IV. souverains pontifes*, trans. Abbé Chanut, 3rd ed. (Paris: Sébastien Mabre-Cramoisy, 1686), 35, 43, 48.

43. For an overview of the main doctrinal and institutional currents of post-Tridentine Catholicism, see *Le Temps des confessions*, vol. 8 of *Histoire du Christianisme des origines à nos jours*, ed. Jean-Marie Mayeur et al. (Paris: Desclée, 1992), 241–246. On the relationship between religious individualism and Catholic Reformation spirituality, see Louis Cognet, *Crépuscule des mystiques, Bossuet–Fénelon*, new ed., with preface by J. R. Armogathe (Paris: Desclée, 1991), 185–203, and Michel de Certeau, *The Mystic Fable*, vol. 1: *The Sixteenth and Seventeenth Centuries*, trans. Michael B. Smith (Chicago: University of Chicago Press, 1992), 12–19.

44. Melchior Cano, *Tratado de la victoria de sí mismo* (1550), trans. Maurice Legendre as *La Victoire sur soi-même* (Paris: Revue des jeunes, 1923), 31–34, 42–48, 185–188; quotations, 48, 185.

45. *Catéchisme du Concile de Trente*, trans. Emmanuel Marbeau and A. Carpentier (Grez-en-Bouère: Dominique Martin Morin, 1984), 130–131, 134–135.

46. Julien Cain, ed., *Nouvelle histoire de France*, vol. 12: *Les Églises ennemies: La Réforme et les guerres de religion, 1547–1589* (Paris: Tallandier, 1966), 1419–1420.

47. On the reception of Tridentine reform in France, see *Temps des confessions* (cited n. 43 above), 443–444, and Victor Martin, *Le Gallicanisme et la Réforme catholique: Essai historique sur l'introduction en France des décrets du concile de Trente (1563–1615)* (1919; repr., Geneva: Slatkine, 1975), xi, xiv, 345–395.

48. On the theological differences between Jansenism and devotion at court, see Van Kley, *Religious Origins of the French Revolution*, 52–65.

49. Blaise Pascal, *Les Pensées*, ed. Francis Kaplan (Paris: Éditions du Cerf, 2005), 154, 252.

50. On this point, see Hans Blumenberg, *The Legitimacy of the Modern Age*, trans. Robert M. Wallace (Cambridge, Mass.: MIT Press, 1985), 125–226, and Gauchet, *Disenchantment of the World*, 47–97.

51. See Jean S. Yolton, ed., Introduction to *John Locke as Translator: Three of the Essais of Pierre Nicole in French and English* (Oxford: Voltaire Foundation, 2000), 1–8.

52. Pierre Nicole, *L'Esprit de M. Nicole sur les vérités de la Religion*, in Nicole, *Essais de morale* (1733–1771; repr., Geneva: Slatkine, 1971), 4: 713. All volume and page references are to the reprinted edition.

53. Nicole, *Essais de morale*, 1: 208.

54. Ibid., 208–209.

55. Ibid., 240.

56. Ibid., 241.

57. Ibid., 251.

58. Ibid., 253.

59. Nicole, *Esprit*, 781–782.

60. Jacques Esprit, *La Fausseté des vertus humaines* (Paris: G. Desprez, 1678), 1: 1–7, 447–459, 2: 14, 15, 548–552; quotations, 1: 4–5, 2: 15.

61. Pascal, *Pensées*, 215.

62. Lawrence Dickey, "Pride, Hypocrisy, and Civility in Mandeville's Social and Historical Theory," *Critical Review* 4, 3 (Summer 1990): 387–431, and E. J. Hundert, "Bernard Mandeville and the Enlightenment's Maxims of Modernity," *Journal of Intellectual History* 56, 4 (October 1995): 577–593. On Jansenist influences on mercantilist political economy, see Lionel Rothkrug, *Opposition to Louis XIV: The Political and Social Origins of the French Enlightenment* (Princeton, N.J.: Princeton University Press, 1965), 54–56.

63. Antoine Montchrétien, *Traicté de l'économie politique* (Paris: Plon, 1889), 37–44; quotations, 39 and 42.

64. On Colbert's system, see C. W. Cole, *Colbert and a Century of French Mercantilism* (New York: Columbia University Press, 1939).

65. *Le Tableau de la Vie & du Gouvernement de Messieurs les Cardinaux Richelieu & Mazarin, & de Monsieur Colbert, representé en diverses Satyres & Poësies ingenieuses* (Cologne: Pierre Marteau, 1694), 245.

66. Jacques Savary, *Le Parfait négociant, ou Instruction générale pour ce qui regarde le Commerce de toute sorte de Marchandises* (Paris: Jean Guignard, 1675), 1–2.

67. For a discussion of the French ideal of *doux commerce*, see Albert O. Hirschman, *The Passions and the Interests: Political Arguments for Capitalism before Its Triumph* (Princeton, N.J.: Princeton University Press, 1977).

68. Antoine de Courtin, *Nouveau traité de la civilité* (Paris: L. Josse & C. Robustel, 1728), 17–32. See also Gordon, *Citizens without Sovereignty*, 86–128.

69. C. M. D. Contière, *Élémens de la politesse ou les secrets de l'art de plaire*, new ed. (Liège: Guilleaume Destrez, 1702), 11–12, 34.

70. René Descartes, *Les Principes de la philosophie*, in id., *Œuvres et lettres*, ed. André Bridoux (Paris: Gallimard, 1987), 574. On the relatively circumscribed bounds of the *cogito* at its inception, see Seigel, *Idea of the Self*, 56–63.

71. Descartes, *Méditations*, in id., *Œuvres et lettres*, 278.

72. Descartes, *Discours de la méthode*, in id., *Œuvres et lettres*, 152, 144, 168.

73. Descartes, *Principes de la philosophie*, 587–588; quotations, 588.

74. On the origins and implications of Descartes's view of divine transcendence, see Blumenberg, *Legitimacy of the Modern Age*, 137–203, and Stephen Gaukroger,

Descartes: An Intellectual Biography (Oxford: Oxford University Press, 1995), 195–210.

75. On Descartes's commitment to Copernicanism as reflected in the *Discours,* see Gaukroger, *Descartes,* 290–292, 308–309, and Seigel, *Idea of the Self,* 65–72.

76. Descartes, *Discours de la méthode,* 155–156.

77. Ibid., 169.

78. Descartes, *Principes de la philosophie,* 587.

79. Descartes, *Passions de l'âme* (1649), in id., *Œuvres et lettres,* 722–795; quotations, 725 and 728.

80. Descartes, *Discours de la méthode,* 143.

81. Descartes to Christina of Sweden, November 20, 1647, and to Elizabeth of Bohemia, September 1, 1645, in Descartes, *Œuvres et lettres,* 1284 and 1202–1203.

82. On Descartes's family's hopes for his career, see Gaukroger, *Descartes,* 22–23, 135; John R. Cole, *The Olympian Dreams and Youthful Rebellion of René Descartes* (Urbana: University of Illinois Press, 1992), 89–110; and Philippe-Jean Quillien, *Dictionnaire politique de René Descartes* (Lille: Presses universitaires de Lille, 1994), 15–17.

83. Descartes, *Discours de la méthode,* 129, 131. On Descartes's internalization of aristocratic values, see Taylor, *Sources of the Self,* 152–155.

84. Descartes, *Passions de l'âme,* 768, quoted in Quillien, *Dictionnaire politique de René Descartes,* 18–19.

85. Descartes to Marin Mersenne, November 1630 and February 1634, in *Œuvres de Descartes,* ed. Charles Adam and Paul Tannery (Paris: J. Vrin, 1974–1986), 1: 181–182 and 281.

86. Descartes, *Discours de la méthode,* 141.

87. On the reception of Cartesianism, see, e.g., François Azouvi, *Descartes et la France: Histoire d'une passion nationale* (Paris: Fayard, 2002), 29–94; *Receptions of Descartes: Cartesianism and Anti-Cartesianism in Early Modern Europe,* ed. Tad M. Schmaltz (London: Routledge, 2005), and Nicholas Jolley, "The Reception of Descartes' Philosophy," in *The Cambridge Companion to Descartes,* ed. John Cottingham (Cambridge: Cambridge University Press, 1992), 397–407.

88. On Malebranche and Descartes, see Henri Gouhier, *La Pensée métaphysique de Descartes* (Paris: Vrin, 1926); Ferdinand Alquié, *Le Cartésianisme de Malebranche* (Paris: Vrin, 1974); and Jean-Christophe Bardout, "A Reception without Attachment: Malebranche Confronting Cartesian Morality," trans. Sarah A. Miller and Patrick L. Miller, in *Receptions of Descartes,* ed. Schmaltz, 41–62.

89. On Cartesianism and early modern arguments for gender equality, see Siep Stuurman, *François Poulain de la Barre and the Invention of Modern Equality* (Cambridge, Mass.: Harvard University Press, 2004), quotation, 94, and Katherine J. Hamerton, "A Feminist Voice in the Enlightenment Salon: Madame de Lambert on Taste, Sensibility, and the Feminine Mind," *Modern Intellectual History* 7, 2 (July 2010): 209–238.

90. On Descartes and the *Querelle,* see Azouvi, *Descartes et la France,* 55–59 and Dan Edelstein, *The Enlightenment: A Genealogy* (Chicago: University of Chicago Press, 2010), 40–41.

91. On the rise and fall of institutional Cartesianism, see Israel, *Radical En-*

lightenment, 477–493; Israel, *Enlightenment Contested: Philosophy, Modernity, and the Emancipation of Man*, 1670–1752 (Oxford: Oxford University Press, 2006), 362, 700–701; and Asouvi, *Descartes et la France*, 82–113.

92. See, e.g., Jacques Bénigne Bossuet, *De la Connaissance de Dieu et de soi-même*, new ed., ed. Émile Charles (Paris: Eugène Belin, 1875), and Benoît Sinsart, *Recueil de pensées diverses sur l'immatérialité de l'ame*, . . . *ou, Réfutation du matérialisme* (Colmar: Imprimerie royale, 1756).

93. *Encyclopédie*, s.vv. "Cartésianisme" and "Locke," 2: 719 and 9: 626.

94. Among the attempts to resituate Locke in his theological and political contexts, see John Dunn, *The Political Thought of John Locke* (Cambridge: Cambridge University Press, 1965); James Tully, *A Discourse on Property: John Locke and His Adversaries* (Cambridge: Cambridge University Press, 1980); and Ian Harris, *The Mind of John Locke: A Study of Political Theory in its Intellectual Setting* (Cambridge: Cambridge University Press, 1994).

95. On Locke's influence in France, see Yolton, *Locke and French Materialism*; Jørn Schøsler, *John Locke et les philosophes français: La Critique des idées innées en France au dix-huitième siècle*, Studies on Voltaire and the Eighteenth Century, vol. 353 (Oxford: Voltaire Foundation, 1997); and Israel, *Enlightenment Contested*, 370–371, 716–719, 755–759. 765–780.

96. Locke, *An Essay Concerning Human Understanding*, ed. with intro. Peter H. Nidditch (Oxford: Clarendon Press, 1975), 48–121, 163–166.

97. Jerrold Seigel has pointed out that Locke's adversaries, such as Joseph Butler, bishop of Durham, did not spare him the charge that the *Essay* left no place for stable personal identity. See Seigel, *Idea of the Self*, 89. Jan Goldstein also argues that Lockean personhood was too porous to external influences, and too potentially varied, to qualify as a truly unified self. See Goldstein, *Post-Revolutionary Self*, 107–112.

98. Locke, *Essay Concerning Human Understanding*, 108–117; quotations, 115, 117.

99. Ibid., 328–348; quotations, 341, 345.

100. On the relationship of the *Essay* to the *Second Treatise*, see Tully, *Discourse on Property*, 3–34.

101. Quoted in Tully, *Discourse on Property*, 7.

102. Locke, *Second Treatise of Government*, 267–268, 270–271; quotations, 271.

103. Ibid., 287.

104. Ibid., 298.

105. On this debate, see Macpherson, *Possessive Individualism*, 197–229; E. J. Hundert, "The Making of *Homo Faber*: John Locke between Ideology and History," *Journal of the History of Ideas* 33, 1 (January–March 1972): 3–22; and James Tully, *An Approach to Political Philosophy: Locke in Contexts* (Cambridge: Cambridge University Press, 1993), 71–136.

106. See Tully, *Approach to Political Philosophy*, 115–121.

107. See Israel, *Enlightenment Contested*, 756–760, on Voltaire's efforts to convince Tournemine that Locke and Newton were right, and Yolton, *Locke and French Materialism*, 44–50, on his failure to do so.

108. *Édit du Roi, Portant suppression des Jurandes & Communautés de Commerce, Arts & Métiers*, 5.

109. Louis-Claude Bigot de Sainte-Croix, *Essai sur la liberté du commerce et de l'industrie* (Amsterdam: Lacombe, 1775), 2–3; quotation, 3.

110. Delacroix, *Mémoire à consulter, sur l'existence actuelle des six corps, & la conservation de leurs privilèges*, 7–10. See also Leroy de Montécly, *Observations présentées par les maîtres composant la Communauté des graveurs, ciseleurs de la ville & fauxbourgs de Paris* (Paris: P. de Lormel, 1776), 3.

111. Birn, "Profits of Ideas," 145–146.

112. Henri Bremond, *Histoire littéraire du sentiment religieux en France* (Paris: Bloud & Gay, 1915–1936), 2: 105–109, and Cognet, *Crépuscule des mystiques*, 21.

113. Bremond, *Histoire littéraire*, 11: 171–185.

114. Cognet, *Crépuscule des mystiques*, 23–30, and Bremond, *Histoire littéraire*, 1: 320–321, 2: 135–168.

115. Bremond, *Histoire littéraire*, 2: 192–322.

116. Pierre Bérulle, *Discours de l'état et des grandeurs de Jésus*, in *Œuvres complètes de Bérulle*, ed. Abbé Jacques-Paul Migne (Petit-Montrouge: J.-P. Migne, 1856), 167–178. On Bérulle's doctrine and career, see Yves Krumenacker, *L'École française de spiritualité: Des Mystiques, des fondateurs, des courants et leurs interprètes* (Paris: Éditions du Cerf, 1998), 125–210, and Bremond, *Histoire littéraire*, 3: 43–110, 197–215, 222–279.

117. François de Fénelon, *Instruction pastorale . . . sur le livre intitulé: "Explication des maximes des saints"* [1697], in *Œuvres complètes de Fénelon*, ed. Jean-Edme-Auguste Gosselin (1848–1852; repr., Geneva: Slatkine, 1971), 2: 317–318. Fénelon's admiration for François de Sales is also discussed in Jeanne-Lydie Goré, *La Notion de l'indifférence chez Fénelon et ses sources* (Paris: Presses universitaires de France, 1956), and Madeleine Huillet d'Istria, *Le Père Caussade et la querelle du pur amour* (Paris: Aubier, 1964), 12 and 23.

118. Camus, *Théodoxe, ou De la Gloire de Dieu*, 15–18, 41–57; quotations, 41–41 and 57. On the Camus–Sirmond debate, see also Henri Bremond, *La Querelle du pur amour au temps de Louis XIII: Antoine Sirmond et Jean-Pierre Camus* (Paris: Bloud & Gay, 1932).

119. Jacques Sirmond, *La Déffense de la vertu* (Paris: Sébastien Huvré, 1641), 12–15, 16–17, 32–65; quotations, 26 and 57.

120. Ibid., 69–90; quotations, 69 and 88.

121. Camus, *La Déffense du pur amour* (Paris: Robert Bertault, 1640), 98, 178.

122. Augustine, *De Doctrina Christiana*, ed. and trans. R. P. H. Green (Oxford: Clarendon Press, 1995), 14–17; quotations, 15.

123. Ibid., 178–9, 495.

124. Camus, *Homélies des États-Généraux (1614–1615)*, ed. Jean Descrains (Geneva: Droz; Paris: Minard, 1970), 232. On the crown's broken promise to abolish venality, see Descrains, introduction to Camus, *Homélies*, 89n67, and Doyle, *Venality*, 9.

CHAPTER 2. THE CHALLENGE OF MYSTICISM

1. On the condemnation of Molinos, see the bull *Coelestis pastor*, issued November 20, 1687, and printed in *Décret de la sacrée et générale Inquisition de Rome où sont rapportées fidellement en Italien et François les LXVIII propositions condamnées de Michel de Molinos* (Rome: Chambre apostolique, n.d. [1687]).

2. Ibid. 11, 13, 17.

3. Miguel de Molinos, *Guía espiritual*, trans. Paul Drochon as *Guide spirituel* (Paris: Éditions du Cerf, 1997), 168; see also 199–200.

4. François de Sales, *Introduction à la vie dévote* (Paris: Victor Lecoffre, 1894), 22–58; quotations, 23 and 51.

5. Bérulle, *Discours de l'état et les grandeurs de Jésus*, 263.

6. Innico Caracciolo, "Lettre de M. le Cardinal Caraccioli à sa Sainteté, écrite de Naples le 30 Janvier 1682," in Bossuet, *Actes de la condamnation des quiétistes*, published with *Instruction sur les estats d'oraison* (Paris: J. Anisson, 1697), iv. On Caracciolo and the reaction against Molinos in Naples, see Romeo de Maio, *Società e vita religiosa a Napoli nell'età moderna (1656–1799)* (Naples: Edizioni scientifiche italiane, 1971), 161–178. As Jacques Le Brun has noted, the cardinal was the first to use the term "Quietist." See Le Brun, "Le Quiétisme entre la modernité et l'archaïsme," in *Modernité et nonconformisme en France à travers les âges*, ed. Myriam Yardeni (Leiden: E. J. Brill, 1983), 87.

7. See Jaime de Palafox y Cardona, "Lettre de M. Palafox Archevesque de Seville, au Pape Innocent XI," Jean d'Arenthon d'Alex, "Lettre de Monseigneur l'Evesque de Genève, aux Curez du Chablais," and François de Harlay de Champvallon, *Ordonnance de Monseigneur l'Archevesque de Paris*, in Bossuet, *Actes de la condamnation des quiétistes*, xlix–lxv. For Innocent XI's role in the trial of Molinos, see Cognet, *Crépuscule des mystiques*, 87.

8. On the "Church-state alliance" under the Old Regime, see John McManners, *Church and Society in Eighteenth-Century France* (Oxford: Oxford University Press, 1998), 1: 29–94.

9. Voltaire, *Le Siècle de Louis XIV*, in *Œuvres complètes de Voltaire*, ed. Louis Moland, new ed. (Paris: Garnier, 1877–1885), 15, 2: 64. On the reception and influence of Guyon's writings, see Elizabeth Goldsmith, "Mothering Mysticism: Mme Guyon and Her Public," in *Women Writers in Pre-Revolutionary France: Strategies of Emancipation*, ed. Colette Winn and Donna Kuizenga (New York: Garland, 1997), 127–139; Marie-Florine Bruneau, *Women Mystics Confront the Modern World: Marie de L'Incarnation (1599–1672) and Madame Guyon (1648–1717)* (Albany: State University of New York Press, 1998), 136, 147–148, 157, 193; Pierre-Maurice Masson, *La Religion de Jean-Jacques Rousseau* (Paris: Hachette, 1916), 1: 68–70; and Albert Cherel, *Fénelon au XVIIIe siècle en France (1715–1820): Son Prestige—Son Influence* (1917; repr., Geneva: Slatkine, 1970), 589–592.

10. On Guyon's early life, see Françoise Mallet-Joris, *Jeanne Guyon* (Paris: Flammarion, 1978), 98–126 and Louis Guerrier, *Madame Guyon: Sa Vie, sa doctrine, et son influence* (Paris: Didier, 1881), 7–52.

11. Jeanne-Marie Guyon, *La Vie de Madame J. M. B. de la Mothe-Guyon, écrite par elle-même*, new ed. (Paris: Libraries associés, 1791), 1: 72–81; quotation, 78. On the chronology of the text, see Nicholas Paige, *Being Interior: Autobiography*

and the Contradictions of Modernity in Seventeenth-Century France (Philadelphia: University of Pennsylvania Press, 2001), 272, n. 70.

12. Guyon, *Vie*, 1: 88–91.

13. Ibid., 94.

14. Ibid., 185.

15. Ibid., 3: 238–239.

16. Ibid., 1: 159–163, 168–169, 210–220, 260–272.

17. AN, L 22, no. 15, Guyon to Père Dominique de la Motthe (n.d.), pp. 10–13; quotation, 11. On Guyon's fortune at the time of her father's death, see Bruneau, *Women Mystics Confront the Modern World*, 124. Her almsgiving during this period is described in Guerrier, *Madame Guyon*, 64.

18. On Guyon's leaving her family, see Guerrier, *Madame Guyon*, 63–64.

19. AN, L 22, no. 15, pp. 12–15; quotation, 15.

20. Guyon, *Vie*, 2: 1–28.

21. Guyon, *Règle des associés à l'Enfance de Jésus, Modèle de Perfection pour tous les états* (Cologne: Jean de La Pierre, 1705), in *Les Opuscules spirituels de Madame J. M. B. de la Mothe Guion* (Cologne: Jean de la Pierre, 1712), 2: 19–20. This work has frequently been attributed to Guyon, but Jean Orcibal has noted the possibility that she assembled the text from pre-existing sources. See Orcibal, introduction to Guyon, *Les Opuscules spirituels* (Hildesheim: Olms, 1978).

22. Guyon, *Règle des associés à l'Enfance de Jésus*, 28–50; quotations, 42, 45, 49, 50.

23. Ibid., 63–73; quotation, 69.

24. Ibid., 52–54; quotation, 53.

25. Guyon, *Lettres chrétiennes et spirituelles* (London, 1767), 2: 374–375.

26. Ibid., 1: 364.

27. Ibid., 4: 316–319; quotation, 319.

28. Ibid., 3: 571.

29. Ibid., 4: vii–viii.

30. Ibid., 5: 178.

31. Ibid., 181–183.

32. On mysticism and the "clericalization" of religious practice after the Council of Trent, see Certeau, *Mystic Fable*, 12–19.

33. *Le Secret de l'oraison mentale, où l'on découvre la parfaite idée de La Méditation, les grands avantages qu'on en reçoit, et un moyen facile de la faire* (Dijon: J. Ressayre, 1680), 3–5, 38–64; quotation, 4 and 55.

34. Guyon, *Le Moyen court et très-facile de faire oraison que tous peuvent pratiquer très-aisément*, in *"Le Moyen court" et autres écrits spirituels*, ed. Marie-Louise Gondal (Grenoble: Jérôme Millon, 1995), 74–75; quotation, 74.

35. Ibid., 64.

36. Guyon, *Lettres chrétiennes*, 5: 557.

37. Guyon, *Moyen court*, 65, 71–74, 84–85, 118.

38. Ibid., 62, 79.

39. Ibid., 121–125; quotation, 122.

40. François La Combe, *Maximes spirituelles*, in Guyon, *Opuscules spirituels*, 2: 112–125; quotations, 113–114, 117, 124–125.

41. On the arrest and imprisonment of Guyon and La Combe, see Guyon, *Vie*, 3: 1–37; Guerrier, *Madame Guyon*, 144–162; and Mallet-Joris, *Madame Guyon*, 192–206.

42. Guyon, *Vie*, 6 and 41; quotation, 41.

43. Guerrier, *Madame Guyon*, 155–170.

44. On Fénelon's early life and career, see Agnès de La Gorce, *Le Vrai visage de Fénelon* (Paris: Hachette, 1958), 9–86, and Sabine Melchior-Bonnet, *Fénelon* (Paris: Perrin, 2008), 25–76.

45. On Fénelon's refutation of Malebranche, see Patrick Riley, *The General Will before Rousseau: The Transformation of the Divine into the Civic* (Princeton, N.J.: Princeton University Press, 1986), 66–78.

46. See Carolyn C. Lougee, "*Noblesse*, Domesticity, and Social Reform: The Education of Girls by Fénelon and Saint-Cyr," *History of Education Quarterly* 14, 1 (Spring 1974): 87–113, and Lougee, *Le Paradis des Femmes: Women, Salons, and Social Stratification in Seventeenth-Century France* (Princeton, N.J.: Princeton University Press, 1976), 173–201.

47. On Guyon's role as spiritual director, see also Goldsmith, "Mothering Mysticism," 129–135.

48. Guyon to Fénelon, November 1688, in Guyon, *Correspondance*, ed. Dominique Tronc (Paris: Honoré Champion, 2003–2005), 1: 227. N.B. Following Tronc's usage, approximate dates will be given when the exact month or day of the letter was left unspecified.

49. Guyon to Fénelon, October–November 1688, in ibid., 229–231; quotation, 229.

50. Cognet, *Crépuscule des mystiques*, 97–101.

51. Guyon to Fénelon, April 1689, in Guyon, *Correspondance*, 1: 289–90.

52. Fénelon to Guyon, April 1689, and Guyon to Fénelon, April 25 and 30, 1689, in ibid., 293–294, 300; quotation, 300.

53. Fénelon to Guyon, May 1689, in ibid., 300–306; quotations, 305–306.

54. Fénelon to Guyon, April 25–May 15, 1690, and Guyon to Fénelon, April 25–May 5, 1690, in ibid., 510–512; quotations, 510–511.

55. Guyon to Fénelon, Autumn 1690, in ibid., 542–543; quotation, 543.

56. See Laurent Angliviel de Beaumelle, *Mémoires et lettres de Madame de Maintenon*, quoted in H. L. Sydney Lear, *Fénelon, Archbishop of Cambrai: A Biographical Sketch* (London: Longmans, Green, 1907), 92.

57. On Fénelon's associates during this period, see Ludovic Navatel, *Fénelon: La Confrérie secrète du pur amour* (Paris: Émile-Paul frères, 1914), and Albert Delplanque, *Fénelon et ses amis* (Paris: J. Gabalda, 1910).

58. Guerrier, *Madame Guyon*, 191–231.

59. La Gorce, *Vrai visage de Fénelon*, 154–181.

60. Fénelon's stature on the eve of the Quietist affair is documented in Lear, *Fénelon, Archbishop of Cambrai*, 105–107.

61. See, e.g., Hyacinthe Robillard d'Avrigny, *Mémoires chronologiques et dogmatiques, pour servir à l'histoiree ecclesiastique depuis 1600 jusqu'en 1716* (n.p., 1720), 4: 123–128, and Raymond Schmittlein, *L'Aspect politique du différend Bossuet-Fénelon* (Baden-Baden: Éditions Art et Science, 1954).

62. Voltaire, _Siècle de Louis XIV_, 68. On the Augustinian, and specifically Jansenist, influences on Bossuet's moral thought, see also Charles Urbain, _Du Jansénisme de Bossuet_ (Paris: Letouzey & Ané, [1899]).

63. Nicole, _Réfutation des principales erreurs des quiétistes_ (Paris: Elie Josset, 1695), 40, 41, 44, 360.

64. Bossuet, _Traité de la concupiscence_ (Paris: Garnier frères, 1879), 6–7.

65. See Pascal, _Pensées_, 252.

66. Bossuet, _Traité de la concupiscence_, 69, 70, 102.

67. The work was first published, anonymously, in 1722. See Thérèse Goyet, "Autour du traité posthume de Bossuet, «De la connaissance de Dieu et de soi-même»," _Revue d'Histoire littéraire de la France_ 67, 3 (July–September 1967): 518–528.

68. Bossuet, _De la Connaissance de Dieu et de soi-même_, 212, 192.

69. Ibid., 203, 225.

70. Bossuet, _Instruction sur les estats d'oraison_, 107–108.

71. Ibid., 457–463; quotations, 461 and 463.

72. Ibid., 113.

73. Among historians of theology, Henri Bremond is notable for minimizing the doctrinal differences between Fénelon and Bossuet; see Bremond, introduction to Jean-Pierre de Caussade, _Bossuet, maître d'oraison: Instructions spirituelles en forme de dialogues sur les divers états d'oraison_, ed. Bremond (Paris: Bloud & Gay, 1931), XXVIII–XLI. For criticisms of Bremond on this point, see Michel Olphe-Galliard, introduction to Caussade, _Traité sur l'oraison du cœur: Instructions spirituelles_, ed. Olphe-Galliard (Paris: Desclée de Brouwer; Montreal: Bellarmin, 1981), 7, and Istria, _Père de Caussade_, 13.

74. Quoted in Bossuet, _Instruction sur les estats d'oraison_, 387–388, 395.

75. Bossuet, _Ordonnance et Instruction pastorale de Monseigneur l'Eveque de Meaux, sur les estats d'oraison_, in Bossuet, _Actes de la condamnation des quiétistes_, lxvi–lxxvi; quotations, lxix–lxx and lxxv.

76. Paul Godet des Marais, _Ordonnance et instruction pastorale de Monseigneur l'Evesque de Chartres_, in Bossuet, _Actes de la condamnation des quiétistes_, xci, cxvi.

77. Bossuet, _Instruction sur les estats d'oraison_, 388.

78. On the period following the Articles of Issy, see Guerrier, _Madame Guyon_, 300–324, and La Gorce, _Vrai visage de Fénelon_, 178–190.

79. Fénelon, _Explication des maximes des saints sur la vie intérieure_, in id., _Œuvres_, ed. Jacques Le Brun (Paris: Gallimard, 1983), 1: 1017.

80. Ibid., 1008–1012; quotations, 1008 and 1111.

81. Ibid., 1021. For the condemnation of Molinos, see Fénelon, _Explication et réfutation des LXVIII Propositions de Molinos condamnées par le Pape Innocent XI_, in id., _Œuvres_, 2: 230–247.

82. Fénelon, _Explication des maximes des saints_, 1021.

83. Ibid., 1049–1050.

84. Ibid., 1051.

85. Guyon, _Moyen court_, 74.

86. Bossuet, _Instruction sur les estats d'oraison_. Noailles and Godet des Marais provided approbations (ii–vii).

87. Ibid., 72, 80, 115, 141, 464; quotation, 72.

88. On Fénelon's cited influences, see *Explication des maximes des saints*, 1116–1117. For extended discussions of Fénelon's sources, and the orthodoxy of his position, see Bremond, *Histoire littéraire*, 7: 3–139, and Jeanne-Lydie Goré, *L'Itinéraire de Fénelon: Humanisme et spiritualité* (Paris: Presses universitaires de France, 1957), 399–450. On novelty as a common charge in theological polemics in general, and on the status of Quietism in particular, see Jacques Le Brun, "Quiétisme," 86–98.

89. Bossuet, *Instruction sur les estats d'oraison*, 72–80, 107–115; quotations, 80, 107, 111, 115.

90. Ibid., 464.

91. Ibid., 82–84; quotation, 82.

92. Ibid., 458–465; quotations, 461, 462 465.

93. Gabriel Joppin, *Fénelon et la mystique du pur amour* (Paris: Beauchesne, 1938), 213–214.

94. Bossuet, *Instruction sur les estats d'oraison*, 194.

95. Guerrier, *Madame Guyon*, 346–380.

96. See *Relation des Actes et Deliberations concernant la constitution en forme de bref de N. S. le Pape Innocent XII. du douziéme Mars 1699* (Paris: François Muguet, 1700), 13–17.

97. Fénelon, *Instruction pastorale de Monseigneur l'archevêque duc de Cambrai sur le livre intitulé: "Explication des maximes des saints,"* in id., *Œuvres complètes*, 2: 286–328.

98. See Louis Cognet, "Fénelon," in *Dictionnaire de spiritualité ascétique et mystique, doctrine et histoire*, ed. M. Viller et al. (Paris: Beauchesne, 1932–1995), 5: 169–161.

99. Godet des Marais, *Lettre pastorale de Mgr l'évêque de Chartres au clergé de son diocèse sur le Livre intitulé: "Explication des maximes des saints"* (Lyon: Veuve A. Tomas, 1698), and Louis-Antoine de Noailles, *Instruction pastorale de Monseigneur l'Archevesque de Paris, sur la Perfection Chrétienne & sur la vie interieure*, 2nd ed. (Paris: Louis Josse, 1698).

100. Noailles, *Instruction pastorale sur la vie intérieure*, 66.

101. Ibid., iii–iv.

102. Ibid., 66.

103. AN, L 22, no. 7, piece 5, *Extrait d'une lettre de Dom Hilarion Monier, Bénédictin, Prier de l'Abbaye de Luxeuil en Franche Comté, sur le livre de M. de Fénelon, Archevêque de Cambrai*, 14.

104. AN, L 22, no. 5, *Lettre du pur-amour*, 1–2.

105. Bossuet, *Relation sur le quiétisme* (Paris: J. Anisson, 1698), 144.

106. Guerrier, *Madame Guyon*, 403–410, 457.

107. "Condamnation et Prohibition Faite par nostre tres-Saint Pere le Pape Innocent XII du livre imprimé à Paris l'an MDCXCVII. qui a pour titre: *Explication des Maximes des Saints sur la vie interieure*, &c.," in *Relation des Actes et Deliberations*, 26.

108. *Relation des Actes et Deliberations*, 7–8, 39–41, 88–93; quotation, 92.

109. Guerrier, *Madame Guyon*, 473, 490.

110. "Condamnation et Prohibition," 24–36; cf. Cognet, "Fénelon," 162.

111. Robillard d'Avrigny, *Mémoires chronologiques et dogmatiques*, 4: 137. On Albani's role, see Cognet, "Fénelon," 162.

112. *Relation des Actes et Deliberations*, 56–57.

113. Fénelon, *Sentimens de piété, où il est traité de la nécessité de connoître & d'aimer Dieu* (Paris: François Babuty, 1713), 139.

114. Ibid., 54–92; quotations, 56, 72, 82, 92, 93.

115. Ibid., 10–11, 127.

116. Ibid., 130, 133–135.

117. Fénelon to Maintenon, October 1690 and late 1689–early 1690, in id., *Œuvres complètes*, 8: 489 and 485–486.

118. Fénelon to Maintenon, n.d., in id., *Œuvres*, ed. Le Brun, 1: 606. The letter was most likely written during Fénelon's time as the spiritual director at Saint-Cyr from 1689 to 1694.

119. Fénelon to Guyon, August 11, 1689, in Guyon, *Lettres chrétiennes*, 5: 317–318.

120. The date of composition of *La Nature de l'homme* remains uncertain, though Henri Gouhier has placed it around 1688. The work did not appear in print until 1904, when it was published by Eugène Griselle in the *Revue de philosophie* under the title "Fénelon métaphysicien (Œuvres inédites)"; see Fénelon, *Œuvres*, ed. Le Brun, 2: 1633.

121. Fénelon, *La Nature de l'homme*, in id., *Œuvres*, ed. Le Brun, 2: 833–838; quotations, 833.

122. On the dates of composition of the Fénelon's *Traité de l'existence et des attributs de Dieu*, see Denise Leduc-Fayette, "Fénelon et 'infini véritable,'" in Jean-Marie Lardic, *L'Infini entre science et religion au XVIIe siècle* (Paris: J. Vrin, 1999), 95.

123. On Fénelon's engagement of Spinoza, see also Bruschvicg, *Spinoza et ses contemporains*, 225–236, and Vernière, *Spinoza et la pensée française*, 270–278.

124. Fénelon, *Traité de l'existence et des attributs de Dieu*, in id., *Œuvres complètes*, 1: 59–62; quotations, 60–61.

125. Ibid., 62–82; quotations, 63, 76, and 82.

126. Ibid., 68–69, 72, and 79.

127. As Michel de Certeau has pointed out, "mystic science" invariably exhausts the lexicons employed in the process of formulating it; see *Mystic Fable*, 141–144.

128. See also Gilbert Gidel, *La Politique de Fénelon* (1906; repr., Geneva: Slatkine, 1971), 89–90, and Alain Niderst, "Le Quiétisme de *Télémaque*?" in *Fénelon mystique et politique (1699–1999)*, ed. F.-X. Cuche and J. Le Brun (Paris: Honoré Champion, 2004), 208–214. Niderst's article led me to the reference to Noailles cited in the following note.

129. Noailles, *Instruction pastorale sur la vie intérieure*, 166.

130. Fénelon, *Troisième Lettre à M. l'Archevêque de Paris, sur son Instruction pastorale*, in id., *Œuvres complètes*, 2: 495–497.

131. Fénelon's efforts to manipulate dynastic politics is elaborated in Sanford B. Kanter, "Archbishop Fénelon's Political Activity: The Focal Point of Power in Dynasticism," *French Historical Studies* 4, 3 (Spring 1966): 320–334.

132. On the success of *Télémaque*, see Cherel, *Fénelon au XVIIIe siècle*, 24–30,

and Patrick Riley, "Fénelon's 'Republican' Monarchism in *Telemachus*," in *Monarchisms in the Age of Enlightenment: Liberty, Patriotism, and the Common Good*, ed. Hans Blom et al. (Toronto: University of Toronto Press, 2007), 81.

133. Fénelon to the duc de Bourgogne, January 1702, in id., *Œuvres complètes*, 7: 233. The dating of these letters is approximate.

134. Fénelon, *Les Aventures de Télémaque*, in id., *Œuvres complètes*, 6: 426.

135. Rothkrug, *Opposition to Louis XIV*, 67–69, 87–110. See also Peter Burke, *The Fabrication of Louis XIV* (New Haven, Conn.: Yale University Press, 1992), 85–91, and Jean-Marie Apostolidès, *Le Roi-Machine: Spectacle et politique au temps de Louis XIV* (Paris: Éditions de Minuit, 1981).

136. Fénelon, *Télémaque*, 426, 478–480; quotation, 426.

137. Gidel, *Politique de Fénelon*, 13–14.

138. Fénelon, *Lettre à Louis XIV*, in id., *Œuvres complètes*, 7: 509–513; quotations, 511–512.

139. On Fénelon's activities during the War of the Spanish Succession, see La Gorce, *Vrai visage de Fénelon*, 264–287.

140. Fénelon, *Mémoires sur la Guerre de la Succession d'Espagne*, in id., *Œuvres complètes*, 7: 167. On Fénelon's opposition to French hegemony in Europe, see Klaus Malettke, "Fénelon, La France et le système des états européens en 1699," in *Fénelon mystique et politique*, 469–480.

141. On the composition of the *Tables de Chaulnes*, see Gidel, *La Politique de Fénelon*, 68–82.

142. Guyon to Fénelon, August 18, 1689, in Guyon, *Correspondance*, 1: 396.

143. Quoted in La Gorce, *Vrai visage de Fénelon*, 273.

144. Fénelon, *Plans de gouvernement [Table de Chaulnes]*, in id., *Œuvres complètes*, 7: 182–188.

145. Riley, "Fénelon's 'Republican' Monarchism," 78.

146. Fénelon, *Examen de conscience sur les devoirs de la royauté*, in id., *Œuvres complètes*, 7: 101.

147. Fénelon, *Télémaque*, 561.

148. Fénelon to the duc de Bourgogne, January 17, 1702, in id., *Œuvres complètes*, 7: 233. On this point, see also Niderst, "Quiétisme de *Télémaque*?" 206–215, and Riley, "Fénelon's 'Republican' Monarchism," 86–92.

149. Fénelon to Charles Auguste d'Allonville, marquis de Louville, October 10, 1701, in id., *Œuvres complètes*, 7: 548.

150. Fénelon, *Examen de conscience*, 85.

151. See Bossuet, *Sermon sur nos dispositions à l'égard des nécessités de la vie* (1660) and *Sermon du mauvais riche* (1662), in *Politique de Bossuet*, ed. Jacques Truchet (Paris: Armand Colin, 1966), 216–219 and 223–224, and *Politique tirée des propres paroles de l'Écriture sainte*, ed. Jacques Le Brun (Geneva: Droz, 1967), 317–328.

152. Bossuet, *Politique*, 72–77, 317–328, 386–392; quotation, 73.

153. Lucien Jaume, "Fénelon critique de la déraison d'État," in *Raison et déraison d'État: Théoriciens et théories de la raison d'État aux XVIe et XVIIe siècles*, ed. Yves Charles Zarka (Paris: Presses universitaires de France, 1994), 399–402. See also Rothkrug, *Opposition to Louis XIV*, 296–297.

154. Bossuet, *Politique*, 177, 74.

155. Fénelon, *Examen de conscience*, 102.

156. Fénelon, "Sur le pur amour," in *Œuvres spirituelles de Messire François de Salignac de la Mothe-Fénelon* (Anvers: Henri de la Meule, 1718), 1: 266.

157. Fénelon, *Dissertation sur les oppositions véritables entre la doctrine de M. l'Év. de Meaux et celle de M. L'Arch. de Cambrai*, in id., *Œuvres complètes*, 2: 402–403.

158. On this point, see Niderst, "Quiétisme de *Télémaque?*" 209–211.

CHAPTER 3. THE CURSE OF QUIETISM

1. For a classic statement of this position, see Michel Vovelle, *Piété baroque et déchristianisation en Provence au XVIIIe siècle*. Arguments for the decline of mysticism after Fénelon's fall are featured in Certeau, *Mystic Fable*, 76–77, 204–205, and Jacques Le Brun, *Dictionnaire de la spiritualité*, s.v. "Quiétisme," 2838–2839. The few scholarly monographs dealing explicitly with eighteenth-century mysticism have focused on the Jesuit theologian Jean-Pierre de Caussade (1675–1751), who attempted to revive the mystic tradition by reconciling the doctrines of Fénelon and Bossuet. Caussade made his case most notably in *Instructions spirituelles, en forme de dialogues sur les divers états d'Oraison* (Perpignan: Jean-Baptiste Reynier, 1741). On Caussade's life and works, see Michel Olphe-Galliard, *La Théologie mystique en France au 18e siècle, le Père de Caussade* (Paris: Beauchesne, 1984), and Istria, *Père de Caussade*. More recently, historians have produced brief analyses of Quietist scandals in Dijon and Provence. See B. Robert Kreiser, "The Devils of Toulon: Demonic Possession and Religious Politics in Eighteenth-Century Provence," in *Church, State, and Society under the Bourbon Kings of France*, ed. Richard M. Golden (Lawrence, Kan.: Coronado Press, 1982), 173–221; Mita Choudhury, "'Carnal Quietism': Embodying Anti-Jesuit Polemics in the Catherine Cadière Affair, 1731," *Eighteenth-Century Studies* 39, 2 (2006): 173–186; Choudhury, "A Betrayal of Trust: The Jesuits and Quietism in Eighteenth-Century France," *Common Knowledge* 15, 2 (Spring 2009): 164–180; and Jason Kuznicki, "Sorcery and Publicity: The Cadière-Girard Scandal of 1730–1731," *French History* 21, 3 (2007): 289–312.

2. On the rise of public opinion in eighteenth-century France, see Maza, *Private Lives and Public Affairs*, and Baker, *Inventing the French Revolution*, 167–199. Choudhury, "Betrayal of Trust" and "Carnal Quietism," and Kuznicki, "Sorcery and Publicity," explore the role of Quietist trials in the formation of a public sphere.

3. Robillard d'Avrigny, *Mémoires chronologiques et dogmatiques*, 4: 118–141; quotations, 123 and 141.

4. [Jean Phélypeaux], *Relation de l'origine, du progrès et de la condamnation du quiétisme répandu en France* (n.p., 1732), 1: "Avertissement" and "Préface," 2: 152–154.

5. Habermas, *Structural Transformation*, 24, 56.

6. The term "new Quietist" is taken from Philippe Hecquet, *Le Naturalisme des convulsions dans les maladies de l'épidémie convulsionnaire* (Soleure: Andreas Gymnicus, 1733), 183.

7. *Arrest de la cour de Parlement rendu contre Maistre Philibert Robert*, 3–5;

quotations, 3–4. On Robert's life, see [Hubert Mauparty], *Réponse à l'apologie en forme de requeste presentée à l'official de Dijon* (Zell [Reims]: Henriette Hermille, 1703), 33–38. Other copies of this text bear an alternate title: *Histoire du Quillotisme, ou ce qui s'est passé à Dijon au sujet du quiétisme.*

8. *Sentence contre Me Philibert Robert* (Paris: Claude Nego, [1698]), 7. On the legal status of spiritual incest, see *Nouveau Dictionnaire civil et canonique de droit et de pratique* (Paris: Augustin Besoigne, 1697), s.v. "Incestueux," 513.

9. *Arrest de la cour de Parlement rendu contre Maistre Philibert Robert*, 5–6.

10. [Mauparty], *Réponse*, 4–5, and Pensa, *Sorcellerie et religion*, 183–186.

11. *Arrest de la cour de Parlement rendu contre Maistre Philibert Robert*, 6–7.

12. Pensa, *Sorcellerie et religion*, 169–173.

13. McManners, *Church and Society*, 1: 364–370.

14. BMD, Ms. 335/MIC 528, f. 4

15. *Extraits des Registres de Parlement* (Dijon: Jean Grangier, 1700), 1–4, from ibid., ff. 50–52. On the backgrounds of the accused, see [Mauparty], *Réponse*, 38–43.

16. For the date on which the trial began, see [Mauparty], *Réponse*, 25.

17. Bossuet to Noailles, August 4, 1698, in *Œuvres complètes de Bossuet*, ed. F. Lachat (Paris: Louis Vivès, 1862–1875), 29: 528. On how the Dijon case influenced Bossuet's conduct, see Henri Chérot, *Autour de Bossuet: Le Quiétisme en Bourgogne et à Paris en 1698* (Paris: Victor Retaux, 1901), 7, 14–15. For a report on how Bossuet's camp exploited the proceedings, see l'abbé de Chanterac to Fénelon, September 13, 1698, in *Correspondance de Fénelon*, ed. Jean Orcibal, with the collaboration of Jacques Le Brun and Irénée Noye (Paris: Klincksieck; Geneva: Droz, 1972–2007), 8: 161–163.

18. BMD, Ms. 333/MIC 527, f. 1–3, 19; quotations, 1–2. On the popularity of Quietism in the region, see also Pensa, *Sorcellerie et religion*, 171–172, and Elisabeth François de Lacuisine, *Le Parlement de Bourgogne depuis son origine jusqu'à sa chute* (Dijon: Loireau-Feuchot; Paris: A. Durand, 1857), 2: 332.

19. Fénelon to Chanterac, September 27, 1698, in *Correspondance de Fénelon*, 8: 179–180; also cited in Chérot, *Autour de Bossuet*, 49.

20. BMD, Ms. 333/MIC 527, f. 17–23.

21. On the eroticization of the mystical tradition, see also de Certeau, *Mystic Fable*, 4–6, 97–98.

22. BMD, Ms. 333/MIC 527, f. 5.

23. Ibid., 5. On Prudence's alleged role in the affair, see also BMD, Ms. 334/MIC 527. f. 48, and [Mauparty], *Réponse*, 6, 38, 49.

24. BMD, Ms. 333/MIC 527, ff. 6–7; quotations, 7. Cf. Song of Solomon 2:16.

25. BMD, Ms. 333/MIC 527, ff. 7–9; quotations, 7.

26. Ibid., ff. 9–17; quotations, 13 and 14.

27. On Quillot's life, see Pensa, *Sorcellerie et religion*, 201–203, and F. X. de Feller, *Dictionnaire historique, ou histoire abrégée de tous les hommes qui se sont fait un nom par leur genie, leurs talens, leurs vertus, leurs erreurs ou leurs crimes*, 8th ed. (Lille: L. Lefort, 1832–1833), s.v. "Quillot (Claude)," 11: 190.

28. BMD, Ms. 333/MIC 527, f. 36–43; quotations, 39–41.

29. *Sentence de Monsieur Fijan* (Dijon: Jean Grangier, 1700), 4.

30. *Extraits des Registres de Parlement* (1700), 1, in BMD, Ms. 335/MIC 528, f. 39, 50; quotation, 50. The magistrates' votes are reported in Pensa, *Sorcellerie et religion*, 224–225.

31. *Sentence de Monsieur Fijan*, 4.

32. [Mauparty], *Réponse*, 84, and Pensa, *Sorcellerie et religion*, 225–227.

33. *Extraits des Registres de Parlement*, 3–4. On Rollet's flight from justice, see Pensa, *Sorcellerie et religion*, 228.

34. I consulted the version of the text at the Bibliothèque de l'Arsenal, which carries the title *Réponse à l'apologie en forme de requeste presentée à l'official de Dijon* (see n. 7 above). For the author's claims of irregularities in the trial, see 25–30, 74–83. On the history and attribution of the work, see also Pensa, *Sorcellerie et religion*, 239–248, and Choudhury, "Betrayal of Trust," 171–172.

35. *Ordonnance de Monseigneur l'Eveque Duc de Langres Pair de France. Portant Condamnation d'un Livre intitulé: "Histoire du Quillotisme ou de ce qui s'est passé à Dijon au sujet du Quiétisme"* (Langres: C. Personne, 1703), and *Extraits des Registres de Parlement* (Dijon: Jean Grangier, 1703), in BMD, Ms. 335/MIC 528, f. 69.

36. See Van Kley, *Religious Origins of the French Revolution*, 77–85, 128–248; Van Kley, *The Jansenists and the Expulsion of the Jesuits in France, 1757–1765* (New Haven, Conn.: Yale University Press, 1987); and Catherine Maire, *De la Cause de Dieu à la cause de la Nation: Le Jansenisme au XVIIIe siècle* (Paris: Gallimard, 1998). On the religious collapse of absolutism, see also Jeffrey Merrick, *The Desacralization of the French Monarchy in the Eighteenth Century* (Baton Rouge, La.: Louisiana State University Press, 1990).

37. This account is drawn from Van Kley, *Religious Origins of the French Revolution*, 51–53.

38. Louis Richeome, *L'Immortalité de l'âme* (Paris: Sébastien Cramoisy, 1621), 88, 445. For an overview of Richeome's theology, see Bremond, *Histoire littéraire*, 1: 18–67.

39. On this point, see Dale Van Kley, "Pierre Nicole, Jansenism, and the Morality of Enlightened Self-Interest," in *Anticipations of the Enlightenment in England, France, and Germany*, ed. Alan Charles Kors and Paul J. Korshin (Philadelphia: University of Pennsylvania Press, 1987), 69–85, esp. 72.

40. Richeome, *Immortalité de l'âme*, 117–127; quotations, 117, 121–122. In contrast to this view, Van Kley suggests in *Religious Origins of the French Revolution*, 54–55, that Fénelon's doctrines bore significant resemblance to the Molinism of the Jesuits.

41. See Nicole, *Réfutation des principales erreurs des quiétistes*, 354–373, 395–402.

42. On this theme, see Lucien Goldmann, *The Hidden God: A Study of Tragic Vision in the "Pensées" of Pascal and the Tragedies of Racine*, trans. Philip Thody (New York: Humanities Press, 1964).

43. For related interpretations on the rise of human autonomy, see Baker, "Enlightenment and the Institution of Society," 108–120, and Bell, *Cult of the Nation*, 22–49.

44. On the Jesuits' dealings in Rodez, see *Mémoires de la Société des lettres*,

sciences et arts de l'Averyron (Rodez: Société des lettres, sciences et arts de l'Aveyron, 1838–1964), 5: 750–790.

45. *Seconde Dénonciation de la doctrine des Jesuites de Rodez, à Monsieur l'évêque de Rodez. Traité des actes humains* (n.p., n.d.), 1, 4–7, 19–20; quotations, 5. See also *Dénonciation à Monseigneur l'évêque et comte de Rodez, du "Traité des actes humains"* (n.p., [1721]).

46. *Dénonciation à Monseigneur le Procureur général du Roy au Parlement de Toulouse & contraire à l'obeissance & au respect due aux Magistrats* (n.p. 1722). See also *Mémoires de la Société des lettres, sciences et arts de l'Averyron,* 5: 793–802.

47. *Ordonnance et Instruction pastorale, pour la condamnation du "Traité des actes humains"* (Rodez: N. Le Roux, n.d.) and *Arrest de la cour de Parlement de Toulouse. Qui annulle un Decret de l'Inquisition de Rome, du 14 Juillet 1723* (Toulouse: Claude-Gilles Lecamus, 1723).

48. *Remontrances des curez de Rhodés, à Monseigneur leur évêque. Contre plusieurs propositions quiétistes & autres injurieuses aux SS. Pères* (n.p., 1732), 1–2; quotation, 2. For the Jesuit reaction to the clerics' previous attacks and mention of their Jansenist sympathies, see *Lettre de Mr. le marquis de *** au R. P. Recteur des Jesuites de Rodez* (n.p., n.d.).

49. *Remontrances des curez de Rhodés,* 3.

50. Ibid., 5. The quotation is taken from Lamejou's unpublished Latin treatise on the theological virtues.

51. Ibid., 5–6, 8–11; quotation, 8.

52. Ibid., 7, 13, 16.

53. Ibid., 18, 19–20.

54. Ibid., 20–24; quotations, 21 and 23.

55. Ibid., 32–39; quotation, 39.

56. Henri Bremond coined the phrase *humanisme dévot*; see *Histoire littéraire,* 1: 187–385.

57. Fénelon, *Explication des maximes des saints,* 1012.

58. *Remontrances des curez de Rhodés,* 26–32.

59. *Requeste présentée au Parlement pour Marguerite-Catherine Turpin* (Paris: Ph. Nic. Lottin, 1735), 3–9; quotation, 9.

60. Ibid., 9–10; quotation, 9.

61. After heated debate, the Parlement dismissed the subject of the *requête* as beyond its legal competence, so Turpin remained in prison. On the initial support for the Pâris cult among the Parlement's magistrates and their subsequent ruling on the case of Turpin and other *convulsionnaires,* see B. Robert Kreiser, *Miracles, Convulsions, and Ecclesiastical Politics in Early Eighteenth-Century Paris* (Princeton, N.J.: Princeton University Press, 1978), 223–224, 336–338.

62. Kreiser, *Miracles, Convulsions, and Ecclesiastical Politics,* 152–155, 336; Daniel Vidal, *Miracles et convulsions jansénistes au XVIIIe siècle: Le Mal et sa connaissance* (Paris: Presses universitaires de France, 1987), 194–198; and Maire, *De la cause de Dieu à la cause de la Nation,* 250–253, 261–265.

63. Kreiser, *Miracles, Convulsions, and Ecclesiastical Politics,* 93–98.

64. *Pensées sur les prodiges de nos jours* (n.p., 1734), 6–9 and [Abbé de Saint-

Jean], *Lettre d'un ecclesiastique de province, à un de ses amis, où il lui donne une idée abregée de l'œuvre des convulsions* (n.p., 1733), 8–10.

65. Jacques Vincent d'Asfeld, *Vains efforts des mêlangistes ou discernans dans l'œuvre des convulsions, pour défendre le systême du mêlange* (Paris, 1737), 127.

66. Kreiser, *Miracles, Convulsions, and Ecclesiastical Politics*, 13–68. See also Van Kley, *Religious Origins of the French Revolution*, 97–100.

67. See Jan Goldstein, "Enthusiasm or Imagination? Eighteenth-Century Smear Words in Comparative National Context," in *Enthusiasm and Enlightenment in Europe, 1650–1850*, ed. Lawrence E. Klein and Anthony J. La Vopa (San Marino, Calif.: Huntington Library Press, 1998), 29–49.

68. On the *convulsionnaires* and the problem of the hidden God, see Maire, *De la cause de la nation à la cause de Dieu*, 306–314.

69. On Pâris's life, see Kreiser, *Miracles, Convulsions, and Ecclesiastical Politics*, 81–90.

70. *Recueil des miracles operés au tombeau de M. de Pâris diacre* (Utrecht, 1733), 1: 5–10, 14–34.

71. Ibid., 301–308; quotation, 306.

72. Kreiser, *Miracles, Convulsions, and Ecclesiastical Politics*, 125–128, 130–160, 173–176.

73. [Pierre Boyer], *Coup d'œil en forme de lettre sur les convulsions* (Paris, 1733), 4.

74. *Procès Verbaux de plusieurs Medecins et chirurgiens, . . . , au sujet de quelques personnes soi-disantes agitées de Convulsions* (Paris: Veuve Mazieres & Jean-Baptiste Garnier, 1732), 2, 4, 7–8, and Kreiser, *Miracles, Convulsions, and Ecclesiastical Politics*, 208–209.

75. Quoted in Kreiser, *Miracles, Convulsions, and Ecclesiastical Politics*, 181.

76. Ibid., 320–347.

77. *Consultation sur les convulsions* (n.p., 1735), 9–12. On the meanings of the term *aliénation*, see *Dictionnaire de l'Académie française*, 1st ed., s.v. "Aliéner" and 4th ed., s.vv. "Aliénation" and "Aliéner."

78. *Consultation sur les convulsions*, 5.

79. *Nouveau plan de réflexions sur la Consultation des Docteurs contre les convulsions* (n.p., n.d.), 8–14; quotations, 11, 13, 16.

80. On the figurist tradition, see Kreiser, *Miracles, Convulsions, and Ecclesiastical Politics*, 245–250; Vidal, *Miracles et convulsions*, 289–313; and Maire, *De la Cause de Dieu à la cause de la Nation*, 286–320.

81. [Saint-Jean], *Lettre*, 7, 8, 11. The abbé claimed to have spent seven weeks in Paris gathering firsthand information on the *convulsionnaires*. According to his count, in 1733, there were as many as 400 practicing convulsionists in Paris, 270 of whom he observed personally. Furthermore, the abbé noted a significant gender disparity in the movement: in the groups he visited, 211 were women or girls, and only 59 were men.

82. Despite his initial enthusiasm, Boyer would soon grow disillusioned with Augustin; see Kreiser, *Miracles, Convulsions, and Ecclesiastical Politics*, 326–328.

83. Boyer, *Coup d'œil*, 6–13, 15–20; quotations, 7, 13, 19.

84. Ibid., 9; cf. [Saint-Jean], *Lettre*, 12.

85. [Saint-Jean], *Lettre*, 9–20; quotation, 20.

86. Boyer, *Coup d'œil*, 20.

87. [Saint-Jean], *Lettre*, 20.

88. Boyer, *Coup d'œil*, 16, 26.

89. On d'Asfeld's shifting views on the *convulsionnaires*, see Joseph Dedieu, "L'Agonie du jansénisme (1715–1790). Essai de bio-bibliographie," *Revue de l'histoire de France* 14: 184, and Kreiser, *Miracles, Convulsions, and Ecclesiastical Politics*, 288–289.

90. D'Asfeld, *Vains efforts*, 13, 121.

91. Ibid. 13–15, 43–44, 120.

92. Jean-Baptiste Poncet Desessarts, *XIII. Lettre de Monsieur P*** à une de ses amis sur les convulsions* (n.p, n.d.), 1–9; quotations, 4–5.

93. D'Asfeld, *Vains efforts*, 136–149; quotations, 136, 142–143, 146.

94. Ibid., 13–14.

95. Desessarts, *XIII. Lettre de Monsieur P****, 46.

96. Jacques Fouillou, *Réponse à un mémoire en forme de plainte; faite au nom de la convulsionnaire nommé Charlotte* (Paris, 1735), 4–9, 16–20, 25–29; quotations, 9 and 29. For additional details on this case, see *Requeste présentée au Parlement par Charlotte de la Porte* (Paris: Ph. Nic. Lottin, 1735).

97. Hecquet, *Naturalisme des convulsions*, 183.

98. Hecquet, *Le Mélange dans les convulsions confondu par le naturalisme* (Soleure: Andreas Gymnicus, 1733), 40.

99. Hecquet, *Naturalisme des convulsions*, 4, 7, 119.

100. On Hecquet's life and career, see *Encyclopédie méthodique: Médecine*, vol. 7 (Paris: H. Agasse, 1798), s.v. "Hecquet (Philippe)," 77–79, and L. W. B. Brockliss, "The Medico-Religious Universe of an Early Eighteenth-Century Parisian Doctor: The Case of Philippe Hecquet," in *The Medical Revolution of the Seventeenth Century*, ed. Roger Kenneth French and Andrew Wear (Cambridge: Cambridge University Press, 1989), 191–221.

101. Hecquet, *Naturalisme des convulsions*, 14, 17, 116.

102. Ibid., 21, 189–194; quotation, 21.

103. Ibid., 1, 43–45, 184; quotations, 1, 184.

104. Ibid., 7.

105. On the mounting persecution and gradual decline of the *convulsionnaires*, see Kreiser, *Miracles, Convulsions, and Ecclesiastical Politics*, 388–394.

106. Hecquet, *Naturalisme des convulsions*, 176. See also 148, 160, 183, 193–194.

107. On this view, see Kreiser, "Devils of Toulon," 174–175; Choudhury, "Carnal Quietism," 174–175, 182–183; and Kuznicki, "Sorcery and Publicity," 291–294, 307–308.

108. *Justification de Demoiselle Catherine Cadière*, in *Recueil général des pièces concernant le procez entre la demoiselle Cadiere; de la Ville de Toulon; Et le Pere Girard, Jesuite* (The Hague: Swart, 1731), 1: 3–18; quotations, 7–10.

109. *Parallèle des sentimens du Pere Girard, avec ceux de Molinos* (n.p., n.d) and *Mémoire Instructif pour Demoiselle Catherine Cadière*, in *Recueil général*, 2: 10–11, 72–88.

110. See *Confession faicte par Messire Louys Gaufridi Prestre en l'Eglise des Accoules de Marseille* (Aix: Jean Tholozan, 1611), 3–5.

111. *Mémoire instructif pour le Pere Jean-Baptiste Girard* (n.p., n.d. [1731]), 35, 66–67; quotation, 35.

112. *Copie du prononcé de l'Arrest de la cour du Parlement de Provence, Au sujet de l'Affaire du Pere Jean-Baptiste Girard, Jesuite; & de Catherine Cadière* (n.p., 1731). On the Parlement's deliberations, see also Kreiser, "Devils of Toulon," 190–194.

113. On the popularity and literary significance of *Thérèse philosophe*, see Robert Darnton, *The Forbidden Best-Sellers of Pre-Revolutionary France* (New York: Norton, 1996), 63–64, 89–114.

114. *Thérèse philosophe*, in *Œuvres anonymes du XVIIIe siècle*, ed. Michel Camus (Paris: Fayard, 1985–1987), 3: 54–59, 98–115, 174–180; quotations, 58, 99, 108, 175, 179.

115. Among other pornographic works featuring Quietism, see *Histoire de Dom Bougre* (1741), in *Œuvres anonymes du XVIIIe siècles*, 1: 29–236.

CHAPTER 4. SPINOZA'S GHOST

1. *Correspondance littéraire, philosophique et critique*, ed. Maurice Tourneux (1877–1882; repr. Nendeln, Liechtenstein: Kraus, 1968), 10: 342, 344.

2. *Arrest de parlement, qui condamne le nommé Humain, . . . & le nommé Bourdeaux* (Paris: P. G. Simon, 1774), 1–2. On the legal punishment of suicide, see John McManners, *Death and the Enlightenment: Changing Attitudes to Death among Christians and Unbelievers in Eighteenth-Century France* (Oxford: Oxford University Press, 1985), 409–410, and Albert Bayet, *Le Suicide et la morale* (Paris: Félix Alcan, 1922), 605–633.

3. See L. P. L. D. [le P. Laliman, dominicain], *Moyens propres à garantir les hommes du suicide* (Paris: Benoît Morin, 1779).

4. See Gay, *Enlightenment*, 3–10; quotation, 8.

5. Israel, *Radical Enlightenment*, esp. v–vii and 6–13; quotations, vi.

6. Montesquieu, *Lettres persanes*, ed. Paul Vernière (Paris: Garnier frères, 1960), 123.

7. See, e.g., Kwass, "Ordering the World of Goods"; John Shovlin, "The Cultural Politics of Luxury in Eighteenth-Century France," *French Historical Studies* 23, 4 (Autumn 2000): 577–606.

8. Voltaire, *Questions sur l'Encyclopédie*, s.vv. "Dieu, Dieux," in id., *Œuvres complètes*, 18: 366. Although the text is presented under the generic title *Dictionnaire philosophique*, which is a compilation consisting of the publication of the same name along with other works that Voltaire organized alphabetically, it first appeared in *Questions sur l'Encyclopédie*; see Voltaire, *Œuvres complètes*, 18: 365n1.

9. Gottfried Wilhelm Leibniz, "Considerations on the Doctrine of a Universal Spirit," in *The Philosophical Works of Leibnitz*, trans. George Martin Duncan (New Haven, Conn.: Tuttle, Morehouse, & Taylor, 1890), 139–148; quotation, 139–140. See also Émilienne Naert, *Leibniz et la querelle du pur amour* (Paris: J. Vrin, 1959), 97–100.

10. On the circulation and impact of Spinozist ideas in France, see Israel, *Radical Enlightenment*, 565–598 and 684–720; Ira O. Wade, *The Clandestine Organization and Diffusion of Philosophical Ideas in France from 1700 to 1750* (Princeton, N.J.: Princeton University Press, 1938), 265–269; and Vernière, *Spinoza et la pensée française*. On the liberalization of the book trade, see Chartier, *Cultural Origins of the French Revolution*, 50–53. The *Encyclopédie*'s intellectual ambitions are discussed in Robert Darnton, "Philosophers Trim the Tree of Knowledge: The Epistemological Strategy of the *Encyclopédie*," in *The Great Cat Massacre and Other Episodes in French Cultural History* (New York: Basic Books, 1984), 191–214.

11. Albert Monod, "Mouvement de l'apologétique de 1670 à 1802," in id., *De Pascal à Chateaubriand: Les Défenseurs français du Christianisme de 1670 à 1802* (1916; repr., Geneva: Slatkine, 1970).

12. Baruch Spinoza, *Ethics*, in *The Collected Works of Spinoza*, ed. and trans. Edwin Curley (Princeton, N.J.: Princeton University Press, 1994), 1: 408 [ID3]. In addition to the discussions in Israel and Vernière, my reading has been informed by Jonathan Bennett, *A Study of Spinoza's "Ethics"* (Indianapolis, Ind.: Hackett, 1984); Richard Mason, *The God of Spinoza: A Philosophical Study* (Cambridge: Cambridge University Press, 1987); Pierre-François Moreau, *Spinoza et le spinozisme* (Paris: Presses universitaires de France, 2003); and Roger Scruton, *Spinoza* (Oxford: Oxford University Press, 1986).

13. Spinoza, *Ethics*, 410–424, 433–434; quotations, 420, 434 [IP1–15, 29; quotations, IP15 and IP29].

14. Ibid., 425–429, 435–439; quotation, 435 [IP17–20, 32–33; quotation, IP32C1].

15. Ibid., 420–424, 454–456; quotation, 456 [IP15, IIP10–11; quotation, IIP11C].

16. Ibid., 498–512, 563–568 [IIIP6–30, IVP35–37]. See also Bennett, *Study of Spinoza's "Ethics*," 25.

17. Cf. Scruton, *Spinoza*, 52.

18. Spinoza, *Ethics*, 604–606; quotation, 604 [VP17–20; quotation, VP19].

19. This quotation is taken from Spinoza's supplement to the *Ethics*, published as *Dieu, l'homme et la béatitude*, trans. Paul Janet (Paris: G. Balière, 1878), 124.

20. Spinoza, *Ethics*, 605–606; quotation, 606 [VP20; quotation, VP20S].

21. Spinoza, *Ethics*, 611–613 [VP32–36].

22. Ibid., 544 [IV Preface].

23. On Fénelon's engagement with Spinoza, see Vernière, *Spinoza et la pensée française*, 270–278. Keep in mind that Spinoza came under direct attack in Fénelon's *Lettres sur divers sujets de métaphysique et religion*, in id., *Œuvres complètes*, 1: 121–122, 128–129.

24. Fénelon, *Traité de l'existence et des attributs de Dieu*, in id., *Œuvres complètes*, 1: 60–61.

25. Ibid., 61–62.

26. Ibid., 64.

27. I have adapted this expression from Adam Sutcliffe, *Judaism and Enlightenment* (Cambridge: Cambridge University Press, 2003), 133–147.

28. Voltaire, *Dictionnaire philosophique*, s.v. "Athéisme," in id., *Œuvres complètes*, 17, 1: 474.

29. Étienne Bonnot de Condillac, *Traité des systèmes*, in id., *Œuvres complètes* (1821–1822; repr., Geneva: Slatkine, 1970), 2: 166, 250.

30. Montesquieu, "Continuation de quelques Pensées qui n'ont pu entrer dans le *Traité des Devoirs*," in id., *Œuvres complètes*, ed. Roger Caillois (Paris: Gallimard, 1949–1951), 1: 1137–1138.

31. Ibid., 1138. Chilperic was a Merovingian king notorious for his brutality.

32. See Guyon, *Vie*, 2: 238–239; cf. chap. 2 above.

33. Montesquieu, *Esprit des lois*, 2: 797–798, 800–803; *Défense de "l'Esprit des lois*," in Montesquieu, *Esprit des lois*, 2: 1199–1228.

34. Montesquieu, *Esprit des lois*, 828–831.

35. On this point, see Hirschman, *Passions and the Interests*, 12–20, 69–81; Van Kley, "The Morality of Enlightened Self-Interest," 69–85; and Dickey, "Pride, Hypocrisy and Civility," 387–431, esp. 411–412, 416–418.

36. On the history of the *Traité des trois imposteurs*, see Silvia Berti, "The First Edition of the *Traité des trois imposteurs* and Its Debt to Spinoza's *Ethics*," in *Atheism from the Reformation to the Enlightenment*, ed. Michael Hunter and David Wootton (Oxford: Clarendon Press, 1992), 183–220; B. E. Schwarzbach and A. W. Fairbairn, "History and Structure of Our *Traité des trois imposteurs*," in *Heterodoxy, Spinozism, and Free Thought in Early Eighteenth-Century Europe: Studies on the "Traité des trois imposteurs*," ed. Silvia Berti et al. (Dordrecht: Kluwer, 1996), 75–130; and Israel, *Radical Enlightenment*, 694–700.

37. *Traité des trois imposteurs* (n.p., 1771), ed. Pierre Rétat (Saint-Étienne: Universités de la région Rhône-Alpes, Centre interuniversitaire d'éditions et de rééditions, 1973), 4–6; quotations, 5–6.

38. Ibid., 6–15; quotations, 6, 13–15.

39. Ibid., 17–25; quotations, 19, 17, 20, 23.

40. Ibid., 27–79; quotations, 27–28, 78.

41. Ibid., 80–92; quotations, 80 and 91.

42. See Schwarzbach and Fairbairn, "History and Structure of our *Traité*," 111–115; and Vernière, *Spinoza et la pensée française*, 275.

43. The phrase "société de gens de lettres" appears on the title page of the *Encyclopédie*. On the organization of the philosophe movement, see, e.g., Goodman, *Republic of Letters*, and Frank A. Kafker, *The Encyclopedists as a Group: A Collective Biography of the Authors of the "Encyclopédie"* (Oxford: Voltaire Foundation, 1996).

44. Monod, *De Pascal à Chateaubriand*, 8.

45. Darrin M. McMahon, *Enemies of the Enlightenment: The French Counter-Enlightenment and the Making of Modernity* (Oxford: Oxford University Press, 2001).

46. On this point, see Israel, *Radical Enlightenment*, 488–491.

47. Sinsart, *Réfutation du matérialisme*, 269–270, 277.

48. Ibid., 8.

49. François-André-Adrien Pluquet, *Examen du fatalisme* (Paris: Didot, 1757), 1: i–v; quotation, v.

50. Laurent François, *Preuves de la Religion de Jésus-Christ, contre les spino-sistes et les deistes* (Paris: Veuve Estienne & fils, 1751), 1: 276–280; quotation, 278.

51. Guillaume de Maleville, *La Religion naturelle et la révélée, établies sur les principes de la vraie philosophie, et sur la divinité des écritures* (Paris: Nyon, 1756–1758), 1: 277; 2: 46, 49.

52. Ibid., 125–127; quotation, 127.

53. Ibid., 144, 173. See also Sinsart, *Réfutation du matérialisme*, 289–291.

54. François, *Preuves de la Religion*, 1: 143–145, 366–368; quotation, 367.

55. Ibid., 368–378.

56. See McMahon, *Enemies of the Enlightenment*, 28–42.

57. François, *Preuves de la Religion*, 1: 370–379; quotations, 371, 378.

58. Pluquet, *Examen du fatalisme*, 2: 500–515; quotations, 500.

59. Sinsart, *Réfutation de matérialisme*, 13–16, 43–44, 125–161; quotations, 14, 43, 144.

60. Ibid., 203.

61. *Encyclopédie*, s.v. "Providence," 13: 514.

62. Ibid., s.v. "Bonheur," 2: 322–323.

63. Voltaire, *Épitre à l'auteur du nouveau livre: "Des Trois Imposteurs,"* 1–2. On Voltaire's relationship with Spinozism, see Vernière, *Spinoza et la pensée française*, 495–527, and Ira O. Wade, *The Intellectual Development of Voltaire* (Princeton, N.J.: Princeton University Press, 1970), 708.

64. To cite one instance, *Épitre aux matérialistes* (Amsterdam, 1779).

65. Athanse-René Mérault de Bizy, *Voltaire apologiste de la religion chrétienne* (Paris: Perisse frères, 1838), Avant-propos.

66. Ibid., 394.

67. Ibid., 13.

68. On the similarities between Christian and Enlightenment writers regarding self-interest, see Lester G. Crocker, *An Age of Crisis: Man and World in Eighteenth-Century French Thought* (Baltimore: Johns Hopkins University Press, 1959), 256–281.

69. Mérault, *Voltaire apologiste*, 239. On Voltaire's wavering opinion of religion, see Crocker, *Age of Crisis*, 23–26, 384–386.

70. Ernst Cassirer, *The Philosophy of the Enlightenment*, trans. Fritz C. A. Koelln and James P. Pettegrove (Princeton, N.J.: Princeton University Press, 1951), 187.

71. See, e.g., Vernière, *Spinoza et la pensée française*, 374–375, 413, 528–529; Israel, *Radical Enlightenment*, 704–713; and *Spinoza au XVIIIe siècle*, ed. Oliver Bloch (Paris: Méridiens Klincksieck, 1990).

72. *Encyclopédie*, s.vv. "Spinosa, Philosophie de" and "Spinosiste," 15: 463–475. On the borrowings from Bayle in the first article on Spinoza and Diderot's authorship of the second, see Israel, *Radical Enlightenment*, 712, and Vernière, *Spinoza et la pensée française*, 596–597.

73. *Encyclopédie*, s.v. "Spinosiste," 15: 474.

74. On Enlightenment vitalism, see Elizabeth Ann Williams, *A Cultural History of Medical Vitalism in Enlightenment Montpellier* (Aldershot: Ashgate, 2003), and

Peter Hanns Reil, *Vitalizing Science in the Enlightenment* (Berkeley: University of California Press, 2005).

75. For a more in-depth discussion of the function of memory in materialist epistemology, see Perkins, *Concept of the Self in the French Enlightenment*, 42–56.

76. Alan Charles Kors, *D'Holbach's Coterie: An Enlightenment in Paris* (Princeton, N.J.: Princeton University Press, 1976), 41–91, 120–146. See also Jean-Claude Bourdin, *Les Matérialistes au XVIIIe siècle* (Paris: Payot & Rivages, 1996), 16–18.

77. Denis Diderot, *Essai sur les règnes de Claude et Neron*, in id., *Œuvres complètes*, ed. Herbert Dieckmann et al. (Paris: Hermann, 1975-), 25: 246–249, and Paul Henri Dietrich, baron d'Holbach, *Système de la nature, ou Des Loix du monde Physique & du monde moral*, new ed. (London, 1771), 2: 381–382. In the text and in the following notes, I use the modern spelling of the d'Holbach's work (*Système de la nature*). On La Mettrie and materialist critiques of his work, see Ann Thomson, *Materialism and Society in the Mid-Eighteenth Century: La Mettrie's "Discours préliminaire"* (Geneva: Droz, 1981), 5–20, 181–185, and Pierre Naville, *D'Holbach et la philosophie scientifique au XVIIIe siècle* (Paris: Gallimard, 1967), 361–368.

78. On Vaucanson's flute-player, see Jacques Vaucanson, *Le Méchanisme du fluteur automate* (Paris: Jacques Guerin, 1738), and *Encyclopédie*, s.v. "Androide," 1: 448–451.

79. Julien Offroy de La Mettrie, *L'Homme-machine*, in *Œuvres philosophiques de La Mettrie*, new ed. (Paris: Charles Tutot, 1796), 3: 119–141; quotation, 139.

80. La Mettrie, *L'Art de jouir*, in id., *Œuvres philosophiques*, 3: 229–230, 246.

81. On La Mettrie's Jansenist influences, see Ann Thomson, *Materialism and Society*, 60–68.

82. La Mettrie, *Anti-Sénèque, ou Discours sur le bonheur souverain*, in id., *Œuvres philosophiques*, 2: 163, 175, 218.

83. On La Mettrie's political views and motives, see Thomson, *Materialism and Society*, 52, 182–183, and Kathleen Anne Wellman, *La Mettrie: Medicine, Philosophy, Enlightenment* (Durham, N.C.: Duke University Press, 1992), 246–266.

84. D'Holbach, *Système de la nature*, 2: 381–382. On Mandeville's debt to Jansenism, see Dickey, "Pride, Hypocrisy and Civility," 387–431.

85. Kors, *D'Holbach's Coterie*, 13, 83–84; Darnton, *Forbidden Best-Sellers*, 25–28, 48–49, 63–66.

86. D'Holbach's scientific work and its relationship to vitalism is discussed in Reill, *Vitalizing Nature*, 81–82, and Williams, *Cultural History of Medical Vitalism*, 129–131, 173–175. On d'Holbach's scientific endeavors more generally, see Naville, *D'Holbach*, 185–203.

87. D'Holbach, *Système de la nature*, "Préface de l'auteur."

88. Ibid., 1: 1–3, 11–29; quotations, 1–3, 25.

89. Ibid., 1: 55–75; quotations, 55, 58, 73.

90. Ibid., 1: 77–82, 93–94; quotations, 80–81, 93–94.

91. Ibid., 1: 96–224; quotation, 219.

92. Ibid., 1: 54, 79, 231, 342–361; quotations, 54, 231, 361.

93. Nicole, *Essais de morale*, 3: 132–143. For d'Holbach's critique of the doctrine of original sin, see id., *Système de la nature*, 1: 230, 349–352.

94. D'Holbach, *Système de la nature*, 1: 241–273; quotations, 241, 253, 258, 260, 262, 273.

95. Ibid., 2: 443.

96. Ibid., 2: 443–449; quotation, 445.

97. Ibid., 1: 12. For a refutation of the view that Diderot had a direct hand in d'Holbach's work, see Virgil W. Topazio, "Diderot's Supposed Contribution to d'Holbach's Works," *PMLA* 69, 1 (March 1954): 173–188.

98. D'Holbach, *Système de la nature*, 2: 453.

99. Ibid., 2: 188–193. For a more detailed discussion of the relationship between d'Holbach and Spinoza, see Vernière, *Spinoza et la pensée française*, 630–642, and Jacques Moutaux, "D'Holbach et Spinoza," in *Spinoza au XVIIIe siècle*, 151–167.

100. *Réquisitoire sur lequel est intervenu l'Arrêt du Parlement du 18 Août 1770*, in d'Holbach, *Système de la nature*, 2: 465–500; quotations, 469, 473. Séguier's remarks were themselves condemned for including excessive paraphrases from the books he aimed to ban. See Kors, *D'Holbach's Coterie*, 240–241.

101. Voltaire, *Questions sur l'Encyclopédie*, s.v. "Dieu, Dieux," in id., *Œuvres complètes*, 18, 2: 369–381; quotations, 375–376.

102. Voltaire to d'Alembert, July 16, 1770; to Bernard-Joseph Saurin, November 10, 1770; and to Frederick William of Prussia, November 28, 1770; in id., *Œuvres complètes*, 47, 15: 139, 250, 265.

103. Laliman, *Moyens propres à garantir les hommes du suicide*, 9–30, 126–138; quotations, 29, 36, 126. On the incidence of suicide during this period, see Louis-Sébastien Mercier, *Tableau de Paris* (Amsterdam, 1782), 1: 196, and McManners, *Death and the Enlightenment*, 429–437.

104. Laliman, *Moyens propres à garantir les hommes du suicide*, 38.

105. *Correspondance littéraire*, 10: 346.

106. Laliman, *Moyens propres à garantir les hommes du suicide*, 139–148; quotation, 142. Laliman took this expression from Luke 21:19.

107. On Bergier's life and career, see Kors, *D'Holbach's Coterie*, 113–116, and Didier Masseau, *Les Ennemis des philosophes: L'Antiphilosophie au temps des Lumières* (Paris: Albin Michel, 2000), 165–169.

108. On the strategies associated with this renewed offensive, see Masseau, *Ennemis des philosophes*, 157–171.

109. Nicolas Bergier, *Examen du matérialisme, ou Réfutation du systême de la nature* (Paris: Humblot, 1771), 1: 3–5, 110–115; quotation, 110. Cf. d'Holbach, *Système de la nature*, 1: 75.

110. Bergier, *Examen du matérialisme*, 1: 115–257; quotations, 132, 137, 142, 229.

111. Ibid., 1: 133.

112. Ibid., 2: 232.

113. Cf. *Dictionnaire de l'Académie française*, 4th ed., s.v. "mystique."

114. On the government's efforts to open up the grain trade, see Steven Laurence Kaplan, *Bread, Politics and Political Economy in the Reign of Louis XV* (The Hague: Martinus Nijhoff, 1976).

115. On this point, see Shovlin, "Cultural Politics of Luxury," 580–590.

116. Rousseau, *Discours sur l'inégalité*, 167–168.

117. Kaplan, *Bread, Politics and Political Economy*, 676–693.

118. Horkheimer and Adorno, *Dialectic of Enlightenment*, 84.

119. Foucault, *Discipline and Punish*, esp. 195–228; quotation, 217.

120. For a recent statement of this position, see Jonathan Israel, *A Revolution of the Mind: Radical Enlightenment and the Intellectual Origins of Modern Democracy* (Princeton, N.J.: Princeton University Press, 2009), ix.

121. D'Holbach, *La Politique naturelle, ou Discours sur les vrais principes du gouvernement* (London, 1773), 1: 3–5. On d'Holbach's political thought, see also Everett C. Ladd Jr., "Helvetius and D'Holbach: 'La Moralisation de la Politique,'" *Journal of the History of Ideas* 23, 2 (April–June. 1962): 221–238, and T. C. Newland, "D'Holbach's Political Ambivalence," *Journal of Eighteenth-Century Studies* 4, 2 (September 1981): 184–190.

122. D'Holbach, *Système social, ou Principes naturels de la morale et de la politique* (London, 1773), 1: 1–16, 58–75, 105–112; 3: 63–83; quotations, 1: 62, 107; 3: 76, 84–85.

CHAPTER 5. THE SLEEP OF REASON

1. *L'Art de se rendre heureux par les songes* (Frankfurt, 1746), 167–168, 119–124, 2, 38–42, 77–78; quotations, 167–168, 119, 78.

2. The expression "mystic materialism" is adapted from Paolo Casini, *Diderot "philosophe"* (Bari: Laterza, 1962), 291–292.

3. *Encyclopédie*, s.v. "Philosophe," 12: 509–510. The article is an abridgement and revision of a tract first published in 1743. On Dumarsais, see Frank A. Kafker, in collaboration with Serena L. Kafker, *The Encyclopedists as Individuals: A Biographical Dictionary of the Authors of the "Encyclopédie,"* (Oxford: Voltaire Foundation, 1988), 121, and *Le Philosophe*, in Voltaire, *Œuvres complètes*, 29: 41, n. 1.

4. On Voltaire's love of coffee, see Voltaire, *Défense du mondain*, in id., *Œuvres complètes*, 10: 91.

5. On Enlightenment sociability, see Goodman, *Republic of Letters*, 90–135; Gordon, *Citizens without Sovereignty*, esp. 43–85, 86–128; Steven Kale, *French Salons: High Society and Political Sociability from the Old Regime to the Revolution of 1848* (Baltimore: Johns Hopkins University Press, 2005), esp. 1–45. Antoine Lilti, in contrast, places far greater stress on the hierarchical power relations at play; see *Le Monde des salons: Sociabilité et mondanité à Paris au XVIIIe siècle* (Paris: Fayard, 2005), 148–158, 169–186, 207–222.

6. Goodman, *Republic of Letters*, 102.

7. Quoted in ibid., 103.

8. On literary property and authorial identity, see, e.g., Chartier, *Cultural Origins of the French Revolution*, 53–61; Carla Hesse, "Enlightenment Epistemology and the Laws of Authorship in Revolutionary France, 1777–1793," in *Law and the Order of Culture*, ed. Robert Post (Berkeley: University of California Press, 1991), 109–137; Gregory S. Brown, *A Field of Honor: Culture and Public Theater in French Literary Life from Racine to the Revolution* (New York: Columbia University Press, 2005); Brown, *Literary Sociability and Literary Property in France*; and Turnovsky, *Literary Market*.

9. On the reform of the book trade, see also Birn, "Profits of Ideas," and David Pottinger, *The French Book Trade in the ancien régime, 1500–1791* (Cambridge, Mass.: Harvard University Press, 1958), 234–237.

10. Diderot, *Lettre historique et politique sur le commerce de la librairie*, in id., *Œuvres complètes*, 8: 509–510.

11. Diderot to Sophie Volland, August 15, 1762, in id., *Correspondance*, ed. Georges Roth (Paris: Éditions de Minuit, 1955–1970), 4: 105.

12. Diderot to Madame Riccoboni, November 27, 1758, in id., *Correspondance*, 2: 96–97; quotation, 97. In *Paradoxe sur le comédien* (1769), Diderot further refines this logic. In playing a role, the actor should not attempt to take on the feelings of a character within himself. Rather, Diderot explained, he "is often obliged to strip it [his sensibility] away, and this abnegation of self is impossible without an iron will." See Diderot, *Paradoxe sur le comédien*, in id., *Œuvres complètes*, 20: 60–64, 109–110; quotation, 63.

13. Robert Darnton, *The Literary Underground of the Old Regime* (Cambridge, Mass.: Harvard University Press, 1982); quotation, 1. On the commodification of culture in eighteenth-century France, see also Julia Simon, *Mass Enlightenment: Critical Studies in Rousseau and Diderot* (Albany: State University of New York Press, 1995).

14. Descartes, *Méditations*, 268, and Locke, *Essay Concerning Human Understanding*, 113. On this position, see also Michel Foucault, *Madness and Civilization: A History of Insanity in the Age of Reason*, trans. Richard Howard (New York: Vintage Books, 1988). For a noted criticism of Foucault's argument, see Jacques Derrida, "Cogito and the History of Madness," in *Writing and Difference*, trans. Alan Bass (Chicago: University of Chicago Press, 1978), 31–63.

15. Louis-Antoine de Caraccioli, *La Jouissance de soi-même* (Utrecht: H. Spruit, 1759), 293.

16. For an overview of the vast scholarship on this theme, see John O'Neal, *The Authority of Experience: Sensationalist Theory in the French Enlightenment* (University Park: Pennsylvania State University Press, 1996); David J. Denby, *Sentimental Narrative and the Social Order in France, 1760–1820* (Cambridge: Cambridge University Press, 1994); Anne C. Vila, *Enlightenment and Pathology: Sensibility in the Literature and Medicine of Eighteenth-Century France* (Baltimore: Johns Hopkins University Press, 1998); and Jessica Riskin, *Science in the Age of Sensibility: The Sentimental Empiricists of the French Enlightenment* (Chicago: University of Chicago Press, 2002).

17. On vitalist medicine during the Enlightenment, see Elizabeth Williams, *The Physical and the Moral: Anthropology, Physiology, and Philosophical Medicine in France, 1750–1850* (Cambridge: Cambridge University Press, 1994), and Williams, *Cultural History of Medical Vitalism*.

18. This point is expounded upon in revealing detail in Vila, *Enlightenment and Pathology*.

19. Diderot, *Salon de 1767*, in id., *Œuvres complètes*, 16: 230.

20. Steven F. Kruger, *Dreaming in the Middle Ages* (Cambridge: Cambridge University Press, 1991), 17–56.

21. On the status of dreams in eighteenth-century Christian thought and devo-

tion, see Vesna Petrovich, *Connaissance et Rêve(rie) dans le discours des Lumières* (New York: Peter Lange, 1996), 14–15, 50–51, and Kay S. Wilkins, "Some Aspects of the Irrational in 18th-Century France," in *Studies on Voltaire and the Eighteenth Century*, 140 (Oxford: Voltaire Foundation, 1975), 109–111.

22. *L'Art de faire des songes* (n.p., n.d., [ca. 1750]), 5, 7.

23. *Art de se rendre heureux par les songes*, "Avertissement," 2–3. The guide has been attributed to Benjamin Franklin, in part because of his authorship of the similarly entitled *The Art of Procuring Pleasant Dreams*. On the work's problematic status in Franklin's bibliography, see Léopold Derôme, *Causeries d'un ami des livres: Les Éditions originales des romantiques* (Paris: Édouard Rouveyre, 1886), 1: 218–220. For Franklin's text, which was available to eighteenth-century French readers, see *L'Art d'avoir des songes agréables*, in *Vie de Benjamin Franklin, écrite par lui-même, suivie de ses œuvres morales, politiques et littéraires* (Paris: F. Buisson, Year VI), 1: 346–357.

24. *Art de se rendre heureux par les songes*, "Avertissement," 5 ff.

25. Ibid., 39–52.

26. Ibid., 1–6.

27. Ibid., 78, 82, 92.

28. Ibid., 119–150; quotations, 119, 138.

29. Ibid., 161–162.

30. Ibid., 172–173.

31. On Augustine's views, see id., *On the Literal Meaning of Genesis*, trans. John Hammond Taylor (New York: Newman, 1982), 197–198.

32. *Art de se rendre heureux par les songes*, 175–185.

33. Ibid., 207.

34. Ibid., 208–210; quotation, 210.

35. Jean-François Lavoisier, *Dictionnaire portatif de médecine* (Paris: Aux Dépens de P. F. Didot le Jeune, 1764), s.vv. "Rêve" and "Délire," 2: 113 and 1: 194.

36. Condillac, *Essai sur l'origine des connaissances humaines*, in id., *Œuvres complètes*, 1: 12–13, 27–74; quotations, 65 and 67. Cf. Condillac, *Traité des sensations*, in id., *Œuvres complètes*, 3: 91–92.

37. Voltaire, *Dictionnaire philosophique*, 20: 434.

38. Louis Levade, Jean-Louis-Antoine Reynier, and Jacob Berthout van Berchem *fils*, *Rapport fait à la Société des Sciences Physiques de Lausanne sur un somnambule naturel* (Lausanne: H. Vincent, 1788), 52–53.

39. Ibid., 8–42; quotations, 7 and 17.

40. Ibid., 43–49; quotations, 43.

41. Cf. Condillac, *Traité des systèmes*, 60.

42. Levade et al., *Rapport sur un somnambule naturel*, 49–50, 58–60; quotation, 49 and 60. On the spiritual aspects of the Mesmerist movement, see Robert Darnton, *Mesmerism and the End of the Enlightenment in France* (Cambridge, Mass.: Harvard University Press, 1968), 47–81, 127–128.

43. P.F.L.M., *Du Sommeil* (The Hague: Pierre-Frederic Gosse, 1779), 21–35 78–82, 99, 130–135; quotations, 22, 79–80, 99, 131–132.

44. Ibid., 101–102, 136–141, 16–17; quotations, 101, 136, 138–140, 17.

45. For a contrasting view, see Denby, *Sentimental Narrative and the Social Order in France*, 86–89.

46. P.F.L.M., *Du Sommeil*, 141–142.

47. See, e.g., Keith Thomas, *Religion and the Decline of Magic: Studies in Popular Beliefs in Sixteenth- and Seventeenth-Century England* (New York: Scribner, 1971), and Lorraine Daston and Katharine Park, *Wonders and the Order of Nature, 1150–1750* (New York: Zone Books, 1998). For a provocative overview of recent scholarship on modern enchantment, defined as "one that enchants and disenchants simultaneously," see Michael Saler, "Modernity and Enchantment: A Historiographic Review," *American Historical Review* 111, 3 (June 2006): 692–716 (quotation, 702), and *The Re-Enchantment of the World: Secular Magic in a Rational Age*, ed. Joshua Landy and Michael Saler (Stanford, Calif.: Stanford University Press, 2009).

48. John Lough, *The "Encyclopédie"* (London: Longman, 1971), 61.

49. On the production of the *Encyclopédie*, see Jacques Proust, *Diderot et l'Encyclopédie* (Paris: Armand Colin, 1962), 47–58.

50. On the significance of the Prades affair for assessing the religious origins of the Enlightenment, see Burson, *Rise and Fall of the Theological Enlightenment*.

51. For an overview of the publication history of the *Encyclopédie*, see Lough, "*Encyclopédie*," 17–136 and Robert Darnton, *The Business of the Enlightenment: A Publishing History of the "Encyclopédie," 1775–1800* (Cambridge, Mass.: Harvard University Press, 1987), 4–17.

52. Darnton, "Philosophers Trim the Tree of Knowledge," 191–209; quotation, 205.

53. Israel, *Enlightenment Contested*, 732–862; quotation, 747.

54. *Encyclopédie*, s.v. "Anthropophagie," 2: 498.

55. Kafker, *Encyclopedists as Individuals*, 176–177 (quotation, 177); Kafker and Kafker, *Encyclopedists as a Group*, 65–68, 74–77.

56. *Encyclopédie*, s.v. "Encyclopédie," 5: 635–635A.

57. *Dictionnaire de l'Académie française*, 4th ed., s.v. "Distraction"; cf. *Encyclopédie*, s.v. "Distraction (Jurisprudence)," 4: 1061.

58. *Encyclopédie*, s.v. "Rêve," and *Dictionnaire de l'Académie française*, 4th ed., s.v. "Aliénation."

59. *Encyclopédie*, s.v. "Distraction," 1061.

60. Ibid.

61. *Encyclopédie*, s.v. "Rêver," 14: 228.

62. On the etymology and shifts in usage of *rêve, rêverie, songer*, and their linguistic relatives, see Robert Morrissey, *La Rêverie jusqu'à Rousseau: Recherches sur un topos littéraire* (Lexington, Ky.: French Forum, 1984), 34–35, 104–107, and Petrovich, *Connaissance et Rêve(rie)*, 6–7.

63. On the ecclesiastical campaign against popular forms of superstition and the role played by enthusiasm, see Wilkins, "Some Aspects of the Irrational," 109–117, and McManners, *Church and Society*, 2: 189–238.

64. The secularizing tendencies of the campaign against enthusiasm are featured in Michael Heyd, *"Be Sober and Reasonable": The Critique of Enthusiasm in the Seventeenth and Early Eighteenth Centuries* (Leiden: E. J. Brill, 1995), 274–

279. Arguments that complicate this position abound in *Enthusiasm and Enlightenment*, ed. Klein and La Vopa.

65. *Encyclopédie*, s.vv. "Songe (Métaph. & Physiol.)," 15: 354–358, and "Songer," 15: 358–359. On Formey and Jaucourt's respective roles, see "Songe," 357, and Petrovich, *Connaissance et Rêve(rie)*, 64.

66. Morrissey, *Rêverie jusqu'à Rousseau*, 30–35, 108–109.

67. *Encyclopédie*, s.v. "Songe (Métaph. & Physiol.)," 15: 357.

68. Locke, *Essay Concerning Human Understanding*, 113.

69. *Encyclopédie*, s.vv. "Songe (Métaph. & Physiol.)," 354, and "Songer," 358–359.

70. *Encyclopédie*, s.v. "Songe (Métaph. & Physiol.)," 355; cf. Locke, *Essay Concerning Human Understanding*, 111–112.

71. *Encyclopédie*, "Songe (Critique sacrée)," 15: 357–358.

72. Lenglet's relationship with Bossuet is discussed in Geraldine Sheridan, *Nicolas Lenglet Dufresnoy and the Literary Underworld of the Ancien Régime* (Oxford: Voltaire Foundation, 1989), 11–14, 148–149.

73. See Sheridan, *Nicolas Lenglet Dufresnoy*, 20–24; Petrovich, *Connaissance et Rêve(rie)*, 19–26; and Wilkins, "Aspects of the Irrational," 116–117.

74. Nicolas Lenglet Dufresnoy, *Traité historique et dogmatique sur les apparitions, les visions et les révélations particulières* (Paris: J.-N. Leloup, 1751), 1: viii, 3–8; quotations, 7, 8. Cf. Lenglet Dufresnoy, *Recueil de dissertations, anciennes et nouvelles, sur les apparitions, les visions et les songes* (Paris: J.-N. Leloup, 1751–1752).

75. Lenglet Dufresnoy, *Traité historique et dogmatique*, 1: 11–34, 255–291; quotations, 255, 289.

76. Jérôme Richard, *La Théorie des songes* (Paris: Estienne frères, 1766), xiii–xxi; quotations, xv–xvi, xxi. On Richard's espousal of Enlightenment ideals, see also Petrovich, *Connaissance et Rêve(rie)*, 27–30, and Caroline Jacot-Grapa, "Rêve et identité: Autour de la *Théorie des songes* de Jérôme Richard (1766)," in *Songes et songeurs (XIIIe–XVIIIe siècle)*, ed. Nathalie Dauvois and Jean-Philippe Grosperrin (Quebec: Presses de l'Université de Laval, 2003), 235–243.

77. Richard, *Théorie des songes*, 16–25, 46–50, 66–88, 120–137; quotations, 16–17, 19, 22, 77, 80, 50, 123.

78. Ibid., 229–240; quotations, 239–240.

79. *Encyclopédie*, s.v. "Quiétisme," 13: 709.

80. Richard, *Théorie des songes*, 241.

81. See Voltaire, *Siècle de Louis XIV*, 63.

82. *Encyclopédie*, s.v. "Imagination," 8: 561–562.

83. Jan Goldstein, "Enthusiasm or Imagination? Eighteenth-Century Smear Words in Comparative National Context," in *Enthusiasm and Enlightenment*, ed. Klein and La Vopa, 29–49. See also Daston, "Enlightenment Fears, Fears of Enlightenment," in *What's Left of Enlightenment? A Postmodern Question*, ed. Keith Michael Baker and Peter Hanns Reill (Stanford, Calif.: Stanford University Press, 2001), 116–123.

84. On Cahusac's life, see Kafker, *Encyclopedists as Individuals*, 79–81.

85. *Encyclopédie*, s.v. "Enthousiasme," 5: 719–720.

86. Ibid. 720–721.

87. Ibid., 720, 722.

88. *Encyclopédie*, s.v. "Génie," 7: 583. Of course, Diderot was a great admirer of Shaftesbury, and his first major work was a translation of the earl's *An Inquiry Concerning Virtue and Merit*, which appeared in 1745. See Diderot, *Essai de M. S.*** sur le mérite et la vertu* (1745), in id., *Œuvres complètes*, 1: 287–428, and Arthur Wilson, *Diderot* (New York: Oxford University Press, 1972), 50–52.

89. *Encyclopédie*, s.v. "Théosophes," 16: 260.

90. *Encyclopédie*, s.v. "Éclectisme," 5: 276.

91. Ibid., 272, 281, 288, 289. Not incidentally, the prominent Neoplatonist Proclus provided the philosophical inspiration for the early Christian mystic known as Pseudo-Dionysius, whose theological views Fénelon would later defend. See Fénelon, *Explication des maximes des saints*, 1067.

92. *Encyclopédie*, s.v. "Éclectisme," 281, 270.

93. Ibid., 289.

94. *Encyclopédie*, s.v. "Délicieux," 4: 784.

95. Ibid.

96. Fénelon, *Sentimens de piété*, 134.

97. *Encyclopédie*, s.v. "Délicieux," 784.

98. See *Dictionnaire de l'Académie française*, 4th ed., s.v. "Quiétisme" and *Encyclopédie*, s.v. "Quiétisme." The ARTFL database contains records of 39 occurrences of the term for the years 1689 to 1789; the vast majority (31 occurrences) refer explicitly either to the Quietist controversy in particular, or more generally, to heretical forms of Christian mysticism; the others allude to states of disinterestedness and abandon associated with the theology of Fénelon and Guyon.

99. On these developments, see, e.g., Elena Rousso, *Styles of Enlightenment: Taste, Politics, and Authorship in the French Enlightenment* (Baltimore: Johns Hopkins University Press, 2007); Thomas E. Crow, *Painters and Public Life in Eighteenth-Century France* (New Haven, Conn.: Yale University Press, 1985); Chartier, *Cultural Origins of the French Revolution*, 20–66; and Simon, *Mass Enlightenment*, 2–14, 147–155.

100. See Crow, *Painters and Public Life*, 7–22, and Michael Fried, *Absorption and Theatricality: Painting and Beholder in the Age of Diderot* (Chicago: University of Chicago Press, 1980), 35–61.

101. Fried, *Absorption and Theatricality*, 7–8, 35, 92–107; quotation, 107.

102. On Dubos, see Fried, *Absorption and Theatricality*, 73–76; David Marshall, *The Surprising Effects of Sympathy: Marivaux, Diderot, Rousseau, and Mary Shelley* (Chicago: University of Chicago Press, 1989), 13–39; and Alfred Lombard, *L'Abbé Du Bos: Un Initiateur de la pensée moderne (1670–1742)* (1913; repr., Geneva: Slatkine, 1969).

103. Jean-Baptiste Dubos, *Réflexions critiques sur la poésie et sur la peinture*, new, rev. ed. (Utrecht: Étienne Neaulme, 1732), 1: 4–5, 14–15; quotations, 4 and 14. Cf. *Encyclopédie*, s.v. "Ennui," 5: 693–694.

104. Dubos, *Réflexions critiques*, 2: 3–11, 177–179; quotations, 8, 178–179. On Diderot's arguments for artistic self-command, see *Paradoxe sur le comédien*, 50–41.

105. Diderot, *Essai sur la peinture*, in id., *Œuvres complètes*, 14: 389; also quoted in Daniel Brewer, *The Discourse of Enlightenment in Eighteenth-Century*

France: Diderot and the Art of Philosophizing (Cambridge: Cambridge University Press, 1993), 149.

106. On this point, see also Jay Caplan, *Framed Narratives: Diderot's Genealogy of the Beholder* (Minneapolis: University of Minnesota Press, 1985), 89–90, and Herbert Dieckmann, "Diderot et son lecteur," in id., *Cinq Leçons sur Diderot* (Geneva: Droz, 1959), 17–39.

107. Diderot, *Éloge de Richardson*, in id., *Œuvres complètes*, 13: 193. On the publication history of the text, see Jean Sgard, introduction, ibid., 181, 190–192.

108. Roger Chartier, "Richardson, Diderot et la lectrice impatiente," *Modern Language Notes* 114 (1999): 654–655.

109. Diderot, *Éloge de Richardson*, 195.

110. It should be noted as well, however, that in his article "Charité," Diderot took the side of Bossuet over Fénelon on the question of disinterested love, arguing that the self is incapable of renouncing its desire for happiness, even in seeking such a renunciation. See *Encyclopédie*, s.v. "Charité," 3: 205–207; quotation, 206.

111. Diderot, *Éloge de Richardson*, 206. On Richardson's popularity and *anglomanie*, see Aslög Anund-Tråvén, *Étude quantative de cinq traductions françaises du XVIIIe siècle basées sur les romans anglais de Samuel Richardson, à savoir "Pamela," "Clarissa", et "Sir Charles Grandison"* (Göteborg: Kompendiet, 2000), 1–5.

112. Diderot, *Éloge de Richardson*, 200–206; quotation, 200. On the sacralization of authorship, see Chartier, "Diderot, Richardson, et la lectrice impatiente," 664–665.

113. Annette Lorencau, introduction to Diderot, *Salon de 1767*, 34–36; Fried, *Absorption and Theatricality*, 138, 181, 231–232; and Crow, *Painters and Public Life*, 7–15.

114. Diderot, *Salon de 1767*, 64–78, 177–179; quotations, 71, 179.

115. Ibid., 58–62, 164–169; quotations, 62, 167. For Diderot's views on luxury, see also *Observations sur le Nakaz*, in Diderot, *Œuvres politiques*, ed. Paul Vernière (Paris: Garnier frères, 1963), 411–412.

116. For an extended discussion of Diderot's philosophical and aesthetic writings as a response to commodification and alienation, see Simon, *Mass Enlightenment*, 123–168.

117. Fried, *Absorption and Theatricality*, 104–136.

118. *Encyclopédie*, s.v. "Absorber, Engloutir," 1: 43.

119. Diderot, *Salon de 1767*, 183–184; also cited in Fried, *Absorption and Theatricality*, 125.

120. Ibid., 191–192; also cited in Fried, *Absorption and Theatricality*, 126.

121. *Encyclopédie*, s.v. "Jouissance," 8: 889. Cf. *Dictionnaire de l'Académie française*, 4th ed., s.v. "Jouissance."

122. Caraccioli, *Jouissance de soi-même*, xvii, xix–xx, 6.

123. Diderot, *Salon de 1767*, 192, 200, 273; cf. 214–216, 451–453.

124. Ibid., 186–188; quotation, 186.

125. On Diderot's intellectual development toward materialism, see Wilson, *Diderot*, 59, 559–570, 659–673, and Israel, *Enlightenment Contested*, 785–790, 818–824.

126. Cassirer, *Philosophy of the Enlightenment*, 90.

127. While Diderot first composed the *Rêve* in 1769, it went unpublished until 1831. On the text's publication history, see Varloot, introduction to *Le Rêve de d'Alembert*, in Diderot, *Œuvres complètes*, 17: 25–27. Wilson notes that a version of the *Rêve* appeared in the *Correspondance littéraire* in 1782 (*Diderot*, 570).

128. On Diderot's relationship with d'Holbach, see Wilson, *Diderot*, 174–177, 373–374; Naville, *D'Holbach*, 32–40, 58–62; and Kors, *D'Holbach's Coterie*, 14, 82, 85.

129. Diderot, *Pensées sur l'interprétation de la nature*, in id., *Œuvres complètes*, 9: 26; Diderot, *Essai sur les règnes de Claude et de Néron*, 246–249; and Diderot, *Encyclopédie*, s.v. "Spinosiste," 15: 472. See also Vernière, *Spinoza et la pensée française*, 2: 560–610, and Israel, *Enlightenment Contested*, 818–822.

130. On Diderot's relationship to Marx, see Simon, *Mass Enlightenment*, 104–115.

131. Diderot, *Rêve de d'Alembert*, 89–113.

132. D'Alembert and Jeanne-Julie-Eléanore de Lespinasse (1732–1776) lived together for nearly ten years, in what was likely a platonic relationship (despite persistent rumors to the contrary), until her death in 1776. See Goodman, *Republic of Letters*, 60, 74–76.

133. On Bordeu, Diderot, and medical vitalism, see Williams, *Cultural History of Medical Vitalism*, 130–131, 154–162, 172–177.

134. Diderot, *Rêve de d'Alembert*, 117.

135. Ibid., 120–122; quotations, 121 and 122.

136. Ibid., 123.

137. See also, Wilma C. Anderson, *Diderot's Dream* (Baltimore: Johns Hopkins University Press, 1990), 65–66.

138. Diderot, *Rêve de d'Alembert*, 133.

139. Ibid., 127–128; quotation, 128.

140. Guyon, *Vie*, 3: 238–239; cf. Montesquieu, "Continuation de quelques Pensées qui n'ont pu entrer dans le *Traité des Devoirs*," 1138.

141. Diderot, *Rêve de d'Alembert*, 127–129; quotation, 129.

142. Ibid., 134.

143. Ibid., 135, 137–139.

144. Ibid., 140–141, 154–155, 175–176; quotations, 140, 154, 175.

145. Ibid., 157–163; quotations, 157–159.

146. Ibid., 163.

147. Ibid., 171–185; quotations, 171, 179, 182, 185.

148. *Encyclopédie*, "Discours préliminaire," 1: xv.

149. Diderot to d'Alembert, end of September 1769, in *Correspondance*, 9: 156–158. On Lespinasse's and d'Alembert's reactions, see also Wilson, *Diderot*, 569–70.

150. Diderot to Volland, September 11, 1769, in id., *Correspondance*, 9: 140.

CHAPTER 6. THE POLITICS OF ALIENATION

1. Rousseau, *Lettres à Malesherbes*, 1: 1135–1136, and *Les Confessions*, 351, in id., *Œuvres complètes*.

2. Rousseau, *Julie, ou La Nouvelle Héloïse*, in id., *Œuvres complètes*, 2: 440–470; quotation, 467.

3. Charles-Joseph Panckoucke to Rousseau, February 1761, and a reader of *La Nouvelle Héloïse* to Rousseau, March 1761, in *Correspondance complète de Jean-Jacques Rousseau*, ed. R. A. Leigh, vol. 8 (Oxford: Voltaire Foundation; Geneva: Institut et Musée Voltaire, 1969), 77–78, 261. See also Darnton, "Readers Respond to Rousseau: The Fabrication of Romantic Sensitivity," in *Great Cat Massacre*, 215–256, and Claude Labrosse, *Lire au XVIIIe siècle: "La Nouvelle Héloïse" et ses lecteurs* (Lyon: Presses universitaires de Lyon, 1985).

4. On Rousseau's appeal to provincial elites, see Shovlin, *Political Economy of Virtue*, 24–26.

5. Voltaire to d'Alembert, June 23, 1760, in Voltaire, *Œuvres complètes*, 40, 8: 437; d'Alembert to Voltaire, April 9, 1761, in Voltaire, *Œuvres complètes*, 41, 9: 262; and Diderot, *Réfutation de l'ouvrage d'Helvétius intitulé "L'Homme,"* in *Œuvres complètes de Diderot*, ed. Jules Assézat and Maurice Tourneux (Paris: Garnier frères, 1875–1877), 2: 292.

6. Bergier, *Le Déisme réfuté par lui-même: ou Examen, en forme de Lettres, des Principes d'incrédulité répandus dans les divers Ouvrages de M. Rousseau*, 5th ed. (1771; repr., Paris: J. Vrin, 1981), 5, and Maleville, *Examen approfondi des difficultés de M. Rousseau de Genève contre le christianisme catholique* (Paris, 1769), 379.

7. Rousseau, *Ébauche des Rêveries*, in id., *Œuvres complètes*, 1: 1165.

8. The most perceptive and detailed study of Rousseau's attempts to intervene in Genevan politics is Helena Rosenblatt, *Rousseau and Geneva: From the First Discourse to the Social Contract, 1749–1762* (Cambridge: Cambridge University Press, 1997).

9. Mark Hulliung, *The Autocritique of the Enlightenment: Rousseau and the Philosophes* (Cambridge, Mass.: Harvard University Press, 1994), 1–37.

10. James Swenson, *On Jean-Jacques Rousseau, Considered as One of the First Authors of the Revolution* (Stanford, Calif.: Stanford University Press, 2000), ix–xi, 171–226.

11. For readings of Rousseau as an individualist, see Ernst Cassirer, *The Question of Jean-Jacques Rousseau*, 2nd ed., trans. Peter Gay (New Haven, Conn.: Yale University Press, 1989), 38, 51–52, 55–56; Alfred Cobban, *Rousseau and the Modern State*, 2nd. ed. (London: George Allen & Unwin, 1964), 8; and Gay, *The Science of Freedom*, vol. 2 of *The Enlightenment: An Interpretation*, 534. On Rousseau as a collectivist, see C. E. Vaughan, introduction to *The Political Writings of Jean-Jacques Rousseau* (Cambridge: Cambridge University Press, 1915), 1: 1–5, 111–114; and Stephen Ellenburg, *Rousseau's Political Philosophy: An Interpretation from Within* (Ithaca, N.Y.: Cornell University Press, 1976). On Rousseau as an agent of oppression, and even of proto-totalitarianism, see Hippolyte Taine, *L'Ancien régime*, pt. 1 of *Les Origines de la France contemporaine* (Paris: R. Laffont, 1986 [1876–1894]), 183, 186 (quotation); and J. L. Talmon, *The Origins of Totalitarian Democracy* (London: Secker & Warburg, 1953), 40–45.

12. On this approach, see Jean Starobinski, *Jean-Jacques Rousseau: Transparency and Obstruction*, trans. Robert J. Morrissey (Chicago: University of Chicago Press, 1988); Bronisław Baczko, *Rousseau, solitude et communauté,*

trans. Claire Brendhel-Lamhout (Paris: Mouton, 1974); and Dumont, *Essais sur l'individualisme*, 112–120.

13. Rousseau, *Les Rêveries du promeneur solitaire*, in id., *Œuvres complètes*, 1: 1013–14. In addition, other favorable allusions to Fénelon are scattered throughout *Émile*, *Rousseau juge de Jean-Jacques*, and *Les Confessions*. However, Rousseau appeared less charitable toward Guyon, whom Madame de Wolmar upbraids in *La Nouvelle Héloïse* for neglecting her domestic responsibilities "to go and compose books of devotion, to argue with bishops, and to have herself placed in the Bastille for reveries that no one can understand" (Rousseau, *La Nouvelle Héloïse*, 697). On Madame de Warens's spirituality, see Masson, *Religion de Jean-Jacques Rousseau*, 1: 69–72, and Albert Metzger, *La Conversion de Madame de Warens* (Paris: Fetscherin & Chuit, 1886).

14. Rosenblatt, *Rousseau and Geneva*, 11–17, 24–27, 82–83; quotation, 15.

15. Rousseau, *Émile, ou De l'Éducation*, in id., *Œuvres complètes*, 4: 594.

16. Rousseau to Matthieu Buttafoco, March 24 1765, quoted in Masson, *Religion de Jean-Jacques Rousseau*, 2: 209. For Rousseau's vacillations between Protestantism and Catholicism, see 1: 26–37, 1: 150–157, 2: 162, 2: 206–212.

17. Jean-Henri Bernardin de Saint-Pierre, *La Vie et les ouvrages de Jean-Jacques Rousseau*, ed. Maurice Souriau (Paris: E. Cornély, 1907), 108, 123. Bernardin de Saint-Pierre (1737–1814) failed to complete his biography of Rousseau, which he began shortly after the latter's death in 1778. It was first published in 1836. On Fénelon's influence on Rousseau, see also Masson, *Religion de Jean-Jacques Rousseau*, 1: 100–104, 273–274, 2: 206–212, and Cherel, *Fénelon au XVIIIe siècle*, 393–400.

18. On the popularity of *Télémaque*, see Riley, "Fénelon's 'Republican' Monarchism,'" 81; on that of *La Nouvelle Héloïse*, see Darnton, "Readers Respond to Rousseau," 242.

19. See Rousseau, *Émile*, 849.

20. Shovlin, *Political Economy of Virtue*, 17–29, 32–42.

21. André-François Boureau-Deslandes, *Lettre sur le luxe* (Frankfurt: Joseph-André Vanebben, 1745), 45.

22. Jean-François Melon, *Essai politique sur le commerce*, in *Économistes-financiers du 18e siècle*, vol. 1 of *Collection des principaux économistes*, ed. Eugène Daire (1841–1852; repr., Osnabrück: O. Zeller, 1966), 709, 742.

23. Voltaire, *Le Mondain* (1736), in id., *Œuvres complètes*, 10: 83–88; quotation, 83–84.

24. Jean-François de Saint-Lambert, *Essai sur le luxe* (n.p., 1764), 73 (cf. *Encyclopédie*, s.v. "Luxe," 9: 763–771); Diderot, *Observations sur le Nakaz*, 411–412.

25. See *Encyclopédie*, s.v. "Encyclopédie," 635–635A.

26. See Carol Blum, *Strength in Numbers: Population, Reproduction, and Power in Eighteenth-Century France* (Baltimore: Johns Hopkins University Press, 2002).

27. For an overview of these developments, see Didier Terrier, *Histoire économique de la France d'Ancien Régime* (Paris: Hachette, 1998), 4–15; Joël Cornette, *Absolutisme et Lumières, 1652–1783*, 4th ed. (Paris: Hachette, 2005), 176–199; François Crouzet, "Angleterre et France au XVIIIe siècle: Essai d'analyse

comparée de deux croissances," *Annales. Économies, Sociétés, Civilisations* 21, 2 (March–April 1966): 254–291; and David R. Weir, "Les Crises économiques et les origines de la Révolution française," ibid. 46, 4 (July–August 1991): 917–947.

28. See Crouzet, "Angleterre et France au XVIIIe siècle," 279; Jan de Vries, "Purchasing Power and the World of Goods," in *Consumption and the World of Goods*, ed. Brewer and Porter, 107–121; and Jones and Spang, "Sans-culottes," 45–46.

29. Daniel Roche discusses the scope of indebtedness in *The People of Paris: An Essay in Popular Culture in the Eighteenth Century*, trans. Marie Evans and Gwynne Lewis (Berkeley: University of California Press, 1987), 83–85.

30. On the consumer revolution and its relationship to general economic trends, see, e.g., Jones and Spang, "Sans-culottes," 42–52; Fairchilds, "Populuxe Goods," 228–231; and Roche, *Culture of Clothing*, 44–64.

31. Mercier, *Tableau de Paris*, 7: 163.

32. See Roche, *History of Everyday Things*, 202–205.

33. Shovlin, "Cultural Politics of Luxury," 579–588, and Mercier, *Tableau de Paris*, 7: 161.

34. Chaussinaud-Nogaret, *French Nobility*, 22–35, 90–108, and Jay Smith, *The Culture of Merit: Nobility, Royal Service, and the Making of Absolute Monarchy in France, 1660–1789* (Ann Arbor: University of Michigan Press, 1996), esp. 1–9, 180–188.

35. For an insightful discussion of this controversy, see Shovlin, *Political Economy of Virtue*, 58–65.

36. Gabriel-François Coyer, *La Noblesse commerçante*, new ed. (Paris: Duchesne, 1756), 9–36, 39–92, 133–151; quotations, 133, 148.

37. Philippe-Auguste de Sainte-Foix, comte d'Arcq, *La Noblesse militaire, ou le Patriote françois* (n.p., 1756), 2–40, 60–67; quotations, 34, 37–38, 65, 63, 65–66.

38. Shovlin, *Political Economy of Virtue*, 61–63.

39. Rosenblatt, *Rousseau and Geneva*, 17–29, 76–77, 84–171, 215–219.

40. Shovlin, *Political Economy of Virtue*, 25–26.

41. *Mercure de France*, October 1749, 153–155 (repr., Geneva: Slatkine, 1968–1970), 57: 213–214; cf. Rousseau, *Discours sur les sciences et les arts*, in id., *Œuvres complètes*, 3: 1.

42. Rousseau, *Discours sur les sciences et les arts*, 9–10. On Fénelon's influence on this work, see Patrick Riley, "Rousseau, Fénelon, and the Quarrel," in *The Cambridge Companion to Rousseau*, ed. Riley (Cambridge: Cambridge University Press, 2001), 81–89.

43. Rousseau, *Discours sur les sciences et les arts*, 10–23; quotations, 15, 22.

44. Ibid., 7–8.

45. Ibid., 17–18, 21, 28, 30.

46. McMahon, *Enemies of the Enlightenment*, 32–53; for references to Rousseau, see 34–35, 51–52.

47. Friedrich Melchior Grimm to Johann Christoph Gottsched, November 25, 1752, in *Correspondance complète de Rousseau*, 2: 202; also quoted in Maurice Cranston, *Jean-Jacques: The Early Life and Work of Jean-Jacques Rousseau* (London: Allen Lane, 1983), 234.

48. Guillaume-Thomas-François Raynal with Diderot, *Histoire philosophique*

et politique du commerce et des établissements des Européens dans les deux Indes (1981; repr., Paris: La Découverte & Syros, 2001), 75.

49. Rousseau, *Discours sur les sciences et les arts*, 15; *Encyclopédie*, "Discours préliminaire," xxxiii.

50. Charles Borde, *Discours sur les avantages des sciences et des arts, prononcé dans l'Assemblée publique de l'Académie des Sciences & Belles-Lettres de Lyon, le 22 Juin 1751* (Geneva: Barillot & fils, 1752), 8–9, 24–25, 48–49, 56–58; quotation, 58.

51. Johann Heinrich Samuel Formey, *Examen philosophique de la liaison réelle qu'il y a entre les sciences & les mœurs* (Avignon, 1755), 1–4, 22–24, 31–33, 40–50, 53–55; quotations, 24, 32–33.

52. Georges-Marie Butel-Dumont, *Théorie du luxe* ([Paris: J.-F. Bastien], 1771), pt. 1: vii–viii.

53. Ibid., 1: vii–xx, 1–8, 31–44, 100–111, 177–183; quotations, vii, 2, 31, 103–104, 182–183.

54. Ibid., 1: 46–62, 107–124; quotations, 46, 59, 61.

55. Ibid., 1: 72–104; quotations, 72, 81–82, 89–90.

56. Kwass, "Ordering the World of Goods," 91–93, 100–109.

57. Butel-Dumont, *Théorie du luxe*, pt. 1: 93–100.

58. Ibid., 1: 96.

59. See chapter 2 above.

60. Butel-Dumont, *Théorie du luxe*, pt. 1: x, 85; pt. 2: 2, 9.

61. *Mercure de France*, November 1753, 65–66, in *Mercure de France*, 55: 242. Rousseau's text was first published in 1755.

62. On the rise of direct, theoretically universal taxation, see Michael Kwass, *Privilege and the Politics of Taxation in Eighteenth-Century France: Liberté, Égalité, Fiscalité* (Cambridge: Cambridge University Press, 2000), 33–38.

63. Robert Derathé, *Jean-Jacques Rousseau et la science politique de son temps*, 2nd ed. (Paris: J. Vrin, 1970), 28–33. On the natural rights tradition during the Enlightenment, see also Dan Edelstein, *The Terror of Natural Right: Republicanism, the Cult of Nature, and the French Revolution* (Chicago: University of Chicago Press, 2009), 45–124.

64. On physiocracy, see Catherine Larrère, *L'Invention de l'économie: Du Droit naturel à la physiocratie* (Paris: Presses universitaires de France, 1992); Philippe Steiner, *La «Science» de l'économie politique* (Paris: Presses universitaires de France, 1998); and Elizabeth Fox-Genovese, *Origins of Physiocracy: Economic Revolution and Social Order in Eighteenth-Century France* (Ithaca, N.Y.: Cornell University Press, 1976).

65. On this point, see also Rétat, "Jouissance physiocratique," 185–189.

66. François Quesnay, *Dialogue sur les travaux des artisans* (1766), in *Physiocrates: Quesnay, Dupont de Nemours, Mercier de La Rivière, l'Abbé Baudeau, Le Trosne*, vol. 2 of *Collection des principaux économistes*, ed. Daire, 192.

67. Victor de Riqueti, marquis de Mirabeau, *Leçons œconomiques* (Amsterdam, 1770), 10–16, 25; quotations, 10, 25.

68. Pierre-Paul Le Mercier de La Rivière, *L'Intérêt général de l'État, ou La Liberté du commerce des blés* (Paris: Desaint, 1770), 30–37, 41–49, 98–103; quotations, 35 and 49.

69. Quesnay, *Maximes générales du gouvernement économique d'un royaume agricole*, in *Physiocrates*, ed. Daire, 81.

70. Ibid., 82–99; quotation, 83.

71. Rousseau to Mirabeau, July 26, 1767, in *Correspondance complète*, 33: 239–240.

72. See, e.g., Delacroix, *Mémoire à consulter sur l'existence des six corps*, 14–25; quotation, 25. On the liberalization of the grain trade and Turgot's reforms, see Kaplan, *Bread, Politics and Political Economy*, 1: 90–151, 2: 409–520, 611–670, and Robert Perry Shepherd, *Turgot and the Six Edicts* (New York: Columbia University Press, 1903).

73. On Rousseau's state of nature, see also Christopher Kelly, "Rousseau's 'Peut-Être': Reflections on the Status of the State of Nature," *Modern Intellectual History* 3, 1 (2006): 75–83.

74. Rousseau, *Discours sur l'inégalité*, 121–134; quotations, 123, 125, 134.

75. Ibid., 132.

76. Thomas Hobbes, *Leviathan*, ed. Richard Tuck (Cambridge: Cambridge University Press, 1991), 86–90; Richard Cumberland, *A Treatise of Laws of Nature*, trans. John Maxwell (London: R. Philipps, 1727), 83–85; Samuel Pufendorf, *On the Duties of Man and Citizen According to Natural Law*, ed. James Tully (Cambridge: Cambridge University Press, 1991), 115–119.

77. Rousseau, *Discours sur l'inégalité*, 159–160.

78. Ibid., 131–145, 152–155; quotations, 132–133, 154.

79. Ibid., 125–145; quotation, 143.

80. Ibid., 125, 148, 153–155, and Rousseau, *Émile*, 505.

81. Rousseau, *Discours sur l'inégalité*, 219n15. Translators disagree on how to render Rousseau's use of the term into English; see Graeme Garrard, *Rousseau's Counter-Enlightenment: A Republican Critique of the Enlightenment* (Albany: State University of New York Press, 2003), 139–40n15.

82. On Rousseau's approach to theodicy and his rejection of the Christian doctrine of original sin, see Cassirer, *Philosophy of the Enlightenment*, 156–157.

83. Rousseau, *Discours sur l'inégalité*, 146–152, 156–166; quotations, 156, 151, 161, 162.

84. Ibid., 164.

85. On this point, see also Patrick Coleman, "Property, Politics, and Personality in Rousseau," in *Early Modern Conceptions of Property*, ed. Brewer and Staves, 256–257.

86. Rousseau, *Discours sur l'inégalité*, 164–172; quotations, 164, 167–169, 171.

87. Ibid., 171–174; quotations, 171, 174.

88. Ibid., 174–175.

89. Ibid., 176–191; quotations, 184–185, 191.

90. Ibid., 193.

91. Abbé Pilé, *Lettre à M. Jean-Jacques Rousseau, citoyen de Genève, à l'occasion de son ouvrage intitulé: "Discours sur l'origine & les fondements de l'inégalité parmi les hommes"* (Westminster, 1755), 3, 8, 21, 12, 31, 72–73. On Pilé's profession, see Antoine-Alexandre Barbier, *Dictionnaire des ouvrages*

anonymes et pseudonymes, 3rd ed., ed. Olivier Barbier et al. (Paris: Paul Daffis, 1872–1874), 3: 1108.

92. Voltaire to Rousseau, August 30, 1755, in Voltaire, *Œuvres complètes*, 38, 6: 446–447.

93. Voltaire, *Questions sur l'Encyclopédie*, s.v. "Homme," in id., *Œuvres complètes*, 19, 3: 378–379. Cf. Pilé, *Lettre à Rousseau*, 47.

94. Voltaire, "Homme," 380.

95. Voltaire, *Questions sur l'Encyclopédie*, s.v. "Propriété," in id., *Œuvres complètes*, 20, 4: 292–293 (quotation, 293), and *Lettres philosophiques*, in id., *Œuvres complètes*, 22: 109–111. On Voltaire's politics, see also Wade, *Intellectual Development of Voltaire*, 748–753.

96. On Diderot's dealings with Frederick and Catherine, see Wilson, *Diderot*, 466, 642–648.

97. Rousseau, *Confessions*, 389. On Diderot's contributions to the *Second Discourse*, see Diderot, *Morceau de Diderot inséré dans le "Discours sur l'inégalité,"* in *Œuvres complètes de Diderot*, ed. Assézat and Tourneaux, 4: 100–104.

98. Rousseau, *Rousseau juge de Jean-Jacques*, in id., *Œuvres complètes*, 1: 662. On Rousseau's break with the philosophes, see also *Confessions*, 346–488, and Maurice Cranston, *The Noble Savage: Jean-Jacques Rousseau, 1754–1762* (Chicago: University of Chicago Press, 1991), 55–88.

99. Rousseau, *La Lettre à d'Alembert sur les spectacles*, in id., *Œuvres complètes*, 5: 3–7; quotation, 7. For a more detailed account of the polemics surrounding Rousseau's *Lettre*, see Margaret M. Moffat, *Rousseau et la querelle du théâtre au XVIIIe siècle* (1930; repr., Geneva: Slatkine, 1970).

100. Rousseau, *Lettre à d'Alembert*, 53–60; quotations, 57, 59.

101. Ibid., 69–74; quotations, 73, 74.

102. Rousseau, *Émile*, 484.

103. Ibid., 248–250.

104. Ibid., 330–333; quotations, 331, 332–333.

105. Coleman, "Property, Politics, and Personality in Rousseau," 266–267.

106. Rousseau, *Émile*, 486, 487, 547, 551.

107. Ibid., 855–856.

108. Ibid., 550–558, 570–585; quotations, 570, 579, 585.

109. Ibid., 589–594; quotations, 593–594.

110. Ibid., 594–633; quotations, 594, 600, 602, 607.

111. *Arrest de la cour de Parlement qui condamne un imprimé ayant pour titre, "Emile, ou de l'Éducation"* (Paris: P. G. Simon, 1762), quotations, 3. See also Christophe de Beaumont, *Mandement de Monseigneur l'archevèque de Paris, portant condamnation d'un livre qui a pour titre "Émile, ou De l'Éducation,"* in *Œuvres de Jean Jacques Rousseau* (Amsterdam: M. M. Rey, 1762–1763), 3, 2: 3–45. Rousseau's response is found in *Lettre à Christophe de Beaumont*, in id., *Œuvres complètes*, 4: 927–1007.

112. Rousseau, *Confessions*, 583–656; Cranston, *Noble Savage*, 360–369; and Cranston, *The Solitary Self: Jean-Jacques Rousseau in Exile and Adversity* (Chicago: University of Chicago Press, 1993), 1–159.

113. Bergier, *Déisme réfuté*, 1: 45–47; 2: 111–122; quotations, 1: 45 and 2: 118.

114. Ibid., 2: 23–27; quotations, 23, 26–27.

115. Maleville, *Examen approfondi*, 63 and n. 1., 347–348.

116. Rousseau, *Émile*, 363, 855, 867–868.

117. Rousseau was writing *Les Solitaires* when the controversy over *Émile* broke out in 1762. The sequel remained unfinished at Rousseau's death and was first published in 1780. On the publication history of the text, see the introduction to it in Rousseau, *Œuvres complètes*, 4: CLXVII–CLXVIII.

118. Rousseau, *Émile et Sophie, ou Les Solitaires*, in id., *Œuvres complètes*, 4: 917.

119. On the tension between the appearance and reality of freedom in *Émile*, see Diane Berrett Brown, "The Constraints of Liberty at the Scene of Instruction," in *Rousseau and Freedom*, ed. Christie McDonald and Stanley Hoffmann (Cambridge: Cambridge University Press, 2010), 168–173.

120. Seigel, *Idea of the Self*, 215–228.

121. Rousseau, *Émile*, 825 and 840.

122. See Cranston, *Solitary Self*, 2, 6–7, 77, 214.

123. This theme is elaborated in rich detail in Van Kley, *Religious Origins of the French Revolution*, 135–248.

124. Keith Michael Baker, *Inventing the French Revolution*, 86–152, and "Transformations of Classical Republicanism in Eighteenth-Century France," *Journal of Modern History* 73 (March 2001): 32–53. The position and functions of classical republicanism in French political culture remain a fertile subject of historical scholarship. See Johnson Kent Wright, *A Classical Republican in Eighteenth-Century France: The Political Thought of Mably* (Stanford, Calif.: Stanford University Press, 1997), and, for the subsequent period, Andrew Jainchill, *Reimagining Politics after the Terror: The Republican Origins of French Liberalism* (Ithaca, N.Y.: Cornell University Press, 2008).

125. Riley, *General Will*, 3–63, 181–250.

126. On Riley's position that Rousseau's understanding of *généralité* remains individualist, see ibid., 249.

127. For Rousseau's use of this expression, see *Du Contrat social, ou Principes du droit politique*, in *Œuvres complètes*, 3: 361.

128. Ibid., 360.

129. Ibid. 352–358. On the function of alienation in natural law theory and Rousseau's critique, see Derathé, *Jean-Jacques Rousseau et la science politique de son temps*, 25–27, 142–150, 245–271.

130. Rousseau, *Du Contrat social*, 360–372; quotations, 361, 364.

131. Ibid., 371–377; quotation, 372.

132. Ibid., 365–367; quotations, 365, 367. On the nature of property rights in Rousseau, see also Vaughan, introduction to *Political Writings*, 104–110; James I. MacAdam, "The Moral Dimensions of Property," in Howard R. Cell and James I. MacAdam, *Rousseau's Response to Hobbes* (New York: Peter Lang, 1988), 107–128; and Coleman, "Property, Politics, and Personality in Rousseau," 254–274.

133. Étienne Gabriel Morelly, *Code de la nature, ou Le Véritable esprit de ses lois* (Paris: Paul Masgana–H. Fournier, 1841), 57. On Morelly, see also Nicolas Wagner, *Morelly: Le Méconnu des lumières* (Paris: Klincksieck, 1978), and Nicole

Dockes, "Un Ordre communautaire du XVIIIe siècle: Morelly," in *Ordre, nature, propriété*, 63–118.

134. On their correspondence, see André Robinet, *Dom Deschamps: Le Maître des maîtres du soupçon*, 2nd ed. (Paris: J. Vrin, 1994), 22–41.

135. Léger-Marie Deschamps, *Le Vrai système, ou Le Mot de l'énigme métaphysique et morale*, ed. Jean Thomas and Franco Venturi (Paris: Droz, 1963), 71–87, 117–127; quotations, 117, 118, 84. On Deschamps's relationship to mysticism, see Deprun, *Philosophie de l'inquiétude*, 117–120.

136. Rousseau, *Discours sur l'économie politique*, in id., *Œuvres complètes*, 3: 263.

137. Rousseau, *Du Contrat social*, 391. On Rousseau's dealings with the independence movement in Corsica, see *Confessions*, 648–652.

138. Rousseau, *Projet de Constitution pour la Corse*, in id., *Œuvres complètes*, 3: 931.

139. Rousseau, *Du Contrat social*, 380–384, 460–469; quotations, 380, 465, 382, 381.

140. Ibid., 381–382, 384.

141. On Diderot's reaction to *Du Contrat social*, see Crocker, *Diderot's Chaotic Order*, 123; for his own use of the concept of general will, see *Encyclopédie*, s.v. "Droit naturel," 5: 115–116.

142. Paul-Louis de Bauclair, *Anti-Contrat social* (1765; repr., Paris: J. Vrin, 1981), 27–30, 80–83.

143. Ibid., 37–39, 44–45; quotations, 37, 44.

144. Ibid., 46, 48, 261; cf. Rousseau, *Du Contrat social*, 465.

145. François, *Réponse aux difficultés proposées contre la religion chrétienne, par J. J. Rousseau, Citoyen de Genève* (Paris: Babuty, 1765), 251–278; quotations, 251–252, 273. See also Maleville, *Examen approfondi*, 364–372.

146. François, *Réponse aux difficultés*, 286–287, 292.

147. Rousseau, *Du Contrat social*, 365.

148. On the details of Rousseau's life during this period, see Cranston, *Solitary Self*, 1–176.

149. Rousseau, *Rousseau juge de Jean-Jacques*, 813; *Rêveries*, 1065.

150. Rousseau, *Confessions*, 22–25, 36–38, 225; quotations, 38 and 225. Among the many other telling events is his encounter with a courtesan named Giulietta, which he described as the "one circumstance of my life that truly portrays my character." While recognizing that "never was such sweet pleasure offered" to him, he lamented not knowing "how to savor it fully and completely for a single second" (320).

151. Rousseau, *Du Contrat social*, 424.

152. Rousseau, *Rêveries*, 999.

153. Ibid., 999. See also Marcel Raymond, introduction to *Rêveries*, XCV, and *Jean-Jacques Rousseau: La Quête de soi et la rêverie* (Paris: Corti, 1962), 150–151. Pierre Masson, in contrast, refers to Rousseau's "Quietism" in his final years as "the submission of a passive soul" (*Religion de Jean-Jacques Rousseau*, 2: 230–232).

154. Rousseau, *Rêveries*, 1010, 1075; quotation, 1075.

155. Joseph Adrien Lelarge de Lignac, *Éléments de métaphysique tirés de l'expérience, ou Lettres à un materialiste sur la nature de l'Ame* (Paris: Desaint & Saillant, 1753), 23. On Rousseau's contributions to the idea of reverie in the eighteenth century, see also Morrissey, *La Rêverie jusqu'à Rousseau*, 148–159; Petrovich, *Rêve(rie) et connaissance*, 143–172; and Raymond, *Quête de soi et la rêverie*, 173–178.

156. Rousseau, *Rêveries*, 1005.

157. Ibid., 1042. On Rousseau's interest in botany, see Lisa Gasbaronne, "De la Partie au tout: La Nature et la machine dans les *Rêveries* de Rousseau," in *Lectures des "Rêveries*," ed. and trans. Anne F. Garreta (Rennes: Presses universitaires de Rennes, 1998), 45–57; Jean Terrasse, "Dieu, la nature, les fleurs: sur une page des *Rêveries*," in *Rêveries sans fin*, ed. Michel Coz and François Jacob (Orléans: Paradigme, 1997), 73–88; and Natasha Lee, "A Dream of Human Nature," in *The Nature of Rousseau's "Rêveries": Physical, Human, and Aesthetic*, ed. John C. O'Neil (Oxford: Voltaire Foundation, 2008), 99–110.

158. Rousseau, *Rêveries*, 1045–1047. The relationship between the self's *sentiment de l'existence* and the experience of divinity during reverie has long captivated Rousseau scholars. See Masson, *Religion de Jean-Jacques Rousseau*, 2: 227–230; Mauzi, *Idée du bonheur*, 295–300; and Raymond, *Quête du soi et la rêverie*, 134–135, 145–151, 183–185.

159. Rousseau, *Rêveries*, 1062–1063.

160. Ibid., 1088.

CHAPTER 7. REVOLUTIONARY REVERIES

1. Joseph Lakanal, *Rapport sur J. J. Rousseau, fait au nom du Comité d'Instruction, suivi des détails sur la translation des cendres de J. J. Rousseau au Panthéon français* (Paris: Imprimerie nationale, Year III), 12–19.

2. Théodore Desorgues, *Hymne à Jean-Jacques Rousseau* (n.p., n.d. [1794]).

3. Mercier, *De J. J. Rousseau considéré comme l'un des premiers auteurs de la Révolution* (Paris: Buisson, 1791). Here and in the discussion that follows, I draw on James Swenson's arguments in *On Jean-Jacques Rousseau*, esp. x, 1–52, 160–226. The scholarship on Rousseau's influence on the Revolution is nearly inexhaustible. For an overview of recent approaches to the problem, see Swenson, *On Jean-Jacques Rousseau*; Baker, *Inventing the French Revolution*, 19–20, 26–27, 123–152, 235–238 241–305; Roger Barny, *L'Éclatement révolutionnaire du rousseauisme* (Paris: Belles Lettres, 1988); Carol Blum, *Rousseau and the Republic of Virtue: The Language of Politics in the French Revolution* (Ithaca, N.Y.: Cornell University Press, 1986); Chartier, *Cultural Origins of the French Revolution*, 3–19, 67–91; François Furet, "Rousseau and the French Revolution," in *The Legacy of Rousseau*, ed. Clifford Orwin and Nathan Tarcov (Chicago: University of Chicago Press, 1997), 168–182; and Nathalie-Barbara Robisco, *Jean-Jacques Rousseau et la Révolution française: Une Esthétique de la politique, 1792–1799* (Paris: Honoré Champion, 1998).

4. Lakanal, *Rapport sur J. J. Rousseau*, 6.

5. Swenson, *On Jean-Jacques Rousseau*, 225–226.

6. Emmanuel-Joseph Sieyès, *Qu'est-ce que le Tiers-État?* (n.p., 1789), 38–39,

88–90, and Baker, *Critical Dictionary of the French Revolution*, ed. François Furet and Mona Ozouf, trans. Arthur Goldhammer (Cambridge, Mass.: Belknap Press, 1989), s.v. "Sieyès."

7. Louis-Antoine-Léon Saint-Just, *Discours de Saint-Just sur la Constitution de la France*, in *Œuvres complètes*, ed. Michèle Duval (Paris: Ivrea, 2003), 416; Saint-Just, *De la Nature*, in id., *Œuvres complètes*, 922–924; and Edelstein, *Terror of Natural Right*, 77, 199–201.

8. *Déclaration des droits de l'homme et du citoyen*, in *Réimpression de l'ancien Moniteur*, ed. Léonard Gallois, 32 vols. (hereafter cited as *Moniteur*) (Paris: Bureau Central, 1840–1845), 9: 312 (no. 218 [August 6, 1791]).

9. On the nationalization of these properties, see Jacques Godechot, *Les Institutions de la France sous la Révolution et l'Empire* (Paris: Presses universitaires de France, 1951), 175–185, 200–202, 403–406.

10. On the Civil Constitution, see Timothy Tackett, *Religion, Revolution, and Regional Culture in Eighteenth-Century France: The Ecclesiastical Oath of 1791* (Princeton, N.J.: Princeton University Press, 1986), 11–16, and Van Kley, *Religious Origins of the French Revolution*, 352–362.

11. *Discours sur le patriotisme* (n.p., 1789), 10.

12. Maximilien Robespierre, "Sur les principes de morale politique," in *Œuvres de Robespierre* (1958; repr., Paris: Phénix, 2000), 10: 357.

13. Sieyès, "Fin de l'état social," in *Des Manuscrits de Sieyès, 1773–1779*, ed. Christine Fauré et al. (Paris: Honoré Champion, 1999–2007), 1: 471, and *Opinion de Sieyès sur plusieurs articles des titres IV et V du projet de constitution, prononcée à la Convention le 2 thermidor de l'An III* (Paris: Imprimerie nationale, Year III), 7.

14. Sieyès, *Bases de l'ordre social*, in *Des Manuscrits de Sieyès*, 1: 508, 510.

15. On the emergence of society as a purely terrestrial entity, see Baker, "Enlightenment and the Institution of Society," 95–120, and Brian C. J. Singer, *Society, Theory and the French Revolution: Studies in the Revolutionary Imaginary* (New York: Macmillan, 1986), 11–22.

16. *Déclaration des droits de l'homme et du citoyen* and *Constitution de 1791*, in Jacques Godechot, ed., *Les Constitutions de la France* (Paris: Garnier Flammarion, 1996), 35, 40–41; quotation, 35.

17. On resistance to the reforms of August 4, and on the subsequent abolition of trade corporations with the d'Allarde and Le Chapelier laws of 1791, see Sewell, *Work and Revolution in France*, 86–91, and Michael P. Fitzsimmmons, *The Night the Old Regime Ended: August 4, 1789 and the French Revolution* (University Park: Pennsylvania State University Press, 2003), 127–128, 207, 219.

18. *Moniteur*, 1: 284 (no. 34 [August 5, 1789]).

19. The following account relies on Fitzsimmmons, *Night the Old Regime Ended*, 1–45, 47–52, 93–98, 137–142, and 173–178.

20. *Moniteur*, 1: 279 (no. 33 [August 4, 1789]).

21. Ibid., 280–290; quotations, 280, 284, 287, 290.

22. On the conceptual tensions built into the declaration, see Marcel Gauchet, *La Révolution des droits de l'homme* (Paris: Gallimard, 1989), 60–101, and Baker, *Inventing the French Revolution*, 269–273.

23. On the social and economic repercussions of the sale of *biens nationaux* and *biens communaux*, see Godechot, *Institutions de la France*, 197–207, 400–403.

24. Jean-Paul Marat, *Plan de législation criminelle* (Paris: Rochette, 1790), 19.

25. Marat, *Journal de la République française*, no. 133 (Februrary 25, 1793), in *Œuvres politiques (1789–1793)*, ed. Jacques De Cock and Charlotte Goëtz (Brussels: Pôle Nord, 1995), 9: 5740–5741.

26. For further discussion of Marat's economic views and their attempted implementation, see Louis R. Gottschalk, *Jean Paul Marat: A Study in Radicalism* (New York: Benjamin Blom, 1927), 100–106, and Jean-Pierre Gross, *Fair Shares for All: Jacobin Egalitarianism in Practice* (Cambridge: Cambridge University Press, 1997), 27–30.

27. Robespierre, "Sur la nouvelle Déclaration des Droits," in *Œuvres*, 9: 459, 461. For an overview of Robespierre's intervention in the debate over the Declaration of the Rights of Man and Citizen, and of his economic views more generally, see Lucien Jaume, *Le Discours jacobin et la démocratie* (Paris: Fayard, 1989), 242–245; Gross, *Fair Shares for All*, 35–40; and Florence Gauthier, "Robespierre, critique de l'économie, politique tyrannique et théoricien de l'économie politique populaire," in *Robespierre: De la Nation artésienne à la République et aux nations*, ed. Jean-Pierre Jessenne et al. (Villeneuve d'Ascq: Centre d'histoire de la région du Nord et de l'Europe du Nord-Ouest, 1994), 235–244.

28. Robespierre, "Déclaration des droits de l'homme et du citoyen," in id., *Œuvres*, 9: 464–466. Cf. "Opinion de Maximilien Robespierre sur les subsistences" (December 2, 1792), in id., *Œuvres*, 9: 109–120, and *Moniteur*, 18: 5–6 (no. 274 [October 1, 1793]).

29. Robespierre, "Sur la nouvelle Déclaration des Droits," 459.

30. Robespierre, "Sur le Marc d'argent et sur le cens électoral," in *Œuvres*, 7: 622.

31. Robespierre, "Opinion sur les subsistences," 112.

32. *La Constitution du 24 juin 1793*, in Godechot, ed., *Constitutions de la France*, 80, 82.

33. William H. Sewell Jr., "The Sans-Culotte Rhetoric of Subsistence," in *The Terror*, ed. Keith Michael Baker, vol. 4 of *The French Revolution and the Creation of Modern Political Culture*, ed. Baker et al. (Oxford: Pergamon Press, 1994), 249–269.

34. On the infighting between the Girondins and the Montagnards, see Gary Kates, *The Cercle Social, the Girondins, and the French Revolution* (Princeton, N.J.: Princeton University Press, 1985), 238–242, 254–256, 268–270.

35. For an overview of the Maximum and other economic controls of the Year II, see Godechot, *Institutions de la France*, 410–417, and Gross, *Fair Shares for All*, 64–92.

36. On this claim and its significance for the question of what constituted luxury, see Sewell, "Sans-Culotte Rhetoric," 266–267, and Jones and Spang, "Sans-culottes," 239–240.

37. Julien-Joseph Souhait, *Discours sur le partage des biens communaux, prononcé à la tribune de la Convention nationale* (Paris: Imprimerie nationale, Year II), 9–13; quotation, 9.

38. Claude-Dominique-Cosme Fabre, *Rapport et projet de décret du citoyen*

Fabre, député de l'Hérault, sur le mode de partage des biens communaux (Paris: Imprimerie nationale, n.d.), 12, 5. On the legislation, see also Gross, *Fair Shares for All*, 101–106.

39. Jacques Nicolas Billaud-Varenne, *Les Élémens du républicanisme* (Paris, Year I), 1–45; quotations, 1, 12, 20, 21. On Billaud-Varenne's critique of individualism, see also Jaume, *Discours jacobin*, 187–191.

40. Billaud-Varenne, *Élémens du républicanisme*, 48–57, 60–118, 129–132; quotations, 53, 54, 57, 74, 102, 130.

41. Saint-Just, "Rapport au nom du Comité de salut public et du Comité de sûreté générale sur les personnes incarcérées," in id., *Œuvres complètes*, 705.

42. On the implementation of the Ventôse decrees, see Gross, *Fair Shares for All*, 115–121.

43. Ibid., 96–97.

44. See Blumenberg, *Legitimacy of the Modern Age*, 65.

45. Fénelon, *Œuvres spirituelles*, 1: 260–271.

46. Marie-Joseph Chénier, *Fénelon, ou Les Religieuses de Cambrai* (Paris: Moutard, 1793), iii–iv; Sylvain Maréchal, *Almanach des républicains, pour servir à l'instruction publique* (Paris: Cercle Social, 1793), 9. On Fénelon and the Revolution, see Cherel, *Fénelon au XVIIIe siècle*, 475–480, 534–581.

47. On d'Holbach and the Revolution, see also Max P. Cushing, "A Forgotten Philosopher," *Monist* 30 (1920): 312–313.

48. These observations draw on Sewell, *Logics of History*, 164–173.

49. On the king's death as sacrifice, see also Daniel Arasse, *La Guillotine et l'imaginaire de la Terreur* (Paris: Flammarion, 1987), 80–85, and Antoine de Baecque, *Glory and Terror: Seven Deaths under the French Revolution*, trans. Charlotte Mandell (New York: Routledge, 2001), 99–100.

50. On this point, and for a broader discussion of the place of the sacred in the political culture of the Terror, see Sophie Wahnich, *In Defence of the Terror: Liberty or Death in the French Revolution*, trans. David Fernbach (London: Verso, 2012), 21–33.

51. Robespierre, "Opinion de Maximilien Robespierre sur le jugement de Louis XVI," in *Œuvres de Maximilien Robespierre*, 9: 121, 130, and Saint-Just, "Second Discours sur le jugement de Louis XVI," in id., *Œuvres complètes*, 400.

52. On Louis's execution and the passage of sacred sovereignty from the king to the people, see Arasse, *Guillotine*, 67–71.

53. Robespierre, "Second Discours sur le jugement de Louis Capet," in id., *Œuvres*, 186.

54. *La Passion de 1790, ou Louis XVI sacrifié pour et par son peuple. Extraits tirés des Évangélistes nationaux* (Paris: Philippe Parabole, 1790), 21.

55. On Le Peletier de Saint-Fargeau's death and funeral arrangements, see Simon Schama, *Citizens: A Chronicle of the French Revolution* (New York: Knopf, 1989), 671–673.

56. Robespierre, "Éloge funèbre de Michel Lepeletier," in id., *Œuvres complètes*, 9: 258.

57. A. C. N. de Closquinet de La Roche, *Discours prononcés . . . à l'occasion de l'inauguration des bustes des Martyrs de la Liberté, Marat & Le Pelletier, & de la*

Fête de la Raison (Paris: Moutard, n.d. [1794]), 13–14. La Roche was a member of the section's Commission de Bienfaisance and author of "several patriotic works," including *Règlement pour la formation permanent des districts et l'administration municipale de Paris* (1789) and *Plan de muncipalité populaire et civique à l'usage de Paris* (1790); see La Roche, *Discours prononcés à l'occasion de l'inauguration des bustes des Martyrs de la Liberté*, 7.

58. Célestin Morel, *Éloge funèbre de Jean Paul Marat* (n.p., Year II), 13–15; quotation, 15.

59. On the observation of the Marat cult, see Jean-Claude Bonnet, "Les Formes de célébration," in *La Mort de Marat*, ed. Jean-Claude Bonnet (Paris: Flammarion, 1986), 101–127.

60. Ibid., 117–118. On the Convention's approval of Marat's pantheonization, see *Moniteur*, 18: 429 (no. 56 [26 brumaire Year II]).

61. AN, DXXXVIII 3, no. 2561, J. Dumas, "Discours prononcé sur l'Autel de la Patrie," in *Procès-verbal et discours prononcés sur l'Autel de la Patrie, & dans la salle de la Société Populaire, lors de la Fête de l'immortel Marat* (Uzès-la-Montagne: Imprimerie du District, Year II), 7, 10.

62. For an overview of this development, see Michel Vovelle, *Religion et Révolution: La Déchristianisation de l'an II* (Paris: Hachette, 1976).

63. Franck Paul Bowman, "Le «Sacré Cœur» de Marat," in *Les Fêtes de la Révolution*, ed. Jean Ehrard and Paul Viallaneix (Paris: Société des études robespierristes, 1977), 155–179.

64. On the use of Catholic imagery, see Bonnet, "Formes de célébration," 120–123.

65. As Thomas Crow has argued, David's *Marat at His Last Breath* (1793) drew upon the *Pietà* completed by his pupil Anne-Louis Girodet in 1790; see Crow, *Emulation: Making Artists for Revolutionary France* (New Haven, Conn.: Yale University Press, 1995), 166.

66. François-Alphonse Aulard, *Le Culte de la raison et le culte de l'être suprême* (Paris: Alcan, 1892), 61, and Albert Soboul, "Sentiment religieux et cultes populaires: Saintes patriotes et martyrs de la liberté," *Archives des sciences sociales des religions* 2 (1946): 78–80. More generally, see Albert Mathiez, *Les Origines des cultes révolutionnaires (1789–1792)* (Paris: Société nouvelle de librairie et d'édition, 1904), 29–38, and L. Bergeron, "Évolution de la fête révolutionnaire: Chronologie et typologie," in *Fêtes de la Révolution*, ed. Ehrard and Viallaneix, 125–127.

67. Jaume, *Discours jacobin*, 245–250; quotation, 245. See also Mona Ozouf, *L'Homme régénéré: Essais sur la Révolution française* (Paris: Gallimard, 1989), 138–145, and Edelstein, *Terror of Natural Right*, 220–225.

68. See, e.g., Ozouf, *Homme régénéré*, 129–130; Bell, *Cult of the Nation*, 75–76, 142–167; and Alyssa Sepinwall, *The Abbé Grégoire and the French Revolution: The Making of Modern Universalism* (Berkeley: University of California Press, 2005), 57–73, 87–108, 130–136.

69. Jaume, *Discours jacobin*, 250–251.

70. Saint-Just, "Discours sur le jugement de Louis XVI," in id., *Œuvres complètes*, 380.

71. La Roche, *Discours prononcés à l'occasion de l'inauguration des bustes des Martyrs de la Liberté*, 12.

72. On the expansion of the cult, see Soboul, "Sentiment religieux et cultes populaires," 80–81.

73. *La Mort pour la patrie. Discours prononcé au nom de la Société-Populaire-Révolutionaire de Dune-Libre, le jour de la Fête des Martyrs de la Liberté* (Dune-Libre [Dunkirk]: Drouilard, n.d. [1794]), 1, 3–5.

74. Ibid., 5.

75. François Peyrard, *De la Nature et de ses lois* (Paris: Louis, 1793), i–iii, lv–lvii, 1–14, 96–101; quotations, lv–lvi, 4, 96, 101.

76. Anacharsis Cloots, *Bases constitutionnelles de la République du Genre Humain* (Paris: Imprimerie nationale, Year II), 4, 33, 35.

77. Ibid., 21, 32, 37.

78. See Aulard, *Culte de la raison*, 52–58, 80–85.

79. Jacques-Antoine Brouillet, *Discours républicain prononcé le dernier décadi frimaire, jour de l'inauguration du Temple de la Raison* (n.p., Year II), 2, 4–5, 16.

80. On these events, see Aulard, *Culte de la raison*, 24–50, 59–67, and Vovelle, *Déchristianisation de l'an II*, 19–80, 147–182, 236–238.

81. Aulard, *Culte de la raison*, 61, and Soboul, "Sentiment religieux et cultes populaires," 85.

82. Aulard, *Culte de la raison*, 200–211; quotation, 211. On Robespierre's mystical sensibilities, see also Henri Guillemin, *Robespierre, politique et mystique* (Paris: Éditions du Seuil, 1987), esp. 7–14, 347–408. On the priestly elements of his role in the festival, see Jean Deprun, "Robespierre, pontife de l'être suprême: Notes sur les aspects sacrificiels d'une fête," in *Fêtes de la Révolution*, ed. Ehrard and Viallaneix, 485–491.

83. Robespierre, "Pour la liberté des cultes," in id., *Œuvres*, 10: 193–201.

84. Robespierre, "Sur les principes de morale politique," 350–367; quotations, 359, 360, 350, 364.

85. Edelstein, *Terror of Natural Right*, 1–4, 170–256; quotation, 3. For other approaches to the influence of the natural law tradition on revolutionary politics, see Florence Gauthier, *Triomphe et mort du droit naturel en Révolution, 1789–1795–1802* (Paris: Presses universitaires de France, 1992), and Robisco, *Rousseau et la Révolution française*, 59–112.

86. Robespierre, "Sur les principes de morale politique," 352–355.

87. Ibid., 356–357.

88. Robespierre, "Sur les rapports des idées religieuses et morales avec les principes républicains, et sur les fêtes nationales," in id., *Œuvres*, 10: 444–445.

89. On the motif of sacrifice in Marat's writings and political career, see Philippe Roger, "L'Homme du sang: L'Invention sémiotique de Marat," in *Mort de Marat*, 141–166.

90. Robespierre, "Sur les rapports des idées religieuses et morales avec les principes républicains," 453.

91. Ibid., 452–453, 458.

92. On this point, see also Mona Ozouf, *La Fête révolutionnaire, 1789–1799* (Paris: Gallimard, 1976), 130–139, 332–338.

93. Robespierre, "Sur les rapports des idées religieuses et morales avec les principes républicains," 454–455. For a discussion of Rousseau's influence on Robespierre's religious views, see also Michaël Culoma, *La Religion civile de Rousseau à Robespierre* (Paris: L'Harmattan, 2010), 211–259.

94. Robespierre, "Dédicace à Jean-Jacques Rousseau," in id., *Œuvres*, 1: 211–212. On the composition and dating of the text, see Guillemin, *Robespierre, politique et mystique*, 348–349.

95. Robespierre, "Sur les rapports des idées religieuses et morales avec les principes républicains," 456–457.

96. Ibid., 457.

97. Robespierre, *Lettres à ses commetans*, 7 (November 29, 1792), in id., *Œuvres*, 5: 99.

98. *Moniteur*, 20: 411 (no. 229 [20 floréal Year II]).

99. Ibid. Several dozen submissions were subsequently published and are available at the Bibliothèque nationale. Other manuscript submissions are held at the Archives nationales, Série DXXXVIII. For a study of the place of songs in revolutionary political culture, see Laura Mason, *Singing the French Revolution: Popular Culture and Politics, 1787–1789* (Ithaca, N.Y.: Cornell University Press, 1996).

100. On the initial reactions to the Cult of the Supreme Being, see Aulard, *Culte de la raison*, 297–206.

101. AN, DXXXVIII, 3, no. 3735.

102. Ibid., 5, no. 3527, "Oraison républicaine à l'Être suprême."

103. Ibid., 3, no. 153, "Cantique à l'Être suprême."

104. Ibid., 7, no. 2924, "Prière à l'Être suprême."

105. Collandière, *Discours sur l'existence de l'Être-suprême et l'immortalité de l'âme* ([Paris]: Renandière, Year II), 10–14; Étienne-Louis Bézout, *Discours sur l'existence de l'Être suprême et l'immortalité de l'âme* (Chaumont: Bouchard, Year II), 8.

106. Collandière, *Discours sur l'existence de l'Être-suprême*, 11; Bézout, *Discours sur l'existence de l'Être suprême*, 18.

107. Bézout, *Discours sur l'existence de l'Être suprême*, 20; Collandière, *Discours sur l'existence de l'Être-suprême*, 19.

108. See Rousseau, *Du Contrat social*, 465–467.

109. Plaisant de La Houssaye, *Hymne à la Nature* (Paris: Demoraine, Debray, & Prault, Year II), 55, 63–65, 67.

110. Ibid., 44 and 71; quotation, 71.

111. *Rituel républicain. Fête à l'Être-suprême* (Paris: Aubry, Year II), 1–6, and *Moniteur*, 20: 653–656, 683–684, 701–702 (nos. 259 [19 prairial Year II], 262 [22 prairial Year II], and 265 [25 prairial Year II]). Quotations from the *Moniteur*, 20: 653, 683. On the festival, see also Albert Mathiez, *Robespierre et le culte de l'Être suprême* (Le Puy: Peyriller, Rouchon & Gamon, 1910); Aulard, *Culte de la raison*, 307–322; and Ozouf, *Fête révolutionnaire*, 172–192. The report of damage to the statue of Wisdom is related in Aulard, *Culte de la raison*, 314.

112. *Rituel républicain*, 7–14; and *Moniteur*, 20: 653–654, 683, 702. Quotations from the *Moniteur*, 20: 683, 702.

113. Ozouf, *Fête révolutionnaire*, 317–340; quotation, 317.

114. Quoted in Pierre-Joseph-Benjamin Buchez and Pierre-Celéstin Roux-Lavergne, *Histoire parlementaire de la Révolution française, ou Journal des Assemblées nationales depuis 1780 jusqu'en 1815* (Paris: Paulin, 1834–1838), 33: 177.

115. On this problem, see also Jaume, *Discours jacobin*, 183–187.

116. Robespierre, "Sur les principes de morale politique," 364.

117. Billaud-Varenne, *Rapport fait à la Convention nationale, au nom du comité de Salut public, sur la théorie du gouvernement démocratique* (Paris: Tribunal révolutionnaire, Year II), 8–9, 27, 29–31. Emphasis added.

118. For further reflections on this conundrum, see Patrice Gueniffey, *La Politique de la Terreur: Essai sur la violence révolutionnaire, 1789–1794* (Paris: Fayard, 2000), 317–326; Lucien Jaume and Georges Labica, "Table ronde. Robespierre: La Politique, la morale et le sacré," in *Robespierre*, ed. Jessenne et al., 431–434; and Jaume, *Discours jacobin*, 237–249, 338–340.

119. On resistance to the Maximum imposed on wages, see Godechot, *Institutions de la France*, 416. On the reception of the Cult of the Supreme Being, see Ozouf, *Fête révolutionnaire*, 130–138, and Aulard, *Culte de la raison*, 323–354.

120. For the text of the law, see *Moniteur*, 20: 697 (no. 264 [24 prairial Year II]).

121. The figure is from Colin Jones, *The Great Nation: France from Louis XV to Napoleon, 1715–1799* (London: Allen Lane, Penguin Press, 2002), 496. This number of deaths, while ghastly in itself, pales in comparison to the 16,600 victims sentenced to death by "legal" means. If one includes "extra-legal" executions as well, but not the casualties of the civil war in the Vendée, the overall number quickly exceeds 40,000. See Gueniffey, *Politique de la Terreur*, 234–237.

122. On the events of 9 thermidor and their immediate aftermath, see Jean Tulard, *Les Thermidoriens* (Paris: Fayard, 2005), 12–26, and François Brunel, *Thermidor: La Chute de Robespierre* (Paris: Éditions Complexe, 1989), 73–126.

123. On these developments, see Godechot, *Institutions de la France*, 385, 396.

124. *La Constitution de 1795 ou de l'An III*, in Godechot, ed., *Constitutions de la France*, 60–61.

125. Quoted in Godechot, *Institutions de la France*, 461, and Jainchill, *Reimagining Politics after the Terror*, 43.

126. *Constitution de 1795*, 63–67, 75–78. On the deliberations that produced the Constitution, see Jainchill, *Reimagining Politics after the Terror*, 26–61.

127. Jean-Baptiste Chemin-Dupontès, *Qu'est-ce que la théophilanthropie? ou Mémoire contenant l'origine et l'histoire de cette institution, ses rapports avec le christianisme, et l'aperçu de l'influence qu'elle peut avoir sur tous les cultes* (Paris: Librairie classique, Year X), 8–10; quotation, 8. On Theophilanthropy, see also Albert Mathiez, *La Théophilanthropie et le culte décadaire: Essai sur l'histoire religieuse de la Révolution (1796–1801)* (1903; repr., Geneva: Slatkine-Megariotis, 1975), and Martyn Lyons, *France under the Directory* (Cambridge: Cambridge University Press, 1975), 110–112.

128. Chemin-Dupontès, *Code religieux et moral des théophilanthropes ou adorateurs de Dieu et amis des hommes* (Paris: l'Éditeur, Year VI), 20–23, 126–130; quotations, 20, 126.

129. Chemin-Dupontès, *Qu'est-ce que la théophilanthropie?* 14–15, 62, 63; see

also Mathiez, *Théophilanthropie*, 81–82, 400–405, and Lyons, *France under the Directory*, 110–111.

130. See Philippe Riviale, *La Conjuration: Essai sur la Conjuration pour l'Égalité dite de Babeuf* (Paris: l'Harmattan, 1994), 94–130, and Lyons, *France under the Directory*, 26–27.

131. On Babeuf's estimation of Robespierre, see Gracchus Babeuf, "Contre la propriété, pour le bonheur commun" (letter to Anaxagoras Chaumette, 18 floréal Year II [May 7, 1793]), and *Le Tribun du peuple*, no. 28 (28 frimaire Year III [December 18, 1794]), in Babeuf, *Textes choisis*, ed. Claude Mazauric (Paris: Éditions sociales, 1976), 170–171, 192.

132. Eric Walter, "Babeuf écrivain: L'Invention rhétorique d'un prophète," in *Présence de Babeuf: Lumières, révolution, communisme*, ed. Alain Maillard et al. (Paris: Sorbonne, 1994), 183–231; quotations, 195 and 219.

133. Babeuf, "Le Manifeste des plébiens," in *Textes choisis*, ed. Mazauric, 227, 229, 230, 231, 233, 235, 236. On the Conspiracy of Equals, see Philippe Buonarroti, *La Conspiration pour l'égalité, dite de Babeuf* (Brussels: Librairie romantique, 1828); R. B. Rose, *Gracchus Babeuf: The First Revolutionary Communist* (London: Edward Arnold, 1978), 226–273; and Lyons, *France under the Directory*, 24–36.

134. Sylvain Maréchal, "Le Manifeste des égaux," in Buonarroti, *Histoire de la conspiration pour l'égalité dite de Babeuf*, new ed. (Paris: G. Charavay Jeune, 1850), 70–74.

135. For a discussion of the aims of the leaders of the conspiracy versus that of their supporters, see Rose, *Gracchus Babeuf*, 235–243 and Lyons, *France under the Directory*, 31–33.

136. *Analyse de la doctrine de Babeuf* (n.p., n.d. [1796]), 1–4; quotations, 1–2.

137. Rose, *Gracchus Babeuf*, 262–326.

138. Maréchal, "Manifeste des égaux," 71. On the divided nature of Jacobin opinion regarding Babeuf, see Isser Woloch, *Jacobin Legacy: The Democratic Movement under the Directory* (Princeton, N.J.: Princeton University Press, 1970), 20–32, 36–47.

EPILOGUE

1. *Code civil* (Paris: Garnery, Year XI–Year XII), 2: 25, 31–33. On the Civil Code and the primacy of property, see also Godechot, *Institutions de la France*, 691–696; Donald R. Kelley and Bonnie G. Smith, "What Was Property? Legal Dimensions of the Social Question in France (1789–1848)," *Proceedings of the American Philosophical Society* 128, 3 (September 1984): 200–201; and Suzanne Desan, *The Family on Trial in Revolutionary France* (Berkeley: University of California Press, 2004), 289–291.

2. *Code civil*, 2: 31.

3. Kelley and Smith, "What Was Property?" 202.

4. Jean-Baptiste-Victor Proudhon, *Traité du domaine de propriété* (Dijon: Victor Lagier, 1839), 1: 2–11; quotations, 4 and 9.

5. Ibid., 1: 21–33; quotations, 21–22.

6. Ibid., 1: 49–78; quotations, 49, 66, 52.

7. Desan, *Family on Trial in Revolutionary France*, 308. As Desan argues, there was nothing inherent in revolutionary ideology dictating that the archetypical citizen

should be coded male. Rather, jurists in the early nineteenth century were reacting to specific conditions—namely, the destabilizing effects of previous legislation on family life and gender relations—in formulating and extrapolating from the Civil Code.

8. Alexis de Tocqueville, *Democracy in America*, trans. Gerald E. Bevan (London: Penguin Books, 2003), 587–589.

9. See, e.g., Joseph de Maistre, "Extrait d'une conversation entre J. de Maistre et M. Ch. de Lavau," in Maistre, *Œuvres complètes* (Lyon, 1884–1886; facs. repr., Geneva: Slatkine, 1979), 14: 286. For a more general discussion of this point, see Lukes, *Individualism*, 13–16.

10. Antoine-Louis-Claude Destutt de Tracy, *Traité de la volonté et de ses effets*, vol. 4 of *Élémens d'idéologie* (Paris, 1801–1815; facs. repr., Stuttgart: Frommann-Holzboog, 1977), 55–59; quotations, 56, 57, 67.

11. Ibid., 71–95; quotations, 73–74, 81.

12. Goldstein, *Post-Revolutionary Self*, esp. 139–232.

13. Ibid., 60–138.

14. Victor Cousin, *Cours d'histoire de la philosophie morale au dix-huitième siècle, professé à la Faculté des lettres, en 1819 et 1820*, ed. Étienne Vacherot and Arsène Danton (Paris: Ladrange, 1839–1842), 2: 14, 19, 23.

15. Ibid., 2: 82–84.

16. Ibid., 1: 10–14; quotations, 12–13.

17. Ibid., 2: 22–25. Goldstein also notes this similarity; see *Post-Revolutionary Self*, 164.

18. Cousin, *Cours d'histoire*, 1: 11.

19. Ibid., 2: 16, 40–42; quotation, 16.

20. Ibid., 2: 30–31.

21. Goldstein, *Post-Revolutionary Self*, 180–181. For Foucault's theory, see Foucault, *Discipline and Punish*, 170. Seigel makes a similar claim, but with more general applications, in *Idea of the Self*, 7–11.

22. Cousin, *Cours d'histoire*, 2: 31. For the passage to which Cousin referred, see Fénelon, *Démonstration de l'existence de Dieu*, 633.

23. Cousin, *Cours de philosophie* (Paris: Pichon & Didier, 1828–1829), 1: 498.

24. See Goldstein, *Post-Revolutionary Self*, 233–268.

25. Pierre-Joseph Proudhon, *Qu'est-ce que la propriété?* new ed., (Paris: Librairie internationale, 1873), 14.

26. Ibid., 46–59; quotations, 52–53.

27. Ibid., 53, 59–120; quotation, 53.

28. Ibid., 202–205, 219–224; quotations, 204, 219.

29. Pierre-Joseph Proudhon, *Théorie de la propriété* (Paris: Librairie internationale, 1866), 127–153, 167–198, 237–242; quotations, 136, 167, 183.

30. Pierre-Joseph Proudhon, *Système des contradictions économiques, ou Philosophie de la misère* (Paris: Librairie internationale, 1872), 1: 342.

31. Pierre-Joseph Proudhon, *De la Justice dans la Révolution et dans l'Église*, ed. Rosemarie Férenczi et al. (Paris: Fayard, 1990), 1495–1498; quotation, 1498. For Proudhon's broader criticisms of Fénelon's rejection of personal virtue, see 1351–1354.

Bibliography

I. PRIMARY SOURCES

A. *Manuscripts*

1. Archives nationales, Paris
Series DXXXVIII 3
Nos. 153, 2561, 3735
Series DXXXVIII 5
No. 3527
Series DXXXVIII 7
No. 2924
Series L22
Nos. 5, 7, 15.

2. Bibliothèque nationale de France, Paris
Manuscrits, Collection Joly de Fleury
Vol. 596, fol. 114
Vol. 462, fol. 112

3. Bibliothèque municipale de Dijon
Fonds Patrimoine, Ms. 335/MIC 528.

B. *Printed Primary Sources*

Analyse de la doctrine de Babeuf, tribune du people, proscrit par le Directory exécutif, pour avoir dit la vérité. N.p., n.d. [1796].

Arcq, Philippe-Auguste de Sainte-Foix, comte d'. *La Noblesse militaire, ou le Patriote françois.* N.p., 1756.

Arrest de la cour de Parlement de Toulouse. Qui annulle un Decret de l'Inquisition de Rome, du 14. Juillet 1723. rendu contre l'Instruction Pastorale de Monseigneur l'Evêque de Rodez, pour la Condamnation du "Traité des Actes Humains," dicté au College de Rodez par le P. Cabrespine Jesuite, l'an 1722. Toulouse: Claude-Gilles Lecamus, 1723.

Arrest de la cour de Parlement qui condamne un Imprimé ayant pour titre, "Émile, ou de l'Éducation"; par J. J. Rousseau, citoyen de Genève, à être lacéré et brûlé par l'Exécuteur de la Haute-Justice. Paris: P. G. Simon, 1762.

Arrest de la cour de Parlement rendu contre Maistre Philibert Robert, Prêtre, Curé de la Ville de Seurre, accusé du Quietisme & d'inceste Spirituel, & l'a condamné à être brûlé vif. Paris: Jean-Baptiste Langlois, 1698.

Arrest de parlement, qui condamne le nommé Humain, Tambour Major au Régiment de Mestre de Camp Général de dragons, & le nommé Bourdeaux, Dragon au Régiment de Belzunce. Paris: P. G. Simon, 1774.

Arrêt du Conseil d'État concernant les 500 lettres de noblesse accordées par l'édit du mois de mars 1696. N.p., n.d [August 1696].

L'Art de faire des songes. N.p., n.d. [ca. 1750].

L'Art de se rendre heureux par les songes, c'est à dire en se procurant telle espece de songes que l'on puisse désirer conformément à ses inclinations. Frankfurt, 1746.

Asfeld, Jacques Vincent d'. *Vains efforts des mêlangistes ou discernans dans l'œuvre des convulsions, pour défendre le systême du mêlange*. Paris, 1737.

Augustine, Saint, bishop of Hippo. *De Doctrina Christiana*. Edited and translated by R. P. H. Green. Oxford: Clarendon Press, 1995.

———. *On the Literal Meaning of Genesis*. Translated by John Hammond Taylor. 2 vols. New York: Newman, 1982.

Babeuf, Gracchus. *Textes choisis*. Edited by Claude Mazauric. Paris: Éditions sociales, 1976.

Bauclair, Paul-Louis de. *Anti-Contrat social, dans lequel on réfute d'une manière claire, utile & agréable, les principes posés dans le "Contrat social" de J. J. Rousseau, citoyen de Genève*. 1765. Reprint, Paris: J. Vrin, 1981.

Beaumont, Christophe de. *Mandement de Monseigneur l'archevêque de Paris, portant condemnation d'un livre qui a pour titre "Émile, ou De l'éducation."* In *Œuvres de Jean-Jacques Rousseau*, 3, pt. 2, 3–45. Amsterdam: M. M. Rey, 1762–1763.

Bergier, Nicolas. *Le Déisme réfuté par lui-même: ou Examen, en forme de Lettres, des Principes d'incrédulité répandus dans les divers Ouvrages de M. Rousseau*. Paris: Humblot, 1765. 5th ed. 1771. Facsimile, Paris: J. Vrin, 1981.

———. *Examen du matérialisme, ou Réfutation du systême de la nature*. 2 vols. Paris: Humblot, 1771.

Bérulle, Pierre de. *Œuvres complètes de Bérulle*. Edited by Abbé Jacques-Paul Migne. Petit-Montrouge: J.-P. Migne, 1856.

Bézout, Étienne-Louis. *Discours sur l'existence de l'Être suprême et l'immortalité de l'âme*. Chaumont: Bouchard, Year II [1794].

Bigot de Sainte-Croix, Louis-Claude. *Essai sur la liberté du commerce et de l'industrie, par feu M. le Président Bigot de Sainte-Croix*. Amsterdam: Lacombe, 1775.

Billaud-Varenne, Jacques Nicolas. *Les Élémens du républicanisme*. Paris, Year I [1793].

———. *Rapport fait à la Convention nationale, au nom du comité de Salut public; Sur la théorie du gouvernement démocratique, et sa vigueur utile pour contenir l'ambition, et pour tempérer l'essor de l'esprit militaire; sur le but politique de la guerre actuelle; et sur la nécessité d'inspirer l'amour des vertus civiles, par des fêtes publiques, et des institutions morales*. Paris: Imprimerie du Tribunal révolutionnaire, Year II [1794].

Borde, Charles. *Discours sur les Avantages des sciences et des arts, prononcé dans l'Assemblée publique de l'Académie des Sciences & Belles-Lettres de Lyon, le 22 Juin 1751*. Geneva: Barillot & fils, 1752.

Bossuet, Jacques Bénigne. *De la Connaissance de Dieu et de soi-même.* 1722. Edited by Émile-Auguste Charles. New ed. Paris: Eugène Belin, 1875.

———. *Instruction sur les estats d'oraison, où sont exposées les erreurs des faux mystiques de nos jours; Avec les actes de leur condamnation.* Paris: J. Anisson, 1697.

———. *Œuvres complètes de Bossuet.* Edited by F. Lachat. 31 vols. Paris: Louis, Vivès, 1862–1875.

———. *Politique de Bossuet.* Edited by Jacques Truchet. Paris: Armand Colin, 1966.

———. *Politique tirée des propres paroles de l'Ecriture sainte.* Edited by Jacques Le Brun. Geneva: Droz, 1967.

———. *Relation sur le quiétisme.* Paris: J. Anisson, 1698.

———. *Traité de la concupiscence.* Edited by Charles Urbain and Eugène Levesque. 1930. Reprint, Paris: Eurédit, 2007.

Boureau-Deslandes, André-François. *Lettre sur le luxe.* Frankfurt: Joseph-André Vanebben, 1745.

[Boyer, Pierre]. *Coup d'œil en forme de lettre sur les convulsions, où on examine dès son principe & dans les differens caracteres qu'elle porte, & on éclaircit ce qui peut s'y appercevoir de désavantageux.* Paris, 1733.

Brouillet, Jacques-Antoine. *Discours républicain prononcé, le dernier décadi frimaire, jour de l'inauguration du Temple de la Raison.* N.p., Year II.

Buonarroti, Philippe. *La Conspiration pour l'égalité, dite de Babeuf.* 2 vols. Brussels: Librairie romantique, 1828.

———. *Histoire de la conspiration pour l'égalité dite de Babeuf.* 1830. New ed. Paris: G. Charavay Jeune, 1850.

Butel-Dumont, Georges-Marie. *Théorie du luxe; ou Traité dans lequel on entreprend d'établir que le Luxe est un ressort non-seulement utile, mais même indispensablement nécessaire à la prosperité des états.* 2 pts. in 1 vol. [Paris: J.-F. Bastien], 1771.

Camus, Jean-Pierre. *La Défense du pur amour, contre les attaques de l'amour-propre.* Paris: Robert Bertault, 1640.

———. *Homélies des États-Généraux (1614–1615).* Edited by Jean Descrains. Geneva: Droz; Paris: Minard, 1970.

———. *Théodoxe, ou De la gloire de Dieu.* Rouen: F. Vaultier, 1639.

Camus, Michel, et al., eds. *Œuvres anonymes du XVIIIe siècle.* Paris: Fayard, 1986.

Cano, Melchior. *Tratado de la victoria de sí mismo.* 1550. Translated by Maurice Legendre as *La Victoire sur soi-même.* Paris: Revue des jeunes, 1923.

Caraccioli, Louis-Antoine de. *La Jouissance de soi-même.* Utrecht: H. Spruit, 1759.

Catéchisme du Concile de Trente. Translated by Emmanuel Marbeau and A. Carpentier. Grez-en-Bouère: Éditions Dominique Martin Morin, 1984.

Caussade, Jean-Pierre de. *Instructions spirituelles, en forme de dialogues sur les divers états d'Oraison.* Perpignan: Jean-Baptiste Reynier, 1741.

Chemin-Dupontès, Jean-Baptiste. *Qu'est-ce que la théophilanthropie? ou Mémoire contenant l'origine et l'histoire de cette institution, ses rapports avec le chris-*

tianisme, et l'aperçu de l'influence qu'elle peut avoir sur tous les cultes. Paris: Librairie classique, Year X [1801].

———. *Code religieux et moral des théophilanthropes ou adorateurs de Dieu et amis des hommes.* Paris: l'Éditeur, Year VI [1797–1798].

Chénier, Marie-Joseph. *Fénelon, ou Les Religieuses de Cambrai.* Paris: Moutard, 1793.

Cloots, Anacharsis [Jean-Baptiste]. *Bases constitutionnelles de la République du Genre Humain.* Paris: Imprimerie nationale, Year II [1793].

Code civil, contenant la série des lois qui le composent, avec leurs motifs et un extrait des rapports faits au Tribunat et des discours prononcés au Corps législatif sur les matières les plus importantes. 2 vols. Paris: Garnery, Year XI [1803]–Year XII [1804].

Collandière. *Discours sur l'existence de l'Être-suprême et l'immortalité de l'âme, prononcé par le Citoyen Collandière, en présence des Autorités de la Commune de Villejuif.* [Paris]: Renandière, Year II [1794].

Condillac, Étienne Bonnot de. *Œuvres complètes.* 21 vols. 1821–1822. Reprint, Geneva: Slatkine, 1970.

Confession faicte par Messire Louys Gaufridi Prestre en l'Eglise des Accoules de Marseille, Prince des Magiciens, depuis Constantinople jusques à Paris. Aix: Jean Tholozan, 1611.

Consultation sur les convulsions. N.p., 1735.

Contière, C. M. D. *Élémens de la politesse ou les secrets de l'art de plaire.* New ed. Liège: Guilleaume Destrez, 1702.

Copie du prononcé de l'Arrest de la cour du Parlement de Provence, Au sujet de l'Affaire du Pere Jean-Baptiste Girard, Jesuite; & de Catherine Cadiere; Nicolas de Saint-Joseph, Carme; Estienne-Thomas, & François Cadiere, Freres. N.p., 1731.

Correspondance littéraire, philosophique et critique. Edited by Maurice Tourneux. 16 vols. 1877–1882. Reprint, Nendeln, Liechtenstein: Kraus, 1968.

Courtin, Antoine de. *Nouveau traité de la civilité qui se pratique en France parmi les honnestes gens.* Paris: L. Josse & C. Robustel, 1728.

Cousin, Victor. *Cours de philosophie.* 2 vols. Paris: Pichon & Didier, 1828–1829.

———. *Cours d'histoire de la philosophie morale au dix-huitième siècle, professé à la Faculté des lettres, en 1819 et 1820.* Edited by Étienne Vacherot and Arsène Danton. 4 vols. (Paris: Ladrange, 1839-1842).

Coyer, Gabriel-François. *La Noblesse commerçante.* New ed. Paris: Duchesne, 1756.

Cumberland, Richard. *A Treatise of Laws of Nature.* Translated by John Maxwell. London: R. Philipps, 1727.

Daire, Eugène, ed. *Collection des principaux économistes.* 15 vols. 1841–1852. Reprint, Osnabrück: O. Zeller, 1966.

Declaration du Roy, Portant Reglement pour les Enregistrements des Lettres de Noblesse crées par Edit du mois de Mars 1696. Paris: Estienne Michallet, 1697.

Décret de la sacrée et générale Inquisition de Rome où sont rapportées fidellement en Italien et François les LXVIII propositions condamnées de Michel de Molinos. Rome: Chambre apostolique, n.d. [1687].

Delacroix, Jacques-Vincent. *Mémoire à consulter, sur l'existence des six corps, & la conservation de leurs privilèges, et Réflexions des six corps de la ville de Paris, sur la suppression des jurandes.* Paris: P. G. Simon, 1776.

Dénonciation à Monseigneur l'évêque et comte de Rodez, du "Traité des actes humains," dicté par le P. Cabrespine, dans le College des PP. Jesuites de la même Ville, la presente année 1721. N.p., n.d. [1721].

Dénonciation à Monseigneur le Procureur general du Roy au Parlement de Toulouse, d'une Doctrine qui autorise les Vols, les Meurtres, l'impunité des Criminels, & contraire à l'obeissance & au respect due aux Magistrats. n.p. 1722.

Descartes, René. *Œuvres de Descartes.* Edited by Charles Adam and Paul Tannery. 11 vols. Paris: J. Vrin, 1974–1986.

———. *Œuvres et lettres.* Edited by André Bridoux. Bibliothèque de la Pléiade. Paris: Gallimard, 1987.

Deschamps, Léger-Marie. *Le Vrai Systême, ou Le Mot de l'énigme métaphysique et morale.* Edited by Jean Thomas and Franco Venturi. Geneva: Droz, 1963.

Desessarts, Jean-Baptiste Poncet. *XIII. Lettre de Monsieur P*** à une de ses amis sur les convulsions.* N.p, n.d.

Desorgues, Théodore. *Hymne à Jean-Jacques Rousseau.* N.p., n.d. [1794].

Destutt de Tracy, Antoine-Louis-Claude. *Traité de la volonté et de ses effets.* Vol. 4 of *Élémens d'idéologie.* 1815. Facsimile, Stuttgart: Frommann-Holzboog, 1977.

Dictionnaire de l'Académie française. 1st and 4th eds. 1694 and 1762. ARTFL Dictionary Project. http://artfl-project.uchicago.edu/content/dictionnaires-dautre fois.

Diderot, Denis. *Correspondance.* Edited by Georges Roth. 16 vols. Paris: Éditions de Minuit, 1955–1970.

———. *Œuvres complètes de Diderot.* Edited by Jules Assézat and Maurice Tourneaux. 20 vols. Paris: Garnier frères, 1875–1877.

———. *Œuvres complètes.* Edited by Herbert Dieckmann, Jacques Proust, and Jean Varloot. 33 vols. projected. Paris: Hermann, 1975–.

———. *Œuvres politiques.* Edited by Paul Vernière. Paris: Garnier frères, 1963.

Diderot, Denis, and Jean Le Rond d'Alembert, eds. *Encyclopédie, ou Dictionnaire raisonné des sciences, des arts et des métiers, par une société de gens de lettres.* 35 vols. 1751–1780. Reprint, Stuttgart: F. Frommann, 1966–1988.

Discours prononcés dans L'Assemblée générale et dans le temple de la raison de la section regénérée de Beaurepaire, à l'occasion de l'inauguration des bustes des Martyrs de la Liberté, Marat & Le Pelletier, & de la Fête de la Raison, les 20 & 25 Nivôse, l'an deuxieme de la République, une & indivisible. Paris: Moutard, n.d. [1794].

Discours sur le patriotisme. N.p., 1789.

Dubos, Jean-Baptiste. *Réflexions critiques sur la poésie et sur la peinture.* New rev. ed. 3 vols. in 2. Utrecht: Étienne Neaulme, 1732.

Édit du Roy, Portant Annoblissement dans nostre Royaume de cinq cens personnes, qui seront choisies parmy eux qui se sont le plus distinguez par leurs merites, vertus & bonnes qualitez. N.p., n.d. [March 1696].

Édit du Roy, Portant création des Offices de Controlleurs de la Marque d'or & d'argent. Paris: E. Michallet, 1696.

Édit du Roi, Portant suppression des Jurandes & Communautés de Commerce, Arts & Métiers. Paris: Imprimerie royale, 1776.

Édit du Roy, Portant suppression des Offices de Visiteurs & Controlleurs de la Marque de l'or & de l'argent, des Offices de Distributeurs du Papier & Parchement Timbré, & de ceux de Vendeurs de poisson d'eau douce. Paris: Estienne Michallet, 1698.

Épitre aux matérialistes. Amsterdam, 1779.

Esprit, Jacques. *La Fausseté des vertus humaines.* 2 vols. Paris: G. Desprez, 1678.

Fabre, Claude-Dominique-Côme. *Rapport et projet de décret du citoyen Fabre, député de l'Hérault, sur le mode de partage des biens communaux.* Paris: Imprimerie nationale, n.d.

Fénelon, François de. *Œuvres complètes de Fénelon.* Edited by Jean-Edme-Auguste Gosselin. 10 vols. 1848–1852. Reprint, Geneva: Slatkine, 1971.

———. *Correspondance de Fénelon.* Edited by Jean Orcibal. With the collaboration of Jacques Le Brun and Irénée Noye. 18 vols. Paris: Klincksieck; Geneva: Droz, 1972–2007.

———. *Œuvres spirituelles de Messire François de Salignac de la Mothe-Fénelon.* 2 vols. Anvers: Henri de la Meule, 1718.

———. *Œuvres.* Edited by Jacques Le Brun. 2 vols. Paris: Gallimard, 1983.

———. *Sentimens de piété, où il est traité de la nécessité de connoître et d'aimer Dieu.* Paris: François Babuty, 1713.

Formey, Johann Heinrich Samuel. *Examen philosophique de la liaison réelle qu'il y a entre les Sciences & les Mœurs; Dans lequel on trouver* [sic] *à la Solution de la dispute de M. J. J. Rousseau, avec ses adversaires, sur la Question proposée par l'Académie de Dijon.* Avignon, 1755.

Fouillou, Jacques. *Réponse à un mémoire en forme de plainte; faite au nom de la convulsionnaire nommé Charlotte.* Paris, 1735.

François, Laurent. *Preuves de la Religion de Jésus-Christ, contre les spinosistes et les deistes.* 3 vols. Paris: Veuve Estienne & fils, 1751.

———. *Réponse aux difficultés proposées contre la religion chrétienne, Par J. J. Rousseau.* Paris: Babuty, 1765.

Franklin, Benjamin. *L'Art d'avoir des songes agréables.* In *Vie de Benjamin Franklin, écrite par lui-même, suivie de ses œuvres morales, politiques et littéraires,* 1: 346–357. Paris: F. Buisson, Year VI [1797–1798].

Godet des Marais, Paul. *Lettre pastorale de Mgr. l'évêque de Chartres au clergé de son diocèse sur le Livre intitulé: "Explication des maximes des saints."* Lyon: Veuve A. Tomas, 1698.

Guyon, Jeanne-Marie. *Correspondance.* 3 vols. Edited by Dominique Tronc. Paris: Honoré Champion, 2003–2005.

———. *Lettres chrétiennes et spirituelles sur divers sujets qui regardent la vie intérieure.* 5 vols. 1717-1718. London, 1767.

———. *Moyen court et très-facile de faire oraison que tous peuvent pratiquer très-aisément.* In *Le Moyen court et autres écrits spirituels,* edited by Marie-Louise Gondal, 61–127. Grenoble: Jérôme Millon, 1995.

———. *Règle des associés à l'Enfance de Jésus, Modèle de Perfection pour tous les états*. Cologne: Jean de La Pierre, 1705. In *Les Opuscules spirituels de Madame J. M. B. de la Mothe Guion*, 2: 4–81. Cologne: Jean de la Pierre, 1712.

———. *La Vie de Madame J. M. B. de la Mothe-Guyon, écrite par elle-même*. 3 vols. 1720. New ed. 3 vols. Paris: Libraries associés, 1791.

Hecquet, Philippe. *Le Mélange dans les convulsions confondu par le naturalisme*. Soleure: Andreas Gymnicus, 1733.

———. *Le Naturalisme des convulsions dans les maladies de l'épidémie convulsionnaire*. Soleure: Andreas Gymnicus, 1733.

Histoire de Dom Bougre, Portier des Chartreux, Écrite par lui-même. In Camus et al., eds., *Œuvres anonymes du XVIIIe siècle*, 1: 29–236.

Hobbes, Thomas. *Leviathan*. 1651. Edited by Richard Tuck. Cambridge: Cambridge University Press, 1991.

Holbach, Paul Henri Dietrich, baron d'. *La Politique naturelle, ou Discours sur les vrais principes du gouvernement*. 2 vols. London, 1773.

———. *Système de la nature, ou Des Loix du monde Physique & du monde moral*. New ed. 2 vols. London, 1771.

———. *Système social, ou Principes naturels de la morale et de la politique*. 3 vols. in 1. London, 1773.

La Combe, François. *Maximes spirituelles*. In Guyon, *Opuscules spirituels*, 2: 112–125.

Lakanal, Joseph. *Rapport sur J. J. Rousseau, fait au nom du Comité d'Instruction, suivi des détails sur la translation des cendres de J. J. Rousseau au Panthéon français*. Paris: Imprimerie nationale, Year III [1795].

La Mettrie, Julien Offroy de. *Œuvres philosophiques de La Mettrie*. New ed. 3 vols. Paris: Charles Tutot, 1796.

Lavoisier, Jean-François. *Dictionnaire portatif de médecine, d'Anatomie, de Chirugie, de Pharmacie, de Chymie, d'Histoire Naturelle, de Botanique et de Physique*. 2 vols. Paris: Aux Dépens de P. F. Didot le Jeune, 1764.

Leibniz, Gottfried Wilhelm. "Considerations on the Doctrine of a Universal Spirit." In *The Philosophical Works of Leibnitz*, trans. George Martin Duncan, 139–148. New Haven, Conn.: Tuttle, Morehouse, & Taylor, 1890.

Lelarge de Lignac, Joseph-Adrien. *Élémens de métaphysique tirés de l'expérience, ou Lettres à un matérialiste sur la nature de l'âme*. Paris: Desaint & Saillant, 1753.

Le Mercier de La Rivière, Pierre-Paul. *L'Intérêt général de l'État, ou La liberté du commerce des blés démontrée conforme au droit naturel, au droit public de la France, aux lois fondamentales du royaume, à l'intérêt commun du souverain et de ses sujets dans tous les temps*. Paris: Desaint, 1770.

Lenglet Dufresnoy, Nicolas. *Recueil de dissertations anciennes et nouvelles, sur les apparitions, les visions et les songes*. 4 vols. Paris: J.-N. Leloup, 1752.

———. *Traité historique et dogmatique sur les apparitions, les visions et les révélations particuliéres*. 6 vols. Paris: J.-N. Leloup, 1751.

Leroy de Montécly. *Observations présentées par les maîtres composant la Communauté des graveurs, ciseleurs de la ville & fauxbourgs de Paris. Sur l'édit de suppression des corps des marchands & des communautés des arts & métiers*. Paris: P. de Lormel, 1776.

Lettre de Mr. le marquis de *** au R. P. Recteur des Jesuites de Rodez. N.p., n.d. Copy in the Bibliothèque nationale, Paris.

Levade, Louis, Jean-Louis-Antoine Reynier, and Jacob Berthout van Berchem *fils*. *Rapport fait à la Société des Sciences Physiques de Lausanne sur un somnambule naturel.* Lausanne: H. Vincent, 1788.

Locke, John. *An Essay Concerning Human Understanding.* 1689. Edited by Peter H. Nidditch. Oxford: Clarendon Press, 1975.

―――. *Second Treatise of Government.* 1689. In *Two Treatises of Government,* ed. Peter Laslett, 265–428. Cambridge: Cambridge University Press, 1988.

Loyseau, Charles. *Les Œuvres de maistre Charles Loyseau.* Latest edition, more accurate than the preceding ones. Lyon: Compagnie des Libraires, 1701.

L. P. L. D. [le P. Laliman, dominicain]. *Moyens propres à garantir les hommes du suicide.* Paris: Benoît Morin, 1779.

Maleville, Guillaume de. *Examen approfondi des difficultés de M. Rousseau de Genève contre le christianisme catholique.* Paris, 1769.

―――. *La Religion naturelle et la révélée, établies sur les principes de la vraie philosophie, et sur la divinité des écritures.* 6 vols. Paris: Nyon, 1756–1758.

Marat, Jean-Paul. *Œuvres politiques (1789–1793).* Edited by Jacques De Cock and Charlotte Goëtz. 10 vols. Brussels: Pôle Nord, 1989–1995.

―――. *Plan de législation criminelle.* Paris: Rochette, 1790.

Maréchal, Sylvain. *Almanach des républicains, pour servir à l'instruction publique.* Paris: Cercle Social, 1793.

[Mauparty, Hubert]. *Réponse à l'apologie en forme de requeste presentée à l'official de Dijon, par Claude Quillot, Prêtre de ladite Ville.* Zell [Reims]: Henriette Hermille, 1703.

Marx, Karl, and Frederick Engels. *The Marx-Engels Reader.* 2nd ed. Edited by Robert C. Tucker. New York: Norton, 1978.

Melon, Jean-François. *Essai politique sur le commerce.* In Daire, ed., *Collections des principaux économistes,* vol. 1, *Économistes-financiers du 18e siècle,* 707–835.

Mémoire instructif pour le Pere Jean-Baptiste Girard. N.p., n.d. [1731].

Mérault de Bizy, Athanase-René. *Voltaire apologiste de la religion chrétienne.* 1826. Paris: Perisse frères, 1838.

Mercier, Louis-Sébastien. *Tableau de Paris.* New ed. 12 vols. Amsterdam, 1782–1788.

―――. *De J. J. Rousseau considéré comme l'un des premiers auteurs de la Révolution.* 2 vols. Paris: Buisson, 1791.

Mercure de France. 89 vols. Reprint, Geneva: Slatkine, 1968–1970.

Mirabeau, Victor de Riqueti, marquis de. *Leçons œconomiques.* Amsterdam, 1770.

Molinos, Miguel de. *Guía espiritual.* 1675. Translated by Paul Drochon as *Guide spirituel.* Paris: Éditions du Cerf, 1997.

Montchrétien, Antoine. *Traicté de l'économie politique.* 1615. Paris: Plon, 1889.

Montesquieu, Charles-Louis de Secondat, baron de. *De l'Esprit des lois.* 1748. Edited by Laurent Versini. 2 vols. Paris: Gallimard, 1995.

―――. *Lettres persanes.* 1721. Edited by Paul Vernière. Paris: Garnier frères, 1960.

―――. *Œuvres complètes.* Edited by Roger Caillois. 2 vols. Bibliothèque de la Pléiade. Paris: Gallimard, 1949–1951.

Morel, Célestin. *Éloge funèbre de Jean Paul Marat, Député à la Convention natio-nale, pronounce à Schiltigheim le 26 Brumaire.* N.p., Year II [1793].

Morelly, Étienne Gabriel. *Code de la nature, ou Le Véritable esprit de ses lois.* Paris: Paul Masgana–H. Fournier, 1841.

Moritz, Karl Philipp. *Anton Reiser: A Psychological Novel.* Translated by John R. Russell. Columbia, S.C.: Camden House, 1996.

La Mort pour la patrie. Discours prononcé au nom de la Société-Populaire-Révolu-tionaire de Dune-Libre, le jour de la Fête des Martyrs de la Liberté. Dune-Libre [Dunkirk]: Drouilard, n.d. [1794].

Nicole, Pierre. *L'Esprit de M. Nicole.* 1771. Reprint, Geneva: Slatkine, 1971.

————. *Essais de Morale, contenus en divers traités sur plusieurs devoirs impor-tants.* 4 vols. 1733–1771. Reprint, Geneva: Slatkine, 1971.

————. *Réfutation des principales erreurs des quiétistes.* Paris: Elie Josset, 1695.

Noailles, Louis-Antoine de. *Instruction pastorale de Monseigneur l'Archevesque de Paris, sur la Perfection Chrétienne & sur la vie interieure. Contre les illusions des Faux Mystiques.* 2nd ed. Paris: Luis Josse, 1698.

Nouveau Dictionnaire civil et canonique de droit et de pratique. Paris: Augustin Besoigne, 1697.

Nouveau plan de réflexions sur la Consultation des Docteurs contre les convul-sions. N.p., n.d..

Ordonnance et Instruction pastorale, pour la condamnation du "Traité des actes humains." Rodez: N. Le Roux, n.d.

P.F.L.M. *Du Sommeil.* The Hague: Pierre-Frederic Gosse, 1779.

Pascal, Blaise. *Les Pensées.* Edited by Francis Kaplan. Paris: Éditions du Cerf, 2005.

La Passion de 1790, ou Louis XVI sacrifié pour et par son peuple. Extraits tirés des Évangélistes nationaux. Paris: Philippe Parabole, 1790.

Pensées sur les prodiges de nos jours. N.p., 1734.

Peyrard, François. *De la nature et de ses lois.* Paris: Louis, 1793.

Phélypeaux, Jean. *Relation de l'origine, du progrès et de la condamnation du quiét-isme répandu en France avec plusieurs anecdotes curieuses.* N.p., 1732.

Pilé, Abbé. *Lettre à M. Jean-Jacques Rousseau, citoyen de Genève, à l'occasion de son Ouvrage intitulé: "Discours sur l'origine & les fondements de l'inégalité parmi les hommes."* Westminster, 1755.

Plaisant de La Houssaye. *Hymne à la Nature.* Paris: Demoraine, Debray & Prault, Year II [1794].

Pluquet, François-André-Adrien. *Examen du fatalisme.* 3 vols. Paris: Didot, 1757.

Pothier, Robert-Joseph. *Traité du droit de domaine de propriété.* 2 vols. Paris: Dubure père; Orleans: Veuve Rouzeau-Montaut, 1772.

Preudhomme. *Traité des droits appartenans aux seigneurs sur les biens possédés en roture.* Paris: Froullé, 1781.

Procès Verbaux de plusieurs Medecins et chirurgiens, dressé par ordre de sa Majesté, au sujet de quelques personnes soi-disantes agitées de Convulsions. Paris: Veuve Mazieres & Jean-Baptiste Garnier, 1732.

Proudhon, Jean-Baptiste-Victor. *Traité du domaine de propriété, ou de la Distribu-*

tion des biens considérés principalement par rapport au domaine privé. 3 vols. Dijon: Victor Lagier, 1839.

Proudhon, Pierre-Joseph. *De la Justice dans la Révolution et dans l'Église.* Edited by Rosemarie Férenczi, Georges Navet, Patrice Vermeren, and Bernard Boyenne. 4 vols. Paris: Fayard, 1990.

———. *Système des contradictions économiques, ou Philosophie de la misère.* 2 vols. Paris: Librairie Internationale, 1872.

———. *Théorie de la propriété.* Paris: Librairie Internationale, 1866.

———. *Qu'est-ce que la propriété?* New ed. Paris: Librairie Internationale, 1873.

Pufendorf, Samuel. *On the Duties of Man and Citizen According to Natural Law.* Edited by James Tully. Cambridge: Cambridge University Press, 1991.

Quesnay, François. *Dialogue sur les travaux des artisans.* In Daire, ed., *Collection des principaux économistes,* vol. 2, *Physiocrates: Quesnay, Dupont de Nemours, Mercier de La Rivières, l'Abbé Baudeau, Le Trosne,* 145–251.

———. *Maximes générales du gouvernement économique d'un royaume agricole.* In Daire, ed., *Collection des principaux économistes,* vol. 2, *Physiocrates,* 79–104.

Raynal, Guillaume-Thomas-François, with Denis Diderot. *Histoire philosophique et politique du commerce et des établissements des Européens dans les deux Indes.* Paris: François Maspero, 1981. Reprint, Paris: La Découverte & Syros, 2001.

Recueil des miracles operés au tombeau de M. de Paris diacre. 3 vols. Utrecht, 1733.

Recueil général des pièces concernant le procez entre la demoiselle Cadiere; de la Ville de Toulon; Et le Pere Girard, Jesuite, Recteur du Seminaire Royal de la Marine de ladite Ville. 5 vols. The Hague: Swart, 1731.

Réimpression de l'ancien Moniteur. Edited by Léonard Gallois. 32 vols. Paris: Bureau Central, 1840–1845.

Relation des Actes et Deliberations concernant la constitution en forme de bref de N. S. le Pape Innocent XII. du douziéme Mars 1699. Paris: François Muguet, 1700.

Rémonstrances du Parlement de Paris au XVIIIe siècle. Edited by Jules Flammeront. 3 vols. Paris: Imprimerie nationale, 1898.

Remontrance des curez de Rhodés, à monseigneur leur evêque. Contre plusieurs propositions quiétistes & autres injurieuses aux SS. Peres, que le P. Lamejou, Professeur Jesuite, enseigne au Seminaire de cette Ville. N.p., 1732.

Requeste présentée au Parlement par Charlotte de la Porte. Paris: Ph. Nic. Lottin, 1735.

Requeste présentée au Parlement pour Marguerite-Catherine Turpin. Paris: Ph. Nic. Lottin, 1735.

Richard, Jérôme. *La Théorie des songes.* Paris: Estienne frères, 1766.

Richeome, Louis. *L'Immortalité de l'âme déclarée avec raisons naturelles, témoignages humains et divins pour la foy catholique contre les athées et libertins.* Paris: Sébastien Cramoisy, 1621.

Rituel républicain. Fête à l'Être-suprême, exécutée à Paris, le 20 prairial, l'an 2e. de la République. Paris: Aubry, Year II [1794].

Robespierre, Maximilien. *Œuvres de Maximilien Robespierre.* 10 vols. 1958. Reprint, Paris: Phénix, 2000.

Robillard d'Avrigny, Hyacinthe. *Mémoires chronologiques et dogmatiques pour servir à l'histoire ecclésiastique depuis 1600 jusqu'en 1716 avec des réflexions et des remarques critiques.* 4 vols. N.p., 1720.

Rousseau, Jean-Jacques. *Œuvres complètes.* Edited by Bernard Gagnebin and Marcel Raymond. 5 vols. Bibliothèque de la Pléiade. Paris: Gallimard, 1959–1995.

———. *Correspondance complète de Jean-Jacques Rousseau.* Edited by R. A. Leigh. 52 vols. Geneva: Institut et Musée Voltaire; Oxford: Voltaire Foundation, 1965–1998.

[Saint-Jean, Abbé de]. *Lettre d'un ecclesiastique de province, à un de ses amis, où il lui donne une idée abregée de l'œuvre des convulsions.* N.p., 1733.

Saint-Just, Louis-Antoine-Léon. *Œuvres complètes.* Edited by Michèle Duval. Paris: Ivrea, 2003.

Saint-Lambert, Jean-François de. *Essai sur le luxe.* N.p., 1764.

Saint-Pierre, Jean-Henri Bernardin de. *La Vie et les ouvrages de Jean-Jacques Rousseau.* Edited by Maurice Souriau. Paris: E. Cornély, 1907.

Le Sainte Concile de Trente œcuménique et général, célébré sous Paul III. Jules III. et Pie IV. souverains pontifes. Translated by Abbé Chanut. 3rd ed. Paris: Sebastien Mabre-Cramoisy, 1686.

Sales, François de. *Introduction à la vie dévote.* Paris, Victor Lecoffre, 1894.

Savary, Jacques. *Le Parfait négociant, ou Instruction générale pour ce qui regarde le Commerce de toute sorte de Marchandises, tant de France, que des Pays Estrangers.* Paris: Jean Guignard, 1675.

Seconde Dénonciation de la doctrine des Jesuites de Rodez, à Monsieur l'évêque de Rodez. Traité des actes humains dicté, l'année 1713 dans cette Ville, par le père Charly, Jesuite. N.p., n.d. [1713].

Le Secret de l'oraison mentale, où l'on découvre la parfaite idée de La Méditation, les grands avantages qu'on en reçoit, et un moyen facile de la faire, Avec sa pratique, sur les plus importantes vérités du christianisme, et sur tous les mystères de la vie de Jésus-Christ. Dijon: J. Ressayre, 1680.

Sentence contre Me Philibert Robert. Paris: Claude Nego, [1698].

Sentence de Monsieur Fijan, Conseiller au Parlement, contre Les Sectateurs & Adherans de Me. Philibert Robert, Pretre ci-devant Curé de la Ville de Seurre. Dijon: Jean Grangier, 1700.

Sieyès, Emmanuel-Joseph. *Des Manuscrits de Sieyès.* Edited by Christine Fauré. Paris: Honoré Champion, 1999.

———. *Opinion de Sieyès sur plusieurs articles des titres IV et V du projet de constitution, prononcée à la Convention le 2 thermidor de l'an III.* Paris: Imprimerie nationale, Year III [1795].

———. *Qu'est-ce que le Tiers-État?* N.p., 1789.

Sinsart, Benoît. *Recueil de pensées diverses sur l'immatérialité de l'ame, son immortalité, sa liberté, sa distinction d'avec le corps, ou Réfutation du matérialisme.* Colmar: Imprimerie royale, 1756.

Sirmond, Jacques. *La Deffense de la vertu.* Paris: Sebastien Huvré, 1641.

Souhait, Julien-Joseph. *Discours sur le partage des biens communaux, prononcé à la tribune de la Convention Nationale.* Paris: Imprimerie nationale, Year II [1794].

Spinoza, Baruch. *Dieu, l'homme et la béatitude.* Translated by Paul Janet. Paris: G. Balière, 1878.

————. *Ethics.* In *The Collected Works of Spinoza,* ed. and trans. Edwin Curley, 408–617. Princeton, N.J.: Princeton University Press, 1985.

Talleyrand-Périgord, Charles Maurice de. *Mémoires du prince du Talleyrand.* Edited by Albert de Broglie. 5 vols. Paris: C. Lévy, 1891–1892.

Le Tableau de la Vie & du Gouvernement de Messieurs les Cardinaux Richelieu & Mazarin, & de Monsieur Colbert, representé en diverses Satyres & Poësies ingenieuses. Cologne: Pierre Marteau, 1694.

Thérèse philosophe, ou Mémoires pour servir à l'historie du Père Dirrag et de mademoiselle Éradice. In Camus et al., eds., *Œuvres anonymes du XVIIIe siècle,* 3: 31–191.

Tocqueville, Alexis de. *Democracy in America.* Translated by Gerald E. Bevan. London: Penguin Books, 2003.

Traité des trois imposteurs. 1771. Facsimile edited by Pierre Rétat. Images et témoins de l'âge classique, vol. 3. Saint-Étienne: Universités de la région Rhône-Alpes, Centre interuniversitaire d'éditions et de rééditions, 1973.

Vaucanson, Jacques. *Le Mécanisme du flûteur automate, présenté à Messieurs de l'Académie royale des sciences.* Paris: Jacques Guerin, 1738.

Vicq-d'Azyr, Félix, ed. *Encyclopédie méthodique: Médecine.* 13 vols. Paris: Panckoucke, 1787–1830.

Voltaire [François-Marie Arouet]. *Œuvres complètes de Voltaire.* Edited by Louis Moland. New ed. 52 vols. Paris: Garnier, 1877–1885.

II. SECONDARY SOURCES

Alquié, Ferdinand. *Le Cartésianisme de Malebranche.* Paris: J. Vrin, 1974.

Anderson, Wilma C. *Diderot's Dream.* Baltimore: Johns Hopkins University Press, 1990.

Anund-Tråvén, Aslög. *Étude quantative de cinq traductions françaises du XVIIIe siècle basées sur les romans anglais de Samuel Richardson, à savoir "Pamela," "Clarissa," et "Sir Charles Grandison."* Göteborg: Kompendiet, 2000.

Apostolidès, Jean-Marie. *Le Roi-Machine: Spectacle et politique au temps de Louis XIV.* Paris: Éditions de Minuit, 1981.

Arasse, Daniel. *La Guillotine et l'imaginaire de la Terreur.* Paris: Flammarion, 1987.

Aulard, François-Alphonse. *Le Culte de la Raison et le culte de l'Être suprême, 1793–1794: Essai historique.* Aalen: Scientia, 1975.

Azouvi, François. *Descartes et la France: Histoire d'une passion nationale.* Paris: Fayard, 2002.

Baczko, Bronisław. *Rousseau: Solitude et communauté.* Translated by Claire Brendhel-Lamhout. Paris: Mouton, 1974.

Baecque, Antoine de. *Glory and Terror: Seven Deaths under the French Revolution.* Translated by Charlotte Mandell. New York: Routledge, 2001.

Baker, Keith Michael. "Enlightenment and the Institution of Society: Notes for a Conceptual History." In *Main Trends in Cultural History,* ed. Willem Melching and Wyger Velema, 95–120. Amsterdam: Rodopi, 1994.

————. *Inventing the French Revolution: Essays on French Political Culture in the Eighteenth Century.* Cambridge: Cambridge University Press, 1990.

————. "Sieyès." In *The Critical Dictionary of the French Revolution,* ed. François Furet and Mona Ozouf, trans. Arthur Goldhammer, 313–323. Cambridge, Mass.: Belknap Press, 1989.

————. "Transformations of Classical Republicanism in Eighteenth-Century France." *Journal of Modern History* 73 (March 2001): 32–53.

Barbier, Antoine-Alexandre. *Dictionnaire des ouvrages anonymes et pseudonymes.* Edited by Olivier Barbier, René Billard, and Paul Billard. 3rd ed. 4 vols. Paris: Paul Daffis, 1874.

Bardout, Jean-Christophe. "A Reception without Attachment: Malebranche Confronting Cartesian Morality." Translated by Sarah A. Miller and Patrick L. Miller. In Schmaltz, ed., *Receptions of Descartes,* 41–62.

Barny, Roger. *L'Éclatement révolutionnaire du rousseauisme.* Annales littéraires de l'Université de Besançon, vol. 378. Paris: Belles Lettres, 1988.

Basdevant-Gaudemet, Brigitte. *Aux Origines de l'état moderne: Charles Loyseau (1563–1627), Théoricien de la puissance publique.* Paris: Economica, 1977.

Bayet, Albert. *Le Suicide et la morale.* Paris: Félix Alcan, 1922.

Becker, Carl. *The Heavenly City of the Eighteenth-Century Philosophers.* New Haven, Conn.: Yale University Press, 1932.

Bell, David. *The Cult of the Nation in France: Inventing Nationalism, 1680–1800.* Cambridge, Mass.: Harvard University Press, 2001.

Bennett, Jonathan. *A Study of Spinoza's "Ethics."* Indianapolis, Ind.: Hackett, 1984.

Berg, Maxime, and Elizabeth Eger, eds. *Luxury in the Eighteenth Century: Debates, Desires & Delectable Goods.* New York: Palgrave Macmillan, 2003.

Bergeron, L. "Évolution de la fête révolutionnaire: Chronologie et typologie." In Ehrard and Viallaneix, eds., *Fêtes de la Révolution,* 125–127.

Berti, Sylvia. "The First Edition of the *Traité des trois imposteurs* and Its Debt to Spinoza's *Ethics.*" In *Atheism from the Reformation to the Enlightenment,* ed. Michael Hunter and David Wootton, 183–220. Oxford: Clarendon Press, 1992.

Bien, David D. "Property in Office under the *ancien régime*: The Case of the Stockholders." In Brewer and Staves, eds., *Early Modern Conceptions of Property,* 481–496.

Birn, Raymond. "The Profits of Ideas: Privilèges en librairie in Eighteenth-Century France." *Eighteenth-Century Studies* 4, 2 (Winter 1970–1971): 131–168.

Bloch, Olivier, ed. *Spinoza au XVIIIe siècle.* Paris: Méridiens Klincksieck, 1990.

Blum, Carol. *Rousseau and the Republic of Virtue: The Language of Politics in the French Revolution.* Ithaca, N.Y.: Cornell University Press, 1986.

————. *Strength in Numbers: Population, Reproduction, and Power in Eighteenth-Century France.* Baltimore: Johns Hopkins University Press, 2002.

Bourdin, Jean-Claude. *Les Matérialistes au XVIIIe siècle.* Paris: Payot & Rivages, 1996.

Blumenberg, Hans. *The Legitimacy of the Modern Age.* Translated by Robert M. Wallace. Cambridge, Mass.: MIT Press, 1985.

Bonnet, Jean-Claude. "Les Formes de célébration." In Bonnet, ed., *Mort de Marat,* 101–127.

Bonnet, Jean-Claude, ed. *La Mort de Marat*. Paris: Flammarion, 1986.

Bowman, Franck Paul. "Le «Sacré Cœur» de Marat." In Ehrard and Viallaneix, eds., *Fêtes de la Révolution*, 155–179.

Bradley, James E., and Dale Van Kley, eds. *Religion and Politics in Enlightenment Europe*. Notre Dame, Ind.: University of Notre Dame Press, 2001.

Bremond, Henri. *Histoire littéraire du sentiment religieux en France*. 12 vols. Paris: Bloud & Gay, 1915–1936.

———. Introduction to Jean-Pierre de Caussade, *Bossuet, maître d'oraison: Instructions spirituelles en forme de dialogues sur les divers états d'oraison*, ed. Bremond. Paris: Bloud & Gay, 1931.

———. *La Querelle du pur amour au temps de Louis XIII: Antoine Sirmond et Jean-Pierre Camus*. Cahiers de la nouvelle journée, no. 22. Paris: Bloud & Gay, 1932.

Brewer, Daniel. *The Discourse of Enlightenment in Eighteenth-Century France: Diderot and the Art of Philosophizing*. Cambridge: Cambridge University Press, 1993.

———. *The Enlightenment Past: Reconstructing Eighteenth-Century French Thought*. Cambridge: Cambridge University Press, 2008.

Brewer, John, and Roy Porter, eds. *Consumption and the World of Goods*. New York: Routledge, 1993.

Brewer, John, and Susan Staves, eds. *Early Modern Conceptions of Property*. London: Routledge, 1995.

Brockliss, L. W. B. "The Medico-Religious Universe of an Early Eighteenth-Century Parisian Doctor: The Case of Philippe Hecquet." In *The Medical Revolution of the Seventeenth Century*, ed. Roger Kenneth French and Andrew Wear, 191–221. Cambridge: Cambridge University Press, 1989.

Brown, Diane Berrett. "The Constraints of Liberty at the Scene of Instruction." In *Rousseau and Freedom*, ed. Christie McDonald and Stanley Hoffmann, 168–173. Cambridge: Cambridge University Press, 2010.

Brown, Gregory S. *A Field of Honor: Culture and Public Theater in French Literary Life from Racine to the Revolution*. New York: Columbia University Press, 2005.

———. *Literary Sociability and Literary Property in France, 1775–1793*. Studies in European Cultural Transition, vol. 33. Aldershot: Ashgate, 2006.

Bruneau, Marie-Florine. *Women Mystics Confront the Modern World: Marie de L'Incarnation (1599–1672) and Madame Guyon (1648–1717)*. Albany, N.Y.: State University of New York Press, 1998.

Brunel, Françoise. *Thermidor: La Chute de Robespierre*. Paris: Éditions Complexe, 1989.

Bruschvicg, Léon. *Spinoza et ses contemporains*. 5th ed. Paris: Presses universitaires de France, 1971.

Buchez, Pierre-Joseph-Benjamin, and Pierre-Celéstin Roux-Lavergne. *Histoire parlementaire de la Révolution française, ou Journal des Assemblés nationales depuis 1780 jusq'en 1815*. 40 vols. Paris: Paulin, 1834–1838.

Burke, Peter. *The Fabrication of Louis XIV*. New Haven, Conn.: Yale University Press, 1992.

Burson, Jeffrey D. *The Rise and Fall of the Theological Enlightenment: Jean-Martin de Prades and Ideological Polarization in Eighteenth-Century France.* Foreword by Dale Van Kley. Notre Dame, Ind.: University of Notre Dame Press, 2010.

Bush, Michael. *Rich Noble, Poor Noble.* Manchester: Manchester University Press, 1988.

Calhoun, Craig, ed. *Habermas and the Public Sphere.* Cambridge, Mass.: MIT Press, 1992.

Cain, Julien, ed. *Les Églises ennemies: La Réforme et les guerres de religion, 1547–1589.* Vol. 12 of *Nouvelle histoire de France.* Paris: Tallandier, 1966.

Caplan, Jay. *Framed Narratives: Diderot's Genealogy of the Beholder.* Minneapolis: University of Minnesota Press, 1985.

Casini, Paolo. *Diderot "philosophe."* Biblioteca di cultura moderna, vol. 567. Bari: Laterza, 1962.

Cassirer, Ernst. *The Philosophy of the Enlightenment.* Translated by Fritz C. A. Koelln and James P. Pettegrove. Princeton, N. J.: Princeton University Press, 1951.

———. *The Question of Jean-Jacques Rousseau.* 2nd ed. Translated by Peter Gay. New Haven, Conn.: Yale University Press, 1989.

Certeau, Michel de. *The Mystic Fable,* vol. 1: *The Sixteenth and Seventeenth Centuries.* Translated by Michael B. Smith. Chicago: University of Chicago Press, 1992.

Chartier, Roger. *The Cultural Origins of the French Revolution.* Translated by Lydia G. Cochrane. Durham, N.C.: Duke University Press, 1991.

———. "Richardson, Diderot et la lectrice impatiente." *Modern Language Notes* 114 (1999): 647–666.

Chaussinaud-Nogaret, Guy. *The French Nobility in the Eighteenth Century: From Feudalism to Enlightenment.* Translated by William Doyle. Cambridge: Cambridge University Press, 1985.

Cherel, Albert. *Fénelon au XVIIIe siècle en France (1715–1820): Son Prestige— Son Influence.* 1917. Reprint, Geneva: Slatkine, 1970.

Chérot, Henri. *Autour de Bossuet: Le Quiétisme en Bourgogne et à Paris en 1698.* Paris: Victor Retaux, 1901.

Choudhury, Mita. "A Betrayal of Trust: The Jesuits and Quietism in Eighteenth-Century France." *Common Knowledge* 15, 2 (Spring 2009): 164–180.

———. "'Carnal Quietism': Embodying Anti-Jesuit Polemics in the Catherine Cadière Affair, 1731." *Eighteenth-Century Studies* 39, 2 (2006): 173–186.

Cobban, Alfred. *Rousseau and the Modern State.* 2nd ed. London: George Allen & Unwin, 1964.

Cognet, Louis. *Crépuscule des mystiques, Bossuet–Fénelon.* New ed. Preface by J. R. Armogathe. Bibliothèque de théologie. Paris: Desclée, 1991.

Cole, C. W. *Colbert and a Century of French Mercantilism.* 2 vols. New York: Columbia University Press, 1939.

Cole, John R. *The Olympian Dreams and Youthful Rebellion of René Descartes.* Urbana, Ill.: University of Illinois Press, 1992.

Coleman, Charly. "Resacralizing the World: The Fate of Secularization in Enlightenment Historiography," *Journal of Modern History* 82, 2 (June 2010): 368–395.

Coleman, Patrick. "Property, Politics, and Personality in Rousseau." In Brewer and Staves, eds., *Early Modern Conceptions of Property*, 254–274.

Cornette, Joël. *Absolutisme et Lumières, 1652–1783*. 4th ed. Paris: Hachette, 2005.

Cranston, Maurice. *Jean-Jacques: The Early Life and Work of Jean-Jacques Rousseau*. London: Allen Lane, 1983.

———. *The Noble Savage: Jean-Jacques Rousseau, 1754–1762*. Chicago: University of Chicago Press, 1991.

———. *The Solitary Self: Jean-Jacques Rousseau in Exile and Adversity*. Chicago: University of Chicago Press, 1993.

Crocker, Lester. *An Age of Crisis: Man and World in Eighteenth-Century French Thought*. Baltimore: Johns Hopkins University Press, 1959.

Crouzet, François. "Angleterre et France au XVIIIe siècle: Essai d'analyse comparée de deux croissances." *Annales. Économies, Sociétés, Civilisations* 21, 2 (March–April 1966): 254–291.

Crow, Thomas E. *Emulation: Making Artists for Revolutionary France*. New Haven, Conn.: Yale University Press, 1995.

———. *Painters and Public Life in Eighteenth-Century France*. New Haven, Conn.: Yale University Press, 1985.

Culoma, Michaël. *La Religion civile de Rousseau à Robespierre*. Paris: L'Harmattan, 2010.

Cushing, Max P. "A Forgotten Philosopher." *Monist* 30 (1920): 312–313.

Darnton, Robert. *Business of the Enlightenment: A Publishing History of the "Encyclopédie," 1775–1880*. Cambridge, Mass.: Belknap Press, 1979.

———. *The Great Cat Massacre and Other Episodes in French Cultural History*. New York: Basic Books, 1984.

———. *The Forbidden Best-Sellers of Pre-Revolutionary France*. New York: Norton, 1996.

———. *The Literary Underground of the Old Regime*. Cambridge. Mass.: Harvard University Press, 1982.

———. "Philosophers Trim the Tree of Knowledge: The Epistemological Strategy of the *Encyclopédie*." In Darnton, *Great Cat Massacre*, 191–213.

———. "Readers Respond to Rousseau: The Fabrication of Romantic Sensitivity." In Darnton, *Great Cat Massacre*, 215–256.

Darwall, Stephen. *The British Moralists and the Internal "Ought," 1640–1740*. Cambridge: Cambridge University Press, 1995.

Daston, Lorraine. "Enlightenment Fears, Fears of Enlightenment." In *What's Left of Enlightenment? A Postmodern Question*, ed. Keith Michael Baker and Peter Hanns Reill, 116–123. Stanford, Calif.: Stanford University Press, 2001.

Daston, Lorraine, and Katharine Park. *Wonders and the Order of Nature, 1150–1750*. New York: Zone Books, 1998.

Dedieu, Joseph. "L'Agonie du jansénisme (1715–1790). Essai de bio-bibliographie." *Revue de l'histoire de France* 14: 161–214.

Delplanque, Albert. *Fénelon et ses amis*. Paris: J. Gabalda, 1910.

Denby, David J. *Sentimental Narrative and the Social Order in France, 1760–1820*. Cambridge: Cambridge University Press, 1994.

Deprun, Jean. *La Philosophie de l'inquiétude en France au XVIIIe siècle*. Paris: J. Vrin, 1979.

———. "Robespierre, pontife de l'être suprême: Notes sur les aspects sacrificiels d'une fête." In Ehrard and Viallaneix, eds., *Fêtes de la Révolution*, 485–491.

Derathé, Robert. *Jean-Jacques Rousseau et la science politique de son temps*. 2nd ed. Paris: J. Vrin, 1970.

Derrida, Jacques. "Cogito and the History of Madness." In Derrida, *Writing and Difference*, trans. Alan Bass, 31–63. Chicago: University of Chicago Press, 1978.

Derôme, Léopold. *Causeries d'un ami des livres: Les Éditions originales des romantiques*. 9 vols. Paris: Édouard Rouveyre, 1886.

Desan, Suzanne. *The Family on Trial in Revolutionary France*. Berkeley: University of California Press, 2004.

Dewald, Jonathan. *Aristocratic Experience and the Origin of Modern Culture: France, 1570–1715*. Berkeley: University of California Press, 1993.

Dickey, Lawrence. "Pride, Hypocrisy and Civility in Mandeville's Social and Historical Theory." *Critical Review* 4, n. 3 (Summer 1990): 387–431.

Dieckmann, Herbert. "Diderot et son lecteur." In *Cinq leçons sur Diderot*, 17–39. Geneva: Droz, 1959.

Dockes, Nicole. "Un Ordre communautaire du XVIIIe siècle: Morelly." In Klotz, ed., *Ordre, nature, propriéte*, 63–118.

Dumont, Louis. *Essais sur l'individualisme: Une Perspective anthropologique sur l'idéologie moderne*. Paris: Éditions du Seuil, 1991.

———. *Homo aequalis I: Genèse et épanouissement de l'idéologie économique*. Paris: Gallimard, 1985.

Dunn, John. *The Political Thought of John Locke*. Cambridge: Cambridge University Press, 1965.

Durand, Yves. *L'Ordre du monde: Idéal politique et valeurs sociales en France, XVIe – XVIIIe siècle*. Paris: Sedes, 2001.

Edelstein, Dan. *The Enlightenment: A Genealogy*. Chicago: University of Chicago Press, 2010.

———. *The Terror of Natural Right: Republicanism, the Cult of Nature, and the French Revolution*. Chicago: University of Chicago Press, 2009.

Ehrard, Jean, and Paul Viallaneix, eds. *Les Fêtes de la Révolution*. Paris: Société des études robespierristes, 1977.

Ellenburg, Stephen. *Rousseau's Political Philosophy: An Interpretation from Within*. Ithaca, N.Y.: Cornell University Press, 1976.

Fairchilds, Cissie. "Marketing the Counter-Reformation: Religious Objects and Consumerism in Early Modern France." In *Visions and Revisions of Eighteenth-Century France*, ed. Christine Adams, Jack R. Censer, and Lisa Jane Graham, 31–52. University Park: Pennsylvania State University Press, 1977.

———. "The Production and Marketing of Populuxe Goods in Eighteenth-Century Paris." In Brewer and Porter, eds., *Consumption and the World of Goods*, 228–248.

Feiner, Shmuel. *The Jewish Enlightenment*. Translated by Chaya Naor. Philadelphia: University of Pennsylvania Press, 2004.

Feller, François Xavier de. *Dictionnaire historique, ou Histoire abrégée de tous les hommes qui se sont fait un nom par leur genie, leurs talens, leurs vertus, leurs erreurs ou leurs crimes.* 8th ed. 13 vols. Lille: L. Lefort, 1832–1833.

Fitzsimmons, Michael P. *The Night the Old Regime Ended: August 4, 1789 and the French Revolution.* University Park: Pennsylvania State University Press, 2003.

Foucault, Michel. *Discipline and Punish: The Birth of the Prison.* 2nd ed. Translated by Alan Sheridan. New York: Vintage Books, 1995.

———. *Madness and Civilization: A History of Insanity in the Age of Reason.* Translated by Richard Howard. New York: Vintage Books, 1988.

———. *The Order of Things: An Archeology of the Human Sciences.* New York: Vintage Books, 1994.

Fox-Genovese, Elizabeth. *The Origins of Physiocracy: Economic Revolution and Social Order in Eighteenth-Century France.* Ithaca, N.Y.: Cornell University Press, 1976.

Fried, Michael. *Absorption and Theatricality: Painting and Beholder in the Age of Diderot.* Chicago: University of Chicago Press, 1980.

Furet, François. "Rousseau and the French Revolution." In *The Legacy of Rousseau,* ed. Clifford Orwin and Nathan Tarcov, 168–182. Chicago: University of Chicago Press, 1997.

Gasbaronne, Lisa. "De la Partie au tout: La Nature et la machine dans les *Rêveries* de Rousseau." In *Lectures des "Rêveries,"* ed. and trans. Anne F. Garreta, 45–57. Rennes: Presses universitaires de Rennes, 1998.

Gauchet, Marcel. *The Disenchantment of the World: A Political History of Religion.* Translated by Oscar Burge. Foreword by Charles Taylor. Princeton, N.J.: Princeton University Press, 1997.

———. *La Révolution des droits de l'homme.* Paris: Gallimard, 1992.

Gaukroger, Stephen. *Descartes: An Intellectual Biography.* Oxford: Clarendon Press, 1995.

Gauthier, Florence. "Robespierre, critique de l'économie, politique tyrannique et théoricien de l'économie politique populaire." In Jessenne et al., eds., *Robespierre,* 235–244.

———. *Triomphe et mort du droit naturel en Révolution, 1789–1795–1802.* Paris: Presses universitaires de France, 1992.

Gay, Peter. *The Enlightenment: An Interpretation.* 2 vols. New York: Norton, 1966–1969.

Gidel, Gilbert. *La Politique de Fénelon.* 1906. Reprint, Geneva: Slatkine, 1971.

Godechot, Jacques, ed. *Les Constitutions de la France.* Paris: Garnier Flammarion, 1996.

———. *Les Institutions de la France sous la Révolution et l'Empire.* Paris: Presses universitaires de France, 1951.

Goldmann, Lucien. *The Hidden God: A Study of Tragic Vision in the "Pensées" of Pascal and the Tragedies of Racine.* Translated by Philip Thody. New York: Humanities Press, 1964.

Goldsmith, Elizabeth C. "Mothering Mysticism: Mme Guyon and Her Public." In *Women Writers in Pre-Revolutionary France: Strategies of Emancipation,* ed. Colette Winn and Donna Kuizenga, 127–140. New York: Garland, 1997.

Goldstein, Jan. "Enthusiasm or Imagination? Eighteenth-Century Smear Words in

Comparative National Context." In *Enthusiasm and Enlightenment in Europe, 1650–1850*, ed. Laurence E. Klein and Anthony J. La Vopa, 29–49. San Marino, Calif.: Huntington Library Press, 1998.

———. "Foucault and the Post-Revolutionary Self: The Uses of Cousinian Pedagogy in Ninetheenth-Century France." In *Foucault and the Writing of History*, ed. Jan Goldstein, 99–115. Oxford: Blackwell, 1994.

———. *The Post-Revolutionary Self: Politics and Psyche in France, 1750–1850*. Cambridge, Mass.: Harvard University Press, 2005.

Goodman, Dena. *The Republic of Letters: A Cultural History of the French Enlightenment*. Ithaca, N.Y.: Cornell University Press, 1994.

Gordon, Daniel. *Citizens without Sovereignty: Equality and Sociability in French Thought, 1670–1789*. Princeton, N.J.: Princeton University Press, 1994.

Gordon, Scott Paul. *The Power of the Passive Self in English Literature, 1640–1770*. Cambridge: Cambridge University Press, 2002.

Goré, Jeanne-Lydie. *L'Itinéraire de Fénelon: Humanisme et spiritualité*. Paris: Presses universitaires de France, 1957.

———. *La Notion de l'indifférence chez Fénelon et ses sources*. Paris: Presses universitaires de France, 1956.

Gottschalk, Louis R. *Jean Paul Marat: A Study in Radicalism*. New York: Benjamin Blom, 1927.

Gouhier, Henri. *La Pensée métaphysique de Descartes*. Paris: J. Vrin, 1962.

Goyet, Thérèse. "Autour du traité posthume de Bossuet, «De la connaissance de Dieu et de soi-même»" *Revue d'Histoire littéraire de la France* 67, 3 (July–September 1967): 518–528.

Garrard, Graeme. *Rousseau's Counter-Enlightenment: A Republican Critique of the Enlightenment*. Albany, N.Y.: State University of New York Press, 2003.

Gross, Jean-Pierre. *Fair Shares for All: Jacobin Egalitarianism in Practice*. Cambridge: Cambridge University Press, 1997.

Gueniffey, Patrice. *La Politique de la Terreur: Essai sur la violence révolutionnaire, 1789–1794*.

Guerrier, Louis. *Madame Guyon: Sa Vie, sa doctrine, et son influence*. Paris: Didier, 1881.

Guillemin, Henri. *Robespierre, politique et mystique*. Paris: Éditions du Seuil, 1987.

Habermas, Jürgen. *The Structural Transformation of the Public Sphere: An Inquiry into a Category of Bourgeois Society*. Translated by Thomas Burger. Cambridge, Mass.: MIT Press, 1989.

Hamerton, Katherine J. "A Feminist Voice in the Enlightenment Salon: Madame de Lambert on Taste, Sensibility, and the Feminine Mind." *Modern Intellectual History* 7, 2 (July 2010): 209–238.

Harris, Ian. *The Mind of John Locke: A Study of Political Theory in its Intellectual Setting*. Cambridge: Cambridge University Press, 1994.

Hazard, Paul. *The European Mind, 1680–1715*. Translated by J. Lewis May. Cleveland: Meridian Books, 1963.

Hesse, Carla. "Enlightenment Epistemology and the Laws of Authorship in Revolutionary France, 1777–1793." In *Law and the Order of Culture*, ed. Robert Post, 109–137. Berkeley: University of California Press, 1991.

Heyd, Michael. *Be Sober and Reasonable: The Critique of Enthusiasm in the Seventeenth and Early Eighteenth Centuries.* New York: E. J. Brill, 1995.

Hirschman, Albert O. *The Passions and the Interests: Political Arguments for Capitalism before Its Triumph.* Princeton, N.J.: Princeton University Press, 1977.

Horkheimer, Max, and Theodor W. Adorno. *Dialectic of Enlightenment.* Translated by John Cumming. New York: Continuum, 1999.

Hulliung, Mark. *The Autocritique of Enlightenment: Rousseau and the Philosophes.* Cambridge, Mass.: Harvard University Press, 1994.

Hundert, E. J. "Bernard Mandeville and the Enlightenment's Maxims of Modernity." *Journal of Intellectual History* 56, 4 (Oct. 1995): 577–593.

———. "The Making of *Homo Faber*: John Locke between Ideology and History." *Journal of the History of Ideas* 33, 1 (January–March 1972): 3–22.

Israel, Jonathan. *Enlightenment Contested: Philosophy, Modernity, and the Emancipation of Man, 1670–1752.* Oxford: Oxford University Press, 2006.

———. *Radical Enlightenment: Philosophy and the Making of Modernity 1650–1750.* Oxford: Oxford University Press, 2001.

———. *A Revolution of the Mind: Radical Enlightenment and the Intellectual Origins of Modern Democracy.* Princeton, N.J.: Princeton University Press, 2009.

Istria, Madeleine Huillet d'. *Le Père de Caussade et la querelle du pur amour.* Paris: Aubier, 1964.

Jacob, Margaret C. *The Radical Enlightenment: Pantheists, Freemasons, and Republicans.* London: George Allen & Unwin, 1981.

Jacot-Grapa, Caroline. "Rêve et identité: Autour de la *Théorie des songes* de Jérôme Richard (1766)." In *Songes et songeurs (XIIIe–XVIIIe siècle),* ed. Nathalie Dauvois and Jean-Philippe Grosperrin, 235–243. Quebec: Presses de l'Université de Laval, 2003.

Jainchill, Andrew. *Reimagining Politics after the Terror: The Republican Origins of French Liberalism.* Ithaca, N.Y.: Cornell University Press, 2008.

Jaume, Lucien. *Le Discours jacobin et la démocratie.* Paris: Fayard, 1989.

———. "Fénelon critique de la déraison d'État." In *Raison et déraison d'État: Théoriciens et théories de la raison d'État aux XVIe et XVIIe siècles,* 395–422, ed. Yves Charles Zarka. Paris: Presses universitaires de France, 1994.

Jaume, Lucien, and Georges Labica. "Table ronde. Robespierre: la politique, la morale et le sacré." In Jessenne et al., eds., *Robespierre,* 431–434.

Jessenne, Jean-Pierre, Gilles Deregnaucourt, Jean-Pierre Hirsch, and Hervé Leuwers, eds. *Robespierre: De la Nation artésienne à la République et aux nations. Actes du colloque, Arras, 1-2-3 avril 1993.* Villeneuve d'Ascq: Centre d'histoire de la région du Nord et de l'Europe du Nord-Ouest, 1994.

Johansen, Karstein Friis. *A History of Ancient Philosophy: From the Beginnings to Augustine.* Translated by Henrik Rosenmeir. London: Routledge, 1998.

Jolley, Nicholas. "The Reception of Descartes' Philosophy." In *The Cambridge Companion to Descartes,* ed. John Cottingham, 397–407. Cambridge: Cambridge University Press, 1992.

Jones, Colin. *The Great Nation: France from Louis XV to Napoleon 1715–1799.* London: Allen Lane, Penguin Press, 2002.

Jones, Colin and Rebecca Spang. "Sans-culottes, sans café, sans tabac: Shifting

Realms of Necessity and Luxury in Eighteenth-Century France." In *Consumers and Luxury: Consumer Culture in Europe, 1650–1850*, ed. Maxine Berg and Helen Clifford, 37–62. Manchester: Manchester University Press, 1999.

Joppin, Gabriel. *Fénelon et la mystique du pur amour*. Paris: Beauchesne, 1938.

Kafker, Frank A. *The Encyclopedists as a Group: A Collective Biography of the Authors of the "Encyclopédie."* Studies on Voltaire and the Eighteenth Century, vol. 345. Oxford: Voltaire Foundation, 1996.

Kafker, Frank A., in collaboration with Serena L. Kafker. *The Encyclopedists as Individuals: A Biographical Dictionary of the Authors of the "Encyclopédie."* Studies on Voltaire and the Eighteenth Century, vol. 257. Oxford: Voltaire Foundation, 1988.

Kaiser, Thomas E. "Property, Sovereignty, the Declaration of the Rights of Man, and the Tradition of French Jurisprudence." In *The French Idea of Freedom: The Old Regime and the Declaration of Rights of 1789*, ed. Dale Van Kley, 300–349. Stanford, Calif.: Stanford University Press, 1994.

Kale, Steven. *French Salons: High Society and Political Sociability from the Old Regime to the Revolution of 1848*. Baltimore: Johns Hopkins University Press, 2005.

Kanter, Sanford B. "Archbishop Fénelon's Political Activity: The Focal Point of Power in Dynasticism." *French Historical Studies* 4, 3 (Spring 1966): 320–334.

Kaplan, Steven Laurence. *Bread, Politics and Political Economy in the Reign of Louis XV*. 2 vols. The Hague: Martinus Nijhoff, 1976.

———. *La Fin des corporations*. Translated by Béatrice Vierne. Paris: Fayard, 2001.

Kates, Gary. *The Cercle Social, The Girondins, and the French Revolution*. Princeton, N.J.: Princeton University Press, 1985.

Kelley, Donald R., and Bonnie G. Smith. "What Was Property? Legal Dimensions of the Social Question in France (1789–1848)." *Proceedings of the American Philosophical Society* 128, 3 (Sept. 1984): 200–201.

Kelly, Christopher. "Rousseau's 'Peut-Être': Reflections on the Status of the State of Nature." *Modern Intellectual History* 3, 1 (2006): 75–83.

Kelly, Duncan. *The Propriety of Liberty: Persons, Passions, and Judgements in Modern Political Thought*. Princeton, N.J.: Princeton University Press, 2010.

Klotz, Gérard, ed. *Ordre, nature, propriété*. Lyon: Presses universitaires de Lyon, 1985.

Kors, Alan Charles. *D'Holbach's Coterie: An Enlightenment in Paris*. Princeton, N.J.: Princeton University Press, 1976.

Kreiser, B. Robert. "The Devils of Toulon: Demonic Possession and Religious Politics in Eighteenth-Century Provence." In *Church, State, and Society under the Bourbon Kings of France*, ed. Richard M. Golden, 173–221. Lawrence, Kan.: Coronado Press, 1982.

———. *Miracles, Convulsions, and Ecclesiastical Politics in Early Eighteenth-Century Paris*. Princeton, N.J.: Princeton University Press, 1978.

Kruger, Steven F. *Dreaming in the Middle Ages*. Cambridge: Cambridge University Press, 1991.

Krumenacker, Yves. *L'École française de spiritualité: Des Mystiques, des fondateurs, des courants et leurs interprètes*. Paris: Éditions du Cerf, 1998.

Kselman, Thomas. "Challenging Dechristianization: The Historiography of Religion in Modern France." *Church History* 75, 1 (2006): 130–139.

Kuznicki, Jason. "Sorcery and Publicity: The Cadière-Girard Scandal of 1730–1731." *French History* 21, 3 (2007): 289–312.

Kwass, Michael. "Consumption and the World of Ideas: Consumer Revolution and the Moral Economy of the Marquis de Mirabeau." *Eighteenth-Century Studies*, 37, 2 (2004): 187–213.

———. "Ordering the World of Goods: Consumer Revolution and the Classification of Objects in Eighteenth-Century France." *Representations*, 82 (Spring 2003): 87–116.

———. *Privilege and the Politics of Taxation in Eighteenth-Century France: Liberté, Égalité, Fiscalité*. Cambridge: Cambridge University Press, 2000.

Labrosse, Claude. *Lire au XVIIIe siècle: "La Nouvelle Héloïse" et ses lecteurs*. Lyon: Presses universitaires de Lyon, 1985.

Lacuisine, Elisabeth François de. *Le Parlement de Bourgogne depuis son origine jusqu'à sa chute*. 2 vols. Dijon: Loireau-Feuchot; Paris: A. Durand, 1857.

Ladd, Everett C., Jr. "Helvetius and D'Holbach: 'La Moralisation de la Politique.'" *Journal of the History of Ideas* 23, 2 (April–June 1962): 221–238.

La Gorce, Agnès de. *Le Vrai visage de Fénelon*. Paris: Hachette, 1958.

Landy, Joshua, and Michael Saler, eds. *The Re-Enchantment of the World: Secular Magic in a Rational Age*. Stanford, Calif.: Stanford University Press, 2009.

Larrère, Catherine. *L'Invention de l'économie: Du Droit naturel à la physiocratie*. Paris: Presses universitaires de France, 1992.

Lear, H. L. Sidney. *Fénelon, Archbishop of Cambrai: A Biographical Sketch*. London: Longmans, Green, 1907.

Le Brun, Jacques. "Le Quiétisme entre la modernité et l'archaïsme." In *Modernité et nonconformisme en France à travers les âges*, ed. Myriam Yardeni, 86–99. Leiden: E. J. Brill, 1983.

Leduc-Fayette, Denise. "Fénelon et 'infini véritable.'" In *L'Infini entre science et religion au XVIIe siècle*, ed. Jean-Marie Lardic, 95–110. Paris: J. Vrin, 1999.

Lee, Natasha. "A Dream of Human Nature." In *The Nature of Rousseau's "Rêveries": Physical, Human, and Aesthetic*, ed. John C. O'Neil, 99–110. Studies on Voltaire and the Eighteenth Century. Oxford: Voltaire Foundation, 2008.

Lehner, Ulrich L. and Michael Printy, eds. *A Companion to the Catholic Enlightenment in Europe*. Leiden: Brill, 2010.

Lilti, Antoine. *Le Monde des salons: Sociabilité et mondanité à Paris au XVIIIe siècle*. Paris: Fayard, 2005.

Lombard, Alfred. *L'Abbé Du Bos: Un Initiateur de la pensée moderne (1670–1742)*. 1913. Reprint, Geneva: Slatkine, 1969.

Lossky, Andrew. *Louis XIV and the French Monarchy*. New Brunswick, N.J.: Rutgers University Press, 1999.

Lougee, Carolyn C. "*Noblesse*, Domesticity, and Social Reform: The Education of Girls by Fénelon and Saint-Cyr." *History of Education Quarterly* 14, 1 (Spring 1974): 87–113.

———. *Le Paradis des Femmes: Women, Salons, and Social Stratification in Seventeenth-Century France*. Princeton, N.J.: Princeton University Press, 1976.

Lough, John. *The "Encyclopédie."* London: Longman, 1971.

Lukács, Georg. *History and Class Consciousness: Studies in Marxist Dialectics*. Translated by Rodney Livingston. Cambridge, Mass.: MIT Press, 1971.

Lukes, Steven. *Individualism*. Oxford: Basil Blackwell, 1973.

Lyons, Martyn. *France under the Directory*. Cambridge: Cambridge University Press, 1975.

MacAdam, James I. "The Moral Dimensions of Property." In Howard R. Cell and James I. MacAdam, *Rousseau's Response to Hobbes*, 107–128. New York: Peter Lang, 1988.

Macpherson, C. B. *The Political Theory of Possessive Individualism: Hobbes to Locke*. Oxford: Oxford University Press, 1962.

Magee, Glenn Alexander. "Quietism in German Mysticism and Philosophy." *Common Knowledge* 16, 3 (Fall 2012): 457–473.

Maio, Romeo de. *Società e vita religiosa a Napoli nell'età moderna (1656–1799)*. Naples: Edizioni scientifiche italiane, 1971.

Maire, Catherine. *De la Cause de Dieu à la cause de la Nation: Le Jansenisme au XVIIIe siècle*. Paris: Gallimard, 1998.

Mallet-Joris, Françoise. *Jeanne Guyon*. Paris: Flammarion, 1978.

Marshall, David. *The Surprising Effects of Sympathy: Marivaux, Diderot, Rousseau, and Mary Shelley*. Chicago: University of Chicago Press, 1989.

Martin, John. *Myths of Renaissance Individualism*. New York: Palgrave Macmillan, 2004.

Martin, Victor. *Le Gallicanisme et la Réforme catholique: Essai historique sur l'introduction en France des décrets du concile de Trente (1563–1615)*. 1919. Reprint, Geneva: Slatkine, 1975.

Mason, Laura. *Singing the French Revolution: Popular Culture and Politics, 1787–1789*. Ithaca, N.Y.: Cornell University Press, 1996.

Mason, Richard. *The God of Spinoza: A Philosophical Study*. Cambridge: Cambridge University Press, 1987.

Masseau, Didier. *Les Ennemis des philosophes: L'Antiphilosophie au temps des Lumières*. Paris: Albin Michel, 2000.

Masson, Pierre-Maurice. *La Religion de Jean-Jacques Rousseau*. 3 vols. Paris: Hachette, 1916.

Mathiez, Albert. *Les Origines des cultes révolutionnaires (1789–1792)*. Paris: Société nouvelle de la librairie et d'édition, 1904.

———. *La Théophilanthropie et le culte décadaire: Essai sur l'histoire religieuse de la Révolution (1796–1801)*. 1903. Reprint, Geneva: Slatkine-Megariotis, 1975.

———. *Robespierre et le culte de l'Être suprême*. Le Puy: Peyriller, Rouchon & Gamon, 1910.

Mauzi, Robert. *L'Idée du bonheur dans la littérature et la pensée françaises au XVIIIe siècle*. 1960. Reprint, Geneva: Slatkine, 1979.

Mayeur, Jean-Marie, Charles Pietri, André Vauchez, and Marc Venard, eds. *Le Temps des confessions*. Vol. 8 of *Histoire du Christianisme des origines à nos jours*, ed. Marc Venard. Paris: Desclée, 1992.

Maza, Sarah. *Private Lives and Public Affairs: The Causes Célèbres of Prerevolutionary France*. Berkeley: University of California Press, 1993.

McMahon, Darrin M. *Enemies of the Enlightenment: The French Counter-Enlightenment and the Making of Modernity*. Oxford: Oxford University Press, 2001.

————. "Happiness and *The Heavenly City of the Eighteenth-Century Philosophers*: Carl Becker Revisited." *American Behavioral Scientist* 49, 5 (2006): 681–686.

McManners, John. *Church and Society in Eighteenth-Century France*. 2 vols. Oxford: Clarendon, 1998.

————. *Death and the Enlightenment: Changing Attitudes to Death among Christians and Unbelievers in Eighteenth-Century France*. Oxford: Oxford University Press, 1985.

Melchior-Bonnet, Sabine. *Fénelon*. Paris: Perrin, 2008.

Mémoires de la Société des lettres, sciences et arts de l'Averyron. 28 vols. Rodez: Société des lettres, sciences et arts de l'Aveyron, 1838–1964.

Merrick, Jeffrey. *The Desacralization of the French Monarchy in the Eighteenth Century*. Baton Rouge: Louisiana State University Press, 1990.

Metzger, Albert. *La Conversion de Madame de Warens*. Paris: Fetscherin & Chuit, 1886.

Moffat, Margaret M. *Rousseau et la querelle du théâtre au XVIIIe siècle*. 1930. Reprint, Geneva: Slatkine, 1970.

Monod, Albert. *De Pascal à Chateaubriand: Les Défenseurs français du Christianisme de 1670 à 1802*. 1916. Reprint, Geneva: Slatkine, 1970.

Moreau, Pierre-François. *Spinoza et le spinozisme*. Que sais-je? no. 1422. Paris: Presses universitaires de France, 2003.

Morrissey, Robert. *La Rêverie jusqu'à Rousseau: Recherches sur un topos littéraire*. Lexington, Ky.: French Forum, 1984.

Mousnier, Roland. *Les Institutions de la France sous la monarchie absolue*. 2 vols. Paris: Presses universitaires de France, 1974.

————. *La Venalité des offices sous Henri IV et Louis XIII*. Paris: Presses universitaires de France, 1971.

Moutaux, Jacques. "D'Holbach et Spinoza." In Bloch, ed., *Spinoza au XVIIIe siècle*, 151–167.

Naert, Émilienne. *Leibniz et la querelle du pur amour*. Paris: J. Vrin, 1959.

Navatel, Ludovic. *Fénelon: La Confrérie secrète du pur amour*. Paris: Émile-Paul frères, 1914.

Naville, Pierre. *D'Holbach et la philosophie scientifique au XVIIIe siècle*. Paris: Gallimard, 1967.

Newland, T. C. "D'Holbach's Political Ambivalence." *Journal of Eighteenth-Century Studies* 4, 2 (Sept. 1981): 184–190.

Niderst, Alain. "Le Quiétisme de *Télémaque*?" In *Fénelon mystique et politique (1699–1999)*, ed. F.-X. Cuche and J. Le Brun, 205–216. Paris: Honoré Champion, 2004.

Olphe-Galliard, Michel. Introduction to Jean-Pierre de Caussade, *Traité sur l'oraison du cœur: Instructions spirituelles*, ed. Olphe-Galliard. Paris: Desclée de Brouwer; Montreal: Bellarmin, 1981.

———. *La Théologie mystique en France au 18e siècle: Le Père de Caussade*. Paris: Beauchesne, 1984.

O'Neal, John. *The Authority of Experience: Sensationalist Theory in the French Enlightenment*. University Park: Pennsylvania State University Press, 1996.

Orcibal, Jean. Introduction to Jeanne-Marie Guyon, *Les Opuscules spirituels*. Hildesheim: Olms, 1978.

Ozouf, Mona. *La Fête révolutionnaire, 1789–1799*. Paris: Gallimard, 1976.

———. *L'Homme régénéré: Essais sur la Révolution française*. Paris: Gallimard, 1989.

Palmer, R. R. *Catholics and Unbelievers in Eighteenth-Century France*. Princeton, N.J.: Princeton University Press, 1939.

Paige, Nicholas. *Being Interior: Autobiography and the Contradictions of Modernity in Seventeenth-Century France*. Philadelphia: University of Pennsylvania Press, 2001.

Pensa, Henri. *Sorcellerie et religion: Du Désordre dans les esprits et dans les mœurs aux XVIIe et XVIIIe siècles*. Paris: Félix Alcan, 1933.

Perkins, Jean. *The Concept of the Self in the French Enlightenment*. Histoire des Idées et Critique littéraire, vol. 94. Geneva: Droz, 1969.

Petrovich, Vesna. *Connaissance et Rêve(rie) dans le discours des Lumières*. The Age of Revolution and Romanticism Interdisciplinary Studies, vol. 15. New York: Peter Lange, 1996.

Plongeron, Bernard. *Théologie et politique au siècle des lumières (1770– 1820)*. Geneva: Droz, 1973.

Pottinger, David. *The French Book Trade in the ancien régime, 1500–1791*. Cambridge, Mass.: Harvard University Press, 1958.

Porter, Roy, and Mikuláš Teich, eds. *The Enlightenment in National Context*. Cambridge: Cambridge University Press, 1981.

Proust, Jacques. *Diderot et l'Encyclopédie*. Paris: Armand Colin, 1962.

Quillien, Philippe-Jean. *Dictionnaire politique de René Descartes*. Lille: Presses universitaires de Lille, 1994.

Raymond, Marcel. *Jean-Jacques Rousseau: La Quête de soi et la rêverie*. Paris: Corti, 1962.

Reil, Peter Hanns. *Vitalizing Science in the Enlightenment*. Berkeley: University of California Press, 2005.

Rétat, Pierre. "La Jouissance physiocratique." In Klotz, ed., *Ordre, nature, propriété*, 179–211.

Riley, Patrick. "Fénelon's 'Republican' Monarchism in *Telemachus*." In *Monarchisms in the Age of Enlightenment: Liberty, Patriotism, and the Common Good*, ed. Hans Blom, John Christian Laursen, and Luisa Simonutti, 78–100. Toronto: University of Toronto Press, 2007.

———. *The General Will before Rousseau: The Transformation of the Divine into the Civic*. Princeton, N.J.: Princeton University Press, 1986.

———. "Rousseau's General Will." In *The Cambridge Companion to Rousseau*, ed. Patrick Riley, 124–153. Cambridge: Cambridge University Press, 2001.

Riskin, Jessica. *Science in the Age of Sensibility: The Sentimental Empiricists of the French Enlightenment*. Chicago: University of Chicago Press, 2002.

Riviale, Philippe. *La Conjuration: Essai sur la conjuration pour l'Égalité dite de Babeuf.* Paris: L'Harmattan, 1994.

Robinet, André. *Dom Deschamps: La Maître des maîtres du soupçon.* 2nd ed. Paris: J. Vrin, 1994.

Robisco, Nathalie-Barbara. *Jean-Jacques Rousseau et la Révolution française: Une Esthétique de la politique, 1792–1799.* Paris: Honoré Champion, 1998.

Roche, Daniel. *The Culture of Clothing: Dress and Fashion in the 'ancien régime.'* Translated by Jean Birrell. Cambridge: Cambridge University Press, 1994.

———. *France in the Enlightenment.* Translated by Arthur Goldhammer. Cambridge, Mass.: Harvard University Press, 1998.

———. *The History of Everyday Things: The Birth of Consumption in France, 1600–1800.* Translated by Daniel Pearce. Cambridge: Cambridge University Press, 2000.

———. *The People of Paris: An Essay in Popular Culture in the Eighteenth Century.* Translated by Marie Evans in association with Gwynne Lewis. Berkeley: University of California Press, 1987.

Roger, Philippe. "L'Homme du sang: L'Invention sémiotique de Marat." In Bonnet, ed., *Mort de Marat,* 141–166.

Rose, R. B. *Gracchus Babeuf: The First Revolutionary Communist.* London: Edward Arnold, 1978.

Rosenblatt, Helena. *Rousseau and Geneva: From the First Discourse to the Social Contract, 1749–1762.* Cambridge: Cambridge University Press, 1997.

Rothkrug, Lionel. *Opposition to Louis XIV: The Political and Social Origins of the French Enlightenment.* Princeton, N.J.: Princeton University Press, 1965.

Rousso, Elena. *Styles of Enlightenment: Taste, Politics, and Authorship in the French Enlightenment.* Baltimore: Johns Hopkins University Press, 2007.

Saler, Michael. "Modernity and Enchantment: A Historiographic Review." *American Historical Review* 111, 3 (June 2006): 692–716.

Schama, Simon. *Citizens: A Chronicle of the French Revolution.* New York: Knopf, 1989.

Schmaltz, Tad M., ed. *Receptions of Descartes: Cartesianism and Anti-Cartesianism in Early Modern Europe.* London: Routledge, 2005.

Schmittlein, Raymond. *L'Aspect politique du différend Bossuet–Fénelon.* Baden-Baden: Éditions Art et Science, 1954.

Schneewind, J. B. *The Invention of Autonomy: A History of Modern Moral Philosophy.* Cambridge: Cambridge University Press, 1998.

Schøsler, Jørn. *John Locke et les philosophes français: La Critique des idées innées en France au dix-huitième siècle.* Studies on Voltaire and the Eighteenth Century, vol. 353. Oxford: Voltaire Foundation, 1997.

Schrader, Hans-Jürgen. "Madame Guyon, le piétisme et la littérature de langue allemande." In Joseph Beaude et al., *Madame Guyon: Rencontres autour de la vie et l'œuvre de Madame Guyon, Thonon-les-Bains, Château de Ripailles, septembre 1996,* 83–130. Grenoble: Jérôme Millon, 1997.

Schwarzbach, B. E., and A. W. Fairbairn. "History and Structure of Our *Traité des trois imposteurs.*" In *Heterodoxy, Spinozism, and Free Thought in Early-*

Eighteenth-Century Europe, ed. Sylvia Berti, Françoise Charles-Daubert, and Richard Popkin, 75–130. Dordrecht: Kluwer, 2010.

Scruton, Roger. *Spinoza*. Oxford: Oxford University Press, 1986.

Seigel, Jerrold. *The Idea of the Self: Thought and Experience in Western Europe since the Seventeenth Century*. Cambridge: Cambridge University Press, 2005.

Sepinwall, Alyssa. *The Abbé Grégoire and the French Revolution: The Making of Modern Universalism*. Berkeley: University of California Press, 2005.

Sewell, William H., Jr. *Logics of History: Social Theory and Social Transformation*. Chicago: University of Chicago Press, 2005.

———. "The Sans-Culotte Rhetoric of Subsistence." In *The French Revolution and the Creation of Modern Political Culture*, ed. Keith Michael Baker, François Furet, Colin Lucas, and Mona Ozouf, vol. 4, *The Terror*, ed. Keith Michael Baker, 249–268. Oxford: Pergamon Press, 1994.

———. *Work and Revolution in France: The Language of Labor from the Old Regime to 1848*. Cambridge: Cambridge University Press, 1981.

Shank, J. B. *The Newton Wars and the Beginning of the French Enlightenment*. Chicago: University of Chicago Press, 2008.

Shepherd, Robert Perry. *Turgot and the Six Edicts*. Studies in History, Economics and Public Law, vol. 18, no. 2. New York: Columbia University Press, 1903.

Sheridan, Geraldine. *Nicolas Lenglet Dufresnoy and the Literary Underworld of the Ancien Régime*. Studies on Voltaire and the Eighteenth Century, vol. 262. Oxford: Voltaire Foundation, 1989.

Shovlin, John. "The Cultural Politics of Luxury in Eighteenth-Century France." *French Historical Studies* 23, 4 (Fall 2000): 577–606.

———. *The Political Economy of Virtue: Luxury, Patriotism, and the Origins of the French Revolution*. Ithaca, N.Y.: Cornell University Press, 2006.

Simon, Julia. *Mass Enlightenment: Critical Studies in Rousseau and Diderot*. Albany, N.Y.: State University of New York Press, 1995.

Singer, Brian C. J. *Society, Theory and the French Revolution: Studies in the Revolutionary Imaginary*. New York: Macmillan, 1986.

Smith, Jay. *The Culture of Merit: Nobility, Royal Service, and the Making of Absolute Monarchy in France, 1660–1789*. Ann Arbor, Mich.: University of Michigan Press, 1996.

Soboul, Albert. "Sentiment religieux et cultes populaires: Saintes patriotes et martyrs de la liberté." *Archives des sciences sociales des religions* 2 (1946): 73–87.

Sorkin, David. *The Religious Enlightenment: Protestants, Jews, and Catholics from London to Vienna*. Princeton, N.J.: Princeton University Press, 2008.

Starobinski, Jean. *Jean-Jacques Rousseau: Transparency and Obstruction*. Translated by Robert J. Morrissey. Chicago: University of Chicago Press, 1988.

Steiner, Philippe. *La "Science nouvelle" de l'économie politique*. Paris: Presses universitaires de France, 1998.

Stuurman, Siep. *François Poulain de la Barre and the Invention of Modern Equality*. Cambridge, Mass.: Harvard University Press, 2004.

Sutcliffe, Adam. *Judaism and Enlightenment*. Cambridge: Cambridge University Press, 2003.

Swenson, James. *On Jean-Jacques Rousseau, Considered as One of the First Authors of the Revolution.* Stanford, Calif.: Stanford University Press, 2000.

Tackett, Timothy. *Religion, Revolution, and Regional Culture in Eighteenth-Century France: The Ecclesiastical Oath of 1791.* Princeton, N.J.: Princeton University Press, 1986.

Taine, Hippolyte. *L'Ancien Régime.* Part One of *Les Origines de la France contemporaine.* Paris: R. Laffont, 1986.

Talmon, J. L. *The Origins of Totalitarian Democracy.* London: Secker & Warburg, 1953.

Taylor, Charles. *Sources of the Self: The Making of Modern Identity.* Cambridge, Mass.: Harvard University Press, 1989.

Terrasse, Jean. "Dieu, la nature, les fleurs: sur une page des *Rêveries.*" In *Rêveries sans fin,* ed. Michel Coz and François Jacob, 73–88. Orléans: Paradigme, 1997.

Terrier, Didier. *Histoire économique de la France d'Ancien Régime.* Paris: Hachette, 1998.

Thomas, Keith. *Religion and the Decline of Magic: Studies in Popular Beliefs in Sixteenth- and Seventeenth-Century England.* New York: Scribner 1971.

Thomson, Ann. *Materialism and Society in the Mid-Eighteenth Century: La Mettrie's "Discours préliminaire."* Geneva: Droz, 1981.

Topazio, Virgil. W. "Diderot's Supposed Contribution to d'Holbach's Works." *PMLA* 69, 1 (March 1954): 173–188.

Tulard, Jean. *Les Thermidoriens.* Paris: Fayard, 2005.

Tully, James. *An Approach to Political Philosophy: Locke in Contexts.* Cambridge: Cambridge University Press, 1993.

———. *A Discourse on Property: John Locke and His Adversaries.* Cambridge: Cambridge University Press, 1980.

Turnovsky, Geoffrey. *The Literary Market: Authorship and Modernity in the Old Regime.* Philadelphia: University of Pennsylvania Press, 2009.

Urbain, Charles. *Du Jansénisme de Bossuet.* Paris: Letouzey & Ané, [1899].

Van Kley, Dale. "Christianity as Casualty and Chrysalis of Modernity: The Problem of Dechristianization in the French Revolution." *American Historical Review* 108, 4 (2003): 1081–1104.

———. *The Jansenists and the Expulsion of the Jesuits from France, 1757–1765.* New Haven, Conn.: Yale University Press, 1975.

———. "Pierre Nicole, Jansenism, and the Morality of Enlightened Self-Interest." In *Anticipations of Enlightenment in England, France, and Germany,* ed. Alan Charles Kors and Paul J. Korshin, 69–85. Philadelphia: University of Pennsylvania Press, 1987.

———. *The Religious Origins of the French Revolution: From Calvin to the Civil Constitution of the Clergy, 1560–1791.* New Haven, Conn.: Yale University Press, 1996.

Vaughan, C. E. Introduction to Jean-Jacques Rousseau, *The Political Writings of Jean Jacques Rousseau,* 1: 1–117. Cambridge: Cambridge University Press, 1915.

Vernière, Paul. *Spinoza et la pensée française avant la Révolution.* Paris: Presses universitaires de France. 1954. Reprint, Geneva: Slatkine, 1970.

Vidal, Daniel. *Miracles et convulsions jansénistes au XVIIIe siècle: Le Mal et sa connaissance.* Paris: Presses universitaires de France, 1987.

Vila, Anne C. *Enlightenment and Pathology: Sensibility in the Literature and Medicine of Eighteenth-Century France.* Baltimore: Johns Hopkins University Press, 1998.

Viller, M., F. Cavallera, J. de Guibert, A. Rayez, A. Derville, and A. Solignac, eds. *Dictionnaire de spiritualité ascétique et mystique, doctrine et histoire.* 17 vols. Paris: Beauchesne, 1932–1995.

Vovelle, Michel. *Piété baroque et déchristianisation en Provence au XVIIIe siècle: Les Attitudes devant la mort d'après les clauses de testaments.* Paris: Éditions du Seuil, 1978.

———. *Religion et Révolution: La Déchristianisation de l'an II.* Paris: Hachette, 1976.

Vries, Jan de. "Purchasing Power and the World of Goods." In Brewer and Porter, eds., *Consumption and the World of Goods,* 107–121.

Wade, Ira O. *The Clandestine Organisation and Diffusion of Philosophical Ideas in France from 1700 to 1750.* Princeton, N.J.: Princeton University Press, 1938.

———. *The Intellectual Development of Voltaire.* Princeton, N.J.: Princeton University Press, 1969.

Wagner, Nicolas. *Morelly: Le Méconnu des lumières.* Paris: Klincksieck, 1978.

Wahnich, Sophie. *In Defence of the Terror: Liberty or Death in the French Revolution.* Translated by David Fernbach. Foreword by Slavoj Žižek. London: Verso, 2012.

Wahrman, Dror. *The Making of the Modern Self: Identity and Culture in Eighteenth-Century England.* New Haven, Conn.: Yale University Press, 2004.

Walter, Eric. "Babeuf écrivain: L'Invention rhétorique d'un prophète." In *Présence de Babeuf: Lumières, révolution, communisme,* ed. Alain Maillard, Claude Mazauric, and Eric Walter, 183–231. Paris: Sorbonne, 1994.

Watt, Ian. *Myths of Modern Individualism: Faust, Don Quixote, Don Juan, Robinson Crusoe.* Cambridge: Cambridge University Press, 1996.

Weir, David R. "Les Crises économiques et les origines de la Révolution française." *Annales. Économies, sociétés, civilisations,* 46, 4 (July–August 1991): 917–947.

Wellman, Kathleen Anne. *La Mettrie: Medicine, Philosophy, Enlightenment.* Durham, N.C.: Duke University Press, 1992.

Wilkins, Kay S. "Some Aspects of the Irrational in Eighteenth-Century France." In *Studies on Voltaire and the Eighteenth Century,* 140: 107–201. Oxford: Voltaire Foundation, 1975.

Williams, Elizabeth Ann. *A Cultural History of Medical Vitalism in Enlightenment Montpellier.* Aldershot: Ashgate, 2003.

Williams, Elizabeth Ann. *The Physical and the Moral: Anthropology, Physiology, and Philosophical Medicine in France, 1750–1850.* Cambridge: Cambridge University Press, 1994.

Wilson, Arthur. *Diderot.* New York: Oxford University Press, 1972.

Wingertszahn, Christof. *Anton Reiser und die "Michelein": Neue Funde zum Quietismus im 18. Jahrhundert.* Hannover: Wehrhahn, 2002.

Woloch, Isser. *Jacobin Legacy: The Democratic Movement under the Directory.* Princeton, N.J.: Princeton University Press, 1970.

Wright, Johnson Kent. *A Classical Republican in Eighteenth-Century France: The Political Thought of Mably.* Stanford, Calif.: Stanford University Press, 1997.

Yolton, Jean S., ed. *John Locke as Translator: Three of the Essais of Pierre Nicole in French and English.* Studies on Voltaire and the Eighteenth Century. Oxford: Voltaire Foundation, 2000.

Yolton, John W. *Locke and French Materialism.* Oxford: Clarendon, 1991.

Index